THE COMPENSATION HANDBOOK

FIFTH EDITION

A STATE-OF-THE-ART GUIDE TO COMPENSATION STRATEGY AND DESIGN

LANCE A. BERGER *and* **DOROTHY R. BERGER**

New York   San Francisco   Washington, D.C.   Auckland   Bogotá
Caracas   Lisbon   London   Madrid   Mexico City   Milan
Montreal   New Delhi   San Juan   Singapore
Sydney   Tokyo   Toronto

*The **McGraw·Hill** Companies*

1 2 3 4 5 6 7 8 9 0   DOC/DOC   0 9 8

ISBN: 978-0-07-149675-9
MHID: 0-07-149675-0

This publication is designed to provide accurate and authoritative information in regard to the subject matter covered. It is sold with the understanding that neither the author nor the publisher is engaged in rendering legal, accounting, or other professional service. If legal advice or other expert assistance is required, the services of a competent professional person should be sought.

> *— From a Declaration of Principles jointly adopted*
> *by a Committee of the American Bar*
> *Association and a Committee of Publishers*

McGraw-Hill books are available at special quantity discounts to use as premiums and sales promotions, or for use in corporate training programs. To contact a representative please visit the Contact Us pages at www.mhprofessional.com.

Library of Congress Cataloging-in-Publication Data

The compensation handbook / [edited] by Lance Berger and Dorothy Berger. -- 5th ed.
    p. cm.
  Includes bibliographical references and index.
  ISBN-13: 978-0-07-149675-9 (alk. paper)
  ISBN-10: 0-07-149675-0 (alk. paper)
 1. Compensation management--Handbooks, manuals, etc. I. Berger, Lance A. II. Berger, Dorothy R.
HF5549.5.C67H36 2008
658.3'2--dc22

                                 2007046249

Contents

Preface

THE COMPENSATION HANDBOOK HAS BEEN recognized as the most authoritative reference book in the compensation field for over 35 years.

The book's success has resulted from:

- Identifying the most significant issues impacting compensation and human resources practitioners

- Providing the best straightforward, comprehensive, and understandable solutions to deal with issues

- Presenting the thoughts and research of respected and prestigious compensation leaders

- Offering unique and innovative approaches not found elsewhere

- Building on the strong foundation of past editions

- Imparting the best historical and current compensation tools, methods, and diagnostics for compensation and human resources professionals to align their programs with key issues

Each edition of the book has its own novel foundation. The first three editions focused on the evolution of new compensation techniques and methodologies as they applied to the business and social environment of their eras. The fourth edition is based on a framework of compensation diagnostics. It structures prior and current approaches into a cohesive set of guiding principles that helps practitioners to select the most appropriate compensation methodology.

The fifth edition's objective is to demonstrate to human resources and compensation professionals how they can address a dramatically changing set of human capital issues. These include:

- New strategies for winning the talent wars
- Addressing the retirement of the baby boomers, the greatest talent management issue of the twenty-first century
- Responding to a multicultural, multigenerational workforce
- The globalization of human capital

Thanks to the contributions of 64 compensation specialists, 45 of whom are new authors to *The Compensation Handbook*, this edition contains new, updated, or revised chapters. This "linkage" to talent management issues provides common threads and a roadmap for developing a comprehensive approach to compensation program design and implementation. The fourth edition's structural integrity is maintained because our readers have expressed their appreciation of consistency when seeking updated information and solutions to compensation issues.

We again, as we did for the fourth edition, dedicate this book with appreciation and affection to Milton L. Rock, consummate compensation and business guru, whose vision spearheaded the first through third editions of *The Compensation Handbook*.

Dorothy R. Berger

Lance A. Berger

About the Editors

Lance A. Berger is CEO of Lance A. Berger & Associates, Ltd., a Bryn Mawr, Pennsylvania management consultant firm specializing in compensation, talent management, and change management. A former general partner for the largest compensation practice worldwide at The Hay Group, he cowrote *Management Wisdom from the New York Yankees' Dynasty* and *Deengineering The Corporation*, and cowrote and coedited the third and fourth editions of *The Compensation Handbook, The Talent Management Handbook*, and *The Change Management Handbook*.

Dorothy R. Berger is Managing Director of Lance A. Berger & Associates, Ltd. She coordinates all organizational activities for the firm and is also a talent management consultant. She cowrote *Management Wisdom from the New York Yankees' Dynasty*, and cowrote and coedited *The Compensation Handbook*, fourth edition, *The Talent Management Handbook, The Change Management Handbook*, and *Deengineering The Corporation*. Dorothy has over 20 years' experience in the field of education.

Contributors

Kenan S. Abosch   Broad-Based Compensation Practice Segment Leader, Hewitt Associates, LLC, Lincolnshire, Illinois (*Chapters 12 and 19*)

Richard L. Alpern   Principal, Frederic W. Cook & Company, Inc., New York, New York (*Chapter 29*)

Linda E. Amuso   Senior Vice President, Radford Surveys & Consulting, An Aon Business, San Francisco, California (*Chapter 17*)

Summer F. Barnes   Senior Consultant, Sibson Consulting, Los Angeles, California (*Chapter 39*)

Dorothy R. Berger   Managing Director, Lance A. Berger & Associates, Ltd, Bryn Mawr, Pennsylvania (*Chapter 5*)

Lance A. Berger   Chief Executive Officer, Lance A. Berger & Associates, Ltd, Bryn Mawr, Pennsylvania (*Chapters 1 and 43*)

Mark Graham Brown   President, Mark Graham Brown & Associates, Manhattan Beach, California (*Chapter 38*)

Tim Brown   Vice President, Radford Surveys & Consulting, An Aon Business, San Jose, California (*Chapter 9*)

Seymour Burchman   Managing Principal, Semler Brossy Consulting Group, LLC, Los Angeles, California (*Chapter 30*)

Ted Buyniski   Senior Vice President, Radford Surveys & Consulting, An Aon Business, Southborough, Massachusetts (*Chapter 24*)

Mark D. Cannon, Ph.D.   Associate Professor of Leadership and Organizational Studies, Peabody College, Vanderbilt University, Nashville, Tennessee (*Chapter 41*)

Paul Coleman   Senior Consultant, ORC Worldwide, London, UK (*Chapter 49*)

Jerome A. Colletti   Colletti–Fiss, LLC, Scottsdale, Arizona (*Chapter 20*)

Paul Davis President, Scanlon Leadership Network, East Lansing, Michigan (*Chapter 23*)

Bruce R. Ellig   Author and retired Corporate Vice President, HR, Pfizer Inc., New York, New York (*Chapter 33*)

Christian M. Ellis   Senior Vice President, Sibson Consulting, Los Angeles, California (*Chapter 39*)

Mary S. Fiss   Colletti–Fiss, LLC, Scottsdale, Arizona (*Chapter 20*)

Iain Fitzpatrick   Reward Information Services General Manager, Hay Group, Philadelphia, Pennsylvania (*Chapter 10*)

Luis R. Gomez-Mejia, Ph.D.   Professor of Management, W.P. Carey School of Business, Arizona State University, Tempe, Arizona (*Chapter 21*)

David E. Griffith President and CEO, Modern Group Ltd, Bristol, Pennsylvania (*Chapter 15*)

Steven E. Gross   Worldwide Partner and Segment Leader, Broad-based Performance and Rewards Segment Leader, Mercer Human Resources Consulting, Philadelphia, Pennsylvania (*Chapter 2*)

Dick Grote   President, Grote Consulting Corporation, Dallas, Texas (*Chapter 36*)

Myrna Hellerman   Senior Vice President, Sibson Consulting, Chicago, Illinois (*Chapter 7*)

Robert L. Heneman, Ph.D.   Professor of Management and Human Resources, Max M. Fisher College of Business, Ohio State University, Columbus, Ohio (*Chapter 11*)

Jeffrey S. Hyman, Esq.   Exequity LLP, Wilton, Connecticut (*Chapter 25*)

Bernard Ingster, Ph.D.   Consultant, Human Resources Management, Philadelphia, Pennsylvania (*Chapter 8*)

Randy Jayne   Managing Partner Global Aerospace, Defense, and Aviation Practice, Heidrick & Struggles, McLean, Virginia (*Chapter 26*)

Blair Jones   Managing Principal, Semler Brossy Consulting Group, LLC, Los Angeles, California (*Chapter 30*)

David Knopping   Vice President, Radford Surveys & Consulting, An Aon Business, San Francisco, California (*Chapter 17*)

James Kochanski   Senior Vice President, Sibson Consulting, Raleigh, North Carolina (*Chapter 7*)

Geoffrey W. Latta   Executive Vice President, ORC Worldwide, New York, New York (*Chapter 48*)

Gerald E. Ledford, Jr., Ph.D.   President, Ledford Consulting Network, LLC, Redondo Beach, California (*Chapter 11*)

Kathleen M. Lingle   Director, Alliance for Work–Life Progress, WorldatWork, Scottsdale, Arizona (*Chapter 44*)

Susan Malanowski   Principal, Wilson Group, Inc., Concord, Massachusetts (*Chapter 34*)

Robert L. Masternak   President, Masternak & Associates, Medina, Ohio (*Chapter 22*)

Robert Mattson Product Marketing, Workscape, Marlborough, Massachusetts (*Chapter 50*)

Marvin A. Mazer Senior Vice President, Radford Surveys & Consulting, An Aon Business, Atlanta, Georgia (*Chapter 24*)

Nora McCord Consultant, Steven Hall & Partners, New York, New York (*Chapter 32*)

Steven T. McGuire Manager, Human Resources, GlaxoSmithKline, Philadelphia, Pennsylvania (*Chapter 16*)

Thomas D. McMullen Vice President and Reward Practice Leader, Hay Group, Chicago, Illinois (*Chapter 10*)

Pearl Meyer Senior Managing Director, Steven Hall & Partners, New York, New York (*Chapter 32*)

Leslie Moody Senior Vice President of Human Resources and Administration, Pennsylvania Academy of the Fine Arts, Philadelphia, Pennsylvania (*Chapter 14*)

Jerry M. Newman Distinguished Teaching Professor and Chair Department of Organization and Human Resources, State University of New York at Buffalo, Buffalo, New York (*Chapter 47*)

Paul R. Niven President, The Senalosa Group, Inc., Ramona, California (*Chapter 37*)

Erin C. Packwood Principal, Mercer Human Capital Consulting Group, Houston, Texas (*Chapter 18*)

Johannes M. Pennings, Ph.D. Department of Management, The Wharton School, University of Pennsylvania, Philadelphia, Pennsylvania (*Chapter 27*)

Shelley Peterson Senior Associate Broad-based Performance and Rewards, Mercer Human Resources Consulting, Philadelphia, Pennsylvania (*Chapter 2*)

James F. Reda Managing Director, James F. Reda & Associates, LLC, New York, New York (*Chapter 35*)

Deborah Rees Director, Innecto Reward Consulting, Woodborough, UK (*Chapter 42*)

Andrew S. Rosen Vice President, ORC Worldwide, New York, New York (*Chapter 6*)

John A. Rubino President, Rubino Consulting Services, Pound Ridge, New York (*Chapter 46*)

Aino Salimäki Researcher, Helsinki University of Technology, Helsinki, Finland (*Chapter 11*)

Dow Scott, Ph.D. Professor of Human Resources, Loyola University Chicago, Chicago, Illinois (*Chapter 23*)

Allan Schweyer   President and Executive Director, The Human Capital Institute, Quebec, Canada (*Chapter 4*)

Rodger D. Stotz   Vice President and Managing Consultant, Maritz, Inc., Fenton, Missouri (*Chapter 13*)

David N. Swinford   President, Pearl Meyer & Partners, New York, New York (*Chapter 31*)

David Turetsky   Director of Product Management, Workscape, Marlborough, Massachusetts (*Chapter 50*)

Frank P. VanderPloeg, Esq.   Partner, Employee Benefits and Executive Compensation, Sonnenschein Nath & Rosenthal, Chicago, Illinois (*Chapter 28*)

Melissa Van Dyke   Consultant, Maritz, Inc., Fenton, Missouri (*Chapter 13*)

Theresa M. Welbourne, Ph.D.   Adjunct Professor of Executive Education, Ross School of Business, University of Michigan, Ann Arbor, Michigan; President and CEO, eePulse, Inc., Ann Arbor, Michigan (*Chapter 21*)

Fred Whittlesey   Principal Consultant, Compensation Venture Group, Inc., Bainbridge Island, Washington (*Chapter 40*)

Thomas B. Wilson   President, Wilson Group, Inc., Concord, Massachusetts (*Chapters 3 and 34*)

Martin G. Wolf, Ph.D.   President, Management Advisory Services, Inc., Jalisco, Mexico (*Chapter 45*)

Don York   Senior Vice President, Radford Consulting & Surveys, An Aon Business, San Jose, California (*Chapter 9*)

PART 1

Introduction

EMPLOYEE PAY: A RIDDLE WRAPPED IN A MYSTERY INSIDE AN ENIGMA

Lance A. Berger, Chief Executive Officer

Lance A. Berger & Associates, Ltd

TO MOST EMPLOYEES WINSTON CHURCHILL could have been describing their pay package instead of Russia when he said that "it was a riddle wrapped in a mystery inside an enigma." The purpose of this chapter is to solve the riddle by unwrapping the mystery and explaining the enigma.

To employees the most recognizable deliverable in a compensation program is their own pay package. It is essential to the organization that this deliverable be transparent. To the practitioner the challenge is to ensure transparency by rationalizing the employee's pay package as the end result of an unambiguous, disciplined, and explainable thought process based on a coherent business and human resources strategy. We will explain the enigma (how the pay components are derived) by unwrapping three layers of mystery.

LAYER 1: A WINNING BUSINESS STRATEGY BEGINS WITH A DEFINITION OF STRATEGY

A strategy is a risk management program for allocating major resources today where the identified competitive opportunities and returns are in the future. Lance A. Berger & Associates research indicates that a winning business strategy is based on allocating major resources to accomplish the three goals outlined in Figure 1.1.

Successful organizations seek to answer the following three questions when they develop action plans to address the three goals.

1. *Continuous stakeholder satisfaction*: Are the customers, employees, shareholders, suppliers, and vendors satisfied that their own goals have been and will continue to be met?
2. *Perpetual competitive advantage*: Did the organization stay in the top three of its competitive comparison group over time?
3. *Sustained "employer of choice"*: Do employees and candidates prefer the organization to others as a place to work? Are turnover rates relatively low? Does the organization have a performance-driven culture?

To help an organization answer these questions and achieve these goals, we need to engage in strategic thinking from a human resources perspective. What is strategic thinking? Strategic thinking is the application of intuition, creativity, synthesis,

FIGURE 1.1   A winning business strategy

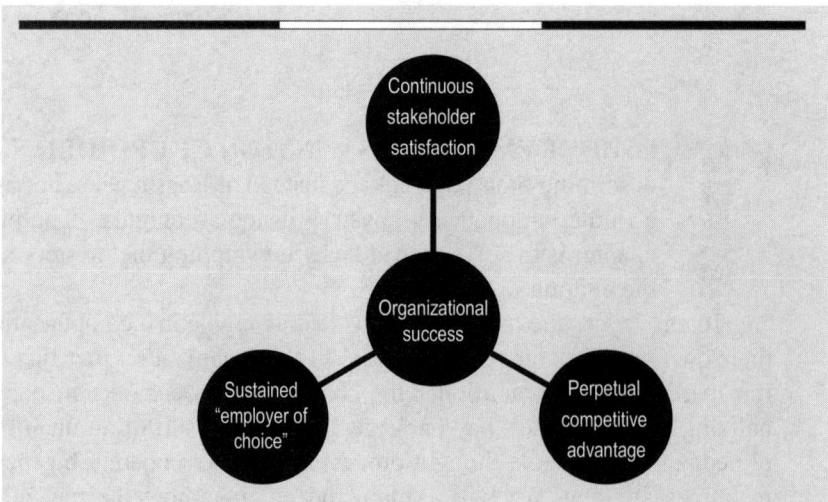

and judgment to design a strategy. In this case we are applying strategic thinking to create a human resources environment that supports the three objectives of a winning business strategy.

LAYER 2: THE HR STRATEGY THAT SUPPORTS THE WINNING BUSINESS STRATEGY IS BASED ON THE CREATION OF A WINNING CULTURE

Before exploring the elements of a winning culture we must first define the meaning of culture. We define culture as the shared knowledge, experience, emotions, beliefs, values, attitudes, meanings, and concepts developed, acquired, and transmitted by the people in an organization. Culture determines whether business strategies can and/or will be supported at an employee's personal risk level and what reward systems will actually work in the culture. In our highly competitive world the only acceptable culture is one that drives business excellence defined by strategic goals. A culture of excellence is one in which people have shared knowledge, experience, emotions, beliefs, values, attitudes, meanings, and concepts that contribute to business, group, and personal success now and in the future. Cultural excellence enables an organization to be an "employer of choice," perpetually achieve competitive advantage, and continuously generate stakeholder satisfaction. There are three dimensions and several components of cultural excellence. The three dimensions, expressed as competency clusters, are shown in Figure 1.2.

FIGURE 1.2   The three dimensions of cultural excellence

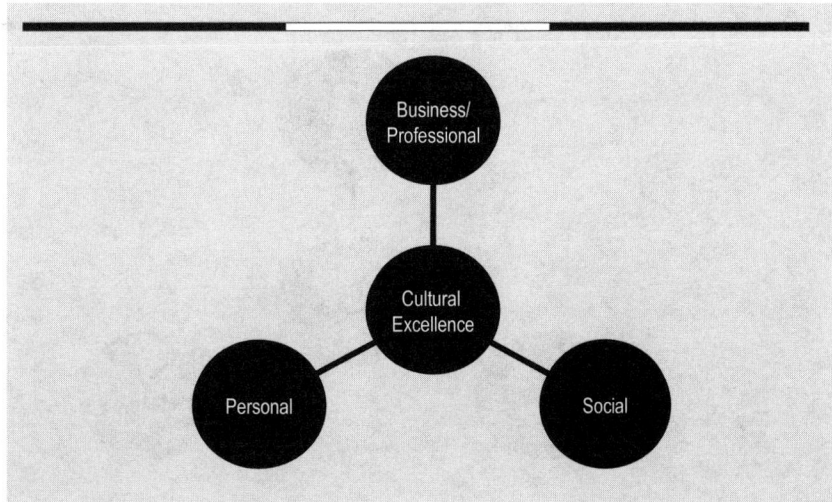

Copyright Lance A. Berger & Associates, Ltd.

The competencies (organizational and personal success factors) that comprise these clusters are:

- *Business/professional*—knowledge-based competencies needed to produce a product or service (technical, functional), customer orientation, and results orientation
- *Social*—leadership, interpersonal skills, teamwork, citizenship (ethics and morality)
- *Personal*—creativity, communications, and risk tolerance

In many organizations culture evolves in a happenstance way largely through a mosaic of unconnected and nonstrategic processes that affect how people are hired, promoted, developed, and terminated. Culture is transmitted through bureaucratic and perfunctory policies, processes, and employee manuals designed to mechanically regulate daily work and employee behaviors. In a highly competitive world, however, organizations cannot let culture evolve in a haphazard way. Companies must manage the creation, development, and sustenance of a culture of excellence based on the behaviors associated with competency clusters such as those cited above. It is only when employee behavior is connected to organizational success that its talent pool spawns a culture of excellence. All human resources and compensation strategies must be transparently focused on driving behaviors associated with a culture of organizational excellence.

Three talent management strategies drive the culture of excellence. These strategies are shown in Figure 1.3.

FIGURE 1.3   Three talent management strategies

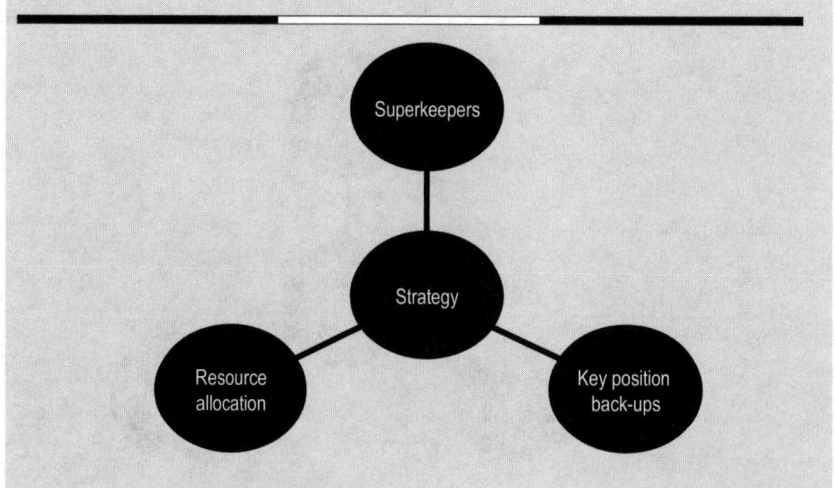

Copyright Lance A. Berger & Associates, Ltd.

The three talent management strategies are defined as follows:

- Cultivate a *Superkeeper*™ pool—the keepers of the flame for the culture of excellence (2–3 percent of the workforce)

- Enhance incumbents and handcuff strong backups in key/mission critical positions (8–12 percent of positions are critical)

- Allocate *TREADs* (training, rewards, education, and development) based on current and future employee contribution (actual and potential achievement)

In order to allocate resources in accordance with a talent management strategy such as that outlined above, an organization must be able to classify every member of its workforce based on her actual and potential contribution to success. Our research generated the following employee classifications.

1. Superkeeper™—demonstrates superior accomplishments; inspires others to superior accomplishment; serves as the embodiment of organizational competencies (about 2–3 percent of the workforce)

2. Keeper—exceeds expectations for performance; can lead others; exceeds expectations on organizational competencies (about 20 percent of the workforce)

3. Solid citizen—meets expectations for performance; can work with others; meets expectations on organizational competencies (about 70 percent of the workforce)

4. Misfit—does not meet expectations for performance; does not work well with others; does not reflect institutional competencies (about 7 percent of the workforce)

Most successful organizations generate their employees' classifications based on some combination of three types of assessment. These are: performance, competencies (current and future), and potential.

Performance. This is a measurement of actual results achieved within those areas for which the employee is held accountable. All individual and group performance measures must be woven into the fabric of organizational success measures in order to connect the employee to institutional achievement.

Core/Institutional Competencies. These are behavioral/skill expectations that are crucial to the success of each employee and to the success of the entire organization. Our research has determined that most organizations use between seven and eleven institutional competencies in their assessment process. Typical core competencies can be communications, innovation, critical judgment, customer orientation, interpersonal skills, leadership, teamwork, and technical/functional expertise.

An example of an organization's competency definition may be:

> *Communication*: communicates well both verbally and in writing. Effectively conveys ideas and shares information with others. Listens carefully and understands different points of view. Presents ideas clearly and concisely and understands relevant detail in presented information.

Competency definitions can further be differentiated into glossaries of behaviors associated with each level of the organization. This provides amplification, clarity, and greater specificity to the definition. As an example, when considering communications all employees are required to clearly and appropriately express their desires and needs, whereas in addition supervisors are expected to adapt communications to audience requirements to optimize understanding, managers are required to actively present information and ideas to all appropriate levels and lead others to do the same, and individuals in top management are required to promote open expression of ideas and encourage communication without retribution, assuming that they have mastered the behaviors outlined for lower-level employees.

Potential.   This is a prediction of how many levels (organization or job) an employee can progress through based on their past/current/projected performance appraisals, training and development needs, career preferences, and actual and projected competency levels. Underlying the assessment of potential is the employee's desire to improve, need to achieve tangible results, probable acceptance by higher peer levels, self-confidence, and emotional stability.

LAYER 3: THE ORGANIZATION'S PAY STRATEGY IS DEVELOPED AND IMPLEMENTED TO SUPPORT ITS TALENT MANAGEMENT STRATEGY BUILT UPON ITS EMPLOYEE CLASSIFICATION SYSTEM

In order to transparently deliver pay to each employee, in accordance with the human resources strategy defined above it must first be filtered through a set of principles known as a pay strategy. The five elements that compose a pay strategy are: philosophy, pay/talent market, competitive level, mix, and contribution. The definitions of rules for a pay strategy are discussed below.

Compensation Philosophy.   Organizations customize their compensation philosophy based on their particular business and human resources requirements. Most commonly, these philosophies focus on delivering pay, based on institutional affordability, in a way that enables them to attract, retain, and reward employee performance in an equitable, competitive, and legal way. To complete the statement of philosophy, organizations are now adding the goal of "allocating pay based on business and human resources strategies" such as those described above.

Pay/Talent Markets. In order to determine the competitiveness of pay associated with a given position, an organization must survey its pay, or talent, market. A pay/talent market consists of incumbents in institutions that have or will provide a source of talent for, or would pirate talent from, an organization. The surveyed compensation for people in benchmark (commonly found) jobs in a chosen talent market should be the basis for establishing pay in an organization. The best surveys are those that accurately measure a pay market derived from sources of recruitment and exit interviews. Positions within a talent market that have no survey counterpart can derive their value from a comparison of relative organizational worth with those jobs that can be surveyed. Note that pay/talent market competitors may not necessarily be in the same business.

Competitive Level. Within each pay/talent market and within the organization as a whole, management must determine the competitive level of total human resources costs it can afford to pay to attract, retain, and reward its employees. Competitive level is generally expressed as a percentile in surveys associated with a given pay/talent market (25th, 50th, 75th). The total affordable pot of money is the basis of allocation of pay. It is possible that the characteristics of different pay/talent markets (supply and demand) will necessitate different pay structures and competitive levels. Regardless, individual employees should be paid at competitive levels that reflect their own current and projected contribution (value) to the organization.

Mix. The percentage of total pay targeted for each pay component (base salary, annual incentives, and long-term incentives) defines its mix. Furthermore, within a total pay package, there may be different competitive levels targeted for base, annual incentives, long-term incentives, and total compensation. The greater the amount of variable or non-base pay, the more leverage (upside opportunity) or risk (non-guaranteed pay) becomes a factor in an employee's compensation package. In general, the level of risk or leverage decreases in employee pay packages as organizational financial strength evolves from that of a perilous start-up to that of a secure established organization. Within an organization the amount of leverage in a pay package also reflects the risk and accountability associated with a given position. Senior management and line positions typically have more variable pay than staff positions. Figure 1.4 illustrates the typical mix of pay in organizations at different stages of growth.

Contribution. This refers to the employee's classification, based on her assessed current and future organizational value, derived from factors such as those previously defined (performance, competencies, and potential). The final pay package architecture for a single employee is now in place. The employee's mix and competitive level of pay based on the characteristics of her own talent market and consideration for her personal contribution can now be expressed in

FIGURE 1.4   Pay mix and stage of business growth

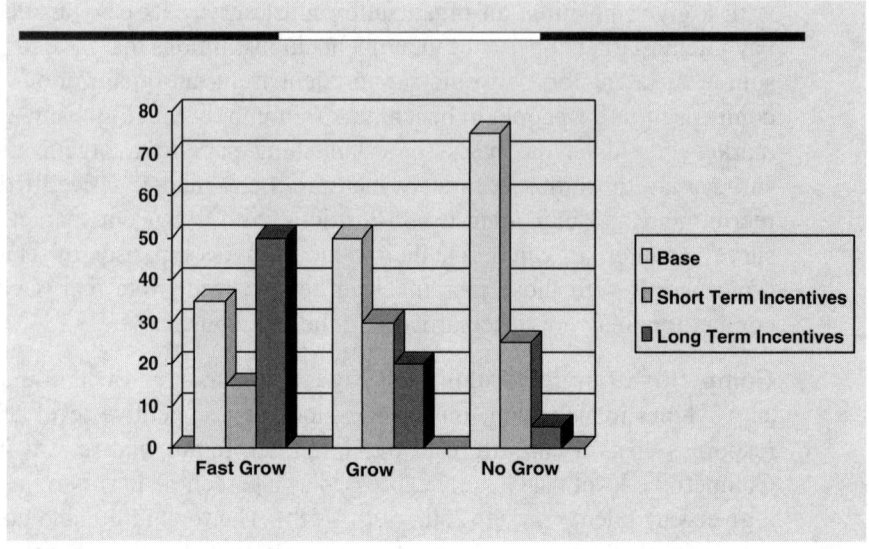

Copyright Lance A. Berger & Associates, Ltd.

TABLE 1.1   Application of Employee Classification and Compensation Strategy

Employee Classification	Pay/Talent Market Position	Compensation Competitive Level	Compensation Mix
Superkeeper™	Top 3%	Accelerate much than pay markets	Strong use of long-term incentive devices
Keeper	Top 20%	Accelerate faster than pay markets	Use of long-term incentive devices
Solid citizen	Middle 70%	Accelerate at pace of pay market	Consistent with pay/talent market

categories such as those defined below. In every case there may be an additional pay premium for each employee whose pay category is projected to increase to or remain at a higher contribution level over time. Like the batting averages of baseball players, an employee's classification must be re-earned each year.

Table 1.1 illustrates the application of an individual employee's contribution level (classification) to an organization's pay strategy (philosophy, pay/talent market, competitive level, and mix). We now have the answer to the "riddle wrapped in a mystery inside an enigma."

2

TOTAL REWARDS AND THE FUTURE WORKFORCE

Steven E. Gross, Worldwide Partner and Segment Leader, and
Shelley Peterson, Senior Associate Broad-based Performance and Rewards

Mercer Human Resources Consulting

ALTHOUGH THE CONCEPT OF COMPENSATION has changed a great deal in recent decades—moving from a traditional base pay and bonus structure to a broader "Total Rewards" approach—its evolution is hardly complete. The years to come will see continued change in market and workforce dynamics. A new employment model is evolving, as organizations face pressure to perform domestically and globally in a tightening labor market while balancing cultural and generational differences in employee wants and needs along with long-term sustainability of employment costs. Adapting to a new model requires the creation of alternative employment arrangements that recognize the role of flexible work plans, contingent staff, and nonlinear careers. Optimizing the new model requires Total Rewards strategies to be changed, or finite resources to be strategically allocated across unique workforce segments with holistic yet customized approaches.

THE NEW EMPLOYMENT MODEL

The evolving employment model is driven not by one dominant perspective, as in the past—a perspective typically founded on the employer's capacity to draw from a deep labor pool and rely on long-tenured workers happy to have jobs—but by multiple perspectives. Now, the employer perspective recognizes an emerging shortage of labor skills, knowledge, and experience (in part driven by the aging of the baby boomer population in mature economies) in a less company-loyal, more geographically mobile workforce. The employee perspective is marked by changing cultural and generational attitudes, needs, and wants when it comes to work. The cost perspective is that of increasing employment costs and their sustainability—driven largely by the ever-inflating cost of health care (primarily) and other benefits, along with the competitive cost of paying for skilled talent in a tightening global job market.

Though operating in an increasingly global marketplace, employers are often recruiting from a smaller qualified workforce, as statistics show that the level and quantity of technical education is not keeping pace with demand. At the same time, the loss of experienced workers to retirement—a phenomenon that will only accelerate as the baby boom generation moves out of the workforce en masse in the coming years—results in a loss of institutional knowledge that cannot easily be replaced simply by adding new hires. Not only do less-experienced workers need more on-the-job training, forcing organizations to invest more energy and resources, but today's and tomorrow's employees question a one-company career. In the United States, for example, median years of tenure with current employer is 1.7 years less across age groups in 2006 versus 1996 (U.S. Bureau of Labor Statistics), reflecting the general decline of historical lifetime-employment and job-security covenants. Human resource professionals around the world consistently and repeatedly cite attracting and retaining talent as the number one rewards challenge (Mercer's 2006 global snapshot survey, *Measuring the Return on Total Rewards*). Labor dynamics suggest that employers will continue to face the daunting task of engaging a diverse new workforce so that it joins, grows its own institutional knowledge, and stays with the organization.

Myriad employee perspectives of this diverse workforce are illustrated in Mercer's 2006 *What's Working* global employee survey of workers' perceptions and attitudes toward their organizations. When asked to rank the factors that influence their commitment and motivation at work, survey participants in North America, Asia, and Western Europe put "Being treated with respect," "The type of work that you do," and "work/life balance" among the top three (only Asian participants cited "base pay" as the primary factor). But the cultural context of employee perspectives often varies. "Being treated with respect" may mean promotion and rewards based on performance in one country or seniority in another. Different generations also have different priorities. The traditionalist, 60-plus generation values security and company loyalty, and wants its expertise and experience to be recognized; hard-working baby boomers (ages 43–60) want their hard work to be valued; Generation X (ages 30–42) seeks work/life balance and wants the company to value its contributions; while the so-called millennials (ages 18–29), a technology-savvy generation that values work/life balance and changes jobs most frequently, want to value their *own* contributions, living and working with a strong sense of purpose outside a specific company's value system. Balancing the attitudes, wants, and needs of a diverse employee population adds complexity and cost to workforce management.

In fact, assessing the sustainability of current costs for employers points disturbingly to the escalating price of providing Total Rewards. Suppose an organization's total cost of pay and benefits equaled 60 percent of revenue in 2007, with a projected annual 2 percent growth in employee headcount and 5 percent growth in revenue. At the same, the annual cost of pay and benefits is increasing at 3.5 and 12 percent, respectively. In 2012, five years later, the total cost of pay and benefits would equal 67 percent of revenue. This realistic estimate points to the very real risk that employment costs pose to an organization's sustained financial success. Adding to the cost dilemma is the fact that for most businesses—especially those operating in a global context—workforce requirements vary over time and location. For example, the traditional model of permanent, full-time employees is not flexible or cost-efficient in addressing periods of under-capacity or over-capacity of staff.

Cost and flexibility pressures, changing employee demands, and the challenges employers face in attracting, engaging, and motivating talent are the realities of the new employment model that promote the growth of alternative employment arrangements.

ALTERNATIVE EMPLOYMENT ARRANGEMENTS

The workforce of the future demands a suite of employment arrangements that meet employer, employee, and cost concerns. Traditional, long-term, permanent, full-time positions will always have a role in delivering organizational success. But employers and employees will see an expanded range of work arrangements, from long-term to contingent. Long-term employment is typically traditional permanent full-time or part-time work. The visible shift in long-term arrangements is the increasing demand for flexible work plans. Contingent employment is a more varied mix of nonlinear, multicompany work experiences, including short-term employment that may be structured as temporary/full-time or part-time; temporary-to-hire; specific project employment structured as temporary/full-time or part-time; and contractor arrangements, including consultants and the self-employed. Including contingent workers in an organization's staffing model allows it to optimize the number and cost of permanent headcount while adding resources as required to meet fluctuating capacity demands (see Figure 2.1).

FIGURE 2.1   Fluctuating capacity requirements

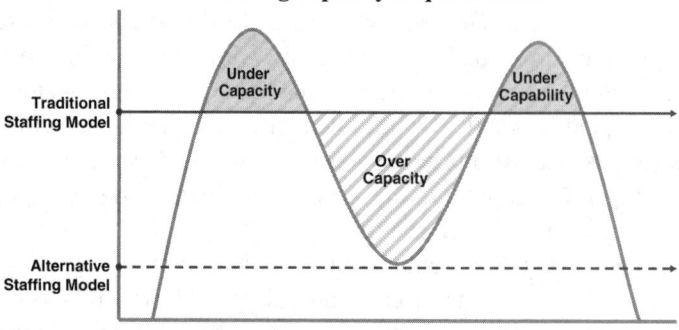

Long-term employment with flexible work options can include flexitime, telecommuting, job sharing, compressed work weeks, sabbaticals, and generally a greater level of employee autonomy in scheduling and delivering work. Growth of flexible work plans speaks to what employees want and need and how employers are rising to the challenge. Surveys on workplace policies and practices conducted by Mercer over the years reveal some material changes—for example, only about 30 percent of surveyed companies had telecommuting arrangements in 1999, but by the 2006 survey, more than 65 percent had telecommuting arrangements for professional staff. The prevalence of flexitime arrangements grew from less than 60 percent in 1990 to more than 90 percent of survey respondents in 2006. A 2005 *National Study of Employers* conducted by the Families and Work Institute showed that more than 20 percent of workplaces had employees who moved from full-time to part-time status and back to full-time, along with rising numbers of phased-retirement and temporary workers.

Taking "flexible" one step further, the growth of temporary/contingent labor is expected to outpace total employment growth over the next decade, according to the most recent *Temporary Jobs Guidebook: Niche Market Opportunities for Staffing Firms* (2007, Staffing Industry Analysts Inc.). While total employment is expected to grow by 1.2 percent, the contingent workforce is expected to triple that, at 3.8 percent. Shifting employment patterns are further underscored by the growth of one-person businesses, which increased by more than one million in the U.S. between 2002 and 2003.

As a result, the contingent-workforce phenomenon will modify such traditional patterns as those seen in Figure 2.2 in career paths, where long-term career growth is predicated on a typically linear progression from job A to jobs B, C, and ultimately D. Contingent-workforce careers tend to move nonlinearly from job A to modified work arrangements (lateral jobs B1, and then B2, for example) before acceding to next-level jobs C or D. Ultimately, organizations will have to recognize and respond to different views of career paths—that of permanent,

FIGURE 2.2 Linear and nonlinear career paths

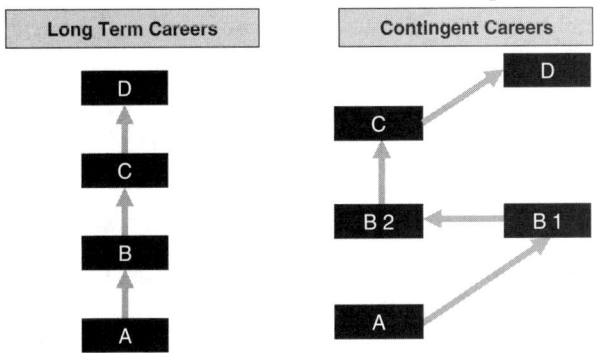

long-term workers who see a career path within the firm and contingent workers who see a career path moving from firm-to-firm.

Increasing demands for alternative employment arrangements such as flexible work plans and contingent staff along with the changing view of "career path" require organizations to re-think workforce management for the future.

WORKFORCE SEGMENTATION

Clearly, in this one-size-doesn't-fit-all employment universe, businesses require a strategic solution to managing the workforce, one that encompasses the realities of generations and geographies, emerging nontraditional staffing models and pressure to produce return on human capital investments. That strategy begins with the identification of unique workforce segments. There are four important aspects of segmentation to consider:

- *Business life cycle*—a company's position on the business life cycle curve; whether it is experiencing rapid, moderate or declining growth. A young start-up will have different characteristics than a mature firm in a flat market.

- *Business design*—a company's business model; how the entity is organized and types of competencies required to create value. There may be one overall design or different emphases for units or divisions within the company.

- *Geography*—a company's geographic breadth and complexity as well as its need for cross-border interconnectedness and mobility.

- *Brand reputation*—the extent to which a company's brand is an asset or liability in attracting and retaining both customers and employees.

Once the portfolio of workforce segments is identified, it is important to assess the contribution each segment makes to organization success. Segments may include:

- *Performance drivers*—segments that create value for the organization, such as marketing in consumer products companies, research scientists in pharmaceutical organizations, or China operations in a globally expanding manufacturing firm

- *Performance enablers*—segments that support value creation, such as staff (HR, IT, accounting, etc.), and workers who play an important role in facilitating the efficiency of performance drivers

- *Legacy drivers*—segments (skill sets) that historically created value for the organization but no longer drive competitive advantage, e.g., production and circulation functions in a media organization may become legacy drivers as content is increasingly delivered online.

It is critical to emphasize that different job families, geographies, and skills sets are not universally categorized as performance drivers, performance enablers, or legacy drivers, since their role in value creation depends on organization and even business-unit profit models. A good example would be a single group of information technology (IT) professionals that might play a different role in value creation for different organizations. How? To a buyer of IT outsourcing services that relies on IT to support its operations, those IT professionals function as performance enablers, but to the IT outsourcing vendor that sells their services, they are performance drivers. In other words, workforce segmentation requires an organization-specific view of value creation.

The rewards challenge for each workforce segment is often different. For performance drivers, the value proposition must succeed in attracting, engaging, and retaining these value-creators through an optimal mix of base pay, incentive compensation, benefits, and career-development offerings. For performance enablers, the rewards mix must ensure that these workers continue to effectively support the business. And for legacy drivers, appropriate rewards depend on the value of retaining their institutional knowledge.

Complex organizations are complex compilations of workforce segments. If an organization does not rigorously identify and qualify its workforce populations, it cannot act on differences in relative value-contribution or design programs that reflect varying workforce needs and performance goals. Workforce segmentation is required to ensure Total Rewards resources can be strategically, intentionally allocated across the organization to promote the greatest opportunity for success.

TOTAL REWARDS STRATEGY

Strategic allocation of Total Rewards means taking both a holistic (recognizing all the tools in a rewards toolkit) and customized (using the right tool for the right job) approach.

Considerable strides have been made in shifting both employee and employer focus from disparate pay components to a holistic Total Rewards approach that encompasses:

- *Compensation*, which includes base pay, short-term and long-term incentives, and recognition awards

- *Benefits*, comprising health and other group benefits, retirement plans, work/life programs, and perquisites and

- *Careers*, including training and development, stretch assignments, and other career opportunities, and formal career and succession planning

According to Mercer's 2006 global snapshot survey, *Measuring the Return on Total Rewards*, this paradigm shift has occurred globally, with approximately two-thirds of companies in Asia, Europe, and North America now taking a comprehensive view of rewards as a blend of compensation, benefits, careers, and other intrinsic factors (such as working conditions). In a competitive and cost-conscious environment, employers know they must utilize and communicate the value of the full rewards package provided. But a universal holistic approach can (see Figure 2.3) lead to over-rewarding or under-rewarding specific workforce segments—or, worse, inappropriately rewarding all segments. Strategic Total Rewards means THAT organizations must make tactical decisions in customizing programs for unique workforce segments. A good example is the case of the global energy company which identified multiple business models: in one, profit is generated through a premium, long-term position in global exploration; and in another, profit is generated through low-margin, intensely competitive, local retail market share transactions. This organization needed to distinguish two workforce segments and build tailored Total Rewards approaches. One design, relating to the firm's global

FIGURE 2.3 Regional, total rewards data

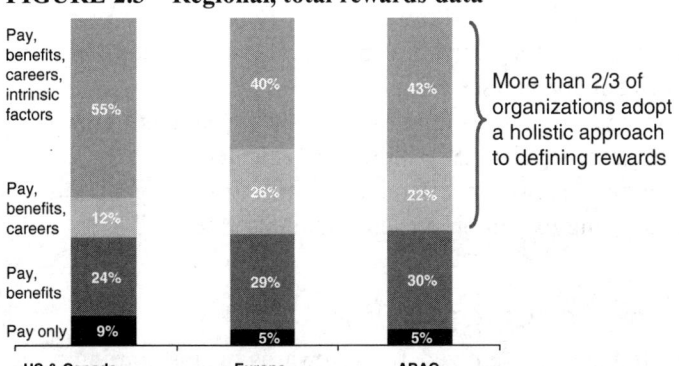

Source: Mercer's 2006 Snapshot Surveys "Measuring the Return on Total Rewards" (APAC, Europe, US & Canada)

organization, involved paying above-market salaries for "hot" skills; building talent from within the organization through a Total Rewards program that emphasized career-based rewards, nondifferentiated, corporate performance awards, and a focus on learning and development; and centralized decision making. The other approach, keyed to the local, retail end of the business, involved paying market price for talent (and "buying" it on the open market rather than "building" it from within the organization); spot rewards and differentiated performance awards; less emphasis on learning and development; and entrepreneurial decision making. While this may seem like a mix-and-match, one-from-column-A, two-from-column-C approach to Total Rewards, it reflects the need for a holistic yet customized Total Rewards strategy that aligns with different business models.

Segmentation helps organizations understand where customization of Total Rewards will drive business performance, but organizations cannot forget that in the new employment reality there are likely to be multiple work arrangements across or even within workforce segments. This dimension further refines how and where a company should target its rewards spending to attract, engage, and retain diverse employee populations. All the elements of Total Rewards play a role. The question is where to place the greatest emphasis. Long-term, permanent performance drivers, for example, should be engaged by career opportunity, offered through access to quality training and development, leading edge projects, international assignments, etc. Contrast that with long-term, permanent legacy drivers. Unfortunately, these employees operate in an area of business that is no longer a growth engine or source of competitive advantage. The organization should not invest in career opportunity or promote career opportunity as a means of motivating or retaining these employees. Emphasis on short-term incentives which reap the remaining benefits of legacy market share or transferred institutional knowledge is a better and more realistic allocation of funds. For contingent workers, current cash is often the driving factor. This is particularly true for traditionalist or baby boomer employees that may consider cash the primary reason to remain in the workforce as they may be unable to retire in the lifestyle they desire. Contingent Generation X and millennials may be more forward-looking. For performance drivers in this group, the opportunity for potential full-time employment holds significant appeal (see Figure 2.4).

Addressing alternative employment arrangements and unique workforce segments requires significantly more sophisticated Total Rewards strategies than those of the past. However, effectively defining strategy is not the only hurdle. Initial and ongoing execution presents challenges as well.

CHALLENGES OF STRATEGIC TOTAL REWARDS
Executing strategic, customized Total Rewards means coming to grips with institutional attitudes and operations that need to change—and change again. One of

FIGURE 2.4   Rewards offers by work arrangement and workforce segment

		Performance drivers	Performance enablers	Legacy drivers
Employment Arrangement		**Permanent**	**Contingent**	**Permanent**
Long-term		▪ Career ▪ Alternative work arrangements	▪ Base pay ▪ Benefits	▪ Short-term incentives ▪ Alternative work arrangements
Contingent	▪ Traditionalists ▪ Baby boomers	▪ Cash ▪ Benefits	▪ Cash ▪ Benefits	▪ Cash
	▪ Generation X ▪ Millennials	▪ Cash ▪ Potential full-time employment		▪ Short-term incentives

the most widespread struggles is addressing organizational views of equity and fairness. By definition, segmented, differentiated Total Rewards programs treat people differently—some perhaps better than others. And though organizations often vary rewards in response to market pressures, skill shortages, and so on, a strategy of explicit differentiation-based employment arrangement and/or value creation is a difficult approach for organizations to adopt and communicate. When an organization seeks change, it may be a difficult undertaking. Systems, processes, and people must adapt; compensation management systems may need to accommodate multiple base pay and incentive programs, compensation, training and development, recruiting may need to make trade-offs across historically silo budgets, and managers will need to handle more challenging conversations about an individual's compensation, benefits, and career. Once an organization has changed, it must be prepared to change again. Business strategies continuously evolve. If Total Rewards strategy does not keep pace, costly misalignments can occur, hindering business progress and diminishing return on investment. Overcoming these challenges requires leadership support, pragmatic segmentation (recognizing meaningful differences in workforce segments), and comprehensive implementation and communication change management with an eye on both today's and tomorrow's change.

SUMMARY

The workforce of the future is taking shape now, as the new employment model continues to evolve to address changing employer, employee, and cost dynamics.

More and more, today's and tomorrow's employees will be re-thinking traditional employment arrangements and taking a nonlinear, multicompany, individually driven attitude towards career success. Organizations need to take steps to better understand their workforce—the cultural and generational differences of the people they employ, the emerging alternative work arrangements they demand, and the relative value creation of unique workforce segments in the business models they advance—and strategically design and invest in holistic and customized Total Rewards programs for that workforce.

These differentiated strategies recognize the role of each Total Rewards component but emphasize the element that best meets employer and employee needs for various combinations of employment arrangements and workforce segments. It is a challenging task that requires organizations to think differently about the definition of fairness and strategic Total Rewards in order to create sustainable employment costs while driving performance now and engaging the workforce of the future.

C H A P T E R

TOTAL REWARDS STRATEGY

Thomas B. Wilson, President

Wilson Group, Inc.

EVERY ORGANIZATION WANTS TO ATTRACT, retain, and motivate employees. Many think that this is the primary purpose of the total compensation and reward programs. These companies then define their compensation strategy as being at "X" percentile in their industry, with the belief that this will enable them to attract and retain desired talent; motivation is achieved by the belief that their "pay-for-performance" program works. It would be interesting to determine if other systems within the organization are viewed in such a simple manner.

Recent changes in the regulations for disclosure of executive compensation require public companies to describe their compensation philosophy in detail. In the past, boards of directors (and executives as well) would use boilerplate statements to describe their programs in general, vague terms that provided little insight for the reader. This change in regulation has many compensation committees, boards, executive managers and human resource directors looking for verbiage that does not require them to invest too much effort or divulge too much information. Some companies are using this situation to examine their fundamental philosophy and requirements, while others are missing a critical opportunity.

While one can appreciate the need to keep specific compensation information confidential, the inability to define the firm's basic philosophy in meaningful and substantial ways often leads to haphazard decisions and undermines the confidence of shareholders and employees alike.

Consider.   What would happen if your marketing department presented to executive management a strategy that positioned a new key product to be the same as your competitors—in the price, features, and value proposition? How would your executives respond? Then, why does a company seek to make their compensation and reward programs "the same" as other firms in the market? Is it better for your compensation programs to conform to the market or be distinctive?

Why should someone come to work for your company, remain with your company, or buy your company's products, services or stock? What is different about your organization that would compel one to work for your company? Furthermore, how much money does your organization spend on compensation? What is compensation as a percentage of revenues or operating income? Does the company apply the same level of strategic and operational thought to expenditures for compensation as it does to other major expenditures or investments? When an organization spends (or invests) its dollars, it should know what it is paying for and seek to maximize the "value" from these expenditures. Addressing these issues is the value a reward strategy provides to an organization.

PURPOSE OF A TOTAL REWARD STRATEGY

To understand what a Total Reward strategy is, let us start with a definition. "Total Rewards" are those policies, programs, and practices that provide employees of a company (or organization) with something of value in return for their contributions to the mission and goals of the organization. These can include salary and variable cash compensation programs, employee benefits and services, stock options and other equity awards, and special recognition, promotions, etc. Therefore, the *purpose* of a Total Rewards strategy is to provide the objectives, guidelines, and principles necessary to design and operate the company's reward programs consistent with its core requirements.

Fundamentally, this means that the reward strategy should:

- Reinforce the core mission, values, and critical success factors of the company in terms that reflect the role of reward programs and practices

- Define what are (or will be) the key elements that will create a strong competitive advantage for the company in the marketplace for talent

- Provide sufficient clarity and guidance to key decision makers so they can assess the effectiveness of current programs and practices, and determine what actions are needed to improve their effectiveness

- Answer "why" a particular program is designed or functions in a particular manner

We have found that, while the words may appear similar from one organization to another, the real value is the meaning the reward strategy has to the members of the organization. The words become reality when they are effectively translated into action through policies, programs (or systems) and practices. The result is simple—an effective framework to allocate resources and create strong capabilities to influence desired behaviors (i.e., performance) of people.

KEY ELEMENTS OF THE TOTAL REWARD STRATEGY

Developing a reward strategy that meets these requirements is a real challenge for many organizations. An increasing number of companies realize that their performance is truly based on the talents and actions of their people, and that these programs in fact exert significant influence on behaviors by the messages they send, the opportunities they provide, and the needs they meet for the workforce. An organization's culture is not shaped by its stated values and communication, but by what and how *actions are encouraged, rewarded, and punished*. A reward strategy translates a company's strategy and core values into policies, programs, and practices that *directly* influence the performance of people.

The reward strategy statement needs to include these elements:

1. Establish the context for the total reward philosophy, especially if the organization is facing particular challenges or has implemented a fundamental change in the way programs have been managed in the past
2. Provide a unifying statement of philosophy (or principles) that connects reward programs to the core mission, strategy, and values of the organization
3. Express the importance of these programs to the company's ability to attract and retain people, as well as develop talent and reward desired performance
4. Define the primary programs and their basic purpose or focus, including base salaries, variable cash compensation and equity participation, employee benefits and services, and workplace opportunities for development, careers and recognition, etc.
5. Identify the primary drivers of these programs—the competition for talent, corporate/unit/individual performance, the infrastructure to make sound decisions, desired types of behaviors and support for strategic change

A Total Reward strategy is therefore a statement that sets the stage for specific policies and programs, and defines the requirements and impact desired from them. Here is an example:

> IBM has significantly reoriented its reward strategy, focusing more of its compensation investment on programs that recognize results than on those that reflect only tenure. Today, IBM's overall compensation strategy is designed to deliver market-based, performance driven pay in all segments of our business portfolio, and to reward appropriately our highest contributors. We do this through a

combination of base salaries and variable performance-driven bonuses. Our goal is nothing less than to sustain and renew the highest performing, most cost effective culture in business. To do that, we seek to hire, measure and reward the individuals who create that culture every day.[1]

DETERMINE THE RIGHT REWARD STRATEGY

Carl Sagan once said that, in order to make an apple pie, we must first create the universe. Without going into this level of design, the reward strategy is fundamentally based on the strategic and organizational requirements the organization has for its people. This process involves addressing four primary areas. As these are understood, the task of developing a reward strategy that makes sense and is effective for the organization becomes significantly easier. These areas are shown in Figure 3.1.

Define the Organization's Philosophy

To develop the total rewards strategy, the first stage is to understand the organization's business model, vision, and strategy as well as its critical success factors. One needs to know the leadership philosophy, values, and desired culture, whether or not it is written into a formal document. The following questions may be helpful in defining this philosophy:

- Is the organization focused on broad markets or specific niches or market segments?
- Is the core competence of the company stronger in creating innovative solutions to meet customer's needs or in providing low-cost, efficient services to customers?
- Is growth achieved through organic, market expansion or through acquisitions, joint ventures, and business networks?

FIGURE 3.1   Defining the Total Reward strategy

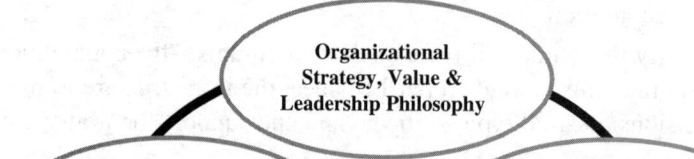

- Do the firm's leaders have a particular philosophy, values, and operating principles by which they lead the organization, and seek to create its position in the marketplace?

- Is the organization facing pressures to adapt to changing market conditions or transform itself into a different business model or marketing strategy?

Examine the Organizational Structure *plus* its Guiding Principles

The response to these questions provides the context and frames the challenges facing the organization from both a talent management and performance perspective. This information should provide insights on why the organization is structured and operates as it does, as well as the types of rewards that will be most effective in supporting the long-term strategy of the organization.

The next stage is to articulate how the firm is organized to implement the strategy and operate within the constructs of the firm's values and leadership philosophy. This goes beyond examining the structure of the organization (i.e., who reports to whom), and identifies the guiding principles by which the organization functions.

Questions that may be important to understand this stage are:

- Is the company organized around markets (i.e., geographic, industry, or customers), functions (i.e., sales, operations, engineering, etc.) or independent business units? Why?

- Does the culture of the organization emphasize collaboration and teamwork or individual initiative and accountability? Does it emphasize short-term, concrete results or long-term development? Does it foster transactions or long-term relationships? How and why?

- Are decisions made in a highly centralized, well-controlled manner, in a highly decentralized, entrepreneurial manner, or in a cross-functional, collaborative manner? Are there differences in how specific types of decisions are made (e.g., financial, operational, customer, capital investment, etc.)? Why?

This information is important to forming a reward strategy because it defines how much flexibility various reward programs will foster as well as the process for making decisions related to goal setting, performance assessments, staffing levels, and hiring agreements.

Determine Employee Groups with Unique Reward Requirements

The third stage is then to define the groups of employees where reward policies or programs should be distinct or specifically tailored to unique requirements. These groups may be by business unit, function (e.g., sales, engineering, manufacturing, corporate services), level (e.g., executives, senior management, managers and supervisors, professional and technical contributors, administrative and operational employees), or where "special attention" is needed (e.g., high potentials, key contributors, technical/product specialists, diversity groups, recent acquisition). By identifying specific groups of employees and understanding what they may want or need as well as what the organization needs from them, the reward strategy becomes more pragmatic and grounded in the realities of the organization.

Create Specific Reward Policies

The next stage is to identify the specific reward policies, programs (or systems) and practices the organization will employ to achieve short- and long-term requirements. While this can be defined for specific groups (based on the previous stage), it can also be framed for the entire organization. We have found that it is useful to categorize reward programs according to dimensions that reflect their inherent function and impact. To be more specific, there are reward programs that are:

- Available to virtually everyone because they are employed by the organization (or for a specific level or group within the organization). These programs provide a foundation for the employment relationship.

- Based on performance or meeting other requirements of individuals or groups to which they belong. In these types of programs not everyone receives these rewards, and the amount depends on many factors related to the design of the specifications of the particular policy or program.

   Furthermore, there are programs that are:

- clearly compensation based (e.g., salaries, variable cash compensation, equity based plans, etc.), and

- meet the personal needs of individuals (e.g., employee benefits, services, recognition award programs, promotions, career opportunities, training and development, etc.).

These two sets of dimensions provide a simple framework for understanding and organizing reward programs according to their primary function or inherent purpose. Figure 3.2 shows this framework and illustrates the types of reward programs that correspond to these dimensions.[2]

As the organization conducts its own "inventory" of reward programs using this framework, it creates a portfolio of rewards that can be analyzed and refined to specific employee groups. People within an organization often have different needs and values; this "portfolio approach" enables the organization to target specific programs to address the unique needs and expectations of population segments within their organization, similar to how a company targets products and services to specific market segments. Using this framework, the organization can develop a strategy that is consistent with its strategic objectives and the requirements it has for key groups within the organization.

FIGURE 3.2 Compensation strategy and performance reward programs

	Foundation Programs:	*Performance Rewards:*
Total Compensation	**SALARY & WAGES** • Job or market based pay • Competency based pay • Salary ranges/Broad bands • Career path based pay • Geographic differentials • Merit/Market increases	**CASH & EQUITY BASED VARIABLE PAY** • Individual variable pay • Team/unit variable pay • Company profit sharing • Stock options/restricted • Long-term cash or phantom share plans
Workplace Opportunities	**EMPLOYEE BENEFITS & SERVICES** • Health and life insurance • Retirement and investment • Disability and long-term care • Training and education • Company events/parties • Employee discounts/services	**DEVELOPMENT & RECOGNITION** • Public/private recognition • Verbal/informal recognition • Personal item rewards • Special award bonuses ($) • Promotions • Professional development

Develop the Reward Strategy

Once the organization has identified its formal and primary informal reward programs and practices, the final stage is to address several important questions to develop the reward strategy.

1. What current programs is the organization primarily using? Which ones are most important to the overall organization and why?

2. How competitive are these programs in the external marketplace for talent? Where does the company need to lead or be distinctive in the market and where does it need to follow or meet basic levels? Why?

3. Which of these programs are the most important to specific groups of employees and why?

4. Where (among the types of programs or services) does the organization spend the most money? Where does it spend the most time and effort, and why?

5. Which of these programs are the most and least effective in supporting the mission, strategy and culture of the organization? Why?

Based on this information and insights, the company can develop a strategically based Total Rewards framework that is consistent with its core mission, business, and strategy. The statement of requirements for each program (or type of program) should include the following elements:

- The purpose and key objectives of the specific reward program

- The most important requirements for these programs to be successful

- The marketplace and desired position the program needs to achieve in order to be meaningful to the relevant individuals

- How these programs will directly support the needs of the organization and the individual.

These strategy statements not only define the purpose and requirements for specific programs, they reinforce the universal principles necessary for achieving alignment with a firm's core strategy and leadership philosophy. Therefore, the corporate philosophy captures the primary themes that are important to the entire enterprise, while the reward strategy defines the requirements for key programs. The effective implementation of its policies, programs, and practices will significantly strengthen the firm's competitive advantage and market leadership.

Consider another example from a rapidly growing medical devices company:

> The purpose of our total reward programs and practices is to provide the company with strong competitive advantages to attract, retain and effectively utilize the talent we need to achieve sustained market leadership.

The primary principles for all our reward programs are to:

- Strengthen our ability to drive desired business results

- Support the growth of our business globally

- Expand the capabilities of our people, from both attraction of new talent and developing current talent, to sustain high performance

- Make effective decisions in utilize our people and our resources to the benefit of the company, the people we employ and the people we serve.

This company went on to define the primary purpose of each category of rewards as follows:

- **Base Pay Programs:** They provide the structure and pay guidelines for the company to attract, retain and reinforce the development of personal capabilities. The pay structure will enable us to be competitive with the median of our key market, both globally and locally, where the grade level reflects one's job scope and responsibilities and the pay range reflects the external market for talent. Pay increases are based on both the growth of responsibilities and competencies and the demonstration of these practices in what and how results are achieved.

■ **Variable Pay Programs:** We will utilize a weighted blend of individual, team and key business unit goals to provide clear performance expectations, encourage achievement and reward results. Our cash-based variable pay will focus on those results that provide critical contributions to and achievement of key annual business objectives tied to the corporation's overall objectives; our equity-based awards will reward those who make significant contributions to results that build the long-term value of the corporation—to our shareholders and our customers.

■ **Employee Benefits and Services:** These are a variety of programs, services and opportunities for individuals that provide needed security to one's personal obligations and ability to receive highly valued benefits at a lower cost because of our combined participation. Because we as a company value our differences, individuals will have the greatest flexibility possible in selecting those that are most meaningful and important to oneself and one's family.

■ **Performance Recognition:** In order to recognize individuals and teams who clearly made a difference to our customers and to our organization, we offer a wide variety of formal and support for informal appreciation programs. While these are often defined by the particular business unit within the company and provide awards that are personally meaningful to the individual, they each reinforce important values of the company—collaboration, commitment, responsiveness, integrity, respect, and performance.

The company uses the philosophy and principles implied by these descriptions as the framework for designing, managing and communicating their reward programs.

APPLYING THE TOTAL REWARD STRATEGY

A Total Rewards strategy statement works because it enables the organization to make better decisions and focus actions on those areas that create a sustained competitive advantage. It facilitates an assessment of current programs and practices, and identifies where the organization may need to invest resources. So, the reward strategy goes beyond just defining compensation in reference to an external marketplace and strategically positions these programs. For many organizations "how" programs work is often more important than "how much" (in terms of dollars) they provide to employees. Understanding the marketplace and your competitive position is critical to a sound reward strategy.

Once this statement of philosophy and strategy has been defined and applied to existing programs, the challenge of communication will need to be addressed. There are several applications for this information:

■ For meeting SEC *disclosure requirements* for executive compensation, one should select those statements that communicate key messages to the broad audience of investors, employees, and interested parties.

- For *recruiting*, key messages can again be selected and integrated into the materials and initiatives to attract desired talent to the organization; they should support the firm's overall staffing plans and initiatives.

- For *retention* of critical talent, this process has identified the specific groups, their needs as well as the organization's requirements, and the reward strategy can now effectively assesses whether it provides sufficient rewards and opportunities to retain these individuals. The company can create mechanisms to cost-effectively retain this talent.

- For *performance*, the reward strategy can identify the performance metrics that can and should be integrated with reward programs for specific groups of employees—executives, sales, operational, and service employees. Through the application of the guidelines, principles, and messages of the reward strategy, the organization gains a return on its investment in both the development of these statements and the dollars invested through its specific performance-based compensation, benefits and rewards.

The process and the outcomes should move an organization to a new level in its understanding, use, and value received from its reward programs. Rather than imitating what other firms have done in the past, or providing superficial statements that ultimately are not translated into decisions or actions (thereby undermining leadership credibility), a strong reward strategy shapes decisions. This will strengthen the effectiveness of these programs and help build a new, more significant, and important relationship between an organization and its people. By so doing, the organization is more capable of meeting the challenges of a complex marketplace and fulfilling its mission. It is just that simple, and that important.

END NOTES

1. IBM SEC Filing 14A, 2006.

2. Thomas B. Wilson, *Innovative Reward Systems for the Changing Workplace*, 2nd edn, New York: McGraw–Hill, 2003.

THREE TRENDS SHAPING THE FUTURE OF COMPENSATION AND HUMAN RESOURCES

Allan Schweyer, President and Executive Director

The Human Capital Institute

I**N 1798, THOMAS MALTHUS WROTE:** "Population, when unchecked, increases in a geometrical ratio." Essentially, he warned that the population of the world would soon outstrip the planet's capacity to sustain it.[1] Ironically, despite population growth of more than 600 percent since then, concern has recently shifted to too little population growth in much of the world.

Malthus's grim predictions have not materialized because among the population there has always been a talented core that, through the application of human ingenuity, has so far overcome our major challenges to survival. Scarce talent has similarly driven the growth of our economies and businesses. Up until the very recent past, the talented few, combined with plentiful and cheap labor, were sufficient to power our economies and prosperity.

Today, despite global population growth nearly as steep as it has ever been,[2] the demand for talent has reached pandemic levels across much of the world. There is an obvious but important distinction between the thin layer of worldwide talent that can contribute to our increasingly complex, global economy and what is commonly referred to as "labor."

The global market for competent, skilled workers is getting tighter; while at the same time the developed world is shedding as much of the repetitive, "low-end" work as it can. All the while, we raise the bar for talent unrelentingly. In 2000, Thomas Homer-Dixon warned in his thought-provoking book, *The Ingenuity Gap*, "When things happen faster, in greater numbers, and with greater interactive complexity, we need more ingenuity to make the right decisions at the right time."[3]

If education can be used as a proxy for talent, albeit an imperfect one, the situation is dire and worsening. Between May 2006 and April 2007, unemployment among four-year college graduates in the United States averaged just over 1.8 percent,[4] meaning essentially that anyone in the United States with a college degree who wanted a job, had one. Even during the last U.S. recession, roughly between 2001 and 2004, unemployment in this group never went above 4 percent, which is the rate economists consider as full employment.

As economies, business, social problems, science, and health and security issues become more complex, and as our knowledge and information society becomes more globally integrated and sophisticated, ever greater skills and knowledge are required and in larger numbers. Add to this the demographic realities of an aging workforce nearly everywhere in the world, and demand that will continue to come out of developing economies like China and India, and we have the ingredients for a talent crisis.

Without a doubt, organizations that can develop, attract, mobilize, and retain talent will be the winners of the future, and the talent management executives and teams that lead these efforts will be among the most important and strategic parts of any organization. The question then, is what are organizations and the human resources profession in general doing about it?

THREE CRITICAL TRENDS

The human-resources trade long ago proved itself, at best, a necessary evil—and at worst, a dark bureaucratic force that blindly enforces nonsensical rules, resists creativity, and impedes constructive change . . . it is a career graveyard for people who can't make it in other parts of the business. (Keith Hammonds, from "Why We Hate HR," *Fast Company* magazine, August 2005)

Where is HR? Has the profession taken advantage of the tremendous opportunity that our nascent "Age of Talent" presents? As the questions surrounding talent, skills, successors, performance, and leadership consume more corporate board and "C" suite time, in what direction will the HR profession evolve? There are really just two possibilities—up or out. But which outcome is the more likely?

A good place to start is with the shifts and trends that are likely to shape the workplace in the coming years. The ways in which HR anticipates and responds to these changes will largely determine its future. The first of these trends is demographics. The United Nations cites the aging workforce globally as among the three great challenges facing the world today. Nations in Europe and Asia have already begun the painful process of depopulation, and from the United States to China, the fastest growing segment of the population is the over-50 cohort.

But it is not just an aging workforce that is presenting new challenges; the workforce is being transformed through rapid changes in its makeup—more women, more visible and ethnic minorities, more generations in the workforce, and more disparate types of workers—from contingent to virtual. This trend is accelerating faster than most organizations can respond.

The third sweeping trend that will change the business landscape, and the world, is continued and faster-paced globalization. The threats and opportunities it poses to developed world economies and business are as yet barely understood. For Western workforces, globalization accelerates the imperative for innovation, creativity, and productivity. For stewards of talent, it demands a deeper understanding of international economics, laws, and culture as well as a range of new expertise in issues as esoteric as "captive" vs "third-party" offshoring.

These and other forces will shape the evolution of the HR profession, but HR executives must also shape the trends. A daunting set of skills and knowledge will be required for success. The modern talent management (TM) executive will be multidisciplinary: an economist, demographer, strategist, psychologist, sociologist, salesperson, speaker, leader, coach, consultant, and among the organization's most knowledgeable authority on globalization, outsourcing and offshoring, sustainability, corporate social responsibility, talent-related technologies, finance, corporate governance, and measurement. Of course, he or she must also be a master of the organization's business and its industry. This does not sound much like HR and it is not. It is a tall order for anyone, but exciting at the same time. An executive who can demonstrate these competencies will almost certainly take a well-earned position beside the CEO and will be on a par with any senior executive. But advancement is not the point. Increasingly, winning organizations will require world class TM executives. The best from other parts of the business need to be drawn into these ranks and this transformation must come soon.

Trend 1: Demographics

Every day in the United States, 10,000 baby boomers turn 55. By the end of this decade, two experienced workers will leave the U.S. workforce for every inexperienced young one that joins. This is significant in more ways than one. Since the turn of the twentieth century, each new generation of workers has brought more "human capital" to their employers (and hence, more productivity) than the generation of workers exiting the workforce—*despite* the imbalance in work experience. This is no longer true. Mass access to higher education began in the 1960s in North America and has continued ever since. Unfortunately, today's 25-year-old male is only marginally better educated than his predecessor of the 1960s and 1970s. Today's generation of workers brings roughly the same level of education as the baby boom generation. Yet the early boomers are leaving with 30–40 years experience, a legendary work ethic, and incredible reservoirs of knowledge.

This knowledge deficit could not come at a worse time. Some 85 percent of jobs today require education beyond high school compared with just 61 percent fifteen years ago. The trend is only accelerating, yet in the United States today, less than 70 percent of students graduate high school on time and many who graduate are the beneficiaries of exaggerated grades and low expectations such that they require remedial studies before they can enter university-level courses. As of 2007, only 38 percent of Americans held at least a two-year degree; worse, it is estimated that 60 percent of the jobs in North America already require skills possessed by only 20 percent of the population.

> The greatest HR challenge of the coming decades will be to enhance workforce productivity as the availability of skilled workers declines. (Watson Wyatt, 2006)

To underscore the importance of workforce productivity gains, especially in an era that promises perpetual talent shortages, consider that since World War II, the U.S. economy has grown eightfold while the labor force has only grown 2–2.5 times. This means that the average worker is about four times as productive now as they were in 1946. This is partly due to technology but is in greater part due to an increasingly better educated workforce. If the next generation of retirees is replaced by a smaller, less productive cohort, the results will be doubly grave.

Demographically, the United States is in a much better position through 2030 than other Western nations. The U.S. birthrate, in part due to recent immigrants from the south, is at near-replacement rates (i.e., there are enough people being born to replace those dying), compared with Canada and Europe, where the birthrate is far below replacement rates.

However, the United States is, arguably, in the midst of an education crisis, not only at the primary and secondary levels but also in the university and college systems. As noted above, dropout rates are increasing, high school students opting for math and science tracks are decreasing, and many schools themselves are inflating grades, passing almost everyone and producing legions of graduates who are functionally innumerate and illiterate.

Quality post-secondary education remains America's greatest educational advantage, but today some colleges and universities are complicit in catering to the lowest denominator. Classes and tests are dumbed down and passing grades are doled out to anyone who complains. Students who do not show up for classes are rarely censored. Obviously this trend produces graduates without the knowledge, skills, abilities, or discipline to contribute in the modern workplace.

In the past, North America has made up for labor and talent shortfalls by increasing immigration. The United States and Canada are still magnets for people from all over the world and neither has lost the ability to attract the best and the brightest. But this advantage is slipping away quickly. Today's stricter immigration laws in the United States are making it more difficult for firms to bring in foreign skilled workers. Moreover, as the Indian and Chinese economies grow (at three or four times the rate of Western economies), more and better opportunities arise in those countries. Far fewer graduates of the famous Indian Institutes of Technology or their equivalents in China are interested in relocating to the West today and the numbers will only diminish. Moreover, according to experts like Richard Florida and David Heenan, thousands of Indian and Chinese entrepreneurs who built their companies and fortunes in the West in the 1990s, are returning home to launch creative new initiatives there.[5]

Whereas the United States had few competitors for global skilled talent in the past, today demographics have changed the game entirely. Many countries are already experiencing the turmoil of shrinking workforces. For Russia, Japan, Italy, and Spain the wrenching experience of depopulation has begun or will begin by the end of the decade.[6] For them, attracting young, skilled workers is a matter of national urgency. Much of Western and Eastern Europe face only a slightly milder problem. The competition for talent, wherever it resides, will intensify. The United States will be but one competitor. According to recent research conducted by the Human Capital Institute, sourcing and attracting talent remains the greatest challenge faced by HR (see Figure 4.1). HR executives expect this to continue over the coming three years at a minimum (see Figure 4.2).

Global workforce growth, even among developing countries, is already or will soon be in decline. By 2012, China's workforce, which has grown for centuries, will start to reverse. As Figure 4.3 reveals, today only 22 percent of the Chinese population is aged 50 or more. By 2030, that number will jump to 37 percent and by 2050 to 45 percent.

Even more worrisome, in the short term, is the steep decline in worldwide working-age population—a truly bleak picture among developed countries. Combined, the Western economies, including Japan, will see working-age population reductions of more than half. In the developing world, only a few countries— Brazil, India, some Northern African nations (sub-Saharan African populations are held in check by the AIDS epidemic), and some small countries in the Middle East—will register working age population gains through 2025. By 2050, even India will be an aging society if current trends hold.

The final front in this "perfect storm" is the global, inexorable demand for higher skilled, better educated talent. As organizations and nations rush to become

FIGURE 4.1   Talent attraction and sourcing remain the number one current challenge of HR

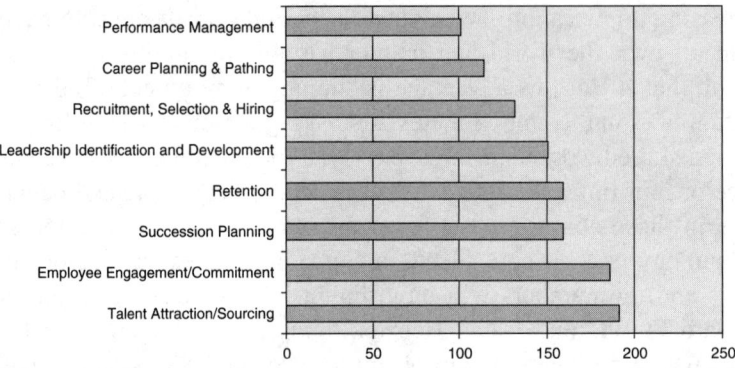

In your organization, which of the following areas represent your
three greatest current challenges? (Top 8)

Source: (Human Capital Institute/Vurv Technologies, October 2007;[7] N=732)

more creative and innovative (so that they can maintain their higher wages and better standards of living), the demand for talent capable of producing in the global economy is placed under greater and greater stress. Billions of people may reside in Asia and Africa, but the percentage capable of working for a firm that operates in the global economy is tiny. Even university graduates in China, India, and Eastern Europe are, in most cases, under-equipped upon graduation to work in the knowledge economy. Simply put, this means that they are not in the global talent pool.

FIGURE 4.2   Specific skills and talent shortages represent a challenge

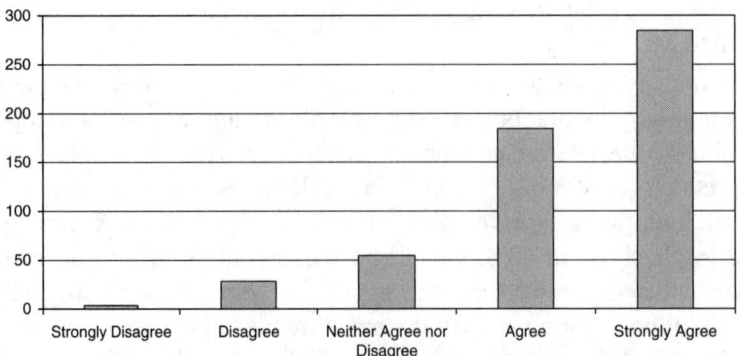

Source: (Human Capital Institute/Vurv Technologies, October 2007;[8] N=732)

FIGURE 4.3   Asia Pacific's demographic transformation: percentage of population aged 50 and above

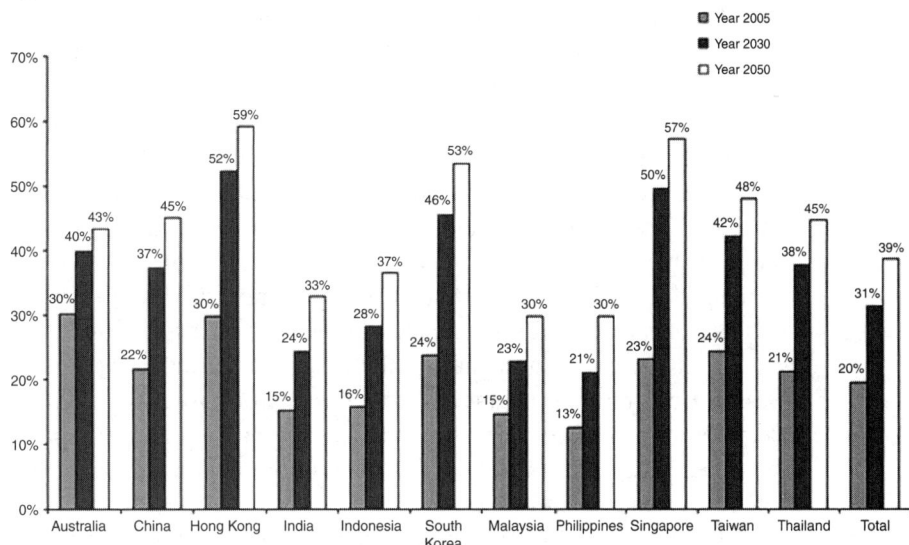

McKinsey estimates that, over the next 10–15 years, China alone will require 75,000 leaders who can manage in global environments; today there are fewer than 5,000. In India, the situation is similar. In mid 2007, *Business Week Magazine* reported that fewer than 8 million of that country's 200 million students make it through high school and even fewer finish college. The article quotes NASSCOM (India's National Association of Software & Services Companies) as stating: "At the nation's 1,200 technical colleges, just 400,000 engineers graduate each year. Among those, only a fourth has the skills to immediately start work at a multinational or major Indian IT firm."[9] Mckinsey has projected that, by this year, 2008, India will not be able to meet its own domestic demand for engineers, let alone supply the West as it has been doing for decades.

To summarize, we are facing everything from declines in workforce growth to outright depopulation in Western nations. At the same time, the young workforce replacing the first waves of baby boomer retirees brings less human capital to the table and therefore (at least theoretically) less productivity to the workforce. Foreign skilled talent, which has been so critical in building the North American economy, is increasingly less likely to emigrate for work. Worse, many thousands of highly skilled and entrepreneurial members of the Indian and Chinese diasporas have decamped and are now applying their creativity and innovations in their countries of origin. For the mobile and virtual global workforce, competition will be intense from all corners of the developed and less developed worlds. Already, Poland, for example, is recruiting Asian workers to replace the million-plus young workers who have left that country (mainly for Western Europe) since the fall of the Soviet Union.

The problems above are not insurmountable. However, like the trends described in the next two sections, global demographics represent a serious challenge. The associated problems will almost certainly lead to economic disruption in some nations and the outright demise of thousands of organizations worldwide. To some degree, the economic laws of demand and supply will correct for part of the problem. Smaller working age populations normally result in less demand for goods and services. Obviously, in some sectors, health care for example, steady growth and demand are likely for decades to come. Inevitably, there will also be recessions in the coming decades. These will offer temporary relief, though the cure, in this case, is perhaps worse than the disease, especially where lack of talent might actually be the cause of prolonged recessions in the future, leading to gradually lower standards of living.

Organizations and governments cannot take a laissez-faire attitude toward the aging population phenomena nor the other demographic issues described above. So what can be done? First and foremost, efforts to encourage older workers to delay retirement must be made. This will have a significant impact if even only a small percentage of the baby boom generation remains in the workforce into their late sixties and seventies.

Unprecedented consumer debt, particularly in the United States, will provide part of the solution—some people will simply have to work longer. For the majority, however, incentives and creative, flexible work options, including phased retirement schemes, will be required.

But organizations must also resign themselves to the fact that they will not have as much talent as they would like. This means investing in labor-saving technologies, more impactful and targeted training, and better management to engage the workforce. As has always been the case, any successful measure to increase workforce productivity will lead to immediate (if not sustained) competitive advantage. Outsourcing and off-shoring will almost certainly accelerate and those organizations that embrace it early and gain experience and deep relationships in developing countries will have the advantage. As will be discussed in more detail below, workforce and succession planning will also take on a new urgency and importance.

Trend 2: Diversity

Diversity used to mean quotas and targets; it used to center on compliance and focus on gender, race, and ethnicity. Today, diversity is a competitive advantage; it is about inclusiveness as opposed to tolerance and affirmative action. It includes most of the population in the sense that it recognizes the differences in talent— from age to lifestyle and from contingent to traditional.

In 2004, Dr Richard Florida unveiled extensive research that compared thriving cities in the United States to those that are stagnant or in decline. Among his findings were that successful cities, including Boston, San Francisco, and Austin, have one consistent trait in common—they tend to be more open and more tolerant of talented individuals who are not part of the mainstream culture for whatever reason. Among Florida's more celebrated work is his "Gay index." By overlaying statistics on the size of the gay population in cities across the United States with data, including unemployment statistics, GDP per capita, and growth, he was able to show a high correlation between cities with larger than average gay populations and success on each of his measures. Florida's point is not that we should deliberately source and hire gay workers, but that talented people, who are different in a variety of ways are drawn to regions and workplaces that are inclusive and that value a person for the skills and talent they bring rather than whether they conform.

It is clear is that the "traditional" North American workforce, whether that means white male or full-time, "on-premises," is only a memory today. Already, more than a quarter of the U.S. workforce in non-white and almost half is female. By 2050, almost half the U.S. workforce will be racial minorities. What this means for employers is that almost all workforce growth in the United States between now and 2050 will be among the diverse, non-white population. For many sectors, including retail and hospitality, the lack of a diversity strategy is already suicidal. Moreover, the "contingent" or alternative workforce, made up of contract, temporary, remote and part-time workers, already accounts for more than 35 percent of the U.S. workforce and is growing at five times the rate of the traditional workforce.

While "attracting, retaining and managing a more diverse workforce" is considered a significant challenge by almost 70 percent of the 560 respondents to the Human Capital Institute's 2007 study on the state of HR transformation, it is not ranked among the top five challenges of today, nor over the next three years (see Figure 4.4).

Increasingly, diversity is also about the young, mid-career, Boomer and senior generations. We have always had a multigenerational workforce but, until recently, we have not recognized the importance and advantages of segmenting it and adjusting our messages, benefits, and motivators to suit groups that are driven by clearly different factors.

Of course the wise talent manager takes diversity to its ultimate advantage. Today, with the capabilities technology brings and by engaging every manager and supervisor as a talent manager, the work experience can be customized and maximized for each and every worker on a one-to-one basis. This goes beyond individual learning plans and individual performance goals to include individualized retention and engagement initiatives, customized total rewards packages and flexible work arrangements that can maximize the performance and commitment of every contributor.

In many ways, and certainly compared to the more complex demographic challenges outlined above, diversity can be seen as the "low hanging fruit" of talent management issues in the coming years. After all, the main requirement in seizing the opportunity is in understanding the benefits of an inclusive, welcoming culture. These include the advantages of disparate thinking, which has been shown

FIGURE 4.4   Diversity not yet considered a top five challenge (ranked 6 of 18 challenges)

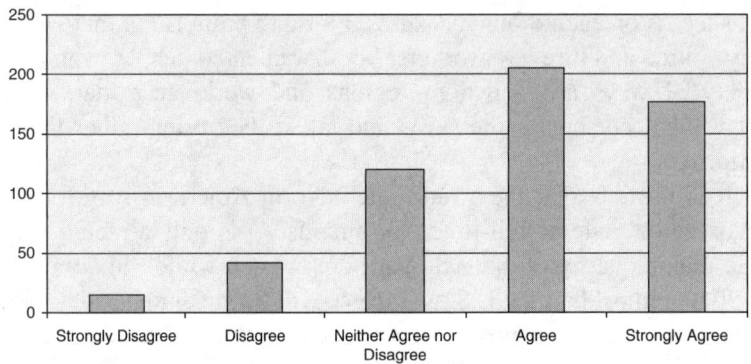

Attracting, retaining and managing a more diverse workforce will be a
significant challenge over the next three years

Source: (Human Capital Institute/Vurv Technologies, October 2007[10])

to foster more creativity and lead to faster innovation; the advantage of reflecting customer diversity in the workforce; and the advantages in recruiting that come from being known as a great place to work for minorities. Each is collectively worth fortunes to organizations. The solution goes far beyond a campaign of cross-cultural training, however. Diversity for competitive advantage must be quickly embraced by companies today so that antiquated attitudes are changed and the new, inclusive workforce can emerge.

Trend 3: Globalization

As hackneyed as the term has become, globalization cannot be ignored as a key trend that will continue to change everything. Trade, economies, standards of living, peace, conflict, health, education, everything is impacted. Among the most publicized disruptions caused by globalization to date is the impact on the work-force. In the 1980s and 1990s globalization resulted in the loss of millions of manufacturing jobs in the West. At the end of the last century, the Internet, Y2K, and the dot-com bust contributed to the emergence of the offshore services industry. Suddenly, white collar jobs started moving from the West to India and Eastern Europe. Despite the fact that net job losses have so far been very modest (relative to those lost in manufacturing), the debate has been heated. Yet good or bad, the process of globalization is unlikely to stop or even slow. Therefore, most organizations are compelled to factor globalization into their strategies.

In late 2006, the Human Capital Institute (HCI) and Development Dimensions (DDI) conducted a survey involving more than 750 talent management leaders. The study revealed that a strong majority foresee, over the next three years, that trade of knowledge and intellectual capital (86 percent) and goods and services (85 percent) across countries will increase. They also see that competition for talent with the skills needed to work across borders will grow fiercer (91 percent).[11]

> Managers will be more virtual and remote. They will have to adapt to an ever-changing workforce . . . Outsourcing will continue to increase as will the need for managers to work in a global setting and be flexible enough to handle any situation. (Survey Respondent)

Old mindsets will not succeed in the global economy. Successful business leaders must move out of their domestic comfort zones and into a more international or worldly way of thinking. Ultimately, a "global" mindset is necessary. Peter Senge, in his groundbreaking work *The Fifth Discipline*, defines mindsets as "deeply ingrained assumptions, generalizations, or even pictures or images that influence how we understand."[12] Successful global managers broaden their mindset such that they look at a business, an industry or a culture from a global perspective. They can see across multiple geographies and perspectives to focus on the commonalities rather than the differences. Top-performing global managers set themselves apart with the ability to keep the entire worldwide business opportunity in mind.

Part of the success in making the realities of globalization an advantage to an organization in the West, is leveraging a virtual workforce. As the competition for critical talent heats up, organizations must rethink the ways in which they attract, acquire, develop, manage, and deploy talent. To begin, one should identify the segments of the workforce that will drive current and future growth and what components of their work need to be done on-site. Given today's economic and demographic realities, more and more talent will be tapped remotely.

The world continues to shrink with greater advancements in technology, while expanding as new business locations and talent pools become viable. The global skilled-labor pool has more than doubled in size in the last 15 years and continues to grow rapidly, though not at a pace fast enough to meet growing demand. The competition for global talent will require organizations to build high-performing *virtual* teams, since moving workers around the world is becoming less practical and less desirable for workers and organizations alike.

Of course, for remote workforce management to succeed, leaders must have the ability to navigate and exploit the complexities of a global business environment. As a starting point, they should understand the capabilities required of global managers. Companies should then select candidates with these competencies while developing existing managers to succeed in a virtual global environment. Managers need to monitor and manage the performance of the remote workforce by instituting simple but effective measurements and processes that are adapted for local and global conditions.

Organizations are also faced with making sure they have the right quality and quantity of global leadership talent. Leaders who are effective when working within the confines of their home country will not necessarily be effective when they have to lead across borders. Underscoring this point is a 2005 Conference Board study in which 97 percent of respondents indicated that general leadership skills are transferable into a global context, but only 50 percent were confident that leaders successful in one setting or region would be equally successful in another.

The impact of globalization will continue to be felt in ways that are impossible to predict. The only certainty is that it will not stop and is likely to accelerate as more economic power shifts east and south. Savvy organizations will see opportunity as more of the world's population becomes consumers of goods and services. To succeed, however, attitudes, outlooks, and mindsets must be adjusted in most organizations, global leaders must be acquired and/or developed and remote, virtual teams must be leveraged, either through outsourcing or by developing a "captive" workforce overseas. Moreover, HR must get involved in the organization's global strategy, particularly where it impacts the workforce. As Figure 4.5 attests, however, HR still remains partially or fully on the sidelines in the majority of organizations.

THE NEW ROLE OF THE HR LEADER

Talent management is distinct from human resources, in part because it is the responsibility of leaders across the organization rather than a discipline that can or should reside in just one department. In May 2006, a report from the Economist Intelligence Unit (EIU) and DDI suggested that CEOs from across industries and throughout much of the world are strong believers in taking direct, personal leadership in recruiting, mentoring, succession planning, talent development, performance management, and retention. Indeed, seven out of twenty CEOs

FIGURE 4.5   HR involvement in global talent management

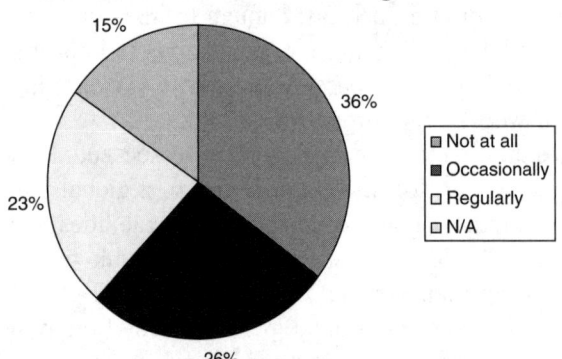

Source: (Human Capital Institute/Vurv Technologies, October 2007[13])

interviewed for the report said they spend more than half of their time on talent management compared with only four who reported spending less than one-fifth of their time in those pursuits.

CEOs and boards of public companies are paying attention to talent these days for two main reasons. First, there is little room otherwise to differentiate from their competitors. Over the past several decades, industry has been successful in ironing out many of the wrinkles in bringing products and services to market. Production efficiencies and supply chain management combined with globalization have increased competition and reduced margins for most products and many services. The result is that products and processes that were once points of differentiation are now often indistinguishable from supplier to supplier. Even the most advanced products quickly become commodities today unless they offer a design or creative appeal beyond their practical purpose or functionality. Today, intangibles, including constant reinvention, innovation, design creativity, marketing prowess, and reputation (through human talent) form the key sustainable advantage for knowledge economy organizations.

Investors and shareholders constitute the second driver. They too have become aware of the importance of hiring and keeping top performers and of maintaining solid succession plans for leaders and those in other critical positions. In 2007, the EIU reported that "human capital risks," related to "loss of key personnel, skills shortages, and succession issues" had become the number one risk to global business operations.[14] Tighter governance rules in many countries mean that boards of directors and CEOs are held responsible for their decisions affecting the health and sustainability of their firms (much of which today rest on the quality and depth of talent). Succession and workforce planning, especially, are areas in which leaders must focus and demonstrate due diligence.

For HR leaders, this is very good news. All 20 CEOs referenced in the EIU/DDI study believe that HR should be responsible for "executing talent management strategy, being custodians of the talent management process and [providing] guidance and fresh thinking about talent management programs." Nineteen of twenty said that their head of HR is part of their "inner circle" of executives, a key person they rely on to help differentiate the firm on the basis of superior workforce strategy. Indeed, HCI's own poll of over 600 HR managers and executives in August 2007 revealed that more than two-thirds of heads of HR report directly to the CEO.[15]

This is a new and welcome development. HR is finally making headway in becoming a "strategic partner." Traditional HR remains vital, but after decades of hard work and progress, most organizations can now rely on and take for granted efficient and effective processes for payroll and benefits administration. Traditional HR has, in a sense, been a victim of its own success in creating repeatable, dependable administrative processes. Today, most firms outsource payroll and benefits administration and a growing number are opting to outsource HR in its entirety. One potential benefit is that this should make room for internal centers of excellence in talent management.

However, to the extent that HR has succeeded in administration, it has generally failed thus far at "strategy." Now that CEOs are demanding workforce strategies, including innovative ways to compete—*for and through*—superior talent, the pressure is on HR leaders to perform like their finance, IT, marketing, and operations counterparts, who, unlike HR, have for years aligned and integrated their work with the highest corporate goals and objectives. A "transformation" is necessary but most HR leaders and non-HR leaders alike agree that generally the profession has not progressed as rapidly as needed. Figure 4.6 demonstrates a disappointing assessment of HR leaders' skills and knowledge across a range of eight talent and general management areas.

The trends outlined above, along with new attitudes among senior executives, present a tremendous opportunity for HR leaders. This is a golden opportunity for HR to move up the organizational and professional ladder. Clearly, though, HR must change in order to respond to the business challenges confronting organizations today. The art of human resources must quickly evolve into the art and science of human capital management (HCM), or talent management. HR executives with their eyes on a bigger role in the business agree that the reputation of HR is so poor today that the profession must be re-branded.

For those involved in managing talent for competitive advantage, new titles and categories are vital. We should begin seeing more 'C' level human capital and talent management professionals heading highly skilled, business-focused teams in the coming years—categories that began emerging in the late 1990s when the primacy of talent in organizations became widely understood for the first time. HR leaders should start this process by first gaining a solid understanding of their

FIGURE 4.6   All respondents (HR and non-HR) assessed HR leaders in their organization as "expert" less than 25 percent of the time

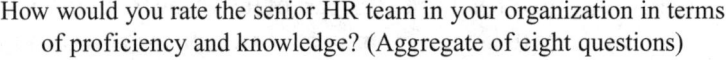

How would you rate the senior HR team in your organization in terms of proficiency and knowledge? (Aggregate of eight questions)

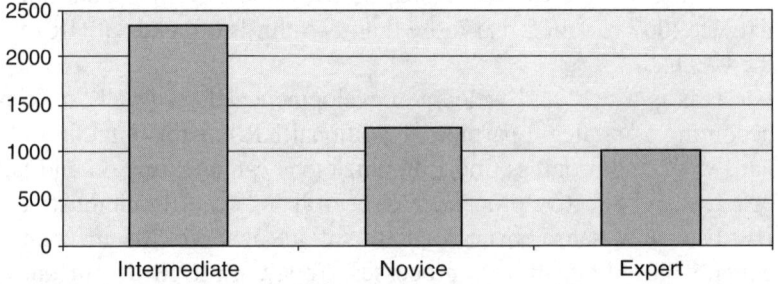

Source: (Human Capital Institute/Vurv Technologies, October 2007[16])

organization's business and then aligning their talent management initiatives toward achieving those goals.

Beyond the name, hardcore change and new skill sets are needed. The modern TM executive must be able to speak in financial terms about the workforce. They must understand the organization's current complement of skills and competencies as well as external local, national, and international workforce demographics. They must be able to advise the "C" suite and the board on whether it makes sense to buy, develop, or borrow talent, and this advice must be presented in financial terms. TM executives must be able to forecast workforce needs aligned with corporate goals, capabilities, and objectives.

The modern TM executive is aware that HR is no longer a one-to-many exercise; that there is no one-size-fits-all benefit program, for example. Recruitment, development, performance management, and retention will increasingly be ongoing, one-to-one activities, and highly differentiated for the greatest possible impact. Thus, traditional "HR," most often characterized by generic programs, is quickly giving way to the more sophisticated methods of talent management. In order for this to succeed, however, TM executives must enlist the support and active involvement of managers and leaders from all parts of the business.

Another critical skill for today's TM executive is in understanding measurement, data, and return on investment (ROI) analysis. Organizations have gone through the discipline of creating measurable processes—a science—around the manufacturing and quality control fields. Unfortunately, this rigor has not yet been applied to the field of human resources.

"The revolution in quality control and manufacturing techniques that has taken place in the last fifteen years was data-driven and systems-driven and statistical-process-control-driven. The U.S. economy has benefited incredibly over the last fifteen years . . . by seriously embracing the science of manufacturing and quality control."[17] When Andy Grove, Chairman and Founder of Intel said these words in a Harvard Business School Press interview in 2003, he was talking about general business strategy and execution.

Jeffrey Pfeffer, a professor of organizational behavior at Stanford University, calls the data-driven approach "Evidence-Based Management." He strongly advocates its application in the field of human capital management. In his book, *Dangerous Half-Truths & Total Nonsense*, Pfeffer says:

> There is compelling evidence that when companies use HR best practices based on the best research, they trump the competition. These findings are replicable in industry after industry, from automobiles to textiles, to computer software to baseball. Yet many companies still use inferior people management practices. The problem isn't just that HR managers know what to do but can't get their companies to do it. Like other leaders, many HR executives hold flawed and incomplete beliefs. They fall prey to second rate evidence, logic and advice, which produce suspect practices, and in the end damage performance and people.[18]

Despite the admonitions of Pfeffer and other luminaries, HR professionals have for years argued that their discipline is an art rather a science and that there is no way of measuring the ROI in talent management initiatives. While talent management may indeed be the most esoteric and difficult of sciences, there are more and increasingly credible indicators available today that clearly demonstrate the link between human capital investment, customer satisfaction, and profit. To earn credibility, but more importantly, to continuously measure and improve, TM executives must know and apply these methods in their organizations.

HR's transformation is also dependent on its leaders having a deep understanding of the organization's business and industry. A talent management division must know corporate plans and objectives and the competitor landscape, it must have deep knowledge of the organization's current talent pool and capabilities, and have a good understanding of local, national, and international talent pools. It must know the company's competitive advantages and differentiators, the comparative costs of training vs recruiting, and where use of the contingent workforce is warranted. It must be able to build a compelling business case to close talent gaps in the most effective manner possible. In short, the TM executive must possess a level of strategic thinking on a par with the CEO and an ability to execute that strategy.

The harsh reality today, however, paints a depressing picture. USC Marshall School of Business professors Ed Lawler and Susan Mohrman found recently that, despite all the talk of HR becoming more strategic, in the 10 years between 1995 and 2004 it actually progressed very little toward a reduced focus on administration and a greater allocation of time toward strategic planning. HCI's own research in 2007 suggests some progress in this area,[19] but it is difficult to argue that a lot has changed in the profession in the past few decades, despite the fact that the "C" Suite and the board now recognize the importance of top talent and the difference that world class talent management can bring.

Ideally, talent management will evolve in much the same way that the finance function has grown into a decision science separate from accounting, or marketing has evolved as a strategic discipline separate from sales. Most HR executives and their teams have a long way to go. Unfortunately, the past three years of unprecedented opportunity for the profession have been more squandered than seized upon. If the profession is to evolve and lead organizations into our "Age of Talent," radical change and transformation are required quickly—our businesses and economies are depending on it.

END NOTES

1. Thomas Malthus, *An Essay on the Principles of Population*, Oxford University Press (1999 first published in 1798).

2. Ibid.

3. Thomas Homer-Dixon, *The Ingenuity Gap*, Knopf Canada, 2000, p. 25.

4. www.bls.gov

5. See David Heenan, *Flight Capital*, Davies-Black Publishing, 2005 and Richard Florida, *The Flight of the Creative Class*, Harper Collins, 2007.

6. See www.globalageing.org: *Depopulation and Ageing in Europe and Japan: The Hazardous Transition to a Labor Shortage Economy*, 2002.

7. "The State of HR Transformation," HCI/Vurv Technologies, October 2007.

8. Ibid.

9. "India's IT Labor Pinch," *Business Week Magazine*, February 2007.

10. "The State of HR Transformation," HCI/Vurv Technologies, October 2007.

11. Rich Wellins and Allan Schweyer, *Talent Management in Motion: Keeping Up with an Evolving Workforce*, Development Dimensions International, 2007.

12. Peter Senge, *The Fifth Discipline*, Doubleday, 1994.

13. "The State of HR Transformation," HCI/Vurv Technologies, October 2007.

14. "Best Practice in Risk Management," The Economist Intelligence Unit, 2007.

15. "The State of HR Transformation," HCI/Vurv Technologies, October 2007.

16. Ibid. (measures assessed were: financial acumen; globalization; change management; HR technology; demonstrating the value of HR to the business; measurement, reporting & data analysis).

17. "The State of HR Transformation," HCI/Vurv Technologies, October 2007.

18. Jeffrey Pfeffer and Robert Sutton, *Dangerous Half-Truths & Total Nonsense*, Cambridge, MA: Harvard Business School Press, 2006, p. 217.

19. "The State of HR Transformation," HCI/Vurv Technologies, October 2007 (respondents reported a focus on talent management over traditional HR 48 percent of the time across 10 scenarios. Lawler and Mohrman's research in 2003 found that HR spent less than 25 percent of its time in strategic activities).

20. Ibid. (respondents reported a focus on talent management over traditional HR 48 percent of the time across 10 scenarios. Lawler and Mohrman's research in 2003 found that HR spent less than 25 percent of its time in strategic activities).

C H A P T E R **5**

DEMOGRAPHICS: THE TEMPEST DRIVING COMPENSATION

Dorothy R. Berger, Managing Director

Lance A. Berger & Associates, Ltd

A N ENCROACHING TEMPEST IS ON the verge of attaining full-blown ferocity. In the very near future a mosaic of business conditions will merge to jeopardize businesses both large and small. A combination of demographic realities and a diverse workforce, possessing a spectrum of values and requirements, will destabilize the business arena. Organizations will not only have to adjust their compensation strategies in order to maintain competitiveness, but will also have to contend with a range of talent management issues. Companies will be faced with realties that require vigilance and preparedness. A seismic shift is approaching and survival measures must be instituted. By 2012, the storm will have attained full intensity. Companies must have talent management and compensation programs in place to attract and retain a shrinking and increasingly diverse pool of workers.

LABOR SHORTAGES COMPLICATED BY INCREASED DIVERSITY

In 2006, 70 percent of the American workforce was between the ages of 25 and 54. In the same year, individuals aged 55+ represented 14 percent of workers. In 2012, the projection is that 66 percent of workers will be in the 25–54 age group, whereas 19 percent will be 55 and over. This represents a 35 percent increase in the number of people aged 55+. In real numbers, there will be 24 million Generation Xers outnumbered by 77 million baby boomers (see Table 5.1). As evidenced by the following comparison between 2006 and 2012, the labor force is becoming increasingly diverse.

Diversity is not as simple as looking at people as black or white, male or female, young or old. It must also include considering the differing ways in which people think, value, and behave. Diversity thinking also must encompass the social realties that the workforce is becoming increasingly dissimilar. Workers dress, speak, value money, time, work, family, and a growing list of other distinguishing characteristics, in an endless spectrum of variation. A trend toward greater diversity is an inevitable aspect of the global and free society. Clearly, a more diverse workforce will be in play when major numbers of baby boomers retire. This increased diversity will dramatically affect sources of recruitment, level of competition, employee expectations and values, and company cultures.

Other sobering statistics demand organizational readiness for a labor force smaller than workforce requirements. According to the Bureau of Labor Statistics and Bureau of Economic Analysis in their Employment Policy Foundation Analysis and Projection, in 2007 the available labor pool is about congruent with labor requirements. By the year 2012, the available labor force will be about 162 million whereas labor needs will be over 165 million workers, a 3 million shortfall. Forecasting beyond 2012, the shortfall continues to grow. Figure 5.1 depicts the escalating imbalance between labor requirements and workforce availability.

The projected point at which tax revenues fall below social security program costs is 2017. The Social Security Trust Fund is projected to be exhausted by 2040,

TABLE 5.1   Labor force changes 2006–2012

Group	Growth Rate
Men	1.0
Women	1.3
White	0.8
African-American	1.0
Hispanic	2.9
Asian	4.2

FIGURE 5.1   Escalating imbalance between labor requirements and workforce availability

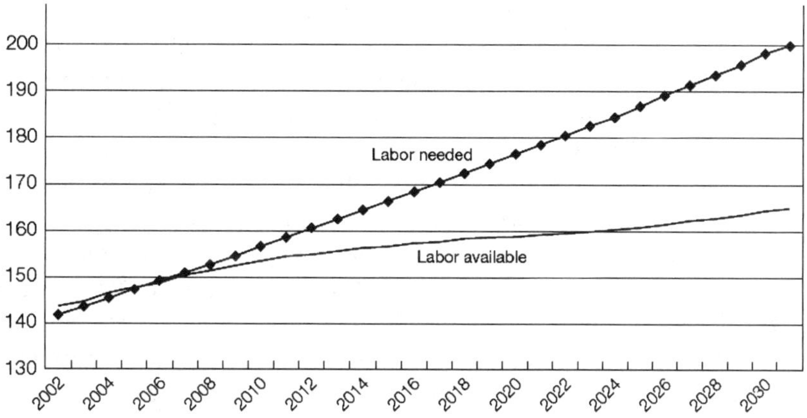

Source: Employment Policy Foundation analysis and projections of Census, Bureau of Labor Statistics, and Bureau of Economic Analysis data

one year earlier than the projection in the previous year's report. Other statistics that companies must consider in preparing for future labor requirements include: the Department of Education states that 60 percent of all new jobs in the twentieth century will require technical skills possessed by less than 20 percent of the current workforce. Industries such as petroleum are coping currently with huge reductions of petroleum engineers graduating from American universities. It is forecast that 40 percent of the manufacturing sector will retire in the next 10 years and 50 percent of government workers will retire within the next five years. Over one-third of companies are currently experiencing some talent shortages and nearly 60 percent of companies expect to somewhat or significantly increase their recruitment of experienced employees immediately. Over 35 percent of companies expect 11 percent or more of their workforce to retire in the next two to three years. Due to probable early retirements of baby boomers starting in 2008, vigilant companies have already started to seek and hire new employees.

The demand for well-educated "knowledge workers" continues to escalate. The proportion of American high school and college graduates is dropping as compared with a rapid rise in comparable students in developing nations. In 2000, three-fifths of the world's college students were from developing nations with the inequity continuing to grow.

U.S. trends indicate that native whites have a low birthrate while minorities and immigrants have a higher birthrate. In 2005, native white males (both well and poorly educated) made up about 38 percent of the workforce, and that percentage is continuously decreasing. The global picture indicates that workers, many of them well educated, will be migrating from developing nations to the United

States. This trend and the birthrate differential within the United States and the academic shortcomings of many Americans mandate that the pool of well-educated workers will be increasingly composed of people who are not native white males. Compensation packages must be carefully constructed to attract and meet the very different expectations and needs of a melting pot of individuals.

In the near future, companies will increasingly have to go to the marketplace to replenish their executives. The number of 35–45-year-olds in the United States is projected to decline by 15 percent by 2015, drastically reducing the pool from which new executives will emerge. The current trend for top executives is to retire earlier. Leadership-starved organizations will try to make compensation packages so attractive that their executives will delay retirement. A countertrend could be that organizations recognize leadership qualities in their young employees and escalate their career paths by moving them quickly to the executive echelons. Again, compensation packages need careful development to keep pace with these young leaders' rapid move up the executive ladder. Compensation must ensure that potential executives will not be pilfered by competing organizations.

Job markets will be more complicated by the acceleration in the growth of small businesses. Over 40 percent of employees work in corporations having fewer than 500 employees. These companies typically have unsophisticated compensation programs but are dealing with the same talent management issues as large companies. These small businesses will, of necessity, become more and more adept at attracting employees through creative compensation and human resources practices.

Yogi Berra, New York Yankee legend, observed, "It's tough to make predictions, especially about the future." Most organizations live by Yogi's philosophy. They exist in the here and now and do little or nothing to prepare for inevitable change. A vast majority of companies are paying little attention to demographic realities. These companies have no formal people processes. The storm is forecast and yet a vast majority of companies disregard the warnings.

ORGANIZATION DISRUPTION: DEMOGRAPHIC REALITIES

Organizations are facing a "demographic domino effect" causing large-scale people movement and shortages of critical skills and experience. Historically workers believed that they had to adapt to their company's culture in order to scale the corporate ladder and garner financial success. However, with growing labor shortages and a shift in worker values, employees assume that corporate cultures will adjust to their expectations. Inevitably, changing corporate cultures will amplify the "demographic domino effect." Turnover, recruitment, and workforce effectiveness issues will be exacerbated. Heightened competition to attract and retain critical area employees is the inevitable outcome as organizations confront shortages of top talent, and skilled and technical employees. Critical skill groups, due to their small relative numbers and high desirability, will predictably become increasingly demanding and sclf-absorbed as companies compete for them. People in these groups will make high demands on employers for pay and special work–life considerations. In this environment, companies, and HR practitioners in particular, will need to stay several steps ahead of the competition in attracting and retaining needed skill workers.

The global economy will continue to broaden. The Internet will be used by more and more people. Internet recruitment will become increasingly more sophisticated and prevalent. Furthermore, salary and benefit information, company reputations, and a host of corporate information will flood the Internet. People worldwide will become increasingly savvy in understanding their position in the global marketplace. Global companies will become more competitive in attracting people to work overseas. Needed talent may leave the United States as European and Asian economies prosper. Immigration policies can shape demographics to either favor American business or place additional hardships on the filling of critical positions. Will government policies relax immigration quotas in countries where American business can compete for talent? Will immigration policies be adjusted to offer easy long-term entrance to individuals possessing key skills?

THE NEW ? GENERATION

Companies will need to prepare for a new generation entering the workforce with its inherent shifts in culture and values. This new Pop Generation, Generation Z, Tech Generation, or whatever it will be called, will challenge organizations anew with work–life issues that are not even on the radar screen currently. HR practitioners will be challenged to determine the values and requirements of each generation through well-conceived and developed culture surveys. It will be critical to survey values by age group to help drive targeted communication. Communications must be adapted to speak to each generation. Culture surveys should have forced choice to determine hierarchy of values for each age group. Moreover, HR departments will need to respond proactively to what the surveys reveal.

Culture surveys done with professional workers in roughly the same positions confirm divergent results from the younger generation as compared to older workers. Surveys indicate that younger workers see paying dues as less important, regard themselves as more self-reliant, and express anti-institutional sentiments when compared to their more mature coworkers. Individuals born from 1975 to 1985 are harder to attract and even more difficult to retain. They are more prone to shifting loyalties and are prone to showing more loyalty to their age group over their elders or corporate superiors.

Generation ? will require ongoing and greater challenges. This generation will be raised on technological stimulation. Young people constantly text messaging, ears glued to a cell phone, or playing with an X-Box or other "toy" are precursors to a workforce more comfortable with technology than people. Unlike the baby boomers, the subsequent generations have been raised with technology and embrace technological innovation. They will welcome opportunities to learn new technologies and will be comfortable in accepting technological challenges. However, these incoming generations have shorter attention spans and companies will be challenged to stimulate and keep these employees focused on the task at hand. Frequently changing, varied assignments in different venues are one means to challenge restless employees but will strain HR departments and management.

HR departments will need to ensure that all workers understand organizational culture and values. Generation ? is more likely to interpret than accept rules, and will be adept at manipulating the rules. Company rules must be presented clearly and succinctly, and written carefully to be understood by all. Corporate values must be unequivocally cascaded throughout the organization with all managers walking the same walk and talking the same talk. Managers will also need to be change-oriented and open to quickly correcting mistakes and changing course to allay misconceptions and misunderstandings.

Companies can demonstrate sensitivity to employee needs for recognition and personal growth by establishing mentoring and coaching programs. Exemplary employees who demonstrate corporate values and behaviors and excel at vital tasks should be linked with new or developing employees as mentors or coaches. This is a way of acknowledging both the mentor and those being mentored. This is a no-cost way of acknowledging and rewarding employees. Younger employees will also respond positively to opportunities for training and development, either in their present job or for future assignments. They want to know that they are being trained and groomed for advancement.

Encouraging baby boomers to stay in the workforce beyond traditional retirement years will be seen by companies as a way to alleviate large numbers making their exodus simultaneously. Phased retirement will enable workers to stay in the workforce and earn more money for retirement as they change their lifestyles by working fewer hours, thereby gradually shifting toward full retirement. Baby boomers will be offered increased pensions based on years of service with incentives to stay with the company beyond the traditional retirement date. Companies will need to deal with the logistics of health insurance for these baby boomers and demands for flexible hours and extended vacation periods.

Retirement security is a reality that will be increasingly used by companies to retain baby boomers. The age at which workers will receive Social Security benefits is already moving beyond historic dates. Companies are moving from defined pensions plans to defined contribution plans for retirement income. Employees who now control where their retirement dollars are invested may not be knowledgeable about investment planning and are subject to the whims of the stock market. Employers offering health care coverage to part-time workers (retirees), even at the employee's expense, are more likely to attain employer-of-choice status.

HEALTH BENEFITS AND WORK–LIFE ISSUES

Offering employees more flexibility in terms of work–life balance is and will continue to be an important workplace issue. Work–life issues will stay at the forefront in attracting and retaining employees. Employers-of-choice for Generation ? will need to offer a smorgasbord of work–life inducements. More companies will embrace such inducements as flexibility in work site (home, car, etc.), extended paternity as well as maternity time, time off to care for aging parents, flexible time to attend children's functions, flexible time to pursue personal interests including sports teams, exercise classes, lectures, or a host of unquestioned reasons to be away from work during traditional working hours. Furthermore, companies will need to expand their view of traditional family by offering comparable benefits to significant others as to traditional spouses.

The current trend is to alter employee health benefit plans to provide for a defined level of employer contributions. This has been true of retirement plans since the latter half of the last century and is spreading to other types of employee benefits. The trend is moving toward defined contribution employee and retiree health insurance plans, and employee-funded reimbursement accounts. This is part of a larger trend toward individual risk assumption. The current administration's goals of encouraging workers to buy their own health insurance through tax incentives and of privatizing a portion of Social Security is part of this trend. These arrangements enable companies to better predict and control their costs. Aligned with the trend to charge employees with more responsibility for retirement savings and other benefits will be a trend to protect employees against the inherent risks. A defined contribution health insurance plan will need to include a set of benefits guarding against catastrophic expenses.

Health benefit costs are an ever increasing chunk of a company's fixed costs; they will continue to outpace inflation and companies will have to make hard decisions on cutting back on benefits in order to stay competitive while also trying to maintain a loyal workforce. Many experts predict that eventually American workers will have to buy many of the benefits they now get as part of their compensation package. Currently, many small companies that cannot afford to subsidize benefits are contracting with insurance companies to offer them at a group discount. Large firms are attempting to offset the pain for employees who are confronting contributing a bigger chunk of their major medical insurance. Many companies realize that paying for preventive care services appropriate for an employee's age group will ultimately result in health benefit cost savings and are encouraging employees to take advantage of this benefit. Yet many of these same companies still need to offset growing health costs with larger employee contributions.

Companies are becoming increasingly aware that programs aimed at maintaining employee health and healthy lifestyles will ultimately result in increased productivity and goodwill. These are win–win incentives for companies and employees. Many companies are stocking their cafeterias with only healthy foods and others are discounting healthy foods much more than less healthy alternatives. Several companies are offering financial incentives for employees attending weight loss and smoking cessation programs. In addition, companies are encouraging workers to join in-house basketball leagues, attend exercise classes, or join a walking group during lunch hours or at other times during the work day. Companies are also paying for annual health exams, and offering in-house health seminars and other benefits such as 24-hour hotlines staffed by registered nurses and services to help their employees manage chronic conditions.

For many years, companies have responded to employee needs by offering backup child care either on- or off-site to employees. However, many organizations are responding to changing workforce demographics, and recognizing the needs of the baby boomer generation. In order to maintain baby boomer vitality in the workforce, about 27 percent of companies now offer some eldercare benefits, and this percentage is steadily increasing. These organizations realize that, just as parents in the workforce could be more productive with assistance like child care, support groups, and free advisory services, there is a growing need for help in caring for parents or grandparents. Companies are responding to the realization that such services could be cost-effective by decreasing employee downtime and consequently increasing productivity. A growing number of employee assistance programs are helping put employees in touch with geriatric care managers and many are paying for this service as an employee benefit. Geriatric care managers help older people and their families navigate through the health system and are also up-to-date on resources available to the aging population.

EXPANDING RECRUITMENT TECHNIQUES

Competing for as well as motivating and retaining opportunity-seeking employees will be a high priority for human resource practitioners. HR professionals will need to continuously assess the right combination of reward elements to ensure that employees remain committed to the organization. Implementing a well-balanced mix of traditional, quantifiable elements, such as competitive salary and benefits, as well as intangible rewards like providing learning and development opportunities, will require ongoing assessment that the organization is getting the "biggest bang for its buck."

HR departments will also need to go deeper into recruiting strategies. High school or college students could be tracked and developed through expanded summer internship programs or corporate seminars held at targeted educational institutions. Corporations could establish mentor programs linking high school/college students with employees. Company employees can become a source of recruitment through incentive programs granting meaningful rewards to employees recommending key hires.

Outsourcing corporate functions will continue to expand. Organizations will be forced to have sharper and more differentiated employee compensation policies based on a decreasing need for potential outsourced positions. Employees in positions that can be outsourced will need to be open to retraining for other positions. HR departments will be challenged to select and develop appropriate employees to move from outsourced positions to needed areas. Talent management systems will need to address every employee's potential for growth in his position, a lateral position, or a higher position. In-house training will become more prevalent and sophisticated as companies attempt to customize training to fit position requirements and control expenditure of training dollars.

EVOLVING COMPENSATION TRENDS: ADHERING TO THE OLD WHILE PERFECTING THE NEW

As demographic and economic issues affect business realities, more organizations will need to adhere to a clear compensation strategy based on the organization's mission, culture, and core competencies in order to maintain competitiveness. Involving key organization decisions makers in discussions on these differentiating areas before putting a pay policy in place will aid the company in making more informed pay decisions. Compensation in the most competitive companies will be aligned with organizational goals, employee performance, and institutional core competencies. Compensation programs will increasingly include variable pay schemes that link pay to individual or group performance and salary plans developed around skills and competencies considered crucial to organizational success. Compensation in the form of stock options and profit-sharing will likely cascade lower and lower into the organization.

However, as late as 2006, Hay surveys report that 80 percent of organizations are still using the traditional fortieth to sixtieth percentile to target base pay. Broadbanding is used by about 9 percent, and 7 percent use a competency-based pay system. Merit increases have gone up slightly, with the 2006 rate at 3.5 percent reported by Watson Wyatt and WorldatWork. Traditional job evaluation techniques such as point factor and whole job systems are used by more than half of all companies. The Hay survey also indicates that the proportions of skill-based pay, career banding, and job family systems are still in the single digits. Broadbanding and competency-based pay may continue to gain popularity as compensation practitioners learn more about best practices in competing firms. HR departments are reluctant to change the status quo when dealing with compensation issues. They are risk-averse and uncomfortable dealing with the inevitable communication issues presented by new systems. Traditional base pay plans are often chosen without consideration of company goals, culture, or institutional competencies.

Merit budgets for most American industries are increasing slightly but are hovering between 3.5 and 4 percent. This means that the pot for pay increases to spread among top performers continues to be small. With this ongoing trend of small merit budgets, it is increasingly urgent to use the merit budget wisely to incentivize the people who are truly top performers and those with the most potential for contributing to organizational success. In addition to using a valid system for core competency assessment as a means for identifying Superkeepers (those who greatly exceed competency expectations, demonstrate superior accomplishments, and inspire others to superior accomplishments, and only constitute about 3–5 percent of the workforce), Keepers (those who exceed competency expectations), and Solid Citizens (those who meet requirements), companies should judiciously divide the merit budget to incentivize Superkeepers proportionately more than Keepers and Solid Citizens. Retaining Superkeepers will be increasingly vital to organizations as the competition for these rare jewels increases.

The percentage of companies offering one or more variable pay plans has increased by 16 percent since 2001, according to a WorldatWork 2004–2005 Salary Budget Survey. Variable pay plans run the gamut from profit sharing, small group incentives, gain-sharing, goal-sharing, lump sum awards, and other incentives. The rationale behind using variable pay plans is that organizations can share their success when performance is good without increasing salaries, a fixed cost, in the future. This approach should become increasingly popular as companies attempt to adapt quickly to changing economic and demographic conditions. The most common variable pay program is a lump sum merit award granted instead of a base pay increase to high performers and employees at the top of their pay range.

The WorldatWork 2004–2005 Salary Budget Survey reports that most nonexempt employees still earn a small amount of their pay in variable pay form, usually about 5 percent of base pay. Exempt employees typically have about 10–12 percent of pay at risk. Although variable pay remains a small portion of salary, more and more organizations understand the psychological effect on employee performance when those incentives are linked to well-communicated organizational outcomes.

Another major trend is customizing compensation to employee needs. This will give employees a choice in assessing what they want or need rather than employers simply providing a standard program aimed at the "average" employee. Employees will make choices among several health care and retirement savings options, flexible work arrangements, and reimbursement accounts. Implicit in employee choice is the responsibility on the part of the employee to make prudent, informed choices. HR practitioners will be challenged to develop programs that adequately educate employees in understanding their options. Dealing with the consequences of poor choices will place added pressure on social and legislative institutions as well as the organization.

INCREASINGLY KNOWLEDGEABLE, SAVVY, AND DEMANDING WORKFORCE

In recent surveys, employees when asked what they considered "very important" in deciding to take their current job responded: (1) open communications;

(2) opportunities to balance life; and (3) meaningful work. Employees want to feel that they have input into and control of their destinies. Obviously, this includes being heard about their tangible and intangible compensation requirements.

More than half of U.S. workers in medium and large companies are in the job market in some capacity. In addition, workers in general are highly informed about their options and the Internet gives them access to job opportunities without risk to their current position. Competing for and retaining opportunity-seeking employees will challenge human resources professionals. Furthermore employees have easily available access to compensation information. The Internet enables everyone to obtain salary survey and other compensation data. This information is not always accurate and it also reflects national salary data adjusted for cost-of-living or average pay rates. However, different parts of the country have unique demands for certain skills sets, resulting in pay rates that do not conform to national averages. HR practitioners will increasingly be called upon to explain salaries to employees who believe they have garnered correct salary ammunition from the Internet. They will need to be prepared with data explaining the employee's salary competitiveness in their pay market. Employees will need ongoing assurance that their company's pay systems are competitive within their industries and adjusted as appropriate.

CONGRESSIONAL ACTION

As long as the Democrats control both Congressional chambers, workplace issues, including those affecting compensation, will probably be legislative priorities. One of the first acts enacted by the Democratic-controlled Congress was to pass a minimum wage law raising the minimum wage for covered, nonexempt employees to $5.15. The Democrats will most likely increase the minimum wage to $7.25 in three phases over the next two years. President Bush ultimately supported the bill with the suggestion that minimum wage legislation include protections ensuring that wage increases do not affect smaller businesses adversely.

Executive compensation is another issue that will fall under legislative scrutiny. Barney Frank, Democrat from Massachusetts, and chair of the House Financial Services Committee, promises to introduce "The Protection against Executive Compensation Abuse Act." His proposal would establish a market-based approach that would allow shareholders to review and approve their company's comprehensive executive compensation plan. The bill would allow for a company policy for recapturing incentive compensation, such as bonuses or stock options to executives for meeting performance targets if it is discovered that this compensation was based on inaccurate reporting.

Senator Ted Kennedy announced that a legislative priority for the Senate HELP committee will be a reintroduction of the Health Families Act. The proposal would guarantee all employees seven paid sick days to care for their own and their families' medical needs. Several Democrats have vowed that paid sick leave and expanded protections under the Family and Medical Leave Act will be legislative priorities.

Disgruntled shareholders are demanding to let management know how they feel about executive pay. As executive pay packages grow and the media brings these packages to public attention, shareholders are demanding their say. The number of companies putting shareholders' proposals relating to executive pay on proxy statements is growing significantly. Members of the House Financial Services Committee led by Barney Frank approved a bill that would give shareholders a nonbinding advisory vote on pay.

SUMMARY

Ultimately demographic realities and shortages in critical skills will force companies to adopt creative and/or jumbo-size compensation packages to maintain competitiveness. The tempest will devour victims if organizations deny it and do not prepare for its approach. No matter what the industry or company size, organizations must put in place compensation programs that will attract, develop, and retain a viable employee pool. Expanding workforce diversity necessitates a common ground for assessing and compensating employees. The logical basis for establishing an equitable compensation system is core institutional competencies. Core competencies are the behavioral/skill expectations that are crucial to the success of each employee and the success of the entire organization. Most companies can identify between seven and eleven competencies through comprehensive input from stakeholders. Typical core competencies are action orientation, communications, customer orientation, critical judgment, and interpersonal skills. Every core competency should be defined as it pertains to the organization. The competency should also be further differentiated into glossaries of behaviors associated with each organizational level. Core institutional competencies can be the common language for recruiting, assessing, and developing a viable workforce.

Base Salary

SALARY ADMINISTRATION

Andrew S. Rosen, Vice President

ORC Worldwide

THE SALARY STRUCTURE IS THE combination of job groupings and salary ranges that make up the foundation of an organization's pay system. On the one hand, it is perhaps the tool most commonly used (and most often taken for granted) for helping organizations build a human resources infrastructure. On the other hand, if crafted carefully and strategically, the salary structure can communicate clearly an organization's cultural values and priorities and serve as a primary building block of a total direct compensation program. Seen in this latter context, the salary structure can be a strong ally in a company's efforts to attract, retain and energize its workforce.

The primary purposes of a salary structure are, in our view, to help ensure that:

1. Jobs are positioned properly within the organization and within in the context of the marketplace

2. Individuals are paid fairly, competitively, and consistently with the goals of the organization

3. People managers and human resources business partners have the tools and the information they need to make effective pay decisions

According to the *WorldatWork Journal*, "A 'structure' serves a useful purpose if it helps managers make rational pay decisions that are viewed as fair and competitive by employees, and if the company views it as useful in retaining and rewarding the right people."[1]

The type of salary structure(s) selected must be consistent with the company's compensation strategy and fit within the context of the total compensation program. This choice will be determined within the context of a number of important program design and policy issues, such as the following:

- How much flexibility is needed for managers to be successful at managing, developing and rewarding their key people? The need for flexibility should be balanced by how much variation the organization can tolerate and/or support in a salary structure.

- Should the organization plan to target pay for each job, job level, and/or employee at the same market level (e.g., at the market average or median)? To help answer this question, the organization must consider whether there are there some areas (job families, locations) where it must pay at higher levels to recruit and retain higher-caliber employees and/or workers who are uniquely skilled, in high demand, or have considerable strategic impact.

- How many salary structures are needed to accommodate the dynamics of the labor markets and the organization's staffing and career management plans? If multiple structures are required, the organization must consider whether all structures would be based on similar concepts and philosophies. As the organization becomes more of a truly global enterprise, it also must consider how to balance a global strategy with regional and/or local structures and practices.

- What form should the salary structure take to support career management plans? For example, will career paths be hierarchical (i.e., based on sequential promotions) or will employees make more lateral-horizontal career moves? Will there be more advancement "by the numbers" or by described job content?

- How will performance be recognized and rewarded within the framework of the salary structure, and should the pay-for-performance philosophy be the same across the system?

ARCHITECTURE

A *salary structure* is, at its most fundamental, the job groupings (sometimes referred to as job clusters) and salary ranges that reflect the hierarchy of jobs and the subsequent delivery of pay to individuals. It is one of the basic building blocks of a base compensation program and, in fact, often of total direct compensation, in which case both short-term incentive and long-term incentive targets are defined and differentiated by job grouping.

The structure is built on a three-part framework: (1) the relative ranking of jobs or roles (typically called *job* or *role evaluation*) according to an organization's internal valuing system; (2) the incorporation of external market values via the process of benchmarking (market pricing); and (3) the clustering of jobs based on both internal ranking or equity and market pay levels. The result is, most often, a series of salary ranges that apply to each similarly leveled cluster of jobs (see Figure 6.1).

A salary range describes the minimum and maximum an organization will pay for a particular job or job grouping, based upon the organization's compensation philosophy. Using a salary range as opposed to a single pay rate provides flexibility for managers to pay in a manner consistent with an individual's experience, performance, competency and business impact, as well as with market pressures connected to a particular job or job family.

The salary structure emerges as salary ranges are assigned to job groupings; however, positioning jobs within the structure often also determines the degree of participation in other programs, such as bonuses, stock awards, additional benefits (such as vacation), supplemental benefits (such as deferred compensation, supplemental life insurance, or disability benefits), and perquisites (such as financial counseling, medical examinations, or club memberships). While giving greater reward opportunities to individuals in "bigger" jobs that have greater impact on the success or failure of the organization is a rational approach, compensation program designers should keep the following in mind.

- A "have vs have not" culture may emerge if employees in the higher-level positions view increasingly "rich" reward opportunities simply as entitlements. To avoid this, each organizational level must be clearly defined, the impact of its jobholders substantiated, and the rewards set accordingly.

FIGURE 6.1 Job evaluation

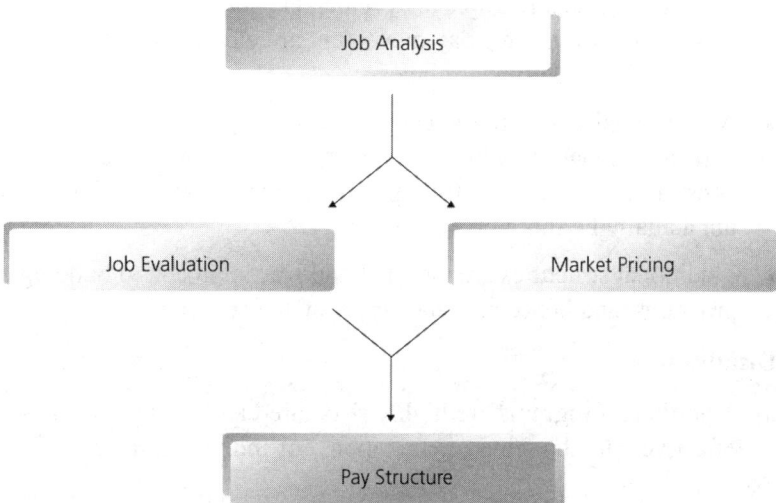

- The more that non-cash offerings are tied to grade level, the greater is the possibility that employees will push to be promoted into the next grade (regardless of the work requirements) and that they will experience dissatisfaction if promotions are not as forthcoming as anticipated. Again, it is important that the total reward package at each level is appropriate to the jobs and their impact on the company.

The following sections review four basic types of salary structure (traditional, flexible, career-based and global), and the advantages and disadvantages of each. Note that, while we treat each type as distinct for the purpose of this discussion, in reality the characteristics of each often overlap considerably.

Traditional Structure

The structures considered most "traditional" are those that are highly layered and technically driven. Highly layered structures use many grades with relatively small distances between adjacent grades/ranges. In technically driven structures, grades are defined primarily by compensation levels, whether market-based or internally focused, rather than career or organizational levels described in terms of job content.

Reasons for Adopting a Traditional Structure.   The reasons for adopting (or maintaining) a traditional structure varies from organization to organization, based on alignment with the organization's strategies. Several common reasons are noted below:

- Traditional structures place emphasis on promotion/career advancement through a hierarchical system; individuals can "see" their promotions in the form of moving from grade to grade (although the line of sight in such designs is less intuitive than in more career-based frameworks)

- Typically, these structures are predictable and easy to administer in that the reasons and timing for pay movement are clearly defined by the structure and associated pay delivery policies

- A traditional structure typically has a strong technical, mathematically derived foundation, which may be viewed as more objective than a less constrained broadband structure recognizing, however, that in reality it may not actually be more objective

- Traditional structures are the tried-and-true approach to building compensation programs, and hence are relatively easy to explain and justify

Disadvantages.

- Traditional programs are highly structured and may not always respond effectively to changing organizational or individual needs.

- They may create perceived or real barriers between or within functional work groups because of differences in perceived value or status as defined by grade levels.

- They may be slow to recognize increased responsibility or competencies unless these changes warrant a promotion to a higher grade.

- Managers may not participate actively in the pay decision-making process; rather, they follow established procedure regarding pay delivery (i.e., promotional, top-of-range, new-hire guidelines).

- Traditional approaches recognize the job more than the individual in the job. The structure accommodates the relative worth of the job as compared to other jobs, and if the job responsibilities change, the placement of the job within the structure may change (i.e., moved up to a higher grade). An incumbent's acquisition of new skills does not typically result in a reclassification of the job within the structure.

Examples. Following are two examples of traditional structures. More specifically, these examples illustrate different approaches regarding salary range symmetry (midpoints vs control points) and of the spacing between salary ranges.

Example 1. Figure 6.2 illustrates a salary structure that reflects a number of characteristics commonly considered to be traditional. These characteristics include the use of midpoints, the "80–120" format, relatively small distances between grades (10 percent), as well as considerable overlap of salary ranges (a function of the small distances between grades as well as the relatively typical range size, 50 percent from minimum to maximum).

FIGURE 6.2   Traditional structure

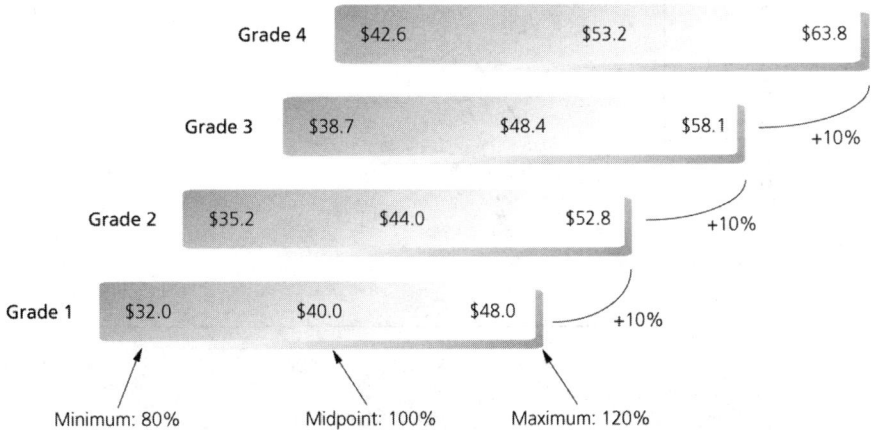

Midpoints. The "midpoint" value is often viewed as the pay level associated with fully competent performance in a job. Typically, the midpoint is the middle of each salary range and is tied to the market target consistent with the company's compensation strategy. This target represents the destination salary (or going rate) for jobs in a particular grade level. The actual value of the midpoint will depend on the organization's compensation philosophy (what to pay within the context of the organization's goals and the local, regional, or national markets) and its selection of pay survey sources.

There are two common methods for determining how midpoints will be used to develop salary ranges: line of best fit and cluster analysis.

Line of Best Fit. By performing regression analyses, a *line of best fit* can be created to represent the intersection of market pay levels and relative job size (whether by job evaluation points, grade levels, or some other measure of internal value). This method is more often used in broadband implementations, but is used by many organizations that take the layered approach common among traditional structures. A similar line of best fit representing internal pay practices can then be developed, and a comparative analysis of the two conducted (see Figure 6.3).

FIGURE 6.3   Line of best fit

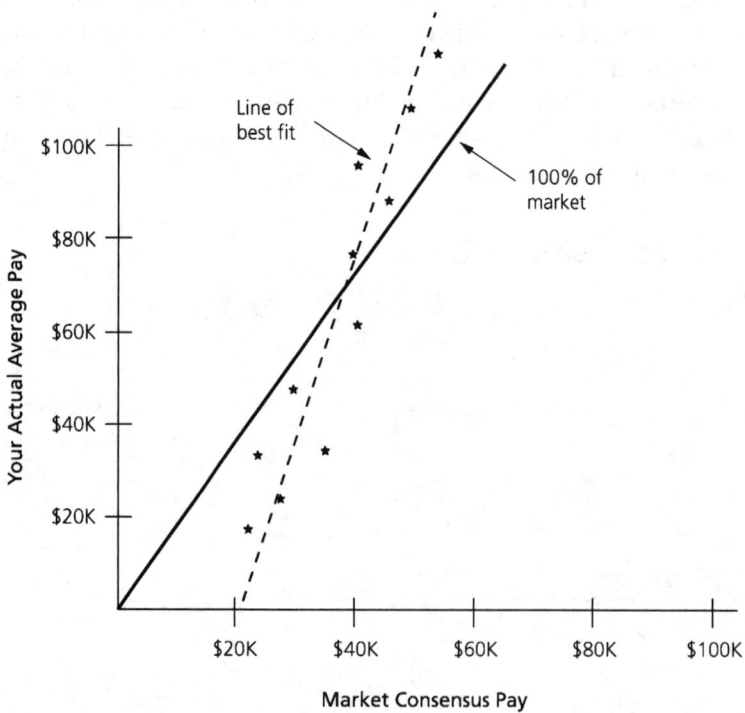

Cluster Analysis. An alternative to the line-of-best-fit approach is the *cluster analysis* method (sec Table 6.1). In this process, market rates for the clustered jobs are reviewed, and target pay levels are developed based on approximate average or median values (or other competitive levels depending, once again, on the organization's particular philosophy).

After creating the preliminary set of grades and ranges based on a market analysis, the compensation analyst places each position in a proposed grade (based primarily on the market findings and secondarily on internal relationships), then compares the market values to the new midpoint.

This preliminary slotting often is quite instructive, as it may show jobs whose market values are farther away from the new midpoints than desired, suggesting a need for repositioning (see Manager of Information Technology in Table 6.1), jobs with titles that sound different but are matched and priced similarly (see Laboratory Associates I and II), or the possible need for additional grades to fill in gaps.

The "80–120" Format. This is a method for establishing salary ranges in which the minimum of each range is set at 80 percent of the midpoint, while the maximum is set at 120 percent of the midpoint. The symmetry of this approach is appealing and relatively easy to understand, but it does not necessarily reflect the realities of the recruiting market. For example, the hiring rates for a particular job may not be at or near the 80 percent mark; they may be either higher or lower. Further, the rigid formula may not match the organization's performance philosophy regarding how much higher than a market target it is willing to pay for extraordinary performance within the boundaries of the job.

Closely Nestled Ranges. Relatively closely nestled ranges ensure that promotions from one grade to the next will not be associated with "windfall" salary increases. This approach also ensures that promotions are viewed more as incremental progressions than significant leaps in responsibility.

Example 2. Figure 6.4 illustrates a structure that looks similar to the structure in Example 1; however, the structure in this example was actually set up in a very different way. Key differences include a much greater inter-range distance (19–22 percent vs 10 percent), progressively greater distance at higher grades, and ranges that are about the same overall size (about 50 percent from minimum to maximum), but that are asymmetrical in design.

Asymmetry. In contrast to the "80–120 format" used in Example 1, the range minima in Example 2 are set at 90 percent of the salary target while the range maxima are set at 130 percent of the target. Some organizations prefer calling the salary targets in such a structure "control points" rather than midpoints since their purpose is less to bisect a range evenly and more to establish a framework for determining pay for individuals within that range.

TABLE 6.1   Cluster Analysis Method

Benchmark Job Title	Target (P50)	Proposed Grade	Proposed Midpoint	Midpoint Difference (%)
Laboratory Associate I	$26,006	1	$25,000	−4%
Laboratory Associate II	$26,967	1	$25,000	−7%
Research Associate I	$30,275	1	$25,000	−17%
Accounting Assistant	$34,484	2	$36,300	5%
Senior Research Associate I	$36,961	2	$36,300	−2%
Research Associate II	$37,628	2	$36,300	−4%
Administrative Assistant	$40,705	2	$36,300	−11%
Engineer Technician I	$42,501	3	$45,400	−7%
Senior Research Associate II	$45,039	3	$45,400	1%
Human Resources Analyst	$49,866	3	$45,400	−9%
Payroll/Benefits Coordinator	$49,866	3	$45,400	−9%
Legal Administrator-Patents	$52,346	4	$56,800	9%
Senior Research Associate III	$55,620	4	$56,800	2%
Supervisor of Process Quality Management	$55,620	4	$56,800	2%
Engineer I	$63,086	4	$56,800	−10%
Unix and Systems Administrator	$63,192	4	$56,800	−10%
Research Scientist	$72,306	5	$73,800	2%
Lead Software Developer	$72,306	5	$73,800	2%
Manager of Accounting	$73,412	5	$73,800	1%
Manager of Human Resources	$76,275	5	$73,800	−3%
Project Leader	$79,822	5	$73,800	−8%
Senior Research Scientist	$92,121	6	$95,900	4%
Manager of Information Technology	$85,035	6	$95,900	13%
Patent Agent	$85,655	6	$95,900	12%
Senior Software Engineer	$86,767	6	$95,900	11%
Database Administrator	$93,442	6	$95,900	3%
Senior Facilities Manager	$99,866	6	$95,900	−4%
Group Leader	$111,510	6	$95,900	−14%

FIGURE 6.4   Traditional structure

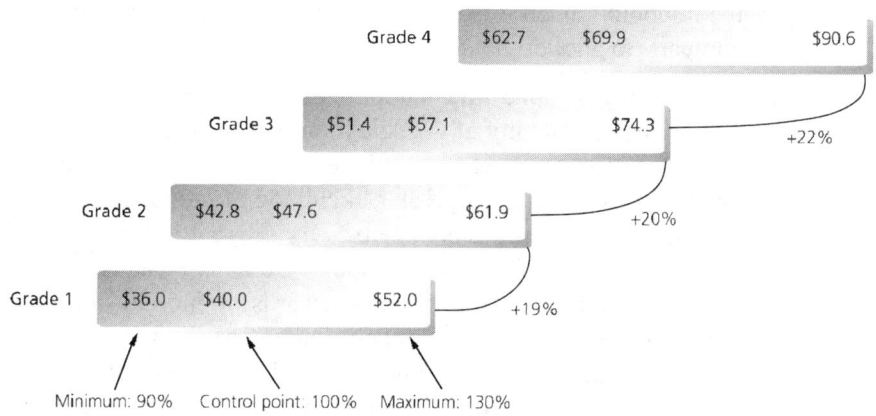

Minimum: 90%   Control point: 100%   Maximum: 130%

There is no inherent rationale for establishing a symmetrical salary range. While range symmetry may appeal to our sense of orderliness, it is more important that salary range frameworks accurately reflect hiring practices, development processes, compensation philosophy, and the degree of linkage between pay and performance. It also is important that employees and their managers understand how ranges work and how the structure affects current and future pay opportunities. Questions to answer in determining how low minima should be and how high maxima should be include:

- How much below target is the hiring rate for a job? Will the organization, in fact, expect to hire qualified but inexperienced people at the minimum or above it? Another way of thinking about this is to ask how long it would take for a newly hired, inexperienced employee paid at the minimum to achieve competence, thereby arriving at market target pay. The longer the expected time period, the greater the distance should be between the minimum and the target. Of course, the answer may differ depending on the job level. For instance, a basic assembler may take weeks or months to get up to speed in the job, while a senior level enterprise architect might take years to gain the technical and organizational knowledge needed to be able to contribute fully. This is why the distance from minimum to control point is smaller for non-exempt/hourly types of positions than for professional and/or management roles in many organizations.

- How much is the organization willing to pay above a market competitive rate for extraordinary performance and/or contribution within the same job? To some extent, the answer to this question may be influenced by how quickly a company is growing. An organization that is expanding rapidly, both from a business and a staffing perspective, will tend to be much less concerned about this issue given the likelihood that many people, particularly top performers, will be promoted into the next level before they come close to the midpoint, much less the maximum. Nonetheless, it is important for the company to answer the question to its satisfaction.

- What should be done when an individual reaches or exceeds the range maximum? The reality of this situation is often hard to deal with, particularly in mature businesses where employees tend to be long-tenured. In such circumstances, there is a greater likelihood of individuals "maxing out" in their ranges. Companies have to be very diligent in communicating their rationales for range caps, in providing alternative means of recognition and reward (e.g., lump sum or incentive awards) to individuals at the top of their ranges who remain significant contributors, and in identifying and helping forge a path to realizing true promotional or developmental opportunities that will expand work challenges and the possibilities of higher pay levels.

Greater Distance between Ranges. Greater distance between salary ranges tends to correlate to more expansive clustering of jobs. In a sense, this is self-evident given that the use of broader grades will result inevitably in fewer grades to hold the organization's populations of jobs. While such a structure is not an actual broadband, it is moving in that direction. It is very likely that employees would spend more time in each grade in the structure shown in Figure 6.4 than they would in the structure shown in Figure 6.2. And given that there is less overlap between ranges, resulting in promotional increases that will tend to be more significant, it behooves management to make sure that their policies and programs around performance management, employee development, and promotion/advancement are well defined and clearly communicated.

Flexible Structure

Let us now take a look at the more flexible structure of a broadband arrangement. "Broadbands are describable clusters of jobs with broadly similar characteristics (e.g., impact, scope, career stage, function, level, etc.) that create a sense of group belonging and career opportunity... Bands themselves are not compensation tools, although pay ranges, pay reference points or pay opportunities may be (and almost always are) nestled within bands."[2]

Many compensation practitioners react to broadband structures with cynicism or outright hostility, and often, unfortunately, for good reason. They might have been through an experience in which broadbanding was viewed as *the* way for their employer to effect cultural and structural change without having to develop and implement the necessary changes in the supporting processes of development, communication, work process or organization structure. Additionally, the company's view of broadbanding may have been that of "super-grades" associated with "super-ranges" of 100–200–300 percent in width. In these incarnations, the salary structure is viewed as endlessly flexible, giving managers adequate rope to make the desired pay decisions (or hang themselves!), and as a way of breaking down all sorts of hierarchical barriers between employees who are in differently graded jobs.

The sad truth is that many such banding implementations have not worked. In fact, they cannot work unless managers have direct and ongoing access to robust external data on market levels by job and individual, as well as valid internal data on performance, experience, dates of hire/promotion, etc. Without such information being readily available, managers need guidelines on where jobs and people fit within the organizational and pay hierarchy and what types of salary increases or target salary levels are appropriate in various situations. On their own, the huge "super" bands just do not have the necessary degree of infrastructure to help managers make effective pay decisions for rewarding and holding onto their "superkeepers."

Thus, while in some instances broadband structures are more flexible than traditional salary ranges, their primary benefit may be in providing a "meta-structure" that contains jobs with similar organizational impact or broad career levels. In fact, they are best established without pay parameters and with a more career-focused purpose.

From this perspective, broadbands are flexible in their function as career groupings, while the salary zones or ranges that serve to anchor the jobs within the bands are often similar in structure to more typical range formats. As discussed in the *WorldatWork Journal*, one of the alternatives to the traditional approaches to banding "would be to define 'market ranges' within a band. The range for each job is centered on the market average or, using one company's jargon, the 'market reference point.' Ranges are defined as plus or minus 20 percent around mean salaries produce a job-specific range that is aligned with the market."[3]

Reasons for Adopting Broadbands. While reasons for adopting a broadbanding approach vary considerably, it is paramount that the structure supports the organization's strategies and not be implemented just because it is the latest trend.

Many organizations that have modified their systems have done so to complement broader organizational changes, such as:

- Reducing the emphasis on promotions and grades
- Providing the organization with the flexibility to respond to changing business needs
- Breaking down the barriers to teamwork and cooperation (i.e., barriers resulting from narrowly defined job duties and responsibilities)
- Providing employees with the opportunity for personal growth and extensive performance recognition
- Placing more human resources decisions in the hands of managers
- Facilitating (and encouraging) lateral job moves
- Reducing the administrative burden of job evaluation

Disadvantages.

- This approach requires significant organizational and supervisory commitment to development, training and communication

- Broadband arrangements may not be worth the commitment of time and money if the change is only superficial (just combining grades)

- Broadbands may be considered too "loose" and lacking definition, which may make them difficult to manage and administer

- Advancing through a band may not afford the individual the same sense of promotion as moving from grade to grade

Examples.   Table 6.2 represents a broadband type of structure within a small banking organization. Note the broad groupings of jobs clustered together and the lack of pay ranges attached to the bands (A–D).

Table 6.3 shows the numbers behind this career-band structure. Each band has multiple "market reference ranges." For example, band A spans the first three ranges. In many banded structures, market-based target rates and ranges are used to separate each band into manageable pay zones. Assuming that benchmark jobs have been accurately matched and market-priced, the expectation is that these ranges reflect reasonable market values for the subsets of jobs in each band. What is interesting is that, although a relatively typical set of market-driven ranges has been created, these ranges are used less as a fully formed salary structure and more as input into the bands. Given that there is no requirement that each band contain a specific and fully overlapping set of pay ranges, this kind of structure tends to be more flexible and less rigid than traditional structures.[4]

Career-Based Structure

Our examination of broadbands has centered largely on their career-based applications. One of the interesting characteristics of career ladder-type structures is how intuitive and commonsensical they are to both employees and their managers. Table 6.4 illustrates a non-broadband, career-oriented structure.

The power of this type of framework starts with the approach to its development. An effective process typically includes considerable employee involvement, uses criteria for job families (i.e., Administrative Support) and levels (AS-1, AS-2, etc.) that are specific to the organization (step 1 on the following list), and allows for the development of levels within each job family (making it highly customized to each work area). Ultimately, this framework provides an integrated salary structure based largely on a formal evaluation of levels (Step 4) and market analysis (Step 6). Key steps typically include:

1. Define job families (roles) and elements of accountability (compensable factors)

TABLE 6.2   Broadband Structure

A Associate	B Technical	C Management	D Leadership
Clerk/Courier	Sr Customer Service Rep.	Purchasing Manager	VP & Auditor
Research Clerk	Sr Sales Rep	Assistant Branch Manager	VP & Corporate Secretary
Teller	DP Operator	Facilities Manager	Controller
Acounting Rep.	Mortgage Lender	Customer Service Supervisor	VP, Consumer Lending
Administrative Assistant	Sr Accounting Rep.	Loan Servicing Manager	VP, Human Resources
Collector	Sr Loan Servicer	Asset Recovery Manager	VP, Marketing & PR
Credit Analyst/Clerk	Commercial Credit Analyst	AVP, Branch Manager	VP, Sales Manager
Customer Service Rep.	Senior Lending Rep.	AVP, Customer Retention	VP, Commercial Lending
Indirect Lending Rep.	Sr Consumer Lender	Branch Manager	VP, Indirect Lending
Loan Servicing Rep.	Assistant Auditor	Compliance Officer	SVP & Treasurer
Receptionist		Human Resources Manager	SVP, Commercial Loans
Sales Rep.		Indirect Lending Officer	SVP, Retail Banking
Consumer Lender		AVP, Information Systems	Executive VP & COO
Facilities Rep.		Commercial Loan Officer	President & CEO
IS Clerk			
Marketing Assistant			
Night Operator			
Proof Operator			

2. Create and validate job family frameworks using content experts from each job family

3. Define each level of work in each job family described in terms of the compensable factors, again using content experts

4. Evaluate each level within each job family to identify the relative hierarchy of work levels

TABLE 6.3   Broadband Structure with Market Reference Ranges

Market Reference Point	Market Reference Range		Bands			
	Low (−15%)	High (+15%)	A	B	C	D
$19,000	$16,150	$21,850	×			
$21,850	$18,570	$25,130	×			
$25,130	$21,360	$28,900	×	×		
$28,900	$24,570	$33,240		×	×	
$33,240	$28,250	$38,230		×	×	
$38,230	$32,500	$43,960		×	×	
$43,960	$37,370	$50,550			×	
$50,550	$42,970	$58,130			×	×
$58,130	$49,410	$66,850				×
$66,850	$56,820	$76,880				×
$76,880	$65,350	$88,410				×
$88,410	$75,150	$101,670				
$101,670	$86,420	$116,920				
$116,920	$99,380	$134,460				×
$134,460	$114,290	$154,630				
$154,630	$131,440	$177,820				×
$177,820	$151,150	$204,490				

TABLE 6.4   Career-based Structure

Job Family	Pay Grades/Job Levels								
	Grade 18	Grade 19	Grade 20	Grade 21	Grade 22	Grade 23	Grade 24	Grade 25	Grade 26
Administrative Support	AS-1	AS-2	AS-3	AS-4	AS-5	AS-6			
Technical and Research			TR-1	TR-2	TR-3	TR-4		TR-5	
Information Technology and Media			IT-1	IT-2	IT-3	IT-4		IT-5	IT-6
Safety and Facility Services		SF-1	SF-2	SF-3	SF-4	SF-5			
Finance			F-1	F-2	F-3		F-4	F-5	F-6
Marketing		M-1	M-2	M-3	M-4	M-4			

5. Map all jobs to the appropriate job family and defined level within the job family (using input from content experts)

6. Conduct competitive analysis on benchmark jobs

7. Establish salary structure by aligning levels and market values.

An additional benefit is the transparency inherent in publishing the leveling matrix, such as the one shown in Table 6.4. This more open communication approach allows employees and managers to see and understand the opportunities for growth, whether by advancing through levels within a family (from M-2 to M-3, for example) or by moving from one family to another (from AS-3 to F-1, for example) to shift functional areas and/or careers.

So long as this system is viewed as a tool for developing careers and promotional opportunities, as well as a guide to the compensation advances that inevitably come along with such development, it can be a powerful aid in engaging employees and improving organizational effectiveness. As with any career-based system, however, to the extent that it degenerates into an entitlement-based give-away, it will lose credibility, add unnecessary labor costs, and may very well hurt morale, particularly among the high-performing or high-potential employees who see that performance and hard work are not necessarily required for advancement.

Dual Career Ladder.   An interesting twist on career structures is the dual career ladder, a framework that exists in many scientific, research, and technically oriented organizations. Similar to the job-family structure and the broadband approaches discussed previously, the value of such configurations is in the intersection of level of responsibility/impact, compensation, and recognition/status.

Figure 6.5 represents a sample dual career ladder from a scientific organization. Dual career ladders came into being and continue to be used as a way to recognize and reward individuals who make increasingly significant scientific contributions without requiring them to move into management roles, thus trying to avoid the downsides of the Peter Principle.

There are a number of reasons for companies to consider this structure. Some of the more common reasons are that dual career ladders:

■ Encourage top scientists, engineers, or developers to continue to focus on their disciplines without requiring them to give up status or reward opportunities, or to assume management positions where many of them may not excel.

■ Facilitate the recruitment and retention of the best technical experts.

■ Reinforce the organization's commitment to research or engineering excellence through consistent recognition, reward and communication. This is particularly important if world-class discovery, research, and development are viewed as core to the business's strategy and market success.

FIGURE 6.5   Dual career ladder

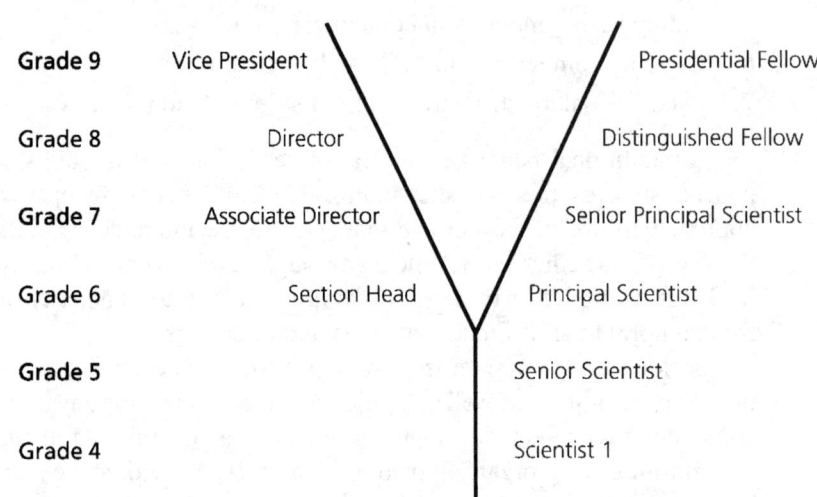

Each dual career ladder must fit the culture, values, and hierarchy of a particular organization. (Figure 6.5, including the titles associated with it, is an illustration only.) Titles are particularly important in technical organizations both as internally and externally discernible indications of achievement and recognition, and as a way of comparing status across the dual ladder. For instance, in Figure 6.5, if vice president on the management side were equated with executive scientific director (as opposed to presidential fellow), there could be a perception that management jobs are more highly valued than scientific ones.

The number of levels below and above the point where the ladder forks tends to be specific to each organization. Key determinants typically include:

- The entry level (grade) for Ph.D. positions. In Figure 6.5, this is the level of the Senior Scientist. The Grade 3 and Grade 4 positions typically require undergraduate and/or "nonterminal" graduate degrees. The more positions suitable to non-PhD workers an organization has, the more levels there typically will be prior to the start of the dual path.

- How layered the organization is and how many viable and necessary levels of work can be identified on the technical and/or management side.

As with any structure or compensation program, it is essential that the actions of the company are consistent with the intent of the dual ladders. For example, compensation *opportunities* (base salary, short-term incentives, stock awards) should be equivalent for employees in the same grades but on opposite sides of the dual career path, recognition *opportunities* should be consistent with the company's business focus and values (mentions in newsletters, acknowledgements in ceremonies, placement on "walls of fame," participation in key scientific initiatives, attendance at/presentation to important conferences, etc.), and staffing proportions (the balance between management staff and scientific staff at each grade) should be appropriate.

Global Structure

Another important consideration in today's business world is whether or not structures should be singular/centralized or decentralized/localized. The number (and type) of structures in an organization depends on many factors, including the following:

- Whether different lines of business are in separate industries, and/or whether different functions require different skills

- Whether various employee groups represent different labor markets and total compensation profiles (e.g., nonexempt, exempt, executive, sales)

- Whether there exist divergent cultures or work environments, which, for example, may range from a customer service organization staffed by self-directed work teams (where a skill-based system within broadbands might be appropriate) to a functionally organized manufacturing plant (in which a more layered, step-based system may be appropriate)

- The extent to which the organization wants to create a seamless, "one-for-all" organization (single structure) vs decentralized, entrepreneurial operations (multiple structures)

Important considerations in determining the ideal number of structures include:

- *The degree to which internal equity is valued.* For instance, how often do people transfer across business units or geographical sites? Are functional specialists located in many or most sites, or has the company established centers of excellence, which may require the "importing" of highly skilled staff from anywhere in the world? To the extent that an organization operates more often using the latter model, it will require a more common structure, to help ensure that people movement is not hindered by grades and ranges that are only applicable locally.

- *The ability of the organization to support and administer a complex array of structures effectively.* One would hope that an organization could create and maintain the structure it needs to support its human resource strategy and needs. In reality, however, sometimes companies do not have the information infrastructure (HRIS, titles, job codes, etc.) that make it easy to translate (and transfer) jobs and employees across geographical boundaries.

Even within a single country, the concept of localization can be relative based on job levels and the variability of employee location. For example, compensation and recruiting professionals typically look to the national labor market for leadership and management jobs and very often for workers in high demand or professionals with rare skills. But for office support and basic production/blue collar jobs, the "local" job market will be much more appropriate.

Given that companies with operations in many areas across the globe are beginning to act like truly global organizations, perhaps the more strategic question is whether or not these companies should adopt global salary structures. If so, what does that mean in terms of salary levels and currency valuation, as well as both cash and stock incentive awards?

Of course, an organization's degree of "globality" can be viewed on a continuum. On the low end of this continuum, we would find organizations in which each country or region or business unit handles its own compensation system in a fairly autonomous fashion. In such instances, while the quality of market data and the objectivity of decisions might be highly variable, more weight still would be given to independent decision making than to corporate control and/or quality assurance. This would be typical in more entrepreneurial organizations or units and/or where the circumstances in each country are unique and/or in flux.

On the other end of the continuum, we find companies that emphasize consistency of treatment, and encourage and/or require the movement of employees across functional silos and sovereign borders. In such instances, a more consistent leveling of jobs is essential to ensure that, for example, a Principal Scientist at a Grade 6 in the United Kingdom does not find herself in Grade 5 after being transferred to the same job in the company's operations in Japan. The issue may be less about pay and more about status and recognition, which are typically matters of great importance in scientific, engineering and academic organizations, the very ones that often have dual career ladders.

In companies that do use global structures, the typical approach is to establish consistent leveling (the Principal Scientist has the same grade, job description, and experience and education requirements everywhere), to provide pay opportunities in alignment with a common pay philosophy (e.g., 50th percentile target salaries and 75th percentile short-term incentive targets), and to ensure that the market data and currencies are localized.

Although it would be wonderfully convenient if a company could just create a single set of salary ranges in its home country and then convert the currency values to arrive at the localized ranges, that approach would be counter to real market conditions and labor markets.

APPLICATION

A key element of a salary structure is how individual employees progress through it, both within ranges and between grades, and how managers make pay decisions

FIGURE 6.6   Salary range with pay zones

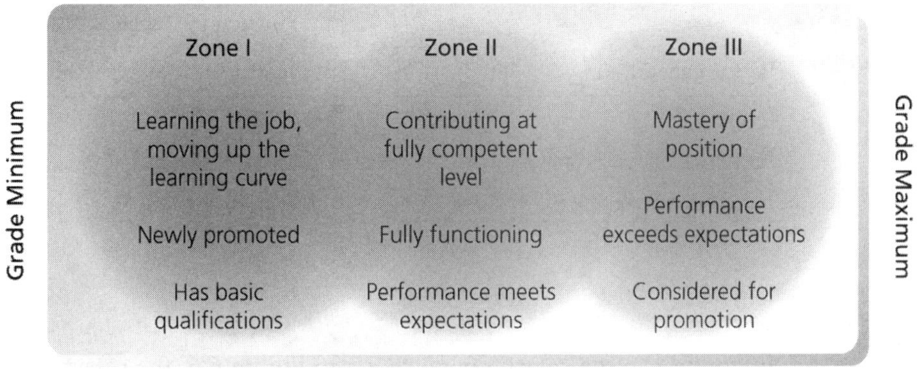

within it. As we noted before in slightly different words, there is no point to having a structure if it does not facilitate pay decision making and job or pay advancement. Figure 6.6 shows a common approach to managing pay within a range, primarily using performance.

Pay Zones Within the Salary Range.   The pay zones are not rigidly defined or mutually exclusive, but they do divide the range into practical segments that are tied to approximate levels of experience, performance, and promotability. This recognizes that pay determination is more an outcome of systematic, informed management judgment than of a scientific process and/or a mathematical formula.

A More Flexible Framework.   This allows companies to take into account market and individual factors. For example, if the market for financial analysts is very hot, it may be difficult or impossible to hire even new college graduates at the range minimum, in which case a zone (as opposed to a single point) at the beginning of the range will allow some individual discretion. If a pharmaceutical company needs to hire a world-class pharmacologist or an engineering company needs a top-notch, highly experienced aerospace engineer, the appropriate salary ranges for these jobs may be wide enough to handle their market-based pay requirements, but the hiring rate may need to be in the upper echelons of the range. So long as the new pay for these individuals does not unduly disrupt internal equity, these higher rates may be justified.

Performance-Based Pay.   A pay-for-performance salary policy fits well with this model, whether it is applied via the more typical "merit matrix" for determining annual salary adjustments (Table 6.5) or a more holistic, but harder to implement, "target pay" approach (Figure 6.7).

TABLE 6.5 Merit Matrix

	Position in Range			
Performance Rating	4th Quartile	3rd Quartile	2nd Quartile	1st Quartile
Exceeds	3–5%	5–7%	7–9%	9–12%
Fully meets	0%	3–5%	5–7%	7–9%
Needs improvement	0%	0%	0%	1–3%

MERIT MATRIX

In contrast to the salary range shown in Figure 6.6, the salary range depicted in Table 6.5 is divided into four quartiles, as opposed to three zones. Both methodologies are widely used and conceptually sound.

TARGET PAY

In Figure 6.7, the midpoint is defined as a market reference point. While the range itself is fairly typical, the approach to pay determination focuses not on what kind of increase the employee should get in a given year, but instead on an appropriate pay level based on her sustained performance or contribution, her experience and perhaps her "rating" on other relevant criteria the organization may have identified.

The pros of the approach shown in Figure 6.7 are that it allows a company to take a coordinated look at the relationship between an individual's overall contribution to an organization and the amount of money she is receiving (establishing an explicit *quid pro quo*), as opposed to looking only at what amount of increase the individual should receive. In the example, Jane's current pay of $27,000 is well below her target pay range of $32,250–34,500, which is predicated on the fact that Jane has significant experience and a sustained track record of making exceptional contributions to the company. Limiting Jane's salary growth to an incremental increase each year may prolong the time it will take for her to reach her target range. The delay could result in Jane feeling undervalued, possibly making her

FIGURE 6.7 Jane's salary

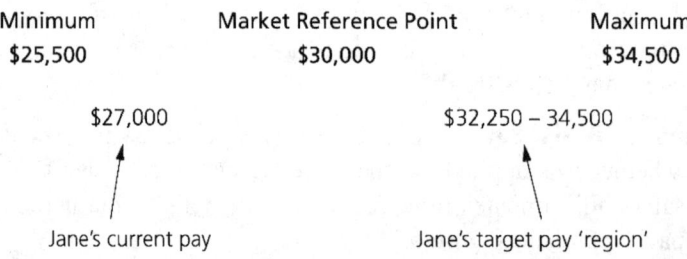

Minimum	Market Reference Point	Maximum
$25,500	$30,000	$34,500

susceptible to offers from other organizations that are willing to pay her in a way that recognizes her value.

The challenges of this approach are the need for company agreement on the key metrics, accurate and accessible data on an individual's contribution, and a confidence in management's ability to make decisions that often have significant cost implications for the company and personal impact on the employee being reviewed. In this example, Jane's manager needs to be able to quantify or at least justify the impact Jane is having on the company in light of how her pay compares to the market target and the significance of the expected increase.

SUMMARY

Salary structures, though often overlooked as high-impact tools, can be strong foundations for companies to communicate their priorities and develop total direct compensation programs that can help recruit, retain, and develop key talent. To allow salary structures to live up to their considerable potential, employers need to:

- Determine the design that will best suit their human resource strategies and cultural values: where on the spectrum behind rigid and flexible; between technically based and career-based; between locally controlled and centrally controlled; between singular and dual career?

- Decide on the basis for their structures: market; internal values; a combination?

- Agree on how to apply the structure to pay decision making: pay zones supported by a merit increase program; target pay levels; other?

The bottom line is that salary structures work best when they are established and administered as living systems in support of the strategic people needs of an organization and not merely as technically correct frameworks for slotting jobs and adjusting pay.

END NOTES

1. Andrew S. Rosen and David Turetsky, "Broadbanding: the Construction of a Career Management Framework," *WorldatWork Journal*, Fourth Quarter, 2002, p. 46.

2. Andrew S. Rosen and David Turetsky, "Broadbanding: the Construction of a Career Management Framework," *WorldatWork Journal*, Fourth Quarter, 2002, p. 48.

3. Howard Risher, "Second Generation Banded Salary Systems," *WorldatWork Journal*, First Quarter, 2007, p. 26.

4. Paraphrased from Andrew S. Rosen and David Turetsky, "Broadbanding: the Construction of a Career Management Framework," *WorldatWork Journal*, Fourth Quarter, 2002, p. 51.

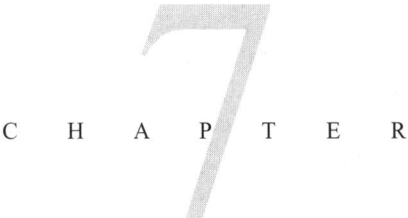

C H A P T E R

MERIT PAY

Myrna Hellerman, Senior Vice President, and
James Kochanski, Senior Vice President

Sibson Consulting

ANNUAL BASE PAY INCREASES HAVE hovered around 4 percent for many years and most year-end bonus pools for the broad-based employee population are small. So, what can organizations do to convince their employees that superior job performance will result in superior pay opportunities? How can employers avoid the "one-size-fits-all" pay increases and bonuses that send the message that individual performance does not count? How can employers encourage pay-for-performance but discourage managers from "gaming the system" for their employees?

Making annual pay actions matter is not easy, but the bottom line is that it is well worth the effort. The key is to improve how an organization thinks and talks about performance. Organizations that tell their employees "*Your* performance matters" will reap the rewards.

THE PROBLEMS WITH A "ONE-SIZE-FITS-ALL" APPROACH

Although the "one-size-fits-all" approach to base salary increases and bonus awards certainly scores points for administrative ease and convenience, it also communicates a very powerful and negative message: "Individual performance doesn't matter here . . . or at least it doesn't matter enough for us to make the effort to differentiate and reward the top contributors to the company's success." This message is likely to cause good performers to disengage, thinking, "Why push myself if I'm going to get the same pay opportunity as everyone else?"

Or look at it this way: Given a 3–4 percent merit increase (as little as $100 per month pre-tax for a $40,000-a-year employee) and a token $500-per-employee bonus, a performance evaluation process may not seem worth the effort. However, consider an organization with 6,000 employees whose average pay is $40,000 per year. A 3.5 percent merit budget adds about $8.4 million to the cost base and a $500-per-employee bonus payment adds another $3 million. To that $11.4 million, add the costs associated with pay-related benefits (e.g., paid time-off, 401(k) plan matches and pension accruals). That is a lot of money to give away because the performance evaluation process does not seem worth the effort.

HOW TO PUT MERIT BACK INTO ANNUAL PAY ACTIONS

Putting merit back into annual pay actions requires tough decisions and it may take several performance cycles to achieve. Nonetheless, meeting the challenge can be worthwhile. Studies show that the existence of pay consequences based on individual performance and impact promotes employee engagement in the success of the organization.

Following are several tested ideas from companies that are getting more bang for the buck in their base pay increase and bonus budgets.

Clearly Define Performance Expectations and Communicate that the Organization Rewards Top Performers. Employers who embrace this approach identify what they expect and what constitutes superior performance—and then reward accordingly through merit pay and incentive opportunities.

Take the case of a multi-billion-dollar retailer that had been teetering on the edge of bankruptcy for several years when a new CEO stepped in. Two years later, he was widely acclaimed by employees and investors alike for having "saved" the company. So it was a bit of a surprise when he made the following statement at a town hall employee meeting: "To help you calibrate this year's performance evaluations and corresponding pay expectations, you should know I am a three [strong contributor] on the five-point performance evaluation scale used for merit increases. That's what the board has told me. In my career I have earned a higher rating only a few times."

The CEO was addressing the fact that, during the company's many years of poor performance, almost all the workforce had been rated a four (outstanding) or five (superior) on the performance scale. As a result, the company had been distributing its limited merit increase pool with little differentiation, which made no sense.

In the end, the CEO's candor served to recalibrate the performance standard for the entire company. "If he's a three after all he has done, how can I justify a four or five?" the employees reasoned. The pay-for-performance message received even more credibility when the board's decisions for CEO compensation were consistent with his performance rating.

In just one performance cycle, the ratings fell into an almost perfect bell curve. The company recognized and rewarded key contributors at all levels and many nonperformers left. Vibrancy and credibility were restored to the pay-for-performance linkage.

Create Employee "Ownership" of the Performance Outcomes that Fund the Base Salary Increase and Bonus Pools. Ideally, employees who receive wage increases and year-end bonuses exhibit superior performance and skill building and make meaningful contributions to the organization's success. This, of course, assumes that they know what they must do to drive the desired business performance outcomes, which, in turn, fund the merit increases and bonus pools.

Some employers say, "Our employees won't understand and can't do anything about all this financial stuff. It's just easier to tell them that we didn't meet our targets and there isn't much money for base salary increases and bonuses." Others, however, see an opportunity to create an economic win–win situation for the company and its employees.

One meat processing company analyzed its business economics and developed sophisticated "value trees" that began with return on capital and flowed through each financial and nonfinancial measure that affected returns. When this analysis led the senior leadership team to conclude that the company would need more belt-tightening (including wage freezes) in order to ensure business success, the senior vice president in charge of plant operations protested the ivy-tower corporate view. "I bet if we can educate my guys on the slaughter floor about how we make money, we can get improvements that will generate money for wage increases and bonuses."

The senior vice president set up a simple financial literacy program for his employee group. It included a discussion of how the company and its customers make money (and how the company can help its customers make more money). After introducing them to a simplified version of the value trees, he asked his employees to work in teams to figure out what they could do in their day-to-day actions to improve the trees' financial outcomes. The "guys on the floor" took ownership of the performance outcomes and identified process improvements and individual skill development opportunities that improved profitability and sustainability—and consistently resulted in "meaty" merit budgets and bonus pools.

Aggregate Merit Budgets and Annual Bonus Pools so that Small Departments can Participate Fully. A growing number of employers combine their merit increase budgets for small departments with those for the next level or create merit budgets that cover at least 30 employees under three or more managers. In this way, the organization can address the concern that small departments with only a few employees cannot differentiate pay.

As an added advantage, the managers of these small departments learn to talk about pay and performance. Through these peer discussions they establish a clearer standard that differentiates top performance from expected performance. Further, groups of managers that the organization holds accountable for allocating a limited merit pool find a way to differentiate performance equitably.

For example, a food distribution company had a multitude of three- to four-employee teams, each with its own manager. These teams, all located at headquarters, provided a specific support service to the field operations. Although the teams were used to thinking of themselves as isolated units, when their merit increase budget was aggregated the managers were forced to think about all of their employees as part of a total service process. In their examination of the total process, it became very apparent which individuals and which teams were carrying more than their load in serving the field. The managers distributed the merit dollars accordingly and also started to revamp aspects of the process that were delivered inefficiently or ineffectively.

Form Groups of Managers to Calibrate Performance Ratings, Merit Increases, and Bonus Pool Allocations to Lessen Manager-to-Manager Differences. One frequently heard employee complaint is: "The system isn't fair because my manager rates tougher than your manager." One way to solve this problem is to convene a group of peer managers to calibrate performance ratings, merit increases, and bonus awards prior to finalization (see Figures 7.1 and 7.2).

Managers bring to this meeting a set of preliminary ratings and merit recommendations. Like the aggregation of budgets approach discussed above, these meetings help define what performance looks like at the highest ratings. Managers learn how to analyze the performance of their subordinates, are more diligent in documenting it, and seek out corporate-sponsored opportunities to learn how to manage it better.

A large multinational manufacturer adopted the group calibration of ratings approach. After the first, very painful, attempt at group calibration there was (and continues to be) an increase in the number of "hits" on the relevant on-line learning modules and increased attendance at company-sponsored training sessions on performance management and calibration.

Calibration also increases employee confidence in the process. Employees who know that managers in addition to their own review their performance have more trust in the fairness of the decisions.

Create Set-Asides to Reward Top Performers Accordingly. A top performer set-aside pool (merit increase and/or bonus) ensures that the organization systematically identifies top performers and sees that they receive greater financial rewards than do average performers. The organization can carve the set-aside pool out of the merit increase and/or bonus pool.

For instance, using the example given earlier in this chapter: If an organization has 6,000 employees whose average pay is $40,000 per year, a 3.5 percent merit budget would produce a merit pool of about $8.4 million. A set-aside of $900,000

FIGURE 7.1   Peer manager base salary calibration

ASSUMPTIONS

- All employees have similar base salary
- All managers have a $7200 merit increase budget
- Rating Scale: Exceptional (E); Outstanding (O); Meets (M); Below Meets (B)

	Manager A (Easy Rater)			Manager B (Tough Rater)			Manager C (Tough Rater with Some Differentiation)			Manager D (Balanced Rater)		
PRE-CALIBRATION	Employee 1	E	$1800	Employee 5	M	$1800	Employee 9	O	$3300	Employee 13	E	$3600
	Employee 2	E	$1800	Employee 6	M	$1800	Employee 10	M	$1300	Employee 14	O	$2000
	Employee 3	E	$1800	Employee 7	M	$1800	Employee 11	M	$1300	Employee 15	M	$1000
	Employee 4	E	$1800	Employee 8	M	$1800	Employee 12	M	$1300	Employee 16	M	$600
	TOTAL		$7200	TOTAL		$7200	TOTAL		$7200	TOTAL		$7200

	Manager A			Manager B			Manager C			Manager D		
POST-CALIBRATION	Employee 1	O	$1500	Employee 5	M	$1200	Employee 9	O	$1500	Employee 13	E	$3500
	Employee 2	M	$1000	Employee 6	M	$1000	Employee 10	M	$1000	Employee 14	O	$1500
	Employee 3	M	$1000	Employee 7	E	$3500	Employee 11	M	$1000	Employee 15	M	$1200
	Employee 4	E	$3900	Employee 8	E	$3500	Employee 12	O	$1500	Employee 16	M	$1000
	TOTAL		$7400	TOTAL		$9200	TOTAL		$5000	TOTAL		$7200

OBSERVATIONS

Pre-Calibration:

- Distribution of Ratings: Exceptional = 5, Outstanding = 2, Meets = 9
- Distribution of Merit Increase: Exceptional = $1800 - $3600
                                     Outstanding = $2000 - $3300
                                     Meets = $600 - $1800

Post-Calibration:

- Distribution of Ratings: Exceptional = 4, Outstanding = 4, Meets = 8
- Distribution of Merit Increases: Exceptional = $3500 - $3900
                                   Outstanding = $1500 (decision made to reward all outstanding performers similarly)
                                   Meets = $1000 - $1200 (decision made to recognize specific capability achieved by two individuals with an additional $200 "premium")

Source: Sibson Consulting

would provide an average additional $1,500 merit increase for the company's top 10 percent of performers and still allow for an average basic merit increase of $1,250 for all 6,000 employees.

Companies that use a set-aside pool find that the allocation determination process is beneficial in itself. For instance, in order to tap into its top performer

FIGURE 7.2   Peer manager annual incentive calibration
<u>ASSUMPTIONS</u>

- Total Bonus Pool: $48,000
- Rating Scale: Exceptional (E); Outstanding (O); Meets (M); Below Meets (B)
- Annual incentive decisions made after base salary and performance recalibration

Manager A			
Employee	**Rating**	**Base**	**AI**
Employee 1	O	$1500	$3600
Employee 2	M	$1000	$1600
Employee 3	M	$1000	$1600
Employee 4	E	$3900	$5500

Manager B			
Employee	**Rating**	**Base**	**AI**
Employee 5	M	$1200	$1600
Employee 6	M	$1000	$1600
Employee 7	E	$3500	$5100
Employee 8	E	$3500	$5100

Manager C			
Employee	**Rating**	**Base**	**AI**
Employee 9	O	$1500	$3600
Employee 10	M	$1000	$1600
Employee 11	M	$1000	$1600
Employee 12	O	$1500	$3600

Manager D			
Employee	**Rating**	**Base**	**AI**
Employee 13	E	$3500	$5100
Employee 14	O	$1500	$3600
Employee 15	M	$1200	$1600
Employee 16	M	$1000	$1600

<u>OBSERVATIONS</u>

- Distribution of Ratings: Exceptional = 4, Outstanding = 4, Meets = 8
- Distribution of Annual incentive: Exceptional = $5100 - $5500
  Outstanding = $3600 (decision made to reward all outstanding performers similarly)
  Meets = $1600 (decision made to reward all "Meets" similarly)
- Managers wanted to give those at the "Meets" level "just enough" to make a difference (amount of award was set at the level it would take to buy a major home appliance)
- Managers wanted "Outstanding" performers to receive at least twice what "Meets" performers received
- "Excellent" performers were to receive at least three times what "Meets" performers received

Source: Sibson Consulting

set-aside pool, one multimillion-dollar service provider requires managers to "nominate" their top performers. Using a simple form with very specific criteria, managers provide "evidence" of superior performance. Both the manager and the nominee must sign the form. The divisional senior management team then reviews the nominations and allocates the top performer set-aside pool among the most meritorious. The company introduced this approach because it wanted to return to a pure merit pay process. However, four years later, it still uses it because of these valuable side benefits:

- *The truly top performers hold their manager accountable for performance discussions and the nomination process.* Employees know they are eligible for nothing more than the across-the-board increase unless their manager gives evidence of their superior performance through a "top performer" nomination.

- *The design of the nomination form helps frame what top performance "looks like."* After the first year (when there was a flood of nominations), managers developed a better understanding of "what it takes" to rate a merit increase from the top performer set-aside pool.

- *Allocating the pool requires "silo-breaking" cross-organization calibration.* It also involves thoughtful senior management discussions about performance expectations.

- *Performance conversations at the senior management team level provide valuable insights into the organization's depth and quality of talent.* They now inform the company's evolving human capital planning process.

Reposition the Organization's Mindset so it Views Merit Increases and Bonuses as Investment Spending. The merit increase budget and annual bonus pools are long-term investments in talent that will drive the organization's sustainable success. Investing in employees who have not demonstrated the level of performance and skill building that the company expects does not make financial sense.

Repositioning the organization's mindset requires consistent and frequent communication with executives, managers, and employees. For example, a mid-sized financial services employer talks the language of its business to its employees. This firm positions all compensation discussions in terms of an investment. Employees understand that decisions with respect to individual merit increases reflect an evaluation of prior-year individual performance and applicable skill acquisition and the expectation of continued further "returns on [the merit increase] investment."

A large insurance company took the "return on investment" concept in a courageous direction. Its go-forward business strategy totally restructured the products offered and the markets served. As a result, the company's talent needs changed dramatically. Unfortunately, there was no increase in merit and bonus dollars to attract, engage, and retain the specialized talent needed to execute the go-forward business strategy. To address the issue of financial resource constraints, the company segmented its talent by business performance impact. The limited merit and bonus dollars were "invested" in the high performers in those roles that were critical to driving long-term sustainable business success, i.e., the high performers in roles with the largest return on investment potential for the company. The company said "no" to any future base pay and bonus investments in those talent segments where skills were no longer aligned with the company's needs.

Simplify the Performance Evaluation Process—Aim for Less Paperwork and More Meaningful Conversation.   Even when merit increase budgets and bonus pools are more robust, many employers still question the time and effort it takes to recognize and reward employees based on differentiated performance. In many cases, the protocols and processes are too complex—and sometimes too depersonalized and mechanical.

A global 25,000-employee engineering firm decided to automate its traditional, highly interactive approach to performance evaluation and pay action determination. An elegant 100 percent online solution replaced the performance-contracting dialog between managers and employees. All interactions were Internet-based. It was a very efficient system: The firm met every payroll deadline associated with merit increases, the merit increase and bonus pools were exactly spent and there were no tough, time-consuming, face-to-face conversations. Everything was on time, on budget, "on spec."

After several years with the online approach, the firm analyzed the outcomes. Among the findings was that managers and employees alike had learned to "game" the system. There was little differentiation of performance (and thus pay increases); almost everyone was a four or five on a five-point rating system. The on-line forms were complicated and time-consuming to complete. Employees and managers saw the process as a burdensome "joke." Even more important for a firm that prided itself on "high performance," its annual performance targets (strategic, operational, and financial) were achieved but not exceeded.

As a result, the firm made several important changes. While it preserved the document trail associated with the online system, it introduced simplified forms and restored face-to-face interactions between managers and employees. The updated approach required specific manager–employee and manager–manager "conversations" as well as cross-unit managerial calibration of performance ratings, merit increases, and bonus determinations.

The most lauded aspect of the new approach was a "Beginning of Cycle" small group meeting where the firm's strategic, operational, and financial performance imperatives for the New Year are reviewed. Employees and managers discussed the performance expectations required to deliver on those imperatives. The employees then used this information to develop their annual individual goals, which were used in future pay action decisions.

While the updated approach was still time-consuming, managers and employees agreed that it took the "black box" out of performance expectations and pay consequences and had re-energized the firm to deliver once again the superior performance that results in superior pay opportunities.

SUMMARY

Small base pay increase budgets and tiny or nonexistent bonus pools have caused many employers to ask themselves: "Can this 'little package' of merit increase and year-end bonus dollars really allow us to differentiate ourselves among employees?" and "Is it worth the time and effort to do so?" Indeed, some organizations are now in the habit of answering "no" to both questions. As a result, almost everyone gets essentially the same annual base pay increase and year-end bonus regardless of how they perform, squandering the opportunity to "make merit matter."

In order to make a difference, increases in an individual's wages and the size of a year-end bonus must be attributable to superior individual performance, effective skill building, and contributions to the organization's success. Employers must clearly define performance expectations, communicate that top performers will be rewarded, and then take the necessary steps to make it happen. Only then will annual pay actions, no matter how small they may seem at first glance, be meaningful.

Although each of the approaches described in this chapter has been used successfully, before an organization adopts any one (or a combination) of them, it should evaluate how it "fits" the organization's current and desired performance culture. Most important, the organization needs to assess its leadership's capability and its willingness to "put its money where its mouth is" and tell its employees, "We'll show you that your performance matters."

C H A P T E R

JOB ANALYSIS, DOCUMENTATION, AND JOB EVALUATION

Bernard Ingster, Ph.D., Consultant

Human Resources Management

IN AN EXTENSIVE REPORT ON the nature and methods of job evaluation, the National Research Council of the National Academy of Sciences defined the process as, "a formal procedure for hierarchically ordering a set of jobs or positions with respect to their *value* or *worth*, usually for the purpose of setting pay rates."[1]

From its beginnings, the process has included three sequential stages: (1) analysis of the job(s) being studied; (2) conversion of the findings of the analysis into a job description; and (3) the development of measurement scales to discern similarities and differences among jobs being evaluated. Historically, a tenet of job evaluation has been that only the job is rated, never the worker.[2]

In the United States, attempts to establish fair methods for setting pay levels of employees can be traced back to the early years of the federal government. In 1838, in response to grievances about pay equity from clerks working in federal departments, the Senate passed a resolution that urged adoption of a method to assign clerks to pay classes based on differences in the responsibilities and required qualifications of their jobs.[3] This was a cry for "internal equity" in the payment of wages.

However, 70 years passed before this rudimentary concept of position classification was elaborated upon and extended much beyond that population. During 1909 and 1910, E. O. Griffenhagen fully developed a classification process that was implemented by the municipal service of the City of Chicago. In 1912, Commonwealth Edison Company—a privately owned Chicago utility—also installed this process to cover 5000 employees.[4] Griffenhagen was the leading influence in a broad adoption of job evaluation for establishing equitable pay for governmental employees, including those in the Dominion of Canada (1919) and the United States Federal Service (1924).[5]

In a short period between 1909 and 1926, the four methods of job evaluation shown in Table 8.1 were developed. They continue to be the dominant techniques used. This chapter describes the principal documentation practices and design characteristics of the four methods and lists some advantages and disadvantages associated with their application.

Until the United States was drawn into World War II late in 1941, the number of employers who adopted job evaluation and related personnel administration practices was very small. However, with wartime regulation of wages under the National War Labor Board—established January, 1942—job evaluation and formal salary administration emerged as a major device to adjust pay inequities without igniting a destructive wartime inflation of wages and salaries. By the end of the war in 1945, vast numbers of employers, labor unions, and employees had

TABLE 8.1   Dominant Methods Used in Job Evaluation

	Method of Analysis Used	
Method of Comparison Used	By Considering the Entire Job	By Considering Job Elements
Comparing job against some scale	Classification Method E. O. Griffenhagen, 1909	Point Method Merrill R. Lott, 1924
Comparing job against job	Ranking Method Arthur H. Young, George Kelday, Early 1920s	Factor Comparison Method Eugene J. Benge, 1926

SOURCE: Table adapted from Eugene J. Benge, Samuel L. H. Burk, and Edward N. Hay, Manual of Job Evaluation: Procedures of Job Analysis and Appraisal (New York: Harper and Brothers, 1941), p. 20 and C. Canby Balderston, Wage Setting Based on Job Analysis and Evaluation, Industrial Relations Monograph No. 4 (New York: Industrial Relations Counselors, 1940), p.11.

become acquainted with the subject of this chapter. That was the impetus for the expansive use of job evaluation in compensation program design since that time.[6]

The chapter also covers a relatively recent job evaluation method that has interested human resources professionals but which has had limited application, the *position analysis questionnaire* (PAQ), as well as contemporary efforts to automate job evaluation through the use of computers. It will briefly discuss a variety of evaluation methods that have come into use based upon a broader focus than the duties of a job. These methods have been built upon studies of jobs with emphases upon worker characteristics. It closes with a brief analysis of the ongoing debate that first erupted in the United States 40 years ago regarding the attempted use of job evaluation to resolve charges of discriminatory pay practices.

JOB EVALUATION AS A TOOL TO ACHIEVE GOOD MANAGEMENT

At the start of the twentieth century, two analysts of workplace management—Frederick Winslow Taylor and E. O. Griffenhagen—were urging differing but related management reforms intended to benefit both employers and employees, and, thereby, society at large. Taylor promoted what he called "scientific management," the objective being to extend to all the potential benefits of living in an industrial society. He offered one of the earliest challenges to a then widely held view that employees and employers were bound in an inherently antagonistic relationship.

Taylor asserted that, in order for *either* group to prosper, the other must prosper as well.[7] Taylor's contribution to the development of job evaluation was his emphasis on management's responsibility (1) to use scientific methods of observation and planning to define and organize the tasks in a job and (2) to recruit and select people who, with continuing training, could perform the required tasks.[8]

While E. O. Griffenhagen also believed in the controlling importance of good definition of jobs in the employment relationship, his emphasis was upon what he termed "personnel administration," which included the following: the processes of formulating policies and exercising managerial functions respecting the selection, compensation, well-being, and conduct of the persons making up the human organization of an enterprise.[9] As did Taylor, Griffenhagen believed strongly that compensation plans were important tools for the general management of an organization.

GRIFFENHAGEN'S CONTRIBUTIONS TO JOB EVALUATION

Griffenhagen was the earliest advocate for the documentation of each aspect of a job evaluation process. A Griffenhagen *compensation plan* consists of three components: (1) a *classification outline* through which the positions in an enterprise are grouped into classes; (2) a *class specification* which identifies qualities of each class of positions that are important for personnel administration; and (3) *classification rules* for applying and administering the plan.[10]

Griffenhagen defined a position as a group of duties "calling for the attention of some one individual for their proper performance."[11] (He preferred the word *position* in place of *job*.) He stipulated that, while an employee may influence the nature of the position, the position not the doer defines what things *should* be done.

That focus on the concept of a position is central to his definition of a *class* of positions, which definition then becomes the keystone for building his method for achieving equitable compensation. A class is a "group of positions that may to all intents and purposes be considered interchangeable."[12] It is possible for a class to include only a single position, a situation common to higher level supervisory positions.

The *classification outline* aspect of the compensation plan consists of a series of documented studies of the positions in the workplace. *Job analysis* is the first task in the studies and involves "ascertaining and examining duties and other attributes that go to define a given position."[13] Griffenhagen describes the process as the "taking apart of a thing, its solution into constituent parts, or elements, and their examination."[14] There is no prescribed format for documentation of the job analysis, with many format variations evident in use among its practitioners at that time.

Upon completing job analysis, a narrative record of the findings of the analysis is prepared as a *position description*, thus enabling others to acquire a succinct, coherent, yet comprehensive understanding of the position.

Finally, with all position descriptions prepared, each position is sorted into an appropriate class level after which a *class specification* is written. That document includes:

1. The title to be applied to the class and all positions assigned thereto
2. A general description of duties common to the positions in the class, together with some illustrations of actual work performed
3. Identification of the qualifications required, which may include both those necessary and those desirable
4. Information regarding lines of promotion, preferably showing next higher and next lower rank
5. Compensation information for the class, including pay scales
6. Other facts or memoranda relating to the class within the personnel administration process[15]

At the risk of some oversimplification, the classification of a group of positions using this method is illustrated conceptually in Figure 8.1.

1. A broad, general category of positions is identified from among other broad categories of positions. For example, an *engineering group* is separated from *physical sciences positions* and *biological sciences positions*, all of which

FIGURE 8.1   Representation of the framework of the classification method

Grades	Professional Positions		Clerical/Technical Support Positions	
	Mechanical Engineering	Civil Engineering	Accounting Clerical	Electronics Technician
1	C			
2	C			
3	C	C		
4	C	C		
5	C	C		
6	C	C		C
7			C	C
8			C	C
9			C	
10			C	

C = A class of positions

Grade 1 contains the position classes of "highest value" among the positions covered

> Prior to assigning specific pay levels to the grades, *class specifications* are prepared for each class.

are in a category of *professional positions* in contrast with *nonprofessional, support positions*.

2. The engineering positions are divided into subdivisions, such as *civil* and *mechanical engineering*.

3. The mechanical engineering positions, for example, are then grouped in a hierarchy through study of the position descriptions prepared after job analysis has been performed. The question being answered in this stage of the process is: considering the position in its entirety, which have (a) the most complex duties *and* (b) the highest level of responsibilities *and* (c) the most demanding qualifications requirements?

4. The process is then applied to the civil engineering positions in like manner, and then extended to all remaining categories of positions.

5. Each hierarchy is then examined separately to determine the number of *classes* into which the positions in each hierarchy should be placed. This effort usually results in a compromise between groupings that are exceptionally homogeneous and narrow and groupings that are loosely inclusive. Neither too few nor too many classes are desirable.

6. Classes are then compared *across* each occupational specialty to determine the number of *levels* or *grades* of work that exist within the entire block of the positions studied. Figure 8.1 illustrates the configuration of the hierarchy at the completion of this step.

While the classification method produces a hierarchy of positions through use of a common sense, nonquantitative approach, compensation analysts who have administered programs based on this method indicate that (1) it is a very complex system, (2) it is very flexible in accommodating an exceptional range of differing types of jobs, and (3) it is prone toward either loose or tight interpretations of language, creating problems in maintaining appropriate grade levels.

Such matters were long recognized by the U.S. Civil Service Commission which had been using the classification method for its General Schedule compensation system since 1924. In 1975 the Commission developed and adopted a point method, named the Factor Evaluation System, for evaluating nonsupervisory positions in Grades 1–15 of the General Schedule.[16]

THE RANKING METHOD

This method is a second type of *whole-job*, nonquantitative grading process. It has been described as a "card-sorting system, because under it jobs are arranged from high to low as are the cards of a playing card deck."[17] Differing jobs are ranked one against the other according to the perceived relative value of each job to the organization. The rankings create groups of jobs that can then be treated in a common manner for purposes of pay determination.

The method was used by Arthur H. Young and George Kelday at the International Harvester Company in the early 1920s, and they are usually considered to be its originators. In their use, judgments of "job value" were made without benefit of any common set of clarifying criteria.[18] However, others who have used the process sometimes introduce criteria to assist the evaluators.[19]

The virtue of the Ranking Method is simplicity. However, unless it is used with the discipline of some definition of differing levels of job worth that the job rankers adopt in common, it is not a good choice for establishing internal equity in a compensation program. On the other hand, in small organizations willing to assure its use in a disciplined, consistent manner with excellent record keeping, it is a viable method for establishing a formal compensation program.

THE POINT METHOD

This method is the most widely used of the four dominant methods under discussion. It was devised in 1925 by Merrill R. Lott when he was superintendent of employment at the Sperry Gyroscope Company, and he described it fully in his book one year later.[20] The Point Method provides a capability to job evaluators of quantifying their judgments about the relative worth of various aspects of jobs by assigning "points" to those judgments. It produces a final statement about job worth expressed as a single total of those points. As with most attempts to quantify attributes of things that are not readily measurable, the Point Method has a tendency to be perceived as being a "more scientific" method than either the Classification or the Ranking Method.

Nearly all applications of a point method of job evaluation require job analysis and the preparation of job descriptions. The methods for analyzing a job and then preparing the description could be similar to those used by Griffenhagen in his classification method.

However, some users of the method—such as the U.S. Civil Service Commission in applying its Factor Evaluation System (FES), as previously noted—merge the job analysis process with the position description preparation process to create a single, distinctive formatted document.

In the FES program, for example, the first section of the position description is titled "Major Duties" and answers the question, "What does the employee do in this position?" Each statement in this section starts with an active verb, as in: "Establishes food standards and plans regular menus complying with nutritional and cost allocations" or "Designs art work for multicolor posters to meet needs of requestors."[21]

In the next section information is developed to be used in assigning point values to each factor. As an illustration for Factor 1, Knowledge Required by the Position, for example, the analyst needs to answer: (1) What kind of knowledge is needed? (2) How is it used?[22] In further illustration, the questions to be answered regarding Factor 4, Complexity, are: (1) What is the nature of the assignment? (2) What facts or conditions does the employee consider in identifying what needs to be done? (3) After considering the facts, what actions or responses does the employee make?[23]

FES instructions are extensive and prescriptive, with many standardized procedures that must be followed without deviation.[24] All of the FES factors listed in Table 8.2 are also widely used in many other versions of point method job evaluation.

In general, there are approximately eight steps in the process of designing a point plan for evaluating jobs.

1. A number of factors are identified as being common to all jobs to be evaluated. These are called the *compensable factors*.

2. The factors are defined and weighted to reflect their perceived importance in the organization.

3. Each factor is analyzed to determine how many different *levels* of job content will probably need to be covered by the factor. These levels are usually called *degrees of the factor*, and they are also defined.

4. The degrees for each factor are quantified using the relative weightings of the factors. Table 8.3 is a representation of a type of evaluation scale that is used in this method.

TABLE 8.2   Factor Evaluation System Factors

Factor 1	Knowledge required by the position
Factor 2	Supervisory controls
Factor 3	Guidelines (for the work)
Factor 4	Complexity
Factor 5	Scope and effect (of the work)
Factor 6	Personal contacts
Factor 7	Purpose of contacts
Factor 8	Physical demands
Factor 9	Work environment

5. The evaluators study a written description of each job. They assign point values for each factor by making judgments about the job content using the predetermined points and job requirements for the degrees of each factor. (No reference is made to the existing wage or salary of the incumbents in the job.)

6. Each job acquires a *total job content* point value.

7. The titles of the positions are hierarchically arranged according to their total point values.

8. Groupings of total points are tested to develop appropriate job grades. The grades can then be converted to pay levels.

Those who have administered point method plans in organizations that inform employees of all of the details of the plan invariably find that most employees understand and find reasonable the principles and rules governing the program.

TABLE 8.3   Representation of a Job Evaluation Scale in the Point Method

Job Requirements	Points
Responsible only for use of own time	15
	30
Must coordinate with crew in a production unit	45
	60
Assures flow of individual processing and meets production schedule for machined parts	75
	90
Develops schedule and assumes joint and supervisory responsibility for work unit	105
	120

THE FACTOR COMPARISON METHOD

This method was developed by Eugene J. Benge in 1926. It is a second method involving the assignment of points to a hierarchy of job content. The concept has been represented as having evolved out of studying the advantages and disadvantages of the three other dominant methods discussed in this chapter.[25] As with all of the other pioneering developers of job evaluation, Benge emphasized the importance of documented job analysis and the preparation of a position description prior to performing the evaluation. These two early steps were to be performed by a job analyst with two essential personal qualities—analytic ability and a pleasing personality. Analytic ability is necessary to separate essential facts from nonessential facts and then to report the data in a manner that keeps significant items in proper relationship. A pleasing personality is necessary because of the need to relate to all levels of employees.[26]

Benge emphasizes that the job analyst should gather information about non-supervisory, wage rate employees' jobs through interview directly with the employee.[27] The job analysis in this method develops information about (1) the general purpose of the work, (2) personal duties and their frequency of performance, (3) instructions received, (4) type of any responsibility, (5) reports prepared, (6) equipment used, (7) contacts with others, including the purpose, (8) minimum education and experience required, and (9) working conditions.[28] Benge supported the use of questionnaires completed by incumbents in supervisory and other salaried positions.[29]

The final position description—which may be called a job specification—is a two-sided form. One side consists of a narrative summary of the job characteristics. The second side summarizes the data collected in job analysis and groups it under one of the five factors used to compare the jobs: mental requirements, skill requirements, physical requirements, responsibility, and working conditions.[30]

The factor comparison method is based upon three key ideas: (1) it assumes that the rates paid for a small number of key jobs in an organization will be found to be in a proper relation to one another; (2) it builds job content measurement scales for each of the five factors just listed from the rates of the key jobs; and (3) it compares each job to each other, factor by factor, and expresses their differing value in terms of similarities and differences in the values of the respective measurement scales. These concepts can be represented as shown in Figure 8.2.

The most significant derivative of the factor comparison method is the *Guide Chart-Profile Method of Job Evaluation* developed by Edward N. Hay and Dale Purves in the early 1950s.[31] Hay had used factor comparison evaluation, and he was a friend and colleague of Benge. Hay's innovations were (1) the elimination of wage rates as the basis for creating measurement scales and (2) the introduction of "profiles" that in effect substitute percentages of job content for the process of allocating a portion of wage rates to each factor. Over more than 60 years, this method has achieved worldwide use in all economic sectors through the consulting organization founded by Hay, currently The Hay Group.

FIGURE 8.2   Building job content measurement scales for the factor comparison method

| Job Title | Current Pay Rate | Factors for Comparing Key Jobs | | |
		Technical Knowledge	Complexity of Work	Responsibility
A	$22.00/h	7.80	5.50	8.70
B	$16.50/h	6.60	4.95	4.95
C	$13.00/h	5.85	4.55	2.60

The job titles are those of key jobs which are a cross section of all jobs and which have current rates considered to be in proper relation to each other.

The factors are considered to be of significance to all jobs. The factors selected *only* for this illustration are:

Technical Knowledge Required to Perform the Work; Complexity of the Work; Level of Responsibility Assigned to the Job

Job analysts are asked to allocate a portion of the current pay rate to each factor according to the analysts' views of the relative importance of that factor in each job. Their differing views are rationalized, and the allocated pay rates can be considered to be like "points" in job content measuring scales for use in evaluating all other jobs.

Thus, a job title "D" would be tested against jobs A, B, and C to determine a "best" selection of a rate from one of the rates shown under each factor. Thus, if D appears to be comparable to job A in Technical Knowledge, it might only be comparable to the B title for Complexity of Work and for Responsibility.

The cumulative values of the three rates for each job would result in a hierarchy that can be grouped into grades.

THE POSITION ANALYSIS QUESTIONNAIRE

There is a traditional admonition given to job evaluators who are using any of the four dominant methods described: neither the *incumbents* in a job being evaluated nor *any characteristic* of those incumbents may be considered during the process.[32] However, this restraint is challenged by the developers of the *position analysis questionnaire* (PAQ), Ernest J. McCormick, P. R. Jeanneret, and Robert C. Mecham.

The PAQ shifts the traditional focus in job evaluation from subjective judgments of the compensable factors that should be measured in jobs to statistical determinations of how the market place is actually valuing worker characteristics. This is accomplished through the use of a structured job analysis questionnaire, developed on the basis of extensive studies that attempted to identify every possible worker behavior. The questionnaire, copyrighted in 1969 by Purdue Research Foundation, is divided into six divisions that cover 187 "job elements." For example, one division consists of 35 job elements measuring the types of information sources which must be perceived by a worker.[33]

There is a substantial amount of published research covering PAQ. All aspects of the questionnaire's administration—from acquiring the instrument through its processing and analysis—are very carefully controlled. I have administered the PAQ in a regulated manner and then interviewed the participants about the experience. There was a nearly unanimous feeling that probably every important aspect of their work had been covered by the questionnaire.

COMPUTER-ASSISTED JOB EVALUATION

The importance of computers to the administration of the PAQ is suggestive of possible automated applications of job-content based job evaluation systems as well. Many consulting organizations offer such systems, some with a preestablished evaluation method and others with customizing opportunities for clients. The installations are frequently built utilizing a point plan similar to that described in this chapter. All involve use of a structured questionnaire for data collection. The formats and types of the outputs vary considerably.

The vendors of the plans invariably cite the following benefits: (1) reduced time in collecting job content data; (2) consistency in the quality of data gathered; (3) the elimination or computer-generation of job descriptions, if desired; (4) the elimination or reduced use of job evaluation committees, which saves executive time; and (5) the ease and relatively low cost of maintenance and updating of the database.

Much of the attraction of computer-assisted evaluation is its potential to maintain current programs with reduced staffing and cost. However, even customized automation may not be able to preserve all desired aspects of an existing program.

HISTORIC AND CONTEMPORARY USES OF JOB DOCUMENTATION

Griffenhagen early recognized that the documentation necessary for job evaluation would have value in other aspects of personnel administration, such as recruitment of new employees.[34] From the 1920s to the present, such documentation has regularly been used for such purposes as orientation of new employees, training, performance assessment and the building of career ladders for advancement and promotion.[35]

For contemporary employers, the need for documentation for job evaluation and for general workplace management is inescapable because of the explosion of laws prohibiting discrimination in employment. That explosion was ignited by the passage of Title VII of the federal Civil Rights Act of 1964. Some of the successor laws—particularly the Americans with Disabilities Act (ADA)—have pushed employers into the detailing of job elements not previously addressed in job analysis. Untangling "essential job functions" to determine if a qualified employment candidate with a disability can be reasonably accommodated has led to a blizzard of paper with a new vocabulary such as "core competencies."

The challenge for human resources managers within this new set of legal requirements is to avoid excessive integration of data into a single document to cover multiple uses. Such integrative efforts could confuse application of the information for a targeted purpose such as job evaluation.

USEFULNESS OF TRADITIONAL METHODS OF JOB EVALUATION

In 2003, Robert L. Heneman reported on a research study commissioned by the U.S. Office of Personnel Management which was seeking guidance for improving its compensation systems.[36] This is an exceptionally extensive examination of published research regarding a very broad array of methods used as a basis for determining equitable payment for work.

In addition to the literature covering the four dominant job evaluation methods described in this chapter, Heneman studied the literature covering methods of compensation built on a foundation of *work evaluation*. The latter includes efforts to pay workers based on: (1) competencies—defined in terms of knowledge, skills, abilities and other attributes of people, including participation on work teams—that can be related to high performance in the workplace; (2) market pricing of jobs; and (3) banding together jobs having common characteristics into separate compensation bands.[37]

He also provides a very useful summary of the variety of perspectives on job and work evaluation held by leading advocates and scholars in compensation management.[38] Finally, his major findings from the literature review include these outcomes:

- Point-factor systems are very reliable

- Total point values are more reliable than point values for each factor

- The validity of work evaluation systems is not well known

- The affective reactions of people to work evaluation systems is not well known

- Competency pay is not used very often

- Skill-based pay works well under certain conditions

- Most work evaluation systems have not been evaluated[39]

CAN JOB EVALUATION SETTLE CHARGES OF DISCRIMINATORY PAY PRACTICES?

If the "true worth of a job" can be determined, a useful process could be developed to address charges that a given pay practice has roots in racial or gender bias. This is essentially the matter that the U.S. Equal Employment Opportunity Commission asked the National Academy of Sciences to study in 1977.

TABLE 8.4 Draft Guidelines for Using Job Evaluation Procedures in a Nondiscriminatory Manner

1. Use a single job evaluation system for all employees.

2. The attributes of jobs deserving compensation should be explicit and public.

3. Factors chosen for factor-based plans should be free of racial or gender bias.

4. Factor scores should be fully consistent with the compensable factors of item 2.

5. Factor weights should not result in adverse impact upon a worker population.

6. The integrity of the job evaluation plan should be protected through:

    a. Clear and complete documentation, distributed for all to read

    b. Good training for all who must use the plan

    c. Regular, documented audits of all aspects of its administration

    d. A formal appeals process open to all employees

    e. Committees that are representative of all employee groups

7. The evaluation of specific jobs should be capable of demonstrated validity.

SOURCE: A working group in which the author participated was convened by the Committee on Occupational Classification and Analysis on May 14–15, 1979 to review a draft of guidelines referenced here. While the draft guidelines were never published, they were fully consistent with the discussion of job evaluation plans in Treiman and Hartmann, pp. 94–95.

The committee appointed to review the matter reached several conclusions related to subjects of this chapter: (1) no universal standard of job worth exists; (2) existing wage rates of labor markets do not provide a measure of relative worth of jobs free of discriminatory practices; and (3) when used under certain guidelines, job evaluation plans can provide measures of job worth useful in identifying and reducing wage discrimination for those covered by a given plan.[40] General guidelines that would be helpful to plan designers are listed in Table 8.4.

While the committee of the National Academy of Sciences did not advocate the universal adoption of job evaluation by all employers, it found continuing experimentation and development of these ideas to be worthy.[41] This is welcome acknowledgment of the socially beneficial contributions of the pioneering developers of job evaluation cited in this chapter.

END NOTES

1. Donald J. Treiman, "Job Evaluation: An Analytic Review," *Interim Report of the Committee on Occupational Classification and Analysis to the Equal Employment Opportunity Commission*, Washington, DC: National Academy of Sciences, 1979, p. 1.

2. Ibid.

3. U.S. Civil Service Commission, *Basic Training Course in Position Classification: Part 1—Fundamentals and the Federal Plan, Personnel Methods Series No. 11—Part 1*, rev. edn, Washington, DC: Government Printing Office, 1965, p. 25.

4. E. O. Griffenhagen, *Classification and Compensation Plans as Tools in Personnel Administration*, Office Executives' Series, No. 17, New York: American Management Association, 1926, p. 17.

5. Ibid., pp. 20–21.

6. David W. Belcher, *Compensation Administration*, Englewood Cliffs, N.J: Prentice-Hall, 1974, p. 92.

7. Frederick Winslow Taylor, *The Principles of Scientific Management*, New York: Harper and Brothers, 1911, p. 10.

8. Ibid., pp. 38–9.

9. Griffenhagen (see note 4), p. 4.

10. Ibid., p. 5.

11. Ibid., p. 6.

12. Ibid., pp. 9–10.

13. Ibid., p. 6.

14. Ibid.

15. Ibid., p. 10.

16. Treiman (see note 1), pp. 19–20.

17. Eugene J. Benge, Samuel L. H. Burk, and Edward N. Hay, *Manual of Job Evaluation: Procedures of Job Analysis and Appraisal*, New York: Harper and Brothers, 1941, p. 23.

18. C. Canby Balderston, *Wage Setting Based on Job Analysis and Evaluation*, Industrial Relations Monograph No. 4, New York: Industrial Relations Counselors, 1940, p. 11.

19. Benge, Burk, and Hay, pp. 23–5.

20. Merrill R. Lott, *Wage Scales and Job Evaluation*, New York: Ronald, 1926.

21. U.S. Civil Service Commission, *How to Write Position Descriptions Under the Factor Evaluation System, PS-27*, Washington, DC: Government Printing Office, June, 1978, p. 8.

22. Ibid., pp. 10–12.

23. Ibid., pp. 19–21.

24. U.S. Civil Service Commission, *FES Position-Classification Standards, Instructions for the Factor Evaluation System, TS-27*, Washington, DC: Government Printing Office, May, 1977, pp. 1–11.

25. Benge, Burk, and Hay, p. 41.

26. Ibid., p. 59.

27. Ibid., p. 64.

28. Ibid. pp. 65–8.

29. Ibid., p. 64.

30. Ibid., p. 77.

31. Edward N. Hay and Dale Purves, "A New Method of Job Evaluation: The Guide Chart-Profile Method," *PERSONNEL Magazine*, vol. 31, no. 1, July 1954, p. 72.

32. Griffenhagen (see note 4), p. 20. This is discussed in his report to the Canadian Government upon the completion of his installation of his method for 60,000 positions in the Dominion of Canada.

33. Robert C. Mecham, "Quantitative Job Evaluation Using the Position Analysis Questionnaire (PAQ); A Description and Comparison with Traditional Job Evaluation Methods," *Personnel Administrator*, vol. 28, no. 6, June 1983, p. 82.

34. Griffenhagen (see note 4), p. 8.

35. U.S. Civil Service Commission, *How to Write Position Descriptions Under the Factor Evaluation System* (see note 21), p. 3.

36. Robert L. Heneman, "Job and Work Evaluation: A Literature Review," *Public Personnel Management*, vol. 32, no. 1, Spring, 2003, p. 47.

37. Ibid., pp. 43–9.

38. Ibid., pp. 54–6.

39. Ibid., p. 66.

40. Donald J. Treiman and Heidi I. Hartmann (eds), "Women, Work, and Wages: Equal Pay for Jobs of Equal Value," *Final Report of the Committee on Occupational Classification and Analysis to the Equal Employment Opportunity Commission*, Washington, DC: National Academy of Sciences, 1981, pp. 94–5.

41. Ibid.

C H A P T E R

SALARY SURVEYS

Don York, Senior Vice President, and Tim Brown, Vice President

Radford Surveys & Consulting

A KEY OBJECTIVE OF THE compensation function is to maximize the return on a company's investment in its people. Achieving that objective requires companies to balance the dual goals of designing pay programs that drive performance, and fulfilling their fiduciary duty to spend money responsibly. Striking this balance requires knowledge of what similar companies pay employees who perform similar jobs, in other words, labor market compensation data. There are numerous sources of compensation data (such as that from labor groups, industry groups, government entities, and third-party, commercial vendors). This chapter discusses the role of commercial, third-party vendor compensation surveys in serving as a basis for pay decisions in organizations today, as well as the issues companies should examine when determining which survey is best for their needs.

CURRENT BUSINESS ISSUES

The business issues facing human resources organizations today have created an environment in which pay data is increasingly critical. The effective use of that data requires increasing sophistication as U.S. employment levels rise, markets continue to expand globally, and demographic trends point to an aging (and in the long-term, contracting) workforce. Organizations are also dealing with stricter regulation related to executive compensation. In the past several years, regulatory agencies and shareholder activist groups have stepped up scrutiny of executive pay, resulting in new requirements for greater disclosure of pay and pay practices for top executives. At the broad-based employee level, changes in the Fair Labor Standards Act and the accounting requirements for stock option grants have meant some significant adjustments for companies' pay practices. Additionally, job definitions have been subject to frequent change, perhaps most visibly in the cases where new technologies render certain job categories obsolete (e.g., "word processor"). Similarly, the complexity of the workplace today has also spawned many so-called hybrid jobs that defy traditional survey job definitions and categories. In addition, work once done by full-time employees is now being shifted to contractors and contingent workforces, two job types for which there is little available credible market data.

THE ROLE OF COMPENSATION DATA

Fundamentally, compensation surveys provide information about how the market (defined in terms of labor competition within an industry and/or geography) values a given job. This data is typically broken down by type of compensation vehicle, including base salary, bonus, commissions, equity, and other forms of compensation. In addition to providing a foundation for creating pay plans that align pay philosophy and business strategy, surveys are used to help companies set budgets. Compensation surveys also help companies understand what competitors are doing with respect to pay practices, for example the frequency of bonus payouts, the vesting for equity, and the target mix of pay. Other roles and applications of surveys include:

- Revealing evolving trends in the labor market (growth in demand for particular jobs, and the shift from stock option allocation to restricted stock, for example)
- Diagnosing compensation issues
- Creating a basis for compensation plan design or redesign
- Establishing market competitive pay mix levels
- Providing the data necessary to effectively communicate a new compensation strategy by showing survey data on current and projected pay positions
- Determining promotional increase plans, merit budgets, salary range movement and salary differentials in various locations
- Establishing and maintaining internal equity
- Establishing how much to offer a new hire and/or determining the appropriate salary grade for a new position

TYPES OF SURVEYS

Compensation surveys are published by a variety of sources, and take numerous forms.

Subscription Surveys. Subscription surveys are typically published by a third-party, commercial survey publisher, which collects, analyzes, summarizes, and reports the compensation data. Participating companies (those providing data) pay a fee, and typically results are only available to participants. Subscription surveys produce both overall results and additional cuts of the data (e.g., geographic, industry, company size, etc.). Participants also often have the opportunity to create custom data cuts (e.g., selecting specific companies to form a peer group-based report). These surveys typically are conducted on an annual basis and have a fairly consistent participant group, which results in meaningful year-over-year data comparisons. A variation on this model allows nonparticipants to obtain overall survey results for a much larger fee than that paid by participants.

Custom Surveys. Custom surveys are often conducted on behalf of a sponsoring company or organization to meet a specific data need. Similar to subscription surveys, custom surveys are often conducted by a third party. However, unlike subscription surveys, custom surveys are limited to a targeted and typically small group of potential participants (such as a specific list of companies, industry niche, geographic area, etc.) and may be conducted on an infrequent basis.

Online Self-Reported Surveys. An emerging survey type is the self-reported compensation survey, often conducted online. As opposed to typical subscription or custom surveys where employers report data for all employees performing specific roles, data from self-reported surveys comes from individuals who directly provide their own pay information. There are several drawbacks to this data, including:

- Most employees are not as skilled as compensation professionals at assessing their job level and matching it appropriately; nor do they typically have access to the full scope of available tools and information to job match effectively

- Data provided by employees cannot be easily verified and validated by the vendor

- Employees typically provide their data on an ad hoc basis, resulting in a less-than-consistent database

- There is an inherent question regarding whether self-reported data is representative of the market overall

Practices Surveys. These surveys typically focus more on "how" companies compensate their employees, rather than "how much." Practices information details the ways in which companies structure and implement the various components of their compensation programs. Comprehensive surveys in this category cover incentive and equity plan types, participation levels, payout or vesting schedules, funding mechanics, equity burn rates, and many more plan design and administrative issues. These surveys may also cover compensation of the board of directors as well as company-wide pay practices, including salary increase budgets and actuals, salary structure adjustments, geographic differentials, shift premium policies, new-hire and retention bonus programs, car policies and turnover.

Pulse or Flash Surveys.   "Pulse" and "flash" are general terms for a topical survey, which is meant to focus on a key area of concern facing organizations. These surveys, partially characterized by the speed with which they are produced, are meant to fill the need for intelligence on how the market is responding to particular events, such as regulatory or accounting changes, emerging practices and/or demand for a particular skill or specialized job type. These surveys often focus on a single topic. Some hot topics or emerging trends become content for future ongoing surveys, but many topics are surveyed only once.

DATA ELEMENTS INCLUDED

Surveys results provide a varying range of data elements. For certain job levels, base salary data alone may be sufficient, because other compensation components are not typically included in the compensation package. However, for many jobs, a more comprehensive picture of the market is essential. In addition to base salary, these surveys cover incentives (both target incentives and actual payouts), equity and long-term incentives in various forms (stock options, restricted stock, performance shares, long-term performance bonuses), and potentially allowances and perquisites. In such surveys, it is important that compensation elements be reported in combination, as well as individually. For example, total cash compensation (base salary plus incentives) is reported as a unit in addition to separate base salary and incentives figures. Since 50th percentile base salary plus 50th percentile incentives does not necessarily equal 50th percentile total compensation, the total cash compensation figure should be calculated in the survey output so that the survey user has a better picture of the market range of cash compensation.

More comprehensive surveys may also report additional data combinations, such as total direct compensation, which combines base salary plus incentive plus equity value, or total remuneration, which adds the value of benefits to the equation.

SURVEY DATA SAMPLE

There is an ongoing potential conflict between the size and the selectivity of the data sample in surveys. Put another way, for a given survey job, is it better to have a larger number of incumbents for a more general cut of the data, or a smaller sample that captures a more narrow market niche? Overall survey results are appropriate for certain types of jobs, but typically companies want to compare their compensation levels to those of companies they compete with for talent. The issue here is that, if the market is too narrowly defined, the size of the data sample yields results that are subject to over-weighting by a relatively small number of companies. In such cases, taking a somewhat broader view of the market renders more reliable and representative results.

Company demographics used to define the market sample can include one or more of the following elements.

Company Size.   Data segmented by company revenue (or assets, market capitalization, or number of employees) is particularly useful for executive level positions, given the general correlation between company size and compensation at that level of the organization.

Geographic Area.   Talent is sourced primarily from the local labor market for lower-level positions, so geography forms the competitive frame of reference for those jobs. By contrast, geography is a less significant driver in professional, management, and executive compensation; in these cases, revenue and industry play a larger role than does geography.

Industry.   Certain jobs are industry-specific, and obtaining data from other companies with the same type of job in the same industry niche can be important. The structure of compensation packages also differs by industry—for example, the high technology and life sciences industries emphasize equity more than other industries. At the same time, industry segmentation (sub-industry) may be less significant for more senior-level positions. Again using high tech as an example, the market sample is best defined by company size rather by type of high tech company (software, hardware, networking, telecomm, etc.) in determining CEO compensation.

Company Type.   Companies can be corporations or subsidiaries, public or private, mature or emerging (and numerous combinations of these). The pay structure differentiations driven by company type are particularly relevant to senior executive positions. For example, compensation levels for general management and finance positions tend to be higher in corporations than in subsidiaries, and equity tends to play a bigger role in emerging, prepublic companies than in public entities.

SURVEY DATA PRESENTATION

Report Types.   Surveys that provide a variety of data presentation vehicles can be a distinct advantage for participating companies. As opposed to the traditional static paper output, surveys are increasingly published using a variety of output vehicles. While many survey providers still publish paper reports, they have augmented those reports with spreadsheet output, online reports, and online access to certain elements of the survey database required for custom reports. Each of these distribution vehicles has advantages and disadvantages. Paper reports provide easy access to answers for specific questions, but are difficult to update frequently, inhibit information sharing among multiple users, and require data entry when additional analyses are necessary. Spreadsheet output will directly interface with a company's HRIS which facilitates salary planning, competitive analysis, and aggregation with other survey databases, but has limitations if the user needs data in a report format that can be shared with senior management or other audiences. Online reports and data access capabilities can be updated on a periodic basis as the database changes, and can also generate downloadable data sets in camera-ready presentation formats. Multiple users in different locations can also access data more easily with online reporting.

Averages and Percentiles.   Most survey reports contain both averages and percentiles; some will also show the absolute high and low range of the data. It is important to analyze the data in a variety of ways. While the average is an appropriate summation of the data for a particular element, it does not convey the range of practices and can be skewed when the data sample is small and there are significant outliers. Using the 50th percentile (median) rather than the average can offset skewing of the data. Percentiles also reflect the range of the data sample, and allow users to more specifically target their competitive position. For example, a company can have a stated competitive position of being "5 percent above the average," without knowing where that places them against their competitors. On the other hand, if the targeted competitive position is stated in terms of a percentile, which in turn is reflected in the survey data, the user has a better sense of what portion of the market it leads or lags.

"Reporting Employees" (Only those for whom the Pay Element Applies—for Example, an Incentive Award) versus all Employees (using Undiluted or Diluted Data).   Different situations dictate where it is best to use "reporting employees" versus "all employees" data. For example, in the case of incentives data, "reporting employees" limits the database to those employees for whom incentive amounts are actually reported. This data is the appropriate frame of reference when users position their employees receiving incentives competitively against other employees receiving incentives. The "all employees" look at the market includes employees not eligible for or receiving incentives, and therefore reduces or "dilutes" the average incentive amount reported. This can be a useful way to look at competitive practices for positions that are not typically incentives-eligible. In such a case a company may want to target the incentives budget across a broader population to be market-competitive (the "all employees/diluted" view) rather than for specific incentives-receiving employees (the "reporting employees/undiluted" view).

EVALUATING SURVEY DATA AND VENDORS

A variety of factors should be taken into consideration when evaluating sources of compensation data, including cost, the time required to participate, validity and reliability of data, survey methodology, confidentiality, and timeliness of the data. The following are issues to consider when evaluating surveys and survey vendors.

Sample Size.   The "N" or number (sample size) is a significant consideration when determining whether or not a survey will meet your company's needs. The size of the sample should be representative of the group you are evaluating. In other words, if you are looking at pay at U.S. auto manufacturers, the "N" will necessarily be low; conversely, if you are evaluating pay practices at high-technology companies, you should expect a sample size that runs into hundreds of companies. The larger the sample size, generally speaking, the more valid the data. Also, surveys with a large participant base tend to have relatively stable participation by the same companies year after year, which results in a better basis of comparison when analyzing data from one year to the next. Some surveys (custom and pulse surveys, for example) will inherently have a small sample size relative to large, established annual surveys. Determining whether a survey has a sufficient number of participants, or whether a particular data set within in a survey has sufficient data, is a function of the compensation questions being posed.

Each survey vendor has its own data sufficiency guidelines for publication (typically at least five companies must submit data for a given job), but users of market data may want even larger quantities of data to ensure adequate data samples are used for compensation analysis. At a minimum, there must be enough data to maintain the confidentiality of participating companies such that antitrust violations are avoided.

Peer Representation.   The sample should be composed of companies that are considered labor market peers. Often these companies are competitors for customers as well as employees. Survey providers typically make the list of participating companies broadly available.

The Age of the Data.   In general, the more recent the data the better. In markets that move quickly (whether with respect to a dynamic pay element such as stock options, or a rapidly changing role such as internet developer), it is preferable to use current data, rather than trust data older than 12–18 months. Older data can be used when there is no alternative with certain entry-level jobs or in certain services industries, where pay is less dynamic.

The age of the data should be clearly stated on survey reports. For "point in time" surveys, where data is collected from all participants at one time, generally the data collection effective date is noted and should be used for aging purposes. Other surveys may be published on a "rolling" data collection schedule, where data is collected from different participants at different times during the year, based upon, for example, the timing of each company's salary increase cycle. These surveys often contain data with different individual effective dates, but the publication date can be assumed as the effective date. Rolling surveys typically are published more frequently than annual surveys, so the publication date is closer to the data effective date than it is during the latter portion of the year with a point in time survey (see Figure 9.1). Irrespective of the age of the data, there are situations where companies elect to "age" the data, or apply a premium to the data that reflects either pay movement not captured in older data or to project future compensation based on current data.

Figure 9.1 is an illustration of the time lapses that occur between changes in payroll, and how those changes are reflected in quarterly vs annual survey reports. The chart assumes a universe where one-fourth of companies conduct pay administration at the start of each quarter and grant 5 percent increases to employees each year. These assumptions are not necessarily reflective of actual market practices; they are used to illustrate the increasing separation that occurs over time between actual market practices and the data reported in annually reported data. While there will always be a gap between actual and reported, the gap between actual practice and reported results remains smaller and is more consistent in quarterly reported data. With annual survey reports the lag can be significant.

Presentation. Ensure that the way the data are presented will be useful for your organization. If for example, company size cuts are presented for companies with $1.0 billion in revenue and above, and your company is a $1.1 billion company, you will need to understand what proportion of the data are coming from companies close to your size. If, in this example, a substantial proportion of companies

FIGURE 9.1   Example of the impact of a rolling survey database on reported survey results versus actual average payroll

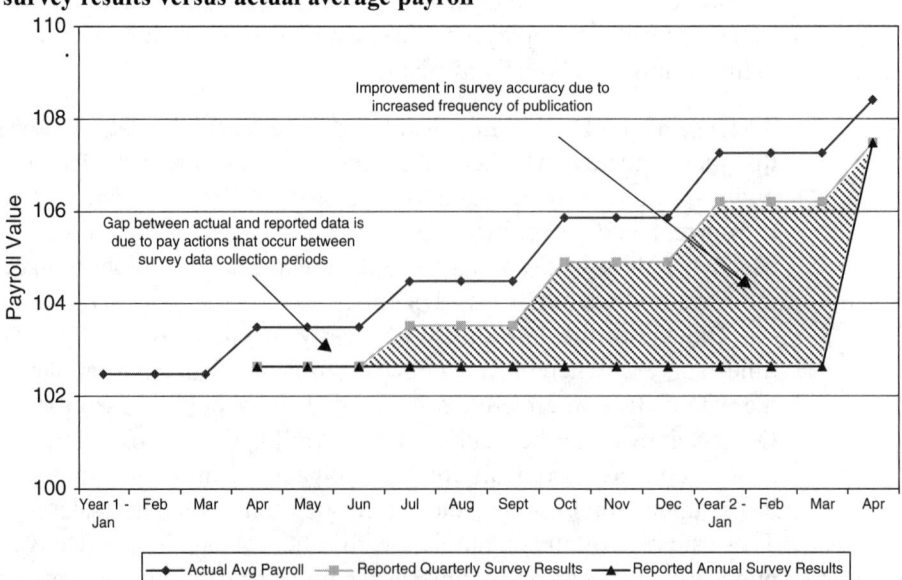

have revenue of $10 billion or more, the data may be less applicable to your company, and customized peer group data will be required.

Data Access. Look for state-of-the-art survey providers that make their data available via secure online environments, allowing for easy access to user-defined special cuts. Electronic output is easily manipulated and analyzed, and greatly mitigates, or eliminates the need for data entry.

Source. Evaluate the source of the data, which should generally be companies, not individual employees. As discussed earlier, employee-reported pay data may not be reliable or representative of the market. Similarly, some vendors offer aggregated data, which is data that comes from numerous sources. Generally speaking, this data is difficult to validate and may be unreliable if the component surveys use different methodologies for leveling jobs, have different effective dates, and use inconsistent definitions for various forms of compensation.

Job Matching.   Participate in job matching sessions and discuss company matches with the survey vendor. Job-level compensation data is only as good as the participant group's common understanding of job definitions and leveling criteria.

Number of Data Sources.   Consider obtaining data from multiple survey sources. Companies commonly rely on more than one source of compensation data. This practice increases a company's assurance in the validity of the data sets it uses to ultimately establish pay levels; however it is important to understand how different survey providers level the various jobs within a survey, and how that process impacts the data reported in the survey.

Costs.   Generally speaking, the cost of purchasing or participating is a minimal expense in relation to the financial stake a company has in ensuring its compensation programs are competitive. Costs for compensation surveys can vary considerably and are typically driven by the size of the data set, the quality of the analysis, the uniqueness of the data and the market demand. Participation in a large-scale annual benchmarking survey can cost several thousand dollars or more. Other, less complex, surveys can be purchased for a couple of hundred dollars or less. Along these lines, when evaluating survey vendors, check to see how customer service and support are delivered to participants, as service levels can vary among survey providers.

Data Validation.   The steps a survey provider takes to ensure the quality of data can vary considerably, and it is important to have a clear understanding of how the provider "cleans" the data it receives from participants, prior to creating reports. Some survey providers have built validation processes into their online submission systems; others manually examine the data and follow up with participants when there are questions about the data. Ideally, survey providers employ a combination of these approaches.

Time.   The time commitment to participate in a compensation survey can be substantial, and as human resources departments have become increasingly taxed, this has become a significant factor in the decision of which survey providers they choose. The more complex the company, and the more the complex the pay approach within the company, the more time is often required to obtain the data needed for participation. While it is important to understand how much time will be required for participation, ultimately it is a balancing act; there is often a connection (or should be) between the time required for submitting data and the comprehensiveness and quality of the data. The value found in the results, their completeness, and their ease-of-use must be considered when evaluating participation costs.

Advisory Groups and Participant Feedback.   Survey providers often seek out the advice of the market when making changes to survey questionnaires and the tools used to gather, analyze, and report data. Participating in this way with survey providers allows companies to "have a say" in the on-going design considerations of a survey and its processes.

Thought Leadership.   Survey providers may also help their participants understand the broader business context within which compensation data are relevant. Survey providers often analyze the data in their databases to produce regular update or trend reports, topical articles or white papers, and presentations for participants. This information not only adds to the breadth of a user's knowledge, it is also a reflection of the thinking behind the survey vendor's design considerations for survey tools and reports.

KEY TERMS TO UNDERSTAND THE EVALUATING OF SURVEYS AND SURVEY DATA

Black–Scholes/Binomial Lattice.   These models are used to determine a potential value for stock options. About 80 percent of companies use the Black–Scholes methodology; survey providers should display the methodology they use in valuing stock options.

Equity.   This term is one of the more difficult compensation elements to survey. While base salaries and incentives use a common "language" (dollars, in the United States), there are various equity vehicles as well as various ways to quantify the size of equity grants. A complete discussion of this topic is beyond the scope of this chapter, but following is a brief discussion of the key issues:

- *Types of equity or long-term incentive plans*—plan types include stock options, restricted stock, performance shares, phantom stock, and cash long-term incentive plans, among others. Since not all equity grants are equal (see below), it is important for a survey to cover equity plan types separately. While combining different types of equity grants can provide a more complete picture of the equity competitive market, certain assumptions need to be made regarding relative equivalencies, and such assumptions need to be clearly stated in the survey report.

■ *Types of grants*—equity grants include those made at or about the date of hire, grants made periodically after hire (on an annual basis for some position levels, sometimes referred to as "ongoing grants") and those made on an unscheduled basis or for special reasons, such as promotion grants, retention grants, grants in connection with a merger or acquisition, etc. It is important that the survey presents data on different types of grants separately so that survey users can evaluate the competitiveness of specific features of their own programs. For example, the size of new hire grants is often a multiple of the size of annual ongoing grants. Combining these two types of grants would dilute the effectiveness of using the survey data for either situation.

Some surveys further segregate equity grants reporting into grant guidelines and actual grants. The former is the equity equivalent of "target incentives," and can be useful in developing a picture of typical equity practices in the market. However, not all companies have guidelines, and those that have guidelines do not always follow them, so it is also important that the survey captures and reports equity grants that have actually been made.

■ *Equity quantification approaches*—there are various ways to quantify the size of an equity grant, ranging from number of shares or percentage of company outstanding shares (which do not attempt to "value" the grant) to starting value or face value (the number of shares multiplied by the stock price at date of grant) to net present value (NPV) or Black–Scholes value, which include the potential future value of the grant, based upon certain assumptions. Different types of equity vehicles lend themselves to one or more of these quantification approaches, and some more comprehensive surveys will report equity data using several different quantification methods. For example, stock option amounts are often reported in terms of NPV or Black–Scholes value, as well as face value or number of shares, while restricted stock amounts are typically reported in terms of face value or number of shares.

■ *Combining equity vehicles*—while it would not be appropriate for a survey to combine new hire grants with ongoing grants (as noted above), it is useful to combine the types of equity vehicles commonly used in the market to provide a more complete picture of the overall value of equity provided in a competitive environment. For example, in the wake of accounting rule changes requiring stock option expensing, the use of restricted stock has become more widespread, often used either in tandem with stock options or in lieu of options. A survey that presents data for options and restricted stock combined, as well as separately, provides a more complete view of the market. However, the value of a stock option and a restricted share are not equal, so certain assumptions need to be made when combining these together. For example, some surveys will combine the "calculated value" of options (using either NPV or Black–Scholes) with the face value of restricted stock to arrive at a combined value. Others may provide a combined number of shares that restates restricted stock in option equivalents, based upon certain conversion ratios. In either case, the survey vendor should clearly state the methodology and assumptions being used. A survey user can then rely on the same methodology and assumptions to quantify his company's own equity grants and make an "apples-to-apples" comparison to the survey data.

International Surveys.   Many companies have employees in more than one country and require data on local competitive practices. This can present a particular challenge when surveys cover different compensation elements across countries, have varying definitions of what is included in a given element, and use different benchmark jobs and leveling schemes. Surveys in each country need to capture all the components of compensation, such as car allowances, housing, meal and transportation allowances, extra months' pay, holiday or festival bonuses, etc. It is important to present the data in a consistent format, suitable for both local and global users. As multinational companies move toward global job leveling, where job X is at the same level from country to country (although pay levels may be different), surveys with consistent global platforms are becoming essential tools in compensation planning.

Mean or Average.   The mean is the average of a set of values, calculated by adding all the numbers and dividing by the number of values. Contrary to the median, averages are more susceptible to the influence of outliers.

Median.   The median describes the midpoint of a range of numbers; half the numbers in a range are above the median, and half below. When there is an even number of numbers in the range, the middle two are added and divided by two to calculate the median. The median is used in working with compensation data to mitigate the impact of pay that is at the extreme highs and lows of the range. It is not unusual to see significant variability between the highs and lows of compensation data, as actual pay can be affected by several factors, including length of service of the incumbent, variability in the responsibility or criticality of the role, and a company's pay approach.

Percentile.   The percentile marks the percentage of the data falling beneath it. For example, if the base salary for a job is $50,000, and that salary is in the 75th percentile of the market, it means that 75 percent of companies pay less than $50,000 for the job. Compensation data is often displayed in quartile buckets using the 25th, 50th, and 75th percentiles; some surveys will include the 10th and 90th percentiles to provide a more complete picture of the range of the data.

Weighted and Simple Average. The weighted average (sometimes also called the "employee" average) takes into account all incumbents in the data sample. Companies matching more employees to a survey job will have a greater impact on the survey weighted average than companies reporting fewer employees. Weighted averages are used in compensation surveys to express the overall market rate for a particular job. On the other hand, a simple (or "company") average weights the data for each company in the sample equally and is essentially an average of each company's average for the data element. Simple averages can be useful when a small number of companies dominate the data sample.

SUMMARY

Salary survey data is always a snapshot of a moment in time, and the application of the data is part art and part science. As labor markets are a consistently changing picture, the limits of even the best pay data should be well understood. Good data leads to more great questions than simple answers. It is tempting to use salary data to find "one number" to the question of "how much should we pay?" or "how should we pay X employee?" However, because the market is always changing, the market will always be defined as a range of values and not a discrete number. Determining the appropriate range—and choosing a value within that range for a specific recommendation—requires a combination of the "science" found in the calculated values and the "art" of using these figures in alignment with an organization's strategy and pay philosophy.

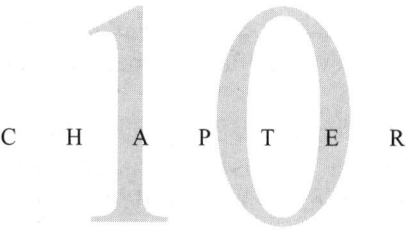

C H A P T E R

BENCHMARKING

Iain Fitzpatrick, Reward Information Services General Manager, and
Thomas D. McMullen, Vice President and Reward Practice Leader

Hay Group

MANY ORGANIZATIONS' REWARD STRATEGIES CAN be summed up as "pay the right people the right amounts for doing the right things." But is it really that simple? Benchmarking compensation levels is a key component in addressing the middle part of this statement: *the right amounts*.

Using surveys to benchmark compensation levels ensures that the pay levels determined by the organization are not extraordinarily misaligned with market practice—i.e., pay is not too low or too high. Determining the appropriate amount of compensation is a balancing act. No organization wants to waste their financial resources by paying too high relative to the market; and those who pay too low risk unwanted turnover from employees looking for a better deal elsewhere.

While compensation benchmarking also provides useful insights on compensation administration and pay delivery practices such as prevalence of practice in the use of different types of compensation, performance measures, performance results, benefits plan design, and compensation administration guidelines, the remaining focus of this chapter is on the foundational activity and processes related to benchmarking cash compensation levels.

COMPENSATION BENCHMARKING ENVIRONMENT

Many times, an organization's compensation costs are the highest component of its total cost structure. As such, those in management positions are increasingly being scrutinized with regard to pay decisions and the level of human resources costs relative to the company's operating revenue (or total operating budget in the case of nonprofits).

Moreover, "one-size-fits-all" compensation policies are not always effective for managing compensation across various businesses, locations, and functions. Market data for jobs, functions, or locations can reflect fluctuating premiums and discounts as labor supply and demand vary. With salary calculation Web sites and newly available data sources (no matter how suspect they may appear to management) accessible to the public, organizations face new challenges in communicating the credibility of their compensation levels to employees.

As a result, managers are demanding better information to validate specific market rates. Also, realize that some managers want to pay more or less for the value of their jobs relative to the reported value in the marketplace. Managers want better and more relevant information about the value of positions within *their* organization. Better compensation information leads to better decisions, clearer messages, and defined expectations. Better information helps to better manage pay.

DEFINING THE LABOR MARKET: THE USE OF PEER GROUPS

Selecting an appropriate peer group (or a comparator group) is a key decision in how an organization compares and sets their pay levels relative to the external marketplace. Peer groups are typically utilized for external benchmark comparisons, in terms of levels of compensation, compensation mix, administrative practices, and performance comparisons. Peer groups are helpful in grounding organization pay decisions.

Shareholder groups are increasingly scrutinizing comparator group selection in executive compensation circles. In broader employee groups, managing compensation toward the selection of an inappropriate peer group can have serious financial consequences as well as send the wrong messages concerning the intent of the organization's reward programs. The selection of the peer group must make business sense and be credible to the organization. The following principles serve as a guide for determining an appropriate and defensible comparator group.

Select a Relevant and Current Peer.   Markets are dynamic and are constantly changing. As a result, a corporation that was an appropriate peer last year may have changed strategy, lines of business, been acquired, divested an important business line, experienced a dramatic change in performance, or even gone out of business. For these and other reasons, a company may no longer truly be a peer to the employer. Accordingly, effort is needed to update the organizations included in any comparator group.

Peers Should Stem from a Reasonably Large Sample.   The ideal peer group typically contains at least 10 organizations. Smaller sample sizes are also susceptible to large year-to-year changes in data if a company changes in the sample.

Peers Should be Consistent in Size and Scope.   A peer should be reasonably aligned with the size and operating characteristics of your organization. The most common factors in selecting peer groups for professional, management, and executive jobs tend to be industry sector and organization size.

While peer group selection and benchmarking are foundations that steer decision making with regard to the establishment of pay practices, they are guidelines. The organization should take the benchmarking information as a reference point and establish a compensation peer group that meets the needs of the business rather than a mechanistic application of market data.

TYPES OF COMPENSATION SURVEYS

Most often, compensation surveys are conducted on a basis of one of the following.

Job Title Matching.   Comparing jobs solely by a job title, while simple, is highly subjective and can lead to the development of erroneous conclusions regarding competitiveness (e.g., recruitment advertisements). This approach may have some use when there is a need for "ball park" estimates in the absence of any other information, but is not recommended for the development of salary structures.

Market Pricing (Job Title and Job Description Matching).   With this approach, benchmark (i.e., representative) job descriptions are used to match an organization's jobs to appropriate survey jobs. While more accurate than relying on job title alone, comparisons are limited to matched jobs in similar industries and are therefore most effective when conducted amongst competitors within market sectors.

To ensure the validity of comparisons in job-based surveys, it is essential that an organization has good job matches. As a general rule of thumb, if the jobholder spends 80 percent or more of their time on the listed major activities, then the job is typically a good match.

To provide the most useful information, benchmark jobs are ones that are typically well represented across the functions and businesses of the organization and span multiple levels or grades. As such, they are a "diagonal slice" of jobs.

Job Evaluation (a Point, Grade or Factor Comparison System).   A large number of jobs cannot be matched to the marketplace. Research suggests that an organization is lucky to be able to have good matches on at least 60 percent of its roles.[1] Often it is the critical positions such as executive, management, and individual contributor roles that cannot be matched to market surveys. These also happen to be roles that might be uniquely designed to provide the organization with competitive advantage in the marketplace. It is important for an organization to have a robust process that ensures that the value of these roles is effectively determined. More often than not, some form of job evaluation is used to ensure that these jobs can be priced using appropriate internal values, which then can be priced in the marketplace.

This method places emphasis on understanding the *content* of surveyed jobs and so overcomes the comparability problems of job title or job description matching surveys. But this extra comparability comes with a requirement for additional inputs and resources. Also, job evaluation-based surveys can be restrictive if specific data are required about particular, unusual, or unique jobs. However, an effective job evaluation system will enable more accurate compensation comparisons, both internally and externally, across any market (e.g., industrial sector, geographic location).

COLLECTING DATA FOR COMPENSATION SURVEYS
Conducting a Survey

If you are planning to conduct a survey, there are a variety of approaches to collecting data. Most surveys will likely consist of one of the following:

- Telephone surveys
- Mailed surveys (or an electronic version of this)
- On-site visits

Although they may provide instant gratification, telephone surveys are typically not the most accurate survey process. While the personal touch can be helpful in gathering information quickly, telephone surveys often yield marginal results, forfeiting quality for immediacy; questions are likely to be inconsistently phrased, and answers are likely to be inaccurate.

Another common approach is the mailed or electronic survey which, compared to telephone surveys, achieves far more consistent results, though rarely is this technique capable of providing a quick turnaround. The mailed or electronic questionnaire can be particularly effective when used in conjunction with telephone surveys and/or personal interviews.

When a survey demands high reliability or has extensive content, an on-site visit may be used to collect data. This has the advantage of ensuring consistent and high-quality data collection since data is collected directly from the source. However, this approach is very time consuming and, therefore, often prohibitively expensive. Table 10.1 provides a guide for the selection of the most appropriate method of data collection for a survey.

SURVEY SCOPE

The scope of compensation surveys varies significantly. However, those of most interest to the Human Resources professionals are likely to fall under one of the three components that comprise Total Rewards:

- compensation
- benefits and
- the work experience

TABLE 10.1   Data Collection Methods

Data Collection Methods	Purpose	Advantages	Disadvantages
Telephone survey	Short surveys collecting simple data about familiar jobs and subjects	■ Fast ■ Inexpensive	■ Questionable reliability ■ Inconsistent
Mail or electronic survey	Used for surveying fairly large numbers of jobs	■ Designed to collect large amounts of data	■ Expensive ■ Time consuming– slower turnarounds
On-site visit	Used when the survey demands high reliability or has extensive content	■ Ensures good job matching ■ Reliable ■ Establishes high levels of understanding	■ Very expensive ■ Very time consuming ■ Involves large amounts of analysis

Compensation Surveys

Compensation surveys typically look to collect one, some combination, or all of the following aggregates.

Base Salary. This is the sum of the basic cash amounts paid for work performed as stated in the employment contract plus all fixed payments that have been awarded to eligible jobholders automatically year over year irrespective of individual, unit or company performance (e.g., fixed bonus, a.k.a. 13th month, bonus, holiday bonus, leave loading, vacation allowance).

Total Cash. This is the sum of *Base Salary* plus short-term variable payments, which are the annualized cash amounts paid that can vary year over year (most typically, these refer to incentive payments that are contingent on discretion, performance, or results achieved).

Total Direct Compensation. The sum of *Total Cash* plus long-term incentive payments (LTIPs), where LTIPs are the economic value to the employee on the date of grant of each long-term incentive vehicle (the values are calculated using a long-term incentive valuation methodology and are annualized and reported as a cash equivalent).

Benefits

Employee benefit programs are complex and multifaceted. Comparison of programs typically requires specific expertise and is difficult to complete without a single common denominator on which all programs are measured. Benefits surveys typically compare programs in one of two ways:

1. *Cost basis*—the employer's cost of a named benefit or perquisite's provision
2. *Value basis*—the perceived value of a benefit to an employee based on the level of benefit received

Cost is clearly the most direct common denominator. However, an organization's cost for a benefits program is subject to numerous variables, such as group demographics, claim experience, geographic location, even how it is funded or accounted for. Thus programs with identical plan provisions and benefits can have widely differing costs from organization to organization, or even from unit to unit within an organization.

Surveys deal with this inherent variation by gaining a sense of a given benefit program's value in order to help the organization understand where to direct its spending—how to get the best "bang for the buck." However, true value is calculated in the "eye of the beholder." For this reason, cash equivalent values for benefits are based on standard assumptions. For benefits that are conditional on the occurrence of an event such as disability, retirement, or death, the cash equivalent is calculated based on the probability of receiving such items using appropriate actuarial assumptions. For perquisites such as cars, loans, and subsidized meals, which have an immediate value, the cash equivalent is calculated on the basis of average replacement cost.

The Work Experience

Extensive research illustrates the importance of intangible reward components (other than direct compensation and benefits) in attracting, retaining, and motivating employees. The five components of the WorldatWork Total Rewards model, specific to the work experience are:

1. *Acknowledgment, appreciation, and recognition*—the extent to which initiatives such as service awards (typically noncash) are used to recognize contribution
2. *Work–life balance*—how an organization uses family programs, nontraditional work arrangements, and other factors to create a perceived higher quality of life inside and outside of work
3. *Culture*—how leadership, diversity, and other factors create a positive work environment
4. *Development*—the extent to which employees receive career development and learning opportunities
5. *Environment*—how the job (e.g., variety), place (e.g., pleasant workspace), and company (well regarded externally) combine to affect an employee's perception of their employer

Increasingly, more reward-related surveys are including measures of the effectiveness of these dimensions on why an employee chooses to work for an organization.

DATA DISPLAYS AND TERMINOLOGY

Surveys appear in myriad forms and formats. Some reports extensively slice and dice the data provided; some adopt a minimal interpretation stance. Remember, though, that the underlying value of a survey is not in the numbers it presents but in the answers you are able to derive from its use.

Most survey data are presented in one of three fashions: tabular displays (numeric), graphic displays (visual), or regression analyses (containing formulas and chart lines that project compensation levels).

TABULAR DISPLAYS

Tabular displays (see Figures 10.1 and 10.2) include arrays, statistical reference points, and frequency distributions.

Arrays

Arrays are high-to-low listings of all data collected in a given category (Figure 10.1). Arrays allow the analyst to inspect each data point reported (often by company code) to see how the data distributes through the range.

Statistical Reference Points

Also called the *arithmetic mean* (or simply the *mean*), the *average* is typically one of the following:

- The *weighted average* is the sum of all salaries (or other compensation values) divided by the number of incumbents reported. [In Figure 10.1, the weighted average is (2 × $60.0) + (5 × $58.7).] This is the best indicator of the real market for a given survey position: large organizations with many incumbents weigh heavily here.

- The *simple (or unweighted) average* is the sum of the averages for each company divided by the number of companies providing information.

FIGURE 10.1   Array with statistical reference points

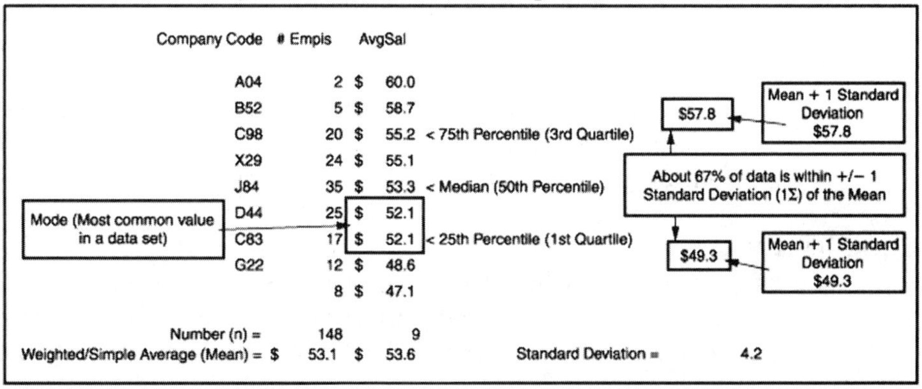

FIGURE 10.2   Pie charts

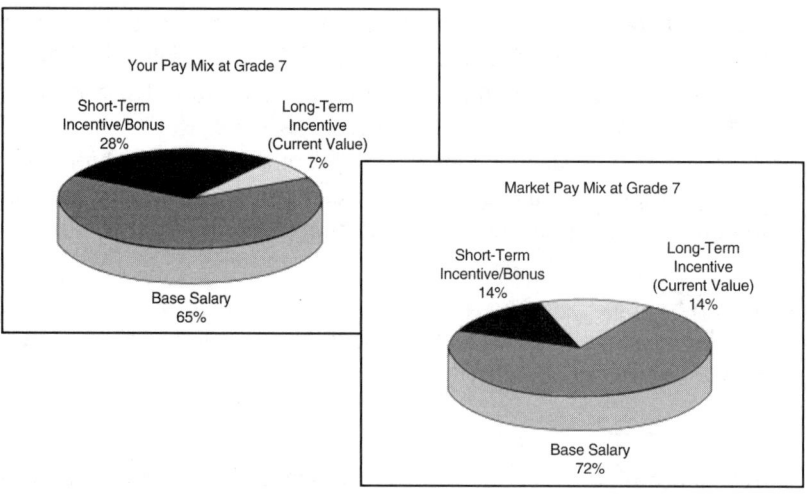

[In Figure 10.1, the simple average is $60.0 + $58.7, etc. (a total of $482.2).]
This number can be used to compare company policy, for example, on
midpoint levels; small companies with few incumbents and large companies
with many weigh evenly here.

- The *standard deviation* is a measure of how widely values are dispersed from
  the mean. The data within ±1 standard deviation cover approximately the
  middle two-thirds of the observations.

- The *median* (also the 50th percentile or second quartile) is the middle of all
  the data points reported. This is commonly referred to as the "market rate."
  Focus on the median when data are erratically distributed, especially when
  you have a small sample.

- The percentiles (also quartiles, deciles, etc.) refer to locations in an array
  below which a certain portion of the data lies. The 75th percentile is frequently viewed by high-paying companies; many analysts prefer to view data
  at the 25th, 50th, and 75th percentiles.

Frequency Distributions

These are often used in lieu of arrays if presenting individual data points strains the
confidentiality concerns of the participants. Table 10.2 shows how many times a salary
is reported within certain ranges of salaries; actual salaries or averages are not shown.

Graphic Displays

Graphic displays include many types of charts (line, pie, bar, and so forth) that can
be used effectively in presenting data, especially to top management, when the big
picture is more desirable than all the detail (see Figures 10.2–10.4).

TABLE 10.2   Frequency Distribution

Range	Frequency
$45.0–47.9	1
$48.0–50.9	1
$51.0–53.9	3
$54.0–56.9	2
$57.0–59.9	1
$60.0–62.9	1

Regression Analysis

Regression analysis (see Figure 10.5) is a very powerful form of presentation that relates two or more data elements and shows, through formulas and charts, the central data relationship tendencies. Based on one or more measures (such as job level, company sales, or time in job), regressions forecast the value of the related measure (i.e., the dependent variable—such as total cash compensation). Regression analysis also correlates the reliability of the information to its dispersal around the line of central tendency. The closer the correlation coefficient is to 1, the greater reliance you can place on the forecast. Regression charts often use logarithms because the range of data covered can be so great and because the formulas often are more accurate when the data relationships are curvilinear.

A few words of caution: regression analysis infers that, if one condition exists, then the other also exists. In addition, when looking at a chart, the eye and mind can lead the untrained observer to conclusions that may or may not be valid. The assumption that you should provide a 35.7 percent incentive opportunity to a $150,000 employee based on Figure 10.5's data is no more valid than if you were

FIGURE 10.3   Bar charts

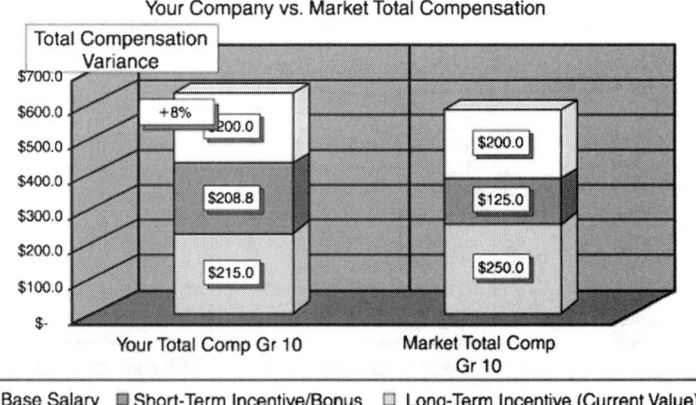

FIGURE 10.4   Line charts

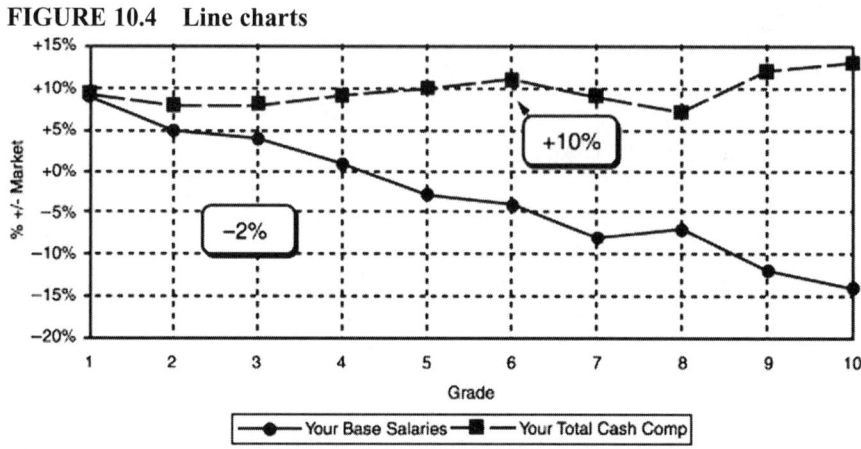

to conclude that $150,000 is the right amount to pay that employee just because that is the peer group average for the individual's position.

HOW TO USE A SURVEY

Competent compensation practitioners assess a survey's reliability and the usefulness of the data before incorporating the information into a spreadsheet or database to be analyzed. All survey data are not as meaningful as you would like them to be. Because people are people and because organizations differ so widely in the way jobs are designed, data quality can vary markedly and should be checked

FIGURE 10.5   Regression analysis

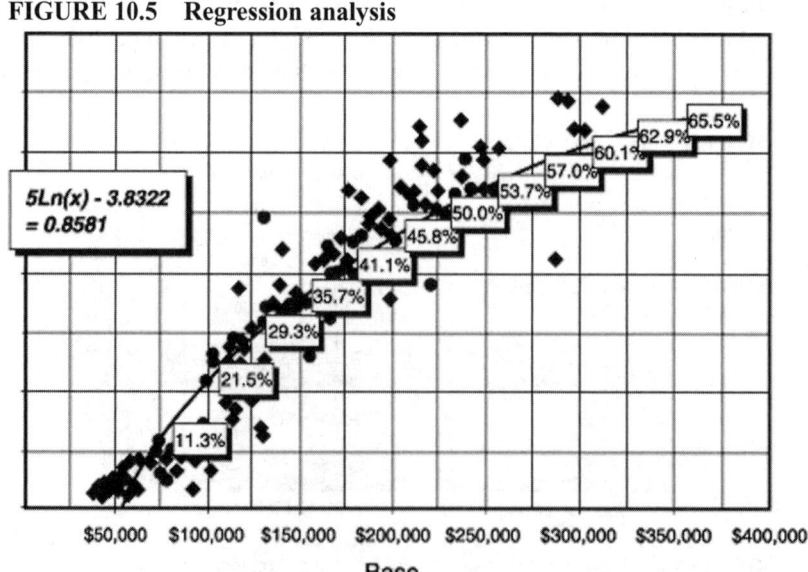

before you decide to base one of your key management decisions on it. When the survey results are published, that is the time to ask two questions, in this order:

1. How can I be sure that the data are meaningful?
2. How similar is our job to the market comparison position?

You can feel comfortable that the data are "meaningful" by following a few guidelines.

■ Choose annual survey sources that contain the majority of the positions and competitors in which your top management is primarily interested. Augment your chief data source with other data and other surveys—do not limit yourself to one source of information. Also, do not overlook the opportunity to compare compensation data from different sources.

■ Do not undermine your efforts by getting only free survey information from recruiters (with their own interests to cultivate), from magazine articles, from free internet sources or anecdotally from others in your organization.

■ Choose survey vendors that are known for their quality and the comprehensiveness of their survey instrument.

Realize that survey costs represent only a small fraction of the human capital investment that benefits from the data they provide. In short, surveys can be one of the highest value-added investments you can make.

So, what if you have taken these steps and the numbers do not agree or if you have only one source with which to work? How do you know that the data are reliable?

You can assess the number of data points. If only a small, unrepresentative sample appears for a given position, you might consider devaluing its importance in your structure development or not using the information at all. The more tightly packed the data distribution, the more confident you can feel about the comparison's validity. Realize, however, that aberrations are common in compensation surveys.

If your data source covers a broad spectrum of positions—upper- and lower-management levels, staff and line functions, multi- and single-incumbent positions—most of the pay relationships should be generally consistent with the compensation program of your organization (see Table 10.3). Most companies try to have overall pay practices within ±10 percent of "their market."

The participant sample should also represent your industry or labor market. Regardless of how odd pieces of data appear in relation to your own, if all of your company's direct and indirect competitors are submitting data, you may have to admit that *you* are out of line with the overall market. On a similar note, realize that the survey becomes more valuable when there is a consistent participant sample from year-to-year and when competitors are covered by your survey. Finally, the survey should describe positions that correspond closely to those in your organization so that you feel confident using the results.

TABLE 10.3   Salary Progression by Position

	Number	Case I Average Salary	Case II Average Salary
Senior-level position	12	$57.0	$57.0
Medium-level position	15	$40.7	$40.7
Junior-level position	*2*	*$29.7*	*$37.9*
Entry-level position	27	$22.4	$22.4

CHARACTERISTICS OF RELIABLE COMPENSATION SURVEYS

Characteristics of reliable compensation surveys include the following:

- Clear and consistent definitions of terms used (e.g., base salary, midpoint, variable cash, benefits values, total direct compensation, etc.)

- A tested and accepted method of relating jobs between organizations that ensures pay is being compared on a like and fair basis (e.g., job models, classification, job size)

- A reasonable representation of the marketplace when determining organizations to include in surveys

- A sample of data representative of all relevant jobs in an organization coded by function, industry, or sector classification, location, and other relevant criteria to facilitate detailed analysis of individual and group positions

- Trends analyzed on the basis of comparing the same organizations at each survey date
  - to establish the exact movement for each level of job size
  - to establish each pay component

- The shortest amount of time possible between the based date of a survey and its publication date

LEGAL CONCERNS ASSOCIATED WITH INFORMATION SHARING

Limited information sharing, such as discussing your company's average wages for a single position with a neighboring company's counterpart, may not seem like a big deal. However, sharing this information directly with competitors and making decisions based on that data can present problems. Using another company's specific compensation data to establish salary levels can be *perceived* as wage setting.

In some countries, businesses must be careful in obtaining compensation survey information. For example, U.S. courts and agencies, such as the Federal Trade Commission (FTC), advise organizations against conducting their own compensation benchmarking surveys, as they could be considered anticompetitive under provisions of the Sherman Anti-Trust Act. These entities have issued opinions regarding the exchange of compensation data between organizations. While not legally binding for all organizations, these opinions can be considered as a best practice in how to use compensation surveys.

For this reason, one of the safest and most efficient ways to obtain survey data is through a disinterested third party—such as a trade organization, consultant, or information survey company—thereby preserving the industrial participants' data confidentiality.

To ensure a successful survey benchmarking process, organizations would be well served by keeping the following points in mind when conducting their compensation studies:

- The survey should be managed by an independent third party (e.g., independent consultant, academic institution, government agency, trade, or professional association)

- Data provided by survey participants must be more than three months old

- The survey must contain data from at least five survey participants, with no individual participant's data representing more than 25 percent of the weighted basis of a given statistic

- Each company must report the results in a way that ensures that no recipient can determine specific participant data (the FTC does allow some exchange of information without a third party, depending upon the use and the anticompetitive effect)

- When conducting a salary survey, companies should seek legal counsel throughout the planning process, execution, and reporting

SOURCES OF COMPENSATION INFORMATION

Organizations should use relevant and reliable market data in benchmarking their compensation programs. It is more credible to use direct market measurement of a market via a credible source of compensation information. Key considerations for sources of compensation information include:

- Coverage of comparator organizations (industry, company size, geography, etc.)

- Coverage of comparator jobs

- Timeliness of information

- Direct and indirect costs of acquisition (i.e., out of pocket costs and time)

- Reliable availability over time

- Measurement of all relevant components of the reward opportunity (e.g., base cash, total cash, total direct cash, total remuneration)

The number of compensation survey providers is growing and the following listing provides some ideas as to where you may find sources of compensation information. The following list is by no means exhaustive. Omission from the list does not impugn a survey's quality nor does inclusion on the list endorse the quality. Consider this merely a starting point in your search for compensation benchmarking information.

- Contact counterparts in your peer group. The surveys they participate in are probably the ones you should also join. Your own functional and line managers may also be aware of surveys covering their particular business or discipline.

- All major compensation and/or human resources consulting firms conduct compensation surveys (i.e., domestic surveys as well as some international surveys as well).

- The U.S. government is a significant surveyor. Contact the Department of Labor, Bureau of Labor Statistics (BLS), Wage and Hour Division. Most major cities have BLS offices. Your state and local Chamber of Commerce may also produce surveys.

- Many regional and local HR and compensation associations conduct surveys. Trade and professional organizations are often good sources as well.

Finally, but perhaps most importantly, several survey bibliographies (e.g., WorldatWork) are periodically published and include extensive lists of available pay surveys.

GETTING THE MOST OUT OF YOUR BENCHMARKING EFFORTS

If you are responsible for using compensation surveys to develop compensation programs in your organization, take the following ideas into consideration to get the most out of your survey investment.

Start by Creating a Survey Library.   Set aside a shared network drive or some other common location where you and other authorized users can access all of your organization's survey data. Alert others in your organization to forward all surveys and requests for survey participation to you so you can respond to them most efficiently.

Be Selective in Responding to Surveys. Limited resources and unlimited day-to-day work requirements often preclude participation in every survey in which a company is asked to participate. You must balance your current and future needs and the ability to get what you want from others. Participate in those studies that benefit your organization and your primary comparator groups.

Consolidate Your Data onto One Spreadsheet or Database. Surveys are often consulted to respond to specific questions from a variety of constituencies. Try consolidating qualified position data from multiple survey sources onto a single electronic spreadsheet or database for more convenient consultation. By arranging your organization's position table alongside the survey data, you have a good tool for developing solid answers during your annual compensation planning and structure review.

Derive a Single Answer from Each Set of Data Presented in a Survey. If you consolidate data from multiple sources or have several views of the data presented in one source, you have a decision to make: of the data available, of the different numbers purporting to be "the market," *what is the single number that best represents the market for your organization?* Practitioners can take different approaches here:

- Some simply aggregate all the data available from all sources, throw out odd data, then assign "company weights" to each data point to replicate what it would cost to staff your company at market rates.

- Some analysts feel certain survey sources are more reliable than others, so they might weight that source differently (say 75 percent) from all other sources (25 percent) as they aggregate and consolidate.

- Others rely on one or two primary surveys and weight those, but have the others available as secondary sources if needed.

Answer All Survey Questions to the Best of Your Ability. Assume that all data requested in a survey have value in the quality of the results and that without certain data from you the survey will be reduced in value to you and to others. This includes doing the best job you can on job matching and perhaps involving others such as HR colleagues or line managers in verifying your job matches to the survey.

While senior management is interested in knowing market levels of pay for jobs in the marketplace, this only tells part of the story they want to hear. Specifically, executives want to know what the market pays for *their* jobs, which takes into consideration role complexity and accountability. They also want to understand what competitors pay for a mix of responsibilities—regardless of organization size or industry segment. That is, the variables that make a job worth more (or less) than market rates and how to link market data to internal career paths. At the end of the day, executives have a limited budget for compensation surveys and they want to spend it as effectively as possible.

Managers will say they want market data that reflects what they would have to pay to hire a competent performer for the marketplace. They do not want market data that does not take into account the role and value of the job at their organization. What managers *really* want is information that allows them to assess pay for their team and assurance that people are paid fairly given their role and value to the company, an ability to manage retention, tools to support accelerated people development, and pay programs that encourage people to take on more.

Compensation decisions are like any other economic buy or sell decision—the more information there is, the sounder the decisions will be. To bring this issue home, consider the following example. If your boss asked you for market information to help her buy a new house in a new area, would you:

- Provide the 10th through 90th percentiles of house price data for all houses in the city?

- Provide the 10th through 90th percentiles of house price data for all houses in the neighborhood area?

- Provide the percentile data for the neighborhood area but increase it by 10 or 20 percent to recognize that your boss is looking at houses that are a little better than the average in the community?

Or would you identify the boss's personal requirements then consider the relative value of homes in different neighborhoods? Examine the selling prices of recently sold homes? Determine the variables that drive value in the housing market? Use the combination of these factors to determine the fair price for that specific house? At the end of the day, pay determination should apply the same rigor. Line executives are interested in understanding not only various rates of market pay (e.g., percentiles of compensation), but what drives the value of jobs. Your role as a compensation professional goes much beyond calculating and reporting statistics from compensation surveys. It needs to include acting as a trusted advisor who can help senior management think through and act on assessing the value of work within your organization and getting the best return on your sizeable investment in your human resources.

SUMMARY

While benchmarking is indeed a core process of the compensation function, realize that benchmarking should be viewed as a reference post for establishing a compensation structure—the going rate of jobs and is not an end result in and of itself. Compensation professionals that blindly follow external market data without fully considering the design of the work as it relates to the marketplace or how the role relates to other jobs within the organization are providing a disservice to their organization. If you are title- and revenue-matching, you are missing an opportunity for an important dialogue about jobs. Title- and revenue-matching provide no help for comparing jobs across countries. Comparing on revenue only may provide misleading information across industries. Effectiveness requires looking both at the market and measuring work internally.

END NOTE

1. Dow Scott, Thomas D. McMullen, and Richard S. Sperling, "Fiscal Management of Compensation Programs," *WorldatWork Journal*, vol. 14, no. 3 (3rd Quarter 2005), pp. 13–25.

11

SKILLS, KNOWLEDGE, AND COMPETENCY-BASED PAY

Gerald E. Ledford, Jr, Ph.D., President

Ledford Consulting Network, LLC

Robert L. Heneman, Ph.D., Professor of Management and Human Resources

Max M. Fisher College of Business, Ohio State University

Aino Salimäki, Researcher

Helsinki University of Technology

COMPENSATION SYSTEMS THAT PAY FOR skills, knowledge, and competencies (SKCs) use a different logic than conventional job-based pay systems. Job-based pay systems compensate for the *job* that an employee is performing at particular point in time. By contrast, systems that pay for skills, knowledge, and competencies reward the employee's repertoire of capabilities. Moreover, compensation typically follows a formal certification that the employee has acquired SKCs. By contrast, the trigger for a change in job-based pay is a change in the employee's job, not a demonstration of capability. In the extreme, the employee's job-based compensation level may change during the course of the workday as the person temporarily changes jobs.

By definition, pay for SKC plans do not reward performance directly. Rather, these plans seek to provide employees with the SKCs that *enable* greater performance. The starting point for establishing an SKC compensation system can be organization-level *core competencies* (making explicit behaviors associated with the core values of the organization), or team-level *role descriptions* (such as multiple roles to be performed by team members), or finally individual-level *SKCs* (see Figure 11.1).

Plans that pay for skills, knowledge, and competencies have become relatively common. The sixth triennial study of human resource practices in Fortune 1000 firms by the Center for Effective Organizations in 2002 found that 56 percent of firms used pay for knowledge or skill, and that this percentage had been relatively constant since 1993.[1] However, the percentage of employees covered by these plans tends to be small. Only 7 percent of Fortune 1000 firms covered more than half of their workforce with these plans. Another survey, conducted in 2003 by Mercer Human Resource Consulting,[2] found that 17 percent of the companies surveyed used, and 9 percent were considering adoption of, skill-based pay, while 15 percent of the companies used, and 12 percent were considering adoption of, competency-based pay. The number of firm considering adoption may portend a future increase in the use of such plans.

The use of pay for skills, knowledge, and competencies has gone global. A 2007 Towers Perrin study[3] of over 600 managers in 21 countries found that salary increases are based on competencies for executives in 27 percent of cases, for managers and professionals in 36 percent, and for nonmanagement in 28 percent.

FIGURE 11.1   Types of skills, knowledge, and competencies

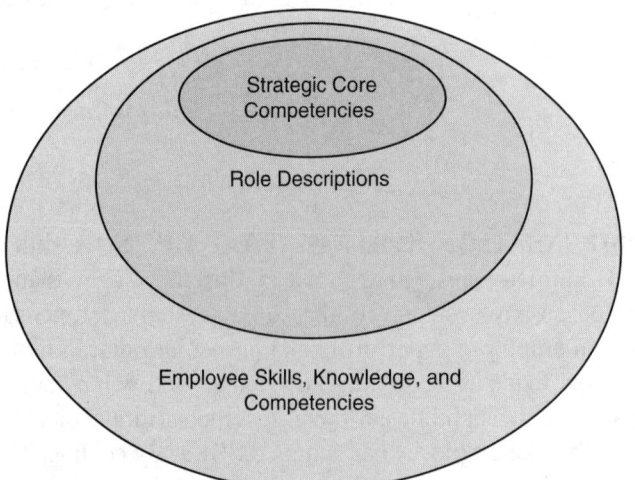

Additionally, increases were skill-based for executives in 9 percent of organizations, for managers and professionals in 15 percent, and for nonmanagers in 18 percent. Skill-based pay plans are even relatively common in the public sector. The International Public Management Association for Human Resources found that 22 percent of public sector organizations surveyed used skill-based pay in 2007.[4]

The available evidence indicates that these plans tend to be successful in general. The users of these plans consistently report a high level of satisfaction with them. For example, a study of 97 skill-based pay plans sponsored by the American Compensation Association found that two-thirds to three-quarters of these plans were rated as successful on a wide range of outcome measures, such as increased workforce flexibility, reduced staffing, and productivity.[5] A rigorous case study reported that skill-based pay in a manufacturing setting resulted in greater productivity, lower labor cost per unit, and favorable quality outcomes.[6]

This chapter will consider two major issues concerning these plans. First, we will examine different types of plans and their applications. Second, we will consider the major issues in the design of these plans, including the infrastructure needed to support them.

VARIETIES OF PLANS TO PAY FOR SKILLS, KNOWLEDGE, AND COMPETENCIES

Plans discussed in this chapter have many names, and they tend to be applied to different groups of employees. However, they share the key characteristic of paying for the employee's repertoire of skills, knowledge, and competencies rather than for the job the employee is currently performing. In this section, we describe the major types of skill-, knowledge-, and competency-based pay approaches, and the conditions in which they appear to work best.

Skill-Based Pay

Skill-based pay originated as a way to reward nonexempt employees for cross-skilling. Organizations may also call these plans pay for knowledge, knowledge-based pay, pay for skills, or pay for applied skills. Although some versions of this approach are ancient, we can trace the modern approach to high-involvement manufacturing plants that Procter & Gamble built in the 1960s. Line managers developed skill-based pay plans to incentivize employees to learn the multiple jobs necessary to support self-managed teams and business involvement. Compared to the other forms of pay for SKCs, skill-based pay systems stick very closely to the specific tasks that employees perform. Characteristics of the original Procter & Gamble plans describe the classic skill-based pay plan still commonly found today. The classic skill-based pay plan has the following characteristics.

1. *Compensation approach*—the classic system is pure base pay, not a set of bonuses or add-ons to base pay.

2. *Design methodology*—the classic system is based on a relatively exhaustive analysis and cataloguing of all the skills necessary to do the work of the organization. The skills identified through this analysis then are packaged into skill blocks that represent compensable units of skill, and employees receive base pay increases for mastering these blocks. Management develops assessment procedures to test whether employees have mastered new skill blocks, and establishes training systems to make it possible for employees to learn new skill blocks.

3. *Most common settings*—classic plans are most common in manufacturing or manufacturing-like service settings, such as back office operations in insurance and financial services. The term skill-based pay continues to be applied primarily to plans that cover nonexempt employees at the lower levels of the organizational hierarchy.

4. *Implicit assumptions*—classic skill-based pay plans require a significant startup investment. Typically, 6–18 months is required to complete the entire design process in a large plant or similar unit. These plans depend on having enough organizational stability to realize a payback on the investment in the design process.

There is far more experience with such skill-based pay plans than with other types of plans that pay for SKCs. The available research suggests that the clear majority of these plans are successful in encouraging multiskilling and in increasing organizational performance, notwithstanding some well-publicized failures (such as one at Motorola). A relatively strong finding in the literature is that these plans work best and are found most often in settings that encourage a high degree of employee involvement, and indeed involve employees in the design and administration of the pay plan. In addition to the typical advantages of employee involvement in the process of organization change, a high involvement system is more likely than a traditional bureaucratic management system to take good advantage of the new skills that employees acquire. A system that adds skills but does not take advantage of new employee abilities simply adds cost without gaining offsetting advantages.

Competency Pay Plans

Competency pay plans evolved from the work of psychologist David McClelland and others on the importance of competencies in determining individual job performance.[7] Competencies are demonstrable characteristics of the person that enable performance, including knowledge, skills, and behaviors. Most of the work in this tradition has focused on the exempt workforce, specifically managers and professionals. In keeping with the nature of the work of these populations, the competencies rewarded in these systems tend to be more abstract and less closely tied to the specific tasks of those on the plan. Cognitive skills (such as analytic thinking), values, self-image (such as self-confidence), motivational patterns, and even personality traits have been used as competencies that are rewarded in pay plans.

Writings about competency pay often include lengthy discussions about what constitutes a competency and about distinctions among different types of competencies. Each author tends to apply his or her own classification scheme. A common distinction is between those competencies that are necessary to perform the job but are not the source of competitive advantage and those that are more difficult to achieve and more strategic in nature, offering the hope of competitive advantage. The former are called, for example, requisite or threshold competencies, while the latter are called for example, strategic or differentiating competencies.

Common characteristics of competency pay systems include the following.

1. *Compensation approach*—the typical competency pay system is pure base pay, not a set of bonuses or add-ons to base pay.

2. *Design methodology*—the most common approach to designing competency pay systems is to study a group of performers who are judged as superior on specified performance criteria, and to collect extensive data to determine how top performers are different from average or poor performers. An extensive battery of tests, interviews, observations, and ratings may be used to discover such differences. The differentiators are packaged into competencies that are then tied to human resource systems, including compensation.

3. *Most common organizational settings*—the term competency pay is most often applied to systems that cover managers, supervisors, professionals (including human resource professionals), and technical personnel. Often, these systems are applied to large numbers of personnel in different positions and locations within a company. When this occurs, the system may not be closely tied to the specific work of covered employees.

4. *Implicit assumptions*—competency pay plans require considerable design and installation effort, and thus these plans make the same assumptions as skill-based pay plans about the organizational stability needed to realize a return on the up-front investment in the plan. These plans also make a strong assumption that performance at the organizational level will increase if more employees emulate the behavior and values of superior individual performers. This assumption is rarely tested, even though a fair amount of research suggests that organizational performance is not merely the sum of individual performance. The problem is that collective behaviors (such as setting a good performance strategy and coordinating effort) may be needed to generate good organizational performance, but not to generate the superior individual performance captured by the competency modeling process.

There is some evidence that plans of this type can have positive effects. For example, a Hewitt study[8] of exemplary firms for executive development found that the use of rewards to reinforce core competencies was related to success. Hewitt found that "Top 20" Companies were twice as likely as other firms to pay for leadership competencies through base pay, annual incentive pay, and long-term incentives; 60 percent or more of Top 20 Companies used each of these compensation tools.

There is little research about the effectiveness of competency pay systems in increasing organizational performance. A 1996 study[9] found too few competency pay cases to draw conclusions about the organizational effects of these plans. A great many validation studies, using industrial psychology methodology, offer encouragement, but these usually validate against individual rather than organizational performance.

A particular concern with competency pay plans is the risk of legal jeopardy for poorly conceived and validated competency pay systems that may illegally discriminate against minorities and other protected groups. This is a special concern with competencies that are based on personality traits and other abstract competencies far removed from the actual work. These may not pass the "face valid" test and may invite court challenges.

Plans Based on Strategic Competencies

The third approach is embryonic. It has been the subject of considerable discussion because of the intense interest in "core competencies" in the business strategy literature and among senior executives during the 1990s.[10] The core competencies approach argues that a small set of technological and organizational skill complexes is a more stable and effective source of competitive advantage than superiority in particular markets or products. Market leadership is fleeting as products evolve rapidly, but competencies remain. For example, Sony's core competencies in miniaturization and precision manufacturing, Toyota's prowess at lean manufacturing, and Wal-Mart's core competencies in distribution, marketing, and information technology, are underlying sources of competitive advantage that remain despite rapidly shifting markets and products.

In many companies, human resource managers and consultants have used executive interest in core competencies as an opportunity to introduce competency-based pay plans. However, it is important to recognize that the "core competencies" of the strategy literature bear no relation to those found in many pay systems. It takes extensive analysis and effort to discover the handful of "core competencies" that business strategists have in mind. In the strategy management literature, sustainable competitive advantage results when a firm develops resources that are valuable, rare, and difficult to imitate. By contrast, "core" in the competency pay literature often means basic or requisite—the opposite of the meaning in the strategy literature. Worse, simply selecting competencies from a consultant's menu of prepackaged choices, a procedure that is far too common, may discredit the plan for strategists and executives who are interested in discovering the unique competencies that gain competitive advantage for the firm.

One of the most positive aspects of the focus on strategic competencies is that it encourages forward thinking. By contrast, the focus in the competency pay approach on identifying why some are superior performers is essentially backward looking, in that it identifies the competencies that have made some people successful in the past. For companies that are about to undergo fundamental change in response to business conditions, reinforcing old successful habits can be a recipe for disaster. Consider IBM or AT&T in 1980, at the dawn of the PC and telecommunications revolutions. If they had paid for competencies, would they have been better served by a forward looking or backward looking system? Many companies believe that their situation today is analogous to that faced by IBM and AT&T 20 years ago.

There are relatively few examples of pay systems based on strategic competencies. Business leaders and authors have devoted little attention to how this approach might be applied to human resource systems, as opposed to business strategy. However, some characteristics of this approach seem clear.

1. *Compensation approach*—the typical system is a base pay compensation system.

2. *Design methodology*—the design methodology is "top down," evolving from the top executive group's identification of the core competencies of the corporation rather than from the current work of employees. This permits identification and rewarding of forward-looking competencies that have not received significant prior attention in the corporation.

3. *Most common settings*—although experience is limited so far, it seems likely that the pay of managers and professionals is most likely to be touched by these plans.

4. *Implicit assumptions*—an important assumption is that highly abstract strategic competencies that may not be within the experience of most employees can serve as the basis for an effective pay plan. This places a heavy burden on management to explain their reasoning and persuade employees of the merits of the strategic competency approach.

The first author has conducted an unpublished study of a plan that fits the strategic competency definition. The plan covered nearly 1000 managers from a variety of functions and levels within a large food company. All were rewarded by movement within a broad band for their mastery of just four competencies that applied to all those covered on the plan. The competencies were closely linked to the business strategy of the firm. For example, one competency supported the customer focus that was important to the company's then new Total Quality Management initiative. The study found that, across the company, the regions that were most effective in implementing and supporting the competency pay plan were the most effective on hard measures of performance (productivity, cost, and quality).

SKC BONUSES

So far, we have considered three kinds of base pay systems for rewarding the acquisition of SKCs. In general, base pay systems are advantageous. Adoption of a base pay system tends to force a relatively thorough analysis of needed SKCs, rather than the casual adoption of a new pay plan. Base pay plans also are relatively difficult to remove arbitrarily. Finally, employees tend to view base pay increases as a desirable and meaningful reward. However, one-time bonuses are an underused alternative to base pay increases, and they make a great deal of sense in two situations.

First, bonuses may help preserve a competitive wage position in the market. If an existing organization is converting to a pay for skills plan, and if base wages are already over market, the organization may not be able to offer additional base wage increases without becoming uncompetitive. It is difficult to see how existing plants in the auto industry, for example, can offer meaningful base wage incentives for skill acquisition, but one-time bonuses may offer an attractive alternative. This is because bonuses do not have the recurring annuity cost of base wage increases.

Second, bonuses are attractive when the organization is experiencing rapid changes in the types and mix of skills, knowledge, and competencies that it needs to be successful. In high technology, for example, the competitive landscape changes so frequently that long-term planning is difficult. The rate of technical obsolescence may be so great that the organization does not have the luxury of devoting a year or two to creating a competency pay plan. The plan might be largely obsolete before the design was complete. Bonuses are an attractive option because they can be developed and implemented very quickly. Such plans can be modified frequently. For example, a new set of bonuses can be adopted each year, changing as business conditions change.

Bonuses have other advantages—and problems. They can be targeted to a select few competencies without upsetting the base pay system. Administrative support is much less than with a base pay system. Sloppy or even poor designs in any given year have fewer negative consequences, because of the absence of an annuity feature. On the other hand, bonuses may have more limited incentive value to employees. Also, these plans are probably more difficult to sustain over time, because management tends to feel more comfortable about terminating bonus plans than terminating base pay plans. The plan may lack credibility with employees if the opportunity for a quickly executed plan becomes an excuse for failing to support it with an adequate communications and training infrastructure.

There is no research about SKC bonus plans, but such companies as Monsanto and Rockwell have used them. Anecdotal evidence is highly encouraging. One engineering-intensive company placed thousands of employees on a competency pay bonus system. All exempt employees negotiated learning contracts with their supervisors in an appraisal cycle set off by six months from the performance review cycle. The plan offered employees a $750 bonus for meeting the negotiated learning contract. The company experienced a five-fold increase in the amount of development activity in the company at a relatively modest cost in bonuses. The tuition reimbursement budget actually experienced a windfall, as technical personnel stopped taking classes that were not directly relevant to their work (and their learning contracts).

THE DESIGN CONTEXT

In designing plans that pay for skills, knowledge, and competencies, managers often seem to have an irresistible urge to jump into the details of skill block design. The first lesson from research and experience is that the fit of the system with its organizational context is far more important than any choice about the design of particular skill blocks. In particular, the system must be carefully married to the business context.

1. *Business-based objectives*—skill-based pay plans, for example, can be especially helpful in increasing employee flexibility, encouraging training, and reinforcing self-management skills. Designers need to think through what specific patterns of behavior are required of employees, whether the proposed pay plan is able to reinforce those skills, and how the intended benefits will be realized. A very important business issue to consider is how much flexibility the organization has to increase average wages levels, which will affect the availability of meaningful incentives in exchange for mastering new skills, knowledge, and competencies.

2. *Organizational structure and technology*—plans that pay for skills, knowledge, and competency can reinforce or undermine organizational structure. For example, if the organization is emphasizing the use of employee teams, cross-skilling within teams may be more appropriate than cross-skilling throughout the entire organization. The organization's production technology often acts as an important constraint, and in some cases, it may need to be modified to support training needs. For example, in customer service organizations, new technology can provide fully trained customer service agents with all the information needed to service a customer fully, rather than sending inquiries to multiple departments. Implementation is usually easier in manufacturing than in service settings. Skill-based pay appears to work best in complex, integrated manufacturing settings that require high levels of employee skill.

3. *Other pay systems*—pay for SKCs is not a complete compensation system, in that it does not reward performance directly. Therefore, it must fit with the overall pay architecture and the performance incentives provided by the organization. Fortunately, pay for SKCs is often highly complementary to

pay systems that reward team and/or organizational results. Group or unit incentives such as gainsharing or goal sharing often make a potent combination with pay for SKCs. Group or unit incentives help overcome the centrifugal force of the individualistic focus on personal SKC development, and encourage a balance between immediate performance requirements and long-term developmental needs. However, individual pay for performance is often problematic in combination with pay for SKCs, because the entire pay system encourages a focus on individual needs.

Organizational Culture

As we have indicated, organizations that adopt pay for SKCs should have or be moving to an open, participative culture. This is one of the strongest predictors of success, in part because cultures with such characteristics are far more likely to take advantage of the new capabilities employees develop through the plan. A hierarchical culture may make it difficult to take advantage of the employee flexibility and self-management capability that pay for SKCs encourages.

Institutional Factors

The economic and social context has a great deal to do with the receptivity to pay for SKCs and its prospects for success. For example, after unions in France lost momentum and wage increases tied to inflation nearly disappeared, institutional pressure has promoted the use of pay based on the person rather than the job. Towards the end of 1990s, about one-fourth of top French companies used some form of skill-based pay.[11] In Britain, competence-related pay is not replacing traditional pay approaches but fusing with them. Such a combination helps to address both the measurement concerns of trade unionists and others and the results-focused orientation of line managers.[12]

THE DESIGN OF COMPENSABLE SKILLS, KNOWLEDGE, AND COMPETENCIES

The design of pay for skills, knowledge and competencies must be based on a holistic human resource management approach, which means that it is closely tied in with training, recruitment and other human resource management systems in the organization. Whatever form the pay system takes, it will be constituted of certain units of skills, knowledge, and competency that the organization is willing to compensate. We address three major issues that must be addressed in the design of compensable units: compensation management, training and development, and assessment.

Compensation Management

First, the architecture of the overall compensation system requires attention. The nature of the SKC blocks will be determined primarily by the type of plan being implemented. A number of questions arise after the basic blocks are defined. How will SKC blocks or units be ordered, indicating career paths, and minimum and maximum advancement opportunities? Decisions about these matters will give employees messages about the sequencing necessary to advance and to remain an employee in good standing. In general, it is best to err on the side of conservatism in these decisions early in the history of the plan. Employees rarely complain if they end up with more career opportunities, easier minimum requirements, and greater maximum earning potential later, but the opposite condition feels like a "take-away" if the plan is modified because it was overly generous.

An important issue concerns the pricing of plans that pay for skills, knowledge, and competencies. Often, it is impossible to price each competency or skill block to the market, in the way that each job in a job-based system can be priced. Rather, the typical procedure is to price the overall system rather than each element of it. The entry rate is set at the level just high enough to get talented people to join the organization. The top rate is set based on market conditions as well. For example, in skill-based pay plans for semi-skilled factory workers, the top end of the range may be placed appropriately near the bottom of the skilled worker classification. Finally, in some cases an average rate pay rate is also set to market, based on labor market or industry benchmarks. Within these anchor points, skill blocks or competencies are assigned value based on their relative degree of difficulty. To take a simple example, assume that the entry rate is $10 per hour and the top rate is $20 per hour, both determined by the market. If there are 10 skill blocks of equal difficulty (as indicated by learning time or some other metric), each block an employee masters might have a value of $1 per hour.

Employees need to have some idea of how long it will take to master competencies or skill blocks. The amount of time required to master a block or competency can vary tremendously, from a few months to several years. In general, it is desirable to break very complex blocks or competencies into several pieces so at least annual advancement is possible on the system. If the blocks or competencies require only a few weeks to master, on the other hand, it is better to group them into a longer and more meaningful grouping or reconsider whether the plan really fits the skill requirements of the organization. The organization does not want too many blocks or competencies because this makes the plan difficult to administer and communicate, and because it sets up the expectation that employees will receive compensation every time they learn anything.

Training and Development

Unless employees have the opportunity to develop the skills and competencies that make up the pay system, they will be frustrated by the incentives they have no opportunity to earn. Experience and research clearly indicate that demand for training greatly increases once employee pay is attached to mastery of skills and competencies.

It is desirable to create a solid training plan in advance of the installation of the pay system. The starting point of the plan is the assessment of the training required to master each skill block or competency in the system, together with an estimate of the likely speed and path of progression of employees through the system. A menu of training courses relevant to the system, a specific schedule of offerings, and the assignment of instructors (which may be peers, vendors, managers, or trainers) are part of the plan. An adequate training budget is essential.

Job rotation is a critical part of the acquisition of many skills and competencies, especially in skill-based pay systems. No classroom training can take the place of the experiences on the job that are needed for mastery of most skills included in the typical system. Rotation issues can become very contentious, and it is best to anticipate the problems and plan for rotation ahead of time. Many issues need to be determined. Who will decide when to rotate, and according to what timetable? How will the organization balance production needs with employee desires for training? How will it handle slow learners and those who refuse to rotate, which can lock up the whole rotation system? Competency systems for exempt employees may require new assignments rather than something analogous to job rotation. However, the same types of issues are relevant.

Assessment of SKC Acquisition

Any system requires some way of determining whether an employee has mastered skill blocks or competencies. The methods and procedures for assessment can be quite contentious if they are not thought through well. The assessment step has no counterpart in job-based pay systems. Unless it is done well in SKC pay plans, however, the plan will deteriorate into a de facto time in grade system, and the organization will receive no value for the increased wages provided under the system.

Part of the design of each skill block or competency is the specification of the standards for determining how we can verify that an employee has mastered it. In skill-based pay plans for nonexempt employees, the process can be fairly elaborate, involving measurement of on-the-job performance, testing, and other methods. In general, management should rely on work samples whenever possible. Work samples are face valid, meaning they have natural credibility with employees. However, work samples may need to be supplemented with oral testing, written testing, or live demonstrations, if it is important to know how the employee would respond to rare or hazardous conditions that are not likely to be encountered during the work sample of a few weeks or months.

In skill-based pay systems, certification may become one of the most time-consuming supervisory duties. Thus, it is important to think through the scheduling of certifications and the procedures for handling those who fail the tests. For example, how soon will they be allowed to retest? Is there any queuing of certification opportunities in the work unit?

Periodic recertification, perhaps annually, seems to be an increasing trend in skill-based systems. This insures that employees maintain the skills for which they receive compensation. Without recertifications, the pay plan can result in increased wages that are attached to skills long lost through disuse.

Competency pay plans tend to incorporate competency assessments into the performance appraisal system. By their nature, most competencies are demonstrated on the job over a long period of time. Increasingly, assessments have a "360 degree" component, with reviews by peers, subordinates, supervisors, and customers who have relevant knowledge of the employee's demonstrated competency.

THE SURVIVAL OF PAY FOR SKCs

Some recent research has explored the reasons why plans paying for skills, knowledge, and competencies not only are successful, but also what explains their survival or termination. The most detailed study[13] examined longitudinal results for 59 plans. It found that the survival of these plans was most strongly associated with organizational characteristics (plans manufacturing was more likely to survive, and a business strategy based on innovation was negatively related to survival). Employee involvement in the design and certain plan characteristics (focus on breadth of skill, number of skill blocks) also predicted survival.

A study of five Finnish cases[14] found that some plans failed due to poor skill definitions and compensation assessment that employees considered unfair. Good training opportunities and clarity of learning goals were critical to the success and survival of these plans.

SUMMARY

We conclude with three summary lessons drawn from our experience and research.

1. The design of the system is important, but the quality of the infrastructure needed to support it (certification, training, ability to move employees among jobs, communication of the pay plan, etc.) is a stronger predictor of success than the elegance of the design.
2. All things being equal, simpler is better. One of the major problems with SKC pay plans is that they tend to become unnecessarily complex, and sometimes are abandoned because management comes to feel that the administrative hassle outweighs any benefit.
3. Communication is even more important than for job-based pay systems. SKC systems are inevitably unfamiliar to most employees, they are complex compared to job-based pay, and they are dependent on employee understanding of certification and training requirements that add complexity.

4. Any SKC pay plan will change over time or it will be abandoned because of its inflexibility and lack of fit with changing conditions. A complete design includes provisions for periodically revisiting the design and its infrastructure, and making revisions as necessary. Such a provision should be very explicit, to increase the chances that employees will greet changes with interest and appreciation rather than resistance.

END NOTES

1. Edward E Lawler III, "Pay Practices in Fortune 1000 Companies," *WorldatWork Journal*, vol. 12, no. 4, 2003, pp. 45–54.

2. Loree Griffith and Steve Gross, "Perspective: Charting a Course Toward Growth: U.S. Compensation Strategies at the Helm," Mercer Human Resource Consulting, October 2003.

3. Towers Perrin HR Services, "Reward Management: Closing a Growing Say/Do Gap," Towers Perrin, 2007.

4. International Public Management Association for Human Resources, "2007 Total Compensation Benchmarking Study," IPMA-HR, Alexandria, VA, 2007.

5. G. D. Jenkins, Jr, G. E. Ledford, Jr, N. Gupta, and D. H. Doty, "Skill-based Pay: Practices, Payoffs, Pitfalls, and Prospects," Scottsdale, AZ: American Compensation Association, 1992.

6. B. Murray and B. Gerhart, "An Empirical Analysis of a Skill-based Pay Program and Plant Performance Outcomes," *Academy of Management Journal*, vol. 41, 1998, pp. 68–78.

7. L. M. Spencer and S. M. Spencer, *Competence at Work*, New York: Wiley, 1993.

8. Hewitt Associates, "Research Highlights: How the Top 20 Companies Grow Great Leaders," Lincolnshire, IL: Hewitt Associates, 2005.

9. American Compensation Association, *Raising the Bar: Using Competencies to Enhance Employee Performance*, Scottsdale, AZ: American Compensation Association, 1996.

10. C. K. Prahalad and G. Hamel, "The Core Competence of the Corporation," *Harvard Business Review*, May–June 1990, pp. 79–91.

11. A. Klarsfeld, D. B. Balkin, and A. Roger, "Pay Policy Variability within a French Firm: The Case of Skill-based Pay in a Process Technology Context," *Journal of High Technology Management Research*, vol. 14, 2003, pp. 47–70.

12. M. Armstrong and D. Brown, "Relating Competencies to Pay: The U.K. Experience," *Compensation and Benefits Review*, vol. 10, no. 1, 1998, pp. 28–39.

13. J. D. Shaw, N. Gupta, A. Mitra and G. E. Ledford, Jr, "Success and Survival of Skill-based Pay Plans," *Journal of Management*, vol. 31, 2005, pp. 28–49.

14. E. Moisio, "Competency Management and Rewarding," *3rd Performance and Reward Conference*, Manchester, 2005, www.business.mmu.ac.uk/newsandevents/parc/moisio.pdf

BROADBANDING

Kenan S. Abosch, Broad-Based Compensation Practice Segment Leader

Hewitt Associates, LLC

BROADBANDING REPRESENTS A SIGNIFICANT DEPARTURE from traditional compensation structures. It is important therefore that human resources professionals have ongoing, accurate, and comprehensive information about how broadbanding approaches are being developed and supported and about their impact on organizations. Such information is critical in helping companies understand broadbanding design and assess the desirability and feasibility of moving to such a compensation structure.

A formal longitudinal study of "early adaptor" companies—those using broadbands for compensation and career management—was conducted from 1994 to 2004.

BROADBANDING DEFINED

Broadbanding refers to a human resources strategy that collapses salary grades into a few wide "bands" for the purposes of managing career growth and administering pay. By eliminating much of the hierarchy associated with a traditional pay structure, broadbands support today's flatter, leaner, more customer-focused organization. The following are characteristics of a broadbanding approach:

- Each band includes a broad grouping of jobs

- Career growth is defined in terms of increased responsibilities, rather than only upward advancement

- Individuals may perform several different jobs that fall within the same band

- Managers and their direct reports may be in the same band

While commonly considered as "just" a compensation approach, more advanced models of broadbanding are more sweeping in scope, encompassing career management and skill mobility.

THE EVOLUTION OF BROADBANDING

When the first companies started what became known as broadbanding in the late 1980s, their purpose was to deemphasize the convention of traditional compensation design and to encourage greater skill development and job mobility. During the 1990s, broadbanding continued to evolve as a way to support organizational changes from internal focus to external focus, to encourage employees toward lateral (versus upward) career growth, and to allow more flexibility in job design and staffing. Broadbanding's continued evolution in the 2000s is moving toward a very strong market focus, in which the ability to respond to the external market quickly and economically is the driving force.

The earliest research established two distinct sets of philosophy and design being applied as broadbanding: broad grades and career bands (see Figure 12.1). *Broad grades* is an approach using few, relatively wide pay levels, but retaining many of the controls found in more conventional salary administration systems (e.g., ranges, midpoints). *Career bands* is an approach that departs more radically from conventional compensation practice by using relatively few bands and significantly wide salary ranges. While both broad grades and career bands are implemented to streamline administration and encourage career development, the career band approach places greater emphasis on skill and competency acquisition.

The latest research has uncovered a further step in the evolutionary process of broadbanding that can be described as pure market. This approach is currently used by relatively few organizations. Companies with pure market have no defined bands, but instead use individual market rates for each job within the organization.

FIGURE 12.1   Evolution of broadbanding over a decade

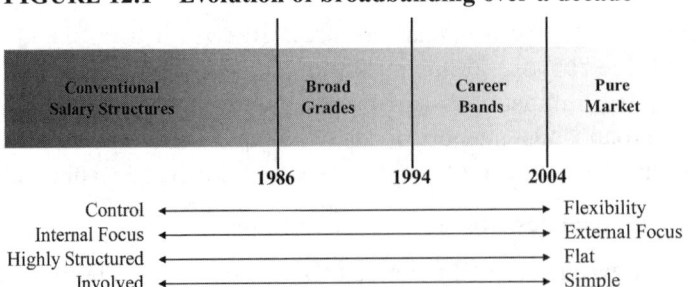

Source: Life With Broadbands II: Reviewing a Decade of Company Experiences With Broadbanding 2004

Jobs are generally compensated based on market-based guidelines, which are allowed to vary depending on the current market value for the particular job.

REASONS FOR USING BROADBANDING HAVE CHANGED

One fascinating aspect of broadbanding has been its adaptability. Those leading the way in broadbanding implementation in the early 1990s were faced with an environment of downsizing and reengineering and the aftermath of a recession. In the late 1990s, companies were in the midst of an economic boom period and could not hire talent quickly enough to keep up with the demand for products and services. In the middle of the first decade of the twenty-first century, political uncertainty, cost containment, and lack of job creation have been key environmental factors for organizations. In spite of this volatility in external conditions, organizations have stayed with their broadbanding systems and most have required only minor modifications to their programs for them to remain viable.

The reason most often cited for using a broadbanding approach has not changed since the 1990s—companies use banding to create organizational flexibility (see Figure 12.2). Yet, while flexibility continues to be the top reason for using bands, other reasons have evolved. For example, in the early 1990s, companies were internally focused—making structural and organizational changes to the company culture. Then, in the late 1990s, companies turned their focus to employees—encouraging them to develop multiple skills, to be flexible, and to develop their careers in nontraditional (nonhierarchical) ways.

Now, in the 2000s, companies' top reasons for using bands are more externally focused—toward the outside marketplace. Today, the most important reasons for using broadbands are to be able to respond to the marketplace quickly and economically.

BAND DESIGN AND COMMUNICATION

Design. Over the course of 10 years, the design and communication of broadbanding programs has changed little. Overall, broadbanding does not seem to be

FIGURE 12.2   Broadbanding evolves to a marketplace focus

1994— *"Structural Focus"*		1998— *"Employee Development Focus"*		2004— *"Marketplace Focus"*
1. Create organizational flexibility		1. Create organizational flexibility		1. Create organizational flexibility
2. Support new culture	→	2. Encourage skill development	→	2. Deemphasize hierarchy
3. Deemphasize hierarchy		3. Emphasize career development		3. Respond to changes in job/work design

Source: Life With Broadbands II: Reviewing a Decade of Company Experiences With Broadbanding 2004

going deeper into the company, but instead, is being deployed more widely (including globally). Broadbanding programs are still used mainly for executives and exempt employees.

Communication. Most companies provide little to no communication about their broadbanding programs (only about one-third communicate much at all, while about 10 percent provide no communication about their programs). This is probably due to the fact that most of these companies have had broadbands in place for some time. Organizations living with broadbands for 9 years indicate that lack of communication is a problem. The most common response to the question "What is the one thing you would do differently?" has been "We would communicate more. And better." This is not surprising, as most compensation professionals (and perhaps human resources professionals) are inherently more comfortable with plan design and implementation, not communication.

> One organization reviewing their experience with broadbands summed it up this way: Communication is the key for a successful experience with broadbanding. You cannot over communicate. Share the facts with managers and employees. Explain the program/system to them—what is it, why we have it, how it works, and how it impacts people. Companies thinking about going to broadbanding should know that about 50 percent of their efforts need to be focused on communication.

Communication methods (when used) have changed greatly over time. In the past, in-person communication (via supervisors or department meetings) was most prevalent, followed by printed material (a print brochure or booklet).

FIGURE 12.3   Bands by employee group and spreads for exempt employees

Number of Bands by Employee Group

	Now	Then	Conclusion
Executives	1–3 bands	1–2 bands	Companies are slightly expanding the number of
Other Exempts	3–5 bands	3–4 bands	bands, for all employee groups
Nonexempts	2–5 bands	1–3 bands	

Band Range Spreads for Exempt Employees

	Now	Then	Conclusion
No Ranges	29%	31%	This has not changed significantly in 2004 from prior
50%–75%	6%	0%	practices
76%–100%	29%	31%	
Over 100%	36%	38%	

Source: Life With Broadbands II: Reviewing a Decade of Company Experiences With Broadbanding 2004

Today personal communication approaches are still used, however printed material has been replaced by electronic means (internal or database sites and e-mail).

MYTHS AND REALITIES

From its inception in the late 1980s, the concept of broadbanding has raised concerns with some human resource professionals. Figure 12.4 shows what is known about the most common broadbanding myths from companies who have had banding in place for at least 10 years.

Broadbanding is Effective

As a whole, broadbanding is viewed as effective by a substantial number of companies who have lived under bands. Only a minority of organizations indicates that broadbanding is "ineffective" and no organizations with broadbanding for a decade or more indicate that it has been "very ineffective" (see Figure 12.5).

In addition to broadbanding being effective, virtually all companies said that their organizations are better off for having implemented broadbands than if they had not. Broadbanding's effectiveness was rated highest in the following five areas:

1. It is flexible
2. It is fair
3. It is simple
4. It is understandable
5. It enhances employees' earning potential

Figure 12.6 shows how companies assessed the impact of broadbanding in their companies in 15 areas.

FIGURE 12.4   Myths and reality

Broadbanding Myths	Reality
1. "It will be expensive—payroll costs will skyrocket without the controls of a well-defined salary structure."	*Not True*. While a disappointingly large number of companies do not know/measure their labor costs, among those that **do**, over 90 percent say their banding program has been cost neutral.
2. "We will be unable to defend it legally."	*Not True*. Companies that have been audited by government agencies (e.g., DOL Wage/Hour Division, OFCCP), have reported that no legal or mandatory corrective actions were required as a result of broadbanding.
3. "Managers and employees will not understand it."	*Partially True*. Companies with broadbands report that while employees are able to understand broadbanding, they do so less often than their managers or supervisors. Interestingly, human resources' understanding is said to be about the same level as managers and supervisors.
4. "We will lose the ability to match jobs and get market data."	*Not True*. Companies are able to set market benchmark matches for the majority of their overall job population. None of the respondents reported that banding is an impediment to managing their compensation program closely to market. Very few broadbanding companies find that it is difficult to **submit** data to surveys. Most say that they do not have difficulties in **applying** survey data to the company.

Source: Life With Broadbands II: Reviewing a Decade of Company Experiences With Broadbanding 2004

FIGURE 12.5   Overall effectiveness of broadbanding on the organization

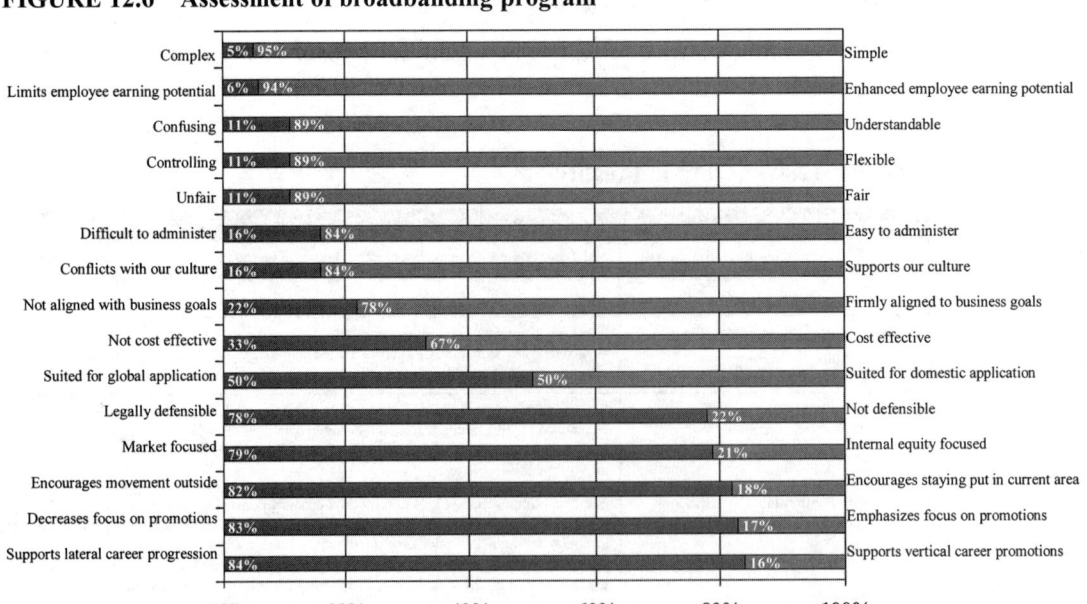

Effective
74%

Very Effective
36%

Ineffective
26%

Effective
64%

Source: Life With Broadbands II: Reviewing a Decade of Company Experiences With Broadbanding 2004

After living with broadbands for a decade, a reasonable question to ask is how well broadbanding is satisfying the objectives that led to introducing it in the first place. Figure 12.7 reveals that most objectives have been achieved to a very high degree.

COMPANIES WOULD DO IT AGAIN

Broadbands are part of the outgrowth of companies' needs to better manage their business in an increasingly fast and global marketplace full of challenging economic conditions. Companies need their employees to constantly adapt in ways that contribute to business success. This is a significant change from the past employment

FIGURE 12.6   Assessment of broadbanding program

Left label	Value (left)	Value (right)	Right label
Complex	5%	95%	Simple
Limits employee earning potential	6%	94%	Enhanced employee earning potential
Confusing	11%	89%	Understandable
Controlling	11%	89%	Flexible
Unfair	11%	89%	Fair
Difficult to administer	16%	84%	Easy to administer
Conflicts with our culture	16%	84%	Supports our culture
Not aligned with business goals	22%	78%	Firmly aligned to business goals
Not cost effective	33%	67%	Cost effective
Suited for global application	50%	50%	Suited for domestic application
Legally defensible	78%	22%	Not defensible
Market focused	79%	21%	Internal equity focused
Encourages movement outside	82%	18%	Encourages staying put in current area
Decreases focus on promotions	83%	17%	Emphasizes focus on promotions
Supports lateral career progression	84%	16%	Supports vertical career promotions

0%   20%   40%   60%   80%   100%

Source: Life With Broadbands II: Reviewing a Decade of Company Experiences With Broadbanding 2004

FIGURE 12.7   Effectiveness ratings of reasons given for broadbanding

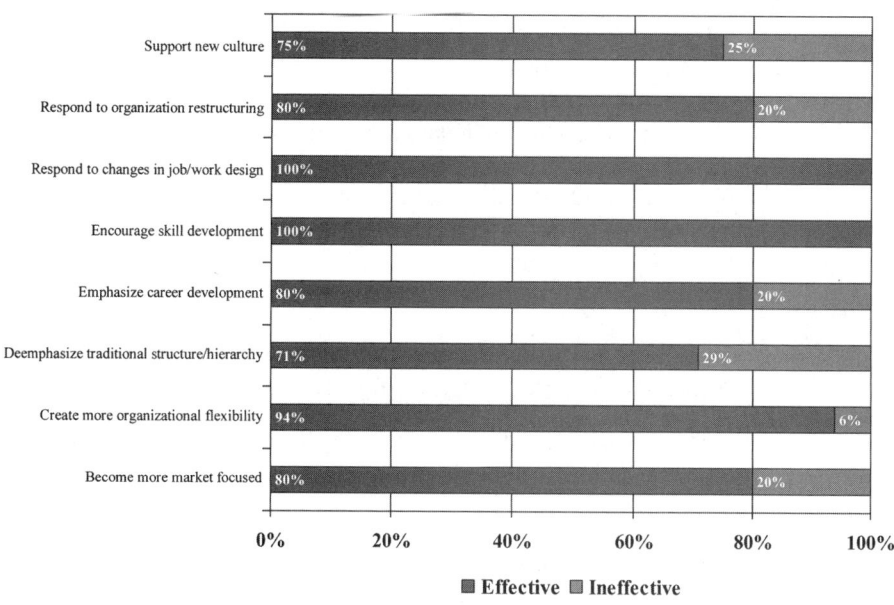

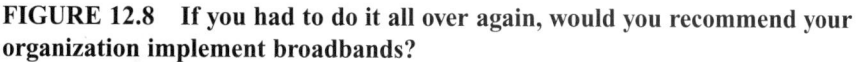

Source: *Life With Broadbands II: Reviewing a Decade of Company Experiences With Broadbanding 2004*

relationship, which was characterized by employees' reliance on job security, steady promotions, and lifetime company loyalty. For these reasons, the use of broadbanding in all its different forms has grown rapidly in the first decade of its existence.

Perhaps the ultimate test of effectiveness might be whether companies would implement broadbanding again or recommend that others implement it. When asked, if they had to do it all over again, would they recommend that their companies implement broadbands, the vast majority of companies said that they would (see Figure 12.8).

FIGURE 12.8   If you had to do it all over again, would you recommend your organization implement broadbands?

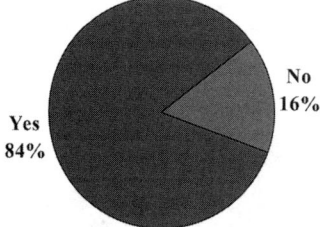

Source: *Life With Broadbands II: Reviewing a Decade of Company Experiences With Broadbanding 2004*

"Broadbanding has been well accepted and is viewed as consistent with our business strategies," according to one company. An HR professional says:

> It is meeting the goals for success and expectations. Broadbanding has introduced the needed flexibility in the workforce, and has greatly streamlined the amount of time spent analyzing and classifying jobs. Broadbanding nicely pulls in market rates for pay levels, and has, to a noticeable degree, reduced hiring new people from the outside at salary range minimums. This results in more market-focused pricing thereby increasing the caliber of new hires.

REFERENCES

Abosch, K. and Hand, J., *Broadbanding Design, Approaches, and Practices*, Scottsdale, AZ: American Compensation Association, 1994.

Abosch, K. and Hand, J., *Life with Broadbands*, Scottsdale, AZ: American Compensation Association, 1998.

Abosch, K. and Hand, J., *Life with Broadbands II: Reviewing a Decade of Company Experiences With Broadbanding*, Lincolnshire, IL: Hewitt Associates, 2004.

13

NONMONETARY AWARDS

Rodger D. Stotz, Vice President and Managing Consultant,
and Melissa Van Dyke, Consultant

Maritz, Inc.

T HE PAST DECADE HAS WITNESSED a significant growth in the market value of corporations' intangible assets by the financial markets. In fact, some studies show that the percentage of a company's market value attributed to intangible assets has risen from 0 to 20 percent in the 1990s to 60–80 percent today. This has resulted in new strategies for investing in human capital and its capacity to affect intangible assets such as productivity, customer service, and branding.

Whereas the primary focus of employee work rewards used to be pay, there is now a growing focus on a balanced use of both cash and nonmonetary awards. A key turning point came in 2000 when the American Compensation Association changed its name to WorldatWork. This change was driven by two trends—globalization and the growth of nonmonetary awards—and resulted in the creation of the WorldatWork Total Rewards Model, which includes Compensation, Benefits, and Work–Life.

The use of work rewards beyond cash compensation is still an evolving and expanding field. In tandem, as we will see in this chapter, nonmonetary awards are growing in importance. In fact, employers that only offer cash compensation as a work reward are not only at a disadvantage for recruiting and retention, but are also often choosing a more costly Total Rewards plan.

The emerging arena of employee experiences is a great example of how far the Total Rewards trend has already evolved. The many studies of the Generation X and Generation Y workers have identified a different set of personal values than found in previous generations. These newer generations are expressing their desire and expectation for work experiences beyond pay. Flex-time, telecommuting, professional development, access to leadership, recognition, and mentoring are just a few of the growing list of experiences and nonmonetary awards.

In this chapter we will explore the new and review the well-established nonmonetary rewards. We look first at the evolution of nonmonetary rewards followed by the reasons organizations are including nonmonetary rewards in the Total Rewards Framework. We then present a discussion of the types of nonmonetary awards. Next, the key elements of plan design and specific plan design strategies are covered. After a review of tax and global implications, we conclude with examining why nonmonetary awards are effective.

EVOLUTION OF NONMONETARY AWARDS

Nonmonetary awards have been a part of U.S. business for decades, historically used as awards for length of service or tenure. In the 1950s and 1960s, the use of nonmonetary awards expanded to certificates, trophies, and mementos for nonsales employees, and to merchandise and travel awards for sales employees. In the 1970s and 1980s, the use of nonmonetary awards expanded again, with small "plateau" award catalogs offered to nonsales employees who met safety, cost reduction, and productivity goals.

From the 1990s to the present, this trend of nonmonetary awards for nonsales personnel has continued to increase, as has the variety of award types. The current choices being offered include: award certificates, credit and debit cards, award catalogs, retail options, individual travel, lunches, dinners, and paid time off, for example.

As we look to the future, a trend for more choice and more focus on "experiences" is quickly emerging. While the classic merchandise and travel options are still popular, the following additional offerings are finding a receptive audience:

- *Unique travel experiences* (spas, biking the Rockies, attending a spectacular theater or athletic event, participating in an archeological dig, flying a MIG jet, attending a race car driving school, etc.)

- *Supplemental professional development* (skill-building conferences, business etiquette, access to organizational leadership and/or experts and formalized mentoring)

- *Personal development* (cooking school, golf lessons, sabbaticals, wine classes, etc.)

The trend of ever increasing choice and diversity in the consumer marketplace is being reflected in nonmonetary awards. Since the value of any award is ultimately determined by the emotional attachment and perception of the recipient and since the values of the recipients are continually changing, nonmonetary award offerings must change correspondingly to maintain their relevance and motivation.

However a note of caution is appropriate: too often the focus on recognition and incentive plans is on awards without adequate attention to the "presentation." Any award is just that, an "award," not a "purchase." This requires the award to be positioned as something special, something earned based on significant achievement. The opportunity to promote these nonmonetary awards beforehand sets them up as goals in themselves and along with proper presentation and recognition is what separates them from normal compensation.

BENEFITS FROM USING NONMONETARY AWARDS IN THE TOTAL REWARDS FRAMEWORK

As more organizations acknowledge the need for a broader reward offering by embracing the Total Rewards Framework, there is an increased focus on nonmonetary awards. Some of the reasons organizations choose to use nonmonetary awards include:

1. *To supplement a fair compensation plan.* In organizations with fair compensation plans, nonmonetary awards are a great way to reinforce performance towards specific objectives. Although nonmonetary awards should never be used in place of competitive compensation plans or as a replacement for effective cash incentive plans, organizations can create supplemental plans with different criteria using nonmonetary awards focused at separate but specific objectives and performance measurements.

2. *To ease the transition to an organizational unit incentive plan.* As even small amounts of cash quickly become embedded in employees' expected compensation, nonmonetary awards are a good way to test a new incentive plan and refine it. After several periods of tweaking the exact measures and historical reference points, organizations can choose to continue it as is, convert the plan to cash or extract it altogether with less negative employee reaction than a cash program would create. Often, once the targeted behavior has become adopted, the reward level will be reduced to a sustenance level and the difference is reinvested in achieving another performance objective.

3. *To "fine tune" employee performance.* Many times, even small changes in cash compensation have the tendency to "overcorrect" behaviors. Nonmonetary awards can produce a more appropriate, moderate response. As an example, raising the cash sales commission for a particular product can have the effect of cannibalizing efforts put toward other products in the

line. The addition and deletion of nonmonetary awards can add emphasis without "tipping the scales" in either direction.

4. *To help introduce an objective-driven, cost reduction or gross profit enhancement plan.* Nonmonetary awards are an effective way to focus employees on cost reduction, gross profit enhancement, or other team-based objectives. If the organization has or is implementing a gain-sharing plan, nonmonetary awards are also a good way to differentiate between the productivity objective of the existing cash gain-sharing plan and the other objectives. Using cash for everything reduces the ultimate effectiveness of all the plans. However, when introducing new plans, mixing award types (cash for gain-sharing, nonmonetary for objective driven programs) is not a good idea. Most organizations cannot adjust quickly enough to absorb and act upon new plans and different types of awards all at the same time.

5. *To recognize outstanding performance.* When properly presented, nonmonetary awards have the added element of recognition. They can be displayed with pride and discussed openly with colleagues, family and friends; the nonmonetary award in essence becomes a "trophy" that increases the object's value, by providing a lasting reminder of the employee's achievement and contributing to an employee's positive feelings toward the company.

6. *To address additional work–life issues.* The market influx of two-earner families, single-parent households, and a new generation of workers has caused organizations to investigate how work–life related offerings can enhance their Total Rewards offerings. This has caused an increase in the use of nonmonetary awards that organizations offer, such as: mentoring, professional development, personal development, unique travel experiences, etc. Organizations offer these awards because they have a much higher perceived value by the recipient than the equivalent cost in cash.

7. *To create organizational attribution versus legally required compensation.* Cash compensation is a legal requirement of the employee–employer contract. Therefore, employees believe the organization owes them the agreed upon cash compensation and any subsequent use of the cash is not attributed to the organization. The employee simply spends her money on bills, etc. and does not give it another thought. Nonmonetary awards, however, are unique since organizations must choose to offer them over and above cash compensation. When a nonmonetary award is received as recognition, the employee attributes it to their incremental performance and achievement and credits additional generosity to the organization. As organizations in today's competitive labor market try to differentiate themselves, this attribution to the organization can be incredibly valuable, particularly to employee prospects who know they are outstanding performers.

8. *Recognition, incentives, perquisites, team-building.* Nonmonetary awards have a variety of applications. Not only are they used in recognition and incentive plans, but also as perquisites and to support team-building. This widening use of nonmonetary awards requires plan administrators to play close attention to the tracking of the award usage and the measurement of their plan's impact. In some organizations, budgets for recognition awards are used to fund perquisites and team-building awards. While these awards and efforts contribute to the culture of the organization and generally to the morale of the employees involved, they are not recognition awards and are not perceived by the employees as such. The outcome is that the reallocated recognition funds tend to diminish the desired impact of the recognition plan.

TYPES OF NONMONETARY AWARDS

To understand and implement a nonmonetary award program, it is important to understand the difference between a full-service performance improvement agency and a fulfillment source. In addition to supplying merchandise, travel and symbolic awards, *full-service performance improvement agencies* offer research, training, communications, promotion, program rules structures and reward systems design. *Fulfillment sources* on the other hand are limited to only supplying awards. For example, a *merchandise fulfillment source* might be the incentives division of a merchandise manufacturer, a *travel fulfillment source* might be a local travel agency, and a *symbolic award fulfillment source* might be a local advertising or promotional products provider.

The choice of whether or not to use a full-service agency or fulfillment source depends on two factors: (1) the goals of the nonmonetary awards strategy and (2) the availability of internal staff to do administrative and technical support. Generally, as the scope of the nonmonetary awards strategy increases or as the availability of internal support decreases, the need for support from a full-service performance improvement agency increases. Good information on selecting an agency or fulfillment source can be found on the Incentive Marketing Association Web site, www.incentivemarketing.org.

It is also important to understand the difference between recognition and incentive as the type of rewards and level of rewards may vary.

■ Recognition is primarily focused on reinforcement of corporate values and desired culture. It is discretionary, such as peer-to-peer or manager spot recognition, or competitive—top performer or role model structures such as top 5 percent of sales performers or project manager of the month. The focus is on psychic value, and the act of recognition and presentation of recognition is more important than the actual award.

- Incentive is primarily focused on organizational improvement and on achieving specific objectives. Structures are formula-based and preannounced: achieve this and earn that reward. The emphasis is heavier on the reward as the reward is the stated consequence for achieving the goal and must be valuable enough to the participant to capture their attention and discretionary effort.

Many performance improvement initiatives do use a mix, but it is important to know whether the emphasis is on recognition or incentive when selecting rewards. One nonmonetary reward that should always be considered is information recognition.

INFORMAL RECOGNITION

Informal recognition that can be used to raise morale may include: a pat on the back, a simple "thank you," a show of respect, new training, a short written note, the opportunity to mentor, etc. With the cost of these being nothing, the return is limitless. Unfortunately, many managers do not take advantage of these simple, yet effective opportunities. To encourage managers to incorporate these types of awards into their everyday management practices, organizations should help managers become more comfortable with this type of award by providing managerial education on the importance and practice of informal recognition. A good source of information regarding recognition is Recognition Professionals International at www.recognition.org.

MERCHANDISE AWARDS

Organizations looking to offer merchandise as part of their nonmonetary awards offering have two primary options: award catalogs and retail award cards or certificates. Both options typically include the ability for employees to order awards through an online shopping experience or a printed catalog. These options, however, are not mutually exclusive as some incentive agencies allow their award cards to be used with both national retailers and their awards catalog. For either award type, the organization must clearly communicate what performance an individual or team must achieve to earn a certain award level. Additionally, each option has slightly different requirements for administration, service, and billing. Following is a detailed description for comparative purposes:

Award Catalogs

Description.   Awards catalogs in support of recognition and incentive programs are available from full-service performance improvement agencies. The items included in an award catalog have been specifically selected and promoted for their ability to become tangible rewards worth striving for. Upon receipt, the selected items will create a memorable and rewarding experience called "trophy value." Award catalogs are also a key way to promote goal setting in performance improvement programs by allowing employees to focus on earning specific items they find highly motivational.

Catalogs can be small booklets of 15 items grouped by value levels or comprehensive catalogs with over 2000 high-quality items selected for their appeal to a broad range of tastes. Coffee table-type awards catalogs also have the advantage of being strong promotional vehicles engaging the entire family when they are sent to the home. Catalogs also stimulate early goal-setting which is very important in engaging the emotional part of the brain and enhancing the desire to change behavior and increase effort. For these reasons, they often have more motivational appeal than cards or certificates.

Administration. Full-service performance improvement agencies provide the online and offline catalogs along with a price for each award listed in points or award credits. The agency is responsible for issuing points based on the performance information provided by the organization or employees. To issue points, agencies either mail award credit checks or deposit points electronically into a personal point bank account. If the agency uses checks, the checks are printed with the appropriate number of award credits or points and mailed directly to the award recipient.

If the agency uses an award point bank system, the agency will deposit all points electronically into the employee's point account which the employee can then view online. Once issued into their accounts, the employees can then redeem the checks or points immediately or accumulate them for a larger award. The majority of employees will accumulate the checks or points until they have enough buying power to get the award they have selected as a goal. The agency also handles all performance tracking, statements, tax reporting, management reporting, order entry, shipping, customer service, auditing, and billing.

Service. When employees earn an award, they naturally have higher expectations in product quality, delivery, and customer service than when they are making a cash purchase at a retail store. They have worked hard to earn the award, and therefore want to receive it as soon as possible with little to no hassle. Service then becomes an important issue for nonmonetary awards. If problems arise and employees do not receive quick, attentive service, they will hold the sponsoring organization, rather then the agency, responsible.

To ensure this level of service, a good agency will have the most requested items on hand and in stock for fulfilling orders. They should also have well-staffed and highly trained customer service centers. As some items such as furniture and large appliances must be shipped directly from the factory, organizations should be aware that the size and buying power of the agency will have a large bearing on the level of service that award earners experience.

Some agencies also offer a special service to find desired items not available in the awards catalog. Nearly as important as the actual fulfillment of the award is the customer service available for achievers who have a question or concern about their order. It is important that customer service representatives understand that they are working with important award earners and treat people accordingly to ensure the entire experience is truly rewarding.

Billing.   Agencies have two billing methods: "bill on issuance," where billing occurs when the points or checks are issued, and "bill on redemption," where points or checks are billed only after they have been redeemed by an employee for an award. Billing on issuance has the advantage of allowing the organization to account for all nonmonetary awards in the year for which they are budgeted. Bill on redemption means the organization may be subject to a large outstanding liability that needs to be paid when outstanding points or checks are redeemed, but it also offers a cash flow advantage since the billing for awards may occur months or even years after issuance.

Shipping and sales tax are either paid by the employee or billed directly to the organization. Some agencies also roll the fixed costs of project management, technology, and administration into the variable cost of the awards. When choosing an agency, organizations should be sure to identify where the agency accounts for these costs to ensure they are accurately calculating their employee's buying power and the full cost of their nonmonetary awards program.

Retail Options (Award Cards and Certificates)

The second type of merchandise awards come from traditional retail outlets and include some of the nation's largest retailers, including catalog merchants, department stores, and specialty stores. These awards are usually in the form of award cards or award certificates and have become an increasingly popular option for all types of incentive programs. Some full-service incentive agencies have also started offering retail cards and certificates as part of their award portfolios.

Advantages of retail offerings include allowing incentive program participants to redeem their points at competitive prices (including sales) and the ability of the sponsoring firm to have an infinite variety of award choices whereby participants can shop for their awards in store, online or by catalog. The disadvantages of retail gift cards or gift certificates include that they are often hard to distinguish from cash points, can be redeemed for many small items that reduce the trophy value, and often have state-mandated expiration date restrictions and late usage fees.

Certificates.   Organizations using this option send award earners the appropriate denomination of merchandise certificate that can be redeemed at one or more retail locations. Most organizations include a free catalog along with the merchandise certificates. Organizations often choose certificates because they can be easily sourced and awarded "on the spot" to employees.

On the downside, however, the lack of fraud control, the need to source from many retailers to accommodate diverse tastes and the inability to easily replace lost or stolen certificates makes them a challenge to use for any sizable program. In addition, if the retailer is not well known or not easily accessible online or in the employee's home town, the organization may face diminished interest in the program.

Retail Award Cards. The advent of the retail award card has attracted a large percentage of programs that traditionally used certificates. The retailer's card fits neatly into the wallet and can be customized with the organization's logo, which provides a continual opportunity for branding every time the participant opens their wallet. These cards can be purchased with a set denomination and some can be set up as reloadable cards for longer-term programs. The drawback of retail award cards is that they can only be used in that retailer's stores or through their Web site.

Stored Value Cards. There are two main types of stored value cards—open or filtered. The open-ended stored value card allows the participant to shop at any retailer that accepts the award card supplier (American Express, MasterCard, Visa, Discover, etc.), and may be used for such things as gas, which holds little trophy value. The filtered card directs the award earner to only the vendors selected, and has the advantage of ensuring that the award is memorable and special, and that it aligns with the organization's brand and values.

Administration. While most retailers who offer award cards or certificates can give some degree of assistance with such things as tracking, promotion, and administration, these services usually are not their specialties. Certificate issuance, record keeping of participants' performance, stop payments, tax reporting, and all the other administrative demands of a program are usually the responsibility of the organization using the card or certificates. Stored value card administration services can vary depending on who is issuing them from a do-it-yourself provider to a full-service agency that can handle all the details.

Service. Service levels and details need to be carefully reviewed as retail card and certificate suppliers provide a wide range of levels of customer service which, good or bad, will reflect on the program and the sponsoring organization.

Billing. Merchandise cards and certificates are billed on issuance and may include an additional processing fee when the awards are issued.

TRAVEL AWARDS

Travel has an almost universal appeal, especially when it is a popular or unique destination. Add to this appeal one's ability to earn it as an award for performance and it is easy to see why year after year organizations use travel awards.

Travel awards can be either an individual or group experience. Although they both involve travel, these are two very different types of awards.

Individual Travel

Individual travel awards provide the award earner with the opportunity to enjoy the travel experience by themselves, with family or with a significant other. From an employee's point of view, this experience is very similar to a personal vacation without all, or at least a major portion of, the expense. When compared to group travel, additional employee benefits include flexibility in scheduling and the ability to have individual experiences without conforming to a group schedule. The downside is the lack of networking, the lack of group events, and the absence of the extra level of service provided by on-site travel directors.

Individual travel awards generally come in the form of travel certificates, travel vouchers, award points in an awards bank account, or stored value award cards, all of which can be redeemed for travel. These awards can cover only the major aspects of the trip (i.e., airfare and hotel) or they can be all-inclusive to include meals, beverages, transfers, and activities. Travel awards can be obtained from local travel agencies, on the Internet, or through full-service incentive companies.

Group Travel

Group travel awards are generally used as top performer awards for channel partners and sales forces. Recently, the use of group travel has been expanded to also include nonsales personnel, i.e., service personnel, individual contributors, and/or special project teams. The group travel experience provides the award earner the opportunity to enjoy the destination, to network with peers and executives, and to enjoy the on-site travel activities with other top performers. With group travel, unique and special events and activities can be included that are not easily replicated by individuals, making this award especially valuable and memorable. Learning opportunities can also be included with group travel by having workshops and/or bringing in experts to provide training.

The many benefits for the sponsoring organization and the employees are accompanied by the realities of any group event: fixed dates, group transfers, and preset agenda. Also, company-sponsored group travel is a business event, not a vacation, and as such attendees are in a business, albeit casual, environment.

SYMBOLIC AWARDS

The use of symbolic or logoed awards is widespread, especially as recognition to acknowledge and express appreciation for participation in corporate projects and events. Many organizations have created unique representations of individual or organizational achievement, and include premium items with logos as diverse as clothing, crystal, desk sets, and unique, one-of-a-kind trophies. One example is commissioning a graphic characterization or comic strip reflecting on the uniqueness of the individual or group, and the challenges they overcame on their path to achievement.

The advantage of symbolic awards comes from the ability to personalize the award both in terms of the sponsoring company and the individual recipient. Many organizations have created a catalog, either in print or online, which facilitates the administration of these awards. A variety of organizations such as ad specialty, recognition award, and full service performance improvement agencies supply these types of catalogs and award fulfillment.

EARNED TIME OFF

An always popular reward is paid time off. This reward has grown in preference over the past decade as the pace of business has accelerated and the hours spent at work by salaried employees have increased. Adding to this desire for time off is the growing value placed on leisure time by employees.

There are several important considerations when time off is used as a reward:

- Labor law—always check with your human resources contact or legal advisor to ensure that time off conforms to legal requirements and corporate policy. Be especially aware of the law regarding "comp time" for nonexempt employees.

- Administration—how is the time off recorded and tracked? How is pay calculated for the time off?

- Costs—will the cost of this reward be determined and reported? If so, how?

- Impact on award earner—what is the impact on the recipient's work load upon return to work? Will the time off cause an increased work load upon their return?

- Impact on the company—the cost–benefit must be carefully studied when taking the most productive people off work.

- Time off for a team—can the organization afford to have the team off at one time or is the team's time off taken by the team members at different times?

Time off is popular with employees and in certain cases a very powerful and appropriate reward. However, if an organization is experiencing a labor shortage or already has significant holiday, vacation, and/or paid time off policies, additional time off can have a negative effect on the business. As with any reward choice, the business implications and the recipients' preferences need to be understood and balanced.

PERSONAL AWARD PROFILES

One constant question regarding nonmonetary awards is: "what is the most motivating award?" This search for the "silver bullet" of awards has gained even more momentum in recent years as the award offerings have expanded. However, to answer this question the focus turns from "what award to use" to "what do the recipients prefer and value?"

To determine what individuals prefer for recognition awards, Maritz Inc. conducted a study[1] of 1,003 adults working full-time. These individuals were asked to repeatedly rank types of awards. The end analysis created hierarchies of award types that fell into six different categories of individuals. Each of these six categories of employees had similar award preference traits. The six categories were labeled based on the award preferences—Awards Seekers, Nesters, Bottom Liners, Freedom Yearners, Praise Cravers, and Upward Movers.

Awards Seekers (22 Percent[2])

Awards Seekers are those who want incentives that have both monetary and trophy value associated with them. These individuals are highly motivated by things such as awards cards and travel awards. *Awards Seekers* also place higher value than most others on status awards. They are far less motivated by things that might take time away from their normal routines such as the opportunity to mentor other employees, the opportunity to work with people outside their own area, or the opportunity to take on particularly challenging new projects.

Awards Seekers were disproportionately female (58 percent). This group was also younger than other segments, with higher proportions of those in the lower age categories (e.g., less than 25 years; 25–34 years) and lower proportions of those in the older (45+) age categories.

Nesters (20 Percent)

This group is defined by what they find demotivating as much as anything else. *Nesters* are turned off by incentives that take them away from home. Travel awards and the opportunity to attend conferences are least appealing to this group. Nesters are far more likely to enjoy days off, flexible scheduling, and a reward of a meal with their family than those in the other segments.

A slightly higher percentage of males fell into this category (54 percent). *Nesters* also tended to be older (45+). They want to go home after a hard day of work and enjoy their families, rather than going on trips that take them away from their loved ones. Achieving a good balance between work and personal life is especially important to *Nesters*.

Bottom Liners (19 Percent)

In many ways, *Bottom Liners* resemble *Awards Seekers* in that *Bottom Liners* have less concern about trophy or award value and are really only concerned about the monetary value of rewards. This group places the highest importance on receiving a bonus. They also value awards, such as 'point programs,' that they can accumulate, as well as the opportunity for paid days off. They place little emphasis on receiving praise. In short, these employees are pretty much 'in it for the money.'

This group had the highest proportion of females (59 percent) than any of the other segments. They were not defined as much by age or income as they were by their attitudes toward their jobs and companies. This group had high job dissatisfaction and low long-term commitment to their companies. In short, these employees 'work to live' rather than 'live to work.' They show up to work every day to earn a paycheck.

Freedom Yearners (17 Percent)

Freedom Yearners are less materially motivated, with limited interest in things like award cards and cumulative award programs. *Freedom Yearners* are best rewarded by giving them flexibility. This includes offering flexible hours, the freedom to choose how to best achieve their goals, the ability to choose interesting and challenging projects, as well as the opportunity to attend conferences.

Freedom Yearners had a higher proportion of men (55 percent), were older (55 percent were over 45 years of age), and had the highest proportion of people making over $100,000 (22 percent). *Freedom Yearners* are often people that have already achieved a certain level of financial success and security and are now more focused on doing work that is personally meaningful without an excessive amount of management interference.

Praise Cravers (16 Percent)

These individuals value any type of praise more than other award segments. This praise may be given verbally, written, formal, or informally given by peers. These people have a higher desire to have their work acknowledged, with or without an accompanying award of monetary value. These people also have the least interest in taking days off or flexible scheduling, suggesting that they achieve a great deal of personal satisfaction from a job well done at work that is recognized accordingly.

Although the *Praise Cravers* segment has a slightly higher percentage of males (54 percent), there is not a great deal otherwise to distinguish this segment demographically. It is likely more of a reflection of some personalities that desire a higher degree of affirmation. Among these persons, simple stated recognition of good work will have a greater impact than most other rewards.

Upward Movers (8 Percent)

The smallest segment is perhaps the most interesting. *Upward Movers* are undoubtedly the most satisfied and committed among all of the employee segments. They are the least interested in cash bonuses, days off, and flexible scheduling. These people love their jobs and want to move up within their companies. Among all of the segments, this group places the most value on meals with their company management, as well as with their departments. They place the highest importance on business-related status awards, the opportunity to mentor other employees, and the opportunity to work with people outside their own areas. Since their greatest gratification comes from greater opportunities to serve their own companies, it is no surprise that they rate their companies the highest of any of the segments on providing consistent, meaningful recognition.

Over two-thirds (68 percent) of this group was male. They were also younger, with 42 percent being 34 years of age or less. In many cases, these individuals have already achieved higher levels of responsibility within their companies, with two-thirds (66 percent) indicating that they managed direct reports and 30 percent describing themselves as an 'executive' at their companies. Interestingly, 20 percent had never worked anywhere else prior to joining their present companies. In short, these persons found a company that was a good fit and have enthusiastically committed themselves to making the company successful.

The study results offer additional insights into the types of awards, particularly nonmonetary awards, an individual values. However, the challenge still remains: which award should be offered? The emerging answers are choice and inquiry. The first approach involves providing a broad choice of awards that allows the individual to choose. This approach acknowledges the diversity of award preferences and engages the recipient in the process. The second approach is to observe and inquire as to the individual's unique recognition preferences.

The one finding of this study is that these six profiles are not static—they do not definitively describe a specific population. They are general descriptors of preferences, which can be exhibited by individuals in every demographic. As an individual's situation changes, so do his or her preferences. The birth of a child, divorce, career change, or other change in circumstances can alter the preferences, placing more or less value on monetary awards. The primary lesson is to be aware of the variation among individuals and to not assume that your recognition preference is shared by others.

PLAN DESIGN

In *Incentives, Motivation and Workplace Performance: Research and Best Practices*, the International Society for Performance and Improvement and the Incentive Research Foundation detail the Performance Improvement by Incentives or PIBI model. Based on extensive research, this model provides a guide to the design and implementation of all nonmonetary awards programs. A brief description of PIBI's eight steps [or "events"] is outlined below:

- *Event 1: identify unrealized work goals* ("It's necessary")—to identify the unrealized work goals that can be improved through an incentive program, organizations should first assess the gaps between the organization's strategic or cultural goals and employees' current performance or behavior. Goals that are nonspecific, unclear, or perceived as unchallenging often go unrealized by the workforce. Additionally, employees may avoid goals if they view them as undesirable or as less important than other tasks. The identified work goals must be assigned by a trusted authority who adequately establishes specific expectations and delegates ownership while expressing confidence in the team's ability and providing feedback on their progress.

- *Event 2: identify Incentive System Design* ("It's appropriate"): the next step is for organizations to identify the recipients, format, type, and time span of the improvement system. Although the details will be highly dependent on the organization involved, the Incentive Research Foundation found that successful performance improvement plans tend to:

  - include tangible awards and intangible recognition
  - last for longer than a year
  - involve employees in the design

- *Event 3: establish task value* ("It's worth it")—individual employees will perform their own cost–benefit analysis to determine whether the communicated awards are worth the effort of changing or redirecting their behavior. If they believe the new task or behavior is worth the effort of the award, they will focus on the newly identified tasks.

- *Event 4: establish efficacy* ("I/We can do it")—once employees have established that the new task or behavior is worth the effort they will evaluate their personal capabilities. The more employees have faith in their personal capabilities and the capabilities of their team, the more likely they are to commit to the new goal, task or behavior.

- *Event 5: establish agency* ("It will work")—employee confidence in management's ability to fairly implement and manage the new system is paramount. After establishing that they are capable of the new task, employees will evaluate the organizational support of the program; the greater their level of confidence that the organization will provide the resources, support structures, and incentives necessary to achieve program success, the greater their willingness to ensure the plan succeeds.

- *Event 6: consider mood* ("It feels good enough")—the current emotional state of employees, both collectively and as individuals, will impact the organizational level of commitment to the new program.

- *Event 7: active choice/persistence/effort* ("We've started, are persisting, and getting smarter")—once installed, organizations should gage the success of the new system by evaluating if employees actively started to do something differently than before (active choice), if they are doing more of what is desired (persistence), and if they are bringing more innovation to their work on the incentivized goal (mental effort).

■ *Event 8: performance improvement* ("I/We did it and it was worth the cost")—as a final event, organizations should evaluate if the choice, persistence, and effort exhibited by employees have closed the necessary gaps in performance. If so, the organization should evaluate if the benefits of the program outweighed the cost; if not, the organization should evaluate both the goal and the program structure behind it.

"TOP PERFORMER" VS "MOVE THE MIDDLE" REWARD STRATEGIES

Many sales force incentive plans emphasize top performers, employing the classic focus on the "80–20" rule. While this reward is appropriate for recognizing and retaining the top sales people, if the program rules are not constructed properly the vast majority of the sales force may perceive these awards as out of reach. This may actually demotivate some as they are constantly reminded through the program's communications of an opportunity for which they have no chance of qualifying.

A solution to this potential negative reaction by the "middle" performers in the sales force is to add earners in each of a series of volume groups, a supplemental second tier incentive plan that provides every sales person with the opportunity to be rewarded for increased performance. The plan design is often called "Move the Middle."

An example of this plan design is for each sales person to have a nonmonetary incentive for reaching and exceeding goal or quota. This plan may offer each sales person award points redeemable for merchandise for achieving quota. In addition, they might earn increasing levels of award points for significantly exceeding quota. The specific plan design and rules must take into account the organization's unique financials and the sales force's characteristics and environment.

Where this dual approach of top travel awards and quota-based nonmonetary incentives has been implemented, the sales increase over top-award-only plans has ranged from 20 to 40 percent. Even with these results, plan designers often get push-back from sales management. The feeling is that "I already pay them a commission and it is their job to hit quota." The unfortunate truth is that the current "commission only" plan frequently does not achieve the desired or potential performance.

The realized results of this "move the middle" approach are testimony to the value and power of nonmonetary rewards as one component of the overall reward strategy. In sales incentive programs where commissioned sales people can earn ever-higher compensation for increased sales, time and again the addition of nonmonetary rewards results in increased effort and results.

TAXES AND NONMONETARY AWARDS

As a general rule, most nonmonetary awards are taxable. It is therefore important to seek legal and tax advice before implementing any size or type of nonmonetary awards program. To ensure employees do not feel demotivated or cheated by the tax bill associated with their nonmonetary awards, most organizations choose to "gross up" the awards by adding the amount of applicable income taxes to the amount that is reported on the employee's W2. Many organizations include federal, state, local, and FICA taxes in the calculation. As long as the nonmonetary awards do not push an employee into a higher tax bracket, grossing up awards ensures there is little or no tax cost to the employee. Listed below is an example formula for gross-up calculations:

$$X = Y + wX, + sX + lX + fX$$

where X = gross award value in \$, Y = new award value in \$, w = federal tax rate, s = state tax rate (percent), l = local tax rate (percent), f = FICA tax rate (individual percent).

If the tax rate estimates are 28 percent for federal, 3 percent for state, 1 percent for local and 7.65 percent for FICA, then the calculation for a \$100 award item is as follows:

$$X = \$100 + 0.28X + 0.03X + 0.01X + 0.0765X$$
$$X = \$100 + 0.3965X$$
$$0.6035X = \$100$$
$$X = \$165.70$$

In this example, a nonmonetary award worth \$100 has a gross award value of \$165.70. To ensure an employee receives the full buying power of a \$100 award, the organization must fund \$165.70.

There are two exceptions specifically addressed in the (current) tax code related to award taxation on certain length of service awards and safety achievement awards. Both of these award types may have tax advantages, based on a number of parameters and restrictions. Some of these considerations are listed below; however, consult your tax advisor for the specific application of these to your organization:

- The maximum amount an employer can deduct for a single employee in a single tax year for both service and safety awards is \$400. This per employee amount may increase to \$1,600 if the award is given under a qualified plan.

- Among other things, a plan will be qualified if it is an established written plan and if the average combined value of service and safety awards per employee in the given tax year does not exceed $400.

- The awards must be "tangible personal property." Award certificates, cards or award credits are not eligible unless they are redeemable only for tangible personal property. Travel, special events tickets, meals, and lodging awards are not considered tangible personal property and are therefore always taxable.

- Length-of-service awards may be given tax-free to an employee only upon her fifth anniversary and then only once every five years thereafter.

- Safety achievement awards may be given tax-free to no more than 10 percent of eligible employees in any one year.

- Productivity awards are never eligible for tax benefits.

- Many other restrictions apply.[3]

In addition to taxation, heavily regulated and public companies should review all significant nonmonetary expenditures to ensure their compliance with the Sarbanes–Oxley Act of 2002.

GLOBALIZATION

The perspective provided by this chapter so far is primarily North American. However, nonmonetary awards, like business in general, have become global. The trend from a U.S.-centric point of view is being driven by the globalization of American companies and their desire to extend reward and recognition plans throughout their multinational organization. This push for consistent plans and rewards has led to the need for global nonmonetary award redemption and fulfillment. In response, some incentive agencies have developed the technology platforms, infrastructure and global partners to provide the desired awards.

A full-service incentive agency with significant global experience and/or an in-country fulfillment partner should be considered for international programs. This can help avoid significant difficulties such as this lesson learned from an early attempt at international fulfillment: an American business contracted with an American award supplier for recognition awards in Mexico. Unfortunately, neither addressed the custom and duty requirements for shipping merchandise from the U.S. to Mexico. The awards entering Mexico were held at the border pending the payment of significant duties for which neither party accepted responsibility.

Using a global supplier with in-country fulfillment not only eliminates duties but also facilitates tracking, delivery, and currency conversion, as well as providing country and culturally appropriate awards.

The advantages realized by those businesses using a global platform and award fulfillment include greater accountability and a consistency of their offering in an ever more transparent world. Global companies which are thinking globally and acting locally can now extend this philosophy to their nonmonetary rewards.

WHY NONMONETARY AWARDS WORK

When used appropriately within the Total Rewards framework, nonmonetary awards are more effective than cash in accomplishing business goals for several reasons. In a research paper titled "The Benefits of Tangible Non-Monetary Incentives," Scott Jeffrey, Ph.D., a professor at the University of Waterloo in Ontario, identified four psychological processes that give nonmonetary awards an advantage over cash in incentive or recognition programs.

- *Evaluability*—when participants cannot directly assign a cash value to an award, research shows that, if the award is properly presented and marketed, a person will focus more on the positive aspects of the award rather than the negative aspects. Therefore a person assigns the award a higher perceived value than its cash equivalent.

- *Separability*—because noncash awards are not included in an individual's paycheck, people are more likely to mentally separate the award from normal compensation. Nonmonetary awards ensure that the award is viewed separately and does not become part of expected compensation, making it easier to start, stop, and revise these award programs where and when necessary.

- *Justifiability*—because nonmonetary awards are separated from cash compensation, employees experience less guilt when choosing a "splurge" award. Nonmonetary awards therefore offer a more pleasurable experience than cash because there is no guilt associated with diverting income into something special that is not a necessity.

- *Social reinforcement*—in most cultures, it is not acceptable to publicly discuss the amount of cash compensation a person receives. Noncash awards therefore offer greater promotability and family involvement because employees can more easily publicly acknowledge the award. Discussing a firm-sponsored award in public with friends and family also creates greater alignment between the employee and the organization.

In addition to these reasons, research also shows that noncash awards are more memorable than cash awards, with employees remembering why they earned a noncash award months, even years, after the event. In contrast, employees often forget the size and expenditure of a cash award within weeks. This memorability factor, coupled with the ability to speak more openly about noncash awards, creates an advantage for the organization that is trying to create greater buzz and emotional commitment among employees.

There is also a note of caution for those deciding to use nonmonetary awards. Employees can be demotivated if they do not value the awards they received, as outlined in the section on award profiles. As with any award, cash or nonmonetary, an award perceived as insufficient for the effort or accomplishment will be ineffective at best. Always consider the recipient and the award value when selecting a nonmonetary award, or offer a broad choice of awards of an appropriate value.

SUMMARY

The past decade has seen an accelerated evolution in the business world and society and nonmonetary awards continue to effectively respond to these changes. The growth of the Internet has allowed incentive plans and their awards to be real-time and more easily administered. The selection of award types continues to expand, reflecting the increasingly diverse individual preferences in the consumer marketplace. Globalization of business is moving organizations to provide rewards globally and seek a level of consistency in the offering location to location.

The efficacy and value of nonmonetary awards, which has been questioned in the past, is now being validated by research and results from practical application. More companies are realizing their human capital's potential by building their own business case for the use of nonmonetary awards. By including a spectrum of rewards that meet both business and individual needs, organizations are verifying that nonmonetary awards are a necessary and effective component of today's Total Rewards Strategy.

END NOTES

1. Maritz Inc., "Award Preference Study," 2006.

2. Percentage of study population fitting this profile.

3. IRS Circular 230 Disclosure: to ensure compliance with requirements imposed by the IRS, we inform you that this written advice was not intended or written to be used, and cannot be used, for the purpose of avoiding penalties under the Internal Revenue Code.

14

SALARY ADMINISTRATION AT A PRESTIGIOUS CULTURAL INSTITUTION: PENNSYLVANIA ACADEMY OF THE FINE ARTS

Leslie Moody, Senior Vice President of Human Resources and Administration

Pennsylvania Academy of the Fine Arts

PENNSYLVANIA ACADEMY OF THE FINE ARTS has been training America's artists for more than 200 years. Steeped in history, the Academy has a growing list of famous alumni and a faculty of working professional artists who sustain the tradition of excellence in the studio arts of drawing, painting, printmaking, and sculpture.

In addition to its prestigious educational programs, the Academy has world-class museums and galleries. Recently it opened a new building that tripled the organization's exhibition space as well as substantially enlarging its teaching and learning facilities.

The Academy's workforce is drawn from people with strong credentials in teaching studio art, a wealth of experience in art museum and gallery management, professional knowledge of functional and operating disciplines, and proficiency in the management of large scale arts organizations. Its workforce is unique and diverse but united in its loyalty, passion, and commitment to the organization's goal of continuing excellence in the fine arts. It is a group of people who thrive in an environment of collegiality, are willing to take on challenges, and are cognizant of the financial limitations of a not-for-profit institution.

The Academy's salary administration program had not been recently updated. The expansion of its facilities, combined with ongoing changes in organization structure and staffing, made it imperative the institution to create a new program that would attract and retain talented employees. The program needed to do so in an equitable and competitive way, take into consideration the realities of affordability constraints, and be easy to maintain.

The Academy engaged in an organization-wide study that:

- established an institutional pay strategy

- documented all positions

- measured the relative worth of each job within the organization

- determined the relative value of each job in its own pay market
- reconciled internal worth and external value

- established a salary administration approach that linked pay strategy with salary practice and individual performance

- communicated all information to all employees and

- created a set of procedures to maintain and update the salary program

The study of the Academy's current compensation practices and the development of a new pay strategy and salary administration program were successful in achieving the criteria listed above. Several important lessons were learned from the exercise that will benefit others in not-for-profit organizations that have similar concerns and issues.

1. *A pay strategy is the starting point.* Every salary administration program must be based on a pay strategy. The Academy's pay strategy, or the way in which it invests in its employees, is based on how much the Academy can afford, the potential for turnover in its workforce, its ability to attract new employees, relevance to internal worth, and employee performance. The Academy studied its sources of recruitment, potential competition for its employees' skills, current budgets and existing pay practices. The Academy found that it participated in two pay markets with different characteristics: art education/museums and executive/functional. It also determined that hiring, turnover rates, and existing practices necessitated that it select the 50th percentile as its compensation strategic goal for each distinct pay market.

2. *Solid documentation on jobs is mandatory.* To assess a job's internal worth and external value and establish the basis for performance, the job must be documented in a way that enables job evaluators to credibly set its worth, match content to appropriate survey jobs, and link it to the value it provides to the organization. In addition, the Academy found that the process of job documentation had an important motivational and cultural impact because it required supervisors and their employees to share and critically review the content of jobs and areas of accountability, as well as mutually establishing the basis for performance measurement. It also enhanced employee self-esteem by making their contribution an important part of the process.

3. *One job evaluation system does not fit all.* Early in the Academy's review of compensation practices, it was clear that the frames of reference for establishing the worth of job content were different in the school of fine arts and other parts of the organization. A study indicated that nonacademic jobs could be measured on the basis of traditional factor comparison and job ranking approaches. The traditional job factor approach was used by the consultants to independently assess jobs while the senior staffs used the ranking approach. The two approaches were then reconciled to yield a credible hierarchy of job worth. A separate and unique job evaluation system was developed for the academic institution based on the "roles" of staff members. A "role" was assigned to individual staff members based on their personal profile. The profiles had five factors (quality or credibility of work, external recognition, teaching qualities, discipline of expertise, and stage of career). Factors had dimensions and subdimensions. The dean of the school placed all faculty members in a nine-point role ranging from Lecturer 1 to Distinguished Professor 9. The accurate development of a job evaluation structure enabled the Academy to establish viable programs for career development and promotion. It was also perceived as credible because its rigor assured a high level of fairness. Because all aspects of the program were easily understood and accepted by its employees, it was simple for the Academy to maintain the job evaluation program.

4. *A survey can make or destroy a compensation program.* The Academy's pay strategy required it to base its salary structures on surveys that were composed of organizations with whom it competes for talent. The Academy used surveys from the art and museum worlds and local and national studies for executive and functional positions (finance, human resources, IT). The result was two separate pay structures. The Academy also paid close attention to the survey benchmark jobs. They were matched to its own jobs based on comparable scope.

5. *Reconciling the market value and internal worth of jobs is not a problem.* When the Academy matched salary survey data with internal rankings it found little difference, within each of the separate pay structures, between market and internal value. Small adjustments were made based on individual situations.

6. *Performance systems must include both results and the way results are achieved (competencies).* Staff interviews focusing on organization culture and mission made it clear that performance had to be defined both in terms of results achieved and the success factors that enabled the results to be achieved. The salary administrations system was based, therefore, half on results and half on institutional success factors, or competencies. To assure that fairness was integral to the process a second factor, position in range, was added to performance as a determinant of salary. Higher performance levels and lower positions in range yielded the highest salary increases; higher salaries and lower performance resulted in the lowest salary increases.

7. *Training and communications are necessary for the compensation program to succeed.* The human resources department trained managers so that they could clearly understand the mechanics of, and communicate, the new salary administration program. Supervisors and employees both greatly benefited from a thorough understanding of discipline of salary administration because it created the opportunity for them to engage in constructive discussions on pay, establish job accountability, and define performance and improve their capability for working together. The training and communications programs also elevated the professional credibility of the human resources function, thereby enabling it to serve as counselor rather than a monitor of pay.

Pennsylvania Academy of the Fine Arts has been a preeminent cultural institution for over 200 years. It will continue its mission of excellence in the fine arts and will continually adapt its institutional strategy and human resources processes to insure that its mission will be realized. The developed compensation system will help the Academy stabilize, and adapt to change, because of its quality, fairness, efficiency, and credibility with employees.

COMPENSATION PRACTICES IN A MIDDLE MARKET COMPANY

David E. Griffith, President and CEO

Modern Group, Ltd

We believe that fundamental to our company's performance is the linkage of mission, goals, strategy, talent, and reward; facilitated and supported through technology to drive information and communications and a core belief in open door/open book management.

MODERN GROUP LTD IS A BRISTOL, Pennsylvania-based holding company with interests in the material handling, construction, rental, power generation, and municipal industries. Founded in 1946 with a single location in Philadelphia, Modern is today one of the nation's largest distributors of industrial equipment and services with 22 locations and about 640 employees. Representing such lines as Hyster forklifts, JLG aerial work platforms, New Holland construction equipment, and Generac power systems, the company's revenue streams include sale of new and used equipment, service, parts, training, and rental of industrial equipment.

In 2000, Modern was ranked as one of the best places to work by the Pennsylvania Chamber of Commerce and in 2003 became a 100 percent employee-owned company through its ESOP. For 60 years the company has averaged a 10 percent plus annual growth in share price while at the same time sharing over 50 percent of the retained earnings with the employees through ESOP contribution, 401K match, and outright year end cash bonus. At the same time, Modern maintains an exceptionally strong balance sheet, cash flows, and reputation with customers and suppliers. Essential to the company's success is its focus on people, process, and product. This chapter will review Modern's core values, the role of technology, the planning processes that underpin the operations of the company, and how compensation reinforces Modern's drive to results.

IT STARTS WITH A MISSION STATEMENT

Modern's mission statement is printed on a laminated card. The card is carried by every employee. The CEO promotes the mission at every new employee orientation. The mission statement reads:

> Our objective is to satisfy our customers by exceeding their expectations.

We focus on equipment sales, service and rentals, specializing in material handling, construction, and maintenance products. We accomplish our objectives while maintaining high employee morale, revenue growth, and return on investment.
The card also describes Modern's basic beliefs:

1. Outstanding customer service in everything we do
2. A dedication to high ethical and legal standards in all aspects of conducting business
3. A dedication to teamwork and partnership with our customers, suppliers and employees
4. A culture of continuous improvement and innovation
5. Respect for the individual, family, and community
6. Growth through performance and acquisition of quality organizations that fit Modern's vision

These simple statements are the basis for how Modern conducts its business. They are also reflected in the processes Modern uses to assess the performance of its employees.

STRATEGIC PLANNING PROCESS DRIVES ACTION

The strategic plan spans three years and has very specific annual outputs and action items. These outputs are incorporated as targets in the long-term incentive plan. The strategic plan starts with the establishment of goals with the board, followed by a SWOT (strengths, weakness, opportunity, and threats) analysis of

Modern's markets, products, company, and economy. These then feed a preliminary budget to which the established goals are compared, and a gap to goal analysis develops. Annual specific action plans are created to drive results and to close the identified gaps. The annual goals are the basis for the annual incentive plans.

Modern's Goals Fall into Three Categories, Financial, Focus, and Cultural

Financial.

1. Achieve, and then exceed, *NEBT goal of 5.0 percent* of sales by 2009, less internals, exclusive of ESOP compensation expense (loan).
2. Maintain a debt to equity ratio, before ESOP debt, of *not greater than 2.5:1.*
3. Grow our business annually *5 percent greater than inflation.* Inflation measure comes from consumer price index U.S. Department of Labor, Mid-Atlantic office, United States percentage.
4. Maintain the 10-year compound growth rate of Modern *stock at historical level of 10 percent.*
5. Achieve specific annual *cash flow budget as defined by management and board* tuned to annual objectives.
6. Fund the ESOP at the established loan repayment formula level plus an additional 5 percent of total compensation (normal contribution) over the strategic period of time for a total of *approximately 8 percent of total compensation.*

Market Focus.

1. Establish Modern as the *premier regional service, parts, and rental company.*
2. Establish and maintain a product mix to obtain financial goals with an objective such that no one vendor accounts for *>20 percent of total sales of the group.*

Culture.

1. Maintain a work environment and culture through Modern's values that makes *Modern an outstanding place to work.* This includes salary at a competitive range, hourly wages at competitive regional rates, competitive benefits, competitive variable compensation, education programs, as well as an ESOP and 401K retirement programs.
2. Establish and *maintain a superior management team.* Develop company-wide succession and education plans to sustain the company.
3. Maintain senior company *management in industry and community leadership positions.*

All company goals are reviewed with every employee.

TALENT MANAGEMENT

Modern's mission statement, values, and planning processes can only be realized by a qualified and motivated workforce. The "open door policy" is central to developing a culture that recognizes that success is linked to honesty and trust between the company and its employees. The open door policy means that employees can have direct access to higher levels of management if their needs are not met at lower levels.

Part of the open book policy is a set of compensation and measurement tools that support the mission statement and Modern's goals. The open book means Modern shares all of its numbers. Once a month all employees receive an e-mail, identical to the information that the board receives, that reviews the company's results. The results are also posted on the company's share-point site which is available 24/7 to all employees. Once a year I, as the CEO, and our CFO meet with every employee in a roundtable format with the agenda driven by the employee. Annually a meeting takes place at which results are reviewed, goals presented, and recognition and rewards handed out. Each location holds a monthly meeting where results are reviewed with senior management and employee questions answered.

COMPENSATION AND EMPLOYEE EVALUATION

Modern has some specific benefits and compensation strategies that are tied to its internal assessment and hiring processes. Every employee, and candidate for employment, is evaluated against seven basic competencies. These core Modern competencies were established by modeling outstanding employees within Modern and the industry, benchmarking other well-run companies, and by working with a compensation consultant. The Modern core competences are shown in Table 15.1.

These seven core competencies define what Modern is looking for in an employee. It also has behavioral maps that are contained within each competency that have specific definitions that are grade-specific to define performance in each of these areas. For example, the definition of leadership is different for a rental coordinator than it is for a company president; both get evaluated in terms of the leadership competency but the behavioral metric is specific to a given level.

In addition to these seven attributes and underlying grade-specific behaviors, the employee is also evaluated against specific goals and objectives for their department and function. These goals are subsets of the company's overall goals and action plans and financial targets. In theory every employee's goals roll up to their company and in return the group. The combination of these two measurement areas allow Modern to establish the annual raise percentage, which is then applied against the midpoint of the grade or level. The midpoints represent the competitive rates within each of Modern's three pay markets. The pay markets are the companies where Modern recruits for talent and measured in salary surveys. Midpoints move annually based on salary survey information on these pay markets.

In addition to a structured evaluation and salary administration practice, Modern is deeply committed to variable pay. Variable compensation consists of

TABLE 15.1   Modern Core Competencies

Business, Technical, Professional Expertise: Possesses the appropriate depth and breadth of business, technical, and professional skills to successfully perform one's job.

Communication: Communicates well both verbally and in writing. Effectively conveys ideas and shares information and ideas with others. Listens carefully and understands diverse points of view. Understands relevant detail in presented information.

Customer Focus: Recognizes importance of placing high value and priority on customer needs (external and internal). Listens to customers (internal and external), builds customer confidence, increases customer satisfaction, assures commitments are met, sets appropriate customer expectations, and responds to customer needs.

Ethics: Demonstrates honesty and candidness in personal and business relationships. Exhibits integrity and develops trusting relationships with others.

Leadership: Motivates, empowers, inspires, collaborates and encourages others to reach Modern's and personal goals. Possesses high energy and sense of urgency, and makes tough calls when necessary.

Results Orientation: Continuously demonstrates behaviors, actions, and activities that support the delivery of measurable results consistent with or exceeding expectations.

Talent Management: Helps Modern maximize the contribution of its human resources to meet Modern's organizational requirements. Able to motivate self and others to develop core competencies, career plans, and learning objectives.

several elements. All salaried employees are on an annual bonus that ranges from 8 to 50 percent of their compensation. These bonuses are paid against specific financial goals that tie to the annual operating plans. In addition, selected senior managers participate in a long-term compensation program tied to driving shareholder interests. All employees also receive an annual cash bonus that can range form 1 to 5 percent of annual compensation based on the overall company's performance. The company provides a significant employee match with the company's 401K plan.

Finally as an employee owned company, every employee participates in the company's ESOP. Depending on company performance an employee can receive a cash contribution that averages 8 percent of total compensation. For the 60 years that Modern has conducted business, over 50 percent of the retained earnings have flowed to the employees through year-end cash, 401K, and ESOP.

EDUCATION PERMEATES TALENT MANAGEMENT

Talent management is more than activities linked to direct remuneration at Modern. Education is an important part of Modern's total talent management package. Modern targets a minimum of 40 hours of formal education every year for each employee. Every employee has an education plan based on their assessment against goal accomplishment and competencies. The plan becomes part of Modern's employee talent management base.

Modern University was created as a vehicle to implement its education program. All current and potential managers attend at least four classes over 2 days taking a curriculum consisting of basic HR training, evaluation, and talent management skills (including salary administration), leadership development, accounting, standard operating procedures, benchmarking skills, and company and product overviews. Modern has a strong tuition reimbursement policy that augments its internal educational programs.

TECHNOLOGY SHARPENS THE COMPETITIVE ADVANTAGE

For Modern's financial model to work efficiently, it needs to achieve 10 percent productivity per year. Modern also needs to have the flow of information be as efficient as possible. Modern has embraced the use of technology to help with its processes. Specifically, Modern uses the Web and its internal e-mail system to support the open door and open book process and practice. Company results, schedules, handbooks, and forms are posted 24/7 on share-point for employee availability. Every employee has Web and e-mail access and Modern regards PC literacy as a core competency. Senior management can communicate quickly and in a structured format with all stakeholders, and more importantly all stakeholders can communicate with senior management. The flow of information, best practices, plans, goals, recognition, accountability, and the ability to react quickly to customers and employees is enabled by the presence of a robust network and easy to use, stable tools. The ability of employees from any location to access product, tools, business applications, customer information, and training is a powerful tool. The fact that they can share information and knowledge is a key driver to productivity objectives. Modern's compensation programs, planning, hiring, evaluation, skills training, operating procedure, and training are all network available and enabled. Modern believes that the return on these investments is significant and clearly drives productivity objectives.

Modern operates in an industry where margins are razor thin. Its talent management processes have enabled it to create an employee culture that has enabled Modern to thrive in this environment. Modern's compensation program is an integral part of our talent management program.

My father, Charlie Griffith, gave me some simple advice: "Great people, given the right tools and information, focused, measured and given the opportunity to shape their own reward, will do extraordinary things." Modern's founder, Joe McEwen, and I adhere to this belief.

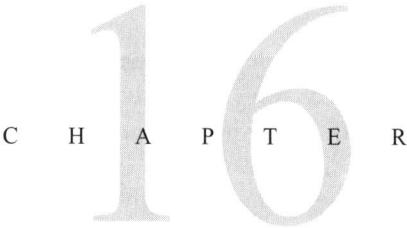

A VISION FOR INFORMATION TECHNOLOGY IN COMPENSATION

Steven T. McGuire, Manager, Human Resources

GlaxoSmithKline

I N RECENT YEARS, THE ROLE of the HR function has changed significantly, moving from a function expected to handle transactional and task-oriented work to one that provides strategic contributions that impacts company financials. These changes have forced companies to be more efficient and productive with the resources they allocate and utilize. In order to achieve necessary efficiencies and productivity, companies have relied heavily on information technology (IT). Compensation is one area in the HR function where IT is critical in shaping and administering compensation processes. IT is used in all aspects of compensation design and administration, including compensation program design, salary administration, variable compensation, performance management, and communication.

REAL LIFE CASE 1

Cheryl receives an email reminding her that self-appraisal of her performance is due by next week. Attached is the electronic form to complete. Planning to complete it at home, she e-mails the form to her home computer. At the same time, her boss, Craig, receives a notice that his appraisal of Cheryl and her compensation recommendation are due the week after next. Attached are the electronic forms for both.

When Cheryl finishes her self-appraisal at home, she logs on to the Internet and sends the data to her computer at work. The following day, she signs onto the company intranet to post her self-appraisal. The system e-mails it to Craig and stores a copy in her personnel file. Cheryl also checks the database to identify the current salary range for her position, noting that she is in the lower third of the range and has plenty of room for an increase. She also checks her last self-appraisal and Craig's appraisal at the time to see how similar they were. Five other appraisers assess Cheryl and she checks their appraisal as well. While she is online, she updates her benefits information, increasing her life insurance coverage and adding her new husband as a beneficiary. She also adds him to her health-care policy as a dependent and switches to the coverage option that includes maternity.

Meanwhile, Craig has completed a draft of his appraisal of Cheryl. He reviews the assessments of other appraisers and uses them as input for his own review. After logging onto the company Intranet, he checks Cheryl's compensation history and her previous appraisals. He also calls up the local and national salary survey data for her position, noting that the demand for her specialty has resulted in an 8 percent increase in market value last year, while the salary range for her position went up only by the XYZ Company's standard 3.5 percent. He also checks what the average pay is at XYZ for others with Cheryl's education and experience, noting that she is paid a little more than others with similar experience but noticeably less than others with the same experience and her advanced degree from Prestige University.

After they meet and discuss her performance, Craig finalizes the appraisal and enters it into the system. Based on Cheryl's performance and her salary level vs both the external market and the internal structure at XYZ, he recommends a 10 percent increase for her, noting his reasoning on the electronic form he completes. The system automatically aggregates Cheryl's appraisal with that of others within Craig's group and his entire business line. Based on the current performance distribution, Cheryl's increase would be outside the parameters of the compensation policy and budget.

The recommendation and the performance appraisal are automatically emailed to Nancy, Craig's boss. She reviews the data and authorizes the full amount based on her determination that Cheryl's potential for growth is high enough to elevate her merit increase beyond her current performance level. Adam, the Compensation Director, calls up the relevant data on his computer and makes the final approval of the increase. The system updates the payroll records to reflect the new salary level and e-mails Craig to that effect. Craig then meets with Cheryl and communicates her salary increase.

REAL LIFE CASE 2

A company decided to integrate its position classification, performance, competency and potential assessment, and compensation processes. First, appropriate competencies for the unique organization were selected. All employees were evaluated by their managers both in terms of their present competency levels, as demonstrated by their job performance, and in terms of their potential on these same dimensions. Customer software was developed using a commercial PC-based database program to collect and analyze this data. In a parallel process, jobs were classified into grades based on a job evaluation methodology. Spreadsheet analysis of survey data was employed to price the grades. Then the employee's present salary and position in the new ranges (compa-ratio) were compared to their performance and potential ratings. Based on the actual distribution of compa-ratios and performance levels, a salary increase matrix was developed that totaled to the organization's budget. The budget was monitored throughout the year based on the actual amounts paid based on the current and forecast future contribution.

The amount of data involved would have defied analysis without a computer. Yet it was possible to develop a package for ongoing program administration and maintenance that was easily handled by the PCs and inexpensive software available to this low-tech, limited-budget, nonprofit organization.

REAL LIFE CASE 3

Company XYZ is evaluating the current sales incentive plan for their 500 sales representatives. The company's product offerings have recently changed, resulting in a need to alter the direction and priorities of the sales force. A new sales incentive plan needs to be developed so sales representatives' objectives and activity align with company strategy, thereby helping drive sales of the new product. A sales incentive compensation system has been implemented to assist in the design, modeling, analysis, administration, and communication of the plan to the sales representatives. The system functions to design different plan options, review potential costs associated with each option, and show the range in incentive payments to the sales representatives.

Modeling is used to determine if the new sales incentive plan aligns to the company's compensation philosophy and allocated budget. Once the new sales incentive plan is finalized, a memo is automatically e-mailed to the sales representatives to communicate changes to their plan. Representatives are then able to go onto the company Intranet to develop a model for their sales incentive payment based on projected sales. Sales representatives will then receive pay statements detailing how they were paid based on the criteria set forth in the incentive plan. Payouts are sent to payroll to compensate the representatives on the allocated date communicated to them during the plan roll-out.

The sales incentive compensation system allows the company the flexibility to review and quickly modify incentive plans, and the confidence to make decisions knowing the company has the ability to react quickly and change the priorities of the sales force.

USES OF IT IN COMPENSATION

Analysis of the outlined cases helps define five important uses of information technology in compensation.

1. A compensation system's goal is to link employee rewards to performance. Performance is measured against set business goals and core competencies by the system. Technology manages compensation programs via effective and efficient data collection, comprehensive analysis and modeling, collaboration in decision making, communication, and program administration.

2. IT in compensation allows organizations to collect, store, and access large amounts of employee-specific information. Current and historical compensation information including employees' salary and bonus payouts, employee performance reviews, market information, and job-related information can be accessed at any time. Access can be controlled by the owner of the information through security settings. Restricted access to information ensures confidentiality and integrity of sensitive information. Employees with approved access to compensation information can use this information effectively and efficiently to analyze and model information for decision making purposes.

3. Data collection can be a time-consuming administrative activity. Efficient data collection allows users to spend less time collecting, storing, and accessing information and more time on strategic contributions.

4. IT enhances reliable and accurate data collection. Ensuring reliable and accurate input provides users with the confidence to make informed decisions.

5. Data stored in compensation information systems can be used for analysis, forecasting, and modeling. This allows for the creation of "what if" scenarios to analyze and model options for potential outcomes. Models can be constructed quickly to provide decision makers with accurate information, allowing them to make sound real-time business decisions. Analysis and models provide decision makers with the ability to review the potential impacts on financial budgets and other metrics. Ongoing analysis and measurement can be constructed to ensure business decisions are having the

intended impact and provide decision makers with necessary information to modify decisions. Analysis is also critical to evaluate how compensation programs are being utilized and if they are leading to consistent and fair decisions across the organization. Completing complicated and large-scale analysis and modeling would require significant resources and time without the use of systems.

Fosters Collaboration throughout the Organization

Compensation information systems help foster collaboration in the decision making process. Compensation information flows through all levels in the organization, across business functions, and through vendors to ensure compensation programs are administered correctly. These groups need to collaborate when working through processes, decision making, and when ensuring compensation elements are paid to employees at the right time for the appropriate performance. IT fosters collaboration within the organization through easy access to information, providing detailed process flows of the compensation programs, sharing analysis and modeling, and showing the potential impact of decisions. Compensation information systems can be designed to notify and detail clear action steps as users go through the process. Clear action steps result in an understanding of the process, definition of deliverables, and the assurance of required approvals to complete the process.

Compensation decisions require multiple levels and cross functional approvals. Identifying accountability is critical to achieve necessary approvals in a timely manner. Information systems can be designed to automate the approval process detailing who is responsible and when approvals are completed. Information systems maintain integrity and consistency by creating guidelines when additional information or higher level approvals are required. IT assists in quickly identifying breakdowns in the approval process, thus allowing processes to function efficiently to accomplish target outcomes in ample time.

Plays Integral Role in Communication

Compensation information systems play an integral role in manager and employee communication. For example, compensation information can be posted to the company Intranet site for managers and employees to easily access and view. Companies can provide employees with unlimited access to various types of compensation programs such as base pay, incentive pay, paid leave, and other company perks and benefits. Notifications via e-mail can be automated to communicate important information on plan objectives, required behaviors, potential rewards, and timing. Generated letters can be created to notify plan participants of compensation payouts and benefits. These examples provide clear details to plan participants on how their behaviors and performance can be rewarded.

The larger the number of plan participants, the more automation is required to communicate a clear and consistent message about the compensation programs to drive intended performance. Effective communication is the key to success for any compensation plan. If an employee does not know how he or she impacts a plan's success, the plan cannot be considered effective.

Ensures Compliance with Compensation Processes

Administration of compensation processes can require large amounts of resources to ensure consistency and accuracy of information, processes, and decisions. Compensation programs are often reviewed and modified annually. It can take months to change a company's processes in administering the changes to the compensation programs. Compensation information systems standardize the handling of transactional and administrative responsibilities, and allow for flexibility and the ability to change compensation programs quickly and efficiently.

IT can ensure processes are adhered to. Guidelines and check steps can be included in the system so users follow processes and notify appropriate people when decisions are outside of established guidelines.

IT is critical to compensation through data collection, analysis and modeling, collaboration, communication, and administration. Effective implementations and utilization of IT in compensation allows for access to information, provides efficient and effective process management, ensures reliable and accurate information, drives communication and decision making, and frees up HR resources for strategic contribution.

Variable Compensation

17

INCENTIVE COMPENSATION PROGRAM DESIGN

Linda E. Amuso, Senior Vice President, and David Knopping, Vice President

Radford Surveys & Consulting

S HORT-TERM INCENTIVE PAY IS variable compensation that rewards achievement of specified results, typically measured over a period of 12 months or less. As one component of a company's Total Rewards program (including base salary, cash incentives, equity, benefits, and learning and development), incentives can be the most effective form of compensation in building and maintaining a strong pay-for-performance culture. By placing pay at risk through the use of incentives, companies help ensure compensation dollars are optimally utilized to reward and motivate the behaviors that drive specific company operational success and build shareholder value. Because the best incentive plan designs are directly tied to achievement of business objectives, companies can expect that total compensation expense will be higher when overall performance is strong and lower in times of weaker company performance.

This material is intended to assist practitioners in developing effective incentive programs by examining design considerations and best practices for incentive plans, within the context of a renewed focus on the war for talent and increased shareholder activism aimed at improving the alignment between executive compensation and company performance. While there are numerous forms of incentive compensation, including spot awards, profit-sharing, sales incentives, and others, this material will focus on incentive plans typically targeted at management and/or key employee populations. See Table 17.1 for a description of incentive plan types and their characteristics. The Table outlines the characteristics of various incentive plan types, including the amount of pay at risk, who the plans are designed for, and the frequency of payout and performance measurement. Management and key employee incentives are an important component of total rewards systems at companies committed to building a strong pay-for-performance culture. Companies often use more than one type of incentive plan, based on their overall business and human resources strategy and compensation objectives.

Once limited to the executive suite, more companies implement incentive compensation throughout the organization to better align business results and priorities with companywide pay programs. This shift is in part a reflection of the

TABLE 17.1   Incentive Plan Features

Plan Type	Plan Description	Participants	Measurement Period	Range of Pay at Risk (% of Salary)
Profit sharing	Company-wide program rewarding for improved profits	All full-time employees	Quarterly, semi-annual, or annual	3–10%
Broad-based	Company-wide program rewarding individual contributors for their contribution to company results	All employees below management	Semi-annual and annual	5–15%
Project-based	Focus on rewarding specific projects milestones or results	Dedicated team members	Just-in-time	5–50%
Management/ Key employee	Targeted at management and key positions/ personnel to align specific performance and behaviors	Management and key individual contributors (exempt professionals)	Semi-annual, annual	7–100%
Sales	Targeted at sales staff responsible for selling the company's products and services	Sales professionals and management	Monthly, quarterly	20–100%

SOURCE: Radford Surveys + Consulting.

power of incentive compensation to direct specific behaviors (and their outcomes), and in part an effort to mitigate an employee mentality of entitlement to base salary increases, a form of compensation that does little to distinguish good from poor performance and little to motivate specific behaviors required to drive organizational success.

CURRENT ISSUES IN INCENTIVE COMPENSATION

Pay-for-performance practices have been under intense scrutiny since the beginning of the decade and that scrutiny shows no sign of abating, as shareholders demand that boards of directors improve the link between company results and executive compensation. Shareholder activist groups, like Institutional Shareholder Services and Glass–Lewis, and some large institutional funds, cite pay-for-performance as a critical measure of a company's overall performance, and of the performance of the compensation committee. Increasingly, shareholders are holding boards of directors accountable for ensuring that pay is aligned with company results and are issuing "no" votes for directors they deem out of synch with these ideals. Certain groups are arguing for "say on pay" programs that would allow shareholders a nonbinding vote in determining the compensation of executives. Whether this initiative becomes practice remains to be seen, but it is clear at this point that board members, specifically compensation committee members, are focused on incentive plan designs that ensure rewards are based on company performance.

DESIGN CONSIDERATIONS

Incentive plans (as is the case with all compensation plans) invariably reflect an organization's culture. However, the extent to which an incentive plan supports the *desired* culture is determined within the plan design. In other words, incentive plan design is undertaken within the context of a company's total rewards philosophy, and has a specific role in supporting that philosophy. Companies focusing on stable business growth and long-term performance may place less emphasis on short-term incentives, compared to companies seeking consistent near-term delivery of specific outcomes.

Successful plan design and implementation is predicated on a company's ability to identify its key business objectives, employees' capacity to affect the achievement of those objectives and management's commitment to measure results and determine awards based on the precepts and conditions of the plan.

Incentive compensation typically accounts for approximately 8 percent (ranging from 4 to 12 percent, at the 25th and 75th percentiles, respectively) of a company's compensation expense, according to Radford's Overall Practices Report (2006). Therefore, ensuring that incentive plans are effectively designed is crucial given their economic impact on the business. Design considerations begin with questions associated with the plan objectives, such as: What are the strategic and financial objectives within the Board-approved business plan? Which objectives are priorities for the organization? How do these business objectives translate into key results for the plan? What behaviors and outcomes does the company want to motivate or direct with incentive compensation?

Although there are various types of plans, the fundamental elements of plan design remain the same and include:

1. Funding and affordability
2. Metrics and measurement frequency
3. Eligibility and participation in the plan
4. Award opportunities tied to the total rewards philosophy
5. Administrative rules

Plan Funding and Performance Metrics

The financial considerations and implications of incentive plan design are dealt with most directly in the determination of which plan funding approach is selected, and which measures will be used to calculate how (or whether) incentive payments are awarded.

Plan Funding.   There are typically two approaches to plan funding: the self-funding incentive pool approach, and the budget approach. Self-funding incentive pools emphasize "the big picture," where company or group performance is used to determine the amount of funds available for the incentive pool. Self-funded plans usually require a specific profit contribution level be met prior to an allocation of additional dollars into the incentive pool. The advantage of self-funding pools is that they emphasize corporate and/or group performance based on financial results, which tend to protect the interests of the shareholders prior to rewarding plan participants. This approach also reinforces the greater good of the team, given that incentive payments are tied to overall company and/or business group or unit performance. The disadvantage of self-funding is that there is often less "line-of-sight" for employees because plan funding is based on broad financial metrics that not all plan participants can directly impact. This can result in a given business unit, for example, receiving no award despite exceeding its objectives, because the company did not meet overall targets.

The budget approach, in which companies factor the overall cost of the incentive plan in their annual operating budget, provides the opportunity for each segment of measurement (e.g., company, business unit) to operate independently. For example, a corporate award can be earned even if group achievement is below plan. Most budgeted plans are designed to ensure the achievement of the annual board-approved business plan. The advantages of this approach are that it emphasizes goal achievement on multiple levels and provides more direct "line-of-sight" to the goals. This is balanced with the fact that this approach can require a stronger performance management culture at all levels of the company. In some instances, depending on the plan design, significant incentives can be paid even when company goals are not entirely achieved, due to the performance of one group over another. This potentially adverse consequence can be managed by the design of the leverage curve, which is described later in the article.

Irrespective of how the plan is funded, companies must decide what financial hurdles must be met to trigger release of the funds for the various levels of incentive payments. These hurdles and accelerators are frequently referred to as plan leverage, defining the downside protection, and upside opportunity in the plan. Virtually all companies set threshold, target, and maximum levels of company and/or group performance when determining plan funding. (Threshold describes the minimum level of performance under which there is no payout associated with the plan.)

Moreover, companies must determine if the threshold level of performance will be defined the same for all levels of participants, or if senior executives will be held to a higher level of performance. For example, with a revenue growth goal of 15 percent, executives may not receive an incentive if less than 70 percent of that goal is met, while the plan for lower-level employees could fund once 60 percent of that goal is achieved. Plan thresholds support sound governance by providing protection to shareholders when company performance is below objectives.

Likewise, placing maximums or caps on the amount that a plan will pay out, irrespective of the degree to which goals are exceeded, provides predictability in the funding and budgeting process. Most companies cap the amount of award payouts at 150–200 percent of target plan funding.

Performance Metrics.   The measures a company selects to gage performance under the plan are a critical factor in determining the success of the program. This is perhaps the most difficult aspect of plan design, as companies must select metrics that are easily understandable, reportable and for which there is reliable data. Key considerations of metric selection include an understanding of:

- The company's business objectives and priorities, and how each specific measure helps to achieve those objectives within the desired time frame

- The appropriate number of measures required to ensure the plan emphasizes the desired behaviors and results; too many measures can fragment an employee's attention and can be a challenge to administer; too few metrics will likely ignore key business drivers

- The relative importance of each metric, and thus the weighting of the measures and how this might change by different levels of authority and influence to drive behaviors

- How short-term measures impact longer-range corporate goals

- How the measures selected are impacted by the employees to whom they apply

Line-of-sight is an important factor when considering metrics. Holding employees accountable for results they cannot influence will likely produce a situation where goals are not met and employees are dissatisfied with the plan.

Ultimately, the measures chosen will help to drive certain behaviors, and companies need to be alert for "unintended consequences" of plan design (e.g., overemphasis on expense management may motivate layoffs that could otherwise be avoided; a drive to hit short-term milestones could erode long-term result, etc.)

The process for setting performance metrics, as well as the performance levels chosen for the senior executive plan, has, as alluded to earlier in the chapter, become an area of intense focus by shareholders and shareholder activist groups. In the wake of changes in the Securities Exchange Commission's proxy filing requirements, companies are required to disclose the details of their named executive officer compensation plans, including how metrics are established and weighted, in addition to how executives performed against the specific objectives upon which specific awards were based.

Companies have also had to adjust to increased involvement by the compensation committee in the selection of measures used to determine the level of achievement required for plan funding, as well as the leverage designed within the plan to motivate overachievement and protect against underachievement. As compensation committees assume a greater role in the policy decisions and design of these plans, they are taking a much more active role in selecting the metrics and ensuring that the performance goals associated with them are neither too low nor unrealistically aggressive. Table 17.2 examines the range of corporate-level measures typically used to drive specific incentive plan outcomes.

ELIGIBILITY AND PARTICIPATION

As incentive pay has increasingly been pushed down from the executive ranks to the broad employee population, eligibility has been most often determined by salary level or job grade or title. A company's culture plays a key role in determining eligibility in the incentive plan. More entrepreneurial and/or egalitarian organizations, for example, may seek to make all employees eligible under the incentive plan. Other companies might elect to shield their employees from the economic risks inherent in these incentive arrangements and deliver substantially all compensation for most employees via base salary.

While a company can designate a relatively large segment of the employee population as "plan eligible," typically not all of these eligible employees will ultimately participate (e.g., receive an incentive award) during the course of the plan cycle. Table 17.3 shows, on average, the percentage of employees that are eligible for incentive pay, and the percentage of those that receive a payout.

For example, in the above table, 88 percent of the companies indicated that the manager level is eligible for the incentive plan, and 87 percent of managers actually received an award under the plan.

TABLE 17.2   Typical Measures of Company Performance for Incentive Design

Performance Measures	% of Companies
Sales/Revenue	45%
Operating profit	29%
Profit before Interest, Taxes and Depreciation/Amortization (e.g., EBIT, EBITDA)	17%
Achievement of other specific company objectives	16%
Profit before taxes	9%
Earnings per share	7%
Customer satisfaction	6%
Free cash flow	6%
New product introduction/development	5%
Quality	5%
Return on investment/equity/assets (e.g., ROI, ROE, ROA)	4%
Profit after taxes	3%
Reporting Companies	587

SOURCE: Radford Surveys + Consulting, Overall Practices Report, 2007.

INCENTIVE AWARD OPPORTUNITIES

The central questions in determining award opportunities include:

- What is the company's target total cash (salary plus on-target incentives) pay position?

Table 17.3   Percentage of Employees Eligible for Incentive by Level

Level	Percent Eligible for Incentives	Percent of Eligible Employees Actually Receiving
CEO	91%	100%
Executives (SVP, VP)	97%	98%
Directors	96%	93%
Managers	88%	87%
IC—Staff/Principal	76%	93%
IC—Career/Senior	64%	87%
IC—Entry/Intermediate	55%	90%
IC—Support	48%	91%

SOURCE: Radford Surveys + Consulting Overall Practices Report, 2006.

- How are total compensation levels and pay mix currently positioned against the market?

- How much can the company afford?

Target Awards.   Award opportunities are generally based on the employee's level and the criticality of his position. Typically, award opportunities are expressed as a percentage of base salary, however determining the appropriate award opportunity across organizational levels is an art, and is largely tied to what a company can afford and its pay philosophy. That said, as a generality, lower-level employees have lower award opportunities, with targets of around 5–10 percent of base salary, and senior level executives have target opportunities closer to 30–100 percent of base salary (see Table 17.4). Market data from surveys reflecting labor market practices are typically taken into account when setting award opportunities.

Once award opportunities are determined, companies often struggle with where to set the bar for performance; in other words, what, for example, constitutes target (and thus threshold and maximum) and how are individual payout opportunities set relative to performance? Typically some portion of a participant's award is tied to company performance, in addition to their business group and/or department, as well as individual contributions. Individual performance measurement faces many of the above-referenced design challenges as companies seek to define the varying levels of individual performance required to receive payment. At a minimum, most companies require an employee to be in good performance standing to receive an award. Individual awards typically range from 0 to 200 percent of target (source: Radford Overall Practices Report, 2006), depending on the actual plan funding. Most companies manage the plan to a fixed pool, thus, for any participants receiving above-target awards, other participants must receive below-target awards in order to manage to the approved budget or pool funding.

TABLE 17.4   Average Target Incentive Award as a Percent of Base Salary

Level	Award Opportunity as Percent of Base Salary
CEO	75%
Executives (SVP, VP)	40%
Directors	25%
Managers	15%
IC—Staff/Principal	13%
IC—Career/Senior	10%
IC—Entry/Intermediate	8%
IC—Support	7%

SOURCE: Radford Surveys + Consulting Overall Practices Report, 2006.

TABLE 17.5   Incentive Plan Payout Frequency

Formal Incentive Plans—Distribution Schedule	% of Companies
Annualy	63.0%
Quarterly	18.0%
Semi-annually	17.0%
Other	3.0%
Reporting Companies	611

Source: Radford Surveys + Consulting Overall Practices Report, 2006.

Award Frequency.   The frequency of award payouts depends on several factors. Some companies can set goals only one or two quarters in advance, and so payouts are made on a quarterly or semiannual basis; other companies set annual goals tied to their business plan and financial objectives and align payouts accordingly. How far a company can look into the future is determined by its business and product development cycles and the features of its performance management system. Typically companies set plan payouts on an annual schedule, which closely aligns with most company's planning cycles and performance management processes (see Table 17.5). As a guideline, the tighter the timeframe between goal achievement and award, the more powerfully the incentive motivates future behavior.

ADMINISTRATIVE RULES

Adjustments to the Plan.   Effective incentive plan design is predicated on management buy-in of the plan and on the company's commitment to use it to drive performance. Making midcourse adjustments to the plan undermines its effectiveness and can lead to an entitlement mentality. Changing the rules of the game can also insulate employees from negative events. This practice is generally met with skepticism by shareholders and others who monitor the link between executive pay and company performance. There are situations where adjustments are justifiable and advised, including during acquisitions and divestitures, in the wake of asset additions or disposals in capital-intensive markets and in reaction to volatile foreign exchange fluctuations. However, plans with rules established at the beginning of the year are more likely to be perceived as fair amongst employees, and certainly create a stronger governance structure for the plan.

Communication.   Communication is an often overlooked aspect of incentive plan implementation; however, it is also one of the most critical aspects of ensuring plan effectiveness. As is the case with many aspects of design, how (or whether) a company communicates the plan details to participants reveals (and in part, determines) a company's culture. The goals, processes, opportunities, and rationale of incentive compensation plans should be communicated clearly and frequently, whether that comes in the form of centralized communication, communication from line managers, or some combination of the two. Companies rely on a number of forms of communications including:

1. Summary plan descriptions
2. Training and educational sessions
3. Total compensation statements
4. Individual performance management feedback sessions
5. Business updates to keep participants informed of goal alignment and performance

Prior to plan execution, participants should have a very strong understanding of what the company, and they individually, must do in order to achieve or exceed the plan and maximize their income potential. In addition to a sound outbound communication strategy for incentive plans, employees should also have the opportunity to communicate their perspective on the plan, via survey or some formal type of communication that creates data that management can use to improve program design from year to year.

SUMMARY

To determine if your plan is designed with market best practices, we have provided a top 10 list of common plan characteristics from high-performing companies.

1. The plan includes realistic and meaningful performance objectives and associated payouts
2. There is demonstrated support for the plan by senior management
3. A willingness exists within the company to accept different types of contributions and "winners"
4. Above-market awards are granted to a limited population (10 percent) of high performers
5. There is differentiation of incentive awards relative to other forms of awards (solid performance can earn cash incentives but not additional awards; e.g., mentoring, training, equity, access to senior management, autonomy, and other development opportunities)
6. Performance management ratings or distribution are managed to fund above-market awards for overachievers
7. Top performers are tracked more directly by cross-functional management to plan their futures and celebrate their contributions
8. Companies establish a strong and dynamic link between the goal-setting process and the company's performance management philosophy
9. Companies understand, and measure, the return on investment of their incentive plan dollars
10. There is definition of plan rules up front to avoid surprises to participants when awards are issued

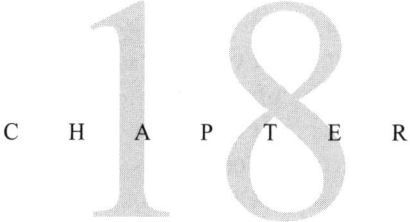

USING VARIABLE PAY PROGRAMS TO SUPPORT ORGANIZATION GOALS

Erin C. Packwood, Principal

Mercer Human Capital Consulting Group

HUMAN RESOURCE PROFESSIONALS ARE ALWAYS looking for ways to ensure that employees are contributing to organizational success and that the right people are in the right roles doing the right things. To facilitate this, they are continually evaluating potential additions to their rewards toolkits. When used effectively, each reward—whether a benefit program, a compensation plan, or other means of recognizing employee contribution—supports the achievement of an employer's business objective in some way.

One of business's more versatile reward tools is variable pay. While variable pay is not new, particularly among the executive ranks, it has become much more widespread in recent years, as employers realize the impact it can have on employees throughout an organization and on how they perform their jobs.

VARIABLE PAY AS AN ATTRACTION TOOL

Even before an employee joins a company, variable pay can have an impact, especially if it is part of a thoughtfully developed compensation strategy derived from a broader human-capital approach which outlines the type of employee the company deems necessary to accomplish its business goals. This talent profile may have been defined for the company's entire population or for a particular segment of the workforce. However, the fact that the company includes variable pay in its mix of rewards is usually because leadership has concluded that employees who fit the desired profile will see value in the program and will be motivated to realize the full potential of the additional rewards available to them. The program then becomes part of the selection process by attracting employees who appreciate this particular type of reward.

Depending upon the nature of the program, variable pay can say a lot to an employee about the type of company he or she is joining. Is it an organization that openly shares financial success with its employees? Does the company value teamwork and/or individual contributions? If so, does it demonstrate this in a way that the prospective employee values?

"Variable pay" generally refers to all forms of ongoing cash compensation other than base pay that employees receive during their employment. These programs take various forms, as described later in this chapter.

In a highly competitive market, the ongoing variable-pay programs available to employees can also play a critical role in attracting talent by enhancing the competitiveness of the compensation package in relation to those offered by other potential employers. As mentioned earlier, while variable pay has long been a key component of compensation for senior management and executive employees, it is now used by the majority of employers to reward employees at all organizational levels.

According to research conducted each year by Mercer, the percentage of U.S. employees eligible for variable pay has increased significantly since 2000 (see Figure 18.1). When compared to base pay increase trend data for the same period, it is interesting to see that the notable rise in the prevalence of variable pay coincides with the first major decline in base pay increase budgets that the United States had seen in over 10 years. During this period, many were inclined to attribute this trend to the economic downturn impacting the country at the time. While this may partially explain the trend, a closer look at the data shows that employers were beginning to face significant annual increases in the costs of their health care benefits. These two factors together were, in fact, prompting employers to evaluate the affordability of all reward programs and to seek ways to ensure that their spending in each area was sustainable.

When looking for ways to better manage reward expenditures, variable-pay programs emerge as one of the most controllable expenses. Unlike many other alternative reward investments, properly designed variable-pay programs can contribute to business performance and profitability by linking employees' rewards to

FIGURE 18.1 Ten-year trend chart

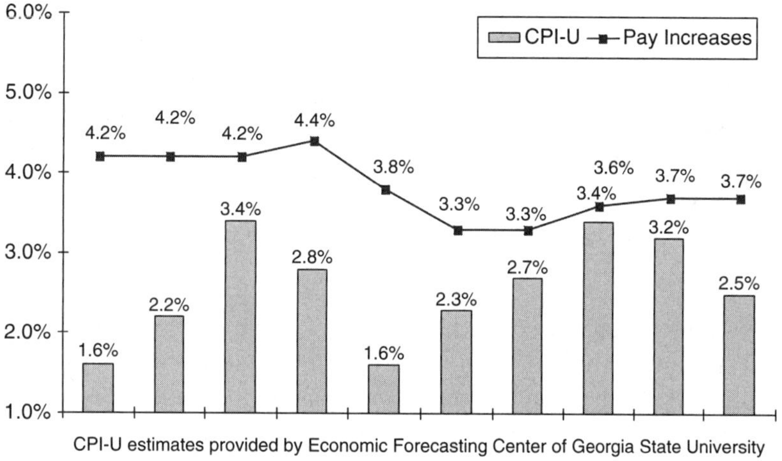
6.0%
5.0%
4.0%
3.0%
2.0%
1.0%
CPI-U
Pay Increases
4.2%
4.2%
4.2%
4.4%
3.8%
3.3%
3.3%
3.6%
3.7%
3.7%
1.6%
2.2%
3.4%
2.8%
1.6%
2.3%
2.7%
3.4%
3.2%
2.5%
CPI-U estimates provided by Economic Forecasting Center of Georgia State University

Source: 2006/2007 US Compensation Planning Survey, Mercer Human Resource Consulting

the activities expected of them. These are among the key reasons that variable-pay programs have become so common since 2001.

As variable-pay eligibility increases and additional cash compensation opportunities become more popular, employees have taken notice and have begun to place greater importance on their availability. Thus, variable pay has become an increasingly effective attraction tool in its perceived potential to provide highly competitive and attractive total-cash compensation to employees who have confidence in their ability to succeed.

So, what sort of variable-pay opportunity is considered competitive? Mercer's research indicates that, where variable-pay programs are present, the expected individual award, or target, is at least the equivalent of one month's pay, or 8.3 percent of an employee's annual salary.

VARIABLE PAY AS A MOTIVATION TOOL

Just as variable pay opportunities must be considered significant in order to be attractive to prospective employees, so must they be in order to have any motivational impact once new hires become active employees. In addition, the requirements that an employee must fulfill in order to receive the awards must be viewed as realistic and achievable. When employees view performance expectations as reasonable, and the reward for such effort is perceived as material, they will strive to earn the additional rewards available to them.

What is considered material? In general, an amount equal to at least one month's pay is considered sufficient to be meaningful to an employee and sufficient to attract his attention. Perhaps not coincidentally, this tends to be the lowest targeted award level for employees who are eligible for variable pay (see Figure 18.2).

FIGURE 18.2   Target versus actual chart

Incentive plans offered?	Executive	Management	Technical / Professional	Nonexempt Clerical / Technician	Trades/ Production /Service
% offered	86%	84%	71%	56%	48%
Median 2007 target %	42%	22%	13%	8%	7%
Average payout based on 2006 performance (as % of base pay)	47%	22%	13%	8%	9%

Source: 2007/2008 US Compensation Planning Survey, Mercer Human Resource Consulting

At an average of somewhere between 3 and 4 percent of base pay, managers and human resource professionals often struggle to find ways to maintain competitiveness in their pay programs and still provide meaningful rewards to employees for desired results through annual base pay increases. In some instances, the traditional annual pay adjustment seems too far off into the future to effectively motivate employees. However, when annual base pay adjustments can be combined with variable pay, total cash rewards can have a much greater impact.

Compensation professionals generally subscribe to the idea that you will get the behaviors and results you reward. Thus, it is important that a variable-pay plan be carefully designed so as to reinforce what is important to the company and to motivate the right things. If properly designed, a variable-pay program can focus employees on business drivers that are within their control. The effectiveness of such a program is dependent upon how the plan is designed and how it is communicated to employees.

VARIABLE PAY PLAN VS BONUS PLAN

When most people think of variable pay, they think of "bonus" plans. But bonus plans can take many forms. In fact, some people use the term "bonus" to refer only to purely discretionary awards that are not directly linked to performance. Variable-pay plans that are clearly driven by performance are commonly called "incentive plans." It is worth noting that bonuses generally award performance which is assessed after the fact, while incentive pay rewards performance objectives that are set in advance.

Variable Pay Plan Design Elements

The ultimate form of bonus or incentive plan is determined by its unique design features. There are seven core features of a variable-pay plan, as illustrated in Figure 18.3.

Eligibility.   Once the decision has been made to implement an incentive-compensation plan and the objectives of the plan have been clearly defined, among the first criteria to address in designing the plan is *eligibility*. Which employees

FIGURE 18.3   Incentive plan type

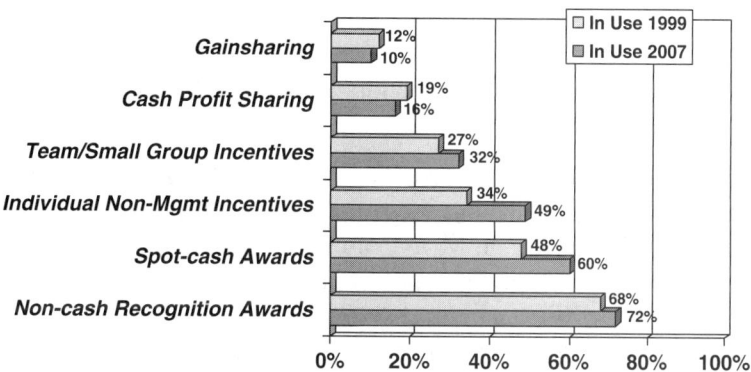

Source: 1998/1999 and 2007/2008 US Compensation Planning Survey, Mercer Human Resource Consulting

will participate in the plan? A common practice is to include everyone in the plan who contributes to achieving what have been defined as the objectives of the plan. In many cases, this may be every employee. In others, the objectives of the plan may suggest that eligibility should be limited to just a portion of the workforce, such as all employees with a certain level of managerial responsibility or all employees in a certain function or department.

Payout Timing and Frequency.   How often will awards be paid, and when? The frequency of the awards (e.g., monthly, quarterly, annually) can be influenced by many drivers, including how often the performance rewarded by the plan can be measured and how frequently such performance should be reinforced through rewards. These considerations will also drive the timing of the award payment.

Funding.   Funding incentive awards is an important design component, as it determines the total amount available to be distributed to eligible employees. Will the incentive awards be funded based on a predefined financial formula (i.e., self-funding), or will they be budgeted using an assumed performance level that can be either financial or nonfinancial? Alternatively, the "pool" used to fund incentive awards may be determined on a purely discretionary basis at the end of the per-formance period. Depending upon the objectives set out for the incentive plan, one approach may be more effective than the others.

Performance Measurement.   Just as the eligibility and award timing will be driven by the objectives of the incentive-compensation plan, the ways in which "success" will be measured, or *performance measurement*, will be dictated by the desired outcomes. Will performance be measured at the corporate level (e.g., year-over-year revenue growth, profitability, etc.), the department level (e.g., achieving a certain level of cost savings, completion of a major project, etc.), or the individual level (e.g., fulfilling specific performance objectives, closing a particular number of transactions, etc.)? Selecting the right performance measures is a critical component in ensuring the incentive plan is aligned with organizational objectives, driving the right behaviors and, thus, achieving the highest return on the variable-pay investment.

Performance Mix. The level at which performance is measured—and rewarded—can say something about an organization's culture and what the organization considers important. Many companies use incentive compensation to reinforce multiple types of performance by placing weight on a number of performance measures. The *performance mix* determines how much each metric will factor into the variable-pay award. For example, corporate performance criteria may drive 50 percent of the award, while the achievement of departmental and individual goals may each contribute 25 percent. The decision as to the appropriate mix of performance measures used to determine the award is typically driven by the degree to which the eligible employee can influence each measure. Senior executives may have an incentive award based entirely on corporate results, as they are the group held accountable for corporate performance, while staff employees may have incentive awards based primarily on their individual activities, as they are among the farthest removed from the achievement of overall corporate objectives.

Award Levels. Award levels provided for in the incentive-plan design specify the award opportunity each participant in the plan will have. We have already established that, in order to be considered meaningful and to drive behavior, an individual award generally should be targeted to be at least 8 percent of the employee's annual base pay, or about one month's pay.

However, the significance of the award should also increase with the level of accountability, which is generally why variable pay is more significant and award "targets" are higher for more senior roles (see Figure 18.2). In addition to establishing target award levels, the incentive plan should also account for the amount of variable pay that is warranted in circumstances where objectives are only partially met but are still worthy of reward (also known as "threshold" performance) and in circumstances where objectives are significantly exceeded (also known as "superior" performance). In other words, how much should the targeted award be discounted in the case of threshold performance? And, what is the maximum amount warranted in the event of superior performance?

Allocation. The final element of an incentive plan is *allocation*, or how the incentive-award pool will be distributed to individual participants once the size of the pool has been determined, or funding has occurred. The allocation approach is typically linked to *performance mix*. However, depending on the funding approach outlined by the plan, individual awards may not be determined using a precise formula. Instead, a more subjective or modified approach to allocating incentive awards may be warranted, taking into account individual performance and targeted award levels. For example, and depending upon the provisions of the plan, the incentive-award pool may be divided among different groups (e.g., divisions, business units, etc.) disproportionately. In such instances, the plan should also indicate whether managers should allocate the funds using a formula which takes into account the variables that impact the size of the pool provided for their group, or whether the funds should be allocated in another way.

Types of Variable Pay Plans

Given the myriad possible design options, the type of plan that is appropriate for one organization may not be appropriate for another. Different approaches to variable pay have characteristics that often make them suitable for very different environments.

Profit Sharing.   For instance, one form of variable pay plan, the *profit sharing* bonus, emphasizes profitability—an overall company performance indicator—as a success measure. Typically, a profit-sharing bonus plan provides for a common award level, either a fixed amount or a percentage of base pay, that will be paid to all eligible employees upon achieving a certain level of profitability. This basic framework makes profit-sharing bonus plans among the simplest to administer.

Profit-sharing plans are used by many organizations in a wide variety of industries, and often are credited with contributing to a low employee-turnover rate. While most profit-sharing plans are similar in the type of performance they are trying to reward and the measures considered most important, there are still some variations. For example, a profit-sharing bonus program at one high-technology company pays out a percentage of net income or pretax margin (whichever is greater) twice yearly. Another large manufacturing organization calls its profit-sharing plan a "wage dividend" program. This plan reportedly provided payments that ranged from 2 to 8 percent of an employee's earnings each year over a five-year period.

By their design, these types of bonus plans also tend to communicate a strong emphasis on organizational performance rather than individual performance. As a result, profit-sharing bonus plans are considered less effective than other forms of variable pay in motivating specific individual behaviors because they have a less direct line of sight to results. For this reason, other forms of variable pay have become more popular in recent years.

Gainsharing.   Another form of variable pay plan that emphasizes group or organizational achievement is the *gainsharing* plan. Gainsharing plans are, as the name implies, intended to share the financial gains achieved above a certain threshold or benchmark level with employees who contribute to creating those gains. In their truest form, gainsharing plans are self-funded: a percentage of the incremental operational or financial gains above a stated minimum measure are used to create the bonus pool. Gainsharing plans can be effective in supporting the achievement of operating efficiencies and in engaging employees in controlling costs. In a typical gainsharing environment, there is pressure within workgroups for each employee to do whatever they can to ensure a high level of productivity, to manage expenses, and to otherwise identify process improvements.

Gainsharing plans are most common in production or production-oriented environments (e.g., logistics, manufacturing, call centers, etc.) and are used to similarly reward all employees in a group for achieving predefined benchmarks. For example, in 2007, a leading automotive manufacturer announced that it would pay bonuses to its salaried and hourly employees in the United States and Canada as a result of quality and cost-cutting improvements achieved in 2006. Nonmanagerial employees reportedly earned bonuses that ranged from $300 to 800 each.

Other industries, such as retail, may use a gainsharing bonus program to encourage warehouse workers to achieve certain productivity targets. When the productivity targets are achieved, employees' weekly wages can increase 5–10 percent.

While some might argue that there is always room for more efficiency, gainsharing plans can start to lose their motivational value as incremental gains over prior performance periods start to diminish. In fact, financially rewarding continued gains can come at other costs, such as neglecting to reinvest in the necessary maintenance of equipment or compromising quality as employees look for additional cost savings. Therefore, true gainsharing plans are often most effective when viewed as a temporary incentive tool. Once optimal productivity levels and efficiencies are achieved, it may be appropriate to shift to another form of variable pay that can be more effective in focusing employees on maintaining the performance levels realized under the gainsharing model. However, as technology and processes evolve and new production techniques come into play, gainsharing continues to be a useful variable-pay tool.

Group or Individual Incentives.   Depending upon their specific design parameters, traditional incentive plans can take the form of either *group (or team) incentives* or *individual incentives*. The funding vehicle, performance mix, and allocation model of the plan will dictate whether variable pay should reward the performance of groups or teams within the organization or individuals, rather than reward overall organizational success.

As organizations seek to improve the linkage between individual behaviors and their financial rewards, group incentives and individual incentives have become increasingly popular. Furthermore, when incentive awards are based on measures that employees feel are at least partially within their control, either as an individual contributor or as a member of a work group, then the opportunity to receive the award becomes a more effective motivational tool.

An example of a group-incentive plan is the program implemented by a large aerospace organization in 2001, which ties performance to team goals. In this example, teams can range in size from 60 to 900 employees. Each team's

FIGURE 18.4   Incentive plan type prevalence chart

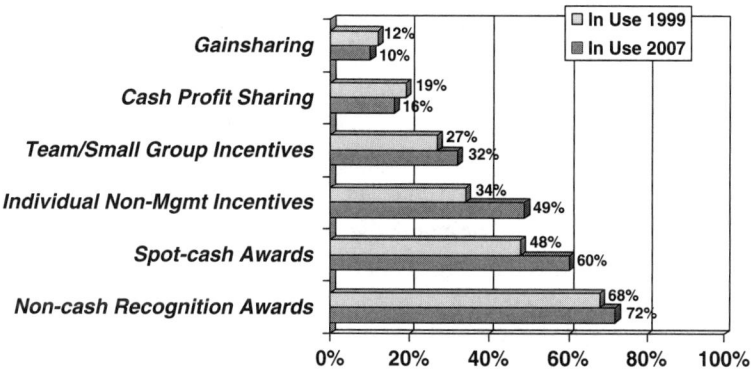

Source: 1998/1999 and 2007/2008 US Compensation Planning Survey, Mercer Human Resource Consulting

performance is based on achieving an overall profit objective and a team "scorecard" rating, although specific scorecard criteria vary by unit. If company profit objectives are not met, partial payouts may be awarded based on the team's scorecard rating. The incentive awards can be as much as $1,500 per year, with a preliminary mid-year payout of up to $500 if the team is performing well.

Individual-incentive plans are widely accepted today and most of them contain provisions that encompass corporate and group objectives. But what makes them truly *individual* incentive plans is the fact that the actual awards to employees are differentiated based on individual performance criteria. For example, a global chemical company's "Performance Award Program" is designed to share the company's financial success with employees. But individual employee awards are determined based on a combination of how the individual, her team, function or business, and the company have performed relative to predefined performance objectives.

Similarly, a global financial-service organization's "Annual Incentive Award" program for management employees is based upon individual and business performance, as well as the successful achievement of specific goals. Individual performance ratings, which reflect the extent to which the employee either meets or exceeds performance expectations, are used to determine an individual's incentive payout. At other companies, the individual-incentive compensation program rewards employees in such areas as marketing, sales and finance for their individual performance in support of the achievement of the company's goals.

Another form of individual cash incentive award is the *spot award*. Spot awards generally refer to one-time cash rewards that are awarded at any time, rather than upon the completion of a predefined performance period. Spot-award programs are typically funded by a budget that is set aside for recognizing employee contributions throughout the budget year. Among the primary benefits of such an approach is the fact that awards can be given promptly following the behavior or event that is being rewarded, thus increasing the perceived linkage between the reward and the activity. The amounts of such rewards can also vary, depending upon the significance of the activity.

MULTIPLE INCENTIVE PLANS CAN BE IMPLEMENTED

The different types of variable-pay plans in use today have different strengths and weaknesses. Some might look at the strengths of each approach and see some benefits to all of them. As a result, it is not uncommon to see multiple types of incentive plans being used within a single organization. Tailoring the incentive approach to the unique needs of various segments of the workforce can actually improve the alignment of employee behaviors with organizational goals. As an example, a leading U.S. bank's profit-sharing bonus plan includes only employees in certain roles whose salaries are less than $100,000 per year and who do not otherwise participate in a commission or other variable pay plan.

On the other hand, where multiple objectives are considered important to highlight, it is feasible that employees could participate in multiple incentive plans. For instance, where an organization desires to focus the efforts of an employee on the handful of specific activities they can control and which have been deemed to have an impact on organizational success, the employee may participate in an individual-incentive plan. Meanwhile, in an effort to also signal to employees the need to collaborate with others in the achievement of their goals or the goals of the organization, they may also participate in a profit-sharing plan.

Where each incentive-award opportunity is, by itself, considered significant, a layered approach like the example described above can help focus the employee on multiple inter-related goals. It is important, however, not to overly diffuse the focus of the individual employee so that multiple performance objectives become too numerous and confusing. Ideally, the number of goals an employee should be tasked with achieving—both individual and organizational goals—should be limited to no more than five.

OTHER VARIABLE PAY CONSIDERATIONS

Aside from the design and administration issues that must be carefully considered in order to ensure that variable pay supports an organization's attraction and motivation objectives, sufficient planning is also required around communicating the plans to employees and monitoring their effectiveness over time. Experience has shown that, for an incentive compensation plan to effectively motivate employee behaviors, employees must understand (1) how their actions impact the success of the organization and (2) how their performance will impact their rewards. Thus, the communication strategy cannot be underestimated as a key to the success of a variable pay program.

For instance, in the aforementioned example highlighting a firm's group-incentive plan, it was mentioned that the incentive awards are based on a combination of achieving financial objectives along with team scorecard objectives. To maintain employee focus on these criteria, the company posts information indicating progress toward achieving the performance objectives in each work area for all employees to see. In addition, the team scorecards are available on the company's intranet.

Finally, it is important to continually evaluate the impact the variable-pay plan is having on the organization's performance and its culture. Is it getting the expected results? Are there objectives that have been overly influenced or, perhaps, neglected as a result of the increased employee focus on specific measures? And has the emphasis on selected criteria resulted in unintended negative consequences in other areas considered important to the business? Periodic evaluation of the variable-pay plan and the results to which it is contributing will help to ensure the program is delivering the desired return on the financial investment in the plan.

SUMMARY

As illustrated in the various incentive-plan examples described in this chapter, each plan has different elements or plan features which impact their effectiveness in supporting business objectives by attracting the desired talent and motivating employee behaviors. In choosing the type of variable-pay plan that is appropriate, an organization should consider its compensation philosophy and strategy. What is the expected role of variable pay? What type of program is right for your business? Different approaches will support the fulfillment of an organization's efforts to attract and motivate talent in different ways.

As an attraction tool, variable pay can assist in ensuring the competitiveness of the rewards an organization can offer to prospective employees. It can facilitate the attraction of high-quality talent by allowing for greater compensation in order to make the employment proposition more compelling than that of the average employer. And variable pay can facilitate the attraction of employees whose values are consistent with those of the employer.

As a motivational tool, variable pay can support the achievement of organizational goals by focusing employees on business drivers that are within their control and rewarding them for the desired behaviors and results. If their employer's performance expectations are considered realistic and attainable, they will take steps to earn the additional rewards available to them, thus contributing to organizational objectives.

Before closing this chapter, it is worth noting that in addition to being a widely used attraction and motivation tool, variable pay, when combined with other reward programs, can help to reinforce just about anything that is considered important to the employer, including the desired corporate culture. It can communicate certain things about the organization's priorities, such as the importance placed on team or individual performance. Variable pay can also aid in the retention of highly valued employees by providing greater rewards to those who most demonstrate the desired behaviors or make significant contributions to the company's success. Finally, variable pay can effectively leverage an organization's compensation spending, creating greater rewards when business results are better and lower rewards when business results are below expectations.

C H A P T E R

RATIONALIZING VARIABLE PAY PLANS

Kenan S. Abosch, Broad-Based Compensation Practice Segment Leader

Hewitt Associates, LLC

ATTRACTING, MOTIVATING, AND RETAINING TALENTED employees have always been a priority for organizations hoping to create and deliver satisfactory results to their stakeholders. Doing so successfully in an era where more employees are nearing retirement, fewer workers are entering the workforce, and top performers are a hot commodity has created unique challenges. One emerging response to this talent predicament is the increasing use of variable pay. Increased funding, greater flexibility in delivery choices, potential upside in earning opportunity, and greater employee attention to organizational goals are making variable pay the preferred pay-for-performance approach at a growing number of organizations.

SHIFT AWAY FROM MERIT-BASED PAY FOR PERFORMANCE

Pay for performance for the mainstream employee has traditionally meant an increase to their base salary—usually in the form of a merit increase. Organizations have created merit increase budgets and have striven to allocate those budgets by giving larger increases to their better performers and smaller increases to employees who are not contributing in a meaningful way. Many human resource practitioners and subject-matter experts today have come to the realization that this approach has not been—and may not be capable of being—an effective mechanism for rewarding for performance. Salary increases are not differentiated by level of performance, spending on merit increases has been declining, and managers and employees are expressing significant frustration about the time and effort required and yet resulting in the failure to achieve true pay for performance.

In fairness, merit-based pay for performance has never been very popular with managers or employees. Complaints about not having enough funding, and an inability to ensure that differentiated increases were awarded to the performers who truly deserved them is not a recent occurrence. The forerunner to the merit increase—the across-the-board or general salary increase—was less controversial and easier to administer, but lacked the ability to reinforce performance outcomes. What is different today is the intensity of dissatisfaction with this approach.

It is not uncommon to hear executives proclaim that this process is not worth the time or effort required given the minimal degree of differentiation in rewards. CEOs believe that their managers spend a lot of time and effort working this process and the net result is an employee getting only a few hundred dollars more than another. A typical comment is, "It's not worth all the effort—I'd rather see managers spending the time focusing on bonuses because there's more leverage and flexibility."

In theory, it should be possible to provide differentiated merit increases to employees. This concept assumes a bell-shaped performance curve like the one

FIGURE 19.1 "Normal" performance distribution

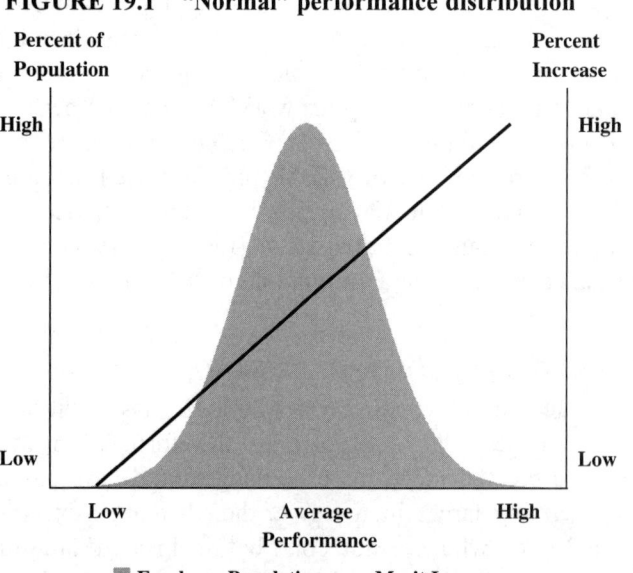

illustrated in Figure 19.1. The bell shape requires a normal distribution of performance—with just as many performers on the low end of the curve as there are on the high end. Since merit budgets are fixed in size, they must be allocated to employees based on the results of the performance curve. With a normal distribution, it is possible to award an average-sized merit increase to the bulk of the population and a significantly larger merit increase to the limited number of high performers on the right end of the curve. The funding source for these higher performers' increases comes from a similar number of low performers on the left end of the performance curve.

The bell-shaped performance curve is rarely seen in practice. Without some intervention such as forced ranking or rating calibration, the typical organization's performance curve looks like the one shown in Figure 19.2. This curve reveals very few, if any, low performers, a sizeable number of solid performers, and many high performers. This outcome occurs when organizations do not set high achievement goals and/or when manager capability and accountability is weak in honestly assessing and communicating employee performance. The net result of this performance curve is a flat merit-increase pay line with little differentiation for high and low performers—and a demotivating performance–rewards relationship.

The scapegoat for this disappointing outcome has been the size of the merit budget. The argument has been that having more money would allow for greater differentiation in merit increases. A review of the last 20 years of merit increase practices—including merit budgets that were nearly three times larger than those seen today—reveals that merit increases were not allocated any differently in the past than they are today as a percentage of the overall budget. This result can be seen in Figure 19.3.

FIGURE 19.2   "Typical" performance distribution

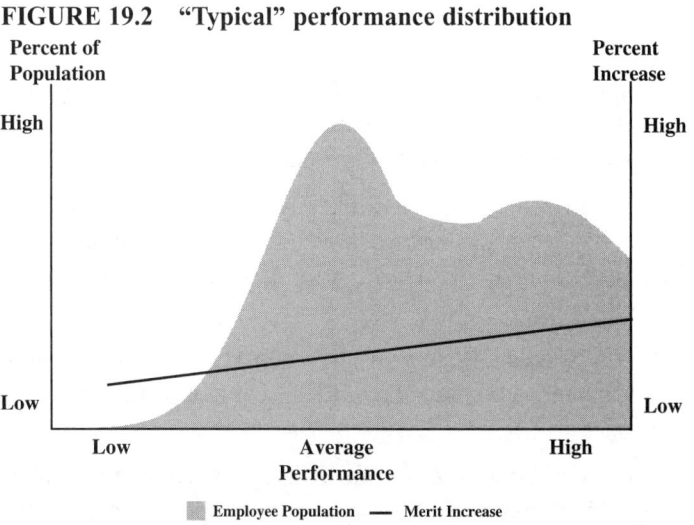

FIGURE 19.3   Allocation of merit increases by performance level

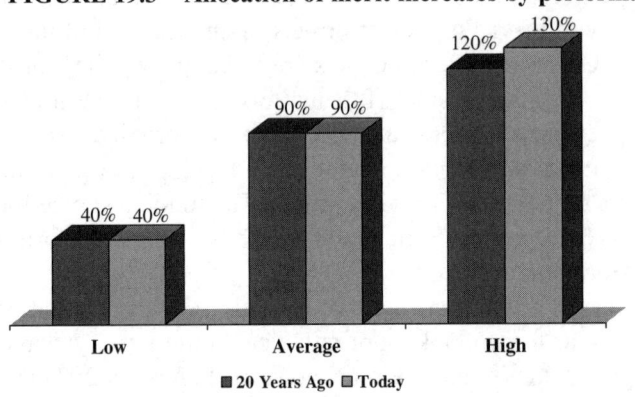

■ 20 Years Ago □ Today

Organizations are not able to, or are not willing to, pay for performance using merit increases. The perceived impact of shrinking merit funding, the reality that fixed merit budgets require a zero-sum game allocation, and the inability to address a skewed performance curve are leading organizations to turn to variable pay as the preferred approach to attracting, motivating, and rewarding talent.

GROWING USE OF VARIABLE PAY

Most organizations today provide at least one variable pay approach for their broad-based employee population. In the early 1990s slightly more than half of all U.S. corporations offered a broad-based variable pay arrangement. Today, over 80 percent of U.S. corporations have implemented a broad-based plan (see Figure 19.4).

Several factors explain this dynamic growth in the use of variable pay:

- Variable pay allows the organization to shift some of its compensation expenses from fixed costs to variable costs, giving it greater flexibility with less ongoing impact on cash flow. In addition, it is typically self-funding, meaning that payments occur when results justify them and do not occur when expected results are not achieved.

- Companies have found that variable pay helps focus employees on important organizational goals and priorities. When employee bonuses are at stake, employees tend to pay greater attention to expected results and required behaviors.

- Variable pay creates a feeling of alignment, with executives and employees working together to create shareholder wealth and sharing in successes or failures.

- Variable pay can build a sense of affiliation whereby employees feel like they have something at stake in how the business operates and performs.

FIGURE 19.4   Use of variable pay increase

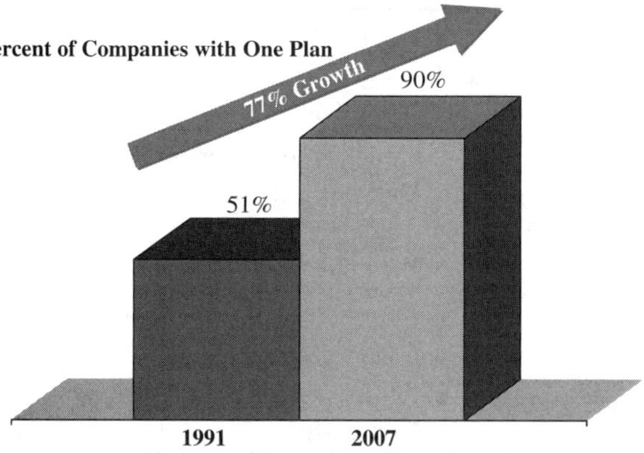

Percent of Companies with One Plan

77% Growth

90%

51%

1991   2007

Source: Hewitt Salary Increase Survey 1990–2007

- Variability in funding along with an increasing use of individual performance in determining bonuses provides an opportunity to send differentiated pay messages to top performers and high-potential employees.

Many of these reasons come from the perspective of the business, yet employees also have expressed a positive reaction to variable pay. Generally employees like the fact that they are eligible for additional compensation beyond their base salaries, they feel a greater degree of control over the determination of their bonuses than with merit increases, and they see an opportunity for upside funding potential for outstanding performance vs a fixed merit increase budget that does not fluctuate based on swings in contribution.

TYPES OF VARIABLE PAY PLANS

There is a wide range of variable pay plan design types that provide organizations with more flexibility in fitting the ideal approach to the needs of the business. Table 19.1 illustrates the range of plan characteristics found in variable pay plans.

Companies considering the implementation of a variable pay plan can select from seven different types of plan design. While some organizations chose to provide only one of these approaches, a growing number of companies are using one or more plan types for either different segments of the employee population or multiple approaches to create different areas of emphasis. This is an increasing trend as variable pay becomes an important element in supporting the business model of an organization.

The seven types of plans are:

- *Business incentives*—plans with combined financial and/or operating measures for company, business unit, department, plant, and/or individual performance.

TABLE 19.1   Range of Variable Plan Characteristics

Measures	■ Financial ■ Qualitative ■ Individual
Focus	■ Organizational performance ■ Unit performance ■ Team performance ■ Individual performance
Frequency of payment	■ Ranges from annual to semi-monthly
Form of reward	■ Cash ■ Equity ■ Non-cash

- *Cash profit sharing*—plans that make equal payment (as a flat-dollar amount or percentage of salary) to all or most employees based on organizational profitability.

- *Individual performance plans*—plans whose payouts are based solely on individual performance criteria. Payout amount typically varies from one individual to another.

- *Gain sharing or productivity plans*—plans designed to share a percentage of cost savings of a group, unit, or organization. The gains are typically shared uniformly among all participants.

- *Team awards*—plans that provide incentives to individuals on a project or work team.

- *Special recognition plans*—plans that are designed to recognize special individual or group achievements with small cash awards or merchandise.

- *Stock option plans*—plans under which stock options are granted to employees below the executive level.

While all of these plan types have been in existence for some time—their use has fluctuated greatly. Figure 19.5 illustrates the current prevalence of each of the plan types and also shows how they have either grown or declined over the last 10 years.

Business incentives are today's fastest growing category due to their use of financial and nonfinancial measures and also their range of coverage from organizational level to unit to individual performance. Individual performance plans are on the rise—especially for organizations that are introducing a plan for the first time. More organizations are also including an individual performance factor in other variable pay plan types. Special recognition has been increasing as a pay plan

FIGURE 19.5   Prevalence of plan type among broad-based employee groups

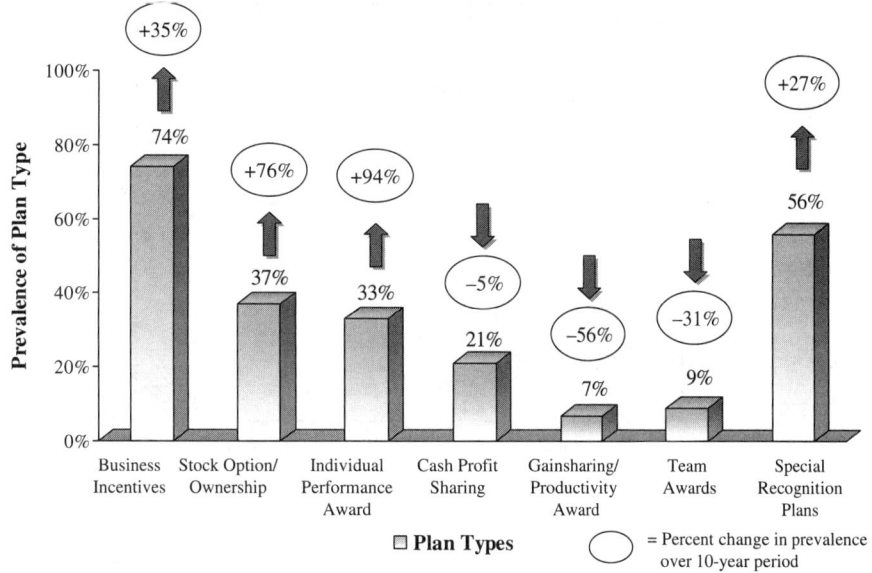

Source: Hewitt 1996–2005 Variable Compensation Measurement ™ Survey

type due to the immediacy of reward, the low cost of rewards, and its ability to reach the new members of the workforce who tend to place recognition high on their list of employment values.

Plans on the decline include gainsharing, team awards, and cash profit sharing. Gainsharing plans eventually run out of incremental improvement opportunities and typically evolve to another plan type. Team awards have created administrative complexities for organizations to track participants and accomplishments. It also has been difficult to determine where a team's impact starts and stops. Cash profit sharing plans are less popular today due to the fact that they have low line-of-sight—employees do not feel like they impact their outcomes. While there has been an overall increase in the use of stock options over the last 10 years, changes in accounting conventions for options have caused most organizations to no longer offer these plans to nonexecutives.

Having awareness of the different variable pay plan types is important in considering which approach to introduce to an organization. Even more critical is knowledge about how each plan type corresponds to different business situations. A company struggling to improve its financial performance might be well served by a plan that focuses on efforts at the lowest common denominator such as team awards or gainsharing plans. These plans focus individuals on very clear and controllable incremental improvements. Alternatively, an organization that is not

FIGURE 19.6   Aligning variable pay programs to the business situation

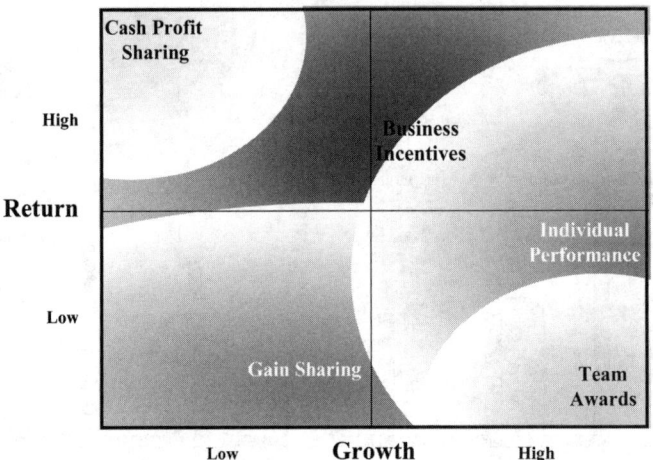

growing rapidly but is highly profitable might find that cash profit sharing is the best way to maintain that position. These relationships have been presented in the two-by-two matrix in Figure 19.6 using a continuum of low or high growth (typically revenues) and low or high return (typically net income). It is essential that an organization analyze its business position relative to its business competitors and select a type of variable pay plan that fits its business situation (see Figure 19.6).

CHANGE IN PAY MIX

Perhaps the most impressive development regarding variable pay is how dramatically the mix of pay has changed for organizations over the last 15 years. Figure 19.7 reveals that 15 years ago the variable pay budget for salaried professionals averaged 3.8 percent of payroll and represented 43 percent of the overall pay increase opportunity. Today, salaried professionals are likely to see an average variable pay budget of 11.1 percent of payroll reflecting 79 percent of the overall increase opportunity. Due to the increased spending in variable pay, the overall pay increase opportunity has grown from an average of 8.8 percent 15 years ago to 14.7 percent today. Employees clearly have more of their earning opportunity at risk and companies have very successfully shifted their compensation expenses from fixed costs to variable costs.

The change in pay mix is particularly critical information for organizations as they try to attract, motivate, and retain talent. With 80 percent of U.S. corporations having variable pay arrangements for nonexecutives and given the shift in pay mix, an organization not offering variable pay to employees is vulnerable in competing for talent. Figure 19.8 illustrates the gap in earning opportunity between a

FIGURE 19.7   Change in pay mix

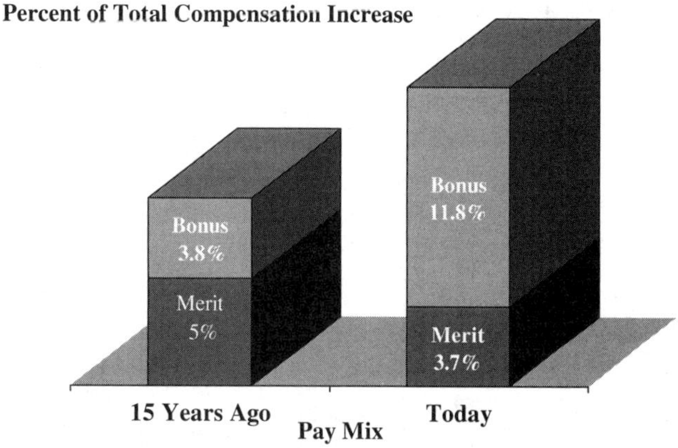

Percent of Total Compensation Increase

Source: Hewitt Salary Increase Survey 1990–2007

FIGURE 19.8   Earning opportunity comparison

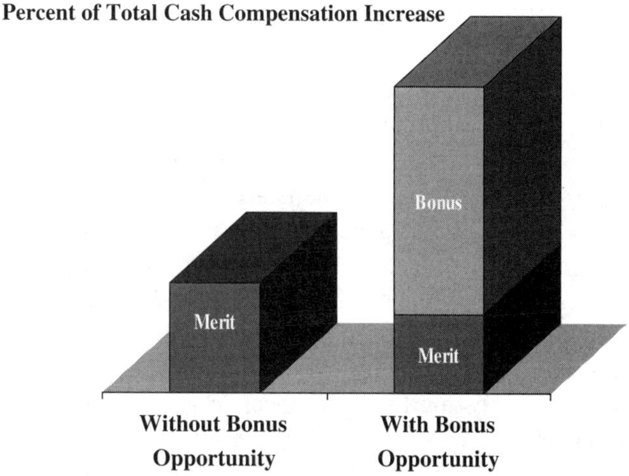

Percent of Total Cash Compensation Increase

Source: Hewitt Salary Increase Survey 1990–2006

company with a variable pay arrangement and one that does not offer such an alternative.

This shift in pay mix has occurred through a steady growth in variable pay budgets and a decline in base salary increase budgets. Organizations have been under intense pressure to decrease costs and labor is typically a top-three expense category for most companies. Figure 19.9 shows how base salary increase budgets have declined from 5.5 percent in 1990 to a stable 3.6 percent of payroll today. Over that same time frame, companies have grown from budgeting 4.0 percent of payroll for variable pay in 1990 to over 11 percent in the mid 2000s.

FIGURE 19.9   Company spending on variable compensation

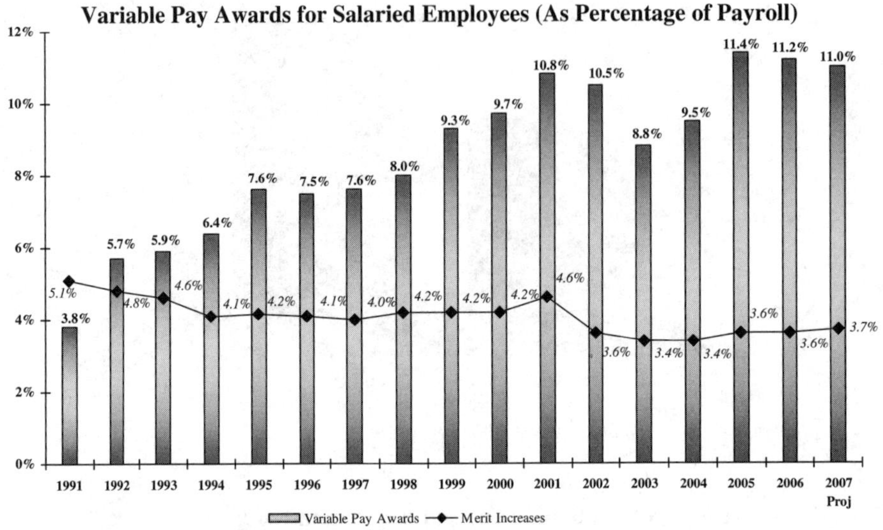

Variable Pay Awards for Salaried Employees (As Percentage of Payroll)

Source: Hewitt 2006/2007 Salary Increase Survey Report

EFFECTIVENESS OF VARIABLE PAY PRACTICES

Organizations that offer a variable pay arrangement to employees stand a much better chance of successfully recruiting, motivating, and keeping talented employees than those without a plan. Not all plans are equally effective and having one that is not effective may be worse than not having a plan at all. Common mistakes organizations make include selecting the wrong metrics, having too many measures, creating goals that employees do not understand or have no way to impact, and providing payouts when results do not warrant them.

A study was conducted recently to identify the characteristics of effective variable pay plans by analyzing the differences in variable pay practices between high- and low-performing companies. High-performing companies were distinguished from low-performing companies using a three-year rolling average of companies' total shareholder return (TSR). Six-hundred public companies were assigned to one of four TSR quartiles and the variable pay practices of companies in the top quartile were compared with those in the bottom quartile. Figure 19.10 illustrates the most significant differences observed in the design and execution of variable pay plans for each group of companies.

The characteristics described will ensure that plans have a better chance to accomplish their intended objectives of improving financial results, focusing employees on critical initiatives, influencing individual behaviors, and creating important organizational synergies so that all employees are working toward a common set of performance expectations. There has been little information on how variable pay plans have actually impacted business results. Skeptics will point to this absence of proof to question whether variable pay plans truly work.

FIGURE 19.10 Comparative variable pay plan characteristics

Highest Performing Companies

- More accurate goal setting
- Realistic goals and targets
- Formal recognition of individual performance when determining incentive awards
- Greater emphasis on communication
  — Communication vehicles
  — Performance targets and updates on projected results

Lowest Performing Companies

- Gaps between projected and actual performance
- Broad measures—low line of sight
- Less leveraged incentive opportunities
- Entitlement-based payouts for poor results (payout ratios)
- Less frequent communication of performance targets
- Fewer communication methods—less likely to communicate

FIGURE 19.11 Plan impact on business results

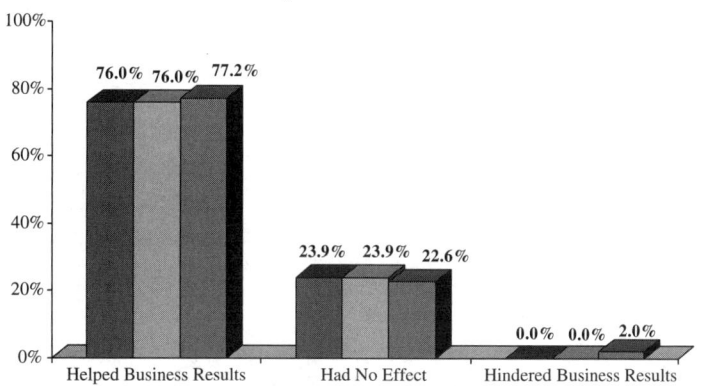

■ 1996-1999 ▨ 2000-2002 ■ 2003-2005

Source: Hewitt VCM 1996–2005

One study has collected 10 years of data regarding the effectiveness of these arrangements. Human resource practitioners were asked the question: "Overall, do you think your variable compensation plan helped to improve business results?" Their answers have been consistently strong over the 10 years and suggest that variable pay plans have a significant positive impact on achieving business results (see Figure 19.11).

REFERENCES

U.S. Salary Increase Survey, Survey Findings: 2006 and 2007, Lincolnshire, IL: Hewitt Associates, 2006.

Variable Compensation Measurement™, the 2006 VCM™ Report U.S. Edition, Lincolnshire, IL: Hewitt Associates, 2006.

SALES COMPENSATION

Jerome A. Colletti and Mary S. Fiss

Colletti–Fiss, LLC

FOR MOST COMPANIES, THE ESSENCE of business success is the ability to attract and retain customers. Because the sales force is a vital link between a company and its customers, it holds the key to business growth and profitability. A properly directed, motivated, and rewarded sales force will make a significant contribution to the achievement of these business measures. The sales compensation plan is one of the company's biggest investments in its sales organization, and one of the more powerful tools available to management to achieve optimal sales force motivation and performance. Sales compensation is very much on the minds of top managers in many companies today.

There are three reasons why this is so. First, our research shows that, depending on the industry, sales compensation makes up between 30 and 70 percent of the selling expense budget. The magnitude of this expense is large enough for concern on the part of top managers about the proper return on compensation investment regardless of the economic business cycle. In one recent research study, 86 percent of participating companies reported that how to determine sales compensation return on investment (ROI) is their number one priority.[1] Second, the sales compensation plan is a powerful "signaling system" to the sales force about what it is important to focus on. A well-designed plan rewards a sales force for achieving business objectives that top management desires. However, when the plan is out of sync with business objectives, the consequences can be as disastrous as a plan "in sync" can be positive. As reported in the business press, CA's (formerly known as Computer Associates) highly publicized negative experience with sales compensation should be a strong incentive for top managers to focus attention on the behavior and performance that their company plan elicits.[2] Three things occurred. First, the lack of internal controls and paying multiple sales employees for the same sales resulted in added commission costs of $70 million in fiscal year 2006. Next, the issue of backdating sales contracts to achieve quarterly revenue targets led to the former head of sales being sentenced to seven years in prison after pleading guilty to that scheme. Finally, CA's former CEO was sentenced to 12 years in prison for his role in creating a "35 day month" to book extra revenue after a quarter ended.

Finally, sales compensation plans do grow obsolete over time. Plan obsolescence is largely a function of the changes that take place in how customers buy or in the way they expect the purchasing process to work. Demands placed on sales roles change as a result of new buying patterns; however, compensation plans either do not change or are changed too late to reflect the new requirement for successfully selling to and interacting with customers. Industries dramatically impacted by the Internet—media advertising, retail automotive, residential real estate, and stock brokerage are but a few examples—have had to fundamentally rethink how they compensate for sales success.

As a recent study reported, the human resources professional can have a meaningful impact on a company's business performance.[3] These sales compensation challenges offer an opportunity for HR practitioners to contribute to business success by strengthening their involvement with plan design, implementation, and on-going management. The overall objective of this chapter is to discuss how HR practitioners can capitalize on and fulfill the need that their companies have for their expertise in this important area of compensation. We believe that HR practitioners should be equipped to make significant and meaningful contributions in this area of compensation because attracting, hiring, and retaining sales talent is the number one challenge faced today by companies in most parts of the world. The right people in the right sales jobs make the difference between business success and failure. Thus, there is perhaps no greater contribution that HR can make to a business than ensuring that sales compensation plays a pivotal role in attracting and retaining the right talented people.

THE NEED FOR INCREASED HR INVOLVEMENT

In recent years, we have surveyed top managers to ask them to identify the work that HR professionals could do that would be valued when they are involved with sales compensation. The four most prevalent responses were:

- Help clarify the business objectives that the plan should support
- Provide benchmarking data on pay levels and practices

■ Gather market intelligence on change—who is making changes to their plans, to what and why?

■ Conduct analyses and provide interpretation of plan effectiveness particularly pay versus performance results

Figure 20.1 provides comments from representatives of leading companies that are illustrative of top management's expectations of HR involvement with sales compensation that add color to these prevalent responses.

We believe that HR's involvement with sales compensation is significantly greater today than was the case in previous years for three reasons.

1. *Sales talent.* In most companies, top management looks to the compensation plan to help attract and retain the caliber of people it needs to successfully sell to and interact with customers. According to a recent Manpower survey, attracting and retaining top-notch sales talent is the most serious challenge faced by companies on a global basis.[4] Manpower surveyed approximately

FIGURE 20.1   Comments

Benchmarking helps top executives cut through the noise around needing to pay more for this position or that position, and allows them to see where our company stands on a Total Cash basis compared to our competitors for talent.
The in-depth knowledge and use of Best Practices is invaluable to top executives in that it allows them to simply convey the company's key drivers for the upcoming year, while having confidence that the Sales Compensation team will build them a plan around those key drivers that will have the greatest impact for their investment.
          Steve Long, Leader – Sales Policy and Planning, D&B, Short Hills, NJ

Our sales executives, CEO and Compensation Committee expect HR to work with our sales comp consultants to develop plans that are attuned to the business and drive the behavior of our sales people in a manner that supports the strategic and operational objectives of the Company.
In addition, they expect us to deliver clear information of how our practices compare to other companies in our space. Relevant, accurate market intelligence is essential to our understanding how to attract and retain talent as well as to assure appropriate management controls and oversight of our compensation practices.
          Mike Major, Vice President, HR AMCC Corporation, Sunnyvale, CA

Concise analytical data thaprovides a clear path for decisions in two areas:
1) Competitive intelligence on market pay and plan design practices; how much money do we pay and how do we deliver it?
2) Diagnosis of actual selling behavior vsplan intent, a.k.a., what plan features show them the money?
          Pete Gardner, Senior Manager, Compensation, Philips Medical Systems, Bothell, WA

37,000 employers in 27 countries. Forty-one percent of the employers indicated they were having difficulty hiring employees and the number one most difficult position to recruit and hire was sales representative. Because a strong sales force is a major competitive advantage, particularly in markets where product commoditization is occurring, HR can make a major contribution to a company's business by partnering with sales leadership to shape compensation plans that attract and retain talented people to sales jobs. Doing so will help sales leadership overcome one of the most serious challenges to business growth, that is, fielding talented, experienced, and well-qualified individuals who can work effectively with customers.

2. *Cost.* In the last couple of years, particularly in North America where, in many industries, the rate of growth has been slower than elsewhere in the world, top managers express concern that the sales compensation plan may be "too rich." A variety of factors could contribute to this situation. For example, in a financial services company that found its sales compensation costs were growing at a rate four times greater than revenue, the architecture of the compensation was largely the reason for that result. Pay levels were set at the 75th percentile for all sales jobs rather than the sales jobs that were chartered to sell new business that supported aggressive revenue growth goals. In the interests of being "fair," mix and leverage ratios were also the same for all sales jobs. Finally, sales crediting practices which allowed multiple sales and sales support roles to be "credited" for the same dollars of sales further contributed to the cost–productivity problem at that company. Fortunately, at that company, when asked by sales leadership to do so, the HR staff possessed both the knowledge and experience to step in and to formulate a change management effort to bring sales compensation costs in line with future financial requirements. What the HR practitioners did at that company is essentially what all HR practitioners involved with sales compensation must know how to do. Specifically, an HR practitioner should be capable of assisting sales leadership with a careful examination and assessment of:

   a. Pay levels, mix and leverage

   b. Performance range, i.e., threshold, quota and excellence levels

   c. Quota performance, particularly percentage of sales force achieving or exceeding quota

   d. Overachievement incentive pay, i.e., ratio to target incentive pay and percentage of sales people earning it

   e. Sales crediting, i.e., the number of sales people and their managers receiving credit for the same dollar of sales.

3. *Audit and compliance.* In 2002, Congress passed the Sarbanes–Oxley Act as a response to accounting and finance scandals occurring in major, publicly

held corporations. Essentially, the act is intended to protect investors by improving the accuracy and reliability of corporate disclosures. While the provisions of that act do not specifically address sales compensation, nonetheless there has been a "trickle-down" effect because companies and their Boards have increasingly become concerned about all forms of compensation and the adequacy of controls to monitor it. With that background in mind, we observe that top management is mandating annual audits of sales compensation plans for compliance with specific rules and requirements. In one example of this, a leading global software company has defined decision making about sales compensation as either centralized or localized. Centralized or corporate decisions are made about roles and job eligibility, performance measures, some formula mechanics (e.g., use of bonus versus commission), quota-setting processes, crediting rules, and key policies concerning employee status. Localized or country level decisions are made about pay levels, salary and incentive ratios, leverage ratios, some formula mechanics (e.g., how to structure the pay for performance relationship within the preferred incentive plan), individual quotas, and pay frequency. Under this type of arrangement HR, typically working hand in hand with finance, is responsible for ensuring that the division of accountabilities is executed as prescribed.

KNOWLEDGE AND SKILLS REQUIRED FOR INCREASED INVOLVEMENT

The degree of an HR practitioner's involvement with a sales compensation plan varies from company to company. In some companies, HR's involvement is actively sought and encouraged by the top sales executive. In other companies, HR has no involvement. To better understand the prevalence and types of HR involvement with sales compensation, we regularly survey companies across many industries. As illustrated in Figure 20.2, in about two-thirds of the companies we surveyed, HR's role ranges from intimate involvement throughout the entire design and administration process to limited involvement at the time of final plan review and approval.

In recent years, we have found that HR practitioners are being asked to play a more active role in plan design and implementation because it uses their expertise in key people management areas. These include ensuring that a company's sales compensation plan is designed to attract and retain the right caliber of salespeople and recognizes and rewards those who achieve the business results management desires. Thus, it is clear that developing and using a compensation plan that helps a company achieve those objectives should draw upon the expertise of its HR professionals.

To make a meaningful contribution to a company's sales compensation plan, an HR practitioner must demonstrate to sales executives that they have the experience and skill to participate in the process. This means that an HR practitioner

FIGURE 20.2   Characterization of involvement

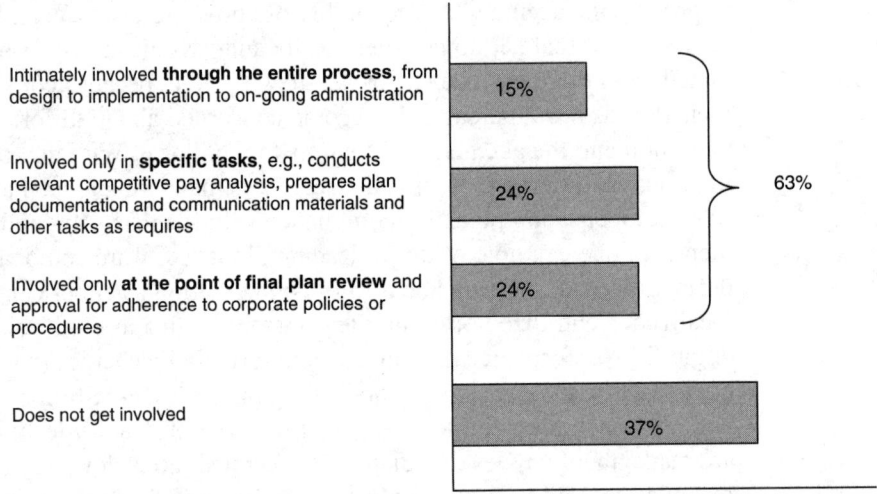

Intimately involved **through the entire process**, from design to implementation to on-going administration — 15%

Involved only in **specific tasks**, e.g., conducts relevant competitive pay analysis, prepares plan documentation and communication materials and other tasks as requires — 24%

Involved only **at the point of final plan review** and approval for adherence to corporate policies or procedures — 24%

63%

Does not get involved — 37%

Source: Colletti–Fiss, LLC Survey, 39 Companies

must win the confidence of the sales leadership team. An appropriate way to do that is by exhibiting an understanding of how the sales organization operates. That understanding includes knowledge of the following:

- Customer markets and the product or service offerings provided
- Sales channels jobs
- Current year's business plan, sales strategies and sales financial goals
- Centralized vs decentralized sales management approach relative to various sales management programs
- Industry competitors and their pay levels and incentive plan practices

HR practitioners who have successfully developed this understanding have done so as a result of building effective working relationships with senior sales leaders and other key staff managers in sales operations, sales finance and IT. Specifically, they do the following:

1. Participate in sales leadership meetings related to the future business planning and, thus, gain insight into the implications for sales compensation change

2. Engage in regular "work withs" with sellers and sales managers to understand the sales processes used to do business with customers and the requirements for success in those sales jobs

3. Join and participate in industry networking groups to understand the challenges faced by others in the industry and their experiences in key practices areas

4. Participate in "job matching" sessions, if enrolled in industry market surveys, to understand job similarities and differences among companies in the industry

5. With sales leaders or sales staff, attend industry trade shows or events to gain insight into current business challenges and opportunities

Meaningful involvement is more likely to take place in a company where the HR practitioner has developed a thorough understanding of how the sales organization operates and has built an effective working relationship with key sales leaders throughout the sales organization. Additionally, HR practitioners must develop and continually improve upon their knowledge of sales compensation principles, practices, and techniques; doing so requires exposure to the practices of other companies that is best gained through active networking. Every HR practitioner that is involved with sales compensation should regularly ask themselves how they can further develop their knowledge base and expertise in tools and techniques related to innovative sales compensation solutions.

ALIGNING SALES COMPENSATION TO BUSINESS STRATEGY

The sales compensation plan needs to support the company's business strategy. Three of the more important elements of business strategy include: business objectives (e.g., financial goals—growth, profit, shareholder return); marketing strategy (e.g., offerings, value proposition, markets targeted, channels used); and sales strategy (e.g., the plan of action that defines how to sell to and interact with customers). The sales compensation plan design effort should follow a series of decision making steps that, when successfully completed, insure that the plan is consistent with business strategy.

Designing a sales compensation plan is a derivative process. That is, the design of the proper plan is derived from the circumstances and objectives unique to that company. Increasingly, the HR practitioner is being asked to play a role in the plan design process. Depending on traditions at a particular company, that role may vary from team member to subject matter expert to process leader. Regardless of the exact role the HR practitioner plays, over the years we have found that the most significant challenge faced by companies during the design process is to understand exactly how to link strategy, jobs, performance measures, and goals, and pay together into an optimal plan. Thus, this requires that the HR practitioner facilitate a process with tools that help those involved in sales compensation design clearly define the type of selling to be performed by the sales force.

We have found the Sales Strategy Matrix[SM] to be a helpful tool to clarify sales jobs and to align those jobs with the company's business objectives. As Figure 20.3 illustrates, there are two variables: buyers and products. Buyers fall into two groups: prospects and customers. Products also fall into two groups: existing and new or additional in line. This two-by-two matrix defines the types of selling opportunities facing a company in each quadrant of the matrix.

FIGURE 20.3   Sales strategy mix

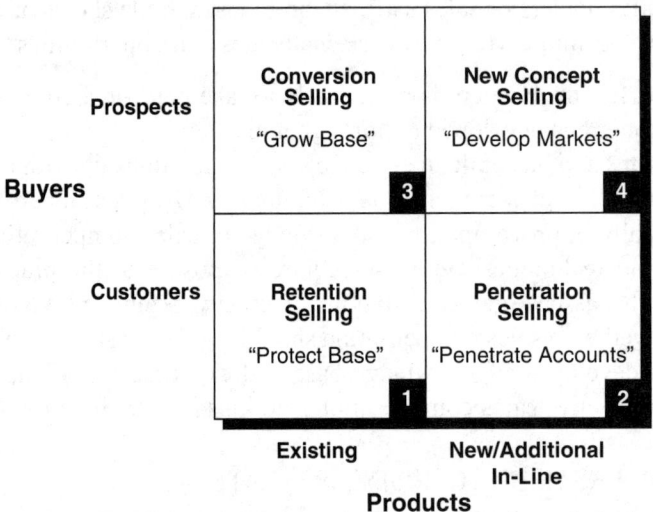

The four selling opportunities are:

1. *Retention selling*—the objective of retention selling is to sell established customers current products on a reorder basis. The sales job is to successfully retain the revenue stream of business with those customers.

2. *Penetration selling*—this type of selling involves maximizing the customer relationship by selling a broader range of products (new or existing) to current customers or selling more to customers within an established account.

3. *Conversion selling*—the objective of conversion selling is to get competitors' customers to switch to the company's products.

4. *New market selling*—this type of selling is probably the most difficult; its objective is to attract new customers to the company by selling new products.

While every situation is individual, one of the principal values of the Sales Strategy Matrix^SM is to provide a framework to define and deploy a company's sales jobs. Figure 20.4 illustrates one likely set of sales jobs that a company could deploy in attracting, retaining, and expanding business with customers.

The four jobs illustrated in this figure are:

1. *Account manager*—our research shows that it is typical for an established company to realize 60–80 percent of its business from selling in-line products to current customers. When this is a company's goal—to retain current business and to expand by selling additional products or new

FIGURE 20.4 Set of sales jobs

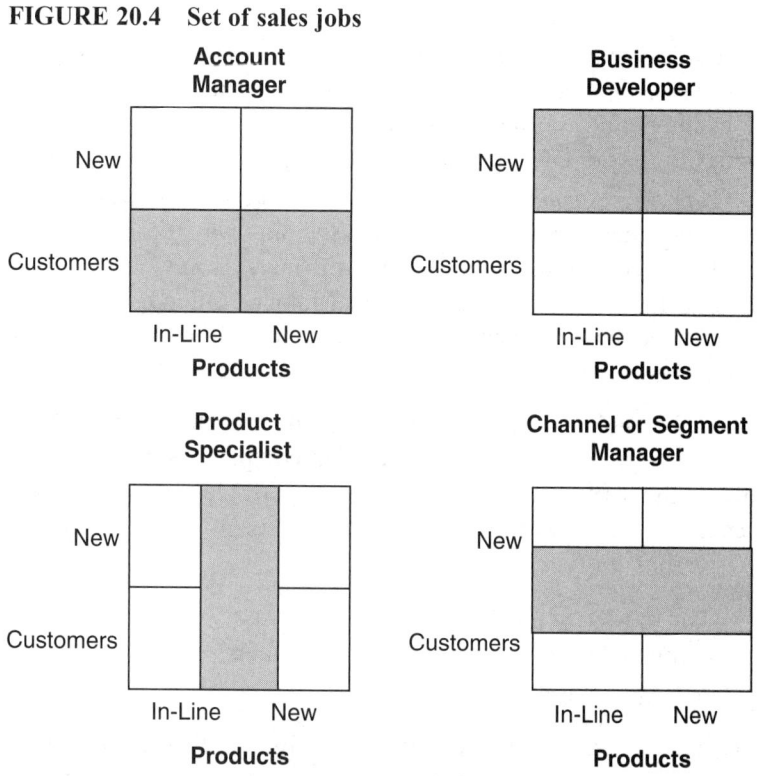

products to buyers within the current account base—an account manager job is established. In recent years, companies have learned that account managers can be deployed in a variety of ways—in an assigned geography, by an assigned industry, by assigned accounts covered telephonically—and, by doing so, the percentage of revenue realized through customer retention can be substantial and profitable.

2. *Business developer*—many companies have discovered that the sales cycle differs by the type of customer. For example, winning business with a new customer often takes three to four times longer than doing more business with a current customer. Thus, some companies adopt a "business developer" job. The focus of that job is to attract new customers to a company by selling current in line products, new products, or both.

3. *Product sales specialist*—a company with a single, large sales force that represents the products of many business divisions often finds that it is impractical for its sales representatives to be "experts" in the application of all products. Thus, one form of sales specialization that is used is the product sales specialist job. This job specializes in understanding a buyer's

(current customer or new buyer) unique requirements and then tailoring the solution with the right mix of a company's products and services. Product sales specialists typically work across a broad slice of a market; however, it would not be unusual for individuals in this job to be dedicated either to a defined set of customers or to targeting new accounts.

4. *Channel or segment sales manager*—as a business grows and matures, management comes to realize that the only way it can address the diversity of sales opportunities available in the markets in which it competes is to consider new routes of access to customers. Often it is more efficient and effective for a company to reach customers through a nondirect sales force channel.

The number and type of sales jobs (and sales channels) derived from applying the Sales Strategy Matrix^{SM} to a particular company is largely influenced by the growth and profit expectations of top managers. Our research shows, however, that when a company is examining the effectiveness of its sales compensation, the top three reasons for doing so are to:

1. Improve sales productivity
2. Improve sales coverage to current customers
3. Grow sales overall profitably

Thus, to achieve these objectives, we observe that companies that are most satisfied with their sales compensation plan start with a review and clarification of the types of sales jobs used to do business with customers.

ESTABLISHING THE "GROUND RULES" FOR PLAN DESIGN

Prior to the actual plan design process, it is critical to establish the basis for decisions about sales compensation plan elements. The two key areas that require management's attention are the company's philosophy of pay, and the principles or rules that establish expectations for the program. Both of these areas will benefit from the HR practitioner's leadership and guidance.

Philosophy of Pay.   In order to develop an effective sales compensation plan, its design should be consistent with an organization's compensation philosophy. Frequently, this philosophy is informal, undocumented, or both. Therefore, we suggest that plan designers discuss with management and then document the company's compensation philosophy, using the following list of key criteria:

1. *Objectives*—confirmation of the strategic purpose of compensation and its elements
2. *Labor market comparison*—identification of relevant companies and job matches
3. *Competitive positioning*—percentile standing for pay levels

4. *Salary/variable pay ratio*—based on the company's philosophy of risk versus reward, competitive practice, and the influence of eligible job(s) in getting and keeping business with customers

5. *Base salary determination*—factors and practices that will be used in setting and adjusting base salary

6. *Short-term incentives*—eligibility and type of incentives considered appropriate

7. *Long-term incentives*—eligibility and type of incentive considered appropriate

8. *Communication*—roles and responsibilities

Confirming this information is the first step to ensuring that the sales compensation plan will be designed to be consistent with other compensation programs in the company.

Compensation Principles.   Typically, the design of a sales compensation plan is influenced by the compensation philosophy and practices used throughout a company. In fact, in many companies' top managers ask human resources or the compensation function to insure that the sales compensation plan is in alignment with the enterprise's programs because employees are moved in and out of the sales organization as part of a company-wide career development initiative. With that background in mind, sales compensation plans should be grounded in core principles that are compatible with those that guide a company's overall compensation and reward system. While there are many publications—including this Handbook—that provide details about the tenets of effective and appropriate compensation, the following briefly summarizes essentials that a sales compensation plan designer should keep in mind:

1. The compensation philosophy must actively reinforce the company's strategy and vision to achieve its objectives.

2. Compensation programs must be consistent with legal and regulatory requirements.

3. Compensation should be consistent with the financial requirements and administrative capabilities of the company.

4. Compensation must be consistent with both internal equity, and external requirements to attract, retain, and motivate talented employees.

5. Compensation program details must be based on clearly defined jobs, and their role within the buying and selling process.

In addition to these core principles, it is generally useful to establish other "ground rules" specific to a company's needs. Consideration should be given to the following topics:

1. *Business objectives*—what objectives are critical for this year? What objectives must the plan reinforce?

2. *Strategy*—what are the company's marketing and sales strategies?

3. *Job definition*—what jobs will be required to achieve the company's strategies?

4. *Performance measurement*—how should performance be defined and tracked over time? How should performance objectives be set? What level of achievement should be expected? What is the range of performance that can be used in sales compensation plan design?

5. *Compensation plan*—who should be involved in the design process? What mechanics are most appropriate to direct and motivate the sales jobs?

6. *Administration*—when should we credit performance for incentive purposes? What is our communication strategy? Who should be involved?

SIX ESSENTIAL COMPONENTS OF PLAN DESIGN

There are six essential components of sales compensation. Figure 20.5 illustrates the relationship of these components to business management considerations addressed prior to plan design. The ideal design process, including the sequence of decisions required, is a derivative process. That is, the design of an effective and appropriate plan is based on the solid foundation provided by business management decisions for the plan year.

In order to address the objectives and strategy of complex business environments, companies generally charter a "design team," or a designated group of

FIGURE 20.5

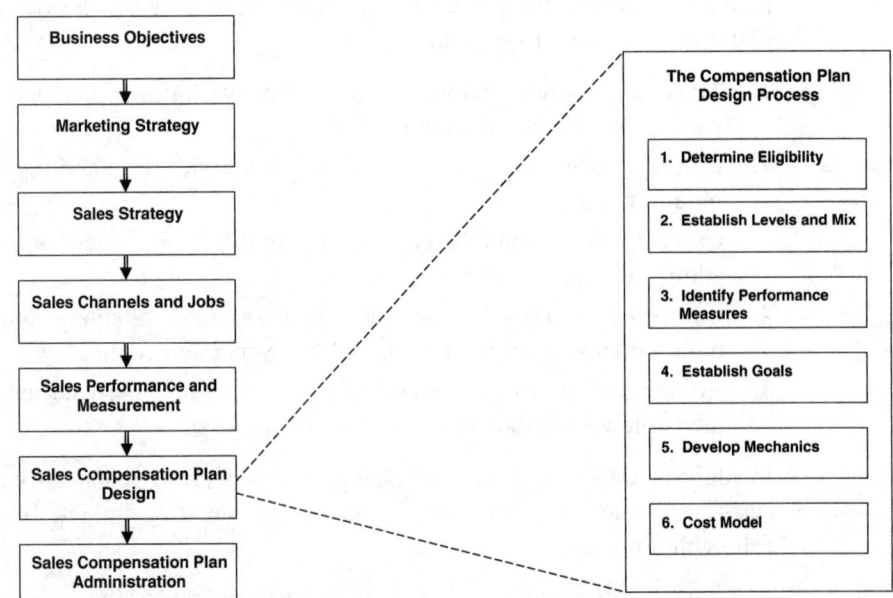

cross-functional resources that bring to the process the necessary knowledge and focus. Increasingly, we see that the responsibility for assembling the team and managing the design process is a key responsibility either assigned to or shared with HR. Functions most frequently represented on this type of team are marketing, sales management, human resources, finance, sales administration, and information systems. A team approach to plan design results in more widespread buy-in to the new sales compensation program, earlier ability of key executives to impact the decision making process, and a plan that is aligned with multiple objectives. Six essential components must be addressed through the design process.

Step 1: Confirm Jobs and Eligibility

Key concept: determine incentive eligibility based on degree of impact in the buying decision and participation in the process to access, persuade and fulfill customer needs.

Typically, these are positions that initiate, persuade, and fulfill in the customer coverage process, and those positions' line managers are eligible to participate in the sales compensation program. Corporate philosophy is also a key determinant in eligibility to participate in a sales compensation program. For example, team members may be eligible for sales compensation only so long as they are on a customer team.

Step 2: Establish Pay Levels and Mix

Key concept: ensure that pay levels are externally competitive, and internally equitable, based on the roles and responsibilities of the job.

The total target cash compensation is the cash compensation (including base salary and variable incentive compensation) available for achieving expected results. Use of market data and application of the company's philosophy of pay result in a reference point for decisions about the level of compensation the company is willing to pay for each job. The total target cash compensation level for each job must be large enough to motivate and to pay for performance to drive business results.

Determination of the pay level for each job serves as a foundation for decisions related to mix (ratio of base salary to incentive opportunity as percentages of the total target compensation; expressed as two portions of 100 percent) and leverage (the amount of "upside" opportunity beyond total target compensation that outstanding performers are expected to earn). The mix is determined by defined criteria, including the type of sale, sales cycle duration, number of transactions in a year, and degree of influence the job has on the decision to buy. The sales compensation plan should provide upside opportunity (leverage) consistent with the job, the company's philosophy of pay, and labor market realities. Outstanding pay should generally be available for excellent performers (i.e., the plan should provide increased dollars on the upside after target performance is achieved).

Step 3: Identify Performance Measures

Key concept: you get what you pay for. Three or fewer measures should be used, based on the key objectives of the organization, and the key accountabilities of the job.

This is perhaps the most critical design component to address effectively. Several decisions are required in order to ensure that the performance measures selected are aligned with the business and the job, as follows:

1. *Confirm business objectives impacted by the job(s).* Examples include growth, profitability, productivity improvement, cost reduction, customer loyalty and retention, or some combination of these five.

2. *Select the indicators that are associated with achievement of those objectives.* Ensure that systems or processes are in place for measurement. If a key indicator cannot be consistently tracked and achievement calculated, potential alternatives must be identified and examined.

3. *Ensure that the measures are consistent with the job.* Measures used in the sales compensation plan should be influenced through reasonable effort and behavior. Measures must be based on job roles, and the salesperson's ability to impact results.

4. *Determine level of measurement.* The unit of aggregation of results (territory, accounts, team, etc.) for the purposes of sales compensation calculation should be based on the level at which results are impacted by the job, and the level to which company systems can accurately track, credit, and report results.

5. *Confirm the relative importance of each measure.* The "weight" of each measure in the plan is based on the strategic importance of each to the achievement of business objectives. As well, the relative weight among measures helps the sales force understand how to deploy its time, based on the plan message and its alignment with management requirements.

The sales function is primarily responsible for the maximization of top-line results. Therefore, a measure of total volume is generally the first consideration for any sales job. The design process determines the appropriate measure of overall volume that can be associated with a sales person's performance. This may mean total sales dollar volume, sales volume from new business, new business and recurring sales dollar volume from regular customer ordering (a measure of retention), revenue derived from volume, or number of units sold. In most plans, one measure should be a volume measure that rewards growth.

Additional criteria should complement the volume measure, communicating what type of volume is best, where the volume should come from, or how it should be achieved. Additional categories to consider include profitability (financial measures), sales productivity (may include both financial and nonfinancial measures), and strategic planning (generally nonfinancial measures).

Step 4: Set Goals

Key concept: assign expectations for key performance measures based on job influence, and a uniform process.

Once performance measures have been selected, many companies assign goals to the sales force for one or all of the selected measures. Particularly for volume or profitability-focused measures, these goals are frequently referred to as a quota. In the past, companies used primarily financial measures of performance in the sales compensation plan, and perhaps 50 percent of all companies established quotas. Many companies simply assigned a uniform percentage or dollar increase across the sales force, based on the growth objectives for the plan year.

In today's competitive environment, many more companies are establishing performance expectations for both financial and nonfinancial measures. The process to arrive at goals varies widely across industries, companies, and types of measures. Regardless of practices, many firms find quota setting to be difficult, and express frustration at both the process and the outcomes. However, giving proper attention to setting goals is essential to the success of the sales compensation plan. Properly assigning goals provides the opportunity to manage for results, allows for maximum flexibility, and visibly aligns the success of field resources with corporate resources.

Once goals are established, attention should be given to the "performance standards" or the performance range associated with incentive payout. The sales compensation plan has varying degrees of payout depending on performance levels. Below a certain level of performance, no payout should occur. A threshold level of performance is used to communicate minimum standards of performance. Above a certain level of performance, many companies provide higher amounts. While a ceiling or "cap" is used in cases where it is difficult or impossible to set realistic ranges, an "uncapped" plan is generally desirable. However, earnings above an "excellence" level should become increasingly difficult to achieve. Some statistical "rules of thumb" for the performance range are based on an optimal performance distribution (e.g., 90 percent achieve threshold, 60–70 percent achieve or exceed goal, 10–15 percent reach or exceed excellence).

Step 5: Develop Incentive Mechanics

Key concept: select plan mechanics based on desired relationship between pay and performance.

"Sales compensation" in its broadest sense includes all elements of remuneration for sales and sales management positions. While base-salary-only plans are appropriate for nonpersuasive selling environments, many companies are moving to putting some percentage of pay "at risk," even for "nonselling" jobs in customer coverage organizations. Therefore, in this final component of plan design, all previous components are aligned through the plan mechanics associated with the incentive (or variable) element of total cash compensation. Mechanics refer to the type of plan, plan formula, and the ways in which incentive elements interact to calculate payment.

Plan Types.   There are two primary plan types, commission plans and bonus plans. Either may be used in conjunction with base salary, or both may be used. As well, either a bonus or a commission may use a quota or goal; however, bonus plans always use some type of goal, while commissions may or may not use a goal or quota as one element in the calculation.

A commission plan provides a percentage share or dollar amount tied to gross dollar sales, product unit sales, or gross profit dollars. Commission programs support absolute measurement systems—the more of a product or service sold, the greater the incentive paid. Commission may be "capped" or "uncapped." This type of plan is most commonly used in new-market selling situations where individual persuasion skills and short sales cycles are key differentiators. Organizations use commission programs to reward individual effort and drive results, with payout directly tied to sales results. In some industries, commissions have typically been used to push new products and gain market share with specialized sales forces.

Bonuses are a percentage of base pay, or a fixed dollar amount, for accomplishing objectives. They are most appropriately used in more complex sales environments, and are always "goal-based," whether the goal is financial (volume, profitability, productivity) or nonfinancial. These programs support a relative measurement system—payout depends on performance against individual goals. They may be "capped" or "uncapped." A salary plus bonus plan manages the amount of incentive payout to a preferred market rate while accommodating goal-based measurement.

Plan Formulas.   Plan formulas may be "linked" or "unlinked." An "unlinked" formula is a series of additive payouts. A "linked" formula means that payout for one measure depends on achievement of another. "Linking" measures together in the formula ensures a clear message that two performance measures must receive the salesperson's attention. There are three ways to accomplish a linkage:

- *Gate (or hurdle)*—hurdles are the minimum performance levels a salesperson must achieve in one plan component to be eligible for variable pay in a different component.

- *Multiplier*—multipliers or modifiers *increase or decrease* the salesperson's earnings in that plan component based on their performance in another measure.

- *Matrix*—the matrix design is used when there are two competing performance measures against which the salesperson must perform. The salesperson has to manage performance between two measures.

Step 6: Cost Model

Key concept: the final design is based on the results of both aggregate costing (effect on the company) and individual plan modeling (effect on individuals).

This step may be completed by finance and human resources, working with sales or sales operations. The results are critical in order to finalize such plan elements as the performance range (threshold and excellence), the upside available at excellence, and the relative weight of each measure. Until this step is complete, the plan cannot be considered "final."

IMPLEMENTATION OF THE SALES COMPENSATION PROGRAM

Even the best designed plans will fail if they are not implemented properly. A successful implementation will test the new plan, gain support throughout the organization, educate the company, and limit transition inefficiencies. Successful implementation uses various principles of adult learning to effectively and efficiently communicate and install a new sales compensation plan. As the implementation plan is developed, the HR practitioner should confirm that four critical elements of learning are addressed:

- *Motivation.* Adults are goal-oriented and want to see the reason for learning what is being taught, e.g., how to succeed under the plan.

- *Reinforcement.* Media and techniques should ensure that the message the company intends the plan to convey is consistently and positively reinforced.

- *Retention.* Adults must see a purpose for what is being communicated. The materials and media should include "practice" sessions to ensure that the participants have direct experience in how the plan works, and how they can affect the payout.

- *Transference.* The information that the media and materials convey must be transferred into positive action on the part of the participant. The participant should be excited, and want to use the information to enhance their current situation.

The thought of change in any aspect of sales compensation is daunting to most salespeople. Successful change management initiatives require an understanding of potential issues in order to anticipate the types of difficulties that may arise when something is new or done for the first time with the sales compensation plan. Typically, HR practitioners have experience and skill in how to structure and roll out change. It is a good idea, therefore, to use a structured change management process to guide planning and decision making tasks related to the implementation of a new sales compensation plan. The objectives of a change process, as it pertains to introducing a new sales compensation plan, are to help:

■ Define specific changes and accountabilities

■ Explain why change is important now

■ Provide a framework for guiding the change process

■ Determine whether desired benefits and improvements are being achieved

■ Provide feedback to work associates who need to remain "in the know" about change results

We have found that a three-step process to address these objectives is required for effective implementation. Briefly, the process involves the following:

1. Field managers who manage with the plan, and headquarters resources that administer the plan should be fully knowledgeable about the company's philosophy of compensation, the principles used to guide plan development, the benefits of the program, and how plan participants can succeed under the plan. As well, all aspects of administration should be thoroughly documented and understood. A special training program for these individuals will contribute significantly to plan success. Electronic "incentive calculators," plan announcement brochures, Q&As, and formal documentation provide managers with the tools to implement and manage with the sales compensation plan. The involvement of the human resources professional is important to ensure that the materials are clear, useful and consistent with company and legal requirements.

2. Once field management and headquarters resources are trained, the program should be introduced to the sales organization. A group presentation that is led by executive management, and individual follow-up sessions to answer specific questions, are both required. Full communication, including detailed descriptions of the reports that will be available to the plan participants, are keys to successful implementation. Note that the calculation of the incentive payment is not, and should not, be the responsibility of the sales department. Calculation is based on information from various systems, and reports should be timely and accurate. Even the best designed plan is likely to be considered a failure if sales people feel they need to constantly "check up" on the accuracy of these reports.

3. A formal assessment process should be completed at least annually. However, an interim evaluation may be undertaken after one or two payout periods to determine the extent to which the plan is supporting the behaviors, and delivering the results for which it was designed. The design team, or designated member of the team, should examine the results of the evaluation and assess any need for change.

SUMMARY

Whether an HR practitioner is considered an internal consultant or a policy gate-keeper, HR involvement with the sales compensation plan is important to business success. Meaningful involvement is most likely to take place in situations where the HR practitioner has developed a thorough understanding of how sales operates and has built an effective working relationship with key sales leaders. Also, HR practitioners must develop and improve upon their knowledge of sales compensation principles, practices, and techniques. That knowledge is critical to making a meaningful contribution to the plan design and implementation process. Because most experienced HR practitioners understand human motivation and how to tap into the workforce to determine root causes of job dissatisfaction, their involvement with sales compensation opens up the opportunity for fresh insights and perspective about how to increase plan effectiveness. The result of that involvement will not only benefit the sales organization but also the company overall.

END NOTES

1. Jerome A. Colletti and Stockton Colt, "Identifying A Complex Sales Environment: Results of Special Member Survey," *Workspan Magazine*, April 2004, pp. 11–14.

2. William M. Bulkeley, "CA Latest Woes Tied to Big Sales Commissions," *Wall Street Journal*, 8 June 2006, p. A4; William M. Bulkeley, "CA Ex-Sales Chief Sentenced to 7 Years," *Wall Street Journal*, 15 November 2006, p. C4; William M. Bulkeley, "Former CA Chief is Sentenced to 12 Year Prison Term, Fined," *Wall Street Journal*, 3 November 2006, p. A3.

3. "HR Departments Have a Substantial Impact on Bottom Line Business Results," *Workspan Weekly*, 31 May 2007.

4. "Talent Shortage Survey: 2007 Global Results," Milwaukee, WI: Manpower Inc., January 2007.

21

TEAM-BASED INCENTIVES

Theresa M. Welbourne, Ph.D., Adjunct Professor of Executive Education

Ross School of Business, University of Michigan and eePulse, Inc.

Luis R. Gomez-Mejia, Ph.D., Professor of Management

W. P. Carey School of Business, Arizona State University

A GROWING NUMBER OF CORPORATIONS are moving away from the long-held belief that individual achievement and success, often through brutal competition with fellow workers, is to be encouraged and reinforced. Instead, there is an emerging emphasis on a more cooperative environment in which employees learn to share their talents and information with each other by working as a team on common tasks. Increased foreign competition, more educated employees, excessive turnover and absenteeism, the aftermath of the social revolution in the 1960s and 1970s, and fewer management positions during the 1980s and 1990s are some of the key factors often cited for this trend.

Redesigning work using a team concept provides the organization with flexibility to blend employees with unique skills and backgrounds to tackle common projects or problems. It also provides workers with more freedom, greater independence, and the ability to improve skills and use talents that might not have otherwise been tapped in a narrowly defined position. Multiple studies conducted since the early 2000s indicate that the use of teams greatly improves worker productivity;[1] induces employees to set challenging and spontaneous group goals;[2] facilitates communication across organizational barriers;[3] improves financial performance for the typical firm;[4] and engenders a social climate that promotes the exchange and combination of new knowledge, leading to the creation of new products and services.[5] Examples of companies successfully employing teams within and across various functional areas include General Motors Corp., TRW Inc., Digital Equipment Corp., Shell Oil Co., and Honeywell Inc.

Many firms also are providing team incentives to reinforce the team concept. These include well-known companies in a variety of industries such as Unisys, Hallmark Cards, Blue Cross–Blue Shields, Rockwell, Motorola, Signicast Corporation, and Smithkline Beecham, among others. Based on a survey of 2,500 corporations in the late 1990s, William Mercer Inc. found that approximately 20 percent of these firms used team-based incentives, and that another 21 percent are considering it.[6] A wide variety of formulas and approaches are used to link incentives to team performance.[7] A 2003 meta-analysis of 45 studies using team incentives found that overall the use of incentives tied to the achievement of group goals resulted in a 22 percent gain in performance. In the words of the study's authors,

> team-directed incentives had a markedly superior effect on performance compared to individually-directed incentives. This effect was not influenced by the location of the study (business, government, or school), the competitive structure of the incentive system (programs where only the highest performers get incentives versus programs where everyone who increased performance receives incentives), the type of study (whether the study was a laboratory experiment or a field study), or the performance outcome (quality, quantity, or both). In these studies, money was found to result in higher performance gains than nonmonetary, tangible incentives (gifts, travel).[8]

Based on our personal experience and interviews with managers, the most common reasons given for redesigning work into teams are:

- Quality—teams are portrayed as the most effective mechanism to improve quality rather than the traditional quality control approaches

- Greater accumulation of knowledge brought to bear on a particular problem—facilitating innovation by breaking down barriers among people and improving the flow of expertise throughout the firm

- Greater flexibility as the organization becomes less dependent on particular individuals—this provides a mechanism to absorb turnover and downsizing because other people can "fill in" as necessary

- Greater cross-fertilization of idea as people from different backgrounds share their views and experiences—this combination of diverse talent can stimulate innovation

- Less dependence on supervisor or formal hierarchies creates more autonomy, discretion, "empowerment," and "emergent leadership" within the firm

- Employees are more committed to the organization if they participate in decision making

- A corporate- or organization-wide perspective is provided so that employees can see how different units or parts of the company fit together

- Better justification for the budget for the awards program—the clearer link to specific performance outcomes, as is the case with many plans, provides the ROI data needed to provide incentives to employees formerly excluded from such plans.

Like any other personnel program, team-based management approaches do not function in a vacuum; they need the support of other human-resources systems to be effective. By putting your money where your mouth is, compensation can play a leading role in communicating the organization's commitment to the team concept. As noted in a recent study by Professor Christina Harbring, nothing can foster communication and cooperation within teams more than the use of incentives linked to the achievement of group goals.[9] Therefore, in addition to the institutional mechanisms by which team-based pay programs are coordinated with other compensation methods, the way group rewards are linked to performance will be pivotal in establishing and maintaining effective team arrangements.

ADVANTAGES AND DISADVANTAGES OF USING TEAM-BASED INCENTIVES

Like any other human resource management program, there is no panacea with the use of team incentives. There is general agreement in the literature that the advantages of team-based incentives outweigh potential problems; nevertheless, it is important to be aware of potential pitfalls so that these can be avoided.

To summarize, key advantages of team based incentives include the following,[10] all of which result in improved performance:

- Reinforcing norms of collegiality and cooperation within groups

- Helping reduce disciplinary and background diversity barriers in cross-functional work teams

- Helping teams to focus on the achievement of project goals and objectives

- Allowing firms to differentially reward teams and groups that are most strategically important

On the other side of the coin, there are some potential disadvantages with the use of team-based incentives. These need to be managed in order to ensure that the advantages noted above are forthcoming. Potential downsides with the use of team-based incentives include the following:[11]

- Free riding, that is, some team members may receive the incentive even if they have made little contribution to the achievement of group goals. This may occur due to lack of effort or perhaps because some team members have much lower ability levels or skills than other team members. To counteract this potential problem, one option is to use peer ratings to assess the contributions of individual team members.

- While team decisions enjoy greater acceptability among team members and generate greater commitment to the achievement of group goals, it is possible that the most talented individuals within the team may come up with better solutions to problems facing the team. To counteract this potential problem, team member need to be trained so that the opinions of individual team members are carefully weighed and the team avoids a rush to reach a decision.

- Difficulty of carving out independent groups for reward purposes due to interdependence. To the extent that the performance of a group is dependent on the performance of other groups, team-based incentives may be problematic since it is not possible to isolate and reward the performance of each group. One approach to deal with this issue is to amplify the size of the team being rewarded, perhaps including all teams that are interdependent with each other.

- Incompatible cultural values. As noted later, the United States is a very individualistic culture so that pushing team-based incentives too far may provoke a negative reaction among employees who believe they should be rewarded for their own personal contributions. One approach to deal with this issue is to offer a combination of individual and team-based rewards, soliciting the opinion from team members as to the appropriate mix.

- Entrepreneurship may suffer if group rewards are pushed too far. Entrepreneurs are often lonely people with their own eccentricities. They tend to be driven by their own personal desire to succeed, and the recognition of personal achievement by others. These people play a critical role in many organizations, and often do not work well in teams. Thus, even when team-based incentives are in place, allowance needs to be made for employees who exhibit a strong entrepreneurial orientation.

REWARDS TIED TO TEAM PERFORMANCE

Team incentives can be based on the concept of either pay-for-performance or pay-for-skills and/or knowledge. Pay-for-performance is the more common design in which outcomes of team effort are used as payment criteria. Objectively measured consequences might include cost savings, number of products manufactured, meeting agreed-upon deadlines, parts rejected, or the team's successful completion of a new product design and successful patent. The goals, methods of measurement, and bonus amount can be determined in advance and communicated to group members, thereby serving as an incentive for the entire team.

Bonus payments can be made in cash, corporate stocks, or through noncash items such as trips, time off, or luxury items. Payment may be distributed equally to all team members or differentially in an effort to reward those who made greater contributions to the team's objectives. If rewards are to be distributed based on the individual's contribution to the team's goals, then the organization must employ a method of individual-based performance measurement. Rather than granting a lead or supervisor the responsibility for evaluating individual contributions, team members may rate each worker's performance, and the group's consensus can be employed for distributing rewards.

When team rewards are distributed differentially to individuals, the element of competition among team members creeps into the team concept. Team bonus payments can easily evolve into simple just one more method of merit pay, and the processes of dividing bonus money among individual members can then be contaminated with the multitude of errors cited in traditional pay-for-performance systems. One also has the added problem of differentiating between true performance and the results of a popularity contest when using peer evaluations.

Team-based pay-for-skills and/or knowledge is a second approach. It is important to differentiate this from other pay-for-skill plans based on individual performance. Manufacturing plants are experimenting with skill-based pay plans in which members of the organization increase their pay when they acquire additional skills and can master new tasks within the plant, usually as a result of extensive cross-training efforts within their team. Although the members might be working in teams, each individual increases his or her pay by improving personal skills. This form of knowledge-based pay is individual-oriented rather than team-based and reinforces individual accomplishments in the same manner that merit pay traditionally rewards workers for self-improvement.

Skill-based pay, at the team level, on the other hand, rewards group members for increasing their ability to work as a team. Cooperation with other teams might be an important criterion for payment; ability to work effectively together on problem-solving assignments might be another. The important distinction is that all team members are rewarded when the skills of the entire team, not just the skills of specific individual members, are improved. Corporations experiencing problems with competition among various teams might find this type of incentive useful to increase cooperation among teams.[12]

This same approach can be used to reward the team when each member has attained new skills. Rather than rewarding one person for learning a new job, the entire team might be compensated when all team members are satisfactorily cross-trained or the team's evaluation can be dependent upon its ability, to bring each team member up to speed. This provides incentives for the more competent employees to assist the struggling employees. It also motivates team members to evaluate each other's performance in a more open, honest environment. Because team members are aware that one person's nonperformance can hinder the rewards to all members, a poorly performing employee is likely to be quickly discovered and dealt with by members of the team.[13]

REASONS FOR CHOOSING TEAM INCENTIVES

Rewards based on team performance will affect the business' ability to attract, retain, and motivate employees and will mold the corporation's culture. Team-compensation plans should be chosen when they are consistent with both the nature of the work and the goal setting of the organization and the team.

Nature of Work

Recent efforts to redesign jobs have focused on enhancing cooperative work relationships among employees to attain desired outcomes, such as improved quality, increased quantity, enhanced communication, and lower costs. Manufacturing programs, such as just-in-time inventories, require constant communication among sales representatives, field engineers, and inventory personnel. Since the nature of much work today requires cooperation among team members, incentive plans that reward the team's performance provide workers with feedback that will reinforce the organization's goals and strategies.

A cooperative work environment was defined by M. Deutsch as one in which the objectives of individual employees are mingled together in such a way that there is a positive correlation among the group member's goal attainment. In other words, no one individual can achieve success without the willingness of coworkers to contribute to the desired performance outcome. This type of work requires compensation programs that emphasize group outcomes rather than individual outcomes.[14]

The concept of individual pay programs stems from economic theories that indicate that individual contracts between employees and the organization are formed in a working relationship. Thus, the sum of all individual employment contracts forms the corporation. This concept has a number of problems associated with it due to the intercorrelated nature of most work. A group of employees independently working on separate goals and objectives is inefficient in an organization that does not have a number of individual goals but rather one objective that requires cooperation among individual workers.

An often-cited example of failure of this concept can be found in traditional sales-commission plans. The sales representative is commonly paid strictly for units sold, representing an individual contract between the salesperson and the employer. Unfortunately, the contract only delineates the amount of money the sales representative receives based on the quantity of goods sold rather than on the quality of information delivered to the customer. This may create a tremendous customer-relations problem that is only realized after the sale. The customer service representatives and field technicians are often extremely frustrated due to the salesperson's disinterest and inability to effectively relay information to either the customer or to headquarters offices. The employment contract between the salesperson and the company specifies only units sold. Therefore, the contractor is not concerned with cooperating with the customer service group, home office, or field representatives. By narrowly defining the jobs, the firms' goal of effective sales and service is not realized. The result is confusion within the organization and a poor image conveyed to the customer. This type of work is intrinsically team-oriented, and team rewards could assist in realizing the organization's true goals, with both volume and quality.

GOAL SETTING

There has been an abundance of research suggesting that goal setting leads to improved performance.[15] Most of the studies have focused on individual goal setting and resulting individual performance, although few studies have considered the issue of group goals and subsequent group performance. In general, it appears that group goal setting does lead to improved group performance when the goals are accepted by the group members.[16] The goals should be difficult, therefore providing a challenge for the team members, but not unattainable.[17] It has also been suggested that group goal-setting processes persuade individuals within the team who have not accepted the team's goals to personalize the group's goals.[18]

Research has also found that linking group rewards to the achievement of group goals has a positive effect on team performance.[19] When combined with consequences, such as rewards, it appears that goal setting has a long-term effect on the team's performance.[20] Compensation programs provide an essential feedback link for the goal-setting process. Pay related to the goals set by the team signifies that the organization is committed to the program, and the feedback provided when regarding the team provides employees with positive reinforcement in addition to an incentive to continue pursuing the team's goals.

TWO EXAMPLES: SELF-MANAGED WORK TEAMS AND RESEARCH AND DEVELOPMENT TEAMS

As the traditional corporate hierarchy continues to evolve into a more egalitarian structure with emphasis on participative management, new organizational forms are being introduced.

Self-managed work teams are currently utilized by manufacturing and non-manufacturing firms that have found the traditional form of supervisor, lead and worker ineffective in promoting autonomous decision making and high levels of cooperation.

Self-managed work teams are formed by a group of employees, usually all at equal status within the hierarchy, who work together in identifying goals and objectives, solving problems, and completing stated performance objectives. The team's responsibility can also encompass personnel matters such as hiring, disciplining, evaluating, rewarding, and firing team members. Such teams are currently being used in many manufacturing firms in which individuals need to closely cooperate to perform tasks. The Sherwin-Williams Co., for example, emphasized work teams in an effort to allow employees to more effectively handle the numerous product changes required in their plant while also maintaining high quality standards.[21] A flat organizational structure with emphasis on operators' contributions to their team's tasks was developed and complemented by an open-plant design allowing workers access to all stages of the production process.

Moving to the concept of team management vs individual workers reporting to a supervisor enhances an environment of close cooperation and allows workers to contribute more effectively to job completion. Employees are more committed to the goals of the group than when individuals are competing under traditional systems. The effectiveness of these teams has been greatly enhanced with the employment of compensation mechanisms that reward the team for accomplishment of team objectives, whether these be performance-based, such as meeting a stated output goal, or process-based, such as improving management skills. The pay system that rewards team members for accomplishment of team goals delivers an important message to workers that management supports team performance and team goals are important to the corporation.

Luis Gomez-Mejia and D. Balkin studied 175 scientists and engineers and found that aggregate rewards were more effective for research and development teams than individual rewards. The nature of research and development work requires teamwork and cooperation by scientists and engineers, who often have competing personal goals due to their scientific training and interest in pursuing strictly research-oriented activities vs customer-oriented projects. Aggregate incentive plans help bring their personal objective into alignment with the organization's needs. These authors found that an additional reason for the effectiveness of team incentives was the absence of adequate individual measures of performance for these professionals. Research and development teams make progress in leaps rather than gradually, and it is hard to measure the contributions of one individual to the team's success in ventures such as designing a new product or creating a unique technology. Team-based bonus programs were also found to provide the organization with more flexibility in timing the reward to match team accomplishments.

Two primary advantages of using team incentives for research and development work rather than individual-based programs or organization-wide plans such as profit sharing were uncovered by Gomez-Mejia and Balkin. First, compensation is more closely tied to performance of the workers within teams that control both the quantity and quality of their research results. Second, pressure can be exerted on individuals to perform their best in alignment with the team's goals.[22] Gomez-Mejia, Balkin, and Milkovich describe the case of a Boston-area high-technology firm that allows engineers to earn up to 25 percent of their salary as a result of successful team performance. The program is administered competitively, and each research and development team is required to submit a written report showing how the team's efforts resulted in significant cost savings or other benefits to the firm. A committee of technical and nontechnical supervisors and managers reviews the proposals and may or may not grant bonus money.[23]

The team approach may also be used to motivate the research and development department to work more closely with individuals within the marketing department. These two divisions traditionally are in conflict due to their responsibilities and training; research and development is interested in pursuing technology while marketing focuses on selling products based on consumer needs and perceptions. Although these two goals are not always in alignment, pay mechanisms can be used to create teams of technical and marketing personnel. The result can be products that are both technologically advanced and marketable.

In a study of 75 four-person teams engaged in a simulated interactive task in which reward structure was manipulated, Beersma et al.[24] note two important things that should be considered in the design of team incentives. The first is that many complex tasks (such as would be the case with R&D teams) embody a speed–accuracy trade-off. Their data suggests that "cooperative rewards promote accuracy, whereas competitive rewards promote speed. Managers may not be able to jointly maximize both aspects of task performance via a single reward structure, and thus they should consider which aspect of a task they want to prioritize before designing the reward structure." The second major finding of their study is that the personality of team members makes a difference in how they react to the incentive. Specifically, they conclude that "our findings show that when teams are composed of extroverted and agreeable members, a cooperative reward structure is a very effective choice."

INTEGRATION

Team incentives can be combined with individual, business unit, and organization rewards programs. The key to success is integrating all of these compensation methods so that they are consistent with the organization's strategy. If they are not developed to be consistent with the business strategy, then each individual method of payment can conflict with each other or the corporation's objectives, therefore transmitting extremely mixed signals to employees. When team incentives are utilized, individuals continue to possess personal goals in addition to their incorporated team goals. The rewards system can be effective in ensuring that individual and team goals are consistent rather than in conflict with each other.

Rewards programs are important for supporting or developing either hierarchical or egalitarian business structures. If the firm is primarily hierarchical and if individual employees know that success comes only after rising through supervisory and management levels, there will continue to be a struggle among team members in an effort for high achievement to ensure that their performance is noticed by upper management. Incentives, in addition to promotional opportunities, must be carefully tailored to anticipate the needs of individuals who desire successful movement within the organization. Tall, hierarchical structures are consistent with individual rewards. Therefore, firms that desire flat organizations must change their rewards methods to be consistent with the desired structural goals.

Organizations must also consider the desired relationships among teams. Teams can work in either a competitive environment, in which teams are competing with each other for performance outcomes and subsequent rewards, or they can work cooperatively on common objectives. The atmosphere will be reflective of the corporation's goals and culture. Team membership can be designed so that only individuals within one department work together on a team, or department members can cross over their traditional boundaries to join teams that are multidisciplinary. Again, the form of the team is dependent upon the goals of the business.

INDIVIDUALISM AS A CULTURAL VALUE

Although many organizations are moving to the team concept, relatively little attention has been given to the nature of the American worker in a team environment, which is foreign to the basic culture from which the employee has emerged. G. Hofstede, in a comprehensive study employing a database with over 116,000 questionnaire responses, found that the United States ranked number one on a construct that he called individualism. High-individualism countries are characterized as places where the culture emphasizes the individual rather than the group. Each individual is expected to care for himself; the organization is not committed to care for individuals on a long-term basis. Pay policies within these countries tend to emphasize individual rather than group performance.

An employee's ability to demonstrate his successful individual achievements to others is important and evidenced by the accumulation of rewards for performance, such as salary, company cars, job title, number of subordinates, and other rewards found in traditional compensation systems. As team concepts are employed, one must ask how the mentality of individualism, which is typical of the American worker, can survive in this atmosphere. The compensation program can be one tool for satisfying both individual and group needs. Awards for outstanding individual performance cannot be ignored in a society so insistent on individual accomplishment, but they must be carefully incorporated within an organizational environment whose survival depends on team rather than individual effort. Turnover should be carefully monitored when a business moves from individual to team programs. This will provide feedback on the types of personnel who are challenged by the team concept and those who are not satisfied within the environment. This information will be essential for future recruitment efforts, succession planning, and program evaluation.

Creative compensation management, in which pay is tailored to the needs of the organization, the nature of work, and the characteristics of the workforce, is playing an important strategic role in organizations. The team concept is rapidly gaining popularity due to the positive outcomes that many organizations have experienced after implementing such programs. Team-based, rather than individual, criteria for pay should be used when the goals of the business are to strengthen the team's performance, not only the individual employee's performance within the team. In a culture so dominated by individual goals and objectives, organizations must strive to be creative in their deployment of effective team-incentive programs that communicate to the worker that group, rather than individual, performance is critical to success.

INNOVATION: MERGING TEAM INCENTIVES WITH EMPLOYEE SURVEYS VIA THE ROI SHARE PLAN

Technology has given way to many different ways of collecting data that can be used to determine bonus amounts. In addition, there is a growing interest in using employee surveys (whether satisfaction surveys, pulse surveys, or engagement surveys) to learn not only attitudes of employees but what ideas workers have for improving performance within their own groups or throughout the organization. Fast retrieval of ideas via surveys opens up new opportunities to merge classic compensation concepts with technology and evolve our thinking about the use of team-based incentives. One such program, currently being integrated into a technology platform,[25] provides an example of such an endeavor. Merging a technology suite that uses pulse surveys and on-line action planning for managers, ROI sharing[26] provides an alternative to other types of team or group-based incentives.

The roots of ROI sharing come from traditional gainsharing plans. Gainsharing programs, usually implemented at the business unit level, have two key components: (1) a financial sharing or incentive system, and (2) an idea program. The logic behind gainsharing is that new ideas result in gains in financial outcomes that are directly under the control of employees. Those financial outcomes are tracked, and a bonus accrues to employees after the "gain" is shared between employees and the organization. The fairness of gainsharing principles and the logic that a bonus is paid for real gains have much appeal. However, the suggestion systems are often cumbersome. ROI sharing provides an alternative that may work for organizations that want a simultaneous focus on overall business unit and team goals. Below is an example of how ROI sharing works:

- The organization sets up a pulse surveying process, asking employees to provide ideas, information on productivity blockers, and more on some frequent basis (suggest bi-weekly or monthly).

- The pulse surveys are kept short (three to five questions); if it is too complex, employees and managers will not stay engaged in the process.

- The system must be one that provides managers with immediate access to the data when the survey closes. Speed in delivering data to managers is essential for managers to be able to engage in the activities needed for the ROI share plan to succeed.

- The pulse survey process also should have an on-line manager action planning tool so that managers can log issues that come through the surveys and then also document their actions and resulting ROI after an action is complete.

- Actions arise from the ongoing data collection and dialogue managers have with employees. Actions lead to results, some of which are quantifiable with a calculated ROI and some that have intrinsic ROI (nonquantifiable).

How is the bonus calculated?

- Incentive plan floor: before any sharing begins, an acceptable ROI for the data collection, reporting and action planning system must be realized. If technology is purchased, this goes into the costs as well as any training and implementation processes that are needed to launch the program. Let us say that senior management agrees that a return on investment of 300 percent is necessary before the incentive plan kicks in.

- After the 300 percent return on program costs (or investment) is accrued, then a bonus pool for employees starts to accumulate value. The criteria for this incentive system will be the actions managers take in response to data that comes in through the pulse survey system. Thus, in a continuous improvement mode, managers drive change for the good of their employee groups.

- The action planning program that the authors have used differentiates actions that are "owned" by individual managers and those that are not owned by the manager (or that are shared with others; owned by other departments or managers). This creates an opportunity for managers to earn a bonus from their individual actions as well as from shared actions. If two managers work together on an action resulting in an ROI, then the ROI is allocated to the employees in both managers' departments. Technology allows for tracking where ideas come from, which manager is taking action, who is working on actions together, and how much ROI is obtained.

■ In our own experience, managers report ROI in two forms: (1) qualitative and less well verifiable; and (2) quantitative and documented. We suggest two separate bonus pools for each form of ROI. One may argue that qualitative (or nonquantifiable) ROI has no place in a bonus system, but our experience proves otherwise. Managers need to be encouraged to take action on items that will improve morale, because although a short-term ROI is not easy to document, multiple research studies show that, in the long-run, employee morale and other "soft" outcomes predict customer service, quality, and other business criteria important for maintaining competitive position. Also, in using these types of ROI "stories" with CEOs, we find that a high level of pride results from some of the most nonquantifiable returns. Thus, both stories and numbers have value in the ROI share plan.

- *Bonus pool 1*—qualitative types of ROI can be entered into a bonus pool for nonfinancial rewards. These types of ROI tend to be sources of pride, less quantifiable but important for communication and story telling. Thus, we suggest that managers be permitted to submit their ROI for senior executive review.

- *Bonus pool 2*—quantitative ROI is submitted to another bonus pool for management review. If the ROI calculations are verified, then some portion of the savings will be shared with the employee team that works for the manager submitting the idea. Managers and employees share equally in this bonus, unless there is a corporate mandate to do otherwise. The split is dictated by the financial situation of the firm and the type of work. It may be that 10 percent goes into the employee pool and 90 percent to the firm, or it could be 50/50.

- Once the bonus pool is determined, the financial split is distributed as a percentage of the employees' salary.

Many parts of this formula are similar to gainsharing plans. The uniqueness is that the program is at the team level of analysis, focused on the managerial team. The process also relies on technology. Lastly, the ROI share process in dependent on individual managers who spearhead the idea generation and action process within their teams and across teams. Managers delegate to employees to help, or they work with peers or their own managers to implement, but because every manager has her own data, then it is the responsibility of the manager to keep the program alive. While gainsharing has committees who shepherd ideas, in ROI sharing, it is the job of the manager to bring their teams into the process.

HOW TO MAKE TEAM-BASED PAY MORE SUCCESSFUL

Compensation is an important aspect of the success of team based work designs, as discussed in this chapter. Figure 21.1 provides a checklist of "best practices" and key issues to consider when linking pay to team performance. We have created this

FIGURE 21.1   Key issues and best practices when designing team-based incentives

- Never forget that you get what you measure and reward!

- Best way to reduce free-riding is through group pressure.

  - Group pressure increases through cohesion.

  - Cohesion increases by providing group rewards.

  - Rewards should go to entire team and not be associated with one person, e.g. "Walter's shop."

- Evaluation and rewards must take into account difficulty of assignment and probability of failure. People will not take risks if they are penalized for taking on difficult assignments and there are easier ways to be recognized.

- Space rewards so that these are linked to different stages of projects to reinforce short-term accomplishments without losing sight of long-term objectives, e.g., from key intermediate landmarks through patenting of innovations through commercialization of project.

- If an employee works for multiple teams, utilize all available inputs for measuring team performance and allocating rewards.

- Identify "internal and external customers" of each group and measure their expectations/assessments of teams.

- Reduce hierarchies (e.g., Technician I, II, II, etc.) as a way for promoting/rewarding people. This creates status/power differentials dysfunctional in a team environment.

- Use "broadbanding" as a flexible way to provide rewards without creating tall career/grade structures.

- Reward team through lump sum payments for landmark accomplishments. These are more noticeable and less contaminated with other things, such as cost of living.

- Identify and reward key contributors through group nomination, utilizing cross-functional groups for evaluation of nominees.

- Be creative to provide non-financial rewards that promote a team spirit such as trips, picture of team in company newspaper, company events, etc.

- Use peer appraisals with supervisor consolidating and integrating this feedback so that it is provided to employee in a manner that is useful.

list based on our own consulting experience and the literature. One important caveat is that effective compensation design is only one aspect that contributes to improved team performance. The firm also needs to consider other important issues in tandem. Additional practices in conjunction with team-based incentives that can enhance team performance are noted in Figure 21.2.

FIGURE 21.2   Internal team organization

- Ensure that each team has an effective facilitator.

- Each individual should have a loosely specified role within the team, thus team composition needs to be carefully thought out, considering both personality and technical issues.

- Recognize major challenge for innovation: Being able to work with people and technical expertise are often at odds with each other. "Mavericks" need to be protected because they are crucial for innovation.

END NOTES

1. C. Ichinowski and K. Shaw, "Beyond Incentive Pay: Insiders' Estimates of the Value of Complementary Human Resource Management Practice," *Journal of Economic Perspectives*, vol. 17, no. 1, 2003, pp. 155–80; G. Hertel, U. Konradt and B. Orlikowski, "Managing Distance by Interdependence: Goal Setting, Task Interdependence, and Team-Based Rewards in Virtual Teams," *European Journal of Work and Organizational Psychology*, vol. 13, no. 1, 2004, pp. 1–28; A. Falk and A. Ichino, "Clean Evidence on Peer Effects," *Journal of Labor Economics*, vol. 24, 2006, pp. 39–57; P. Reilly, J. Phillipson and P. Smith, "Team-Based Pay in the United Kingdom," *Compensation & Benefits Review*, vol. 37, no. 4, 2005, pp. 54–60; O. Kvaloy and T. E. Olsen, "Team Incentives in Relational Employment Contracts," *Journal of Labor Economics*, vol. 24, 2006, pp. 139–69.

2. J. P. Guthrie and E. C. Hollensbe, "Group Incentives and Performance: A Spontaneous Goal Setting, Goal Choice Commitment," *Journal of Management*, vol. 30, no. 2, 2004, pp. 263–84.

3. C. Harbring, "The Effects of Communication in Incentive Systems—An Experimental Study," *Managerial and Decision Economics*, vol. 27, no. 5, 2006, 333–53.

4. J. Devaro, "Teams, Autonomy, and the Financial Performance of Firms," *Industrial Relations*, vol. 45, no. 2, 2006, p. 217.

5. C. J. Collins and K. G. Smith, "Knowledge Exchange and Combination: The Role of Human Resource Practices in the Performance of High-Technology Firms," *The Academy of Management Journal*, vol. 49, no. 3, 2006, 544–60.

6. P. Pascarella, "Compensating Teams," *Across the Board*, 1997.

7. L. R. Gomez-Mejia, D. Balkin and R. Cardy, *Managing Human Resources*. Englewood Cliffs, NJ: Prentice-Hall, 2007.

8. S. T. Condly, R. E. Clark and H. D. Stolovitch, "The Effects of Incentives on Workplace Performance: A Meta-Analytic Review of Research Studies," *Performance Improvement Quarterly*, vol. 16, no. 3, 2003, pp. 46–63.

9. C. Harbring (see note 3).

10. L. R. Gomez-Mejia, D. Balkin and R. Cardy, *Managing Human Resources*. Englewood Cliffs, NJ: Prentice-Hall, 2007.

11. L. R. Gomez-Mejia, D. Balkin and R. Cardy, *Management*. New York: McGraw–Hill/Irwin, 2007.

12. B. E. Garson and D. J. Stanwyck, "Locus of Control and Incentive in Self- Managing Teams," *Human Resource Development Quarterly*, Fall 1997; M. Ezzamel and H. Willmott, "Accounting for Teamwork: A Critical Study of Group-based Systems of Organizational Control," *Administrative Science Quarterly*, vol. 43, 1998, pp. 358–96; M. A. Campion, E. M. Papper and G. J. Medsker, "Relations between Work Team Characteristics and Effectiveness: A Replication and Extension," *Personnel Psychology*, vol. 49, 1996.

13. B. Murray and B. Gerhart, "An Empirical Analysis of a Skilled-Based Pay Program and Plant Performance Outcomes," *Academy of Management Journal*, vol. 41, no. 1, 1998, pp. 68–78; B. Gerhart and S. L. Rynes, *Compensation: Theory, Evidence, and Strategic Implications*, Thousand Oaks, CA: Sage, 2003; Gomez-Mejia et al. (see note 11). Gomez-Mejia et al. (see note 10).

14. S. Johnson, "Plan your Organization's Reward Strategy through Pay-for-performance Dynamics," *Compensation and Benefits Review*, May/June 1998; B. Beersma, J. R. Hollenbeck, S. E. Humphrey, H. Moon, D. E. Conlon and D. R. Ilgen, "Cooperation, Competition, and Team Performance: Toward a Contingency Approach," *Academy of Management Journal*, vol. 46, no. 5, 2003, pp. 572–90; R. Seaman, "Rejuvenating an Organization with Team Pay," *Compensation and Benefits Review*, September/October 1997; C. Harbring (see note 3); S. T. Johnson, "High Performance Work Teams: One Firm's Approach to Team Incentive Pay," *Compensation and Benefits Review*, September/October 1996; M. Erez and A. Somech, "Is Group Productivity Loss the Rule or the Exception? Effects of Culture and Group-Based Motivation," *Academy of Management Journal*, vol. 39, 1996, pp. 1513–37; C. J. Collins and K. G. Smith, "Knowledge Exchange and Combination: The Role of Human Resource Practices in the Performance of High-technology Firms," *The Academy of Management Journal*, vol. 49, no. 3, 2006, 544–60.

15. G. P. Latham and E. A. Locke, "Goal-setting—A Motivational Technique that Works," in R. M. Steers and L. W. Porter (eds), *Motivation and Work*, 1987; E. A. Locke and G. P. Latham, "Building a Practically Useful Theory of Goal Setting and Task Motivation," *American Psychological*, vol. 57, 2002, pp. 705–17.

16. C. R. Gowen, "Managing Work Group Performance by Individual Goals and Group Goals for Interdependent Group Tasks," *Journal of Organization*, 1985; Hamilton, Nickerson & Owan, "Team Incentives and Worker Heterogeneity: An Empirical Analysis of the Impact of Teams on Productivity and Participation," *Journal of Political Economy*, vol. 111, 2003, pp. 465–97.

17. J. Forward and A. Zander, "Choice of Unattainable Goals and Effects on Performance," *Organization Behavior and Human Performance*, vol. 6, 1971, pp. 184–99.

18. J. T. Austin and P. Bobko, "Goal Setting Theory: Unexplored Areas and Future Research Needs," *Journal of Occupational Psychology*, vol. 58, 1985, pp. 289–308.

19. R. D. Pritchard and M. Curtis, "The Influence of Goal Setting and Financial Incentives on Task Performance," *Organization Behavior and Human Performance*, vol. 10, 1973, pp. 175–83.

20. J. T. Austin et al. (see note 18).

21. E. J. Poza and M. L. Markus, "Success Story: The Team Approach to Work Restructuring," *Organization Dynamics*, vol. 8, no. 3, 1980, pp. 2–25.

22. L. R. Gomez-Mejia and D. B. Balkin, "The Effectiveness of Individual and Aggregate Compensation Strategies in an R&D Setting," *Industrial Relations*, vol. 28, 1989, pp. 431–445.

23. L. R. Gomez-Mejia, D. B. Balkin and G. T. Milkovich, "Rethinking your Rewards for Technical Employees," *Organizational Dynamics*, vol. 18, no. 4, 1990, pp. 62–75.

24. Beersma et al. (see note 14).

25. eePulse, Inc. (www.eepulse.com) has integrated this technology into their product suite.

26. ROI share plan is a copyright of Dr. Theresa M. Welbourne.

GAINSHARING OR PROFIT SHARING

Robert L. Masternak, President

Masternak & Associates

MANY PEOPLE CONFUSE PROFIT SHARING and gainsharing. Often companies that install profit sharing have selected the wrong tool for their organization and quickly become disappointed that they have been unable to foster a change in behaviors and to drive performance. The purpose of this chapter is to explain the similarities in profit sharing and gainsharing, the differences, the primary purpose for both systems, and why gainsharing is often the better tool. The chapter begins with a tale about a farmer's good intentions gone astray.

A FARMER'S TALE

Once upon a time there was a farmer in the land of Michigan who held his workers in high regard. He appreciated their dedicated service during the hot and dusty summer days and the cold and dampness of the November corn harvest. He respected their efforts and wished to recognize them for their part in the farm's success. He knew that without his dedicated staff he would not be able to enjoy the prosperity and pride derived from his highly successful farm. He had often thought about ways he could recognize his employees for their efforts. Yes, it was true that he had the annual harvest feast, but that did not seem to be enough.

He had heard of another successful farmer in an adjacent land who had recently installed a profit sharing plan in order to share the financial gains with his workers. The farmer wished to emulate this idea and developed a very simple and understandable profit sharing plan. Basically, the farmer calculated his total revenue from a variety of sources, including the sale of grains, livestock, land leasing, and produce sales at the local farmer's market. From revenues he subtracted all expenses including: the cost of seed, fertilizer, labor, fuel, attorney fees, insurance, depreciation, etc. His result, he called "the bottom line." Then in turn, he designed a formula to share a portion of the profit with his workers. He announced the newly designed profit sharing plan at his annual year-end feast and handed out bonus checks to the workers equal to 6 percent of their annual pay. The average check amounted to $1,200 ($20,000 annual compensation × 6 percent). The workers were delighted with the unexpected bonus and rejoiced in the farmer's generosity.

The farmer explained to his employees that there would be more of the same next year, if the farm continued to prosper. The workers' spirits were high, and they eagerly looked forward to the second plan year.

In year two, the farmer made a strategic decision to plant his entire farm in corn, since the price of corn had skyrocketed to $3.00 per bushel, a record level. The farmer foresaw a great opportunity for increasing production and resulting profits. The farm hands worked especially hard planting, fertilizing, cultivating, and irrigating the corn. As a result of their labors the corn produced a record harvest. The extra irrigation and cultivation had paid off! Unfortunately, other farmers also had decided to place all their land in corn as well. That season's corn production was at a "bumper year" level for every farm. As a result, the selling price plunged to $1.00 per bushel, and the farmer's profits fell to half of the previous year. At the annual harvest feast the farmer passed out the bonus checks, this time only 3 percent of compensation. His people were greatly disappointed, but some compensation was better than nothing. The workers forgave the farmer and looked forward to a better third year.

In year three, the farmer made several strategic business decisions. He acquired more land and decided to boost productivity by investing in a new John Deere tractor. He bought a new truck as well. The tractor was the largest and newest on the market, and he thought it would most likely lead to higher land productivity. The truck was a "4 by 4" with a leather interior and all the added accessories. He knew that the truck was excessive, but after all, he had worked so hard all those years and knew the fancy truck was something he very much deserved. He rejoiced when the bank offered an attractive low interest rate on three loans for the land, tractor, and truck. As luck would have it, however, the new loans had several strings attached, including a variable rate and prepayment penalties. In addition more workers needed to be hired to help with the cultivation and harvest that year, and the spring planting had been especially hectic.

The old workers enjoyed driving the new tractor and managed to do some added cultivation. The new workers were not nearly as impressed, since they had never experienced the discomfort and excessive noise of the older, retired model.

By the end of that fateful year, corn production doubled the previous year's level. The workers grew excited because they had never seen so much corn. Unfortunately, during the course of the year interest rates had taken a dramatic turn. The truck and tractor loan had initially been at only 2 percent, but the loans soared to 12 percent. The new variable rate on the land was so excessive that the farmer had to refinance to a fixed rate, resulting in sizable prepayment penalties and costly refinancing charges. He informed his workers about some of these problems, but their understanding was limited. Their focus was on better corn yield, cultivation, and irrigation. By the end of that disastrous year, profitability had tumbled to "break-even." The farmer's investments had had a devastating effect!

At the annual harvest feast, the workers eagerly looked forward to the announcement of the bonus results, but the farmer distributed a statement of dismal financial results instead of checks. The workers were extremely disappointed. The new workers were especially unhappy. Their expectations were heightened by the human resources manager informing them of the profit share plan. All the workers bitterly complained about the farmer's extravagant purchases and poor financial decisions. They were especially unhappy when they saw the farmer driving his new fancy truck. Employees claimed they had no control over the farmer's shortsighted decisions. Morale and level of trust declined. Some bitter and resentful workers grumbled and plotted against their hapless employer.

The Tale's Moral

Important lessons can be learned from the farmer's story. The farmer's intentions were noble, but the results led to an undesirable outcome. The farmer failed to thoroughly consider what he was trying to accomplish by installing a profit sharing plan. What was the farmer's purpose for the plan? What did he want to accomplish? Was the objective to drive operating performance (yield) or to help instill in the workers the concept of "common-fate?" Was he primarily interested in providing a monetary reward to motivate employees in their efforts, or was he more interested in providing a benefit to recognize loyalty and service? Also, the farmer failed to consider the appropriate rewards system for the culture, growth, and demographics of his workforce. The farm had grown considerably, adding a number of new workers. Unfortunately, the farm had grown so large that the farmer did not even have the opportunity to meet many of his employees. Perhaps he should have considered other options before he jumped into profit sharing. He had heard about a few farmers who had gainsharing plans for their workers. However, he did not take the time to investigate the gainsharing concept, thinking that profit sharing was basically the same concept. Employees have an opportunity to earn a financial reward under both approaches. However, the farmer did not recognize that the similarity ends there. If he had researched the history and evolution of both approaches and their intended purpose, he might have avoided his ill-fated good intentions.

PROFIT SHARING

History

Profit sharing is not a new concept. One of the first documented profit sharing plans in the United States was introduced in 1794 at Glass Works in New Geneva, PA. At the time, the company was recognized by the Secretary of the Treasury under Presidents Jefferson and Madison as applying "the nation's fundamental democratic principles to an industrial operation." However, profit sharing arrangements were far from prevalent until the end of the Civil War. As America became more industrialized, profit sharing begin to grow through the 1920s. Profit sharing companies held the belief that sharing profits would unite workers and management in the pursuit of a common goal. In addition, profit sharing was offered as a means to discourage unionization, but after the Depression many of these profit sharing plans were discontinued.

After World War II there was a rebirth of profit sharing. Most of these plans were deferred compensation plans driven by the desire to avoid a tax on excess income that had been imposed during the war. In other words, companies would place a portion of the profits aside to fund employee retirement plans. This was especially popular among private, "family"-owned companies that saw employees as an extended family. The concept was also one of "common fate." In good times a family would share more, in the bad times less. Employees often spent their entire working career with the same company. There was mutual loyalty on both the employer's and employees' behalf.

In the late 1980s some companies attempted to deviate from the deferred compensation nature of profit sharing. In other words, profit sharing was viewed as incentive compensation rather than a benefit plan. One of the best documented examples was at Dupont's fibers division which employed approximately 20,000 people. The plan's designers intended to develop a program to reward employee contributions, in the belief that sharing the rewards as well as the risks of the division's financial performance would help the business succeed in the market place. The complex arrangement focused on worldwide after-tax operating income and established a "compensation target rate" and a "variable element rate." Basically, DuPont's new pay concept was that employees would place a portion of their normal base compensation at risk. In return, employees had the opportunity to more than offset the "at-risk" monies through a year-end bonus. On the other hand, if profitability was significantly below targeted levels employees would not receive the "at-risk" compensation. The plan could yield a bonus of up to 12 percent of salary in an exceptional year. In a bad year an employee could lose as much as 6 percent of salary. The new "pay-at-risk" system would enable the company to better manage costs by moving to more of an "ability to pay" approach. In addition, the thinking was there would be less workforce pressure for base salary adjustments. The theory was that, since employees would be sharing in the profits, they would feel and act more like stakeholders. The result would lead to positive changes in behaviors and work habits, resulting in even more profits.

When the plan was rolled out in 1989, DuPont employees saw a modest bonus after the first year. However, the second year saw rapidly declining profitability. Profits had declined due to a number of unforeseen business conditions, two of which were the rapid increase in raw material prices and the erosion in the final product's selling price. Profits were "squeezed." As a result, employees lost the portion of their base pay that was placed at risk. The employee loss represented approximately 4 percent of compensation. DuPont experienced a significant rise in employee discontent. Some felt that they were "hoodwinked." A company executive commented, "Employees were not ready for such a program. Employees felt it was fine when they were getting money back, but thought it was not fair when no bonus was paid." As a result the program was abandoned.

The flaw in the "pay-at-risk" form of profit sharing was that employees were asked to put a portion of their pay in jeopardy over something they had little or no control over, profitability. In addition, DuPont is a large, worldwide organization. The sense of employee ownership and identity toward a very large corporation often is less than in a small family-owned business. People have more difficulty trusting the financial data. Clearly most DuPont employees did not like putting their base pay at risk in exchange for the opportunity to share in the profits. Many would say they "preferred to lose money at the casino; at least they would have had some fun and excitement in doing so."

In more recent times, cash profit sharing plans have been installed where no pay-at-risk is involved. These plans are designed to include *all* employees including hourly and salaried, non-exempt employees, not just executives and managers. In other words, all employees have an opportunity to share in the profit pie by having an opportunity to receive a year-end cash bonus (see Figure 22.1).

When profits are up, employees receive a cash payout, if profits are down there is no consequence. Companies that install these plans hope to enable employees to share in the organization's success, to motivate workers to improve profits, and in turn to act in the best interest of the company.

Unfortunately many companies that have a cash profit sharing plan find that workers view the system as an entitlement. People are happy when they get a bonus and are upset when they do not. Employees feel that when they receive a profit bonus they "earned it." When they do not, "it's the company's fault." In lean years, the employee response is often complaining and mistrust in the company.

FIGURE 22.1   Profit sharing pie

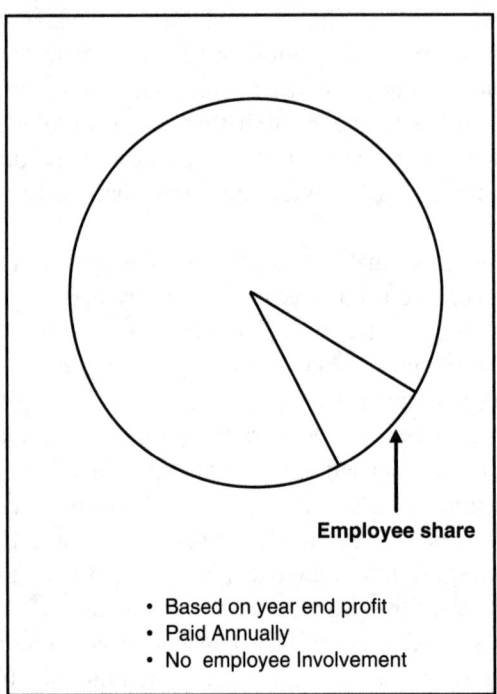

Employee share

- Based on year end profit
- Paid Annually
- No employee Involvement

WHAT WOULD THE FARMER HAVE LEARNED FROM THESE EXPERIENCES?

The clear and simple issues are that for most organizations profit sharing plans provide very little or no "line-of-sight" in terms of what employees do and what they are paid. The general employee population has little understanding of how they directly impact a broad financial measure of profitability. Even those who have an understanding of the financial data find their efforts insignificant in relationship to key management decisions and external market conditions. To make matters worse, some may feel that the company may manipulate the numbers in order to take advantage of tax regulations or influence the investment community. These feelings are further exasperated in large multilocation organizations where employees are distanced from top management. Also these multisite organizations may calculate profit companywide rather than on a location-by-location basis.

So should the farmer further consider profit sharing? It depends on the objective. If the focus is to share the organization's success and to reinforce a sense of ownership, then profit sharing might be the appropriate answer. However, the farmer needs to clearly understand what the result will likely be in terms of impacting employee *attitudes* rather than driving *behaviors*. This is especially true in organizations that have an absence of a high degree of employee involvement.

If profit sharing is the chosen route, should it be a compensation system or a benefit plan, a method to help finance employee retirement years? In most cases, history has demonstrated that the farmer may be better served by incorporating profit sharing into a retirement scheme. In doing so, employees would see their retirement security grow in tune with the company's growth and prosperity. In other words, both employee and employer would share in a "common fate." This would satisfy the objective of sharing in the organization's success. The plan would give employees more of a long-term outlook and strengthen the sense of identity and ownership. On the other hand, if the farmer's objective is to influence not only *attitudes* but to change *behaviors* in terms of teamwork, involvement, and communications, profit sharing most likely will be the wrong answer, particularly if the organization has more than a handful of employees.

GAINSHARING

History

Many people view gainsharing strictly as a bonus or group incentive plan. However, it is much more than a compensation plan. It helps drive culture change. With gainsharing, employees feel that they are more valued and respected. As a result, people develop a higher sense of teamwork, ownership, and identity. People are more engaged, which leads to a higher level of performance.

There are four principles for understanding why gainsharing works. All four are incorporated in the strategy used to install and maintain a successful plan. The four principles address equity, identity, involvement, and commitment. The four principles are interrelated and mutually reinforcing (see Figure 22.2).

In order to fully understand the concept, one must examine its roots. The gainsharing concept dates back to the 1930s when a labor leader, Joe Scanlon,

FIGURE 22.2   Gainsharing strategy

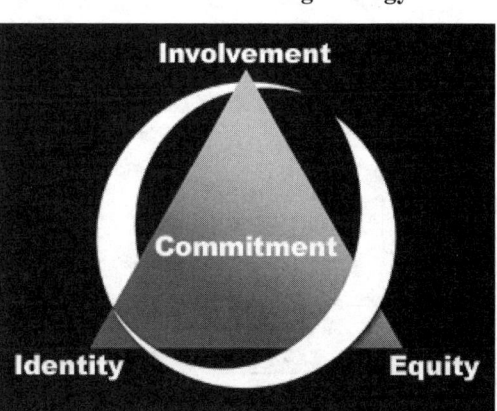

preached that "the worker" had much more to offer than a pair of hands. The premise was that the person closest to the problem often has the best and simplest solution. Moreover, if the worker is involved in the solution, most likely he or she will make the solution work. Scanlon is often credited for developing a system that promotes involvement in the workplace through employee ideas and suggestions.

Basically, employee teams are formed to solicit and review suggestions from other members of the workforce. The teams are permanent groups that meet on a regular basis to discuss ideas and suggestions. The teams are given limited spending authority to approve and implement suggestions. Suggestions that are approved by a team, but are beyond their spending authority, are advanced to a higher level in the organization for final approval. Figure 22.3 is an example of the typical involvement structure.

The involvement structure is intended not only to encourage participation but also to enhance two-way communications regarding company goals and objectives. The idea system helps foster respect and cooperation. In other words, if employees feel their ideas are listened to, are given prompt feedback, and see their ideas promptly implemented, they will feel respected.

FIGURE 22.3   Idea flow

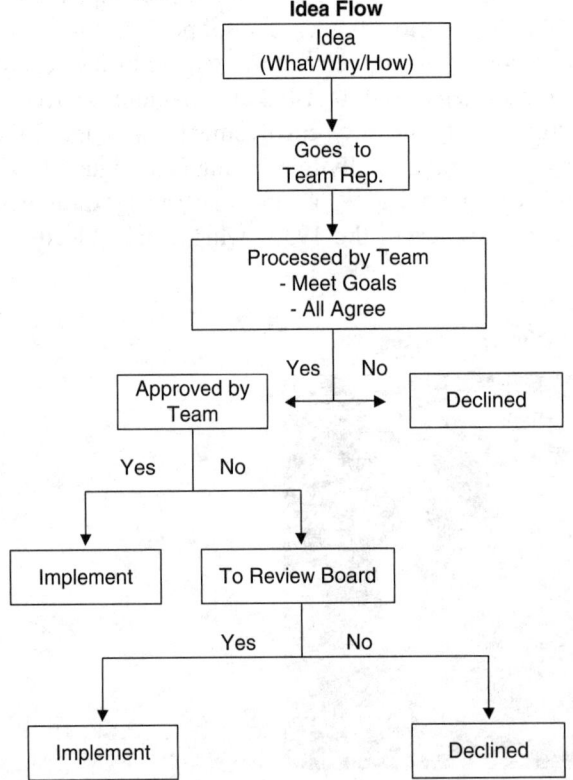

Unlike a traditional suggestion system, Scanlon's system does not provide individual monetary rewards for improvement ideas. The thinking is that the review, investigation, and implementation of employee's ideas are truly a collaborative effort. Suggestion systems that pay individual awards based on the projected savings from the idea promote behaviors in which employees may conceal their improvement suggestions rather than freely share and collaborate with others to advance the idea. Originally the Scanlon approach did not have an employee bonus component. However, a few years after the plan's initial implementation, Scanlon devised an organization-wide bonus formula that provided a more frequent and line-of-sight measurement system than profit sharing. The idea system and other improvement efforts drove the performance measures, and gains (savings) generated through the measurement formula are shared with everyone in the organization. Basically the Scanlon philosophy says, "As we work together to improve the operations, everyone shares financially in the savings."

The Scanlon plan became known as "a frontier in labor-management cooperation." Scanlon went on to work at MIT to help other labor leaders and managers. As a result the Scanlon message gradually spread. In the 1950s Scanlon developed a group of disciples including Frederick Lesieur and Carl Frost. As companies moved forward with the concept, interest in academic and government circles grew. One of the earlier studies was done by the General Accounting Office and was entitled "Productivity Sharing Programs: Can They Contribute to Productivity Improvement?" The 1981 study examined 36 "productivity sharing" firms. The GAO reported that "while productivity sharing plans are not the panacea for every firm in the solution to the Nation's economic problems, they warrant serious consideration by firms as a means of stimulating productivity performance, enhancing their competitive advantage, increasing monetary benefits to their employees, and reducing inflationary pressure." The report was published in the hope of encouraging organizations to implement performance-enhancing tools that better engaged the workforce.

As time passed, the term Scanlon plan changed to gainsharing plan. The Scanlon term mistakenly had become associated with a single bonus formula focused on people productivity. The gainsharing term became more associated with the use of tailor-made measures that focused on the line-of-sight.

CARS

Another hallmark study was published in 1992. The study (one of the most comprehensive studies up until that time) was sponsored by WorldatWork (formerly the American Compensation Association). The group was known as the Consortiums for Alternative Reward Strategies Research (CARS). The study, entitled, "Capitalizing on Human Assets," focused on 2,200 organizations with performance-based reward plans. The findings reported many positive results in both operational performance and employee attitudes. In addition, the study reported better performance in plans that used more line-of-sight measures (gainsharing) than plans using only a bottom-line profit sharing measure. In addition, the study reported that successful plans lead rather than support cultural change.

TQM

In the mid-1990s, the Total Quality Management movement led to further interest in the gainsharing concept. As TQM attempted to involve the workforce, employees began asking; "What's in it for me?" Gainsharing was one answer. More recently interest in gainsharing has again surfaced as companies cycle through lean manufacturing and six/sigma initiates. An important point is that all of these improvement initiatives are nothing more than tools to better engage the workforce and to promote involvement. These tools are an extension to what Scanlon had preached in the 1930s.

Unfortunately many of today's companies that study gainsharing see the concept as an incentive, thinking that if you put a carrot in front of people, you will put "fire in their belly." These organizations focus on the bonus or incentive side of gainsharing, and may lack the understanding and appreciation of the cultural and employee involvement origins of the concept. They believe that a bonus system lacking employee involvement will somehow miraculously lead to a positive result. The problem is that they are putting the *cart* in front of the *horse*, the *incentive* in front of the *involvement*.

LINE-OF-SIGHT AND MEASUREMENT

After focusing on the cultural and employee involvement heritage of gainsharing it is appropriate to turn to the bonus or incentive side. Basically, to provide gainsharing's incentive an organization measures performance through a predetermined formula which, in turn, shares the savings with all employees. The organization's actual performance is compared to baseline performance (often a historical standard) to determine the amount of the gain. The gains and resulting payouts are self-funded based on savings generated by the measurement formula. Some plans may utilize broad financial measures that closely resemble profit sharing. However, it is more common to find gainsharing companies that utilize more narrow operational measures such as productivity, quality, customer service, on-time delivery, and spending. Typically gainsharing plans have multiple measures. In order for a gain to occur, the performance pie must improve (see Figure 22.4).

As the pie expands, the greater the improvement (gain) and the larger the financial benefit for the company and employees. The key point is that there must be an improvement before any sharing occurs. Furthermore, since gains are typically measured in relationship to a historical baseline, employees and the organization must change in order to generate a gain.

FIGURE 22.4 The gainsharing pie

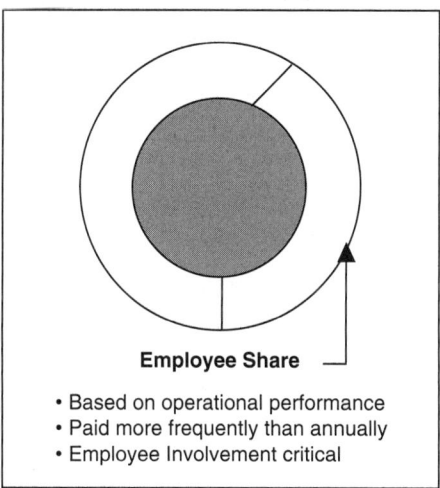

Employee Share

• Based on operational performance
• Paid more frequently than annually
• Employee Involvement critical

A multimeasure system is commonly used which is referred to as a "family of measures" approach. The "family of measures" approach uses three to six drivers of performance. Examples of measures are listed in Table 22.1.

The drivers are measured, and gains and losses are calculated for each respective measure. The gains and losses are shared for each measure and then aggregated into an employee distribution pool.

It's important to point out that employees do not have 100 percent control of any measure. No matter what the measure, there are always outside factors that will influence the result. Employees have *more* control of operational measures than profitability. However, unlike profit sharing and depending on the gainsharing plan's design, employee payouts can potentially occur even during periods of profitability decline. Companies with this type of gainsharing model argue that, even though profits may be down, profits would have further declined if not for the savings generated from the gainsharing measures. In this example the company is sharing "savings" and not necessarily "profits." Figure 22.5 is a good example of a family of measures model.

Another of gainsharing's line-of-sight features relates to employee eligibility. All employees at a site are generally included in the plan, including hourly, salaried, and management. The objective is to improve the line-of-sight by having the plan applied to all employees "housed under the same roof." Alternatively, a profit sharing plan may exclude lower level or hourly employees, or profit bonuses may be paid out on a hierarchical basis. The bonus payout percentage is reduced as profit sharing cascades down the organization.

TABLE 22.1   Examples of Operational Measures

Productivity

Equipment efficiency

Cycle time

Yield

Shrinkage

Scrap

Rework

Spending

On-time shipments

RMAs

Fill rate

PPM returned

Uptime

Inventory turns

Inventory accuracy

Safety

Schedule attainment

Energy usage

Customer complaints

Inventory accuracy

Service satisfaction

Spending

Credits

Collections

The end result could divide the workforce and create feelings of inequity rather than build teamwork and the sense of unity. Gainsharing plans are designed to distribute gains based on an equal percentage of pay or cents per hour worked.

Another gainsharing line-of-sight enhancement is that gainsharing is always paid in the form of a cash bonus. Gainsharing's intent is to be based on the pay-for-performance concept as compared to a benefit or deferred compensation plan. Furthermore, the frequency of possible payout is greater for gainsharing than profit sharing. The payout of profit sharing plans is typically on an annual basis.

Alternatively, gainsharing typically has the potential for a monthly or quarterly payout opportunity. A gain and resulting payout is best described as a score rather

FIGURE 22.5   Family of measures model

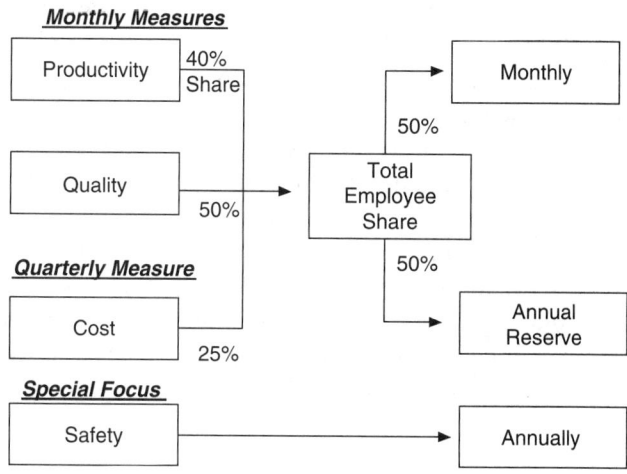

than a bonus. Since everyone in the organization is typically included, the score is a "team score" as compared to an individual one. The score helps give a common focus for employees on measures they can influence and control. Therefore, gainsharing works best in work environments that require collaboration between individuals, work groups, and departments.

Another important feature regarding gainsharing is that typically a portion of the employees share is placed in a reserve account that is paid to all the eligible participants at the end of each plan year. In periods of deficit performance, the employees' share of the loss is deducted from the annual reserve account. Consequently, employees will see consequences for worse performance and longer-term thinking is reinforced. If at the end of the plan year the reserve is negative, a company will typically absorb the loss and start the next plan year at zero. The reserve concept helps further develop a sense of employee identity with and ownership of the organization. For example if a company measured scrap and shared 50 percent of the gain and 50 percent of the loss (through the reserve), in a sense employees would own 50 percent of the financial value of the scrap. Obviously the sense of ownership would drive many new behaviors.

Unlike profit sharing in multisite operations, gainsharing is typically site-specific. The measures and resulting gains are specific to the facility rather than gains being aggregated from multiple locations and in turn distributed across the organization. Again the concept is to increase controllability and the line-of sight. Unlike group incentives, gainsharing typically measures across departments, units or functions. The concept is to build cooperation and communications between departments.

Another distinction between profit sharing and gainsharing relates to the method of plan design and development. A profit sharing plan is typically developed at the top of the organization. In larger corporations the plan may be designed and developed by compensation executives who are granted approval from an executive committee made up of board members.

However, the development of a gainsharing plan often involves employees in many aspects of the plan's design and implementation. Often a cross-functional design team is assembled that mirrors the makeup of the total organization. The design team sorts through a number of issues related to measures, policies, and communication. After executive management's approval, the design team is responsible for conducting all employee kick-off and promotional meetings. The objective is a sense of employee ownership for the plan. In a sense the design team members become disciples of the plan and help lead a process for improvement and change.

GAINSHARING OR PROFIT SHARING?

So should the farmer consider installing a gainsharing plan rather than profit sharing? Again, the same question must be asked. What is the objective? If the farmer's objective is to drive organizational change by influencing attitudes and behaviors, then gainsharing may be the right answer. However, the farmer needs to have the *horse* in front of the cart. He needs to understand that gainsharing is an employee "involvement system with teeth." Simply instituting some type of bonus formula is not enough. A second question is: "Should the farmer consider a broad financial measure of performance or more narrow operational measures?" All things being equal, the use of more narrow "line-of-sight" measures will more likely yield significant changes in behaviors which, in turn, generate positive results. The use of a broad financial-based measure is much more dependent on the level of employee involvement in the organization at the time of the plan's implementation. How open is the company's communication? How knowledgeable are employees about the business conditions? What is the level of trust? How much baggage is the organization carrying from its past?

A gainsharing plan that uses a broad financial measure such as profitability, EBIT, or ROI may be a success if the organization can answer "yes" to the following questions: Is there a high level of company commitment to the concept of sharing? Are employees afforded regular training both in terms of skills and individual development? Is communication ongoing? Are the financial results openly shared? Does the company practice open book management? Are managers willing to admit mistakes? Is the workforce highly engaged? Are people at all levels involved in some decision making? Do employees have a strong understanding of how they influence profitability? Do people identify with the business? Does the company demonstrate loyalty to the workforce? Do employees view themselves as stakeholders? If the answers are "yes" then measuring and sharing profits may work. If not, then it is best to have a plan that focuses on operational, more line-of-site measures. Otherwise, the organization will find itself in the same position as the generous, but disappointed farmer (see Table 22.2).

TABLE 22.2   Gainsharing and Profit Sharing Comparison

	Gainsharing	Profit Sharing
Purpose	To drive performance of an organization by promoting awareness, alignment, teamwork, communication and involvement.	To share the financial success of the total organization and encourage employee identity with company success.
Application	The plan commonly applies to a single facility, site, or stand-alone organization.	The plan typically applies organization-wide; companies with multiple sites typically measure organization-wide profitability rather than the performance of a single site.
Measurement	Payout is based on operational measures (productivity, quality, spending, and service), measures that improve the "line of site" in terms of what employees do and how they are compensated.	Payout is based on a broad financial measure of the organization's profitability.
Funding	Gains and resulting payouts are self-funded based on savings generated by improved performance.	Payouts are funded through company profits.
Payment target	Payouts are made only when performance has improved over a historical standard or target.	Payouts are typically made when there are profits; performance doesn't necessary have to show an improvement.
Employee eligibility	Typically all employees at a site are eligible for plan payments.	Some employee groups may be excluded, such as hourly or union employees.
Payout frequency	Payout is often monthly or quarterly. Many plans have a year-end reserve fund to account for deficit periods.	Payout is typically annual.

Continued

TABLE 22.2 *Continued*

	Gainsharing	Profit Sharing
Form of payment	Payment is cash rather than deferred compensation. Many organizations pay via separate check to increase visibility.	Historically profit plans were primarily deferred compensation plans; organization used Profit sharing as a pension plan. Today we see many more cash plans.
Method of distribution	Typically all employees receive the same % payout or cents per hour bonus.	The bonus may be a larger % of compensation for higher-level employees. The % bonus may be less for lower level employees.
Plan design and development	Employees often are involved with the design and implementation process.	There is no employee involvement in the design process.
Communication	A supporting employee involvement and communication system is an integral element of Gainsharing and helps drive improvement initiatives.	Since there is little linkage between "what employees do" and the "bonus," there is an absence of accompanying employee involvement initiatives.
Pay for performance plan versus entitlement	Gains are generated only by improved performance over a predetermined base level of performance. Therefore, Gainsharing is viewed as a pay-for-performance initiative.	Profit sharing often is viewed as an entitlement or employee benefit.
Impact on behaviors	Gainsharing reinforces behaviors that promote improved performance. Used as a tool to drive cultural and organization change.	Little impact on behaviors since employees have difficulty linking "what they do" and their "bonus." Many variables outside of the typical employee's control determine profitability and the bonus amount.
	Heightens the level of employee awareness, helps develop the feeling of self worth, and builds a senses of ownership and identity to the organization.	Influences the sense of employee identity to the organization, particularly for smaller organizations.

REFERENCES

"Achievement Sharing ... In Business Together," *DuPont Handbook*, 1989.

Coates, Edward M., *Profit Sharing Today: Plans and Provisions*, Monthly Labor Review, April 1991.

General Accounting Office. *Productivity Sharing Programs Can They Contribute to Productivity Improvement*, U.S. General Accounting Office, AFMD-81-22, 3 March 1981.

Lesieur, Fredrick G., The *Scanlon Plan A Frontier in Labor-Management Cooperation.* Cambridge: The MIT Press, 1958.

Masternak, Robert L., "Gainsharing Programs at Two Fortune 500 Facilities: Why One Worked Better," *National Productivity Review*, Winter 1991–1992.

Masternak, Robert L., "How to Make Gainsharing Successful: The Collective Experience of 17 Facilities," *Compensation and Benefits Review*, September–October 1997.

Masternak, Robert L., *Gainsharing: A Team-Based Approach to Drive Organizational Change.* Scottsdale, AZ: WorldatWork, 2003.

Masternak, Robert L. and Camuso, Michael A., "Gainsharing and Lean Six Sigma—Perfect Together," *WorldatWork Journal*, first quarter, 2005.

McAdams J. L. and Hawk E. L., *Capitalizing on Human Assets: The Bench Mark Study.* Scottsdale, AZ: ACA, 1992.

SCANLON GAINSHARING

Paul Davis, President

Scanlon Leadership Network

Dow Scott, Ph.D., Professor of Human Resources

Loyola University Chicago

I N THE NOVEL MOBY DICK, Ishmael signed on for "the three hundredth lay." Providing he survived three years at sea, he would receive one three-hundredth of "the clear net proceeds of the voyage." His friend, Queequeg, was a master harpooner, so he signed on for a ninetieth lay or one ninetieth of the net proceeds. These seventeenth-century whalers were engaged in gainsharing, a concept as old as human history.

SCANLON GAINSHARING:
GROUP REWARDS THAT JUST KEEP GIVING

Gainsharing has stood the test of time, because it meets a fundamental human need for fairness, and it combines a primal understanding of group dynamics with the realities of a business enterprise, i.e., *as we work together we should all benefit according to what we have contributed. Unless we work together to create a "gain" or something of value, there will be nothing to share.* The seventeenth-century whalers were motivated. They faced hardships and considerable danger together and when successful they shared in the rewards that were the result of both their individual talent and the group effort.

Multiple studies by McAdams and Hawk,[1] conducted by the Consortium for Alternative Reward Strategies Research, have shown that gainsharing continues to be a powerful tool for creating high performance workplaces. Gainsharing on average produces a 3 percent increase in pay for employees, and a 134 percent return for the company while fostering teamwork, enhanced communication and improved morale. Edward Lawler[2] notes that "the most important thing we know about gainsharing plans is that they work." Research conducted by Gallup Worldwide[3] shows that two-thirds of employees are not "engaged" in their work. They are waiting to jump-ship, to find more rewarding work. With the retirement of the baby boom generation, reduced immigration, and lower birth rates, the competition for talent will increase.

Compensation will certainly be one important tool to attract and retain talent, but alone it is at best a "blunt instrument." For decades surveys have shown that pay is not the only reason employees are attracted to an organization or decide to stay with an employer. Employees want "open communication with managers," "ability to challenge the status quo," "opportunities for personal growth," "full appreciation of work done," "making a difference," and "job security." Studies conducted by the Saratoga Institute indicate that pay accounts for less than 20 percent of the reason why employees decide to quit.[4] Scanlon principles provide the infrastructure to transform simple gainsharing reward formulas into a powerful engine for increasing productivity and providing both financial and psychological rewards that research shows people want from their job.

As competition increases, organizations are faced with two critical areas that must be managed for survival. First, they must maximize efficiency and productivity by reducing all forms of waste in systems and processes. Traditionally the domain of production area industrial engineers, these "lean" methods are becoming a job requirement in all areas of manufacturing, including office areas. Lean methods are now rapidly spreading to health care and other areas of the economy. The second area that must be managed is innovation. New products and services were once the domain of product development departments. Today the most successful companies tap all employees for ideas about new products and services that can increase the "top line" of an organization.

Scanlon gainsharing is a group reward and participative management system that has been extensively studied, and has proven itself in a wide variety of industries including manufacturing, retail, nonprofit, government, distribution, telecommunications, financial services, telecommunications, hospitality, and health care. Scanlon gainsharing is successful in union as well as nonunion environments, and large and small companies.

THE CROW AND THE CORMORANT

In a Japanese fable, a starving crow watches as a cormorant fills its belly with fish. A cormorant is a black bird that is able to swim and dive underwater to catch its prey.

The crow, reasoning that he too is a black bird, dives into the water, only to drown. The moral of the story is *pay attention to what is truly important and do not be distracted by what is not important.* In the crow's case the ability to swim was more important than the color of his feathers.

Compensation practitioners would be wise to consider this fable as they explore the various gainsharing systems. Gainsharing programs that at first glance may seem similar can, upon closer inspection, reveal critical differences in philosophy, employee engagement, scope, and results. Unfortunately, gainsharing is often defined by the nature of the bonus formula. Just like the crow focusing on the wrong thing, the formula can result in missing what is really important, what drives performance. Years of research has shown that the magic of gainsharing has less to do with the type of formula—single ratio, operational measures, profit sharing—than how the program creates gains, leadership, and how the plan is installed.

The Consortium for Alternative Reward Strategies Research study IV (McAdams, 1992) found:

1. Differences in plan implementation and support drive effectiveness twice as much as differences in plan design
2. The strongest driver of the culture that supports gainsharing is the plant manager
3. The clearest element that separates effective from ineffective gainsharing plans is the employees' understanding of measurement details and how to implement them
4. A key indicator of effectiveness is how much people think about the plan
5. Companies are missing the boat on providing the recognition that employees want from their gainsharing plans

For these reasons, we propose that participative management structure, the commitment to employee development, shared rewards and an unwavering focus on business mandates and purpose as formulated by the Scanlon principles and implementation strategy can substantially improve organizational performance where financial formula-driven gainsharing programs cannot.

THE SCANLON PLAN: SETTING THE RECORD STRAIGHT

Any student of gainsharing inevitably will read about "the Scanlon plan." It is one of the longest lasting and most empirically examined approaches to gainsharing. It also is the only classical approach that is not trademarked or copyrighted by a consulting firm. There are over 400 books in print that cite the Scanlon approach to gainsharing. Unfortunately, some of the information is misleading or simply wrong. Like the crow, they focus on the wrong elements of the Scanlon plan and miss the most important elements. The authors have spent much of their careers studying and installing the Scanlon plan; over 50 years between us. It is our hope that this chapter will set the record straight so compensation professionals will know what aspects of gainsharing plans truly drive organizational performance.

Dr Carl Frost, who spent a lifetime researching and developing Scanlon plans, stated:

> The Scanlon Plan is an innovative management process for total organization development. It consists of a set of assumptions about human motivation and behavior, general principles for the management of organizations based on these assumptions, and specific procedures for implementing these principles.

Scanlon plans are named after Joseph N. Scanlon, a prizefighter, steelworker, cost accountant, researcher, and MIT lecturer who lived from 1899 to 1956. Articles in *Fortune*, *Life*, and *Time* magazines made this modest man "the most sought after consultant in America."[5] Scanlon's radical idea was that the average worker has value and knows his own job better than anyone else in the company. Scanlon believed that the creativity and talent of the majority of workers is not tapped in most companies. He resisted the notion of "the economic man." In other words, Scanlon believed that people are motivated by much more than money. He recognized that people want to do good work, enjoy being part of a team, and have many ideas for reducing waste and improving work. Scanlon believed that lack of business literacy and skills development severely limits the contribution employees can make. He felt that there was too much external competition to encourage internal competition in organizations. Scanlon found that many human resource policies, programs, and systems designed to increase productivity actually prevented people from cooperating and decreased productivity and efficiency. Incentive programs often pitted one group against another to the detriment of the organization.

Based on these beliefs, Scanlon developed one of the most successful models for labor-management cooperation, in the late 1930s, just prior to the United States's entrance into World War II. The war years proved that labor and management could work together cooperatively to increase productivity and improve quality. By the end of the war Scanlon's faction within the Steelworkers Union that advocated cooperation found themselves pushed out, as the unions and management returned to their traditional adversarial relations. Scanlon was invited by Dr Douglas McGregor to join the faculty of MIT as a lecturer, where he continued the work that today is known as the Scanlon plan. At MIT, Scanlon joined Paul Pigors, Charles A. Myers, Douglas McGregor, Paul Samuelson, Walter W. Rostow, George P. Schultz, Robert M. Solow, Charles P. Kindleberger, Fredrick Lesieur and Carl Frost. This interdisciplinary group of scholars engaged in pioneering work in industrial relations. Warren Bennis has described the group as "strange attractors," where very different thinkers bounced ideas off each other.[6] Economists and psychologists contributed ideas to Joe Scanlon and he helped them to see how their theories actually worked in the real world. Scanlon unfortunately was a chain smoker and died from emphysema before being able to see the tremendous impact his ideas had on the world of work.

Douglas McGregor incorporated many of Scanlon's ideas into his book, *The Human Side of Enterprise*, which was extensively studied by the Japanese and incorporated into Japanese management practices. Warren Bennis has stated that "The Japanese took Joe Scanlon's ideas concerning worker involvement . . . and the ideas of W. Edwards Deming . . . now people are adopting Japanese management techniques without knowing that many of them were Scanlon's ideas."[7] McGregor's Theory Y was based on Scanlon's clients, who had different assumptions about human motivation than did traditional managers (Theory X).

In 1951, Dr Carl Frost was invited to bring Scanlon's ideas to Michigan State University which, like MIT, became a center of Scanlon plan-related research. Dr Frost continued to evolve and test Scanlon's ideas in organizations like Herman Miller, Donnelly, Motorola, Bridgestone-Firestone, and Beth Israel Hospital, eventually developing the four principles and a participative implementation strategy which are the basis for Scanlon Plans today.[8]

SCANLON PRINCIPLES

The following four principles are the critical elements of the Scanlon Plan—not the bonus formula.[9]

Identity and Education

Every employee must understand the reality the organization confronts in its business environment in order to make a meaningful contribution and to take ownership of business challenges and opportunities. In addition to financial information about the business, employees need fundamental knowledge of the customer's wants and needs, the strengths and weaknesses of competitors, and the contribution that investors make to the organization's success. As a result, companies committed to the Scanlon principles were practicing open-book management long before it became a popular management strategy. Management is challenged to create a compelling mission and vision for the organization.

Participation and Responsibility

The Scanlon plan is based on the premise that most improvements or gains come from "working smarter, not harder." As a result, to increase productivity, employees must have the opportunity and the responsibility to provide input and influence decisions. Scanlon companies are high involvement organizations and Scanlon leaders use a variety of techniques to encourage employee participation, such as formal suggestion programs, team meetings, special taskforces and focus groups, as described below. Employees are expected to contribute their ideas for improvements; it is just part of the job.

Equity and Accountability

Systems must be developed that insure accountability to the multiple stakeholders, including investors, customers, and employees. Scanlon companies use gainsharing, goal sharing or profit sharing formulas to help focus employees on the critical needs of these stakeholders. Often the formula rewards the contribution of the investors and offers discounts in prices or rewards for customers. However, for employees pay is *not* put "at risk." Employees are paid competitive wages within their industry and labor markets. Equity formulas reward excellence; performance that is beyond what normally can be expected by the company or within the industry. Employees are often involved in calculating the bonus payouts. In some companies the concept of equity includes dispute resolution systems if disagreements occur. As is evident, the equity formula is not just about cash bonus for employees but also about recognizing and rewarding the contribution of important stakeholders.

Competence and Commitment

Everyone must commit to continually improve personally, professionally, and organizationally. Scanlon organizations have learned that employee development is a good investment, especially in a participative work environment where the scope of employee job duties is broader and where employees are expected to offer innovative suggestions for improving organization effectiveness and efficiency. Leaders of companies where Scanlon plans have been implemented often state that higher levels of competence are required than in traditionally managed companies. The Scanlon mantra is "continuous improvement requires continuous learning."

Scanlon principles are believed to be universal. They can be applied in any organization. Processes or applications are flexible and can be changed to meet the unique needs of each organization. For example, the identity principle requires that everyone understand the reality of their organization and business environment. However, the process of *education* is multidimensional and companies employ a variety of methods to help employees become business literate that include face-to-face meetings with management, published financial statements, business games, and posting performance results on bulleting boards and the organization's intranet. As another example, equity is established through a variety of formulas which include labor cost saving, goal sharing economic value added and profit sharing. The combination of universal principles combined with flexible processes has allowed Scanlon plans to create competitive advantage for over 60 years.

IMPLEMENTATION STRATEGY FOR INSTALLING SCANLON PLANS

Carl Frost and subsequent generations of academicians and consultants have developed a very specific process or road map for successfully installing Scanlon gainsharing programs. The roadmap mirrors the high involvement and informed business culture that the Scanlon plan is designed to create. Scanlon gainsharing plans are cooperatively created by the people who will be impacted by the plan. They are not produced by a consultant or compensation professional and then "sold" to the organization as are many traditional gainsharing plans. Implementation of a Scanlon gainsharing program begins with the top leader(s) developing a "mandate." A mandate is a statement that describes what the organization must do to survive and prosper. Just as the Declaration of Independence outlined why the United States sought independence and change, a mandate outlines why an organization must change. Starting with the top leadership team, the mandate is discussed and debated. Eventually a secret ballot is taken among the senior management team. Is the mandate compelling? Is there a critical need to change? Is the leadership team onboard and unanimous in the need for change? Is the leadership team convinced that Scanlon principles and implementation strategy offer the best means for responding to the mandates? If the vote indicates "no," the Scanlon process stops before additional organizational energy is spent or until the senior leadership team unanimously agree.

Assuming that the vote for change is positive, the process continues throughout the various management levels down to the front-line supervisors. This process forces the management team to commit and become aligned before the entire organization is involved. Where a union exists, the mandate is shared with the union leadership and their input is solicited. This part of the Scanlon implementation process is designed to build commitment and vision for the future.

Eventually the mandate is shared with all the employees and they are asked if they would support a design team representing a cross section of employees to develop a Scanlon gainsharing program to respond to the mandate for change. Often management will establish a secret ballot where a supermajority "yes" vote of 80–90 percent of all employees must be achieved or they will not continue to develop a Scanlon plan until the percentage is reached. The supermajority vote forces the leadership and management team to explain in language that the average employee can understand why change and the commitment of the leadership team is necessary. Often the front-line employees know change is needed but do not believe management is serious, focused, and willing to work with them to improve the organization. This phase of the implementation process requires honest communication, a willingness to admit past mistakes, and trust building. If the majority of employees do not vote to proceed, management must take this as sign that employees are not convinced and other change have to be made before employees are willing to commit themselves to Scanlon.

CREATE THE DESIGN TEAM

The next step is to create a design team charged with leading the efforts to create a Scanlon plan adapted specifically for the organization. The design team consists of both elected and appointed members and is chaired by the senior manager of the organization unit for which the program will be installed (e.g., CEO or plant manager). Top leader involvement sends a strong message that the Scanlon initiative is an important priority. The design team has four subcommittees charged with designing the best system(s) to practice the four Scanlon principles.

Identity and Education

The identity–education subcommittee wrestles with the problem of how to insure that everyone knows the critical issues or realities that are important to the organization.

- Who are the organization's customers and investors, and how do they contribute to the success of the organization?

- Who are the competitors; what are their strengths and weaknesses?

- How will information about the organization and the program be shared?

This subcommittee is charged with helping employees understand the business. If employees do not have this fundamental business literacy, their effectiveness and efficiency is limited.

Participation and Responsibility

The participation–responsibility subcommittee has one of the most difficult jobs: tapping into the creativity and improvement ideas of all employees. Participation is key to creating the gains that later will be shared through the financial formula. Research conducted by Daniel Dennison[10] demonstrates that participative organizations have a three times greater return on investment than do traditionally managed organizations. *Identity* creates knowledge about the organization; *participation* puts the knowledge to work improving organizational effectiveness and efficiency.

Since Scanlon gainsharing is based on the idea that "working smarter, not harder" employees must have the opportunity to provide input and influence decisions. The traditional Scanlon plan has a suggestion system that drives organizational improvement. All ideas are recorded and tracked so that no idea falls through the cracks. Employees share their ideas with their immediate work team. If the team likes the idea it can be quickly implemented. If the idea needs the support of other teams or departments or if it requires more money to implement than the team is authorized to spend, the suggestion goes to a "screening team." The screening team is made up of representatives from all the work teams and the top leader. The screening team has the authority and resources to act, allowing improvement ideas to be debated and quickly implemented. Ideas that require additional research are assigned to the necessary resource (e.g., industrial engineering, human resources, or finance department) and are tracked. Because everyone shares in the reward for increased productivity or profits, other employees, supervisors, or management are motivated to make sure good ideas are clearly articulated and quickly implemented.

This classic suggestion approach resulted in over 10,000 ideas at National Manufacturing, resulting in millions of dollars in savings.[11] This approach continues to be used successfully in organizations like Watermark Credit Union.[12]

Scanlon companies have experimented with all forms of participation and employee involvement. Donnelly (now Magna–Donnelly) was one of the first organizations to be totally organized into teams. Self-directed, cross-functional and six-sigma teams, lean cells, and Kaizan events are all used in Scanlon organizations to mine the ideas of employees, to improve productivity, and to reduce waste. In 1991, the average employee in a Scanlon organization contributed over $2,200 per year in cost savings suggestions.[13] Scanlon high-involvement systems are not limited to cost saving ideas. Average employees are also encouraged to submit innovative ideas for new businesses or products. Average employees have suggested new products that have created new billion dollar industries and services through their Scanlon involvement systems.

Equity and Accountability

The equity and accountability subcommittee is charged with designing the system(s) to assure that their organization is accountable to key stakeholders. Accountability to Scanlon practitioners means balancing the needs of all organizational stakeholders, building *valid and reliable measures of* organization performance and taking responsibility for organization performance.

The idea that companies must focus on multiple stakeholders instead of just stockholders is still not universally accepted. One business writer wrote about "stakeholder folly" when describing a public Scanlon company's efforts to balance the needs of multiple stakeholders. His view, shared by many business writers, is that a company does best when it focuses solely on the needs of the stockholders. Yet this is a very simplistic view of business. Rucci et al.[14] showed how wealth is created at Sears. It begins with employees who care about their company and the work they do. This drives employees to meet the needs of customers. Customers shop where their needs are met. When satisfied customers buy products and services, the investor makes more money. Kotter and Heskett[15] found that the Sears experience is not unusual.

> Corporate culture can have a significant impact on a firm's long-term economic performance . . . cultures that emphasized all the key managerial constituencies (customers, stockholders, and employees) and leadership from managers at all levels, outperformed firms that did not have those cultural traits by a huge margin. Over an eleven year period, the former increased revenues by an average of 682 percent versus 166 percent for the latter, expanded their work forces by 282 percent versus 36 percent, grew their stock prices by 901 percent versus 74 percent and improved their net incomes by 756 percent versus 1 percent.

Research is clear; investors who wish to maximize their investment must support employees so employees can create products or services of value for customers.

When organizations are performing and customer and investor needs are being met, employees naturally expect to be treated fairly and to share in the gains (i.e., gainsharing formula). Financial and compensation professionals are usually appointed to serve on the equity team along with the cross section of elected employees to insure the system is fair, economically viable, and meets the requirements of all wage and hour laws.

Early Scanlon plans often used ratio of labor costs to sales as a measure of gains. As the cost of labor was reduced below a historical baseline, gains were shared between the employees and the company. Joe Scanlon used this approach not because he believed it was the only approach, but because it was easy for the average employee to understand and to impact.

The labor to sales formula became entrenched and today this remains the most misunderstood part of the Scanlon plan, with many authors claiming that the formula is the Scanlon plan. Like the crow, their perception is a serious mistake. Scanlon plans are created with every type of formula imaginable. Profit sharing and economic value added are popular financial formulas. Scrap reduction, safety, and quality measures are popular operational measures. The formula is only limited by the equity team's imagination and creativity. The key to a successful formula is the employee's ability to understand how they can contribute to increased performance as measured by the formula.

There are countless books and articles available for the compensation professional on how to design bonus systems, but very little written about why they should create an equity system. Incentive systems focus on the dollars employees can earn whereas an equity system focuses on the relationship between investors, customers, and employees. Each of these important stakeholders must benefit by the program.

The identity principle requires that Scanlon organizations share both good and bad information. Scanlon employees understand that their companies need customers and investors to survive. They understand that sometimes in the life of an organization everyone must be called on to make sacrifices. Scanlon organizations have instituted layoffs, eliminated bonuses, required transfers, turned to outsourcing, etc. to meet the needs of their customers and investors. More often than not these sacrifices are made agreeably because Scanlon employees know why the sacrifices are needed (identity), are involved in creating solutions to the problems (participation), and trust that they will be treated fairly (equity).

Employees at Beth Israel Hospital helped the hospital during an economic crisis by donating blood. Each donation helped the hospital save $200 and prevented layoffs. Employees at Spring Engineering gave up their bonuses so they could save two jobs during a downturn in their business. Faced with huge deficits during a business downturn, Scanlon employees at Herman Miller cooperatively provided millions of dollars of cost saving suggestions. Donnelly Mirror (Magna–Donnelly) employees found ways to save a million dollars during a downturn in business, agreeing to eliminate jobs and accept that no one would receive bonuses during particularly severe business downturns.

Competence and Commitment

The competence and commitment subcommittee is responsible for insuring that all employees have a way to improve personally, professionally, and organizationally. In smaller organizations, the task may be as simple as designating core training competencies and documenting how to obtain them. In larger organizations, it could be as complicated as creating a corporate university. Most often, the task requires identifying available training resources and encouraging employees to use them.

Scanlon practitioners believe that increasing personal competencies ultimately benefits the organization. Atlantic Automotive found that among their minority employees very few were homeowners.[16] The controller provided free classes after work on personal financial management. He then helped the employees complete a mortgage application with the local bank. The increased understanding of business realities (i.e., investors) had a sizable side benefit by dramatically increasing home ownership among hourly employees.

Minutes from subcommittee meetings are shared throughout the organization while the design team works to create the plan. The organization follows the debates as the plan takes form. This part of the Scanlon implementation process requires communication, facilitation, and leadership skills.

Once the draft plan is completed it is taken back to the organization and there is often a secret ballot vote (80–90 percent agreement) to try the plan for a trial period of 1–2 years. The trial period allows those with doubts to test the system before granting their full support. It also allows the design team to analyze what works and what does not. At the end of the trial period, the design team makes any necessary changes and the plan is submitted for a final vote. In most Scanlon companies the Scanlon plan then becomes a way of life and the plan is not subjected to additional votes. Some Scanlon organizations will continue to vote and renew their plans when major changes occur or after a given number of years.

RESOURCES

Anyone can use the Scanlon name, principles, and implementation process without paying royalties or seeking permission. Many Scanlon organizations, much like the open-source software community, have joined together to share best practices. Scanlon-related information is available at no cost from the nonprofit Scanlon Leadership Network at www.scanlonleader.org.

A podcast with Dr William Greenwood on the roadmap process can be downloaded from the Network. Dr Frost's book, *Changing Forever: The Well Kept Secret of America's Leading Companies*, remains the single most definitive book on the Scanlon principles and roadmap process. It is available from Amazon, the Scanlon Leadership Network, or Michigan State University Press. The Scanlon Network sponsors one of the oldest continuing conferences in North America where Scanlon practitioners gather to learn and tour Scanlon organizations. It is usually held in May in the Midwest. Those organizations considering Scanlon are encouraged to attend.

REFERENCES

McGregor, D., *The Human Side of Enterprise.* New York: McGraw–Hill, 1960.

Scanlon, J., The Joseph Scanlon Papers, United Steelworkers of America, Rolls 1550 and 1551. Pennsylvania State University Historical Collection and Labor Archives. University Park, PA, 1941–1945.

END NOTES

1. J. McAdams and E. Hawk, *Organizational Performance and Rewards: 663 Experiences in Making the Link.* Scottsdale, AZ: American Compensation Association and Maritz Inc., 1994; J. McAdams, *Research from the Trenches: Making Incentives Work.* Presentation at the Scanlon Plan Associates Incentive Systems for Effective Organizations Conference, Chicago, IL, 6–7 October 1998.

2. E. Lawler, *The Ultimate Advantage.* New York: Jossey-Bass, 1992.

3. Gallup poll, Employee Engagement Index. Princeton, NJ: The Gallup Organization, 2004.

4. L. Branham, *The 7 Hidden Reasons Employees Leave.* New York: AMACOM, 2005.

5. Anonymous, "The Scanlon Plan," *Time Magazine*, 26 September 1955, pp. 88–90.

6. P. Davis and L. Spears (eds), *Scanlon EPIC Leadership: Where the Best Ideas Come Together.* Scanlon Foundation, 2008.

7. D. Lewis, "At Beth Israel, Workers' Ideas Count for Plenty," *The Boston Sunday Globe*, 1 March 1992.

8. C. F. Frost, *Changing Forever: The Well Kept Secret of America's Leading Companies.* Lansing, MI: MSU Press, 1996; C. F. Frost, J. H. Wakely, and R. A. Ruh, *The Scanlon Plan for Organizational Development: Identity, Participation and Equity.* Lansing, MI: MSU Press, 1974.

9. The four principles can be easily remembered as EPIC Leadership, although the order of the principles is usually listed as IPEC, reflecting the critical importance of identity.

10. D. Dennison, *Corporate Culture and Organizational Effectiveness*. New York: Wiley, 1990, p. 64.

11. P. Davis, *Exploring Scanlon Handout*. East Lansing, MI: Scanlon Leadership Network, 2000, p. 16.

12. D. Scott, P. Davis, and C. Cockburn, "Scanlon Principles and Processes: Building Excellence at Watermark Credit Union," *WorldatWork Journal*, vol. 16, no. 1, 2007, pp. 29–37.

13. J. McAdams, Scanlon Leadership Network Equity Forum, Grand Rapids, MI, 1993.

14. A. J. Rucci, S. P. Kirn, and R. T. Quinn, "The Employee-Customer-Profit Chain at Sears," *Harvard Business Review*, January–February 1998.

15. J. Kotter and J. Heskett, *Corporate Culture and Performance*. Columbus, OH: The Free Press, 1992, p. 11.

16. K. D. Scott, G. Shivers, J. W. Bishop and V. A. Cerra, "Building a Company Culture that Drives Performance: A Case Study," *WorldatWork Journal*, vol. 13, no. 1, 2004, pp. 46–54.

P A R T

4

Executive Compensation

C H A P T E R

EXECUTIVE COMPENSATION STRATEGY

Ted Buyniski, Senior Vice President and Marvin A. Mazer,
Senior Vice President

Radford Surveys & Consulting

HISTORICALLY, EXECUTIVE COMPENSATION STRATEGY **HAS** often been an afterthought. Companies reviewed salaries, set bonuses, granted equity or other long-term incentives, and established executive deferred compensation and retirement plans as discrete, often unconnected events, based on competitive practice, executive direction, and all too often, the flavor *du jour* in the tax and consulting communities, such as the recent romance with restricted stock.

Over the last several years, these practices have changed dramatically as a result of events in the marketplace. First, the institutional investment community has significantly increased its focus on the link between executive pay and performance. While every company has spoken of "pay for performance" as they would of "mom and apple pie," institutional investors are increasingly casting their votes on the basis of performance. Some advisory services routinely recommend "no" votes on equity plans and compensation committee members, based on a perceived negative relationship between pay and performance.

Second, new (2007) proxy reporting rules issued by the Security and Exchange Commission are forcing companies to expose the thought process that goes into their executive compensation plans to an unprecedented degree. The Compensation Disclosure and Analysis ("CD&A"), a newly required section in proxy filings, goes well beyond tabular presentation of executive compensation data, and requires companies to explain the "why" of executive compensation, not just the "what." The result, in some cases, is a great deal of compensation committee consternation as the members review, in some cases for the first time, the totality of what executives have received, as well as the real and potential optics issues created by processes and practices that have driven compensation decisions.

The legal environment, while still granting tremendous latitude for the business judgment of the Board, has, in cases like the *Disney* case[1] highlighted the need for compensation committees to elucidate clear standards and processes in structuring executive compensation. Further, the stock option backdating scandals of 2006 have demonstrated that there are significant procedural issues in executive compensation, which rise to the level of legal liability. Finally, while the extent to which legal limits will be placed on pay is still unclear, and unlikely, there is legislation such as the "The Protection Against Executive Compensation Abuse Act" introduced by Barney Frank (D-MA) in 2007, which would further increase the regulation of executive pay.

Finally, the press continues to focus on executive compensation, generally highlighting the compensation outliers such as Robert Nardelli's exit from Home Depot, and that of United Health's CEO William McGuire.

Given the heightened scrutiny, it is more critical than ever that companies be able to place executive compensation in context by answering the following questions:

- *What* are we paying executives to do?

- *How* do we determine the pay vehicles which will be used?

- *How much* will we pay them?

- *What* impact will there be for different levels of performance and ultimately,

- *Who* is an "executive"?

EXECUTIVE COMPENSATION IN CONTEXT

First though, it is necessary to look at the broadest context in which executive compensation functions (see Figure 24.1).

Executive compensation design takes place, not in isolation, but surrounded by a ring of competing interest groups, each with different, although sometimes overlapping, agendas. *Employees* naturally are focused on whether the strategy provides them with the opportunity to build their wealth and careers better than

FIGURE 24.1   **Strategic perspective**

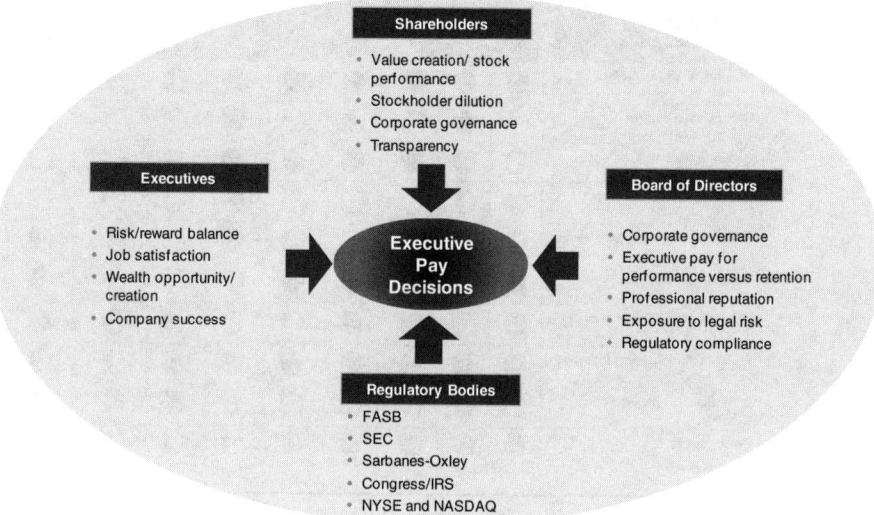

competing offers. *Shareholders* are concerned with whether they are getting suffi-cient "bang for the buck" in terms of pay for performance, and how much their executives are costing them. The *Board* has the unenviable task of keeping execu-tives, shareholders, and regulators satisfied that the proper processes are being observed. Finally *regulators*, from the SEC to the stock exchanges, are charged with maintaining the integrity of the public markets, and as such, are increasingly requiring additional procedural safeguards and disclosures.

Within this context, the compensation committee must develop an executive compensation strategy to meet the company's needs. This, of itself, is a critical change over the past five or so years. This is perhaps the most fundamental change in executive compensation in the last 25 years—the shifting of the balance of power in executive compensation decision-making from management to the compensation committee.

ESTABLISHING AN EXECUTIVE COMPENSATION STRATEGY

So, how should a Compensation Committee go about establishing a company's executive compensation strategy?

Step 1. Know the Goal

Strategy focuses on the achievement of a goal. To paraphrase the ancient proverb, "A journey of a thousand miles does not start with a single step—it starts by knowing where you are going." The company's *business strategy* must drive the

FIGURE 24.2　Relationship of performance measures to business objectives

Business Objective	Cash Flow	TSR	ROE/ROI	ROIC	ROA	Stock price	EPS	Net Income/Earnings	Op Income	Revenue
Increase revenues / sales	●	●	●	●	●	●	◐	◐	◐	○
Manage cash outflow	○	●	◐	◐	◐	●	◐	○	◐	●
Generate cash	○	●	●	●	●	●	●	○	○	◐
Increase income / earnings	◐	◐	○	○	○	●	○	○	○	◐
Increase margins / control costs	◐	●	○	○	○	●	○	◐	◐	●
Increase stock price	●	○	●	●	●	○	◐	◐	●	◐
Increase shareholder return	●	○	●	●	◐	○	◐	◐	●	◐
Promote new business investment	●	●	●	●	●	●	●	◐	◐	◐
Utilize assets efficiently	○	●	◐	○	○	●	●	●	●	●
Raise capital	●	●	●	●	●	◐	◐	◐	○	○

Strong Relationship ● Some Relationship ◐ Little Relationship ○

company's executive compensation strategy. For example, depending on what a company's goals are, there will be significant differences in what the company will want to measure and reward (see Figure 24.2).

The selection of one (or more) of these measures instead of others reflects a variety of factors, including industry, business model, and the stage of the company's life cycle—is it a fledgling pre-IPO biotech company focused on raising money and pushing a new drug through the FDA approval process, or is it a heavy equipment company in a mature industry focused on maximizing its cash flow? We will return to this issue of life cycle again, when we look at how the company chooses to execute its strategy.

Step 2. Know the Tools

Although different elements of executive compensation are more or less attractive at any given time due to changes in taxes (e.g., the decline in deferred compensation post-409A), accounting rules (i.e., stock options post-FAS123R) or institutional concerns (the elimination of pensions for directors), the tools that companies can apply have remained constant: salaries, short-term cash incentives, long-term cash and equity incentives, benefits (both general and executive), and perquisites. Each has benefits and drawbacks, both from the perspective of how they affect the executive and how they affect the company (see Figure 24.3).

Further, they will differ in how they affect the company from the standpoints of cash flow, tax and accounting consequences, and the perceptions of shareholders, the public, and the executives themselves. There are some general tendencies as to

FIGURE 24.3 Purpose of executive compensation vehicles

Vehicle	Attract	Motivate	Retain
Salary	●	○	◐
Annual Bonus	◐	●	○
Long-term Cash	○	●	●
Options	●	●	◐
Restricted Stock	●	○	●
Performance Shares	○	●	○
Qualified Benefits	○	○	◐
Executive Benefits	◐	○	●
Perquisites	◐	○	◐

Strong Relationship ● Some Relationship ◐ Little Relationship ○

how these programs are applied in companies, depending on where they stand in their life cycle (see Table 24.1).

These are general tendencies reflecting competitive market practices, rather than "must follow" rules. For example, a start-up that throws off significant cash flow might have competitive bonuses, while a declining company may consider cutting fixed compensation (salary, benefits, perquisites) to fuel a turnaround.

Step 3. Know the Market

"Knowing the market" boils down to three things. First, you have to know who your "market" is; in other words, the companies you compete with for talent and

TABLE 24.1 Application of Pay Elements to Company Life Cycle Stage

	Life Cycle Stage			
Pay element	Start-up	Growth	Mature	Declining
Salary	Low	Competitive	Competitive/High	High
Annual bonus	Low	Competitive/High	Competitive	Low
Long-term incentives	High	Competitive/High	Competitive	Low
Form of LTI	Options	Options/Performance shares	Performance shares/Restricted stock/Cash	Restricted stock/Cash
Qualified benefits	Low	Competitive	Competitive	High
Executive benefits	None	Low	Competitive	High
Perquisites	None	Low	Competitive	High

market share. Second, you need to know where to position your executive pay strategy relative to the peer group—not only how much the company will pay, but how to it will balance the delivery of that amount across the compensation vehicles (as noted above), relative to its peers. It is only then that you need to know what the market is paying in actual, aggregate dollar amounts. Based on these three points, the company can then make an informed determination of how it wants to actually want to pay *its* executives.

Choosing a Peer Group.   This is one of the most contentious discussions taking place in compensation committee meetings today. Historically, management would present the compensation committee with a list of companies that loosely consisted of those companies management recruited from, or lost people to, or competed with on product. Usually, but not always they would be roughly similar in size. With the advent of the new proxy disclosure rules, companies are applying significantly more rigor to identifying their proposed peers, and are applying multiple screens, including:

- Similar size—for better or worse, the strongest correlation in the marketplace remains that between revenue and salary. But it is important to look beyond just revenue and include the number of employees, market capitalization, assets, and other metrics. Typically, for every doubling in size, there is a 10–15 percent increase in salaries. Therefore as a practical matter, a size-based peer group of 50–200 percent of revenue will generate comparable salaries. As additional size-related characteristics, market capitalization and earnings should also be examined, to find companies that the marketplace considers similar in performance terms as well as complexity.

- Performance—this is typically a thornier issue. Should a company choose peers who: (a) perform comparably; (b) perform at the level the company aspires to; or (c) perform in line with the overall industry? For compensation planning purposes, we would suggest (c) as the benchmark. If we are setting performance *targets*, the focus should be on improving performance from current levels, but to understand the baseline, the focus should be on how the overall industry is performing.

- Similar business—as the markets have evolved, there are definitively different pay structures in some industries, for example, high technology, financial services, and regulated utilities.

- Similar economics—with respect to performance, the analysis might include a review of margin performance, multiyear revenue growth, and even the underlying strategy and value proposition, e.g., value-added reseller versus complete manufacturer.

That said, there are often trade-offs to be made. For many companies, it is not possible to find a sufficient number of companies of the same size in the same business with the same strategy to create a meaningful (usually 15–20 company) peer group. In these cases, judgment must be applied to determine the criticality of each of the criteria, and whether finding a meaningful number of companies takes the "market" too far away from its core. In such cases, weightings can be applied to mitigate the impact of, for example, companies with significantly larger revenue than the median of the peer group.

Positioning.   Critics of executive compensation practices have made much of the "Lake Woebegone Syndrome" of executive pay,[2] in decrying the use of competitive data for determining pay. However, companies still need to determine where, in aggregate and in component, they will pay their executives relative to the market. Generally, there are strategic and market pressures (outlined in the table below) that may suggest paying above, or below the prevailing market for executives, just as for any other employee (see Table 24.2).

TABLE 24.2   Pay Positioning

Positioning	Rationales
Below market	■ Affordability—Company has insufficient cash/equity to pay at the market ■ Company tends to be smaller than most of its peers ■ Company is using other means of attracting and retaining employees (e.g., location, working conditions, corporate mission, etc.) ■ Other pay elements are targeted above market so that total is in line with the market ■ Lack of competition for employees ■ Low turnover, so compensation isn't an issue ■ Local market conditions (e.g., exceptionally low cost of living, or depressed conditions making employer the "best game in town") ■ Low performance expectations
Above market	■ Need to attract/retain executives in a competitive market ■ Company tends to be larger than its peers ■ Pay is the primary motivator in the company's philosophy—e.g., a "no frills" environment ■ Difficult market conditions—e.g., turnaround ■ High turnover ■ Compensates for other elements of pay which are positioned below market ■ High performance expectations

The key is that compensation committees should not simply default to paying "market median." If all companies were alike, everyone could set their targets at median and go home. The potential flaw, against which compensation committees must steel themselves, is the notion that we must set *target pay at least* at market. This naturally leads to an escalation in compensation, generally outstripping the inflation we see in wages overall.

Data.   Finally, once the company determines who the peers are, *and where to pay against those peers*, only then is the actual data discussion relevant. The key becomes finding the "best" data, of which there are essentially two sets of sources:

- *Public data*—sources that essentially trace back to company's public filings with the SEC or other regulatory bodies. This includes proxies as well as companies such as Equilar that collect and disseminate publicly available information. With the new proxy disclosure rules, this has become a much richer source of information, both in terms of the quality of the compensation data and the company practices that generate pay. However, there are three critical limits to using only public data. First, it is generally available only for the "top five" executives. Second, while some jobs are relatively standardized (e.g., comparing chief executive officers across companies will be relatively straightforward) other jobs may not be so easy to compare (e.g., is a "senior vice president global solutions marketing officer" equivalent to a "president sales, marketing and institutional business development"?). Finally, proxy data is always retrospective—it looks at what was done for the last year, not what is being done in the current year. Further, care needs to be taken in mining public data. The new CD&A rules, while providing a wealth of data that has historically been lacking, also provides simple traps for the unobservant—for example, in considering long-term incentives, are we looking at the FAS123R cost for the year, the gain realized, or the FAS123R cost for shares granted? Any of these may be valid for a given purpose, but whoever is collecting the data must be consistent in application.

- *Survey data*—sources that collect confidential data from participants and then analyze and package that data for the use of the survey's participants. These sources address the drawbacks of public data. First, depending on the survey, many more positions are reviewed than are available in public data. Second, because most surveys include job descriptions, and a means of adjusting data for jobs that do not specifically fit the descriptions, they can provide a better "apples-to-apples" comparison for most jobs. Finally, since the data in many surveys is collected more frequently, it is generally "fresher."

Despite these advantages, companies need to exercise caution in using survey data. First, not all surveys are created equal. Care needs to be taken to ensure that the companies in the survey reflect the peers, or potential peers, of the company. Second, there need to be processes in place such that the survey results accurately reflect the market: there are enough companies involved to be meaningful; there is "data scrubbing" to make sure the data submitted is accurate and meaningful. This can be especially troubling with some of the online survey engines, where there is no quality control of data entered by individuals accessing the web site. Third, and relatedly, is the question of the objectivity of the survey—does the sponsor of the survey have an agenda that may color the results? Finally, a potential issue with survey data is its availability—some surveys are available only to participants, and even participation is on an "invitation-only" basis—so-called "club" surveys.

Nonetheless, a judicious use of *both* sources of data is important to ensure that the compensation committee has a well-rounded view of the competitive market. This analysis will provide a baseline. The committee can then determine, based on the relevant market, and the desired positioning vs that market, where to set target pay for target performance. The next step is to determine the opportunities when performance doesn't exactly match plan.

Step 4. Planning for Contingencies

It is a truism in business as in war that "No plan survives contact with the enemy."[3] A crucial part of executive compensation strategy is planning for what *could* happen—either outperforming or underperforming expectations.

In terms of executive compensation strategy this means that any programs must be able to address all scenarios. For example, one increasingly common means of providing long-term incentives is to make performance-based share grants, with the performance measure being based on how a company performs relative to its peers. In the "down" leg of a cyclical market, this can provide an incentive to executives to perform superior "damage control"—minimizing the impact of the cycle. However, if plans are not properly structured, it can lead to counterintuitive results that reflect poorly on the company. For example, one company in the semiconductor space based its annual bonus solely on performance versus peers. In one year, due to strong inventory management and cost-cutting, they saw their performance rise to above the 75th percentile vs their peers, which generated a payout of almost 200 percent of target. From the perspective of the primary objective—getting executives to focus on "damage control," the plan worked. However, at the same time, the company was: (a) losing money, (b) laying off more than 10 percent of its workforce, and (c) suffering a 50 percent decline in its stock price. The result was a public relations conundrum that resulted in the compensation committee deferring part of the bonuses and converting them to restricted stock, both to minimize the economic impact and to defuse employee and shareholder criticism.

Ideally, planning for contingencies needs to take into account a number of factors, including:

■ The likelihood of performance at a level other than at target. How good is management at setting goals? How much of a company's performance is subject to the control of management and how much to the vagaries of the marketplace?

■ How much of the business has a "tail"—is the company fulfilling multiyear agreements, or is it more akin to starting each year at Step 1?

■ At what point do results (either good or bad), move from the realm of good (or bad) execution, to "luck" or "Act of God?"

Essentially, these answers will facilitate both the leverage of plans—e.g., thresholds and maxima—and the vehicles selected (for example, stock options are more volatile than restricted stock, which in turn is more volatile than long-term cash). Finally, the committee, in its planning, must always build in contingency plans that address how they will handle unexpected events such as acquisitions, changes in laws or regulations, etc.

Step 5: What to Pay for What Performance?

Ultimately, all the strategic planning comes together in this step—defining performance, choosing among the different executive compensation tools, examining the market and planning for a range of performance possibilities. In an ideal world, the results will be that pay and performance will align, whether for good or bad performance (see Figure 24.4).

FIGURE 24.4   Aligning pay and performance

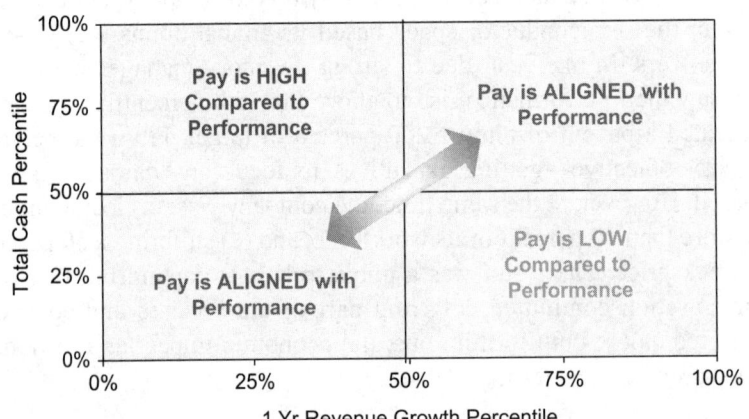

FIGURE 24.5   Pay for performance variables

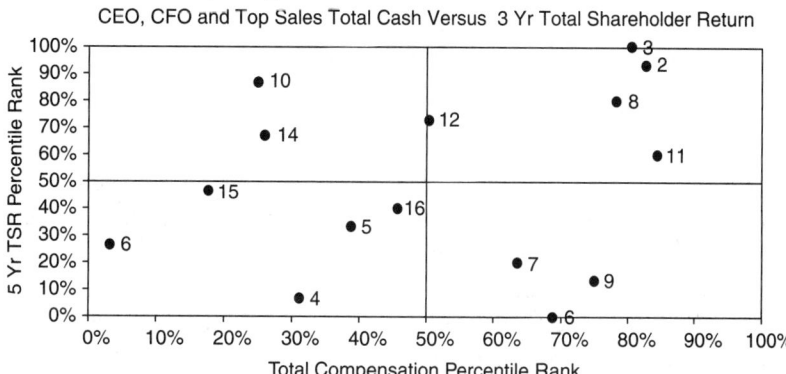

CEO, CFO and Top Sales Total Cash Versus 3 Yr Total Shareholder Return

The reality, of course, is often different, as in a recent analysis (see below) of 16 software companies. While nine of the companies can say their programs are generally working—compensation and performance are at least in the same quadrant—three of the companies are significantly overpaying for performance, while two are likewise significantly underpaying (see Figure 24.5).

This then, is the proof of concept—is the strategy working? If it is, then only fine-tuning may be needed as the company continues to evolve. But if results and compensation are not in synch, or if there is a major strategic change in the company, then the strategy must be reviewed.

Step 6: Defining Executives

The last element of the strategy is to determine what constitutes an executive position for purposes of inclusion in the executive compensation plans. For the top, it is a relatively easy decision—obviously the CEO, CFO, and in fact anyone with a "CxO" designation. But ultimately there is a boundary—where the compensation committee's scope of authority fades, and where the employees' role turns from planning to executing the plans of others. Some companies draw this line between "directors" and "vice presidents." Others may draw the distinction between different types of vice presidents (especially those with large, client-facing sales forces), and still others between vice presidents and senior vice presidents. Regardless of where the line is drawn, there are a number of issues that are highlighted by this differentiation.

- Participation in compensation plans—many companies provide different annual or long-term incentives for executives

- Benefit and perquisite participation—generally participation in "executive" benefits and receiving perks (or different levels of perks) hinges on being "an executive"

- Ownership requirements—with many companies requiring executives to own stock equal to one, two, or more times their salaries, there are downsides as well as benefits to being considered an executive

SUMMARY

Ultimately, there is no single answer. Rather companies need to focus on what distinguishes their executives from their employees, not in terms of pay, but in terms of responsibilities, scope of authority, and impact on the performance of the company, and then build their programs to match.

While the development of the new CD&A and associated tables has been a long and arduous process for many companies, one of the results has been a keener focus on and awareness of the importance of setting a sound and defensible executive compensation strategy that aligns total executive pay outcomes with company success. Following the steps outlined in this article can assist the compensation committee in understanding the key concepts and tactics to successfully navigating through the new proxy disclosure requirements in an informed and thoughtful way.

END NOTES

1. *In re Walt Disney Company Derivative Litigation*, No. Civ. A 15452, 2005 WL 2056651 (Del. Ch. Aug, 2005).

2. Named for the fictitious town in NPR's "A Prairie Home Companion," where "The men are strong, the women are good-looking and *all the children are above average*" (italics added).

3. Helmuth von Moltke the Elder 1800–1891, Chief of the German General Staff.

C H A P T E R

LONG-TERM INCENTIVES

Jeffrey S. Hyman, Esq.

Exequity LLP

IF THE DECADE OF THE 1990s was the era when long-term incentives grew to prominence on the executive compensation landscape, the first decade of the new millennium undoubtedly will be remembered as the time when long-term incentives defined the remuneration package. Spurred by a record-setting bull stock market and ever-increasing demands for enhanced investment value, management increasingly has turned to long-term compensation programs to reinforce value-added mandates and recognize executive contributions to increasing shareowner wealth. As a result, long-term incentives have become one of the most popular—and certainly one of the most publicized—forms of executive compensation today. No treatment of executive compensation is possible without a comprehensive review of long-term incentives.

To understand the extent to which long-term incentives are embedded in the compensation landscape, consider a recent Hewitt Associates survey in which it was reported that 95 percent of all major companies offer their executives at least one form of long-term incentive opportunity.[1] Organizations with more than $1.0 billion in annual sales generally maintain at least two different types of long-term incentive plans, and it is not at all uncommon for executives in these companies to participate in multiple award opportunities, whether in a tandem relationship or independently of one another.

Not only is the prevalence of the long-term component reaching universal proportion, but its relative value within the total executive compensation package has changed, too. What was once considered a relatively incidental fringe benefit has become over the past 25 years a substantial and integral part of the corporate executive's overall pay opportunity. Studies indicate that, while the long-term incentive component was just 16 percent of a senior executive's total pay in 1982, it contributed 31 percent in 1989, 45 percent in 1997, and 60 percent by 2006—quadruple the impact in 25 years.[2] This represents a growth rate of nearly 6 percent per year, far outpacing the rate of increase in cash compensation for most American executives.

CHARACTERISTICS OF LONG-TERM INCENTIVE PLANS

Before choosing a long-term incentive program, careful thought should be given to the overall corporate strategy driving the plan implementation. As is true for all management systems, soundly designed compensation programs should not be structured in a vacuum, so it is essential to understand the purposes for which the long-term incentive plan is being implemented and the specific objectives the program is expected to help satisfy. Well-articulated compensation objectives are instrumental in the process of selecting the long-term incentive program design that best supports the organization's business and human resources needs.

Share the Company's Success with Executives. By allowing executives to share in the company's success, long-term plans serve to focus executive attention on certain key aspects of the company's performance.

Promote Long-Term Thinking. Long-term plans effectively balance the short-term focus of annual incentive plans.

Align Executive Interest with that of Shareholders. By making a portion of an executive's compensation contingent on company performance, long-term plans help correlate management's personal interests with those of shareholders, thereby promoting decision making that enhances the value of the firm's capital investment.

Attract and Retain Talented Executives. Long-term incentive awards often represent a sizable percentage of an executive's total compensation. When these awards are structured so that they vest over a period of years, they can act as an effective retention device. Additionally, the prevalence of long-term incentives in American industry makes it increasingly difficult for companies without such plans to attract and retain talented people.

Supplement Broad-Based, Tax-Qualified Employee Retirement Income Programs. As tax laws continue to limit the benefits that can accrue on behalf of the highly paid, many companies implement long-term incentive plans to supplement the capital accumulation opportunities available to executives under broad-based, tax-qualified retirement programs.

Since the effectiveness of a long-term plan depends largely on how well the program suits the intended objectives, it is important to be familiar with the full range of program designs. Keep in mind, however, that unlike the broad-based benefit programs typically offered to all employees, executive long-term incentive plans generally are not tax qualified (with the exception of incentive stock options) and, therefore, are not usually restricted to a format that complies with stringent legislative regulation. The range of possible program structures is limited only by the creativity and resourcefulness of those challenged with developing the overall plan.

Notwithstanding the flexibility permissible in executive incentive plan design, the format of a long-term program typically falls into one of three categories, depending on the company's primary considerations. Plans that are *market based* relate incentive earnings opportunities to increases in the price of a company's common stock. *Performance-based arrangements*, on the other hand, correlate payout with more internally focused performance targets. *Hybrid formats* incorporate elements of both internal and external performance in determining the value of the earnings available to the plan participants.

Whether a market-based, performance-based, or hybrid plan is right for an organization depends entirely on the operation objectives, overall corporate strategy, and underlying management philosophy of the company itself. Remember, the long-term incentive plan is best characterized as a communication device through which the company identifies for its executives the mission it expects to fulfill, the strategy by which it will do so, and the goals that, when accomplished, will indicate the satisfaction of the corporation's purpose. Consequently, the structure of the long-term incentive is impossible to separate from the objectives it is expected to support.

Many factors affect the choice of an appropriate long-term incentive plan, especially the related tax and financial accounting implications. Given the magnitude of prevailing long-term incentive awards and the breadth of participation in the plans, it is important to consider the impact of charges to the financial statements, the potential for earnings dilution, and the timing and characterization of income and deductions.

Still, the primary consideration when constructing a long-term incentive plan is whether the plan framework supports the organization's objectives. Understanding how these programs can work to deliver the right messages is probably accomplished best by understanding the mechanics of specific program formats. The remainder of this chapter, therefore, characterizes the most frequently used long-term incentive plans, followed by a discussion comparing the different approaches.

MARKET-BASED PLANS

Stock options remain one the most popular forms of long-term incentives offered by American companies. Roughly 80 percent of all major companies have an option program in place. Stock options provide employees with the right to purchase company stock at a stipulated price over a specific period of time. If the stock value appreciates within that time frame, the employee then has the right to acquire the stock at a price below its market value.

There are two types of stock option plans—the nonqualified version and the incentive stock alternative. While the mechanics of both types of plans are similar, they each have distinct characteristics.

Nonqualified Stock Options

The more prevalent of the executive stock option plans is the nonqualified variety. *Nonqualified stock option plans* are the more flexible of the two kinds of stock option programs. They are unfettered by statute or regulation concerning minimum-price requirements, maximum grant periods, or maximum exercise and holding periods. The absence of regulation enables companies to tailor their plans to fit their individual objectives (for example, some companies may wish to limit option exercisability after death or disability, others may wish to extend the term of an option to the duration of an employee's career, and so forth).

Generally, the employee who receives nonqualified stock options incurs no tax liability at the time of the grant. However, at the date of exercise, the excess of the stock's market value over the option price is taxable as ordinary income. Any subsequent appreciation that is realized at the time the acquired share is sold is taxed as a capital gain. Figure 25.1 presents a graph of an employee's tax consequences with nonqualified stock options. With a nonqualified stock option plan, the employer receives a business expense (compensation) deduction in the amount and at the time the employee realizes ordinary income.

Incentive Stock Options

The second type of executive stock option plan is the *incentive stock option*, which is designed to be a tax-favored way to deliver stock to employees. The operational

FIGURE 25.1   Nonqualified stock options and employee tax liability

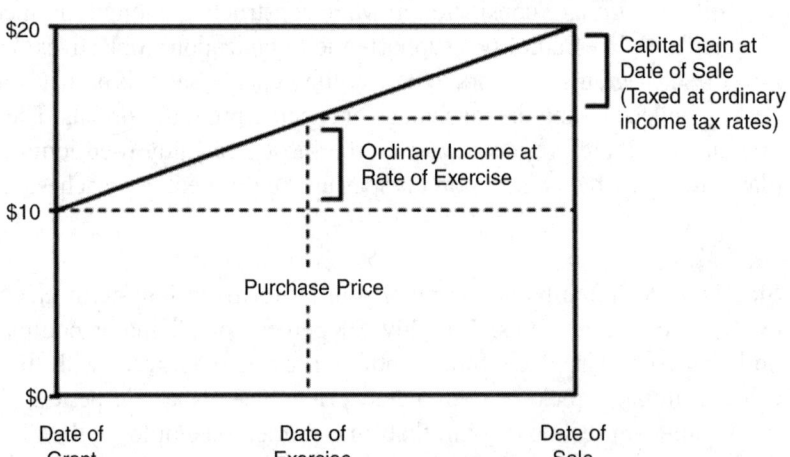

aspects of incentive stock options are largely the same as those of nonqualified stock options, but the employee and the plan itself must comply with several restrictive tax law provisions that have no application to the nonqualified variety of option. If the rules are adhered to, employees benefit in two ways: they avoid taxation both at the grant and the time of option exercise, and any gain ultimately recognizable on the sale of acquired shares is treated as capital in nature rather than as ordinary income.

The rules that ensure favored tax treatment for incentive stock options are delineated in Section 422A of the Internal Revenue Code. In short, the options must be designated "incentive stock options," they cannot be exercised at a price less than 100 percent of the underlying stock's fair value on the option grant date, and no more than $100,000 worth of options can vest in any one year. In addition, a statutory holding period must be satisfied. If the stock is held for at least 1 year following the date of exercise and 2 years from the date of the grant, then when the stock is disposed of, the aggregate difference between the option price and the sale price is taxed as a long-term capital gain.

Essentially, there are two principal advantages to incentive stock options: favorable long-term capital gain tax treatment and the deferral of taxation until the date the acquired shares are sold. However, the *bargain element* (the difference between the option price and the market price) at exercise is a tax preference item subject to the alternative minimum tax. The tax effect of incentive stock options on the employee is shown in Figure 25.2.

For most employees, the tax deferral and capital gain treatment attendant to incentive stock option awards makes them quite appealing. But employers typically object to their issuance because of their less-than-optimal consequences for the company. More specifically, the employer generally earns no business expense

FIGURE 25.2   Incentive stock options and employee tax liability

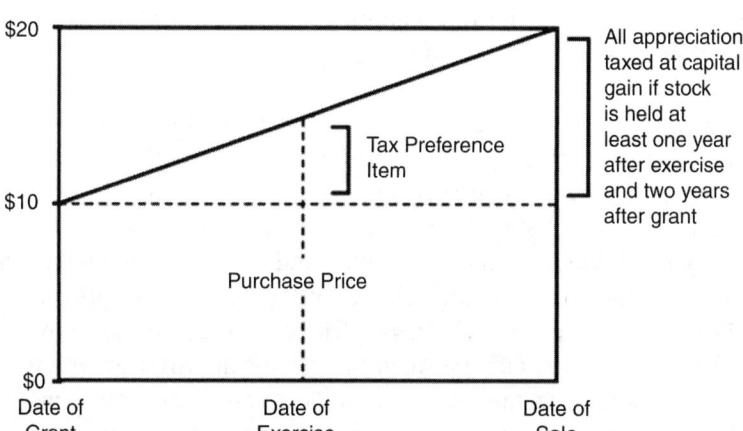

(compensation) deduction on option exercise unless the employee fails the requisite holding-period requirements. In that event, the employee will be forced to recognize any accrued appreciation as ordinary income, and the employer then will become entitled to an offsetting tax deduction.

The manner in which companies account for options has changed recently. For many years, employers typically incurred no compensation expense in association with options granted at fair market value. But the adoption of Financial Accounting Standard (FAS) 123R changed the landscape with respect to accounting for all stock-based compensation awards, and the cost of options (commonly formulated at grant according to a complicated Black–Scholes calculation) now must be charged against earnings and recognized in full over the course of the option vesting period. FAS123R includes an odd, but important, provision requiring that option-related charges cannot be reversed in the event the option expires worthless because the fair market value of the underlying share is lower than the option exercise price at the end of the option term. That means that the option issuer risks incurring accounting costs without conveying any real benefit to the option recipients. To many option critics, that particular inefficiency (which is unique to stock options) is cited as reason to select alternative long-term incentive formats.

Stock Appreciation Rights

Stock appreciation rights (SARs) allow an employee to realize the appreciation in value of a specified number of common shares without making a cash investment in the stock or causing dilution of the employer's shareholder equity. SARs work in the following way.

Suppose an employee is granted 1,000 SARs when a single share of the company's stock is selling for $20. Further assume that the price of a single share appreciates in value by $10 during the exercise period, and the employee exercises all 1,000 SARs when the market value of the stock reaches $30 per share. In this scenario, the employee becomes entitled to a cash award from the company equal to $10,000. It is at this time, when the SARs are cashed out, that tax ramifications materialize.

SARs may be granted alone or in conjunction with nonqualified stock options and/or incentive stock options. When SARs are granted in tandem with stock options, the number of shares covered by the appreciation rights normally equals the number of shares subject to acquisition by option exercise. The exercise of an option typically cancels an SAR account and vice versa. In this manner, the SARs act as a tax offset or financing vehicle for the exercise of options.

When SARs are granted independently of stock options, any appreciation in company stock that occurs between the date of the SAR grant and the date of its exercise is payable to the executive in cash, stock, or a combination. When the SARs are exercised, the employee recognizes ordinary income in the amount

FIGURE 25.3 SARs and employee tax liability

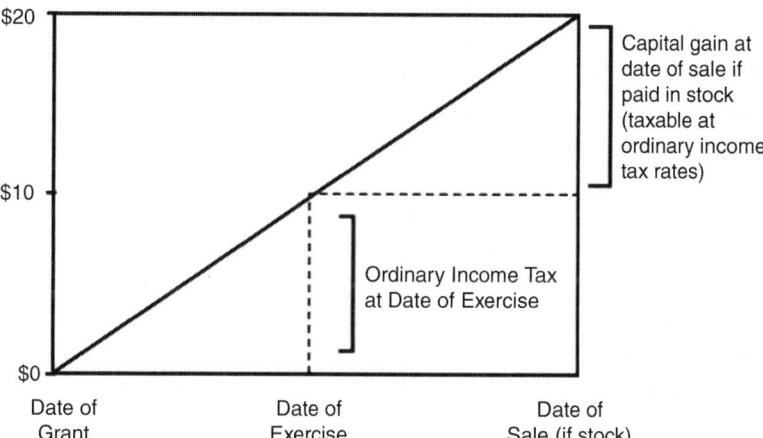

received in satisfaction of the award. If the SARs are settled in shares instead of cash, the recipient becomes, in effect, an investor in the company, So, later on, when the acquired shares are sold, the amount received at sale is subject to tax in accordance with the rules governing the sale of a capital asset. (These results are displayed graphically in Figure 25.3.) Settling SARs in stock can be appealing to a company that is interested in minimizing share utilization in its stock-based compensation program. When SARs are settled in shares, the effect is tantamount to the exercise of stock options, yet stock-settled SARs deplete the share award pool to a lesser extent than stock options do. This enhanced efficiency can make stock-settled SARs an appealing alternative to traditional stock options.

The fact that the employee is taxed at ordinary income rates at the time the SARs are exercised means the employer can claim a business expense (compensation) deduction equal to the amount of the employee's ordinary income in the year that the employee first incurs a tax liability. The employee's subsequently earned capital gain or loss on the disposition of acquired shares has no effect on the company.

The accounting for SARs depends on whether they can be settled in cash or stock. Cash-settled SARs generate variable accounting; they regularly are marked to fair value over the course of their vesting period. In contrast, SARs that can be settled in shares generate earnings charges as if they were stock options. The grant-date cost of the SAR is formulated in accordance with a Black–Scholes valuation, and the cost is expensed over the award's vesting period (see Figure 25.3).

Restricted Stock

Restricted stock programs have proliferated in the past few years to the point where nearly three-in-four companies now maintain one. Restricted stock programs permit the transfer of the employer's stock to an employee, usually free of charge to the recipient. In this sense, restricted stock awards are outright equity grants. Full rights to stock acquisitions are conditional, however, and are predicated on the occurrence of certain events, like the continued employment of the individual for a specified period of time. Some plans provide restricted stock to vest when certain corporate or individual performance goals are met. These variations usually are called performance-based restricted stock awards.

Most restricted stock awards convey to the recipient full shareholder rights during the restricted period, except for the right to sell or transfer stock. Once the conditions placed on the transfer of stock are fulfilled, the recipient owns the stock outright. If the conditions are not satisfied, however, the employee must forfeit the stock in its entirety.

A variation on restricted stock program is a TARSAP, *time-accelerated restricted stock award plan*. The time-accelerated feature allows restrictions to be removed faster than originally scheduled if the executive or the company meets certain performance goals. In this sense, the TARSAP constitutes a hybrid form of long-term incentive award.

For example, if XYZ Company issues restricted stock to executive A, then the stock becomes A's outright if A is in the employ of the company at the end of a five-year period. In an alternative scenario, the company might set up a certain income goal for the corporation. If the company achieves the goal before five years have elapsed from grant, then the vesting period will be accelerated. For example, if the income goal is attained in the third year, the restricted shares will vest with executive A at the end of three years rather than five years.

Another variation among restricted stock plans is a *restricted stock performance plan*. It ties the lapse of transferability restrictions and forfeiture risk on performance results rather than continued employment with the company. For example, executive A may be granted restricted stock that vests in 4 years only if the company generates average earnings per share of $2.00 for the period and the executive is employed at the end of the term. If the performance goal is not satisfied, a smaller number of shares may vest, or perhaps none at all.

Importantly, many companies today substitute awards of *restricted stock units* (RSUs) for restricted shares. RSUs are units of measurement that correspond in value to a share of stock. Like restricted shares, RSUs typically vest some number of years after grant, or, alternatively, on the occurrence of a defined event, such as retirement or termination of service. The decision to grant RSUs in lieu of restricted shares can preserve a degree of flexibility with respect to taxation that might not be available with the granting of restricted stock.

Ordinarily, an executive who gets restricted stock incurs no tax liability at the date of the grant. When the restrictions lapse, however, ordinary income is recognized equal in amount to the current fair market value of the stock, less the employee's cost to acquire the shares, if any. After restrictions lapse, the executive is viewed as an equity investor in the company, so, for tax purposes, any subsequent appreciation or loss is treated as capital in nature.

In the instance where the employee expects there will be a substantial increase forthcoming in the market price of the shares, the employee may elect to pay the tax on the initial bargain value of the restricted grant within 30 days of the grant date. When this election is made, the income recognized is taxed as ordinary income, but any subsequent appreciation is capital gain. Given the disparate treatment accorded ordinary income and capital gain, some employees find this "Section 83(b) election" to be an attractive alternative to the standard tax posture. Figure 25.4 depicts the usual [non-Section 83(b) election] tax consequences for an executive who receives restricted stock.

As is the case in all other nonqualified compensation plans, the employer granting restricted stock becomes entitled to a deductible compensation expense for tax purposes when, and in the same amount as, the employee realizes taxable ordinary income. Typically, this means that the employer gets a deduction when the restrictions on share transferability lapse. In addition, any dividends paid on the restricted shares are tax deductible during the period the restrictions on the shares are in force.

Note that, to obtain this deduction, the company must withhold income taxes on the shares granted. However, the nature of a pure restricted stock program is such that there may be no cash payment from which to withhold. Consequently, the company must either ask the recipient to make a cash payment to the company for the withholding taxes or the company must withhold taxes from other sources, such as salary or bonus compensation, or by withholding shares.

FIGURE 25.4   Restricted stock and employee tax liability

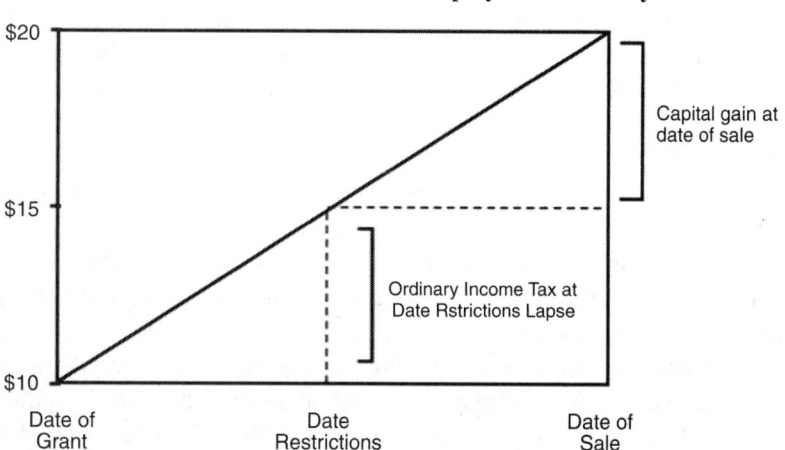

Also consider that the employer obtains a tax deduction equal to the value of the stock at vesting, while the accounting charge is limited to the value of the share on the grant date. This means companies whose stock has appreciated will accrue a tax benefit that is disproportionately high relative to the accounting expense. Any such excess benefit cannot be added to income, however, but instead must be charged to capital.

The compensation-related accounting expense associated with restricted stock is determined as of the date of the initial grant and is not affected by any subsequent appreciation or depreciation in the stock price. The amount of the expense is the cost of the restricted share, measured by the difference between the stock's fair-market-value on the grant date and the price paid for it (if any) by the employee (net of some consideration for potential forfeiture). This amount is amortized for accounting purposes over the vesting period.

Phantom Stock

This form of long-term deferred compensation uses the employer's stock as the measuring device for calculating the value of the ultimate award payment. Designated executives are given units called *phantom stock*, which incorporate a value equal to the price of shares of common equity. Unlike real shares, however, the phantom stock does not represent any true ownership interest in the company. The employer simply credits these phantom shares on its books, and as the company's stock price rises and falls, so does the value of the phantom stock. Typically, phantom shares are "put" back into the company after a stipulated time has elapsed, and the amount of any accrued appreciation during the holding period is paid out in cash. A variation on this theme pays out the full value of the stock plus any accrued appreciation, as opposed to appreciation alone, after the stipulated time frame.

As a rule, the value of one phantom share at any time equals the market price of one share of the company's stock. Nonetheless, when a public market for the company's shares does not exist, the employer may relate phantom stock values to the firm's book value per share. Note also that phantom stock accounts may be credited with any dividends declared on a number of shares of stock equivalent to the number of phantom shares in an executive's phantom stock account.

Sometimes phantom stock plans are used to defer compensation earned from an annual incentive plan. The employee's incentive dollars are used to purchase a number of phantom shares at the then-current value of the employer's stock. At the end of the deferral period, phantom shares are revalued, and final payments are made in cash, in stock, or in a combination of cash and stock. Dividend equivalents may be either credited to the executive's account or paid directly upon declaration.

The tax treatment of phantom stock plans closely resembles that of restricted shares. Participants incur no tax liability on the initial grant of phantom shares. However, final payments in satisfaction of the award accrual are deemed "ordinary

FIGURE 25.5   Phantom stock and employee tax liability

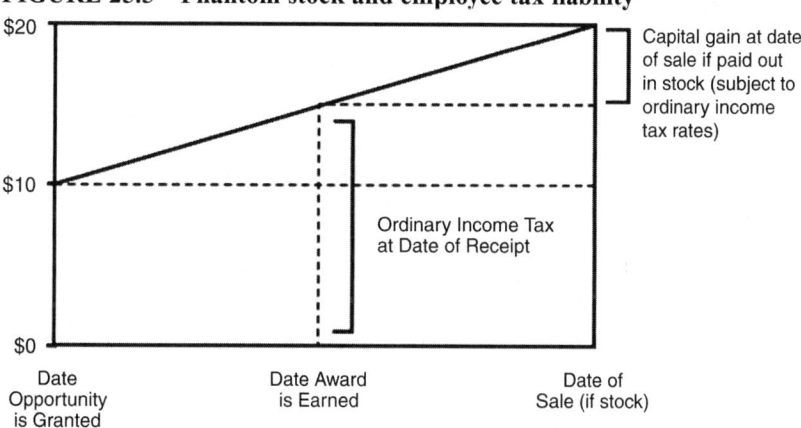

income" in the year paid out, and it is at that time that the employer sees an offsetting deduction. Sometimes dividends are paid to holders of phantom shares. When this happens, the payments are treated as additional compensation and are subject to ordinary income tax when received by the employee. If final phantom stock redemptions are made in stock, subsequent appreciation represents capital gain (see Figure 25.5).

The estimated expense of phantom stock grants needs to be accrued by marking the award to its fair value over the service period. The payment or crediting of dividend equivalents is expensed at the time of payment or credit.

PERFORMANCE PLANS

Performance Shares or Units

Performance share or unit plans are very popular award constructions in today's pay-for-performance environment. Sixty percent of major companies maintain a performance plan of one type or another.

Companies with performance plans typically offer employees awards that are payable in stock or cash and that are contingent on the organization's meeting preset, long-term performance objectives. Generally, an employee receives an unsecured promise from the company to deliver cash or stock at no cost to the recipient. The employer then designates some objective measure of company performance and relates the magnitude of the award opportunity to varying levels of goal achievement. The better the results, the larger the payout. The performance yardstick typically is tied to the fortunes of the entire corporation, but it also could relate to group or division performance.

Commonly, performance is measured over a multiyear cycle (ordinarily a period of three consecutive fiscal years) and is defined in terms of the organization's return on equity, return on assets (or capital employed), or compound growth in earnings. Often, results are defined relative to a standard set by the performance of other companies. It is especially popular to measure performance in terms of total shareholder return relative to the returns generated by a designated benchmark community.

The ordinary performance plan is constructed so that employee earns the right to receive some or all of the promised cash or shares at the end of the performance cycle. The number of performance shares or level of cash to be received depends on the employer's long-term performance. The value of the cash award opportunity is a fixed dollar amount determined at the time of initial grant. The value of the shares, however, is based on the market value of the employer's stock at the conclusion of the performance period.

Accounting for performance awards can be complicated and largely dependent on whether the awards are cash- or stock-denominated. Cash-based performance awards are accounted for variably, marked to fair value over the course of their respective performance periods. When the award is made in shares, on the other hand, FAS123R mandates that the cost of the award be fixed at grant, unaffected by subsequent share price movement, and charged against earnings over the performance period. If the award is earned on the basis of performance against nonmarket-based measures (those unrelated to share price), then the cost of the award is deemed to be the underlying share price at grant adjusted for the likelihood of forfeiture. In the event the award is dependent on achievement with respect to a market-based measure (related to share price), then the cost is formulated in relation to the underlying share price at grant, discounted to reflect the likelihood of goal achievement.

Taxation of performance shares or units is a function of cash-basis accounting. Employers do not get a deduction until they pay out awards, which also is when participants realize ordinary income on the full value of all the amounts received. If final payments are made in stock, then the recipient is an investor with respect to those shares, and any subsequent appreciation in stock price is treated as a capital gain.

Formula-Value Shares

The *formula-value share plan* (sometimes called a book value plan) is a variation on the previously discussed phantom stock program, but this plan is generally applied in private companies or at the divisional level of public organizations. Like the phantom stock concept, the formula-value share plan awards participants with stock-like units priced to reflect a share in the company or division.

Generally, the value of a formulated share is a function of the organization's earnings, revenues, cash flow, or other combination of measures that the market might be expected to consider in assigning value to the company or division.

FIGURE 25.6   Formula-value shares and employee tax liability

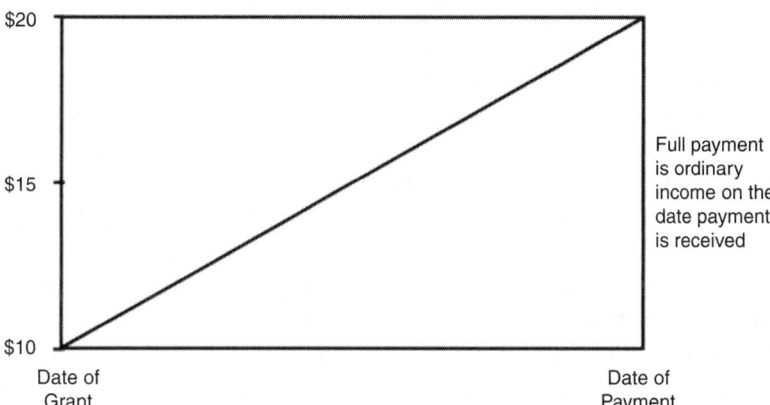

Shares generally are valued at the time of the grant and again after a stipulated performance period, at which point any appreciation in value is paid to the executive in cash. The variable accounting rules associated with stock appreciation rights also apply to formula-value shares. Reserves need to be created over the performance period to reflect postgrant appreciation in award value as it accrues.

Recipients of formula-value shares incur no tax liability when they first receive their shares. When the shares are redeemed at the completion of the performance or measurement period, however, the plan participants realize ordinary income on the amounts received. Figure 25.6 illustrates how an employee is taxed on the receipt of formula-value shares. A tax deduction accrues to the company at the time, and in the same amount as, the participant realizes ordinary income.

MARKET-BASED VS PERFORMANCE-BASED PLANS

After considering the workings of commonly used long-term incentive plan formats, it becomes clear that the selection of a preferred design format depends on balancing the company's objectives in implementing the program with the realities of the operating environment in which the executive group serves. For example, an organization whose management philosophy exhorts its leaders to maximize the value of its shareholders' investment might quickly conclude that any of the market-based programs are well suited for implementation, since the value of the participant's earnings directly relates to increases in the price of the company's stock. This is a logical conclusion to draw, yet it ignores many compelling arguments that suggest that stock prices move in response to many stimuli wholly unrelated to individual executive decision making. If we believe that factors pertaining to macroeconomic events, market psychology, industry cycles, and other external factors strongly impact share value, then introducing a long-term compensation system that relates individual earnings opportunities to stock price appreciation alone may amount to an overzealous and futile attempt to encourage executive activity that enhances shareholder value.

Certainly, the effort to match executive rewards with shareholder value enhancement is an admirable goal, one from which the human resources professional ought not to be distracted. But while market-based plans such as stock options and stocks with appreciation rights can be very effective vehicles for sharing organization success as defined by appreciation in shareholder return, they tend to reward plan participants through a retrospective, after-the-fact view of performance. In this sense, they are passive arrangements that, because of the uncertain connection between management decision making and stock price movement, represent ineffective instruments for communicating the specific goals that are within management's grasp and that the company wants its executive team to achieve.

In many instances then, performance-based awards, such as performance units or formula-value shares, or even the hybrid formats (for example, performance shares or TARSAPs), might offer better approaches to plan structure when the company is clear about its performance targets and confident that goal achievement eventually will drive stock price appreciation. Under this assumption, it is incumbent upon the organization to identify those measures of internal performance that correlate well with share price movement.

As noted earlier, when selecting performance targets, most companies identify earnings, return on assets or investment, or some other reflection of financial performance founded on traditional accounting principles. At the frontier of performance measurement thinking, however, are the advocates of economic-based planning. They argue that, of all the common yardsticks of success, it is the metrics that reflect economic value—measures like net operating profit after tax after capital charges, and discounted inflation-adjusted cash flow and asset growth—that correlate most directly with stock price appreciation.

As a result, organizations that utilize sophisticated financial planning techniques and information systems are increasingly recognizing that there is a profound inconsistency in promoting a management philosophy that advocates shareholder value creation while rewarding executives for maximizing traditional accounting measures. Those organizations are moving away from the more common focus on book earnings and returns on equity and capital. Instead, they are beginning to relate long-term incentive opportunities to value creation models whose foundations rest in economic value-added theory and discounted cash-flow analysis.

SUMMARY

Long-term incentive awards convey substantial value to the overall executive compensation package, and compensation professionals foresee no change in the level of that contribution any time soon. As long as value creation mandates continue to characterize the direction of management initiatives, it should be expected that stock-denominated, long-term incentive plans will maintain their prominence in the compensation landscape.

For the human resources professional, it is very important to possess a clear understanding of how long-term incentives work to help organizations accomplish their operating goals. Part of the challenge is to ensure familiarity with the mechanics of long-term incentive plan design. But equally critical is the ability to discern how the workings of each program type might fit the organization's culture, how effective each can be in promoting the firm's business and human resources objectives, and how well each can support the company's overall management philosophy.

END NOTES

1. Hewitt Associates private survey.

2. Hewitt Associates private survey.

C H A P T E R

EXECUTIVE COMPENSATION: A RECRUITER'S RECOMMENDATIONS

Randy Jayne, Managing Partner Global Aerospace,
Defense, and Aviation Practice

Heidrick & Struggles

FROM THE PERSPECTIVE OF A veteran executive recruiter, much consternation, conflict, uncertainty, and in some cases, even disasters can accompany the compensation-setting process between an executive and a new employer. Highly experienced and competent executives who have been tendered an offer for an exciting new role can be distracted, frustrated, and even derailed by the process of negotiating a compensation package. On the hiring side, an executive team and human resources staff can bring an outstanding new hire to the table, only to have the process falter over negotiations on compensation. To help executive candidates and hiring organizations avoid these unfortunate consequences, this discussion is intended to:

- Clarify the role of the executive recruiter in the compensation-setting process
- Point out potential pitfalls from the perspectives of the candidate, the hiring organization, and third-party participants in the process
- Offer some suggestions that can help candidates better prepare for compensation negotiations

With an understanding of the recruiter's role, a map of potential pitfalls, and candidates willing to do some homework, the path to successful compensation-setting can be far smoother for all parties, resulting in a win–win for the candidate and the hiring company.

ROLE OF THE RECRUITER

First, it is important to clarify the role of the executive recruiter in the process. Success in the recruiting profession, like any other professional service business, demands long-term, sustained accomplishments with clients—in this case, consistently effective executive placements. The effectiveness of a placement, including the executive staying in the new role for a reasonable period, is inextricably tied to compensation. Why? Because if an executive takes a new position with a new company and ultimately feels that he or she has been treated unfairly regarding pay, the chances of a long tenure are slim. Likewise, if the company leadership feels that they were strong-armed into a higher-than-appropriate compensation package, short tenure is also likely. In that case, the company will tend not to reward the new person as well as others, on the grounds that he or she is already overpaid.

Because the recruiter's reputation rests on sustained tenure for placements, two charges, heard repeatedly by those of us in executive search, are misconceptions. We have all heard a client argue that the recruiter is trying to unreasonably increase the compensation package because our professional fees are generally tied to the size of the offer. Conversely, we have heard the candidate complain that the recruiter is beating him or her down on compensation because "you're getting paid by the hiring company, not me."

In the real world of executive search, these are largely urban myths. In fact, the role of the executive recruiter in executive compensation interaction and negotiation is quite simple, and very much neutral in the hiring process. We are, and must always be, the voice of reason and market reality. We must know, and be able to verify, the realistic compensation range for the relevant executive role in that market and industry, for that size company, with that range of job responsibility. Armed with that information, we must then ensure that both our client company and our candidate executive understand and accept this real-world compensation range in the marketplace. Then the only task that remains is to achieve comfort and consensus at a point within that market range. The recruiter's ability to bring this active and neutral expertise to search after search can be tremendously helpful in facilitating long-term tenure of the new hire—a win–win for both the hiring company and their new executive.

PITFALLS AND PROBLEMS

Compensation negotiation and setting for a new hire always involves at least two parties—the hiring organization and the candidate executive—but it can also involve third parties. Executive recruiters, compensation consultants, and sometimes compensation attorneys all potentially could participate. For all of these interested parties and the compensation processes in which they participate, there are specific pitfalls and problems.

The Candidate

For the executive considering an offer and a new role, there are at least five pitfalls that we frequently encounter. Each one, or some combination, can complicate or even derail a particular hiring process.

Perhaps the most common pitfall for executives is a simple lack of knowledge regarding compensation levels in the current marketplace. This gap in understanding can apply to base salary levels, cash and stock annual bonuses, long-term equity award programs, and a host of potential fringe benefits. Such inaccurate or incomplete perceptions can have either of two obvious effects. If the executive has an inflated view of any of these pay and benefit elements, the hiring organization may question her judgment and savvy. The uninformed executive may personally feel that she is being quite reasonable in the negotiation but comes across to the potential new employer as decidedly unreasonable. Conversely, an executive underestimating his own value may accept an offer that significantly undercompensates.

A second pitfall is seen frequently with executives with long tenures in the same organization. These "lifer" executives sometimes place unrealistically high values on elements of their present compensation, particularly when their offer from the new business does not contain an exact equivalent. Examples include defined benefit pension plans, fringes such as car allowances, club memberships, insurance, and extra medical coverage.

Clearly, we can determine a value for each of these elements of compensation, and executives can and should do this themselves in advance of negotiation. The hiring organization should likewise recognize the cash values of these current benefits not included in their offer, and ensure that their cash package and benefits—base salary and annual bonus, and benefits—provide an attractive alternative.

One unrealistically valued element that we see in certain situations involves authorized paid vacation days. Especially for former government employees or those from certain European countries and organizations, too much emphasis can be placed on high numbers—beyond two weeks—of vacation days. In our experience, executives above a certain level tend to have great flexibility in determining leave and vacation, on the one hand. On the other, job demands can automatically limit the realistic number of days annually that can be spent away from the job. An executive overemphasizing vacation days can come across as focusing on the wrong things and cause the hiring team in some instances to view this negatively in the negotiation process.

A third pitfall, related to the first two, is the difficulty or inability of the executive to value accurately the noncash elements of an offer. This is more prevalent when the executive has not previously seen or participated in such elements. Again, the opposite error can also occur—overvaluing something like a defined benefit pension.

These noncash elements—depending on the level of the executive role—can range in value from a few thousand dollars annually to six or even seven figures. At the low end, there are perks like extra life insurance or paid parking. At the higher end are company-sponsored day care, corporate aircraft availability for families, use of company facilities for personal functions, and supplemental 401K or other defined retirement plan contribution matching.

The fourth common pitfall is particularly challenging, both for candidates and hiring executives. Simply stated, we frequently see problems in accurately valuing long-term benefits offered in the new role. Executives struggle to understand the risk and reward aspects of stock option awards, restricted shares, special retirement trusts, and other long-term incentive programs (LTIPs). This challenge is often complicated by the need for comparison of these newly offered equity components to existing long-term (and unvested) elements that our executive would be walking away from to take the new offer.

A common example here, which became a pervasive part of the hiring calculus back in the dot-com boom of the late 1990s, involves major equity awards vesting over four or five years. During the boom, rampant enthusiasm led to widespread overvaluing, with executives understating downside risk and assuming Microsoft- or Google-like future increases in value of newly offered stock packages. Similarly, executives currently holding large equity stakes in smaller, earlier stage companies often seriously overvalue that asset (by failing to discount for risk), particularly when large portions vest two to five years in the future and the company's ability to generate real market value remains uncertain.

The flip side occurs when the hiring company is itself an early stage or troubled turnaround business, offering a major equity element in a total package often characterized by a below-market cash base salary and annual cash bonuses. In these instances, consciously or unconsciously, the offering company can unreasonably hype the value of stock offers.

The fifth pitfall for the candidate is particularly insidious, and it can have highly negative ramifications. In this circumstance, an executive has decided— usually consciously, but sometimes not—that she is not motivated to accept the new job offer. Often the reasons are straightforward—high satisfaction with the status quo, family objections to relocation, risk aversion, and others. In these instances, the candidate genuinely has no intention of making a change but somehow feels obligated to continue the interaction with the potential employer.

Instead of just saying no, the candidate makes ever more inflexible compensation demands. Like the homeowner who puts a house up for sale at a price well above even the top of the actual market, these executives—unmotivated to make a change—are saying "you can have me only if you pay a high premium." Like the homeowner with no real intention to sell, this executive may indeed have no price, regardless of how inflated, that would yield a "yes" answer. Human resources executives and recruiters alike are often surprised, unfortunately, to discover the real motivation behind this behavior. What may initially look like one of our other pitfalls can turn out to be this inability to just say no to an unwanted offer.

PROCESS PROBLEMS

A second set of challenges can arise from the specific processes used by a hiring organization in finding, assessing, developing and offering, and negotiating with a potential new hire. Again, an executive recruiter can be a valuable facilitator— or a contributor to the problem—in these situations. Each of these process issues can affect compensation setting and the closing of the deal.

Incomplete discussions of compensation elements—or failure to discuss in advance—during a hiring process can lead to inaccurate expectations on the part of either party. If a candidate's passing comment like "I really need a cash signing bonus to cover my obligation to repay my current employer an amount forfeited should I leave now" goes unrecognized in the offer, we have an issue. Likewise, a hiring organization's statement that "we do not have any severance agreement plan" may not register for an executive who really wants this new job and comes from a situation with a severance package that includes twelve-month base salary and health coverage.

Lack of full disclosure in either direction can frustrate or derail the compensation-setting process. An executive who outlines current stock options and vesting dates without noting the extent to which those awards are in the money or underwater or who describes an annual cash bonus target without disclosing quarterly payments can create such an issue.

On the hiring side, failure to disclose key aspects of compensation policy can also create problems. The specific rules associated with annual bonuses offer a classic example. An executive may come from a situation where half the bonus target is based strictly on individual goals and performance, independent of division or overall corporate achievement of goals at those levels. If a hiring team fails to mention early in the process that the new company's bonus for all executives can drop all the way to zero if certain corporate financial goals are missed, the problem is obvious.

From the standpoint of both the hiring team and the executive candidate, avoiding this communication shortfall is neither simple nor straightforward. While it is inappropriate to bring detailed compensation elements into the discussion too early, putting it off too long can be equally problematic. When the two parties are reasonably sure that they want the marriage to occur, both should push for detailed exchange on the two obvious pieces—the compensation elements the new executive currently enjoys, and the specifics of the program the hiring organization is offering. If either party is not fully informed on how certain elements work—severance agreement, LTIPs, supplemental retirement plans, hiring bonuses, etc.—then tutorials should occur in both directions. If an executive recruiter or compensation consultant is involved, their marketplace expertise can be put to excellent use in this exchange.

From the perspective of the candidate, the offer process can also be complicated or even threatened by an organizational policy characteristic of many companies and other hirers—the level at which each of the elements of a compensation package can be approved or amended. A hiring manager may agree to a negotiated increase, only to realize that a functional human resources manager, or more senior executive, may have to approve such a change. When stock options or share awards are involved it can sometimes necessitate a board of directors-level approval for change. Clearly, the negotiating executives should try to ascertain how this approval hierarchy might affect the process.

Another process pitfall lies in the potential for a counter-offer from the executive's current employer. By nature, counter-offers can reopen the entire job offer negotiation, by introducing new, higher levels of one or more key compensation elements. To the executive, our recommendation is clear: as you prepare to accept a new offer, anticipate a counter-offer, and be ready and comfortable saying, "I appreciate the counter, but this change is in my best interests for career, responsibility, and family; and this is really not about money." Executives beware—if you say "yes" to a counter-offer and stay in your current role, be alert to your situation changing for the worse simply because you came very close to leaving, especially if a direct competitor was involved.

THIRD-PARTY PROBLEMS

Particularly challenging issues can arise when the executive in negotiation receives excessive or inappropriate help from an interested third party such as an executive recruiter, compensation consultant, or compensation attorney.

With executive recruiters, there are two unfortunate behaviors, previously described here largely as urban myths, that can nevertheless occasionally occur, despite the fact that they are inimical to a recruiter's long-term success and are professionally inappropriate. Because most recruiting fees correlate directly to the size of the newly hired executive's cash compensation package, the recruiter can unreasonably push for higher levels. This phenomenon, resembling real estate transactions in which agents' fees correlate to actual sale price, can have disastrous consequences. It can cause the offerer to pull an offer; or even if the package was increased and the hire made, it can lead to bad feelings in the organization toward the new hire.

Executive recruiters can misbehave in the opposite direction as well. Because the hiring organization pays the recruiter's fee and the candidate pays nothing, the recruiter can become too much the bad cop for the company, persuading the executive to accept a below-market offer. Again, the consequences can be severe—the executive, with a clear sense of her worth in the market, may just walk away. In situations where she accepts the job, she is unlikely to stay long, given the attractiveness of other offers to lure her away. In our view, the executive search professional's role is—as noted above—to be the market expert, helping both parties understand the real range of compensation for equivalent roles.

Compensation consultants can also create problems. Each executive and hiring situation is to some degree unique. Compensation recommendations based on market surveys by necessity aggregate across large sets of companies, with sometimes broad market categories ("technology" or "health care" or "industrial") and equally wide organization ranges ("$100M—$500M revenues" or "over $5B revenues").

That data rarely discriminates across other variables that in turn lead to differing levels of appropriate compensation. Variables such as public vs private, venture capital or private equity funded, normal vs distressed and broadly international vs narrower domestic markets all affect the market value and appropriate compensation packages for an executive role. Given these difficulties in understanding the real market, the process can suffer from the injection of seemingly applicable aggregated data that is not sufficiently focused on this case at hand. Thus, compensation consultants, and even some executive recruiters, can be at a disadvantage in adding value to the compensation-setting process. While search partners in large global firms can have access to dozens or even hundreds of similar recent actual hiring packages, recruiters from smaller firms may lack this perspective and access to current, relevant data.

At very senior levels, executives sometimes retain compensation attorneys to assist them in negotiating. By nature, these lawyers are forceful advocates for their clients. The extent to which they push the executive, and in turn the hiring company, can introduce more contentious elements. The candidate needs to clearly distinguish among the many aspects of the compensation lawyer's potential inputs. In our view, great value can come from these experts' perspectives and advice on key contractual elements—severance, special retirement plans, change of control agreements, postemployment restrictions, and complex equity arrangements. Conversely, serious damage can be done by anyone pushing the executive too far on how and what to negotiate.

SUGGESTIONS FOR SUCCESS

It is always interesting to observe the wide range of knowledge, perspective, and overall comfort in negotiating that we see in candidates as they receive new job offers. For savvier executives, many of the pitfalls and process issues described here are familiar. For executives less comfortable or experienced in compensation negotiation, we suggest taking the following actions to improve the quality of your participation in compensation negotiations and the outcomes of the process.

- *Do your homework.* Learn as much as possible about the offering company, its policies and its programs related to compensation. In the interview process, tactfully ask about these topics. If the company is publicly traded, read the most recent Proxy statement, as it will describe many elements of current executives' compensation.

- *Make yourself an expert on your own market value.* Talk to peers and be comfortable sharing this information. Pay close attention to current compensation survey data. If you have a relationship with one or more executive search professionals, call and ask them two things. First, ask those executive recruiters what they are seeing in the market regarding your specific expertise (sales, manufacturing, finance, etc.) and your chosen sector (consumer goods, financial services, aerospace, etc.). Second, review your current compensation package—salary, bonus, equity, benefits—and seek advice as to how you compare to peer executives in your market sector.

- *Set realistic expectations as to the kind of pay raise a new company could offer you, and determine your own threshold.* Obviously, a person between jobs or in a very unhappy job situation should have a lower threshold than the executive currently in a dream position. Communicate your views on this to the hiring team, and the executive recruiter, if one is involved.

- *Recognize the risks and benefits to you of the longer-term elements of a potential offer and compare them to your current situation.* For example, private equity or venture capital-owned businesses, while sometimes much riskier than other kinds of companies, can return very high long-term wealth through the stock component of compensation. Executives should use a range—often from as low as zero up to a much higher amount—to estimate the future value of equity both in their current situation and for a potential new offer.

- *Seek expert advice on particularly arcane elements of both retirement plans and company stock that may complicate straightforward valuation and comparison.* For example, in many private equity and venture capital situations, the stock offered the executive (as options or RSU's) is in the form of common stock that can have widely disparate values (or lack thereof) depending on the existence of preferred stock holdings by investors.

The math for defining relative value of common and preferred stock in a subsequent liquidity event can lead to very low or even zero value for common shares in some situations. There is a simple prescription here: hiring investors and boards in this situation should not expect senior executive recruits to accept a total equity situation much less favorable than their own. Thus a blended set of stock or options across the various classes of stock is appropriate.

- *Know yourself regarding your personal comfort with taking risks.* If you have been with a single company for many years, determine just how ready and willing you are to accept an outside offer. Sadly, we have seen executives like this go far into an offer and negotiation process, only to pull out in the end simply because they could not bring themselves to leave their current employer. Further, even if they could see themselves leaving, they could not make themselves comfortable with the specific risk associated with the potential new situation. Understanding and acknowledging this individual risk tolerance or aversion early on is of course far preferable. Even those who are not currently "frozen" in their current companies should determine their own risk and reward quotient regarding particularly high-risk new opportunities, for both venture capital-backed very early stage companies and businesses in major distress. The risks to long-term success can be very high. Accordingly, compensation packages—especially the equity components—can be quite large. For some executives, moving into such situations can be quite motivating and exhilarating. For others, the high risk can create severe discomfort and unhappiness.

- *Finally, learn to both value and trade off elements of a compensation package where the new offer's components do not line up one-for-one with your current package.* Perhaps the simplest example is salary vs annual bonus. Some employers put a larger percentage of annual pay at risk, offering lower base salary and much higher bonus payments "at plan." Similarly, some companies' bonuses are strictly cash, some strictly equity (stock options and/or restricted shares), while others offer a blend. Each executive should understand his or her realistic monthly needs and ensure that the salary offer covers those needs. Beyond that, they should understand the future and present values of these various bonus structures.

The executive should not get hung up if a new offer omits—and a potential new employer does not provide—the same perks he or she currently has. A leased car, club membership, day care, parking, supplemental insurance, investment counseling, and many other noncash fringe benefits each have a nominal cash value. Learn how to value them objectively, so that a healthy base salary raise offer, without a car allowance or parking, can quickly and accurately be compared to a current salary plus these fringes.

An interesting and common example of this comparing of apples with oranges occurs with defined benefit pensions. Among "lifers" with decades of service in a single company, we see executives whose pension benefit has both a current value (hypothetically, $3,000 monthly at current age 52) and a higher future value ($8,000 monthly if retirement is deferred until age 65). An offer for one of these executives, without any defined benefit pension, can have a number of components that compare directly to the present and future pension situation. Executives need to both do the math and understand comparable risk. In this example, the age-65 benefit, no less than 13 years in the future, must be assigned some risk (layoff, bankruptcy, disability, etc.). Similarly, we can calculate an annuity value today, or possible new savings profile (and company matching, if offered) that would yield the same cash benefit monthly at age 65. If this executive can leave and take the current age-52, $3,000 pension with him, the amount of new offer cash and equity, growing and compounding over 13 years, may far exceed the $8,000 alternative, with similar acceptable risk. The important thing, obviously, is to do the math and view the comparative risks objectively.

SUMMARY

As you approach a compensation-setting negotiation, all of these suggestions for avoiding the many pitfalls in the process can be boiled down to three essential categories: homework, teamwork, and self-reflection. Doing your homework means learning all you can about your fair market value, about the relative value of various elements of compensation packages, and about the pay of the executives in the hiring company. This is a challenging task, but there is no need to go it alone. Team with seasoned professionals—career mentors, compensation consultants, and, perhaps most pertinent, executive recruiters who know your market space—who deal with matters of compensation daily and who are willing to offer truly independent advice. Use them to confirm or correct your homework about your market value and help you understand and compare compensation elements, especially those related to long-term wealth building. Finally, reflect honestly and carefully on the personal issues that might ultimately affect your response to a compensation package: your current job satisfaction, career ambitions, comfort at differing levels of risk, and economic needs and goals. By being honest with yourself, in addition to doing your homework and engaging in teamwork, you can embark on compensation negotiations from a position of great personal strength because you not only know what you are worth but also what you really want.

27

EXECUTIVE COMPENSATION: AN ACADEMIC'S PERSPECTIVE

Johannes M. Pennings, Ph.D., Department of Management

The Wharton School, University of Pennsylvania

EXECUTIVE COMPENSATION CONTINUES TO BE a matter of controversy among academics and practitioners. Debates continue on how to optimize the incentive structures of top decision makers in organizations. Criticism in the popular business press abounds about senior executives being overpaid, and when benchmarked with peers and their firm's performance, many executives appear to be rewarded at a level that is excessive. Lately such criticism has gained new dimensionality. For example, *The New York Times*[1] reported that, while the pay of top executives continues to swell, the wages of the workforce have grown only piecemeal. The ratio of CEO pay to that of workers grew to 326/1 in 1997, compared to 44/1 only 20 years earlier. Cross-nationally, American CEOs also far out-earn their counterparts in other societies. By way of contrast, we might also argue that, in comparative terms, certain sectors reveal compensation practices that trivialize the outsized compensation of CEOs—for example some hedge fund and private equity managers enjoyed 2006 earnings in excess of one billion dollars. Altogether, the compensation bar has become an example of shifting adaptation levels where our judgments regarding strategically sound pay become fluid and arbitrary.

Furthermore, numerous academic researchers have countered criticism regarding excessive compensation by their findings on the link between pay and performance, even if as little as 1 or 2 percent of the variance in executive pay might be accounted for by differences in accounting or market-derived indices of firm performance. Yet, this skepticism resurfaces if the focus is on strategic performance. Unlike such short-term, relatively unequivocal performance measures, strategic measures are surrounded by a good deal of ambiguity. Executive pay has also become a complex, intricate phenomenon with little transparency, further blurring the pay–performance link.

Executive compensation systems are now widely diffused among U.S. corporations. Usually, they cover a comparatively small number of executives, although in some cases this number might exceed 50 people. The underlying assumption is that these top managers have a disproportionate influence on corporate performance and have the leverage to direct their firm's strategic destiny. Executive compensation plans, therefore, can be labeled as "strategic reward systems." Most of these plans have been devised by compensation consulting firms. Although each firm's system might have its own unique attributes, there is also an increased convergence among corporations in the manner in which these systems are designed. The mechanical features and the formal attributes for making compensation decisions should be distinguished from the behavior and attitudes among those involved. We should ask why firms maintain compensation plans separate from those aimed at other classes of employees.

Compensation plans are often very complex, particularly in the United States, and they raise the question as to whether such plans are truly effective, whether they matter. It boils down to the issue of whether firms in the United States do indeed pay their executives for corporate performance. Such issues acquire an interesting dimension when we make international comparisons and spot determinants of pay that seem to be unrelated to actual performance. In this chapter we explore some of these issues.

CONCEPTUAL ISSUES IN EXECUTIVE COMPENSATION

Linking executive pay to performance is surprisingly difficult because it is not easy to define the proper terms. *Executive pay* includes myriad elements, some of which defy attempts to assign them to a specific time period. Some are entitlements such as a company car or club membership fees, and there is some question as to whether we should include them in executive compensation. Other components can vary temporally. For example, the pay associated with stock options can be measured at the time they are granted. They can also be assessed at the time they are exercised, at the time the exercised options are sold by the beneficiary, at the time of distribution of the stock or cash dividends associated with those stock options when they were exercised but not yet sold, and so on. Valuing the option in the present through some form of discounting further exacerbates the difficulty of determining executive pay. After a stock market correction, many firms adjust the strike price of options, thus further complicating an assessment of this variable component of compensation.

Similar problems exist in the interpretation of "deferred" compensation, pension contributions, and golden parachutes, where one or more executives are to receive a generous cash payment in the event of being forced to resign through some jolt such as a hostile takeover or some palace revolution. Even more difficult to interpret are perks, whose cash value may be small but whose symbolic meaning is highly salient. This latter aspect cannot be sufficiently emphasized. Compensation is only one of a variety of incentives. Power, status, and achievement rival compensation in their prominence for executives. In European and Pacific Basin cultures, such nonpecuniary outcomes may even exceed pay to top executives.

The pay profile of CEOs in different countries varies widely, thus calling into question the benefits of perks, pay components, and other incentives as vehicles for inciting executives. It should therefore also be obvious that one should not only look at the level of compensation but also at the profile. The profile represents the relative size of base salary, bonuses, long-term incentive compensation, stock options, and the perks' cash value. The profile is often depicted with a pie chart, showing the relative magnitude of the various compensation components. The compensation mix has a time-and-risk aspect. The architecture is often depicted with a pie chart in which short-term vs long-term or the fixed vs the variable compensation component is highlighted.

Two ratios are useful in uncovering differences in incentive regimes among firms, industries, or even countries:

$$\text{Compensation risk} = \frac{\text{annual bonus} + \text{long-term compensation}}{\text{salary} + \text{benefits} + \text{perks}}$$

$$\text{Compensation time horizon} = \frac{\text{long-term compensation}}{\text{annual bonus}}$$

The underlying premises can be spelled out in a neoclassical (orthodox economic) way: managers often act in their own self-interest rather than in some altruistic or even corporate interest. Corporations (which are usually not owned by the managers) have divergent objectives regarding R&D, production, and financial decisions. When managers are the owners of the firm, such divergence is often absent.

TABLE 27.1   Computation of Executive Compensation Mix

	Short-Term Time Horizon	Long-Term Time Horizon
High compensation risk	Annual bonus	Long-term bonus
		Stock options
		Restricted stock
Low compensation risk	Salary	Deferred compensation
	Benefits	
	Perks	

Likewise, if managers are the founders and still retain a substantial stake in the firm, we would also assume their interest to be highly overlapping with those of the firm. However, the separation of ownership and control has the potential to create all kinds of problems, which economists refer to as *agency problems* (see Table 27.1).

Sources of conflict between executives and the owners of the firm are manifold. For example, unlike a "regular" investor, executives are constrained in diversifying their wealth. Such constraint might render them risk averse and in fact might induce them to commit to projects that produce low (but highly probable) returns. Many executives do not reach their level of power and compensation until they come close to retirement age and are prone to make commitments that will have a short time payoff. For example, they may refrain from R&D expenditures whose rents do not materialize until after they retire. R&D expenditures suppress internal rates of return. In general, managers might value certain expenditures differently than do owners.

All this also assumes that performance in general, and strategic performance in particular, can be readily articulated, but its antecedents cannot easily be identified. Firms resort to financial, short-term operational and accounting indicators, such as return on investment or return on equity, in choosing the criteria for decisions regarding executive compensation. When trying to endow performance with some strategic meaning, they tend to stretch such indicators over a multiyear period, the assumption being that elongating the time frame renders such performance measures strategic. More recently firms tend to substitute accounting performance measures for (capital) market measures in order to draw executives' attention from short-term to long-term time horizons. Unlike accounting measures, market-derived performance indices are less likely to be manipulated. They also tend to be more future-oriented than historical. Whether such pay bases deserve the label "strategic" is not quite evident, however. Examples of such long-term pay systems are those whereby cost of capital is related to return on equity over a 5-year period—the so-called par line—and the executives are given some long-term bonus (phantom stocks or performance shares) based on the latter's exceeding the former.

Such procedures tend to blur the meaning of performance and can be challenged on their strategic relevance because the essence of "strategic" may reach further than merely the time frame under consideration. The matter becomes far more nebulous and complicated when the issue of tying pay to performance pertains to the marginal contribution to (strategic) performance, which can be attributed to the CEO or any other executive. Economists consider the marginal productivity of labor to be equivalent to compensation: the higher an executive's marginal productivity, the greater his or her pay. It is particularly this issue that confronts the practice and research on executive compensation systems.

The link between pay and corporate strategy can be examined in two distinct ways. Compensation plans might emanate from a firm's strategy, or they may be significant antecedents through which strategic objectives are realized.

Linking pay to strategy, therefore, can be decomposed into two questions: (1) What is the meaning of executive compensation derived from or as part of the firm's strategy? and (2) What role does it play in the implementation of strategic objectives? For example, the adoption of golden parachutes can be construed as part of the firm's strategy to fend off hostile takeovers and to further tie executives to their firm. Yet those golden parachutes may result in conservative choices and discourage executives from taking risks or being innovative.

Strategy formulation entails the long-term decisions about markets, products, customer segments, technology, and human resources. Strategy represents an effort to match corporate resources with environmental opportunities. The strategic choice to operate in a given market with a given technology and other resources is relatively enduring and longlasting, e.g., committing vast resources to a new technology, establishing a solid tradition of lifetime employment and promotion from within such that the firm becomes an "internal labor market," or diversifying to overseas markets all represent significant decisions with profound strategic implications that are mirrored in decisions about executive pay. Compensation practices are part and parcel of such a long-lasting strategic posture.

Strategy implementation represents a set of decisions to preserve ongoing strategic commitments but also to succeed in turning a firm's strategic trajectory around. The reorganization of a firm's design, changes in culture and human resources, and the use of compensation as a lever of strategic change are elements of strategic turnaround. Of course, they can also function as a vehicle for preserving the strategic status quo. The point is that executive compensation systems can have profound strategic unanticipated consequences regardless of whether or not those practices emerged from a given strategic posture. The implication is that executive pay may be the result of a given strategy, or it may be the cause of a strategy.

To better grasp this paradox, it is useful to consider the contribution of Chandler. In his classic 1962 monograph, *Strategy and Structure*,[2] Chandler advocated the argument that strategic changes—such as the move from single-product to multi-product offerings—necessitates changes in organizational structure, planning processes, and staffing; in short, structure follows strategy. In the absence of such restructuring, the firm's strategic turnaround falters. Others have criticized this thesis. Hall and Saias[3] suggested that it is the change in structure, personnel, planning, and other organizational practices that enables a firm to change its strategy; strategy follows structure. Both views might have a kernel of truth in that the firm's strategic posture sets the stage for various decisions regarding people, structure, and planning. Yet, the results of those decisions often acquire their own momentum and have their own consequences.

A similar argument can be developed on the role of executive compensation and strategy. Compensation practices might trigger certain strategic behaviors on the part of those who are governed under a certain compensation system, but those very systems may mirror strategic decisions that are an integral part of the grand strategic design. Separating cause and effect may be tenuous.[4] This chapter further reviews these issues. On one hand, we are exploring questions on the design of executive reward systems, particularly how such designs may reflect a strategic frame of mind. On the other hand, we also are reviewing the strategic implications or consequences of executive compensation. In the first case, one might say that executive pay emerges as part and parcel of the intended or formulated strategy, whereas the consequences of pay can be construed as elements of the strategy as realized or implemented.

STRATEGIC DETERMINATION OF EXECUTIVE COMPENSATION

The strategic posture of the firm and the markets in which it has chosen to compete are crucial to shaping the level and profile of executive compensation. The pay profile is also a function of the degree of strategic diversification and the competitive conditions in the industry. The compensation practices vary a great deal depending on whether firms compete in a discretionary vs constrained industry and on whether they are proactive vs reactive in the strategic orientation they assume. As we will see, they vary also considerably cross-nationally.

Firms reveal different compensation profiles. Those in discretionary industries have a proactive posture stressing variable and contingent pay, such as bonuses and long-term incentive compensation. In contrast, more passive firms in constrained industries tend to stress fixed and noncontingent pay, such as base salary.[5] Ironically, even so-called variable forms of pay, such as bonuses or profit sharing, may be set in such a way that they become a fixed feature of executive pay. Employees and their managers expect the forthcoming bonus to be indeed forthcoming! Likewise, when the stock market goes through a correction, many firms will reset the stock's strike price in order to preserve the option value for managers who may want to exercise their options. The implication is that these variable forms of pay were not at risk, and construing them as "variable" would be somewhat deceptive.

A *discretionary industry* is one in which the firm enjoys a great deal of latitude in crafting its own strategy. Whether or not firms operate in a discretionary industry hinges on their ability to measure and anticipate market developments and, of course, on the degree of regulatory oversight. Thus, marketing research and geopolitical forecasts enable some firms to tune in to strategically important trends and to take anticipatory action. Furthermore, they may enjoy some leverage in shaping consumer demands or diffusing product innovations. Commodity markets or public utility firms tend to have little discretion, whereas firms in the financial services, cosmetics, and entertainment industries have selected relatively free markets. Particularly in such free markets, one would expect strategically aggressive firms to adopt compensation practices with high variations in levels of pay and to differentiate the profile of pay. For example, it has been found that pay levels or pay profiles vary considerably among firms in discretionary industries with a proactive posture.

Diversified firms have the potential to tailor an executive's compensation package to the very market to which he or she has been assigned. This lies at the heart of so-called strategic reward maps, as drawn by strategic compensation consultants such as the Boston Consulting Group and Booz Allen. The strategic product matrix of the firm is mapped on to its compensation plan—taking the general template as described in Table 27.1. Its fixed and variable pay components dovetail with the strategic imperatives of the various product markets. These consulting firms propose to design the firm's compensation profile in such a way as to reflect the riskiness and time horizon of the different marketplaces together with the corresponding strategic intent of the firm. For example, Booz Allen furnishes a two-by-two matrix that is to match the strategic mandate of various divisions.[6] A cash-cow division (large market share, low growth) requires a package with a low-risk posture and short time horizon; the bulk of its executive pay could consist of a salary. The evidence to date suggests, however, that firms are reluctant to strongly differentiate compensation practices by divisions; rather, they adopt a uniform system.

COMPENSATION NORMS IN INDUSTRIES, COUNTRIES, AND EXECUTIVE LABOR MARKETS

A relevant part of a firm's strategy for compensation considerations centers on the recruitment and retention of members. Firms prefer to conform to industry norms of compensation, but, as with strategy in general, human strategies can also be compared on their reactivity. It is likely that conformity to compensation norms is stronger when firms resort to a great deal of external recruitment of executive talent. A strategy of bolstering an internal labor market might render a firm somewhat immune from such norms, which are a key ingredient in strategic choices about human resources and executive labor markets. Compensation consultants such as Booz Allen or Towers, Perrin, Forster, & Crosby, and the Hay Group have a great impact in promoting and institutionalizing certain compensation plans.

They solidify existing practices or disseminate novel ones, thereby setting certain trends. In the management literature such tendencies are referred to as *institutional pressures*: firms are pressured into adopting distinct practices (compensation) plans, procedures for incentivizing executives as a way to signal compliance with sound management and widely held standards of corporate conduct.[7] Such standards differ between industries and societies. There are both industry norms and compensation norms for various societies.

Compensation innovations proliferate, but, as in the world of fashion, the compensation consulting industry has its own designers of pay systems whose diffusion reflects the eagerness of companies and their boards to stay competitive. For example, the adoption of long-term incentive compensation plans by American corporations reveals a certain degree of faddishness. Organization theorists would argue that such limitations are less induced by the desire to create an optimum incentive for strategic behavior than to conform in order to acquire legitimacy and to convey the illusion of sound management. Sophisticated compensation plans, disseminated in 10 K or proxy statements, confer public credibility and preserve the competitiveness in attracting and retaining high-level executives. An even more controversial standpoint would hold that compensation plans represent fossilized practices that have become uncoupled from the actual compensation, serving only to placate the external audience. The announcement of a new compensation plan has often intriguing effects on the short-term fluctuations in stock prices: the announcements produce what financial economists call "abnormal returns" as they cannot be accounted for by systematic or nonsystematic risk.

For high-level executives, such plans disclose how well the firm is in tune with the marketplace for executive talent. The numerous executive compensation surveys have contributed to the specification of the price of managerial labor—both the level and the proportion that is fixed vs variable. They permit a firm to set a pay range with relative, precise bounds for executives in certain industries. A great amount of research remains to be done here, however. For executives as a labor pool, there are issues such as who is in it and who is not, especially if we define the pool to coincide with a firm's industry or its strategic group. Executive search firms, together with compensation consultants, may assist firms in their human resources strategies, but they themselves may blur the boundaries between industries. Also, many firms are reluctant to go to the "external labor market"; they prefer to bolster internal succession. In this case, the firm is more likely to resemble an internal labor market. We know very little presently about whether internal vs external labor markets affect the level or profile of executive compensation. As suggested before, when the firm represents a well-established internal labor market (and its executives have high quitting barriers because their human capital is vested in and idiosyncratic to their firm), compensation may be modest or below the industry norm. Yet, compensation is likely to exceed the level that would be required to retain its executives.

We should also be aware that the recipients of executive pay often have a major impact on the design of the compensation profile, how it is administered, and by whom it is enforced. The CEO is likely to have appointed many if not all the members of the board of directors, and by implication its subset that has responsibility for compensation issues—the compensation committee. The CEO enjoys a good deal of overt and covert power in manipulating the compensation for her own benefit. Overt power derives from such sources as social capital and seniority. The CEO might have recruited board members to whom she owed certain favors or whose very recruitment amounts to a creation of a favor that greatly diminishes their independence. The CEO thus might be surrounded by friends and acquaintances who are unlikely to challenge her (those acquaintances often reciprocate by inviting her on their firm's board). The CEO is the author of her very own social network, enjoys a good deal of structural autonomy, and might in fact broker much of the information or knowledge among the various individuals who surround her, as researched by Barkema and Pennings.[8]

The CEO enjoying considerable leverage in shaping her very own compensation has been amply documented by the retroactive manipulation of the granting of stock options which has been observed in hundreds of firms during the most recent years—a practice which can be compared with betting on a winning horse after the race has been completed. The practice has been observed in both small entrepreneurial start-ups as well as blue chip firms such as Apple and is currently subject to criminal investigations by U.S. law enforcement agencies, as described in a long string of Pulitzer Prize–winning articles in the 2006–2007 editions of the *Wall Street Journal*.

Covert power is associated with more visible sources of power, including ownership and position in the firm. For example, the CEO who founded the firm is likely to enjoy considerable leverage in the firm, especially because most of the individuals in his or her network arrived after the CEO. She is likely to have some ownership stake in the firm. Having a substantial proportion of ownership will make her power even more overt. Under these conditions, we would expect the CEO to manipulate her pay to favor her personal interests, and factors other than performance will determine level and mix of compensation.[9] The significance of these conditions cannot be overstated. That is why the correlation between compensation and performance is often modest, and even infinitesimally small. The correlation is also small in relation to institutional factors such as industry customs and national culture that strongly shape norms about level and mix of executive pay.

The role of institutional (and therefore nonmarket) forces on executive compensation levels or the configuration of executive compensation has diffused from the United States to the EU and other countries. Institutional refers here to normative or "taken-for-granted" as the practice has become widespread and obvious. For example while incentive compensation is common in many private sectors it is largely absent in governmental sectors. In some private sectors we encounter so called "high-powered" incentive regimes with a stronger emphasis on measured performance as driver of compensation. These regimes are more common in US sectors than in their non-US counter parts.

Yet, both level and compensation mix show dramatic convergence across national cultures. The convergence revolves primarily around variable compensation, most notably bonuses, poison pills, and stock options. Some of the legacy differences in compensation practices can be attributed to differences in national culture.[10] The work on national differences in culture has been pioneered by Hofstede.[11] This economic anthropologist identified variations in values such as individualism vs collectivism and the degree to which countries embrace or shun uncertainty and ambiguity. The U.S. system of core values scores highest on the individualism index and manifests also high tolerance for uncertainty. We similarly observe that countries with little tolerance for uncertainty (e.g., Germany) also express little proclivity for compensation profiles with a substantial compensation risk—for example, stock options. Circumstantial evidence now hints at diminished differences in executive compensation practices and previously intrusive governments are reluctant to locally deviate from emerging global practices and marginalize their organizational establishment from the global executive labor markets.

It seems more interesting to consider the strategic implications of the level and profile of executive compensation. After all, executive compensation can be paraphrased as a strategic reward system. Top executives in general and the CEO in particular are governed by a reward system that is usually segregated from the general compensation systems affecting other employees. The reasons for establishing a separate compensation system are numerous. Presumably, executives have an undue impact on the strategic results of the firm. Furthermore, such reward systems are often linked to long-term performance criteria, such as the spread between return on equity vs the cost of capital over a five-year period. Although such criteria are financial and reflect the vicissitudes of the market, many view them as strategic in that the choice behavior of senior executives might be conditioned by such criteria.

There has been a greater deal of research done on pay as a motivator of job performance, but virtually all this effort has been confined to lower-level employees. Thus, we do not know whether executive motivation is different from that of other occupational groups, nor do we know much about the motivational efficacy of executive compensation systems. Theoretical developments among management researchers have also failed to produce comprehensive statements on these issues.

To fully explicate this state of affairs, it may be helpful to highlight two theoretical traditions that are deemed crucial in understanding work motivation and job performance. They are expectancy theory and agency theory.

EXPECTANCY THEORY

Expectancy theory originates in organizational psychology and holds that a person's motivation is a function of two expectancies. The first one is the expectation that a certain level of effort will lead to a given performance level (e.g., "If I try, it is very likely that I will succeed in meeting my sales quota"). The higher this subjective probability; the greater the level of effort.

Performance should be viewed in very general terms. It includes both job performance, such as productivity and return on investment, as well as membership performance. Membership includes decisions about joining or staying, but also other commitment-revealing behaviors such as long working hours.

The second expectancy consists of the subjective belief that performance results in outcomes or rewards having an attractive value to the person. They include pay but also the earlier-mentioned rewards of power, status, and challenge. Crucial is the assumption that individuals differ in their values such that each and every individual may not be equally motivated by the same rewards. Executives might value rewards that are different from those of other groups of employees; even among themselves, there may be differences in values. Yet, most executive compensation systems treat executives in a standardized way, thereby ignoring their differential sensitivity to levels or profiles of pay. They also differ cross-culturally. It may be these differences in values that render the executive compensation systems of Towers, Perrin, Forster & Crosby, and the Hay Group less effective in societies other than the United States.

Apart from the fact that U.S. compensation practices may have limited applicability elsewhere, there are two other issues to consider. First, it is essential that strategic performance criteria be unequivocally related to executive pay. If the time lag between effort and performance is long, the individual is less likely to perceive a clear relationship. Furthermore, under such conditions, factors other than those related to an executive's effort or business acumen may be perceived to affect strategic performance. They may include acts of God, government intervention, technological breakthroughs, executive labor markets, or business cycles. Furthermore, executive compensation plans, including golden parachutes, cover a group of executives in spite of performance accruing from an individual effort. It may be an opportunity for a free ride. These considerations are also at the heart of the question of "whether the CEO makes a difference"—a question that involves a great deal of contemporary research on executive succession and, by implication, executive compensation.

The second issue involves the expectancy that strategic performance is related to pay. As already mentioned, strategic performance is a complicated phenomenon. Apart from financial performance indicators that have been stretched out over a long time period, most firms have tried little to expand the criteria by which strategic performance can be gaged. Financial performance bases of compensation are tied to either accounting measures, such as the efficient use of corporate or divisional assets, or to market measures, such as those that link shareholder wealth with equity cost of capital to the well being of the executives. Other nonfinancial criteria could include the development of successors, the creation of embryo businesses, or a sustained level of technological innovation and the nurturing and commercial introduction of new products or services. Such performance yard-sticks are not necessarily embedded in short- or long-term measures of financial performance.

"Corporations get the behaviors they reward" is an often-heard lament of expectancy theorists, and in principle, this should also hold for executives. If corporations like to entice executives to certain types of behavior and performance, they should make sure that such performance is feasible and convey a clear connection between certain performance criteria and pay. Also crucial is the assumption that pay itself should have a strong inducement, or "valence"—whether symbolic or by virtue of its buying power. Accounting criteria-based incentive plans tend to direct managerial motivation to short-term behaviors to improve perfor-mance on the indexes chosen. Furthermore, such indexes are susceptible to accounting bias and manipulation. In contrast, market-based performance indica-tors, such as five-year earnings per share, could induce executives toward high-risk decisions, particularly those involving external debt financing.

A study by David Larcker is particularly intriguing.[12] This accounting researcher found that the adoption of long-term performance plans led to subse-quent increases in capital expenditures. The effect disappeared, however, after the first year of adoption. From an expectancy theory standpoint, this suggests several concerns. First, it is important to have a sustained and unabating link between rewards and motivated behaviors and performance. Second, it is important to preserve the immediacy and saliency between rewards and performance. Long time periods or routinization of compensation decisions may dissipate the initial trigger that a new compensation plan has brought about. Third, long-term perfor-mance plans may be flawed in that the market does not always recognize the strate-gic strength of the firm. Ultimately, the firm (or its board of directors) seeks to reward those behaviors or performances that it considers most desirable, which may be at variance with executives' behaviors or performances, due to the execu-tives' motives.

AGENCY THEORY

According to *agency theorists*, executives are controlled by a "contract" drawn up between them and the board of directors. The contract can pertain to behaviors (for example, implementation of strategic budgets) or to performance (for example, maintaining return on assets for certain markets or augmenting earnings per share). Such contracts are fraught with all kinds of difficulties. For example, the senior executives may have knowledge to which the board has no access. Agency problems can be alleviated by establishing more elaborate information systems.

Also, and here executive pay considerations come in, the board makes the executives part of the payoff structure in the form of contingent rewards systems. Such contracts alleviate the need for highly sophisticated monitoring devices, but they also result in the sharing of risks between shareholders and executives. The interests of shareholders and executives may not always be congruent. Unlike the former, the latter do not enjoy much flexibility in diversifying their risks. Particularly when executives hold large amounts of stock or their pay profile shows them to be heavily saddled with risk, they may be tempted to shun risky alternatives, even though pursuing them may be in the best interests of the shareholders.

Jensen and Meckling have indicated that senior executives, the CEO not excluded, often avoid risk because they attempt to preserve their status and tenure in the company.[13] By modifying the pay profile, these authors believe that risk-taking behaviors can be encouraged. In contrast, the level of pay may be dysfunctional for motivating certain behaviors or results. Although the evidence to date is scant, there appears to be support for such an opinion. Rapoport showed, for example, a direct relationship between the magnitude of long-term incentive compensation and the amount of research and development expenditures.[14] The profile of executive compensation appears to foster specific strategic decisions. Such findings suggest that under certain conditions it is possible to evoke comparatively desirable types of decisions. One should be alert to dysfunctional or strategically undesirable behaviors as well.

The research by Healey is noteworthy here.[15] He found that executives "tinkered" with their information and control system to inflate the size of their bonus payments. By refashioning the way financial results are reported, they were focusing their attention on the management of appearance rather than the management of performance. The research also highlighted a major example of agency problems (e.g., the asymmetry of information between the CEO as "agent" and the board or stockholders as his or her "principal"), which the former may be tempted to exploit for his or her own advantage. As we observed earlier, our own research also suggests that CEOs use their power to manipulate their level and mix of compensation.

EXPECTANCY AND AGENCY THEORIES: A SYNTHESIS
OF EXPLANATIONS FOR EXECUTIVE PAY

This discussion suggests that there is some overlap and complement between expectancy theory and agency theory. Although the former has psychological origins and focuses on the motivational effects of reward systems on the incumbent, the latter has an economic-accounting origin and stresses the contractual relationship with the incentive structure designed in such a way as to align the interest of the executives and the shareholders. It would appear that these two traditions provide enough support for some propositions on the strategic consequences of executive compensation. Expectancy research assumes that individuals are different and will respond differently to a given situation; it would answer questions such as, "What behavior is motivated by a given reward system?" and, "What values and other motivational attributes (e.g., tolerance for risk, need for financial success, and so on) of various executives are present such that their response to a given reward system can be anticipated?" Agency theorists tend to have an economic-rationalistic view of people and assume that each person will respond to an incentive package in a predictable way. Its major advantage is that it forces the questions: What objectives are to be attained in this time horizon? Are they short term or long term? What milestones should be furnished to direct executives toward strategic targets? In concrete terms, such questions translate into specific statements, such as the amount of risk taking desired.

The firm's information and control system provides data on either operational (accounting) and/or strategic (market) performance indicators. The former includes return on equity, return on sales, return on investments, and net cash flow and might pertain to overall corporate performance or group, divisional, or *strategic business unit* (SBU) *performance*. Strategic indicators include five-year earnings per share, book-to-market value, or other measures. Such indicators tend to apply to corporate-level performance only. In other words, they cannot easily be disaggregated into organizational subunits unless one resorts to accounting measures such as research and development/assets, new product development/assets or even softer measures, such as the amount of new management talent nurtured.

Assuming that information and control systems embody a variety of performance evaluation criteria, their link with pay can be represented bidirectionally. The arrows from reward to performance belong to the realm of expectancy theory, whereas the reverse arrows fit agency theory. It should be obvious that these bidirectional linkages should overlap, or should at least be consistent. Only under such conditions will the pay strategy relationship be optimal.

SUMMARY

Under the auspices of expectancy theory, a number of outcomes or rewards can be tied to these performance indicators. Conventional types include salary, short-term bonuses, long-term bonuses, stock options, stocks with appreciation rights, phantom stocks, and performance units. For such rewards to have a motivational impact, it is important that the connection to performance be direct, immediate, and salient. Random fluctuations of the stock price, the tightening of executive labor markets, the influence of national values in setting compensation levels, and compensation profiles tend to diminish the correlation between pay and long-term, comprehensive performance indicators, resulting in a less-than-effective motivational impact.

Expectancy theories stress the importance of individual differences. Such differences suggest the necessity of differences in compensation mix. Some executives might prefer deferred compensation. Others might prefer golden parachutes as a protection against unemployment. Still others might prefer risky stock options. Some executives might even prefer nonfinancial rewards, such as time for family, sabbaticals, and a variety of other perks. Their tax situation might be an important consideration as well. Of course, taxation mirrors the national institutional context in which it exists! Last, but not least, particularly when a firm is a multinational corporation, there is probably even a greater need to customize executive pay systems. Ideally, the executive compensation system should dovetail with the motivational makeup of the executive in order to render it most efficient.

Efficiency of executive compensation systems is, however, not the only issue. The reward system should also yield the type or quality of performance that is strategically desirable. Agency theory spells out the conditions under which this is most likely. Stock options and stocks with appreciation rights, for example, may diminish risk-taking behavior and promote a temptation to stimulate dividend yield. Changes in accounting standards and the infamous Sarbanes–Oxley legislation have altered the cost-free status of options, which now are more commonly treated as expenses. Other long-term incentive compensation tools, such as phantom stocks and performance units, may be too complex and unwieldy, and they may fail, therefore, to align the direction of an executive's efforts with the long-term interests of the shareholders. Such plans require thorough communication and coaching so that the plans become meaningful and significant. It appears that this is the major challenge of current executive compensation consulting and research.

The employment arrangements of America's senior corporate executives have become a favorite topic for the financial press. Coverage of the details of lucrative compensation packages has become commonplace, with special emphasis being placed on the amounts earned by the executives. For example, *Business Week's* May 1999 publication of the results of its forty-ninth annual survey of executive compensation indicated that, for the first time ever, the average annual salary and bonus for CEOs of surveyed companies topped $1 million, and their aggregate annual compensation exceeded $2 million. *The New York Times* frequently invited Graef Crystal, a compensation consultant and corporate gadfly, to articulate the discrepancy between a CEO's actual pay and the pay he or she should have received if pay systems were consistent across firms and within and across industries. Since the turn of the century, growth in executive compensation has continued, even exponentially, and the inclusion of hedge fund managers has pushed the ceiling beyond $1 billion. Among academics, there are authors, such as Murphy, who wonder about the prominence of executive compensation and the success of the compensation consulting industry given that the marginal effect of corporate performance on pay is often trivial. The rise of hedge funds with their diminished transparency has added further fuel to the skepticism regarding pay and performance. The debates continue.

END NOTES

1. "Pressing the Issue of Pay Inequality," *The New York Times*, 7 February 1999.

2. A. Chandler, *Strategy and Structure*. Cambridge, MA: MIT Press, 1962.

3. D. J. Hall and M. A. Saias, "Strategy Follows Structure," *Strategic Management Journal*, vol. 1, pp. 149–63.

4. Johannes M. Pennsings, "Executive Reward Systems: A Cross-National Comparison," *Journal of Management Studies*, March 1993, pp. 261–80.

5. Johannes M. Pennsings and David T. Bussard, "Strategy, Control and Executive Compensation," *Topics in Total Compensation: Fitting the Incentive Plan to the Company*, vol. 1, 1987, pp. 101–12.

6. Louis J. Brandisi, *Creating Shareholder Value: A New Mission for Executive Compensation*. New York: Booz Allen, 1984.

7. Paul J. DiMaggio and Walter W. Powell, "The Iron Cage Revisited: Institutional Isomorphism and Collective Rationality in Organizational Fields," *American Sociological Review*, vol. 48, 1983, pp. 147–60.

8. H. Barkema and J. M. Pennings, "Top Executive Pay: The Role of Overt and Covert Power," *Organization Studies 19*, vol. 6, November–December 1998, pp. 975–1004.

9. Ibid.

10. Johannes M. Pennings, "Strategic Reward Systems: A Cross-National Comparison," *Journal of Management Studies*, vol. 30, No. 2, March 1993, pp. 261–80.

11. Geert H. Hofstede, *Culture's Consequences*. Beverly Hills, CA: Sage, 1980.

12. David Larker, "The Association Between Performance Plan Adoption and Corporate Capital Investment," *Journal of Accounting and Economics*, vol. 5, 1983, pp. 3–30.

13. M. C. Jensen and W. H. Meckling, "Theory of the Firm: Management Behavior, Agency Costs, and Ownership Structure," *Journal of Financial Economics*, vol. 3, 1976, pp. 305–60.

14. A. Rapoport, "Executive Incentives Versus Corporate Growth," *Harvard Business Review*, vol. 56, 1978, pp. 81–8.

15. M. Healey, "The Effect of Bonus Schemes on Accounting," *Journal of Accounting and Economics*, vol. 3, 1985, pp. 85–107.

REGULATION OF EXECUTIVE COMPENSATION

Frank P. VanderPloeg, Esq., Partner, Employee Benefits and
Executive Compensation

Sonnenschein Nath & Rosenthal

R ECENT YEARS HAVE SEEN GROWING public and shareholder
attention to executive compensation, and increased governmental regulation in response to these concerns. As a result, the people involved
in structuring and administering stock option plans and other forms of
executive compensation—the human resource managers, the board of
directors and/or its compensation committee, and their advisors—must take into
account an increasingly intricate set of laws and regulations.

This brief material cannot describe all of the legal and regulatory structures
that may impinge on executive compensation, nor review the tax treatment of
executive compensation generally. Instead it will focus on those laws and regulations (including some federal income tax provisions) that particularly affect the
design and implementation of executive compensation arrangements; and which
therefore need to be considered at the outset in establishing those arrangements.

Most of the regulation (and public and shareholder attention) is directed at public companies, which must disclose the compensation of their senior executive officers. However, many of the best practices for public companies are equally relevant to privately held companies, especially if they may become public companies (or be sold to public companies) in the future. Some of the tax considerations discussed below apply directly to privately held companies.

BACKGROUND

The start of the millennium saw substantial compensation, option gains, and perquisites paid to executives of companies (such as Enron and WorldCom) that went bankrupt; or paid to executives facing criminal prosecution for bilking public companies (such as Tyco, Adelphi, and Hollinger) through excessive or unauthorized compensation arrangements.

Hardly had the dust settled on these developments when a new wave of stock option backdating scandals erupted. Academic studies (soon reported in the financial and public press) revealed that public company stock options were granted at minimum lows in the stock price far more often than would occur by chance. Most options set the option price at (or above) the fair market value of the stock on the date the option is granted. Thus, backdating to a date when the stock price was lower results in the option being issued with an exercise price below the actual date-of-grant fair market value.

Granting an option with an exercise price below fair market value, even by backdating, is not automatically illegal. But the accounting treatment of options varies significantly depending on whether options are granted at (or above), or below, fair market value on the date of grant. (Tax consequences can also differ.) Under accounting rules in force until 2006, the grant of a stock option at (or above) fair market value did not normally generate a financial statement expense. Backdating caused options to lose this favorable accounting treatment. As a result, financial statements became misleading and had to be restated. The misleading financial statements in turn are a potential criminal violation of the Sarbanes–Oxley Act of 2002 and other securities laws, and spawn shareholder lawsuits charging securities fraud. As affected companies restated earnings, their overall market capitalization fell, according to some estimates, by as much as $250 billion.

Outcry over these developments feeds two somewhat different pressures on executive compensation. One source of pressure—perhaps the one felt most keenly in the boardroom—is growing activism by public company shareholders, and particularly institutional shareholders, attacking weaknesses in corporate governance that permit those excesses, particularly when executive pay is not, in the shareholders' eyes, justified by corporate performance.

A second source of pressure—perhaps the one felt most keenly in Congress—is the broader public dismay at the levels of executive compensation generally.

CEO pay is reported to have increased from 28 times average employee pay in 1970 to more than 500 times average worker pay in 2000, remaining at 369 times average pay as of 2007. The fact that many companies reporting significant executive compensation simultaneously hold the line on rank and file wages, restructure their operations, and lay off employees, adds to the public controversy.

These concerns have already led to the passage in 2002 of the Sarbanes–Oxley Act, accounting changes that require expensing of stock options, the new SEC disclosure requirements for executive compensation, enhanced corporate governance standards for public companies promulgated by the major exchanges, and tax law restrictions on deferred compensation.

The tax law restrictions reflect Congress' preference, so far, for indirect regulation of executive compensation through tax disincentives in the Internal Revenue Code (IRC). These include IRC Section 162(m), denying a deduction for nonperformance-based compensation to certain public company executives in excess of $1 million per year; IRC Section 280G, denying a deduction and imposing an excise tax on "excess parachute payments" in connection with a corporate change in control; IRC Section 409A, imposing additional taxes and interest on deferred compensation (broadly defined) that does not meet new standards for the form and time of payment; and IRC Section 4958, imposing an excise tax on certain tax-exempt organizations and their managers that overpay their officers.

Proposals for further regulation abound. These include "say on pay" requirements that would give stockholders a nonbinding (or under some proposals, a binding) right to approve or disapprove executive compensation arrangements. Other potential legislation would add statutory disclosure mandates (building on the SEC's existing regulatory disclosure requirements), require enhanced disclosure of "parachute" payments in connection with corporate transactions, cap executive pay at 25 times the pay of the lowest-paid full time employee, or place a $1 million limit on executive deferred compensation.

The increasing visibility and potential for controversy respecting executive compensation puts a premium on following "best practices" to design, implement, and set benefit levels for executive pay. This is especially vital now because "best practices" today can become standard practices tomorrow, and minimum legal requirements the following day.

SHAREHOLDER RIGHTS AND DIRECTOR OBLIGATIONS

Role of the Board, Compensation Committee, and Management

Corporate law generally provides that the business and affairs of a corporation are managed by or under the direction of the board of directors. The directors in turn hire the officers to actually run the corporation. However, there is an obvious conflict of interest in letting those officers set their own compensation. Accordingly, while the board can seek management's recommendations on compensation, the actual decision on executive compensation is a direct responsibility of the board of directors. Typically, this responsibility will be assigned to a compensation committee of the board that will be composed of independent directors for a public company (in light of various requirements of the SEC, the tax laws, and the exchanges on which shares are listed for trading).

Corporate directors owe the corporation and its stockholders fiduciary duties of care and loyalty. (Law in some states adds a separate duty of good faith). Director business decisions complying with those standards are entitled to the protection of the "business judgment" rule. This is a presumption that in making a business decision the directors of a corporation acted on an informed basis, in good faith, and in the honest belief that the action taken was in the best interests of the company. Acting on an informed basis in turn requires that that the directors have investigated (and understood) all material information reasonably available to them, which may include reports and recommendations from outside consultants (as well as management).

The duty of care emphasizes the procedures that the board uses to inform themselves of the decision before them. Failure to follow appropriate procedures, especially in a case involving the payment of large benefits to an executive, may prevent a finding that directors acted in good faith. It is thus naturally important for the record behind any decision on executive compensation to demonstrate that the members of the board, and particularly the members of the compensation committee, have fulfilled their duty of care. Practices that may contribute to this are set out at the end of this chapter.

Role of the Shareholders

Shareholders may set overall corporate policy but typically have no direct role in managing the corporation (except of course that they can refuse to re-elect directors, or sometimes remove directors, if the shareholders are unhappy with board decisions). The major exception to this principal for executive compensation is that shareholders usually must approve stock option (or restricted stock or similar equity compensation) plans. Some state corporate laws require shareholder approval of option plans. Even where not required, shareholder approval may be necessary in practice to comply with the stock exchange listing requirements, to obtain favorable accounting treatment, to obtain the benefit of exemptions from the insider trading laws, to obtain favorable tax treatment for "incentive stock options" if those will be granted, or to avoid the $1 million limitation on tax deductions under Section 162(m).

Shareholders take a keen interest in equity compensation plans that they are being asked to approve. Firms such as Institutional Shareholder Services review public companies' proxy statements in light of their own criteria for plan features and "burn rate" (the amount of stock that can be issued under option or other awards), and make voting recommendation to their institutional shareholder clients.

With increased shareholder activism, the shareholders of some corporations have passed resolutions requiring the corporation to submit future executive compensation packages to a nonbinding shareholder vote. Some corporations have voluntarily submitted executive compensation to a shareholder vote. Legislation has been introduced as noted above to require this.

SEC DISCLOSURE RULES

The shareholder concerns outlined above drive demands for increased disclosure (and regulation), and disclosure of executive compensation in turn drives increasing public and shareholder concern. The latest round on the disclosure side of this endless feedback loop is the SEC 2006 final rules for disclosure of executive officer compensation in the proxy statements and annual Form 10-K reports of publicly traded companies (the SEC Disclosure Rules).

The SEC Disclosure Rules reflect several recent developments in executive compensation, particularly those regarding stock option grant date practices, postemployment benefits and executive perquisites. They require extensive disclosure of all types of compensation for named executive officers (NEOs) and directors at publicly traded companies. NEOs are generally anyone who served during the year as principal executive officer or principal financial officer, and the three (generally) most highly compensated executive officers (other than the principal executive and financial officers) serving as executive officers at the end of the last fiscal year.

Disclosure begins with a narrative discussion in nonboilerplate, plain English called the compensation discussion and analysis (CD&A). This disclosure is followed by a summary compensation table, assigning all current and deferred compensation (including equity) to one of seven specified columns for covered executive offices. Other tables and related discussion must then report in more detail on equity-based compensation, retirement benefits, and other actual or potential postemployment compensation.

Compensation Discussion and Analysis

The CD&A is a principles-based, narrative overview of the material factors underlying the company's compensation policies and decisions. Under the regulations, it must describe the company's compensation program objectives; the method by which the program incentivizes certain behaviors; each element of compensation; the reason the company chooses to pay each such element; the amount of (or formula for) each such element; and the manner in which each element helps achieve the company's compensation objectives.

In a broad sense, the CD&A should reveal not just what compensation decisions were made, but how and why they were made. Indeed, a good start on drafting the CD&A can be made simply by explaining how the principles in this Compensation Handbook were applied to result in the compensation figures shown in the tables.

According to the regulations, the CD&A should include, among other things, the rationale behind immediate vs long-term compensation and cash vs other compensation; specific items of corporate performance that are relevant; the factors used to determine a material increase or decrease in compensation; the benchmarking undertaken by a company in establishing compensation programs; and the role of executive officers in the compensation process. Other specific items for the CD&A include the manner in which the company determines when stock options and other equity awards are granted; the relationship between one compensation element (e.g., equity awards) and other elements (e.g., retirement benefits); accounting and tax implications; the company's policies and decisions regarding the adjustment or recovery of compensation if financial statements are restated; the company's equity ownership requirements; and the basis for selecting particular events as triggers for certain posttermination payments (e.g., the rationale for a single trigger for change-in-control payments).

Unsurprisingly in light of stock option backdating concerns, the CD&A must include an extensive discussion regarding equity grants. This discussion must reveal any plan or practice of the company to grant options to executives in coordination with the release of material nonpublic information or to time the release of material nonpublic information to affect the value of the award. It must also disclose how option grants to executives fit into the context of option grants to employees generally; the role of the board or the compensation committee in approving or administering a "timing program"; any delegation by the compensation committee to any other persons of any aspect of the administration of a "timing program"; and the role of executives in the timing of option grants.

The Summary Compensation Table

After the narrative CD&A, a summary compensation table will disclose the compensation of the NEOs for the last three fiscal years. Compensation, generally in the amounts determined for financial statement reporting purposes, is disclosed in a stipulated columnar format:

- Salary (both cash and noncash) earned by the NEO during the fiscal year

- Discretionary bonuses (both cash and noncash) earned by the NEO during the fiscal year

- Stock awards, including restricted stock and phantom stock

- Stock option awards, including options and stock appreciation rights

- Nonequity incentive plan compensation, which includes formula-based annual bonuses as well as long-term nonequity performance awards

- The dollar value of the annual change in the actuarial value of all qualified and nonqualified defined benefit pension plans and arrangements, including the incremental value of any above-market or preferential earnings on nonqualified defined contribution plans

- All other compensation, such as compensation costs for certain discount stock purchases, tax "gross-ups," termination or change-in-control payments, company contributions and other allocations to all defined contribution plans (vested or unvested), company paid premiums for life insurance, dividends or other earnings paid on stock or option awards, and perquisites and other personal benefits
- The dollar value of total compensation for the fiscal year

Other Tables

The summary compensation table is supplemented by other tables (and discussion) for particular forms of compensation, depending on the types of compensation actually paid. These include grants of plan-based awards, outstanding equity awards at fiscal year-end, option exercises and stock vested, postemployment compensation, pension benefits, and nonqualified deferred compensation.

Instructions for the tables require additional discussion of some items, particularly payments in connection with the resignation, severance, retirement, or other termination of a NEO, or a change-in-control of the company. Finally the regulations require a director compensation table.

Impact

The SEC Disclosure Rules must be considered in designing executive compensation programs, not only because of the impact of disclosure, but also because companies may want to amend or design their compensation programs to avoid unpleasant or complicated disclosures. For example, companies may want to simplify disclosures by eliminating multiple option grants throughout the fiscal year that lengthen the tables, or by ensuring that compensation arrangements fall clearly into one or another regulatory pigeon-hole in order to avoid ambiguities and reduce the need for lengthy, technical and nuanced narrative explanation. Companies may also reconsider benefits and perquisites where disclosure creates a potential for controversy that outweighs their intrinsic value. Needless to say, the time to consider this impact is when the compensation program is first considered.

THE FAIR LABOR STANDARDS ACT

The Fair Labor Standards Act (FLSA), originally enacted in 1937, is still a cornerstone of federal regulation of employment. The FLSA addresses four areas: minimum wage requirements, overtime pay requirements, restrictions on child labor, and equal pay. Minimum wage and child labor restrictions do not typically affect executive compensation (though the minimum wage requirements should at least be considered when an executive of a start-up company volunteers, or is recruited, to work for nothing, or for vague promises of future compensation or stock options); and a discussion of equal pay and other federal nondiscrimination laws is beyond the scope of this chapter.

It might be thought that overtime requirements also have little application in the executive suite; but the FLSA has some subtleties in this area that cannot be ignored in designing executive pay arrangements. Properly classifying employees as covered by, or exempt from, the overtime requirements of the FLSA is crucial. There are many FLSA exceptions to the overtime requirements, most applicable to specified occupational groups, but the broadest one, which is generally thought of as applying to most management employees, is for individuals employed in "bona fide executive, administrative or professional capacity," as defined by regulations of the Department of Labor.

Those regulations provide several alternative tests for exempt status, but almost all require that employees be paid on a salaried basis for the exemption to apply. Under the FLSA, an individual is salaried if he or she receives a predetermined amount each pay period and the amount is not subject to variation because of quantity or quality of work. The salary requirement means that an individual (other than an attorney) paid on an hourly basis can almost never be exempt. For some companies, particularly in professional or consulting fields, many highly paid employees whose time is charged to clients by the hour are also paid by the hour, and these individuals are subject to FLSA overtime protection.

For all nonexempt employees, the regular hourly rate from which overtime is determined must be calculated. One of the issues arising in this calculation is the treatment of bonuses or other incentive or equity-type compensation. Generally, discretionary bonuses are excluded, while nondiscretionary bonuses are included. In addition, under 2000 amendments to the FLSA, stock purchase plan, stock option, and stock appreciation right benefits are excluded on certain conditions. Compliance with these exceptions (or the increased overtime cost if they are not complied with) must be considered when bonus and equity plans are extended to nonexempt employees.

Additional requirements apply for the actual exemption of salaried employees. These include an executive exemption, which covers individuals paid more than $250 per week in salary and whose primary duties are the supervision of two or more other employees; or paid at least $155 per week in salary and whose primary duties are management of a business or department and who have authority to hire and fire, regularly exercise discretionary authority, and spend more than 80 percent of their time in the above duties. Other sets of requirements in the same vein delineate the statutory exemptions for administrative and professional employees, and further exemptions cover very highly compensated employees, computer systems analysts and programmers, motor carrier employees, commission salesmen, and the like.

There are two major limitations on benefits that employers may derive from these exemptions. First, they typically involve not just an objective salary component, but a more subjective component that evaluates the particular job duties of the person involved. For instance, whether a lower-level executive regularly exercises discretionary authority is something about which two people can sometimes disagree.

More significantly, these are federal exemptions only. Most states have their own FLSA-equivalent laws governing overtime requirements, which may state their exemptions in different terms or not have comparable exemptions at all. State laws that give enhanced protection (require overtime) beyond the federal requirements are *not* superseded by federal law. Since state laws (like the federal FLSA) allow employees to recover unpaid overtime (and usually interest, penalties, and attorneys fees), and the borderline cases where treatment is unclear generally involve relatively high-paid categories of employees, the potential employer liability for misclassifying employees can be severe.

Employers must therefore be aware of state requirements, exemptions, and limitations on exemptions (as well as their federal counterparts) in the states where they do business, and are wise to periodically review the exempt or nonexempt classification of employees, particularly in the borderline situations, for new job classifications, or for jobs whose functional description has changed since the last review.

INDIRECT REGULATION THROUGH THE TAX LAWS

A full discussion of the tax treatment of executive compensation is beyond the scope of this chapter. Instead, this section will focus on four tax rules that affect the design of executive compensation arrangements or procedures for adopting them. Even here, this chapter cannot discuss these provisions in depth. Actual compliance (avoidance of tax penalties) requires careful attention to voluminous details in lengthy regulations. This section can only briefly describe these provisions, with some comments on their broader implications for stock option plans and other forms of executive compensation.

Section 162(m)—Compensation Exceeding $1 Million

IRC Section 162(m) generally denies a deduction for compensation in excess of $1 million in a taxable year paid to a named executive officer (following the SEC definition, with some exceptions) of a public company, unless the compensation is "performance based." As a result, compensation arrangements that are capable of being performance-based are generally designed to meet the requirements of the statute and regulations.

Base salary and time-vested restricted stock will not qualify as performance-based. However, bonus and most other incentive compensation can generally be designed to be performance-based. To be performance based, the compensation must be paid only upon attainment of a predetermined, objective performance goal, which is established by a compensation committee composed solely of independent directors, and the material terms of which are approved by shareholders.

Under the regulations, to be "preestablished," the performance goal must be established not later than 90 days after the start of the period of service to which the compensation relates, must be stated in terms of objective business criteria (stock price, earnings, or the like), and must be part of an objective formula that lets the ultimate compensation be computed based on the performance results. After the end of the period, the compensation committee must certify the level of attainment of the performance goal. In other words, discretion is generally precluded.

As an exception, though, the regulations allow the compensation committee to apply "negative discretion" to reduce the resulting formula compensation downwards (but not upwards). A consequence of this feature is that bonus plans can comply with the letter of IRC Section 162(m) but violate its spirit by providing an objective formula that creates a high bonus based on soft performance targets, with the compensation committee then using "negative discretion" to reduce the bonus to what it really wants to pay.

Under a special rule, stock options and stock appreciation rights are considered "performance based" if the plan states the maximum number of shares for which options or SARs may be granted in a specified period to any employee, and the option price (or SAR strike price) is not more than the fair market value of the stock when the option or SAR is granted. As discussed above, backdating violates this requirement, exposing perpetrating companies that have relied on IRC Section 162(m) to substantial tax deficiencies.

The regulations describe in excruciating detail when directors are "independent" for purposes of Section 162(m). (These may differ from standards for director independence applied for other purposes.) The regulations also specify that the "material terms" that must be submitted to shareholders for approval are the employees eligible to receive the performance-based compensation, a description of the business criteria on which the performance goal is based, and either the formula used to calculate the compensation if the performance goal is obtained, or the maximum compensation that may be paid.

In light of IRC Section 162(m), compensation committees administering bonus or incentive plans under the regulations will usually meet within the first 90 days of the performance period to select the performance criteria from among those in the shareholder-approved plan, establish the threshold, target and maximum goals for the eligible employees, and certify the degree to which goals for the prior year have been attained, and the resulting bonuses payable. Because of the limitations on flexibility under IRC Section 162(m), some companies will have one Section 162(m)-compliant bonus plan solely for the covered executives whose compensation is (or may be) subject to IRC Section 162(m), with a separate (and more discretionary and more subjective) bonus plan for other management.

The relative ease of establishing an arrangement as "performance based" (if the technicalities are observed), coupled with the "negative discretion" feature, means that public companies can generally avoid the deduction limit of IRC Section 162(m) (except for) base compensation and other nonperformance-based (i.e., time vested) compensation. This fact, coupled with the public and Congressional concern with executive compensation levels described in the first section of this chapter, suggests that Section 162(m) may be a prime target for legislative attention.

Section 280G—Golden Parachutes

IRC Section 280G was enacted in 1984 to restrict "golden parachute" benefits. It denies a deduction for "excess parachute payments" paid to a "disqualified individual" as a result of a corporate change of control. A companion provision (IRC Section 4999) imposes a 20 percent excise tax on the individual receiving "excess parachute payments." Unlike IRC Section 162(m), these provisions apply to many private companies as well as public companies.

Generally a "parachute payment" is any payment of compensation that is contingent on a change of control (as defined in the statute and regulations). This can encompass not only traditional "parachute" benefits, but also sale or retention bonuses and similar arrangements. "Disqualified individuals" are 1 percent or more shareholders, officers, or highly compensated individuals, all as more specifically defined (with some exceptions) in the regulations.

IRC Section 280G contains a complicating leveraging feature. The tax penalties apply if (and only if) "excess parachute payments" exceed three times the individual's "base amount." "Base amount" is essentially the individual's average annual taxable income from the company over the five-year period preceding the change of control. But if the parachute penalties are triggered, they then apply to all parachute payments in excess of *one* times the base amount. Thus, a small excess above the three-times-base-amount-trigger can cause a substantial and disproportionate adverse tax impact.

Responses by companies and executives subject to the parachute tax are varied. One response is for the plan or contract to limit potential parachute payments to 299 percent of the "base amount." However, this can have arbitrary and counterintuitive results. Two executives can earn the same salary and bonus and receive the same nonqualified stock option awards throughout the averaging period, but if one of them exercised nonqualified stock options and the other did not, the one who exercised will have higher taxable income and therefore a higher "base amount," and may escape the parachute tax altogether, while the other may be liable for a significant tax.

Another approach is for the company to "gross up" the payment to neutralize the parachute excise tax. But gross-ups can become very expensive (particularly if the marginal tax rate of federal and state income and 20 percent excise tax exceeds 50 percent). In some circumstances a large gross-up payment might end up being made in order to give the executive a benefit that exceeds the three-time-base-amount threshold by only a small amount. More sophisticated formulas may apply a gross-up only if the resulting after-tax benefit to the executive is, say, 20 percent more than the executive would receive if cut back to three times the base amount.

The parachute penalties apply to all public companies and their "disqualified individual" executives. Privately held corporations may benefit from one of two exemptions. First "small business corporations" those eligible to be taxed as "S-Corporations" under IRC subchapter S, are automatically exempt (whether or not they have actually elected to be taxed as S-Corporations). The main requirements for a "small business corporation" are that it does *not* have (1) more than 100 shareholders, (2) any shareholders that are not individuals (or certain permitted estates and trusts), (3) a nonresident alien as shareholder, or (4) more than one class of stock.

Second, other nonpublic companies are exempt if the payment is approved by 75 percent of the shareholders (as determined immediately before the change in control), after adequate disclosure (as specified in the regulations) of all the material facts concerning the payments. Complying with the conditions for this exemption may be difficult. On the one hand, the shareholder vote must actually determine the individual's right to the payment: it is not sufficient for the shareholders to approve a payment to which the company is already contractually bound. On the other hand, many if not most "parachute" (and sale bonus) arrangements are entered into years before any actual change of control. This makes "adequate disclosure" difficult when the ultimate payment amounts are unknown. Nevertheless, it is crucial for nonpublic companies establishing plans or making contracts that call for "parachute payments" as defined in the statute and regulations to consult the regulations and seek shareholder approval at their inception.

Section 409A—New Requirements for Deferred Compensation

The latest foray into regulation by taxation is IRC Section 409A, effective in 2005, with voluminous technical regulations generally effective in 2008. The basic requirements of Section 409A are deceptively simple, and fairly easy to apply to what we commonly think of as deferred compensation.

- The deferred compensation must be payable only upon death, disability, separation from service, change in control or unforeseeable emergency, or pursuant to a fixed schedule

- Payments on separation from service to a "specified employee" (key employee) of a public company must be delayed until at least six months after separation

- The initial decision to defer compensation for a year must be made before the beginning of the year in which the services for which the compensation is earned are performed (with exceptions for the first year of eligibility and elections under a performance-based bonus plan)

- Further changes in the initial deferral decision are restricted, and acceleration of deferred compensation is prohibited

If a deferred compensation arrangement violates these restrictions, the deferred compensation is included in income at the time deferred (or when it becomes vested and nonforfeitable, if later)—i.e., the deferral does not work to defer tax—*and* is subject to an additional 20 percent income tax (over and above the individual's regular tax rate), *and* is subject to interest from the time of deferral (or vesting) at the IRC tax underpayment interest rate plus 1 percent. These taxes are imposed on the employee (or independent contractor), not the company. But the employer is required to withhold these taxes. This tax treatment is sufficiently severe that it is not practicable to provide deferred compensation other than in accordance with the new Section 409A rules.

The complicating problem is that the final regulations define "deferred compensation" extremely broadly. They generally include anything that gives an employee or independent contractor a legally binding right (even though contingent or not yet vested) to compensation that might be paid in a later year. Under the regulations, stock options and stock appreciation rights (SARs) can be deferred compensation. Separation payments (including postemployment reimbursements), nonqualified supplemental executive retirement plans (SERPs) and certain taxable welfare benefits, are also deferred compensation. Even ordinary bonus arrangements may be deferred compensation.

The breadth of the statutory definition focuses attention on the exceptions. Qualified retirement plans, and benefits that would be tax-free under general rules, are generally exempt. Other exceptions may apply to executive compensation arrangements.

One of these exempts property transfers that are already subject to IRC Section 83. This would cover most restricted stock arrangements (awards of shares to an employees that become vested based on performance or time).

Stock option and SAR arrangements are exempt provided the underlying stock is stock of the employer and the option or SAR price can never be less than fair market value on the date of grant. For public companies, grant date fair market value is readily determined from the market (if the options are not backdated!). For closely held companies, the regulations prescribe safe harbor valuation methods, generally requiring either an appraisal or formula value that is applied for all corporate purposes, though the appraisal requirement is relaxed for an illiquid start-up corporation.

A "short-term deferral" exception states that compensation paid within two and a half months of the end of the calendar year in which it became vested is not deferred compensation. Restricted stock unit arrangements (where the award is to transfer shares in the future when vesting requirements have been met) and most bonus arrangements can be designed to fit within this exception if they have no other deferral features.

Another exception covers severance benefits paid on an involuntary termination of employment (or participation in a window program). The regulations allow a limited number of "good reason" termination events consistent with the involuntary termination. The principal requirements (besides involuntary termination) are that the amount paid may not exceed two times the individual's annual compensation (or two times the limit on compensation that may be taken into account for qualified pension and 401(k) plan purposes, if less), and payment must be completed within two years. Under the regulations, the exception applies to otherwise qualifying severance pay up to the amount limits even if the total amount paid will exceed the amount limits. One significant benefit of this exception is that the six-month delay rule for specified employees of a public company does not apply to involuntary termination payments within the limits of this exception.

The regulations cover in detail these and other exceptions, provide special rules (usually subject to limitations) for disputes and refusals to pay, postemployment reimbursements and indemnification and the like, and define crucial concepts. The regulations require all deferred compensation arrangements to be in writing and by their terms comply with the requirements of Section 409A. Therefore the technical requirements of the regulations must be consulted and observed in drafting any deferred compensation arrangement either to comply with the new standards, or to ensure that it is exempt from them.

IRC Section 4958—"Intermediate Sanction" Standards for Tax Exempt Organizations

Tax regulations governing compensation paid by tax-exempt charitable and educational organizations are naturally of paramount importance to those tax-exempt employers. But inasmuch as they require for those tax-exempt organizations the practices and procedures that the regulators see as standard (if not "best") practices in the for-profit sector, they are significant in revealing the regulators' view of what those practices are (or should be).

Section 4958 of the Code imposes so-called "intermediate sanction" excise taxes on "disqualified persons" (insiders) and "organization managers" (board members or comparable persons) of tax-exempt public charities (and civic leagues and social welfare organizations) whenever an impermissible "excess benefit transaction" occurs between the organization and a disqualified person. An excess benefit transaction includes unreasonable compensation paid to a disqualified person. However, the regulations describe the circumstances in which compensation will be presumed to be reasonable.

Under the regulations, an exempt organization has the benefit of the presumption if the board approving the compensation:

- was composed entirely of individuals who are independent and do not have a conflict of interest

- obtained and made its determination based on proper comparability data and

- adequately documented the basis for its compensation decision concurrently with such determination

Comparability data for the second requirement is considered appropriate when, given the knowledge and expertise of the board members, it offers sufficient information for them to determine that the compensation arrangement is reasonable. The board members must take into account the aggregate amount of all compensation and benefits to an individual, including compensation paid by or through related organizations.

Relevant information (for organizations with annual gross receipts of more than $1 million) to consider in determining whether compensation is reasonable includes compensation levels paid by similarly situated organizations, both taxable and tax-exempt, for a functionally comparable position; the availability of similar services in the geographic area of the organization; current compensation surveys compiled by independent firms; and actual written offers by similar organizations competing for the services of a particular individual. Boards must also ensure that any intention to treat benefits provided to executives is contemporaneously acknowledged or treated as compensation.

Documentation is the third element of the presumption, usually in the board's or committee's minutes. Specifically, the minutes must indicate the terms of the transaction that was approved and the date of its approval; the members of the board or committee who were present during the debate or discussion of the transaction that was approved and who voted on the proposal; the comparability data obtained and relied upon and how the data was obtained; and any actions taken with respect to the transaction by any member of the board who had a conflict of interest with respect to the transaction.

Further, if the board determines to pay compensation that is either higher or lower than indicated by the range of comparability data, a record of that fact and the board's or committee's reasons must be part of the minutes. Factors that may be documented (where they exist) in support of above-average pay may include the ratio of the proposed compensation to the organization's revenues and expenses, the executive's track record, competing offers, the difficulty and costs of replacing the executive, or special circumstances for the organization that require the executive's special qualifications and talents.

BEST PRACTICES

Regular Schedule

Boards and compensation committees should have regular schedules and procedures for making compensation decisions. Because of IRC Section 162(m) considerations discussed earlier, the determination of performance bonus goals and targets, and approval of bonuses to be paid already follows (or should follow, at least in public companies) a regular annual schedule. The same should apply to options and other equity awards. That is, they should be granted annually at a fixed time (or fixed board or committee meeting) each year. Ad hoc grants should be avoided (except where compelling business reasons require otherwise—such as the need to make a special grant for a newly hired or newly promoted executive). The timing of grants should be controlled by the board or compensation committee, and not left up to management's discretion.

At least once a year, the board or committee should comprehensively review total compensation postemployment compensation and benefits payable under all foreseeable scenarios. The SEC Disclosure Regulations essentially mandate that a public company calculate and update these potential payments for disclosure on an annual basis.

Tally Sheets for Compensation

Corporate management (or consultants) must ensure that the board or compensation committee has comprehensive "tally sheets" when any significant compensation decisions are made (including approval of employment contracts), or for the annual review recommended above. For employment contracts or other arrangements providing retirement or severance benefits, or the annual review, a spreadsheet should show what the employee will receive under each circumstance that might potentially arise (death, disability, involuntary or good reason termination, voluntary quit, or discharge for cause). The spreadsheet should place a dollar value on all forms of compensation (including pensions, deferred compensation, postretirement perquisites, including the tax cost of nondeductible compensation). Where those amounts vary depending on other events (such as a change in control) or the company's stock value, the tally should include those alternatives.

Where only certain elements of compensation are up for decision (base salary review, bonus, equity awards), the tally sheet should still show all the elements of the affected individual's compensation. This allows the elements being considered to be evaluated in the context of total compensation. It can also identify areas where one element of compensation will swing because of changes in another. For example, a relatively modest increase in base salary may significantly increase SERP benefits, or the company's obligation for a parachute tax "gross-up" in the event of a change of control.

Of course, this data has to be organized and presented in useful form, without information overload. A good place to start is with the format of the tables forming part of the compensation discussion and analysis under the SEC Disclosure Rules. For one thing, this will give a public company a head start on preparing those disclosures. It will also identify problematic issues or practices that might invite criticism and allow them to be addressed in a timely fashion in making the compensation decisions. Some revisions to plans or awards may avoid potentially undesirable disclosures. This may be especially true for severance plans, change-in-control agreements, retirement plans and perquisites. Preparing pro-forma disclosure tables at the time of the compensation decisions also ensures that the board or compensation committee will not be surprised when they review the ultimate disclosures as part of the company's draft proxy statement or annual report.

Consultants

Outside compensation consultants are an integral part of this process for companies of any size. The compensation consultant can provide information to benchmark executive officer compensation, as well as prepare the tally sheets described above. However, outside consultants reports and recommendations are an aid to board or compensation committee decision-making, not a substitute for it. Directors should have a clear understanding of their company's executive compensation strategy and the various metrics and other standards that underpin it.

Compensation consultants should be truly independent. In larger companies where the amounts and stakes justify the duplication, the board or compensation committee may retain their own advisors or consultants independent of management's or the company's consultants. Where one consulting firm reports to both management and the board, they should at least have the ability to meet with the board or compensation committee outside the presence of management, so the directors have the opportunity to ask any questions about their report and recommendations on management compensation. If the consultants have other relationships with the company, this must be disclosed to the board or compensation committee (and consideration should be given to disclosing it to shareholders in the CD&A).

It is particularly important for the board or compensation committee to have independent consultant (and legal) counsel when renegotiating the employment contract or compensation package for an existing chief executive officer or other senior executive.

Executive compensation is almost invariably set in light of (or at least after considering) data on the compensation for similar executive positions at similar companies. Care must be taken in selecting peer companies for this comparison. Adjustments to "raw" comparator data may be needed for the size of the company and the relative experience of the company's executives to those of the comparator companies. If the comparison is to have any objectivity, the list of comparator companies needs to be developed in advance and stuck with, not adjusted to justify a decision on compensation levels already reached for other reasons.

Stock Option Grant Practices

Companies that have not already done so should review their equity compensation plans and stock option grant practices. Granting options on a regular schedule at the same time each year, as recommended above, will help insure the integrity of the grant date; and providing tally sheet estimates of the dollar value of awards (and other compensation) for the individuals being considered, also noted above, will help ensure that the board or committee has appropriate information. The approval of the grant should cover not only the number of shares and exercise price, but also the form of stock option or other award agreement. Optionees should get prompt notice of the award (and a copy of the agreement). Reallocations or adjustments afterward should not be permitted.

Where management recommends stock option (or other equity) awards, the reasons for the recommendations (as well as the recommended number of shares) should be in writing and included with the committee minutes.

Conduct of the Meetings

The records of the board or compensation committee should reflect that they have followed best practices as outlined above. Action should be taken at a meeting, rather than by written consent, to allow for member interaction. Where particularly significant or potentially controversial decisions are to be taken, consider presenting the arrangement for discussion at one meeting and postponing a vote until a later meeting. Tally sheet and other documentation should be circulated well in advance to allow time at the meeting for thorough analysis and discussion. Management and compensation consultants should be available to discuss and explain the recommendations; and as noted above, the consultants should have the opportunity to do this outside the presence of management.

If one or two members of the board or committee have taken the lead in the matters being considered, the information and studies they developed or on which they relied, not just their conclusions, should be shared with the full board or committee membership.

The board minutes must reflect consideration of the matter and the decision taken, including the reports of consultants and or management giving support for the decision; and should be prepared promptly after the conclusion of the meeting.

SUMMARY

Most important, the compensation setting process and decisions have to be viewed as a vital corporate activity, not just a matter of jumping through government-mandated hoops. A basic reason for the regulation discussed in this chapter is to help ensure that the company gets the most actual value for each compensation dollar spent. Even without the government, that should be the ultimate business goal of those responsible for the corporate compensation function.

REFERENCES

Bickley, J. M. and Shorter, G. *Stock Options: The Backdating Issue*. CRS Report, 15 March 2007.

Council of Institutional Investors—National Association of Corporate Directors Task Force, *Looking Back, Looking Forward: Recommendations on Majority Voting, Section 404, and Executive Compensation*. January 2007.

IRC Section 162(m) Regulations: TD 8650, 60 Fed. Reg. 65534 (20 December 1995), codified at 26 C.F.R. § 1.162-27.

IRC Section 208G Regulations: TD 9083, 68 Fed. Reg. 45745 (1 August 2003), codified at 26 C.F.R. § 1.280G-1-4.

IRC 409A Regulations: TD 9321, 73 Fed Reg. 19234 (17 April 2007), codified at 26 C.F.R. § 1.409A-1-4.

IRC 4958 Regulations: TD 8978, 67 Fed. Reg. 3076 (23 January 2002), codified at 26 C.F.R. § 53.4958-6.

Kraus, H., *Executive Stock Options and Stock Appreciation Rights*. Law Journal Press, 2007.

SEC Disclosure Rules: Release Nos 33-8732A, 34-543202A, 71 Fed. Reg. 53158 (8 September 2006), codified at 17 C.F.R. § 229.402.

Section 162(m) Regulations (Certain excessive employee remuneration).

Seltzinger, M. *Executive Compensation: SEC Regulations and Congressional Proposals*. CRS Report, 12 March 2002.

Shorter, G. and Labonte, M., *The Economics of Corporate Executive Pay*. CRS Report, 8 May 2007.

Shorter, G., Jickling, M. and Roab, A., *Excessive CEO Pay: Background and Policy Approaches*. CRS Report, 2 March 2007.

EXECUTIVE EMPLOYMENT AGREEMENTS

Richard L. Alpern, Principal

Frederic W. Cook & Company, Inc.

EMPLOYMENT AGREEMENTS CAN PLAY AN important role in the retention and motivation of executive-level employees. There are many different reasons for entering into employment agreements, e.g., hiring a new executive, promoting an executive, or reassuring an executive in the event of the arrival of a new CEO or other higher level executive, or in the face of corporate upheaval such as the potential sale of the company or a division. In addition, the provisions included in employment agreements are affected by the position of the executive covered by the agreement, i.e., from a lower level vice president to a CEO.

ESTABLISHING THE BASIC RELATIONSHIP

Period of Employment

Depending on the level of the executive and the reason for the agreement, the period of employment specified in the employment agreement (often referred to as the "term" of the agreement), in addition to its legal significance, can serve as a key psychological tool in reassuring the executive of her importance to the company, that she will be fairly compensated while employed, and that she will be appropriately protected in the event of the termination of the employment relationship.

Employment agreements with lower-level executives often have no fixed period of employment. This type of agreement is often described as making the executive an "employee at will" because as a matter of law the agreement (and the executive's employment) can be terminated at any time without providing any severance. As a practical matter this eliminates the retention aspect of the employment agreement due to the absence of severance protection in the event of the termination of the employment relationship. Note, however, that the termination of the employment agreement does not necessarily mean that the executive's employment will be terminated.

More typically, especially for new hires and senior-level executives, employment agreements provide for a fixed period of employment of between one and three years. Furthermore, many employment agreements provide for an automatic extension of the period of employment (often referred to as a renewal of the term) at the end of the initial period unless either party gives advance written notice of nonrenewal. Usually the renewal is on a year-by-year basis, although for certain senior executives the extension will begin at the end of the first or second year of the period of employment, resulting in a perpetual multiyear period of employment in the absence of notice to the contrary.

Position and Duties

The more specific an employment agreement is with respect to the executive's position and duties, the more likely it is that the executive will feel secure in her relationship with the company. Lower level executives' employment agreements often only have a general description of the executive's position (e.g., vice president) and of the executive's duties (e.g., such duties as are assigned by the board of directors or the CEO). Employment agreements with senior-level executives typically have a specific position (e.g., Chief Financial Officer; Senior Vice President for Marketing) and a description of duties that is consistent with the executive's position (either by specific duties or a reference to typical duties for that position).

A related aspect of the executive's duties is the extent to which the executive may engage in other activities while employed. The inclusion of a provision stating (to the extent applicable) that the executive may serve as a director of other public companies, or serve as an officer of, or work on, activities of professional and trade associations and civic and charitable organizations, can foster a positive relationship with the executive while at the same time protecting the company by specifying that these activities may be engaged in only if they do not materially interfere with the performance of the executive's duties.

The description of the position and the ability to engage in other activities are of legal significance as well. A breach of the provision relating to the executive's position with the company can give the executive the right to severance benefits, and a breach of the provision relating to engaging in other activities can give the company the right to terminate the executive's employment for cause without being required to provide severance benefits.

Reporting Relationship

If the employment agreement states the title of the executive to whom the executive is required to report, it will not only provide legal protection to the executive but also reassurance of where the executive stands in the corporate hierarchy. A provision stating the reporting relationship is less typical for lower-level executives; for some senior executives the provision will specify that they report to the chief executive officer and the board of directors.

COMPENSATION

There are a variety of elements of compensation that can be specified in employment agreements. For lower-level executives the agreement is often very general except for specifying the initial salary level. Agreements with senior executives will typically have more details about one or more of the other elements of compensation. To the extent that elements of compensation are specified in the agreement, the company is obligating itself legally to provide them and, if applicable, failure to honor the obligation can give the executive the right to severance benefits. Specific compensation elements in an employment agreement serve to increase the likelihood of retaining the executive, but at the same time may provide less motivation to the executive to increase his or her efforts on behalf of the company.

Salary

As noted, the executive's salary on commencement of employment is often the only compensation element specified in the employment agreement. The company may also agree to review salary annually (which does not provide any legal obligation to actually increase salary), to provide an annual salary increase in a percentage that is no less than the percentage increase in the cost-of-living based on a recognized index (usually one of the various measures of the Consumer Price Index), or to increase the executive's salary by no less than the percentage increase of salary of similarly situated executives.

Annual Bonus

Another common compensation element that is addressed in the employment agreement is annual bonus compensation. Most employment agreements provide no more than a statement that the executive will be eligible to participate in the company's annual bonus plan. A senior executive's agreement often will include a provision that the executive's annual target bonus will be no less than a specified percentage of base salary. Such a provision does not obligate the company to pay the specified amount as an annual bonus since the actual bonus will be determined based on performance or solely in the discretion of the company's board of directors, compensation committee or CEO (as applicable).

When an executive is recruited to join the company, especially a senior executive, the employment agreement often provides for a minimum bonus for the first year of employment (sometimes referred to as a guaranteed bonus). If the executive commences employment late in the company's fiscal year the minimum bonus is likely to be applicable for the first full fiscal year of the executive's employment. In limited circumstances, the employment agreement with a newly recruited senior executive will specify the bonus formula that will be applied for one or more years of employment. The inclusion of a bonus formula may adversely affect the ability of a public company to deduct the annual bonus if the executive's total annual compensation exceeds one million dollars.[1]

Equity Awards

Employment agreements typically only contain general provisions relating to equity awards (stock options, restricted stock, etc.), i.e., a statement that the executive will be eligible to participate in the company's equity plan. Some agreements will be more specific in providing that the annual equity awards to the executive will be no less than those provided to similarly situated executives. Since a specific provision can obligate the company to provide a level of equity awards to the executive that may not be appropriate based on the executive's performance, companies should carefully consider whether to include the provision in the employment agreement. The one million dollar limitation for certain top executives of a public company also needs to be taken into account in including specific equity award provisions.

Employee Benefits

Typically an employment agreement will also be general about employee benefits, i.e., medical, dental, hospitalization and disability benefits, life insurance, and 401(k), profit sharing and other retirement plans. The agreement will commonly state only that the executive will be eligible to participate in the company's employee benefit plans. Since many companies provide additional benefits to executives, especially senior executives, agreements often provide that the executive will be eligible to participate in all plans available to similarly situated executives.

Once again, newly hired senior executives are often able to negotiate for provisions relating to special benefits, such as life insurance coverage for much higher amounts than are otherwise available to other executives or a different type of life insurance.

Perquisites

Although perquisites have received a great deal of negative attention in the last few years, they can be significant in attracting and retaining executives. There are many different types of perquisites, including country club memberships, financial planning, cars or car allowances, and use of corporate aircraft. Generally perquisites are limited to senior-level executives and in many recent agreements have been omitted and replaced by increased salary or other cash compensation.

New Hire Packages

It is often necessary in order to hire a new executive to provide certain compensation on a one-time basis. A "sign-on bonus" is very common and will vary in amount depending on its purpose. In some cases it is a pure inducement for the executive to join the company, particularly for a lower-level executive. For a senior executive the sign-on bonus is more of a "make-up" for bonus or other compensation that the executive will forfeit by leaving his or her current employer.

Another typical form of compensation for newly recruited executives is a specific award of equity-based compensation. Similar to the sign-on bonus, this can be intended primarily as an inducement or as make-up for forfeited equity compensation from the executive's current employer.

A common provision that is not considered to be compensation but can be an important aspect of recruiting an executive is the reimbursement of various types of relocation expenses that an executive will incur in changing jobs. Among the typical relocation expenses are moving costs, house hunting costs, and temporary living expenses.

Agreements with some senior level executives provide for special retirement benefits to make up for benefits that the executive will lose by accepting employment with a new employer. Typically these retirement benefits require the executive to work a certain number of years before becoming vested in the benefits. Special retirement benefits often play a key role in retaining an executive who changes jobs mid-career, especially if there is a vesting requirement based on continued service with the new employing company.

TERMINATION OF THE EMPLOYMENT RELATIONSHIP

Provisions in an employment agreement relating to severance pay and benefits if the executive's employment is terminated under certain circumstances often aid in attracting and retaining the executive, by assuring the executive of a specified amount of posttermination compensation and benefits.

Expiration of the Period of Employment

If the employment agreement specifies a period of employment, the employment relationship can be terminated without any requirement that the company pay severance benefits (assuming that the executive is not covered by a severance plan) by allowing the period of employment to expire and then terminating the executive's employment. Similarly, if the agreement provides for renewals, the company can give notice that the term will not be renewed and after the end of the period of employment it can terminate the executive's employment without paying severance benefits.

Death and Disability

The term of the employment agreement and the executive's employment will usually terminate upon the death or disability of the executive. In many agreements the company must give notice of termination for disability, and the agreement and the executive's employment will then terminate if the executive does not return to employment within a relatively short time (e.g., 60 days).

It is rare for an employment agreement to provide for any severance benefits in addition to the rights the executive has accrued under various compensation and retirement plans maintained by the company. In some cases the agreement will provide for a *pro rata* bonus (based on the period worked during the bonus year) and the vesting of equity awards, especially those made to newly recruited executives.

Retirement

In contrast to death and disability, any employment agreement provisions relating to retirement are favorable to the executive, since a mandatory retirement provision is either not permissible due to age discrimination regulations or viewed so unfavorably that it is usually not included in agreements. Retirement provisions are often based on achieving a combination of age and service and include entitlement to a *pro rata* bonus, vesting of certain equity awards, and entitlement to special retirement benefits.

Other Terminations

If the executive's employment is terminated by the company without cause during the period of employment, a typical employment agreement for a senior executives or a new hire will specify the severance benefits payable to the executive. Many employment agreements for lower-level executives also provide for specific severance benefits, especially for new hire for a limited period of time (e.g., one to two years) following the commencement of employment. Severance benefits in the event of the termination of employment by the executive for good reason (e.g., reduction in salary, demotion, or relocation) are usually limited to more senior executives. The definitions of cause and good reason are, of course, of critical legal importance in determining the executive's entitlement to severance benefits.

Some employment agreements also address the severance benefits to which an executive would be entitled in the event of termination without cause or for good reason during a specified period following a change in control. A discussion of change in control protection is beyond the scope of this chapter, but note that typically higher cash severance and longer benefits continuation are provided.

Cash Severance.   The two key aspects of the provisions in employment agreements relating to the cash severance payable to the executive are the calculation of the amount payable and the method of payment of the amount. Agreements commonly provide that the amount is based either on salary or on a combination of salary and bonus. The bonus component can be expressed in a variety of ways such as: target bonus for the year of termination; average bonus earned for the prior two or three years; and the higher of target or average.

The cash severance amount can be expressed as (i) a multiple of salary (or a multiple of salary and bonus), (ii) the salary (and bonus) payable for the remainder of the period of employment, or (iii) the greater of (i) or (ii), in which case the multiple is usually lower than if only (i) were applicable.

How the cash severance is payable is significant for a variety of reasons. Typically payment is either made in a lump sum or in installments related to the multiple or the remainder of the period of employment. Companies prefer installment payments in order to have the ability to enforce covenants by terminating future payments if a covenant is violated. Executives prefer lump sum payments due to a concern that any remaining payments will cease (at least temporarily) if the company asserts that a covenant has been violated, even if the existence of a violation is unclear.

Benefits Continuation.   The continuation of medical, dental, and hospitalization benefits, as well as disability and life insurance benefits, following termination of employment is typically of great value to executives. Although by law terminated executives must be given the right to elect "COBRA continuation coverage" of medical, dental, and hospitalization benefits, executives greatly prefer the continuation to be at the same cost as would be paid by an active employee, which is much lower than the COBRA cost. Many employment agreements provide for continued benefits coverage at the same cost as an active employee would be charged for a period of time equal to the period that cash severance is payable. The agreement typically provides for benefits continuation to end if the executive is eligible for coverage for the same benefits from a new employer. It is important to be clear whether the cessation of benefits continuation is on a benefit by benefit basis or in the aggregate.

Vesting of Equity-Based Awards.   If a new hire package provides for a specific grant of one or more forms of equity-based compensation (e.g. stock options; restricted stock) the employment agreement may specify whether (and to what extent) the award will vest on a termination that entitles the executive to cash severance. The posttermination exercise period of stock options may also be specified. In the absence of a provision in the employment agreement, the terms of the award agreement will govern the vesting of equity-based compensation.

Covenants

There are several types of postemployment covenant of an executive that are important in protecting the interests of the employing company: noncompetition, nonsolicitation of employees, nonsolicitation of customers, and confidentiality. There is rarely any dispute about a confidentiality covenant and with rare exceptions it will have no time limit.

The other three covenants are often among the most difficult provisions to negotiate in an employment agreement because the company wants them to apply in all events and the executive wants them to apply only in the event that the executive is entitled to cash severance. These three covenants will end after a period specified in the agreement, which is often equal to the period during which cash severance is payable (or the number of years equal to the multiple for a lump sum payment) but subject to a minimum of one year.

No Disparagement

A related covenant that employers find very desirable is the requirement that the executive not make any disparaging remarks about the company, its directors and employees. Since the covenant can be just as desirable for the executive relating to statements about the executive by the company, many employment agreements contain mutual nondisparagement covenants of the employer and the executive.

Dispute Resolution

Finally, many employment agreements contain a provision requiring that any disputes about the agreement be handled through arbitration, which can have advantages to both the company and the executive. Arbitration proceedings are usually closed to the public and thus often preferred by companies because the dispute can be kept out of the media. An advantage for the executives is that an arbitration proceeding is usually concluded much sooner than a court proceeding and also involves lower legal fees. Some companies are not in favor of arbitration because they view arbitrators as likely to reach a decision that is essentially a compromise.

The legal fees and expenses involved in resolving a dispute can be considerable, even if arbitration is used. As a result, employment agreements with senior executives and certain new hires often contain a provision requiring the company to advance or reimburse the executive for legal fees. A critical aspect of such a provision is to what extent the executive must prevail in order to have the company pay the executive's legal fees. There are various standards that are used, with the most typical being (i) payment unless the executive's claim is found to be frivolous or without merit or (ii) payment if the executive prevails on at least one material claim.

SUMMARY

Employment agreement provisions, in addition to having legal significance, can be an important factor in retaining and motivating executives. The circumstances in which the agreement is entered into (e.g., a new hire) and the level of the executive (e.g., lower-level vice president) influence how the agreement is structured, as well as the degree of legal protection provided to the executive, in establishing the basic employment relationship, the executive's compensation, and the termination of the employment relationship (including the severance benefits provided to the executive).

END NOTE

1. The deduction of annual compensation of each of certain top executives of a public company is limited to one million dollars unless the compensation satisfies the Internal Revenue Code Section 162(m) requirements for performance-based compensation.

Compensation and the Board

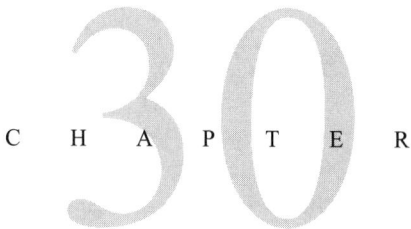

THE COMPENSATION COMMITTEE AND EXECUTIVE PAY

Seymour Burchman, Managing Principal, and
Blair Jones, Managing Principal

Semler Brossy Consulting Group, LLC

IN THE NEW MILLENNIUM, THE role of the compensation committee is being reshaped by converging forces emanating from multiple fronts outside the corporation. As a result, the conversation in the boardroom between committee members and management features a new dynamic and often deeper examination of what executives are paid, as well as why and how.

Compensation committee members do not take on their fiduciary duties lightly. Committees want to do the right thing on behalf of shareholders, the corporation, and executives. Yet increasingly, they find their decisions—and themselves—under a microscope, adding tremendous pressure to an already high-profile role. Corporate scandals and issues such as stock option backdating have had a far-reaching impact: many compensation committees now operate with a risk management mentality, as well as a moderate degree of fear and a desire to keep their personal reputations intact. Changes in the regulatory environment—from the

Sarbanes–Oxley Act, SEC disclosure requirements, FAS123R and 409A—have both broadened and tightened requirements, creating the need for more in-depth education about the myriad issues surrounding executive compensation decision making.

Activism on the part of hedge funds, unions, and organizations such as ISS, CalPERS, and CalSTRS heightens the scrutiny leveled at compensation committees and the members who influence and approve executive compensation packages. Shareholders are not averse to pushing their agendas, and even voting against directors, when they disagree with compensation designs and outcomes. The "say-on-pay" movement, which advocates a nonbinding shareholder vote on executive compensation, is gaining momentum too. Compounding the tension, litigation filed by shareholders and the government is becoming more common.

The media glare is omnipresent: decisions reach far beyond the board room, generating publicity and frequent criticism in the pages of *The New York Times*, *The Wall Street Journal* and *Business Week* as the press has become both more vigilant and strident.

Greater disclosure increases the transparency of not just the outcomes of compensation committee decisions, but also the process and logic for reaching the decisions. A proxy statement's compensation discussion and analysis (CD&A) and the detailed compensation tables open the kimono, requiring a story line that is rational and defensible.

For better or worse, the executive compensation program becomes a litmus test for good governance, placing more attention on the compensation committee and increasing the pressure to "get compensation right." Committees will be well served by partnering with management to ensure the right conversations about executive compensation take place at the right time. Two critical areas for discussion include:

1. *The key accountabilities of the compensation committee.* These include establishing a sound pay philosophy, periodically testing the pay program design to ensure it supports the philosophy, and correcting any breakdowns in design or execution.

2. *The structures, processes, skills and education that will enable the committee to execute its role.* Management and committee members must establish clear expectations about the role and its demands, agree on a calendar that prescribes key conversations and deliverables, and clarify decision rights and accountabilities. Committees also need a solid grounding in executive compensation. Given the rapidity of change in the executive pay arena, they require periodic updates about trends, legislation, regulatory actions, and other issues that relate to and may affect their decisions and their role.

At the bottom line, compensation committee members must be able to draw the link between the business situation and its implications for compensation, and understand the rationale and impact of performance metrics. Equipped with the right skills and appropriate tools and advice, committees and their management team can work together to successfully navigate the challenging issues and manage executive compensation in a way that is right for the business, exhibits effective governance, and yields sound pay–performance relationships.

KEY ACCOUNTABILITIES OF THE COMPENSATION COMMITTEE

Traditionally, the compensation committee is responsible for oversight of the compensation and benefits programs for all senior executives and directors of a company. As such, they have overall authority to establish and interpret the terms of the company's executive salary and incentive plans, benefits and perquisites programs and policies, and other key terms of employment such as contracts. Within this broad scope, the three accountabilities shown in Table 30.1 are arguably the most critical to ensuring the integrity of the executive compensation program. These accountabilities center on establishing the pay philosophy as the foundation for the executive compensation program, periodically testing the program to make sure it is working as the philosophy intends, and identifying any

TABLE 30.1   Key Accountabilities of the Compensation Committee

Accountabilities	Issues to Probe
Establish a sound pay philosophy, which becomes the framework for the program and the basis for the CD&A disclosure.	Does the philosophy reflect the company's business characteristics and talent needs?
	Does it address the key principles of compensation?
	Does it help differentiate the business?
	How does it help attract and retain talent vs competition?
Build out or test the design to ensure the design is aligned with philosophy.	Does the design support the philosophy and business and talent needs?
	How is the program supporting the desired pay/performance relationship?
Identify any break downs in the design or execution.	Do the goals have an appropriate degree of stretch?
	Are the right measures being used?
	Have parts of the program become outdated?
	Does the program have the appropriate mix of fixed to variable pay, short-term to long-term pay, and mix of different long-term incentive vehicles?

issues that are causing the program to break down. These three actions create a common framework that the committee can use to monitor compensation. As questions arise about the program, the committee can return to this framework to test the program's relevance and ensure it continues to serve the interests of all stakeholders.

Working with an objective framework can reduce the awkwardness that often arises when emotions get ahead of facts. It keeps committees focused on the real issue: is the program right for the company, the shareholders and the executives, and does it deliver as designed?

Ensure the Executive Pay Philosophy Represents Business and Talent Needs

An executive pay philosophy should express a company's enduring beliefs about compensation and explain how rewards will align with and support the vision, mission, business strategy, and financial priorities of the company. The philosophy defines the criteria that the company will use to establish compensation programs, providing both a yardstick for retrospective evaluation and a framework to guide program administration and future program design. The philosophy allows the compensation committee and management to make decisions within a mutually agreed-upon framework, rather than face each pay decision as if for the first time.

The committee should ensure the pay philosophy is actionable rather than composed of lofty statements that provide inadequate direction. The philosophy should include the design principles important to that company (see Table 30.2), and it must link to the organization's business characteristics and talent needs.

A pay philosophy can sound all the right notes but ultimately ring hollow. Shareholders want more than promises in the proxy disclosure's CD&A. They want proof that the program design advances company strategy and drives performance.

Table 30.3 illustrates the characteristics that committees should consider in developing a pay philosophy or assessing whether the existing philosophy is sufficiently customized to the company. Too often, compensation programs mirror popular designs or incorporate competitor components that suit the competitor but not others. Such a program may not contribute to better performance; in fact, it could motivate behaviors that diminish results.

Each company must consider its own unique characteristics and determine what implications those business and talent requirements hold for program design. Compensation philosophies cannot remain static; they periodically need tweaking—and even perhaps an overhaul—to ensure the philosophy addresses the business and talent characteristics that are driving strategy and financial results. For example, changes in the market (e.g., customer preferences and competitor actions) may spur the need for a new company strategy, resulting in new business imperatives

TABLE 30.2   Illustrative Design Principles in an Executive Pay Philosophy

Principle	Definition
Pay prominence	The visibility and impact of pay relative to other programs that influence behavior. Prominence is influenced by pay variability, executives' influence over performance results, and the explicitness of communication about the pay–performance relationship.
Emphasis	The role of pay in influencing behavior, i.e., the primary goal of pay (e.g., attraction, motivation, or retention). Typically each component of the compensation program has its own focus.
Comparative framework	The companies used for pay and performance comparison. This involves establishing a peer group of industries or organizations to compare pay practices and performance.
Pay positioning	Targeting pay levels relative to companies in the comparative framework for different levels of performance (e.g., fiftieth percentile vs the fortieth or sixtieth percentile).
Pay mix	Addresses the proportion of fixed and variable compensation components, e.g., what percentage of pay will be delivered in salary vs incentives? What percentage will be based on annual vs long-term results? What is the optimal equity proportion?
Business unit differentiation	The extent to which designs and pay levels might vary based on differences in business unit characteristics.
External/internal balance	The relative influence placed on external market competitiveness in determining pay levels vs internal factors, such as the strategic importance of jobs to the company.
Performance measurement	The measures, standards, and time frames for evaluating performance. Some companies also define the process and criteria for CEO evaluation, and the desired nature and scope of communication.
Stock ownership	Expected guidelines for holding company stock.

and talent requirements. The strategy, the imperatives and the talent requirements should influence the components of the executive compensation program from base salary and incentives to benefits and perquisites.

Implications for Program Design

Business and talent characteristics can influence many aspects of program design. For example, a company's business stage can influence the degree of leverage that should be built into the program. The cyclicality or volatility of the business sector can suggest the need for potential indexing or other mechanisms to control for factors beyond the influence of executives. The company's emphasis on stock price

TABLE 30.3   Business and Talent Needs Influence Pay Philosophy

Key business imperatives	Current performance and prospects for future performance
	Strategy and anticipated shifts in strategy
	Business stage and growth
	Business unit autonomy
Market factors	Total return to shareholders (TRS) allocation strategy (share price appreciation vs dividend)
	Level of stock volatility
	Influence of macroeconomic factors
	Sector cyclicality
Organizational characteristics	Ability to develop financial goals
	Ability to develop peer groups
	Planning time horizon
	Role of equity and incentives generally in employee value proposition
	Employee impact on stock price
	Resource sharing and employee mobility
Talent needs and characteristics	Risk of turnover
	Diversification preferences
	Need to attract or retain talent
	Employee risk and reward profile
	Level of employee motivation
	Desire to change behaviors

appreciation and dividends helps to determine the focus for equity vehicles, i.e., stock price appreciation alone or the inclusion of dividends too. Talent requirements can dictate the type of vehicle as well as vesting considerations: If retention is critical, full-value shares that vest over an extended period may be the answer. Figure 30.1 illustrates how evaluating a company's business and talent characteristics can help a committee develop a perspective on how the characteristics might influence pay design.

Once crafted, the pay philosophy becomes the blueprint for designing the compensation program. Companies with different business and talent characteristics should be designing plans that align with their pay philosophy. For example, consider a mature average performing business that needed to change its strategy to compete in a changing market. The company's first step was to heighten pay prominence by increasing the degree of pay variability and building-in higher leverage. Compensation vehicles were redesigned to be more entrepreneurial.

FIGURE 30.1 Compensation design suggested by company characteristics

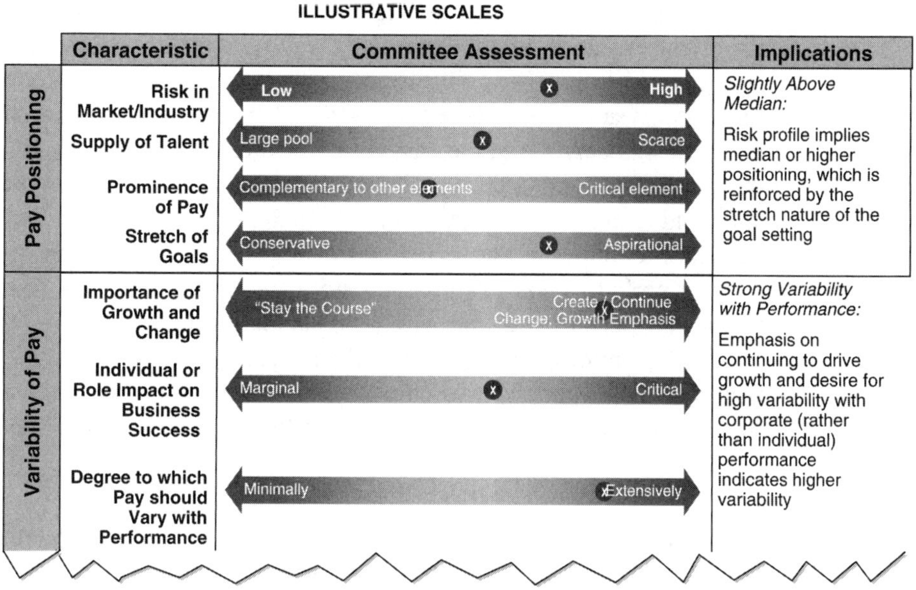

ILLUSTRATIVE SCALES

Next it introduced prescriptive metrics aligned with the new strategy. These focused on growth through differentiating its product offerings. The goal was to drive the specific executive behaviors associated with the desired strategic shift. The company also broadened its comparative framework to include both industry competitors in a similar stage of maturity as well as companies with comparable growth trajectories.

As another example, a company in turnaround required a high degree of behavioral change yet had to tightly retain the executive team, promote unity and improve customer responsiveness. The company modified its program to focus on earnings growth by establishing an approach whereby goals were "ramped up" over time. It also introduced nonfinancial metrics to hit hard on improved customer service. In addition, the company deemphasized the annual plan in favor of long-term equity vehicles with extended vesting because the turnaround would be a multiyear effort.

If business units are where the battle is won or lost, a company's pay philosophy must foster business unit success. The interrelationships among the businesses must be understood and considered in the program design. For example, a highly decentralized company that required strong coordination among its units emphasized business unit results in its annual plan. However, its long-term incentive incorporated both business unit and corporate measures in a 50/50 balance. It also used separate peer groups for each business unit.

Historical Evolution of the Program

To provide useful context, management can help the committee understand the historical evolution of the company's pay philosophy, program design, and pay levels. An historical pay audit, conducted by pay component and overall, can show the compensation committee how pay has changed over time, what factors influenced design changes in the past, and how the design must evolve further to meet current demands arising from changes in the business or the need to attract, motivate, and retain key executives. Figure 30.2 shows an analysis provided to a compensation committee that explained changes in compensation principles over a 10-year period. While pay mix and stock ownership practices held steady during the period, performance measures and standards changed.

With a philosophy in place and the program designed to fit the philosophy, the next level of inquiry focuses on pay–performance alignment. The aim is to ensure that the program is consistent with the philosophy and produces the desired results.

Test the Program

Testing the program requires both qualitative assessment and quantitative analysis. Qualitatively, committees should look for signs that the pay program is meeting its objectives. For example, if retention is an objective, committees might assess whether turnover has abated, or if executive behavior suggests a long-term focus and commitment. If bringing in new talent is paramount, has the program been an asset in attracting the caliber of executive the organization needs? Qualitative success of the program can be determined by interviews with key executives and through keen observation and evaluation of behavior and results. Quantitatively,

FIGURE 30.2   Evolution of compensation philosophy principles

Compensation Philosophy Principle	Plan Year										
	1994	1995	1996	1997	1998	1999	2000	2001	2002	2003	2004
Pay Mix	Incentives represent a significant portion (50% or more) of the total pay opportunity for top executives; actual mix fluctuates from year to year with performance; total pay opportunity cannot exceed utility industry median if incentive targets are not hit										
Performance Measures and Standards	Focus primarily on measurable results Balance of company, team, and individual performance measures Generally, goals set to require maintenance of or improvement over prior year's results										
	Base Salary: Individual performance rating based on role contributions (salary increase matrix anchored by competitive merit budget increase)										
	AIP: Both operational and financial measures						**AIP:** Increased emphasis on EBIT and EPS, to better align measures with the measures used in other competitive industries and further enhance the linkage between executive and shareholder interests				**AIP:** Cash flow for top 2 executives; return to operational measures for all others because their primary focus is excellent operation of the utility
	LTI: ROE relative to RRA companies through 1998; relative ROE and TRS starting in 1999, to enhance the linkage between executive and shareholder interests						**LTI:** Absolute TRS (stock options); relative TRS (2003 long-term cash incentive)				**LTI:** relative TRS vs. S&P
Ownership	LTI programs intended to build ownership over time and historically have done so										

programs must be analyzed both historically and prospectively to test for pay/ performance correlation, value sharing and peer alignment.

Is Executive Pay Well-Correlated with Company Performance and Shareholder Returns?   The aim is to evaluate the extent to which pay varies with performance under varying performance scenarios. Executive pay should show a high correlation[1] with company performance. This test is internally focused, examining whether pay and performance move together. If highly correlated, the more performance increases, the more pay increases (and vice versa). The correlation can be tested by comparing the relationship between changes in total cash compensation (TCC)[2] and company financial results such as earnings and cash flows over time. In addition, changes in both gains on long-term incentives (LTI) and total direct compensation (TDC)[3] over time can be compared with changes in total return to shareholders (TRS).

Are Executives Paid a Reasonable Percentage of Both Company and Shareholder Gains?   This tests whether there is a "fair sharing of the pie." Companies should share an appropriate amount of the value they create with senior executives. Value sharing can be evaluated from three perspectives: (1) the percentage of total value (i.e., earnings and shareholder return) created for shareholders that will be allocated to the top five executives; (2) changes to that percentage given time and circumstances; and (3) a comparison of the value sharing percentage across companies to confirm the sharing relationship is appropriate.

Value sharing does not focus on absolute pay levels, but rather on the split between executives and shareholders. The "right" sharing percentage for a given company should be calibrated according to a company's business circumstances, talent needs, and performance and rewards strategy. Figure 30.3 presents an illustrative (but not exhaustive) list of the types of factors that should influence value

FIGURE 30.3   Types of factors that could influence value sharing rates

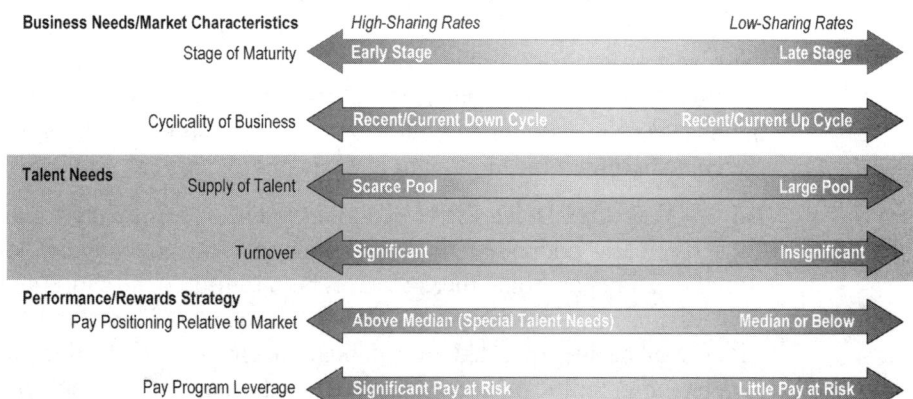

sharing rates. The framework can help committees determine whether their sharing rates might be expected to fall closer to the higher or lower end of the competitive range. Value sharing rates that are high compared to competitors can be caused by poor goal setting, a mix of total pay biased to salary rather than variable incentives, inappropriate leverage in incentive plans, the use of equity vehicles that vary less with performance, unjustified pay positioning vs market, or wrong performance measures in incentive plans (see Figure 30.3).

Are Pay and Performance Well Aligned Given Company and Peer Performance?   For example, when performance has been above median, has pay been above median as well? Relative pay and relative performance compared with a peer group should be aligned. This test helps to determine whether the relative positioning of pay levels for the CEO and other top five executives corresponds to the relative performance positioning when compared with the company's peer group. Alignment means that pay at the median should be backed up by company performance at the median, and pay at the 75th percentile would require performance at the 75th percentile. Historical tests on actual cumulative pay and performance can identify the degree of alignment in the pay programs compared to peers. Total compensation should reflect "actual" cumulative compensation earned during the period, using paper gains for equity vehicles, in order to best assess pay actually delivered for performance.

The three tests help committees assess whether the program is on track with the philosophy and the design intent. If pay and performance are out of alignment, or if the value sharing percentage is not calibrated with the philosophy, the committee must investigate further to ascertain the cause and consider solutions.

Are There Any Breakdowns in the Design or Execution?   If a program shows signs of stress, it may be an indication of inappropriate vehicles, leverage, or pay mix. Additionally, a frequent cause of a breakdown is that the measures are not driving desired results or the goals simply are not tough enough.

Measures should focus on the drivers of TRS (total return to sharesholders, i.e., stock price appreciation plus dividends), represent high priorities for the company, and reflect appropriate targets. Goals must be balanced: they should link to the true drivers of performance and measure performance improvement. Pursuing the answers to the following questions can help committees pinpoint factors that are contributing to misalignment and causing the program to break down.

Do the Measures Drive TRS?   While the ultimate measure for all companies is TRS (typically addressed through long-term incentive plans), other financial, strategic, and operational measures can help reinforce the short- and intermediate-term results that contribute to TRS performance. These additional measures, which can be incorporated into annual incentives, create line of sight and aid understanding of the plan and the goals. Additionally, they also help foster the collaboration necessary at operational levels. In assessing measurement, committees should identify the economic drivers of TRS and the strategic and operational drivers that contribute to financial results. The objective is to identify the key measures that contribute to creating value for shareholders.

Do Measures Represent High Priorities? While many measures may drive TRS, not all of them are critical. The Committee must ensure that the program measures represent those that have the greatest impact on TRS. Sensitivity analyses (i.e., percentage change in economic value, profits, returns associated with a 1 percent change in the measure) plus the review of key analyst metrics and business strategies can provide intelligence on which drivers have the greatest potential to impact TRS. Careful consideration should also be given to determining which measures represent the highest priority areas for improving success with customers, and most importantly, represent an opportunity to improve vs competitors.

Are the Goals Appropriate? When it comes to goal setting, committees should make sure that goals consider and reconcile top-down and bottom-up perspectives. A top-down perspective reflects the company's obligations to shareholders—what a company *should do* to justify its continued independence and management's continued stewardship. A bottom-up view helps to identify what the company *can do* based on their current business model. Reconciliation of the top-down and bottom-up views to determine what the company *will do*. A balanced approach enables companies to establish sustainable goals that are both achievable yet have adequate stretch.

Are Thresholds and Maximums Realistic? Thresholds and maximums are influenced by the company's ability to plan, e.g., the sophistication of the planning processes, the degree to which results are affected by macroeconomic and other external factors, and the toughness of the goals themselves. Other considerations include the proportion of incremental value created for the company that is being shared, performance vs historical results, and peer performance. Ultimately, the plan should build in some leeway if goals are missed, but not so much that executives are rewarded for unsatisfactory results. In addition, it is important to provide adequate incentive so executives strive to beat their goals.

With the disclosure of performance goals in the CD&A, this aspect of compensation design takes on ever greater prominence. Measures that truly drive performance and goals that represent tough hurdles may go a long way in proving to shareholders that the program is delivering on their best interests.

CRITICAL STRUCTURES, PROCESSES, SKILLS, AND EDUCATION

The three committee accountabilities discussed above establish the framework for critical conversation about compensation and performance. Yet robust discussion of pay philosophy and program design can only occur when the committee has sufficient expertise about the issues to pose the right questions and engage in thoughtful analysis and decision making.

Management plays an important role in ensuring committees get off on the right foot. Expectations and accountabilities must be clear. An annual calendar of events will aid planning and decision making. Grounding in executive compensation and regular updates about trends and issues will prepare committee members for their duties.

Set Expectations

The new executive compensation climate can have an impact on the relationship between the committee and management. Previously amicable relationships can become frayed when committee members take on an issue that previously was management's domain, or when the committee feels management is holding back information. Therefore, it is critical to get the committee/management relationship right in order to create an environment that fosters conversation and transparency. From the outset, both parties need to agree on the decision making arena, i.e., what decisions must be made and how the decision making process will work.

A critical first step is to step back and have a candid conversation about expectations. This is a natural conversation to have when a new committee chair comes on board or after the committee's self-evaluation. The objective is to discuss how management and the compensation committee can best work together to achieve the committee's charter. The conversation should focus on questions such as those shown in Table 30.4.

When expectations are clear, management and the committee will have a basis for periodic discussions (at least once a year) of how the relationship is working. Management may choose to have individual conversations with directors first on these matters and then aggregate themes for full committee discussion. Alternatively, a third party might facilitate this process.

Clarify Accountabilities

These discussions can also lead to greater clarity around decision rights, an important outcome. Decision rights define accountability for specific actions and decisions related to compensation, benefits, and perquisites. They guarantee that the policies and practices are in place to ensure the development of management talent, effective corporate governance, and the establishment of competitive and effective management compensation. As shown in Figure 30.4, decision rights specify the governance item (director compensation, CEO compensation, etc.), the specific actions (e.g., initiate, develop, review, approve), and accountabilities of management, the compensation committee, the full board, and the compensation consultant. They also should specify how often the various reviews will take place.

One decision right that is gaining prominence focuses on choosing the compensation consultant and "owning" the consulting relationship. Often in the

TABLE 30.4   Setting Expectations About the Compensation Committee Charter

	Issues for Discussion
Committee charter	What elements of their charter do the compensation committee members consider most important?
	Is the charter still appropriate?
	Does it require modification?
	How well has the committee adhered to its charter? Specifically, what has it done well?
	Where does it need to improve?
	What are the reasons for any shortfalls?
Working relationship with management	How can management best help the committee fulfill its charter?
	To what extent has management been doing this already?
	What is working well?
	What areas could be improved?
	How can the committee help management deliver to the committee's expectations?
Briefings and skill building	Do the committee members feel they are getting the right information in a timely manner in order to fulfill their fiduciary obligations?
Decision making	How do the committee members want to be involved in the making of critical decisions?

past, the compensation consultant was hired by and reported to management. This clearly is no longer the case. An increasing number of compensation committees are hiring the consultant, typically with management assisting in the screening and credentialing. In some cases, a single consultant is hired to serve both management and the committee. In other cases, the committee and management have their own consultants, particularly when a second opinion is sought or when the company's compensation program has come under close scrutiny.

Committees working with a consultant should establish "rules of engagement," or protocols that the consultant will follow in providing independent executive compensation advice and counsel. The purpose is to establish common expectations regarding operating procedures and create an effective working relationship that is consistent with corporate governance standards. The protocols should stipulate the consultant's role and reporting relationship and the responsibility for selecting an advisor, including the authority to retain, terminate, and approve fees. Access to the committee and management should be clarified. For example, while the

FIGURE 30.4   Decisions rights matrix

ILLUSTRATIVE

Principal Duties and Responsibilities: Ensure policies and practices are in place to ensure development of management talent, effective corporate governance, and competitive management compensation.

Governance Item	Description	Decision Roles			Frequency
		Management	Compensation Committee	Corporate Board	
Director Compensation	The compensation, benefits, and perquisites provided to Directors (policy)	Initiate, Develop	Review, Recommend	Review, Approve	Annually
CEO Qualifications	The skills and experience required of CEO	Initiate, Develop	Review, Approve	Review, Approve	Annually (review) As Needed (recommend, approve qualifications)
CEO Compensation and Performance Evaluation	The compensation, benefits, and perquisites provided to the CEO; performance standards and evaluation process	Provide Input and Tools	Initiate, Develop, Recommend	Review, Approve	Annually
CEO Succession Planning	Succession process under various scenarios	Develop	Initiate, Review, Recommend	Review, Approve	Annually (review process) As Needed (develop process)
Officer Compensation	The compensation, benefits, and perquisites	As to compensation, etc.: Initiate, Develop As to	As to compensation, etc: Review, Recommend	Review, Approve	Annually

consultant may have been hired to act as an advisor to the committee, the work will require access to and collaboration with management. Therefore, it is helpful to identify which positions the consultant will have access to and the nature and purpose of the working relationships. The protocol should include periodic assessment of the consultant's effectiveness and specify that performance feedback will be provided.

Discussion of decision rights helps start the conversation about critical issues. It makes sure that all parties are comfortable with the governance items and understand the parameters for discussion and decision making.

Establish a Calendar

Structuring meetings appropriately, including executive sessions, will ensure that committee members' time is well used and that critical topics are covered. A routine annual process detailed in an annual committee calendar will clarify the expectations of each meeting (see Figure 30.5).

Companies often find it helpful to set aside one meeting to examine trends and their relationship to the company's business and talent needs. At the same time, it is helpful to assess how well the compensation program is meeting business needs given organizational changes or shifts in strategy. Management should supply the committee with full information about the impact of executive pay decisions and

FIGURE 30.5   Annual committee calendar

ILLUSTRATIVE

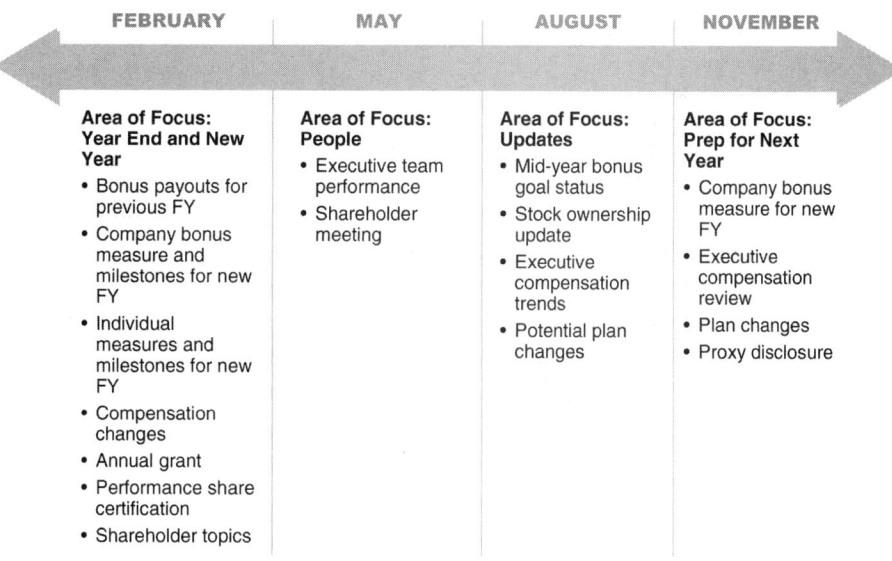

FEBRUARY	MAY	AUGUST	NOVEMBER
Area of Focus: Year End and New Year	**Area of Focus: People**	**Area of Focus: Updates**	**Area of Focus: Prep for Next Year**
• Bonus payouts for previous FY • Company bonus measure and milestones for new FY • Individual measures and milestones for new FY • Compensation changes • Annual grant • Performance share certification • Shareholder topics	• Executive team performance • Shareholder meeting	• Mid-year bonus goal status • Stock ownership update • Executive compensation trends • Potential plan changes	• Company bonus measure for new FY • Executive compensation review • Plan changes • Proxy disclosure

a periodic report card on how the program is working. The calendar in Figure 30.5 shows such a meeting scheduled for August. The timing of the meeting will hinge on the company's fiscal year. Such a meeting should occur at a time when the committee is not facing decisions about payouts, plan changes, or proxy disclosure.

The agenda for each meeting should outline the expected outcomes, and clarify what items are up for discussion and which require decisions. A clear chart or agenda can keep the meeting on track and allow members to focus on the intended outcome. It also is important to provide the right amount of information to members on a timely basis.

Depending on the topic, the right support, including the consultant, HR, and legal, should be available at the meeting to provide appropriate guidance and answer questions. At each meeting, and for longer sessions from time to time, it may be appropriate to schedule an executive session for committee members allowing them to "ask the consultant" without management present.

The committee chair's role in preparing for meetings requires clarification too. Several effective models exist. In some cases, the committee chair fully manages the process, taking accountability for much of the prework and even making some decisions. Other committee chairs take a less active role; they may be briefed in advance about issues, but they defer discussion and decisions to the whole committee. The optimal model for a given company will be influenced by the composition of the committee and the expertise of the committee in working through the intricacies of executive compensation. The better informed and more knowledge-able the committee members are, the more confident they will feel to think through the issues, and, ultimately, the stronger the compensation program will be as a driver of company success.

Keep Current on Executive Pay Issues

The rapidly changing regulatory environment presents challenges for compensa-tion committees. Developing expertise on the rules and regulations—and the many attendant issues—requires a considerable time commitment. Even members who are former CEOs may not have the necessary familiarity with current regulations and the implications they hold for compensation design and reporting. Committee members are often in a position of learning about executive compensation while living with and assessing the current program. Consequently, it is helpful to have members who collectively have the following skills:

- A desire to keep current on trends and issues affecting executive compensation

- Ability to learn quickly and understand the implications of governance rules and regulations

- Strong financial acumen

- HR expertise—it can be helpful to include a former HR executive who has strong business background on the committee

Committee members need regular education and development opportunities. Companies can serve their committees by providing opportunities for education about related issues. Education may include Director's College and similar formal curricula about executive compensation. Annual offsites that cover trends and issues, as noted above, offer a good opportunity for committee members to get up to speed on related issues without the weight of decision making. The board sec-retary or HR should also circulate relevant articles and press briefings on related topics. They should also ensure that various advisors keep the committee informed of changes in the executive compensation environment and their implications for the company.

It is also helpful to brief the committee each year on where the company stands vis-à-vis the evaluation of relevant constituencies, such as ISS, unions, proxy advisors, major institutional shareholders, and regulators.

Scheduling one-on-ones between a committee member and HR and other appropriate members of management from legal and finance affords an opportu-nity for the committee member to ask questions and probe issues outside of the meeting and in a more relaxed atmosphere.

SUMMARY

Making decisions about executive pay can seem challenging and even daunting in the twenty-first century. Management and outside advisors play an important role in ensuring that all committee members are well equipped for their task. Yet committee members have an equal responsibility to build their own knowledge and prepare themselves for the decisions at hand. The best committees create a strong management/committee dynamic through several actions: first they ensure the pay program rests on a solid philosophical foundation. Next, they focus analyses and discussion on how well the rewards address the business situation and talent needs, and achieve the desired pay–performance alignment. They commit to taking corrective action when aspects of the program break down. Finally, they create good relations through ongoing communication, clear expectations, and unambiguous decision rights.

The complexities and challenges of executive compensation can be managed when committee members have the right information, the right skill sets, and operate in an atmosphere that fosters understanding and acceptance of accountability, thoughtful analysis, and vigorous discussion about what serves the interests of all stakeholders.

END NOTES

1. A correlation is a number between -1 and $+1$ that indicates the strength of a relationship between two variables. A $+1$ correlation indicates a perfect correlation (ideal for pay programs), and a -1 indicates a perfect inverse correlation.

2. Total cash compensation (TCC): base salary plus annual incentives.

3. Total direct compensation (TDC): base salary plus annual incentives plus gain on long-term incentives.

NEW DYNAMICS OF CEO PAY

David N. Swinford, President

Pearl Meyer & Partners

A N ONGOING SHIFT IN THE roles played by managements, boards and outside forces over the past five years has transformed the process by which executive compensation programs are developed. Management's longtime leadership in driving the design of pay plans has given way to much closer involvement and more stringent oversight by corporate Boards, who in turn are much more cognizant of the views of critical stakeholders, from activist shareholders and proxy advisory groups to government regulators and elected officials. On the judicial front, the longtime barrier to shareholder interference in the corporate management process has been steadily narrowed, leaving companies and their Boards at increased financial and reputation risk. As companies deal with the fallout from options backdating, spring-loading, accounting restatements, and other pay controversies, new SEC disclosure rules are providing a wider window into the workings of corporate pay programs by requiring that companies articulate both their structure and their underlying philosophy. Yet amidst these pressures to change many pay practices, companies also must accommodate the need to retain the best high-level talent as more baby boom executives head into retirement.

These developments have prompted compensation committees to reassess virtually every aspect of how they discharge their duties. They are holding up long-time pay practices for examination not only in terms of compliance with the letter and spirit of new technical rules, but also for how well they align with heightened good governance standards and drive meaningful longterm shareholder value. Among the major areas of concern are:

- Creating programs to more effectively nurture an internal pool of executive talent

- Ensuring a level of executive stock ownership that is meaningful, without encouraging premature retirement

- Ensuring pay levels are genuinely competitive, by more closely targeting the organization's actual labor market and considering peers' relative performance

- Better defining and calibrating multiple aspects of executive and organizational performance to ensure proportional rewards for direct and measurable results

- Addressing the need to have a clear, defensible rationale for how executive compensation programs are structured

ENSURING A TALENT-RICH ORGANIZATION

As the pool of premium executive talent shrinks, companies are recognizing the need to groom future leadership through programs that attract and retain senior managers with the abilities, integrity, and drive to advance strategic priorities. Numerous boards in recent years have been forced by investor pressure to quickly replace corporate leaders on performance or ethics grounds and have had to provide premium pay and special deals to lure outside talent into the organization. These highly publicized crises drove it home that succession planning is a vital board-level function, requiring that directors put into place a formal planned succession processes to enable a smooth transition of leadership under any termination scenario.

One way in which companies are encouraging retention is by treating equity-based compensation as part of a broader-based strategic policy, rather than on an individual basis. Historically, organizations have tended to offer relatively liberal terms to encourage executives to retire once they have accumulated a sufficient level of wealth, in order to clear the decks for new leadership. However, the unprecedented rise in value during the long bull market enabled some of the very best leaders to retire after relatively few years at the top—well before the succeeding generation was ready. To address the issue, many organizations now are adding restrictions to previously provided retirement incentives; providing senior executives with meaningful restricted stock grants that have multiyear vesting without early retirement accelerators; and offering "career grants" to promising executives in middle management. Stock ownership requirements also are increasingly viewed as a retention device: an executive who receives a disappointing bonus one year, but who holds a significant equity nest egg, is less likely to walk because she still has a long-term investment in the company.

A related dynamic is a growing move to subject top leadership to the same formal evaluation process as other employees. Along with assessing specific financial goals, reviews are more likely to cover "soft" areas of executive performance, such as employee and industry relations, ethics, or customer satisfaction, that impact internal morale and the organization's image. Such a frank performance review not only reinforces the board's preeminent oversight of all managers, including the chief executive, but sends a strong message to employees and shareholders that everyone in the organization will be held to account. It may also inspire CEOs to institute a more rigorous performance review process for their own direct reports.

Compensation planning is also being influenced by recognition of the critical need for organizations to maintain a leadership perspective beyond the current CEO's tenure. Faced with investor pressure to quickly replace corporate leaders who are underperforming or face ethics questions, boards are recognizing that their ability to protect and maximize longterm value for shareholders and to control compensation costs is jeopardized by the necessity to engage in time-pressured negotiations with outside candidates. Toward that end, more organizations are instituting a longterm succession planning process that is based on recruiting, identifying, nurturing, and promoting future leadership from *within* the organization. Many consider General Electric a model of how to identify the organization's key longterm goals and the type of management skills that will be needed to achieve them, and providing promising managers with the coaching, regular feedback and regular opportunities to hone those skills.

At most organizations oversight of talent development has fallen to the compensation committee as a way to make certain the issue receives focused attention, just as nominating committees have assumed new governance-related responsibilities to which the full board cannot devote the needed time and effort. Equally important, having the compensation committee responsible for both functions helps ensure that long-range talent development issues are integrated into—and ultimately enhance—its decisions on compensation issues.

DEALING WITH THE CHANGING LABOR MARKET

One of the most common but controversial tools in executive compensation design is the use of data from a selected group of corporate peers as a yardstick for setting pay levels. In line with the old model of board oversight, directors historically reviewed and approved the general process, but were not involved in the nitty gritty of how or why particular companies were chosen. Critics have long charged that sufficient rigor has not been applied to identifying precisely who the organization really is competing against in the labor market and that the companies chosen often were those with relatively high levels of pay.

In terms of public disclosure, new proxy reporting rules do not specifically require the naming of peer companies or why they were chosen. However, an overall SEC mandate that companies disclose any information "material to the decision-making process" is likely to be interpreted to cover at least some details about the benchmarking process. For that reason, as well as boards' interest in helping shareholders better understand their decisions, members increasingly are scrutinizing the validity and applicability of the peer data being used. As with many other areas of increased board involvement, human resource professionals and the compensation consultant will need to walk members through the analysis and help them understand common issues of concern.

Among the practices directors increasingly are asking about are:

- The inclusion in the peer group of companies in seemingly different businesses or that have revenues from one-half to up to twice the size of the company being compared. The company should specify what, under normal conditions, would be an acceptable range of variation.

- The impact of adding or deleting specific companies from the group, which can point to the sensitivity of conclusions to the specific data points used.

- Whether to consider average pay levels, which are easily skewed by high-paying outliers, or the median, which tends to better reflect typical marketplace practice.

- The pegging of executive pay levels to the 75th percentile of peer pay—often referred to as the Lake Wobegon effect. Directors are increasingly providing pushback to human resource professionals, for whom above-average page is a major recruiting point.

- The failure to factor in what *results* were achieved by peer companies for the payouts they provided. Even if not factored into the final payouts, it provides a context for evaluating the company's own results relative to its competitors.

GETTING MORE PERFORMANCE FROM EXECUTIVE PAY PROGRAMS

Directors increasingly are addressing the need to eliminate overlap and inefficiency among multiple performance incentives by taking a more integrated approach to their decision making. That means not making decisions about individual plan components on an ad hoc basis, but rather in the context of a systematic program review that shows how it fits into and promotes the company's strategic goals.

Companies also are continuing to move more equity value into full-value shares, in line with governance concerns that the overuse of stock options in recent years tended to excessively focus executives on short-term price movement. While most equity awards continue to incorporate traditional time-based vesting, there is growing pressure on companies to find ways to incorporate performance considerations into grants. Performance-based designs have become more attractive since the Financial Accounting Standards Board's decision to impose a charge to earnings for stock options and eliminate "variable" accounting for most equity grants. One common approach is to vest equity awards based on the clearing of certain relative performance hurdles, such as total shareholder returns compared to a peer group.

Boards are also becoming more sensitive to payout issues relative to the particular organization or individual, such as historic company pay trends or the executive's own expectations. For example, payouts in a record year should be reasonably consistent with how outstanding performance was recognized in the past. If performance criteria are not clearly defined, meeting an executive's payout expectations can be just as important as whether they are consistent with the peer data. A small but growing trend is boards' willingness to modify discretionary awards on the downside, and not just the upside, depending on the extent to which results were a function of strategic decisions, operating excellence, or unrelated market conditions. On the one hand, an executive who met performance targets *despite* unexpected obstacles such as a natural disaster might deserve extra recognition. Boards also are less willing to pay out for *missed* targets on the basis of unfavorable external circumstances, on the grounds that executives should share at least some of the same risks as shareholders. Conversely, boards may decide to withhold a windfall incentive payout for superior corporate performance because it was largely unrelated to management, such as record sales volume achieved at a lumber company in the aftermath of a major hurricane. The quality of performance is important, too: boards might not choose to grant the full level of rewards if management met performance targets only by deferring needed maintenance or taking other short-term actions not necessarily in the organization's long-term best interests.

COMMUNICATING PAY PROGRAMS

New SEC rules for the disclosure of executive compensation took effect for the majority of companies in the 2007 proxy season and already have had a noticeable impact on plan design, as companies focus on good optics as well as good governance. It will take some time before companies become fluent in the art of clearly communicating why the company has established its incentive programs, what they are designed to reward, how they are supposed to pay out and how they actually pay out. But companies already have begun to address the need to modify some of the most highly controversial aspects of pay programs.

- *Executive and director perquisites*—among the immediate fallout from the new disclosure rules was the elimination by many companies, of longtime perquisites such as transportation, country club memberships, and private jets, all of which were viewed as excessive and unnecessary by employees and shareholders. In most cases, the value of such benefits was moved into increased salary or performance-based pay opportunities.

- *Special CEO arrangements*—because companies traditionally have avoided creating unique pay packages for individuals, most perquisites to the chief executive eventually have been migrated in some form down the corporate ladder to direct reports. The exception was special benefits such as separate SERPs or corporate apartments provided to a new CEO hired from outside the organization. As with other items that now must be disclosed to shareholders, companies are seeking to avoid special benefits and are pushing new hires instead to accept additional equity or performance-based compensation.

- *Performance-based retirement benefits*—a small but worthwhile trend that can strengthen the link between executive rewards and shareholder value is the replacement of defined benefit SERPs with contributions to such deferred compensation plans that are predicated on achievement of specific performance results.

- *Gross-up provisions*—long a common feature of change-in-control arrangements, the payment of 280G golden parachute taxes by the company is being eliminated or limited at some organizations on the grounds that it is excessive and financially inefficient for the organization.

Companies also are recognizing how critical it is to have a clear understanding of the "Big Picture": the accrued value of all elements of highly complex, multiyear executive compensation programs, particularly components such as deferred compensation, pensions, and equity holdings. When compensation is reviewed on a piecemeal basis, a given pay component in a given year might sound reasonable, but such an analysis ignores the *cumulative* value being provided to the executive and the impact of different termination scenarios. Today, tally sheets have become a standard board tool for explicating the accrued value of compensation programs over the long term, making it less likely that members will be caught off guard by unexpected compensation windfalls.

THE NEED FOR BETTER PROCESS

Many public companies had to struggle to pull together their public filings in 2007, because they lacked access to the greatly expanded documentation required under the new disclosure rules. The problems ranged from incomplete minutes and memories of compensation committee meetings to finding supporting data scattered around the company to the lack of an existing compensation philosophy. A major task has been instituting formal board processes for collecting, presenting, and discussing data and for closely documenting decision making and oversight. As was made clear by the Disney ruling, Boards must be able to provide evidence that their decisions were not arbitrary. Detailed documentation of meetings—which should include minutes of any differences of opinion among members—can serve as good evidence of thoughtful decision making. Other process-related improvements include the creation of formalized annual calendars; clearly designating responsibility for collecting required data among internal finance, human resource and legal staff; better communication among board members; and providing supporting materials to members well in advance of meetings. The latter point is especially important, since directors are hamstrung in their oversight of executive compensation if they lack easy and ongoing access to background materials such as pay data and plan documents.

Compensation programs also are being affected by a reconsideration of how boards can make the best and highest use of outside experts. As part of the move to disengage from a "business as usual" approach to decision-making, more directors are insisting that compensation consultants bring to the table not just data and information on viable alternatives, but a thoughtful point of view and a willingness to try to persuade members of their recommendations. For example, while boards often look to "best practices" in making decisions about pay programs, they expect that the consultant will also ensure that members consider whether typical practices are germane to their company's situation or if a less standardized approach might be appropriate. Additionally, they are looking to their outside advisors to provide for a fresh and critical governance perspective on the quality and effectiveness of accepted Committee practices and processes.

Other approaches to better governance include:

- Conducting an annual proxy post-mortem to ensure that directors follow up on addressing difficult disclosures and questionable decisions

- Establishing new processes to regularly update the value of change-in-control agreements based on updated assumptions

- Developing better strategies for communicating negative aspects of compensation programs that cannot be changed and are likely to create controversy

- Insuring a clear and consistent message and a spokesperson to respond to compensation-related inquiries from the media, shareholders, employees, or executives

- Using technology to streamline and facilitate executive compensation governance

SUMMARY

There will be continued controversy and criticism in regard to the design and level of executive compensation programs. Boards increasingly will need to employ the closer scrutiny and wider perspective needed to make defensible decisions that drive real long-term value creation for investors. But ultimately, better data, best process and adherence to accepted practices will need to be supplemented with the application of reasoned judgment.

32

BOARD COMPENSATION

Pearl Meyer, Senior Managing Director, and
Nora McCord, Consultant

Steven Hall & Partners

DIRECTORS TODAY OPERATE IN A landscape dramatically different than the one they occupied 10 years ago. Far more time and effort are demanded, greater expertise needed, and the risks are higher. The pool of qualified candidates is diminishing, as candidates are unwilling to risk reputations and assume personal liability for board decisions. Additionally, increased time demands have led many organizations to place limitations on the number of directorships that their executives can undertake. Directors also function in the full glare of daylight, subject to far greater oversight by regulators, legislators, and voting advisory services, as well as more active investors, special-interest groups, and a critical media, all of whom scrutinize board decisions. This redefinition of the director role has resulted in a fundamental redesign of director pay.

ROLE OF THE DIRECTOR

In the earliest days of corporate America, directors were founders and investors in the companies on whose boards they served. With the shift to the representative director, a certain gentility, "clubbiness," and prestige, along with nominal payment in gold coin, accompanied "rubber stamp" board service. But today, serving as an independent director means standing in the line of fire—accountable to and under the tough scrutiny of not only the shareholders but also the media, general public, corporate governance activists, voting advisory services, legislators, regulators, unions, and powerful institutions. The responsibilities, risks, and performance expectations associated with independent directorship have risen exponentially in recent years.

This new, more perilous landscape has had a real impact on the way in which directors do their jobs. No longer just a rubber stamp, boards are now called upon not only to provide oversight of a wide range of corporate activities that have traditionally fallen under their purview, such as audit and executive compensation, but also to provide expertise as companies seek directors with skill-sets that are important for compliance purposes, as well as to the achievement of strategic corporate objectives. Coupled with the potential for personal liability for board decisions, this has resulted in a heavier workload; today directors receive large "books" of information a week in advance of the meeting, with the expectation that it will be reviewed and processed beforehand. This increased emphasis on active and strategic leadership on the part of directors has raised the profile of the board, with a degree of transparency largely absent until the past 10 years.

Additionally, currently proposed intervention, both legislative and regulatory, would indelibly alter the U.S. system of corporate governance. Proposals including (i) the right to call special meetings, (ii) shareholder proxy access, (iii) shareholder vote on change in control payouts, (iv) majority election of directors, and (v) an annual advisory shareholder vote on executive compensation all threaten to undermine board authority. This is representative of an ongoing shift in power from boards to special investor and interest groups with diverse agendas.

Prior to the mid-1980s, corporate governance activism—especially with regard to directors—was little more than a gleam in the eyes of a handful of forward-thinking pioneers. Today, influential activists from varied arenas proliferate. To understand how the corporate governance movement has gained momentum, it is helpful to trace the development of American capitalism and the concomitant growth curve of executive compensation.

CAPITALISM AND THE ROLE OF CORPORATE GOVERNANCE

American capitalism originated with small-business owners—bakers, blacksmiths, merchants—who worked hard and reaped the direct financial results of their labors. Equity was in their hands and their hands alone. But, as successful small operations grew into larger enterprises financed by external capital and staffed by multiple layers, the owner–manager disappeared. Chief executives were employees, and the clear correlation between performance and reward dissipated. Stock incentives were then utilized in an endeavor to restore this linkage by shifting into equity a portion of compensation formerly paid entirely in cash.

In the 1950s and 1960s, stock options designed to tie executive compensation to the fortunes of the company and its investors comprised a mere 10 percent of

CEO total pay. With the rise of the pay-for-performance movement, a major cash-to-equity shift was initiated at the senior executive level, causing corporations to move a growing portion of management as well as employee remuneration into company stock to motivate and reward the creation of shareholder value. In 2006, equity vehicles accounted for well over 50 percent of the present value of CEO total remuneration among the top 250 U.S. corporations, and stock options were accompanied by a whole panoply of other equity incentives and stock investment vehicles. With the added boost garnered from share ownership guidelines and holding requirements, the terms CEO and stockholder have again become virtually synonymous.

Once equity became firmly entrenched inside the corporation, governance activists turned their attention to outside directors. Thus began the initial stages of a similar movement to directly align director remuneration with long-term stock performance and, thereby, with shareholder interests. Director compensation has come full circle, with restoration of this all-important ownership stake at the board level.

CORPORATE GOVERNANCE AND THE DRIVE FOR EQUITY

Directors and their compensation—once seemingly beyond reproach—came under attack in the early 1990s from institutional shareholders and activists. It was not how much directors were being paid that was in question, but rather how they were being paid. Bolstered by studies touting the direct linkage between meaningful equity ownership on the part of managers and directors and higher total returns to shareholders, aggressive corporate governance initiatives propelled equity to a position of indisputable prominence in compensating the outside director for board service.

A broad range of constituencies converged upon board pay as a prime target for change. It is no small coincidence that public pension funds, led by the California Public Employees' Retirement System (CalPERS), which invest in broad-based equity index funds, have become powerful governance activists—pension fund assets in the United States have grown almost 10-fold since the mid-1970s to multi-billion-dollar levels. Large union pension funds such as the AFLCIO, AFSCME, and Teamsters also have their eyes on top-level pay practices. For these entities and other activists, pay levels and corporate governance issues are not merely a matter of economics, but also touch on broader agendas driven by the special interests of their membership.

Mutual funds are another important player in the space. With huge investments at stake, it has become increasingly difficult for these funds to unload large holdings if they are unhappy with a company's performance. The potential for negative impact on share price impedes such action. Instead, fund investors have been compelled to work within the system, striving through various means to improve a company's governance and, thereby, hopefully to favorably impact its performance. Mutual fund managers' stock picks are influenced not only by levels of CEO and director pay but also by the amount of pay that is stock-based. Although mutual funds are by far the most passive players in this arena, they are some of the largest. Furthermore, their passivity only adds to the power of proxy voting advisory services.

The rising prominence of voting advisory services is perhaps the most fundamental recent shift in the corporate governance arena. Empowered by a plethora of large institutional investors seeking independent guidance about how to vote shares in the best interest of their clients, advisory firms have stepped in to fill a void. These for-profit entities, armed with proprietary models, have defined new standards of good governance that are validated only by the willingness of large institutional investors to pay for their services. They have been particularly active and successful in regulating share usage levels through the recommendation of no votes on new plans and to identify and chastise disconnects between corporate performance and executive pay through their recommendation of withhold votes for directors on the compensation committee of the offending companies. While some large institutional investors have internal resources to determine how to vote the shares in their control, many as a matter of policy vote their shares in the manner recommended by the voting advisors. As a result, voting advisory services have become a force to be reckoned with.

Companies have responded by creating new executive positions responsible for corporate governance matters, and boards have established corporate governance committees. Varied organizations, such as TIAA-Cref, The Business Roundtable, General Motors, CalPERS, and the National Association of Corporate Directors (NACD) have all issued corporate governance guidelines for executives and directors.

Regarding director compensation, the proactive establishment by the NACD of a blue-ribbon commission to study board pay in December 1994 provided the catalyst needed to set change in motion. The commission's findings, and most importantly, its recommendations, resulted in sweeping alterations in how directors are paid today.

SHIFT IN COMPOSITION OF BOARD REMUNERATION

Board pay has shifted dramatically over the last several decades. As noted earlier, the critical junction was the 1994 recommendations of the NACD blue-ribbon commission, which began the transition from a predominantly cash-based payment system to one with a sizeable equity component and the demise of director pensions. According to an examination of board compensation among the 200 largest U.S. companies in 2006, pensions were extinct and equity compensation represented well over half (61 percent) of the total compensation received for both

FIGURE 32.1 Average total pay mix 2006

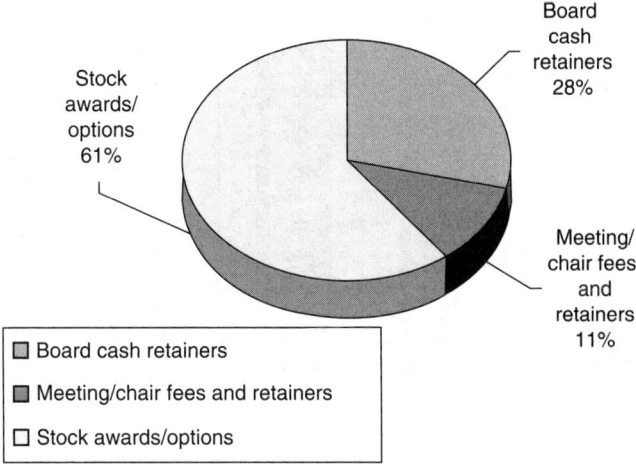

board and committee service. This focus on equity compensation addresses activist shareholder concerns by reinforcing the alignment between the interests of the directors and those of the shareholders, on whose behalf they are elected to serve (see Figure 32.1).

In addition to redesigning the composition of director pay, there has been a steady rise in its level. This increase reflects not only the increasing responsibilities and concomitant rise in workloads, but also the increasingly hostile microscope under which directors are exercising their judgment. For the first time in 2006, director compensation was solidly above $200,000 for directors at the 200 largest U.S. companies. Depending upon the role, director compensation among these companies now ranges between $214,000 and $233,000. However, as compensation approaches the glass ceiling of $250,000, growth in pay is slowing. While total remuneration rose 11 percent from 2004 to 2005, it increased only 5 percent from 2005 to 2006 (see Figure 32.2).

SHIFT FROM OPTIONS TO FULL VALUE SHARES

Whereas equity was previously delivered predominantly in options, director compensation programs have shifted to full value grants, either of restricted stock or the outright award of shares, therefore positioning the director as an owner rather than an optionee. In addition, several well-publicized scandals regarding option pricing abuse have heightened concern that options might focus directors on short-term stock price performance, rather than on strategic progress and long-term shareholder value creation (see Figure 32.3).

From a governance perspective, full-value grants are deemed the more appropriate vehicle for board remuneration. Unlike options, grants place directors in a

FIGURE 32.2   Average total remuneration by role—top 200 companies

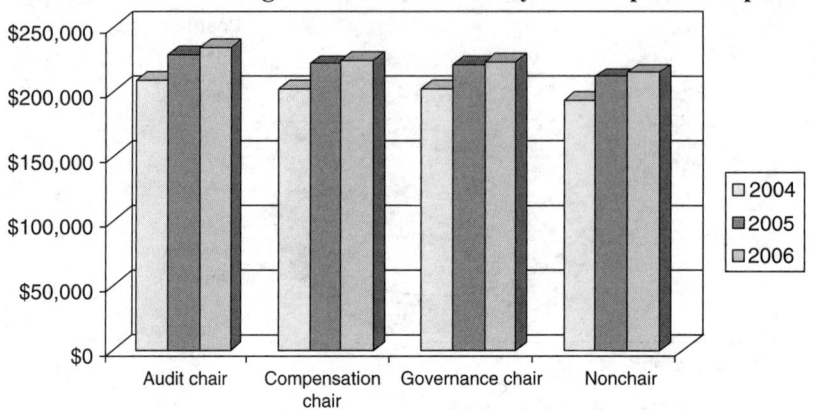

position of immediate ownership with both upside opportunity and downside risk, as well as full voting and dividend rights on a par with stockholders. In addition, stock awards are a boon to the increasing challenge of director recruitment by providing one-time-only, welcome-aboard grants to new board members, as well as ownership at entry, both of which encourage immediate motivation and commitment.

It should be noted that, despite concerns about options, significant option grants are the vehicle of choice—especially as recruitment tools among turn-arounds, pre-IPOs, spinoffs, startups, and high-growth companies. These are clearly identifiable situations in which maximum leverage is needed to attract and compensate desired board talent and in which cash may be in short supply.

FIGURE 32.3   Stock option vs full value awards—average value and prevalence for the top 200 companies

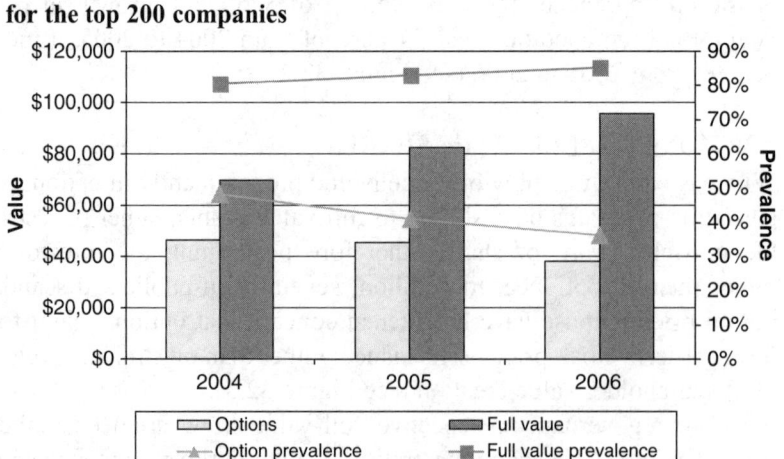

SHORTER VESTING TERMS

Governance concerns have also impacted the vesting terms associated with director equity awards. Whereas awards previously might have vested on the same four-year schedule as management, there is now a drive to shorten vesting terms to correspond more clearly with the elected term of service, or to remove restrictions altogether. Of the top 200 companies in 2006 disclosing equity vesting terms, only 45 percent of them utilized a vesting period greater than the director term. Of those companies with vesting periods greater than the director term, 78 percent had a one-year term. In an age where director independence and the need for responsible oversight are paramount, this trend addresses concern that a director might not leave a board when warranted due to the value of the unvested equity.

PERFORMANCE-BASED EQUITY COMPENSATION

It is also in the equity component of board pay that some have tried to insert a more explicit performance element. The use of more performance-based pay, such as performance contingent vesting, has been criticized for a variety of reasons. When a major consumer products company put in a new program in April 2006, commentary was largely negative, despite the support of renowned investor Warren Buffet. The program creates an all-or-nothing scenario for directors, with compensation totally dependent upon the achievement of predetermined performance goals over a three-year period. Few similar programs have been adopted, in part because of a belief that directors should remain above the short-term interests of the company.

If both the board and management are paid in the same manner and rewarded for the same behavior, the system of checks and balances inherent in an independent board is largely abrogated. Who, the argument runs, will mind the store for the long-term shareholders if both managers and directors are incentivized to achieve predefined, relatively short-term goals? The key to preserving director independence is recognition of the fundamental difference between the duties of a public corporation's board and its management—and the need to reflect those different roles in the design of their compensation. A program that subjects nonemployee directors to the same pay-for-performance standards and pressures as management threatens to undermine outside board members' capacity to act in a truly disinterested manner, especially in setting such standards.

OWNERSHIP GUIDELINES

While performance-based equity pay may be subject to some criticism, there is a widespread consensus that direct ownership of a meaningful number of shares is the most appropriate and effective approach to aligning the interests of shareholders with those of the board. To that end, ownership guidelines have become increasingly common. Stock-based compensation and the requirement to hold a significant number of shares applies the pay-for-performance concept to directors' remuneration by tying the long-term results of their corporate stewardship to the long-term value of their shareholdings and those of all stockholders. In 1998, only 20 percent of companies disclosed ownership guidelines; by 2006, that number had risen to 59 percent. Since such disclosure is voluntary, actual prevalence may be higher. Guidelines are typically disclosed as a multiple of retainer, and in 2006, 86 percent of companies reporting board ownership guidelines required directors to hold shares equal to at least three times their retainer; 52 percent required directors to hold more than three times their retainer. Directors typically have four years to achieve the holding requirement and the average value required is $312,000.

Another positive trend in the alignment of board pay with shareholder interests is offering directors a premium when they elect some form of stock payment in lieu of receiving some or all of the annual retainer in cash. Alternatively, some companies require their directors to receive a specific portion of all fees in stock.

RETREAT FROM BOARD MEETING FEES

Over the last several years, there has been a pronounced shift away from the payment of board meeting fees. While in the past, payment of meeting fees was nearly universal, prevalence in 2006 was 48 percent of the top 200 companies surveyed, down from 52 percent in 2005 and 56 percent in 2004. Interestingly, at companies that do not pay board meeting fees, total compensation received for board service was 12 percent higher, and cash and equity pay 26 percent higher. Examining the shrinking number of companies paying board meeting fees reveals that fees at these companies are actually on the rise, from an average of about $1,900 in 2005 to $2,400 in 2006 after a decline from 2004 to 2005 (see Figure 32.4).

While the movement has been towards the abandonment of meeting fees altogether, there is some evidence that this trend may be reversing. Removing this variable component of board pay can result in dramatic disconnects between the time demanded of directors and the compensation for that time, particularly in special situations like merger and acquisition activity, litigation threats, succession issues, or corporate transitions such as bankruptcy, going public, or going private.

With respect to such situations, boards may delegate responsibility to a special committee empowered to act on its behalf. These committees generally receive additional compensation, either in the form of a large retainer, meeting fees, or a special bonus when the situation is resolved.

COMMITTEE CHAIR COMPENSATION

The committee has become the workhorse of the board, with committee chairs assuming leadership roles with respect to specific areas of board responsibility. Chair fees have increased dramatically over the last several years. From 2004 to

FIGURE 32.4   **Board meeting—average value and prevalence for the top 200 companies**

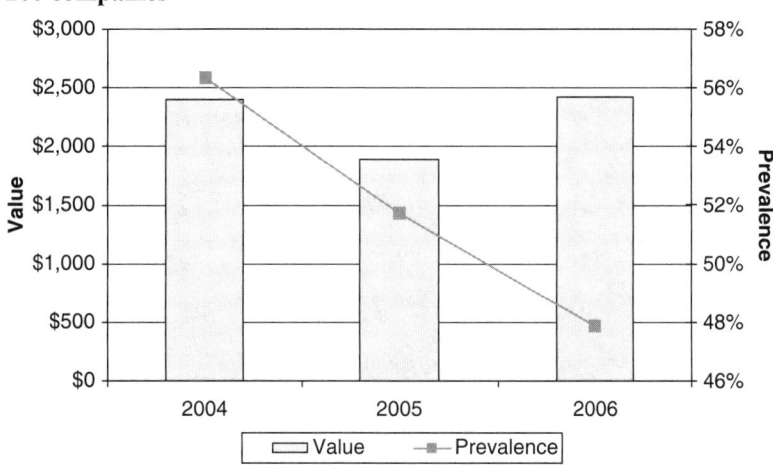

2006, Audit Committee Chair total fees increased by 10 percent while Compensation and Governance and Nominating Committee Chair fees crept steadily up towards Audit Committee levels, growing 6.5 and 5.7 percent respectively. Notably, 37 percent of companies surveyed paid Audit and Compensation committee chairs the same amount, a fact attributable to greater accountability and public scrutiny of executive pay, coupled with the advent of new SEC proxy disclosure rules which place even greater demands on director time.

BOARD DEMOGRAPHICS

Based on 2006 data, the typical board meets nine times annually and comprises 11 directors, nine of whom are independent. The typical director is elected for a one-year term and is retired at age 72 by the 63 percent of survey companies that report mandatory retirement.

THE FUTURE OF BOARD PAY

Going forward, directors will be challenged as never before to provide informed, disciplined, and thoughtful oversight of all facets of the corporation, in addition to guiding its future strategic direction. Directors will be required to master details of the business and engage with management and stakeholders to fulfill their fiduciary duties. All of this will be conducted in an increasingly hostile and transparent environment populated by critical media, politicians, activists, regulators, legislators, investors, and voting advisory services.

BOARD CRITICAL ISSUES IN EXECUTIVE PAY

Bruce R. Ellig, Author and Retired Corporate Vice President, HR[1]

Pfizer Inc.

COMPENSATION PROGRAMS ARE INTENDED TO attract, retain, and motivate executives. The design and administration of those programs for the CEO and other top executives in a company is the responsibility of the board of directors and more specifically its compensation committee. Although the board may be legally liable for inappropriate actions, in accord with Section 162(m) of the Internal Revenue Code it is the compensation committee that must be responsible for final pay determinations of the proxy named executives if the company wishes to take tax deductions permitted, namely up to $1 million annually for each in addition to pay which is performance based. This requirement was introduced with the 1993 Revenue Reconciliation Act, also called the Omnibus Budget Reconciliation Act (OBRA).

Although it is the board's responsibility to hire (and if necessary fire) the chief executive, in addition to approving and monitoring progress on the strategic direction and tactical objections, it is the compensation committee's responsibility to ensure the CEO and other top executives are paid in relation to accomplishing the stated objectives. This responsibility has never weighed heavier on this committee as many critics believe that executive pay for many far exceeds their accomplishments.

The following material will address these issues:

- Excessive executive pay

- Interaction of the board of director and the compensation committee

- Importance of transparency with shareholders and the media

- Composition of the compensation committee

- Compensation committee use of consultants

- Pay-for-performance versus pay-for-position versus pay-for-failure

- Competitive data versus internal equity

- Importance of stock ownership for top executives

- Major issues facing the compensation committee

- Involvement of government in executive pay

EXCESSIVE EXECUTIVE PAY

Generally speaking, this is more of an issue than say five years ago because executive pay then was essentially growing at the same rate as stock prices. But when stock prices took a dive for most companies in 2002, stock holders were alarmed to see that executive pay, especially CEO pay, was not also falling. However, there was a very good reason why it was not declining. Executives were exercising options granted years earlier at far lower prices.

Although the stock market has recovered since the 2002 doldrums, many still believe that executives are overpaid. A recent study by the NACD of board directors revealed that about two-thirds believed CEOs were overpaid (although probably not at their company). And *Directors & Boards* discovered that about the same percentage of their readers believed that executive pay was the hottest topic for the boards—almost twice that of the next concern (board composition and recruitment).

For some, pay packages that look like a telephone number with an area code (i.e. 10 digits) is excessive. But this absolute measurement is not the most appropriate criteria. Pay relative to performance is the best test. High pay can be justified with outstanding performance. And poor performance should dictate low (if any) pay.

Clearly, many shareholders believe that executive pay is inconsistent with company performance, as measured by the price of company stock. Spurned on by shareholder advisory groups, such as Institutional Shareholder Services, they are clamoring for the right to express their concern in a proxy vote, at least in an advisory manner, although a binding vote would be preferable. Congress has moved to adopt such a requirement, but it is unlikely to be approved by a Republican President. Advisory voting by shareholders is not an unknown in Europe where several countries have such a requirement.

Not surprisingly employees who are subjected to givebacks or even worse loss of job believe executives are not subjected to "share the gain, share the pain." Rather they have the philosophy of Gordon Gecko in the 1987 movie "Wall Street" that "greed is good" and executives should also gain from employee pain, receiving added bonuses and stock awards for such cutbacks. However, not all CEOs and top executives fall into this category. Some ensure that jobs of employees are protected and that any cutbacks in pay and benefits also affect executives.

Is the issue receding? Or will this continue to be a problem? The answer is a function of two questions. One, how much incentive is tied to the movement of the company stock price? And two, how will that stock price perform? Compensation committees that do not build in a high downside risk with huge stock awards or stock options that are tied to specific performance targets are likely to extend the issue years into the future.

If shareholders are not satisfied with the compensation committee, they may express their concern as voters to their elected officials. It is not totally impossible that Congress may mandate advisory voting on the CEO pay package, or even mandatory voting on matters such as the compensation committee report.

INTERACTION OF THE BOARD OF DIRECTORS AND THE COMPENSATION COMMITTEE

Best-in-class boards have put in place a governance checklist ensuring it is viewed as a good corporate citizen. This includes:

- Code of responsibility (rank order of stakeholders)
- Code of ethics (how business will be done)
- Code of conduct (how the two above codes will be discharged)

Additionally, it will have developed a pay philosophy identifying the basis and form of reward for meeting performance criteria. It will also have described the duties and responsibilities of the compensation committee (in addition to other committees). And it will have passed a resolution clearly defining the authority and responsibilities of the compensation committee. This would include:

- Suggested changes to the executive compensation pay philosophy, as well as specific plans consistent with the philosophy
- Identification of specific performance objectives and the form and level of pay for each
- Review of competitive pay packages for comparable organizations
- Approved pay packages of executives subject to Section 162(m) as well as proposed actions of others for board approval

- Review and recommendation of approval of appropriate contractual obligations with proxy-named executives and approval of others not subject to board approval

- Engagement of an independent executive compensation consultant that is not subject to CEO approval

This is only an abbreviated listing of both board and compensation committee responsibilities. Essentially, the board must determine what responsibilities it should and/or must retain and what it can delegate to the compensation committee. How it meets both the requirement of Section 162(m) and its own fiduciary responsibilities is the key.

Ever since 1993's introduction of Section 162(m) to the Internal Revenue Code, requiring the committee (not the board) to be fully responsible for the pay of the proxy-named executive officers complying with exceptions to the $1 million per person per year allowable company tax deduction, the committee has taken on added responsibility. This was further enhanced in the same year when the SEC required that a report by the committee be included in the proxy statement.

In 2007, the SEC required that the compensation committee report be replaced by a compensation discussion and analysis (CD&A) stating in plain English the reasons behind the numbers of executive pay. The compensation committee report could continue but would be a "furnished" not a "filed document." The CD&A is a filed document requiring certification by the CEO and CFO. Companies are still working through the process of providing an appropriate CD&A: they range from a few pages to a lengthy document. The committee is accountable for indicating whether the CD&A be included in the proxy and company 10K.

Changes in disclosure requirements are further compounded with possible additional legal requirements and limitations. Some are concerned that what Sarbanes–Oxley did for the auditing committee, a similar piece of legislation could do for the compensation committee and its interaction with the board. This might include requiring that at least one member of the committee be very knowledgeable of executive compensation, just as the audit committee must have at least one member who is financially knowledgeable. Furthermore, the committee may be required to not hire an executive compensation consultant from a firm that also does work for management for at least the same amount of dollars. Perception is as important as reality in this matter.

IMPORTANCE OF TRANSPARENCY WITH SHAREHOLDERS AND THE MEDIA

It was not uncommon until recently for many companies to only provide information when legally required and to obfuscate whenever possible, and then, especially in the proxy, make it virtually unintelligible or very difficult to find.

This opened the door for investigative reporters to dig for the data and when they found misrepresentation to expose it in their writings.

Best practice was to not only provide what was legally required, doing so in an easy-to-understand format, but to also provide additional information to clearly explain executive pay amounts and arrangements.

The SEC dramatically improved this disclosure process with the 2007 requirement for the CD&A report; a dramatic improvement over the previously required compensation committee report. The SEC has indicated that the "analysis" portion requires a clear rationale for the adopted pay policies, as well as the specific pay actions for each named executive. It is expected the report will give not only the formulas used but the extent to which discretion and independent judgment has been applied in the decision-making process. Performance goals and metrics are expected to be disclosed as part of this review, preferably in a tabular form. The reluctance of companies to reveal future performance goals, for competitive reasons, is logical, but that same logic cannot be used for concealing the performance and objectives of the prior year. Reluctance to reveal historical performance in relation to the pay objectives suggests that there are other considerations at work in setting executive pay—considerations the committee apparently would prefer not to reveal.

Five years ago most companies looked at each pay category (e.g., salary, annual, and long-term incentives) separately. Now with the revised summary compensation table, they must look at it all together and the impact of one on the amount reported for total pay. This has introduced the spreadsheet approach, often called tally sheets, once best practice and now commonplace.

Yet there is opportunity to do much more. For example, the required summary compensation table represents company costs, not executive income. Companies would take a giant step toward transparency with both shareholders and the media by including in the proxy a table with identical columns (and for the same named executive officers) to report income to the individuals for the same years. The biggest difference will most likely be in the stock option column. For any year, the company cost will reflect cost for that year of options granted. For the executive it will reflect income received from options exercised (typically granted a number of years earlier).

Best-in-class committees are using spreadsheets, also called tally sheets, for each proxy-named person, reporting the item of compensation on the x-axis and years (earned or paid) on the y-axis. It is expected that this worksheet will become commonplace and the SEC will require a total "walk away" number, the total amount the executive would receive upon leaving.

COMPOSITION OF THE COMPENSATION COMMITTEE

Beginning with the introduction of Section 162(m) in 1993 of the Internal Revenue Code, the committee is not only made up only of outside directors; it must exclude anyone receiving fees from the company, as well as officers of the company. Having a person who is also a member of the audit committee would make sense given the use of financial measures for most incentive plans. However, that may not be practical if both committees meet at the same time.

Just as the audit committee is required to have at least one person fully knowledgeable of finance, so too the compensation committee should have at least one person fully knowledgeable of executive pay programs.

The secretary to the committee is usually not a member of the committee and this provides an opportunity for the committee to use someone with compensation expertise, such as the head of human resources or the internal executive compensation head. But this places that person in a very tenuous position since the individual reports directly or indirectly to the chief executive officer and it takes a brave person (or an understanding CEO) to not put one's job in jeopardy.

It is common to have CEOs of other companies (who sit on the board) on the compensation committee. They are usually more knowledgeable in executive pay matters than nonbusiness directors, but interlocking relationships where CEOs sit on each other's compensation committee should be avoided. Even if everything is at arm's length, the perception is not good.

Due to needed expertise it is not a good idea to rotate compensation committee members off to other committees too soon (if at all). If rotated, it would be best to rotate members only one at a time to provide continuity.

It is important that boards ensure that the composition of the compensation committee is logical, impartial, and knowledgeable. Done right, composition of the compensation committee should minimize claims by shareholders and their advisory groups of inappropriate executive pay. Done poorly, significant negative reactions by shareholders and their advisors can be expected.

COMPENSATION COMMITTEE USE OF CONSULTANTS

Five years ago best practice was for the compensation committee to hire a compensation consultant, who was then asked to work with management but report to the committee. Today, this has become common practice. But an emerging practice is for management to also hire an executive compensation consultant, making him responsible for designing a new plan. In this scenario, the compensation committee consultant would be responsible for commenting on the appropriateness of the management plan. On the surface this sounds logical, but what happens if the two consultants do not agree? Is a third consultant called in to decide the matter? And who hires that consultant? And what role will the third consultant have? Arbitrator or mediator?

Perhaps the initiative for a second consultant is being lead by major consulting firms who provide audit, human resource administration, and other services to the company, and in the minds of many are unable to be completely independent in proposing pay actions for the very management that pays their bills. Having such an organization prepare a study (including the analysis of external pay data) and sending it to the compensation committee consultant impinges on the committee's independence responsibility. If the two-consultant approach makes sense to a company, the final say must belong with the committee consultant, if the company wishes to comply with the spirit of Section 162(m) of the Internal Revenue Code.

A more logical approach would be for the committee consultant [whose proposals would also be subject to board approval, but not in conflict with Section 162(m)], responsible for facilitating the implementation of the plan, including to other parts of the organization. Alternatively, a consultant hired by management could be asked to implement the plan, including extending it beyond the executive ranks.

Since independence from management influence is the rationale for the compensation consultant being hired by the committee, it makes sense that neither the consultant nor the firm the person represents does work elsewhere in the organization. This becomes a problem with major benefit consultant firms who provide pension and other assistance. But if this is the management consultant such as described earlier, this should not be an issue, assuming the committee consultant has no such apparent conflict of interest.

Best practice is to not only identify the consultant(s) in the proxy and to whom they report but also their fees for the year and the fees paid by the company for other services. It is not unlikely that the SEC (or even Congress) will provide further clarification on the matter in the future, including the extent services can be provided to management by an organization also providing executive compensation expertise to the compensation committee.

PAY-FOR-PERFORMANCE VERSUS PAY-FOR-POSITION VERSUS PAY-FOR-FAILURE

These are three major categories of pay that must be rationalized by the compensation committee, assigning dollar values to each.

Pay-for-performance is mainly driven by the short-term and long-term incentive plans. The former is typically an annual payment in cash based on company and, to some extent, individual performance. Company performance may be based on some definition of income (e.g., EBIT, EBITDA, or net), with net income probably the most common. Individual performance may be related to succession planning, shareholder relations or specific personal development requirements. The long-term incentive usually has a three to five year performance period if paid in cash or stock awards. Performance is typically only for company results and may be point-to-point, but more commonly is the compound average for the stated period. For stock options, a 10 year grant has been common, but with the required expensing of stock options some are going to shorter periods because of lower costs. This also permits a faster recovery period in a down market, if option prices exceed market value.

Pay-for-position has nothing to do with performance, other than being sufficient to retain employment. Payment (or the value of the item granted) is based on organizational position and is commonly called perks. These perquisites are benefits only certain executives receive. The most common are personal use of a car and the company plane. Favorable taxing and lack of visibility made these very attractive, but changes in tax rules and proxy reporting are rightfully shrinking these items. Best-in-class companies are increasing the pay-for-performance opportunity and taking away the nonperformance benefits.

Pay-for-position is bad enough but pales by comparison with *pay-for-failure*. These are the severance packages, typically detailed in the employment agreement. The time to challenge these is when the contract is submitted for approval not after the executive has been terminated—then it is too late. Employment contracts for those hired from outside the company may be necessary, but are they really needed for someone promoted from within the company? The latter probably has a significant amount of deferred pay in addition to a lower risk of failure because they are better known than an outside hire. Boards need to do a better job in tightening the eligibility requirements and lowering the amounts, especially where significant stock is held and/or significant deferred pay is owed to the terminated executive.

Best-in-class committees are using spreadsheets, also called tally sheets, for each proxy-named person, reporting the item of compensation on the x-axis and years (earned or paid) on the y-axis. It is expected that this worksheet will become commonplace, and that the SEC will inquire about the use of such a table in setting pay.

COMPETITIVE DATA VERSUS INTERNAL EQUITY

The easiest executive position to view is the pay for CEOs. Consultants use peer company CEO pay data to support increases in salary, incentives, and even perks for a company's CEO. This leads to a never-ending sequence of catch-ups as each company attempts to regain relative position. Because it is not as easy to get comparable data on the other named executives, typically their pay does not move as dramatically. The result is an increasing gap or spread between the CEO and the other officers.

Best practice is to identify CEO relative to performance vs the peer group. Performance at the 50th percentile should result in pay at the 50th percentile, not the 70th. The best way to do this is place the primary emphasis on indexing. For the annual incentive, pay should be based on indexing company performance of the desired objective (e.g., net income as percent of sales) vs pay of the peer groups, CEO pay. If in the 70th percentile, then annual pay should be in the 70th percentile. The same approach should be taken for the long-term incentive plan using performance shares or performance units. This not only ties pay to performance, but also removes the difficulty of developing specific payout targets always subject to management low-balling.

Three important questions need to be answered. What is going to be measured that will drive pay? How will it be measured, and what are the right metrics? And how much pay will be given at each performance rating?

In developing these short-term and long-term peer-based payout schedules it is important to reflect desirable internal rankings. Best practice, which is not SEC required, is to explain the pay differences among the proxy-named executive officers. Some may choose to state the relationship in percentages relative to the principal executive officer, with adjustments for competitive pay data.

Some also look to the "cost of management" approach by examining composite pay for the named officers as a percentage of revenue (or some other financial measure) versus the composite average for the peer group of companies. This can be done for all five named executive officers, as well as the four excluding the CEO. It is another measurement of internal equity. In the future it is likely that emphasis will be placed on a closer balance of external competitive data and internal comparisons.

IMPORTANCE OF STOCK OWNERSHIP FOR TOP EXECUTIVES

Basing a significant portion of an executive's pay on company stock performance is the link between executive and shareholder, but this is only true prior to the executive exercising a stock option and then retaining all or a major portion of the stock received. What incentives does the executive have if all the stock is sold? Unfortunately with its 1991 ruling changing the definition of acquisition date of stock from purchase date to date of grant, the SEC opened the door to same-day-purchase-and-sale of stock options (aka cashless exercises). Not required to even hold the stock for six months after exercising the option, the executive has no downside risk. The person simply waits until the price is right and does a cashless exercise, buying and selling the stock at virtually the same point in time.

Retaining a significant portion of stock acquired has become common practice. The definition of how much varies. A rather common formula is the "multiple of pay." For example, if the CEO's salary is $1 million (some include annual incentive in the definition) and the multiple is 10, then the person must own $10 million of company stock. If the price is $100 a share, this means owning 10,000 shares. The shortcoming of this approach is that some executives view this as a maximum stock ownership position, not simply a minimum, and see no reason to hold more stock. And as the price of the stock increases shares may be sold.

More and more companies are requiring a minimum holding period (e.g., one year) before stock can be sold. Persons may also be required to hold a stated number of shares of stock while an executive officer. These are rather conservative practices; best practice would be to require at least the proxy-named executive to retain the number of shares representing the net after acquisition costs (namely purchase price and taxes). Thus, if an option for 100,000 shares was exercised and the purchase price and taxes represented half of the gross proceeds, then 50,000 shares must be retained until no longer on the proxy.

It is not unlikely that shareholders may become more vocal on the stock ownership issue, voting against committee members that do not require significant ownership positions by the CEO and other named executive officers; and perhaps even introducing shareholder proposals stating stock ownership requirements.

MAJOR ISSUES FACING THE COMPENSATION COMMITTEE

The brighter the light being shone on executive pay, the brighter the light shone on the compensation committee. Shareholder advisory groups are singling out the most grievous committee actions or oversights and recommending withholding votes of these members as directors. But as long as plurality voting (not majority voting) is in place, it will result in no changes. However, best practice even for these companies is to require the resignation of any director who does not receive a majority of the votes cast.

Reducing, if not completely eliminating, the perks associated with pay-for-position is a major issue. Committees will be challenged to defend the continuance of any pay-for-position plans for proxy named executives.

A second major issue is ensuring that pay-for-failure (severance) plans are not inappropriately generous. This means careful examination of the employment contract where one exists (and company policy where it does not). Payments should be scaled back when termination is for reasons within the control of the individual. There are different degrees and conditions of "poor performance." Also, the amount of pension and stock owned should be a consideration. Does a CEO, a person with a lump sum value of $100 million in pension along with $250 million in stock owned, really need a severance payment? Perhaps, but it can be argued it should be far less than a CEO with a $1 million lump sum pension and $2.5 million in stock owned.

Third, the committee needs to regularly revisit the design of the incentive plans to insure they are measuring the right items and payments are appropriate relative to performance.

Fourth, the committee should ensure the CEO and other named executives are retaining an appropriate amount of company stock, thereby linking them to the shareholders.

Boards, although interested in ensuring that the pay of the proxy named executive officers is fair and defensible, need to think carefully about usurping the role of the compensation committee. As previously noted in this material, the interaction between the committee and the board, as well as the use of consultants, must be thoughtfully evaluated before acting.

INVOLVEMENT OF GOVERNMENT IN EXECUTIVE PAY

Philosophers have stated that those who do not learn from history are condemned to make the same mistakes. History has shown that, when voters believe a serious problem exists that is not being solved, the federal government will step in. The most recent business example is Sarbanes–Oxley.

Many shareholders (who are also voters) believe many executives are paid too much and they have no voice in changing it. This has led to proposed legislation (as of yet not enacted) to give shareholders more voice on the issue. Best practice has some companies already permitting an advisory vote on the appropriateness of executive pay. To the extent that the problem remains and business is not voluntarily allowing a shareholder vote, it may become a legislative requirement. A worse case scenario would be a binding vote, at least on CEO pay.

Additionally, it is possible that the SEC may make it easier for shareholders to gain access to the corporate proxy, allowing them to nominate their own candidates for the board.

It may be recalled that in 1993 Congress addressed the problem of excessive executive pay by including section 162(m) in the Internal Revenue Code. It limited company tax deductions to a $1 million per year for each of the proxy-named executive officers unless pay was performance-based. It did not take long for pay experts to figure out how to include virtually everything except perks and salary (so much for merit pay). Instead of curtailing CEO pay, the $1 million limit became a floor for non-performance-based pay and not a ceiling.

A more direct approach to the problem of executive pay is through taxation of the recipient not tax deductibility to the payer. How attractive is millions in pay if almost all goes to paying tax? During the 1960s we had maximum taxes ranging from 50 to 77 percent. In 1950 it was 91 percent and in 1944 it was 94 percent. It is not far from 94 to 100 percent (say at income over $100 million a year). High personal income tax rates are tied to whoever controls Congress and sits in the White House. Companies and executives should be forewarned. Confiscatory personal income taxes could return, if companies and executives do not restrain excessive executive pay.

SUMMARY

The good news is that excessive executive pay is probably not as major an issue now as it has been previously, but the bad news is that it still exists in enough companies to be viewed as a significant issue by a number of shareholders and their advisory institutions. Boards of directors and their compensation committee have a responsibility to address this issue before the legislative and regulatory branches of government intervene to further restrict executive pay. And executives have a responsibility in not accepting outlandish pay rather than suggesting they are forced to take excessive pay packages imposed on them by the compensation committee. Executives need to be vocal in articulating what they believe to be an inappropriate as well as an appropriate pay package for meeting stated objectives. Need not greed should be the prevailing logic.

END NOTE

1. Bruce R. Ellig is a noted compensation expert whose latest book is an updated and revised version of *Complete Guide to Executive Compensation.* New York: McGraw-Hill, 2007.

Performance and Compensation

PERFORMANCE MANAGEMENT BEST PRACTICES

Thomas B. Wilson, President, and Susan Malanowski, Principal

Wilson Group, Inc.

IN ORDER TO REMAIN COMPETITIVE, achieve strategic objectives and provide desired shareholder returns, companies employ strategies that convert concepts into reality. There is increasing evidence that demonstrates that the success of strategic plans is closely linked to the effectiveness with which people are managed. A research study of over 207 companies conducted by John Kotter and James Haskett at Harvard Business School found a very close correlation between the performance of companies and the practices that involve people in goal setting, focusing on results and rewarding performance.[1] This is fundamentally what the performance management process does. Kotter and Haskett referred to these practices as characteristics of the "performance-enhancing culture." There are many other studies that reach the same conclusion. However, in a major national study on the effectiveness of these practices by the Society for Human Resource Management and Personnel Dimensions International, the findings revealed that less than 40 percent of employees felt their performance management system provided clear goals, generated honest feedback, and helped them improve.[2] If performance management is so important, why do organizations and managers struggle with the process?

We will examine "best practices" not in terms of who does what, but examining why some practices work and others do not. If one merely imitates what another company does, with the hope that these "best practices" will bring a similar value, failure is likely. There are many reasons why a particular element of the performance management process is successful. And, while there are many situational conditions that lead to success for some and failure for others, employing well-established principles in the design and operation of one's performance management process will significantly increase the likelihood of success.

KEY ELEMENTS OF THE PERFORMANCE MANAGEMENT PROCESS

The process of performance management is well established. This is shown graphically in Figure 34.1. It contains the following four key stages:

- *Planning and goal setting*—this includes defining the individual's goals and desired performance, using both quantitative and qualitative factors, linked to the performance expectations of teams, departments, and the corporation. This may include a direct line-of-sight to the company's business goals or reflect the specific functions of a business unit or individual job within the organization.

- *Assessment and feedback*—this includes tracking results, discussing how well things are going, and addressing factors that are inhibiting or propelling success. A discussion of results (i.e., what was accomplished) also needs to include the process used (i.e., how they were accomplished). This may occur only at the end of a performance period, at one or two mid-year revues or as part of on-going communication. Finally, the outcomes of this examination

FIGURE 34.1   The performance management process

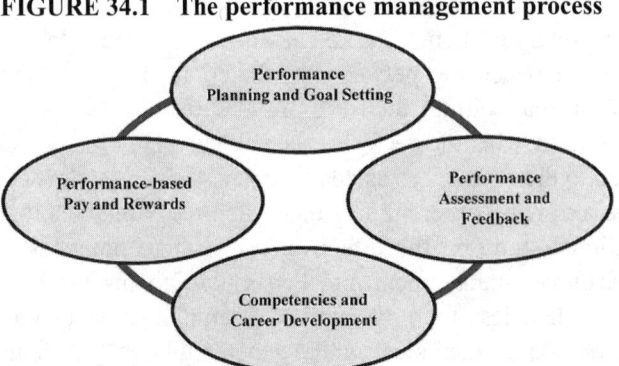

may lead to adjustment of one's priorities and actions, as well as setting the stage for planning goals for subsequent performance periods.

- *Competencies and career development*—included in this stage is examining the effectiveness of the individual's knowledge, skills, and abilities to perform their responsibilities in the organization. The process may focus on strengths and weaknesses in relation to performance and/or responsibilities as well as the degree to which one's unique abilities and competencies are being effectively utilized by the organization. This may also include specific plans for increasing the individual's capabilities, experiences and career advancement opportunities within the organization.

- *Pay and rewards*—the components of this stage include determining the level of rewards appropriate to the individual's performance and contributions. Rewards vary by organization and may consist of pay increases, bonus payouts, special awards, or other ways to directly recognize the degree to which the individual contributed to the company's (or business unit's) overall performance. Those who made little contribution or fell short of key performance goals, but not to the extent that continued employment is in question, will receive less than those who performed better.

These are the common stages of most performance management systems. The difference from one company to another lies in how these elements are performed. To understand the best practices we need to go deeper than just articulating overall elements of this process of management. We will therefore examine the underlying research on the key drivers of performance, and then outline guidelines needed to enhance the impact and effectiveness of the process.

UNDERSTANDING FUNDAMENTAL PRINCIPLES OF PERFORMANCE MANAGEMENT

Examining each stage of performance management process to determine what makes it successful, we find several common characteristics. When these stages are then integrated into a complete "system," then the process of performance management takes on an entirely different look and feel from traditional practices. These characteristics have been summarized into four fundamental principles that are aligned with the stages we identified earlier.

Goal Setting

Effective goal setting is interactive and provides meaningful clarity, connections and commitments.

Goals are useful for defining the purpose of work, providing clear expectations and communicating priorities and focus for actions. They can help the individual see how his work is important to the broader organization and its customers, which is often a critical element of effective motivation. In the context of best practices, goal setting is the process that translates the organization's strategies, key success factors, and priorities into actions that the individual can and should do. In many companies this is regarded as a "cascading" process, where one's goals are based on the performance necessary to achieve the goals of the next higher level organizational unit. This process creates the link between what the organization needs to be successful and how the individual can make an important, meaningful difference (also key to effective motivation).

Research on the setting of goals has provided some very useful concepts that can be applied to the performance management process. In a research study on goal setting, three groups were charged with improving their performance. One group was told to just improve; there was little additional direction. A second group was assigned specific performance goals, and directed to achieve these results. The third group participated in a formal goal setting process where they were given general parameters on performance, but they worked together to set their goals. The results were very clear. The group that participated in goal setting consistently set higher goals than the group where goals were assigned. Further, the participative goal-setting group achieved significantly higher performance. Both participative and assigned goal groups achieved higher performance than the group that was told to "do your best."[3]

Feedback

It works best when it is "real time," objective, provided while in progress and linked to goals and rewards.

In a traditional view, feedback consists of the manager's assessments of an employee's performance. These judgments are often based on subjective criteria, biased conclusions, and inadequate information. In addition, feedback is often given to an employee long after the performance period is over. It is like giving someone the score after the game has ended. It is always frustrating to receive feedback when one can no longer have an impact on the results. In contrast, many sports give individuals feedback about performance *before* they go into a game or event, so they can use this information to win.

To understand what makes feedback work, we turn to another important research study on feedback.[4] This research study examined 126 applications of feedback systems in organizations. The data clearly showed that feedback alone *does not* necessarily improve performance. Performance was consistent when feedback was associated with an effective goal-setting process. However, when feedback was associated with meaningful goals and positive consequences (e.g., pay, recognition, or special awards), performance improved to a much higher level than when feedback was given alone. This research also reveals that rewards will not necessarily drive individuals to higher performance until the feedback indicates that the prospect of receiving the reward is possible.

In the more current view of the performance management, the best kind of feedback is when there is actual data about current performance that is not filtered by the judgments of management, but instead provides information on the causes of the results and highlights factors that are within the individual's control. The data is combined with discussions that focus on the factors that helped and hindered the performance at both the team and individual level. Further, feedback that shows progress toward critical goals has more meaning than just data. A company's use of this real-time feedback is essential if it is ever to achieve better results. Therefore, people need to have objective and interim feedback if they are ever going to be able to win.

Learning

A learning environment where managers coach individuals will lead to performance improvements and individual growth.

A successful organization achieves higher performance in part because it uses its experiences to improve the process, create more innovation, and respond quicker to changes in the external environment. In short, one of the most important elements of effective performance management is the learning process it facilitates.

In a study by the Gallup organization of 101 companies on talent and how well people felt their talents were being used by their organization, only 20 percent indicated they strongly agreed. Research work conducted by Peter Senge and many others found that learning does not occur in an environment of fear and judgment. Rather, it is fostered when people are encouraged to try new things and to succeed or fail in a manner that respects the actions as well as the results. Some organizations have paralyzed themselves by a continuous focus on concrete results without mistakes. In these organizations, employees tend not to take risks or seek to create breakthroughs. In these environments, the negative consequences of "failure" are often more important than positive consequences of "excelling" in performance.[5]

Furthermore, there is exciting research that shows a strong fit between the work one does and capabilities one has of high performance.[6] This means that, when the unique talents of an individual are employed in the work they do, they are very productive; in contrast, little can be done to "motivate" an individual to high performance if what they are asked to do is outside their core competencies. In this context, the role of the manager shifts from being the judge of performance gaps to the coach that both understands and seeks to find the best fit between the requirements of the organization and the talents of the individuals who are part of his unit. The assessment of performance is focused on understanding how one's strengths can be best utilized to accomplish the goals of the organization, and how to minimize or reallocate work that requires one to perform tasks from their weaknesses. If there is a gap for the business unit, then the manager examines and adjusts the staffing to maximize the unit's performance by maximizing the utilization of the people's talents. Mapping talents to tasks leads to higher performance than trying to focus on weaknesses.

Rewards

Rewards work when they are meaningful and truly earned.

There is a common belief that if people are given clear goals and regular feedback, then that is enough to motivate the achievement of high levels of performance. As shown earlier, there is significant research that refutes this assumption. Instead, what works to achieve the best performance from individuals is to link meaningful rewards with the goals and feedback on performance, especially in areas that utilize core talents. If individuals expect that they will be rewarded, intrinsically (by one's own internal criteria) and/or extrinsically (appreciation shown by others), then they will associate positive personal benefits with the work that they do. This is simply called positive reinforcement.

Research on human behavior is very clear and overwhelming: When individuals associate a positive consequence with the goals and feedback and see the probability of achieving this consequence as high, they respond. They often take greater discretionary effort when the consequences are viewed as positive, desirable, and meaningful. However, an entitlement culture emerges when people lose the connection between their performance and the rewards they receive.[7]

In the context of best practices in performance management, we need to look beyond pay raises as the primary reward mechanism, especially since the increase amount is minimal for most organizations (between 3.0 and 5.0 percent of salary). Consider what people really value from their work environment: public recognition, private appreciation, greater job challenges, expanded responsibilities or control over resources, promotion, professional development, work schedule flexibility, bonus payouts, participation in equity programs, etc. If one earns these rewards when they achieve desired results and/or make desired contributions, then they will tend to find more meaning and value in their work. This leads to greater commitment, enjoyment, growth, and success.

INTEGRATING BEST PRACTICES INTO PERFORMANCE MANAGEMENT

If an organization wants to develop a model for performance management based on these best practices principles, it will need to assess the current policies, programs, and practices in light of the information presented above and then implement a design and development process to devise a new model that engages executives, line managers, and employees. While the scope of this chapter does not permit a full discussion of the tactics for achieving this change, the guidelines outlined below offer some assistance to this effort. These guidelines can serve as a decision-making framework for developing an enhanced approach to performance management.

The Purpose and Approach Should Reflect the Company's
Core Strategy and Values

It is common knowledge that executive leadership involvement is critical to the success of any management process. When the performance management process is seen as providing value, a return that far exceeds its requirements, it is more likely to be used effectively. Therefore, the basic design of performance management needs to be structured in ways that resonate with key executives as well as with managers and employees. The approach should resolve several key questions about how performance will be managed within the organization. To be specific, will the process address:

1. Individual or team performance?
2. Results (what) or behaviors and process (how)?
3. Job responsibilities or individual competencies?

In most cases, an organization wants to say "both," e.g., results and process. The challenge is then how to effectively integrate these factors into a process that is simple to understand and use. For example, let us examine the question of results versus process. Most managers want systems to focus on results, but most of the performance problems they face relate to behaviors individuals use to achieve certain objectives. The process needs to find the right balance on each. To understand this parameter, consider the following.

One should place a major emphasis on *results* when:

- The team members are fully competent to achieve the results
- There is a short time duration between the actions of team members and the results
- The results are a clear function of the team members' actions, with limited external influences

One should place a major emphasis on *behaviors* or actions when:

- People are implementing new processes or learning new skills
- There is a long delay between the individual's actions and the results

There are many factors that influence results that are out of the control of the individual.

The Criteria For Measuring Performance Should "Personalize"
the Firm's Strategy, Goals, and Business Priorities

Performance measures and goals are at the heart of every effective performance management process. Without clear and meaningful measures, the effective use of feedback, reinforcement or rewards cannot be provided. In the ideal model, measures provide direction and create opportunities to monitor progress and reinforce achievements. Further, they provide a line of sight between what an individual or team does and the competitive strategy of the business (e.g., revenue growth, customer satisfaction, costs, delivery performance, quality). In this context, the nature of the measures and how they are used need to be determined. Consider the following:

1. Will performance assessment be based on goal achievement or assessed against a set of performance criteria? Objective measures are those that reflect the number of units produced, the time it takes, and the resources (i.e., people, money and materials) used. Judgment or criteria-based measures are those in which someone outside of the team is assessing how well an outcome was achieved. These measures are used for project milestones, the acceptance of a product or service, and to determine whether certain procedures were followed.

2. Will goals be based on improvements from the previous period, in relation to an external reference or standard, or a strategic requirement of the company? This means determining the frame of reference for the goals and measuring performance are critical to creating meaningful, credible expectations.

3. How will people be involved in setting goals? The research shows that involvement leads to commitment, which leads to higher performance. But, in some work settings and jobs, the requirements are very clear and dictated by the commitments of the organization—to customers, to regulators, to shareholders. In other jobs, there is a great deal of flexibility about how work is performed, but the goals need to be met. The key question is how. The level of involvement by individuals should be based on the degree of flexibility permitted by the work—jobs with greater flexibility require people to be highly involved in setting goals and performance standards.

The Timing and Process of Providing Feedback Needs to be Real-Time, Meaningful and Multidimensional

Feedback is essential to providing business units and individuals with information to encourage them to continue or adjust their actions. Feedback means data that is communicated in a manner that is understandable and relevant to individuals and the actions they take. Consider the following issues in determining what and how this information is delivered:

1. Will the feedback be ongoing data (e.g., hourly, daily, or weekly reports on results), be based on critical incidents (e.g., when internal or customer-based problems occur, or milestones are achieved), or a summary of data from a variety of sources?

2. What will be the sources of feedback data? In traditional appraisals, the source is the manager's judgment. In best practices performance management, feedback comes from multiple sources. Many companies are exploring feedback from peers, as well as other staff and subordinates. This is often referred to as 360-degree feedback because the information is coming from all directions. When data comes from multiple sources, it provides rich information for determining achievements and the causes for meeting or missing the desired performance.

3. How will feedback information be provided? Feedback that is data-oriented and generated from reports is usually provided to the team directly and then discussed. This feedback may relate to the quality of products or services, on-time delivery performance, financial performance, or similar information. When the manager summarizes and synthesizes the data, and interprets its meaning or importance, the dialogue will be about what led to achievements or what barriers prevented the achievement of desired performance.

4. When will the feedback be provided? The timing involved in providing feedback should relate to the nature of the data, but the data must be provided as often and quickly as it is available. Obviously, the timing depends on what is being measured. The dynamics that enable timely, effective feedback include the particular level of data that can be shared, as well as the systems within the organization to collect, process, and distribute this information.

The key objective is that feedback must provide employees with information they can use and keep in focus as they do the work. Feedback needs to be linked directly to the goals of the unit and the company. In addition, feedback should create opportunities to reinforce progress, and to learn or pursue alternative actions. Finally, feedback can be the catalyst for important discussions and great fun if used creatively and constructively. This increases the connection between the feedback and reinforcement or positive consequences one receives from examining this information.

Identify Current Learnings and Opportunities for Developing the Person's Unique Abilities

Earlier in this chapter we discussed how the feedback creates opportunities for learning. Reviewing the performance is perhaps one of the most critical aspects of the performance management process. It is where all the feedback data are examined to create understanding, learning, and commitment to action. There are several dimensions to making the "learning" process effective.

1. What is the purpose of review meetings? In the ideal performance management model, the purpose is to analyze the data, learn from the experiences, identify ways to improve performance, and celebrate achievements.

This means they are not just done annually, but are integrated into the communication process of the unit and manager.

2. What should be discussed in review meetings? This depends on what data are available and what is important to the learning process and improving performance. In this new approach, the managers and teams should capture multiple sources of feedback and discuss their meanings and implications. The focus will be on understanding root causes, problem solving, and action planning. The manager's job is to help individuals understand the significance of the information and the strategies for improvement.

3. Should a review meeting include a discussion of ratings, rankings or summaries of performance? Traditional year-end review meetings often focus on a composite of performance. Some organizations use a number, others letters, and still others use words. This single rating is used to determine the merit pay increases. The next section will discuss how to make the pay decision, but at this time, one needs to determine how the performance can be summarized in a manner that supports effective decision making about rewards.

4. What documentation is needed and why? The documentation of review meetings is part of the normal process of summarizing key points, learnings, and commitments. Documentation can be an important reminder of agreements made by the manager and the employee. It should not become a legal document, but care must be taken to insure the information is appropriate if it is reviewed publicly or used for employment decisions.

Link Meaningful Rewards with Contributions and Achievements

Perhaps one of the most difficult, conflicting parts of the performance management process is determining whether and how performance should be linked with compensation. If they are linked, how can this be done so the noncompensation elements can be kept in balance? Let us examine the key decisions to determine the "right approach" to this linkage:

1. Should there be a direct link between performance and pay? If they are linked, the difficulty is that the focus of year-end review meetings is all about justifying the pay increase. If they are not linked, then managers and employees wonder how the performance evaluations relate to pay decisions. Another approach that is gaining interest is to link pay and performance, but separate them in time. In this case the performance reviews are summarized, and a manager makes a recommendation on a performance rating or pay increase (before telling the employee). These ratings or recommendations are then collected, analyzed for their cost impact and justification, and then modified or approved. Then, the manager has another, briefer meeting with

her employees to discuss the pay increase. This allows the organization to make pay increases where a limited amount of dollars can be allocated more effectively than a process where pay guidelines are known up front, and the performance ratings are used to control merit pay increase budget.

2. Should performance be the basis for determining pay increases? In pay systems that base increases on competencies or skills, seniority, cost of living, or the external market, pay is more related to factors other than job performance. In the new model, the manager makes a judgment on the pay increase using a full range of considerations, such as the person's performance, his or her improvement in performance, pay relationships with peers, market competitiveness, and the available budget. The amount is up to the manager, as long as she does not exceed a predetermined budget.

3. How can results-based performance and individual competencies and talent be integrated? Although there are many facets to this question, a simple approach is to tie the base pay increase to a combination of results (i.e., what was accomplished) and individual competencies employed (i.e., how they were accomplished). This technique utilizes a salary-increase matrix with two dimensions—results performance and individual contributions. One dimension summarizes the performance achievements (clear outcomes) of the individual or team. The second dimension summarizes the individual's contributions or use of one's talents. The intersection between these two dimensions provides the "target" pay increase. The actual pay increase may differ because of external factors like spending plans, level in the salary range, etc. Another alternative used by some companies is to use both team or unit and individual performance to determine one's bonus payouts, but use the merit pay to reflect the contributions one made to the group's results or the growth in competencies employed. Hence, these firms integrate the bonus and merit pay systems into their performance management process, but keep the type of measures used by each reward system distinct.

If this process is managed well, it can affect the organization's performance in very positive ways. The combination of factors determines the amount of pay increase that one would receive. This simple approach to adjusting pay increases the linkage between the person and the organization's performance, but uses a broader view of the factors that lead to superior organizational performance. Plus, using the full range of rewards that are meaningful to the particular individual provides a more robust and effective process to linking performance achievements and rewards.

SUMMARY

Albert Einstein once said that we cannot solve our problems with the same thinking we used to create them. Understanding the underlying principles of why things work is essential to building a process that works for the organization. These guidelines to performance management require leadership that goes beyond articulating a vision. This approach involves the active implementation of strategies, plans, and measures that provide a framework for people to receive feedback and be reinforced for their contributions. In short, this presents an action-oriented, "enhanced" model for managing people.

The focus of this effort is not on the outcome or evaluating or appraising performance. Instead, it is about the active management of the process and the ongoing learning opportunity. The process is not about motivation in some carrot and stick fashion, but it is about creating real circumstances where people are valued and rewarded for what they do. It changes the role of manager from judge to coach, the role of human resources from compliance officer to consultant, and the role of executives from goal setters to sponsors and leaders of competitive, purposeful strategies.

The new performance management process has been devised because organizations need the full commitment of their workforce. They need to create conditions that reinforce the workforce's contributions for those aspects of the firm that improve its ability to compete. The organization will thereby achieve or retain its leadership role in the marketplace, and people will feel truly valued for their contributions.

END NOTES

1. J. Kotter and J. Heskett, *Corporate Culture and Performance*. New York: Free Press, 1992.

2. "Performance Management Study," New York: Society for Human Research Management and Personnel Dimensions International, 2000.

3. E. Locke and G. Latham, *A Theory of Goal Setting and Task Performance*. Englewood Cliffs, NJ: Prentice Hall, 1990.

4. G. P. Latham and K. N. Wexley, *Increasing Productivity Through Performance Appraisal*. Reading, MA: Addison-Wesley, 1994.

5. P. Senge, *The Fifth Discipline: The Art and Practice of the Learning Organization*. New York: Doubleday/Currency, 1990.

6. M. Buckingham and D. Clifton, *Now, Discover Your Strengths*. New York, Free Press, 2001.

7. Wilson, T. B., *Innovative Reward Systems for the Changing Workplace*, 2nd edn. New York: McGraw-Hill, 2003.

35

GUIDELINES FOR EFFECTIVE EXECUTIVE PERFORMANCE APPRAISALS

James F. Reda, Managing Director

James F. Reda & Associates, LLC

EXECUTIVES SHOULD BE EVALUATED REGULARLY using a clearly defined process and measurable evaluation criteria. All of these factors should be determined based on each company's goals, objectives, size, compensation philosophy, culture and shared values, and business plan. The information presented in this chapter will assist in designing, implementing, and refining an executive performance appraisal process that will motivate leadership to optimize the organization's competitive advantages, manage talent, and improve economic performance.

As recently as 2003, executive performance appraisal was not a ubiquitous practice. While most companies have an executive performance appraisal process, more needs to be done to improve the process. The performance appraisal process provides an opportunity to capture the attention of every individual in a company, and point each individual toward the goals set for the organization as a whole. Executive talent is the most expensive and most important part of an organization. As such, this precious resource needs to be constantly evaluated, appraised, and encouraged to improve.

The goals, as set by the board and the executive team, are created, ultimately, to grow the company and in turn add value to shareholders. Collectively, the board of directors, the chief executive officers (CEOs) and the executive officers (EOs) are focused on adding shareholder value. Formal appraisals of executive performance are crucial to establishing and ensuring an appropriate balance of power between the board members, the CEO and the executive officers. By making a portion of executive compensation packages contingent upon the results of this evaluation, executives are held accountable for poor performance.[1]

When discussing executive performance evaluations a distinction should be made between the CEO, EOs [those executives with broad policy making authority that typically make up the executives listed as the top-five named executive officers (NEOs) in the company's proxy statement] and all other executives (collectively referred to as the "executives"). The process and oversight of each group of executives are different (see Figure 35.1).

Since CEO performance evaluations are now required as part of the listing requirements of the New York Stock Exchange (NYSE), more and more companies are evaluating the performance of executives. Though this requirement exists, the details of how the appraisal system is designed or implemented are still left unregulated. The NYSE solely requires that such an evaluation be created and that a system be in place for it. Boards are not required to disclose results of the evaluation nor does the evaluation have to be administered in written form.

FIGURE 35.1   Categories of executives

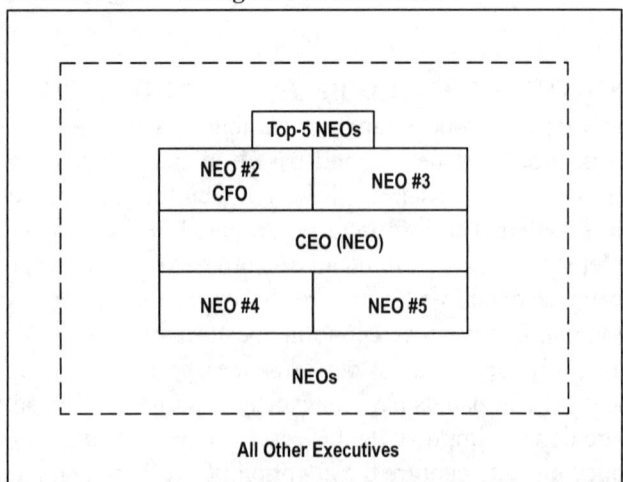

On the other hand, NASDAQ listing requirements remain silent about CEO evaluation. Most NASDAQ companies have CEO evaluations in place because they commonly refer to both exchanges' rules to discern appropriate governance practice. The U.S. Securities and Exchange Commission only requires that CEO compensation be clearly outlined and justified in the Compensation Committee's Report section of their annual proxy statement, and makes no mention of the appraisal process or its implementation.[2]

So, although executive performance appraisal is a cornerstone of good corporate governance and is widely implemented in larger companies, the information it produces is highly confidential and carefully guarded. At the present time, the results of such evaluations are not publicly available unless disclosure is required by subpoena or other imposed process.[3] Although many companies conduct CEO performance appraisals to comply with NYSE requirement, many more do not have a solid process in place to conduct the appraisals. Considering that the potential gains from a performance appraisal process are greatest for high-level executives, it is surprising that appraisals become less structured and regulated as one moves up in the organization.

If the performance appraisal process tends to unravel at the top level of the organization, can increases in compensation of executives continue to be justified? Many share the criticism that executive compensation is excessive. Those in favor of lucrative compensation argue that it is necessary to compete with other companies to attract the best talent and that the return that this talent provides to shareholders is more than enough to justify the compensation packages.[4] Given this debate and the threat of legislation to regulate top executive salaries, the need for organizations to design and implement an effective executive performance appraisal process is obvious.

BARRIERS TO EFFECTIVE GOAL SETTING AND APPRAISAL

A number of factors, from ambiguous goals to the discomfort of evaluating an executive or the executive being uncomfortable about the process, can inhibit the effectiveness of an appraisal. A partial list of inhibitors follows.

- *Discomfort*—some executives (the board in the case of the CEO or the CEO in the case of executive officers) find the executive evaluation process neither enjoyable nor comfortable. The majority of executives being appraised feel the same way.

- *Misunderstood purpose*—some executives misuse the evaluation to find fault rather than providing feedback for constructive purposes.

- *Ambiguity*—this is a major impetus to implementing an effective board evaluation process. Ambiguity can come from a "squishy" statement of the organization's strategic goals, the executive's job description and goals, how the process is designed, or the way that evaluation results are shared with the executive.

- *Low priority*—some managers have the impression that there will be a lack of time and energy to allow for an effective evaluation process.

- *Difficulty rating the executive on qualitative factors*—factors such as the executive's ability to develop the leadership pipeline and a continuously learning organization, should not be included because sometimes the board does not directly observe these activities, or they are difficult to objectively measure.

- *New source of criticism for the executive*—some companies fear the loss of an apparently good executive by the possibility of overly criticizing the executive.

However, when done properly, CEO and executive officer evaluations can create a sense of teamwork, mutual respect, and direct, clear lines of communication that are needed when moving forward with corporate and business goals.[5] An effective executive evaluation system comprises two main components: the actual process and the evaluation criteria.

EXECUTIVE PERFORMANCE EVALUATION PROCESS

As stated earlier, the executive evaluation process needs to be segregated into three parts: the CEO, executive officers, and all other executives. Typically, the board of directors evaluates the CEO and the CEO evaluates her direct reports, and so forth with all evaluations being summarized and reported upward. There is also a typical "two-up rule" that the executive's manager performs the evaluation with the manager's manager reviewing the evaluation (before the evaluation is completed).

On the subject of CEO performance evaluation, the entire board has the final say in most matters. Many other ranks participate in gathering and presenting data, chiefly the compensation committee. Other executives take almost no part in the evaluation process whereas outside advisors have some influence. Note that the corporate governance committee sometimes conducts the evaluation of the CEO, but for the purposes of illustration, we show the compensation committee (see Table 35.1).

We can see a distinct difference in who is evaluating whom clearly from the charts provided. Executive officer evaluation is handled chiefly by the CEO with the aid of the compensation committee and executive officers. The board also has some influence, but other executives have no say (see Table 35.2).

The evaluation of all other executives is quite different from the prior evaluations discussed. The board does not address the assessment of the other executives nor does the compensation committee get deeply involved. The evaluation is nearly entirely in the hands of the CEO with the assistance of the executive officers. In this category, self-evaluation seems prevalent. Outside advisors participate on this level of evaluation as well (see Table 35.3).

TABLE 35.1 Typical CEO Evaluation Process

Group*	Design System	Determine Measures, Set Targets	Gather and Present Performance Data	Appraise Performance	Provide Feedback	Determine Consequences
Entire board	●	●	○	●	●	●
Compensation committee	◑	◑	●	◑	◑	◑
CEO	○	○	○	○	–	–
Executive officers†	○	○	○	–	–	–
All other executives	–	–	–	–	–	–
Outside advisors	○	○	○	–	–	○

* Members of some group categories overlap.

† Includes Top-5 NEOs.

Key: approve (●); recommend (◑); influence (○); no role (–).

TABLE 35.2 Typical Executive Officer Evaluation Process

Group*	Design System	Determine Measures, Set Targets	Gather and Present Performance Data	Appraise Performance	Provide Feedback	Determine Consequences
Entire board	○	○	–	○	–	○
Compensation committee	●	●	–	○	–	●
CEO	◑	◑	●	●	●	●
Executive officers†	○	○	○	◑	◑	◑
All other executives	–	–	–	–	–	–
Outside advisors	○	○	○	–	–	–

* Members of some group categories overlap.

† Includes Top-5 NEOs.

Key: approve (●); recommend (◑); influence (○); no role (–).

TABLE 35.3   Typical Evaluation Process for All Other Executives

Group*	Design System	Determine Measures, Set Targets	Gather and Present Performance Data	Appraise Performance	Provide Feedback	Determine Consequences
Entire board	–	–	–	–	–	–
Compensation committee	O	O	–	–	–	O
CEO	●	●	●	●	●	●
Executive officers[†]	◖	◖	◖	◖	◖	◖
All other executives	O	O	O	O	O	O
Outside advisors	O	O	O	–	–	–

* Members of some group categories overlap.

† Includes Top-5 NEOs.

Key: approve (●); recommend (◖); influence (O); no role (–).

The performance appraisal process also involves determining how the evaluation is administered including: the timing, the form the evaluation will take (written or oral), and feedback to the executive.

Timing

The evaluation process should generally include three main stages: the establishment of the evaluation goals at the beginning of the fiscal year, the mid-year review, and the end-of-the-year performance assessment and approval of compensation package.

There should be multiple evaluation sessions over the year. A meaningful CEO evaluation should contain regular board executive sessions, culminating in a formal annual evaluation. It should be well planned and objective and it should ultimately be tied to the executive's pay package. The executive officer and other executive processes are similar, except that their manager (most likely the CEO in the case of the EO) is in place of the board.

At the beginning of the fiscal year, the short- and long-term objectives that will be used in the executive evaluation should be agreed upon. The establishment of objectives is discussed in the Evaluation Criteria section of this chapter. In addition to their creation, it is important that objectives are given relative weights and that the executive is aware of which objectives are of greater importance (see the sample CEO Evaluation form at the end of this chapter). Along with the targets, the threshold and maximum performance levels and the pay adjustments associated with the diffcrent levels of performance should be discussed and defined.

The mid-year review provides an opportunity to assess progress towards performance targets, isolate and address problems, and determine if the executive is on the right path to meeting or exceeding the objectives. In some cases, it may make sense to adjust performance targets if they are no longer relevant to the company. However, it is not recommended that performance targets be changed unless there are unforeseen, unusual, or extraordinary circumstances. In a more volatile or dynamic industry (such as fashion or apparel), these intermediate reviews may need to be done quarterly or even on a monthly or weekly basis.

The end-of-the year assessment is the most thorough and time-consuming part of the evaluation process. Performance results must be compared to the set targets and the appropriate compensations package must be determined. The final evaluation typically takes place in March following the year in which the work was done, as it takes that long to finalize the financial statements. It is important and prudent that the audited financial statements be completed before the evaluation is completed to provide certainty to the performance data. There have been some recent examples of financial restatements that have highlighted bonuses that should not have been paid or would have been substantially less.

This final evaluation is the formal executive performance appraisal, and should contain the following components:

- Executive completes a written self-evaluation

- Evaluators complete questionnaires assessing performance

- Internal and external data and information are collected

- The committee prepares recommendations

- The evaluators meet and discuss before approving final compensation package

Delivery of the Evaluation

Though it is highly recommended, there is no tax, accounting, security, or legislative rule that requires the evaluations to be in written form, which allows for the option of an oral evaluation. Like the written evaluation, the oral evaluation should also be very detailed and have goals and objectives outlined, and involve a feedback component. The oral evaluation would be conducted by the full board. Oral evaluations eradicate several of the problems with written evaluations, but tend to be less thorough. Oral evaluations are much more prevalent in smaller organizations and in the case of the CEO (particularly in larger organizations that are concerned about the misinterpretation of a CEO evaluation and the discovery of the evaluation in an adverse legal proceeding).

The advantages of oral evaluation are:

- No written comments to be misinterpreted and misused
- May help some directors articulate their opinions
- Take less time than written evaluation

The disadvantages of oral evaluation are:

- Very vocal directors (in the case of the CEO and in some cases executive officers) and executives (in the case of executive officers and other executives) can more easily influence others
- Directors and executives will tend to be less objective and fair if the evaluation is oral
- Tends to be a less in-depth review
- It is very difficult to implement the "two-up" rule
- There will not be a good record to assist in career development and promotional opportunities

Written, documented evaluations are preferred, as a written evaluation allows for tracking of performance over multiple years. The oral process does not lend itself to that. However, CEO evaluation materials are sometimes destroyed because there is no real career development once you are CEO, and records are destroyed to avoid a plaintiff's counsel using these documents in adverse lawsuits of various types.

Feedback to the Executive

Clear communication with the CEO and executives is necessary on the part of the compensation committee. At least two directors should deliver the CEO evaluation. The chairs of the compensation and corporate governance committee should meet with the CEO in private immediately after full-board discussions. The two-person rule is also a good practice to follow with all executives with the immediate manager and perhaps either a representative of human resources or the manager's manager present during the evaluation.

It is paramount that great care for confidentiality be practiced during the evaluation process. The problem of confidentiality is somewhat more difficult in the case of the CEO as the evaluation process involves the completion of evaluation forms by each director. Other executive evaluations are typically completed by the manager and reviewed by their manager.

In the case of the CEO evaluation, all completed evaluation forms by outside directors, board members and other sources should be returned solely to the director or person (sometimes an outside advisor or in some cases the corporate secretary or lawyer working in a legal group) in charge of collection the evaluation forms, and should be disposed of after the summary of the data is collected. The CEO and other executives should never see the raw data. It is easy for data and responses to be misused or misinterpreted. For cogency, a summary of the data is all that the executive should see. It is highly recommended that for further security and confidentiality that outside consultants be utilized to manage the evaluation process.

DEVELOPING EVALUATION CRITERIA

Performance evaluation criteria have evolved in the modern corporation from a trait-based, personality-centric measure to a more specific, results-oriented metric, which includes financial and nonfinancial criteria. This change began in the early 1960s and continues through today as companies review their performance measurement criteria. Until recently, performance appraisals were based on annual "trait" ratings. Certain character traits such as degree of initiative, personality, maturity, judgment, or appearance were assessed because of their supposed relation to executive performance.

Over time, executives became more hostile, defensive, and critical of the system as boards grew more critical in their assessments.[6] This "trait-based" appraisal system was soon replaced with the "overall performance rating." This system, though more comprehensive, was so heavily subjective and lacking in structure that appraisals were easily influenced by insignificant factors such as personality and low golf handicap instead of more relevant factors such as growth and financial performance.[7]

Out of the shortcomings of the "trait-based" and "overall performance rating" came "management by objective." This appraisal system is based on established long- and shortterm objectives or goals that CEOs are expected to achieve in a specified period of time and it measures the degree to which a CEO met, fell short of, or surpassed these objectives.[8]

This appraisal system in comparison to the previous models was more effective because it was:

- simple

- focused on actual work, and not personality

- aligned executive objectives with overall company goals

- far more accepted by CEOs

If the executive participated in the establishment of his objectives it was even more motivating.

Management by objective was revolutionary. Many companies rushed to augment or completely overhaul their performance assessment systems to be in line with this new system. Management by objective is still the most used and most accepted performance appraisal system used by many companies today.

All organizations need to have a well designed and focused performance plan. The performance plan process aggregates individual goals into larger overlapping, collective goals that focus the organization to do more than it would have done. A well-designed performance plan describes the preferred results, how results tie back to the company's results, weighting of results, how results will be measured, and what standards are used to evaluate results.

EXECUTIVE PERFORMANCE MEASURES

As part of the performance plan, executives should set objectives that align with the company's culture, business strategy and compensation philosophy. The objectives set are used to define the performance measures that will be used as evaluation criteria during the performance evaluation (see Figure 35.2). Before executive performance measures can be defined, each of the three contributing factors needs to be defined and understood so that objectives can be developed from each.

Compensation Philosophy

The compensation philosophy takes into account the culture and shared values and business strategy. A compensation philosophy consists of four main components:

- *Peer group comparisons*—who should the company compare themselves against for salary and short- and longterm incentive opportunities?

- *Pay positioning strategy*—how should the company pay their executives in relation to the market levels of pay?

- *Internal vs external pay equity*—the culture and shared values are factored into this part of the compensation philosophy. How much weight should the company place on the internal relationships among executives (internal) versus the market (external)?

FIGURE 35.2   Factors that determine executive performance measures

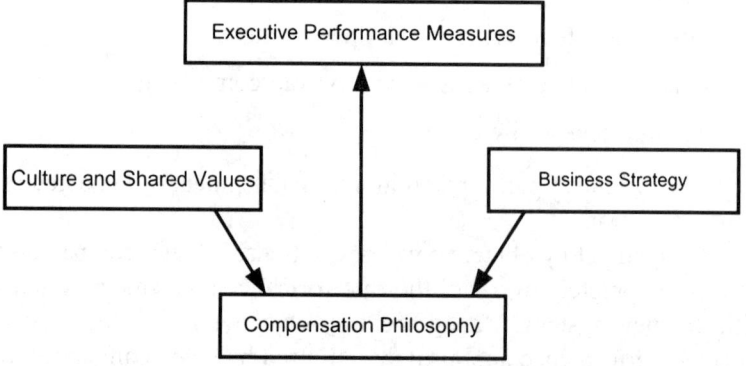

- *Performance alignment with business plan*—specifically, how is the business strategy aligned with the compensation system, particularly the incentive strategy with emphasis on the performance measures?

The compensation philosophy should be reviewed when determining performance goals as it takes some parts from the culture and shared values (internal versus external pay equity) and some parts from the business strategy (performance alignment with the business plan). It is also important to determine the peer group that the company needs to compete with.

Culture and Shared Values

Culture and shared values are naturally included while deciding what criteria will be considered during the conduction of the appraisal process. Some of these values may include: open communications, rewarding competence, preservation of integrity, openness to change, developing talent internally, loyalty, and the belief that goals should be results-oriented and not process-oriented. Identifying a culture and shared values will be of great value when considering how to weigh both quantitative and qualitative measures in the appraisal process. The culture and shared values will vary from company to company, as should their executive performance measures as it should be a reflection of this culture and these values.

Business Strategy

The corporate business strategy which the board of directors and CEOs refer to when developing a performance appraisal system should be taken into account. It is important that these strategies are set and then made clear to the executives so as to guarantee cohesion and unity of ideas and perspective over the course of the year. The appraisal process should assess how successful the executive has been in moving forward with the preestablished business strategy for that year. Mid-year reviews allow for the company to reassess these strategies and alter them if they are proving to be inadequate.

Business success factors should be an extension of the existing business strategy; these tend to be more concrete and narrowed-focused, annual goals. The executive's ability to contribute and their success in achieving these goals should be considered in the appraisal process.

Executive Performance Measures

All of the factors discussed above will be a consideration of the final product, the performance measures used to evaluate executives. Those factors which compose each company's background or identity will determine the route the company will take to assess the executive; it will also determine how much each area is weighted based on the relative importance or value the company believes the criterion to hold.

Because a larger portion of executive compensation has been shifting to variable pay plans, which are linked to performance, companies are placing greater scrutiny on selecting performance measures that actually have an affect on the "bottom line."[9] The most obvious measurable financial results are the principal attributes:[10] profit, total shareholder return, return on invested capital, cash flow, earnings growth, and earnings stability.

Quantitative measures should work in concert with qualitative measures as appraisal criteria.[11] There is no question that qualitative data can be useful during the evaluation process; however, too heavy a reliance on it can lead to a loss of valuable resources such as time, money, and energy. This would, foremost, defeat the purpose of an appraisal as its main objective is to ensure productivity and success.

Every goal specified should be quantified as far as possible so that a third party could review the goal during an evaluation and determine if the executive had indeed achieved the goal. Qualitative information by nature is subjective and quantitative data by nature is objective and thus less subject to evaluator bias. The mix of financial and nonfinancial measures is critical. If the executive evaluation is decoupled from the annual incentive plan (e.g., the bonus is paid independent of the evaluation), then nonfinancial measures should be the predominant part of the evaluation. However, if the executive evaluation is the sole determinant of the bonus, the use of quantitative data should be the main determinate of the bonus to be paid to the executive (see Figure 35.3).

The most effective incentive measures are return on invested capital and total shareholder return. However, these financial measures may not be appropriate for

FIGURE 35.3   Qualitative vs nonqualitative measures

	Quantitative	Qualitative
Financial	• EPS growth • ROIC • TSR	• Better understanding of company strategy in investment community • Achievement of IPO/spin-off/restructuring
Non-Financial	• Employee turnover • Diversity • Employee satisfaction (survey results)	• Milestones • Leadership skills • Strategy implementation • Communication effectiveness

all levels of executives as they may not be directly related to the executive being evaluated.

While there are ad hoc comments made by consultants and others that the achievement of the right nonfinancial goals such as customer satisfaction, customer retention, employee satisfaction, brand recognition, and customer loyalty will improve corporate profitability, there is no definitive proof of such claims. In addition, there are no good metrics as to the relationship between the achievement of nonfinancial goals and financial success. However, the application of non-financial goals is just as important as that of financial goals, particularly lower in the organization.

Nonfinancial goals need to be simple, direct, and measurable. The goals should be results-oriented and not process-oriented—the goal should be expressed as achieving a result that will directly help the organization achieve short- and longterm objectives.

If the performance appraisal is closely linked to compensation, then extreme caution should be exercised on the selection of nonfinancial goals. In this case, a strict financial formula should be used to fund the program to avoid wasting corporate assets in overpaying executives.

OUTCOMES OF THE PERFORMANCE APPRAISAL

Higher qualitative success is usually accompanied by a higher profit margin, which is, of course, the ultimate goal of any company. Qualitative criteria should be used in the executive evaluation process. Unfortunately, IRS Code Section 162(m) does not allow it to be used to set bonus amounts for the NEOs. We recommend that the evaluation process be used as a "negative discretion" element. In other words, the annual executive appraisal can be used to lower the bonus for the NEOs. The treatment of the other executives can vary and may include adjusting the annual incentive upward or downward depending on the executive performance appraisal.

The last and very important part of the evaluation process is to tie the evaluation process into the executive's pay package. This is especially important when corporate success is not synchronous with executive pay. For example, care should be taken to avoid large stock grants, bonus payments, salary increases, and other perceived compensation windfalls when there is an employee layoff, stock slump, or earnings drop.

One of the main objectives of assessing the performance of an executive is to ensure that he is being paid fairly, to gage whether the salary for the performance is justified, over-rewarded, or should be raised. It is important that executives be monitored regularly to ensure that progress is being made. The outcome of the assessment will correlate directly to his salary. Meeting expectations, whether quantitative premeditated ones or goals set relative to competition, should be rewarded.

The current CEO evaluation process is typically de-linked from the CEO bonus decision. This is somewhat true for the NEOs and less true for all executives. The bonus is typically determined using quantitative financial criteria such as EPS growth or EBITDA. The CEO evaluation form, as shown in the example at the end of this chapter is 95 percent nonfinancial and is focused on such areas as leadership, communications, board relations, and management development. Companies are beginning to link these two evaluation processes.

Once performance has been appraised, the results will be considered and then used for decisions in the discourse of action. CEOs are often compared and evaluated in relation to the CEOs of other companies; the reason being that, even if the CEO does meet financial goals, other companies may be doing better. If a CEO does not meet set goals or is falling behind in comparison to other companies, he can be put on probation or more regularly monitored. If the CEO continues to fail to perform in the ways necessary, then a case can be built against him with records from multiple past appraisals and he can eventually be fired. If, on the other hand, he meets or exceeds marks and has put the company in a good place in the market, he may be rewarded with a bonus or other incentives.

Clear communication with the upper management is necessary on the part of the compensation committee. At least two people should deliver the evaluation (two directors in the case of the CEO). The chairs of the Compensation and Corporate Governance Committee should meet with the CEO in private immediately after full-board discussions.

The board alone should have the authority to adjust the CEO's salary and longterm incentive award. In several companies, HR typically gives guidelines as to salary increases. This places HR and management in an awkward position as it may signal an action if the increase is below the recommendation. We recommend that the committee relies on outside advice for recommendations as to the range of the salary increase and long-term incentive (LTI) award.

The salary should not be adjusted as drastically as the LTI award as it is important the CEO be paid according to general market levels with respect to base salary. There is ample amount room to adjust the LTI award opportunity based on the evaluation results.

SUMMARY

There are many factors to consider when designing, implementing, and operating an effective executive performance system. The performance measures (both quantitative and qualitative) are crucial to the success of the organization. In addition, attention must be paid to the related processes for the CEO, NEOs, EOs and all other executives. Finally, the evaluation process should be integrated into the annual incentive plan. The compensation philosophy, culture and shared values, and business plan should be considered carefully when deciding on the performance measures.

APPENDIX: EXAMPLE EVALUATION TOOLS—CEO EVALUATION FORM

XYZ COMPANY, INC.
Chief Executive Officer Evaluation
For the fiscal year ending January 31, 2004

Overview:

The chief executive officer is responsible for the success or failure of XYZ and leads by providing the vision for XYZ. Develops and implements strategic and operational plans to achieve the vision. Oversees the operation of XYZ; develops management, allocates resources and ensures control. Acts as XYZ's chief spokesperson. Works with the board to develop and maintain oversight.

The CEO or any other member of management will not view this form. A summary of your ratings and comments will be prepared that will preserve the confidentiality of your ratings and comments. This summary will be presented to the board at the 2003 board meeting. The CEO will receive a summary of your comments and feedback at the 2004 board meeting.

Please return this form to YOUR CONSULTANT, Address 1, Address 2, City, Sate zip prior to DATE. You can also fax this form to YOUR CONSULTANT at FAX NUMBER.

Each question should be evaluated with the following point system and appropriate comments:

Far Exceeded Expectations/ Exceptional Performance	Exceeded Exceptations/ Superior Performance	Fully Met Exceptations/ Competent Performance	Below Exceptations/ Performance Needs Development	Far Below Exceptations/ Performance Unsatisfactory
1	2	3	4	5

1.   Strategic Planning (Weight 15 percent)   Score: _____

- Ensures the development of a long-term strategy.
- Establishes objectives and plans that meet the needs of shareholders, customers, employees and all other corporate stakeholders, and ensures consistent and timely progress toward strategic objectives.
- Obtains and allocates resources consistent with strategic objectives. Reports regularly to the board on progress toward strategic plan milestones.

Comments:

2.   Financial Results (Weight 20 percent)   Score: _____

- Establishes and achieves appropriate annual and longer-term financial performance goals.
- Ensures the development and maintenance of appropriate systems to protect the Company's assets and assure effective control of operations.

Comments:

3.   Succession Planning (Weight 35 percent)   Score: _____

- Develops, attracts, retains and motivates an effective and unified senior management team.
- Ensures that programs for management development and succession planning have the required resources and direction to grow the future leaders of the Company.

Comments:

4. **Leadership/Communications/Board Relations (Weight 30 percent)**

Score _____

- Develops and communicates a clear and consistent vision of the Company's goals and values.
- Ensures that this vision is well understood, widely supported, and effectively implemented within the organization.
- Fosters a corporate culture that encourages, recognizes and rewards leadership, excellence and innovation.
- Ensures a culture that promotes ethical practice, individual integrity and cooperation to build shareholder value.
- Serves as a chief spokesperson for the Company, communicating effectively with shareholders, prospective investors, employees, customers, suppliers and consumers.
- Effectively represents the Company in relationships with industry, the government and the financial community, including major investor groups and financial services firms.
- Works closely with the Board to keep directors informed on the state of business on critical issues relating to the Company, such as the corporate strategies and the achievement of operating plan and strategic plan milestones.
- Provides effective support for board operations including board materials, and advisory services.

Comments:

Final Summary

A. Overall comments:

B.   Key challenges in year ahead:

C.   Thoughts and concerns:

REFERENCE

Conger, J. A., Finegold, D. and Lawler III, E. E., Appraising Boardroom Performance, *Harvard Business Review on Corporate Governance*. Watertown, MA: Harvard Business School Press (2000) pp. 105–34.

END NOTES

1. G. S. Crystal, The Performance Appraisal Process and Its Relation to Compensation, *Compensating Executive Worth*, ed. Moore, R. F., American Management Association, 1968, pp. 91–105.

2. J. F. Reda, S. Reifler, and L. G. Thatcher, *Compensation Committee Handbook*, 2nd edn. New York: Wiley, 2005, pp. 54–76.

3. Ibid.

4. Hunt, A. R., Letter From Washington: As U.S. Rich–Poor Gap Grows, so Does Public Outcry, *International Herald Tribune: Americas*, 18 February 2007 (accessed 7 August 2007).

5. Reda et al. (see note 2).

6. Crystal (see note 1).

7. Ibid.

8. Ibid.

9. Schneier, C. E. and Shaw, D. G., Measuring and Assessing Top Executive Performance, *The Compensation Handbook*, 4th edn, eds Berger, L. A. and Berger, D. R., New York: McGraw-Hill, 2000, pp. 496–8, 500.

10. Ibid.

11. Ibid.

FORCED RANKING

Dick Grote, President

Grote Consulting Corporation

OVER THE PAST FEW YEARS the procedure called "forced ranking" has gained a great deal of attention from the media, consultants, and academics. The debate over forced ranking began in 2000 with the publication of General Electric's annual report to GE shareowners. CEO Jack Welch both explained and extolled the forced ranking procedure that the company had used for many years. In his report, Welch said, "We break our population down into three categories: the top 20%, the high-performance middle 70%, and the bottom 10%." He went on to argue that the top 20 percent must be loved and nurtured in the soul and wallet while the bottom 10 percent must be removed.

Welch continued by arguing that this removal process must happen every year. Not doing so, he said, "is not only a management failure but a false kindness as well," since eventually a new leader would take out that 10 percent leaving them stranded and having to start over elsewhere. "GE leaders," Welch said, "must develop the determination to change out, always humanely, that bottom 10%, and do it every year. That is how real meritocracies are created and thrive."

Welch's endorsement of a procedure that seemed to pit people against each other rather than against how well they did at meeting predetermined standards and objectives ignited a national argument on the merits of this approach to performance management. The reaction to forced ranking was almost universally negative. Critics argued that identifying and eliminating the bottom 10 percent of an organization every year was not only impractical, it was unethical to "rank and yank" people who had previously been told they were performing at an acceptable level. The press reported stories of class action lawsuits brought by terminated employees against companies that had used a forced ranking process. The implosion of Enron, a company that notoriously celebrated its culture of talent and trumpeted its forced ranking process seemed to offer another argument against the use of the technique.

But while the critics of the procedure were vocal and received a great deal of media attention, the advocates of forced ranking were largely silent. Part of the reason for the negative press is that there have been examples—like Enron—where forced ranking systems were poorly designed and badly executed. In addition, there is probably no subject about which companies are more reluctant to speak. The publicity given to the high-profile lawsuits and the amorphous feeling that forced ranking is not "fair" made those organizations that use the process hesitant to go on record about their practices.

The result is that information about this talent management process, a powerful tool with the potential to offer a great deal of benefit to organizations if it is well designed and well executed, is not widely available. When the only reports are downbeat and pessimistic, good information about how to create and make the most of a forced ranking system are hard to come by. Companies find themselves in the position of having to reinvent the wheel.

A separate difficulty involves the frequent confusion between "forced ranking," a procedure that involves comparing the relative contribution of one employee with the contributions of other employees, and "forced distribution," a mechanism designed to force a more normal distribution curve into performance appraisal ratings. Both are mechanisms companies employ to drive truth into the performance management process. They are completely different procedures; however, getting the maximum benefit from each will be explored.

THE IMPORTANCE OF PERFORMANCE APPRAISAL

If managers met their responsibilities to appraise the performance of subordinates honestly and communicate those assessments straightforwardly, the standard performance appraisal procedure of any organization would probably be sufficient for delivering feedback, managing organizational talent, and making good compensation decisions.

But too many managers flinch at the prospect of having to sit down, face-to-face, and deliver an honest appraisal of a subordinate's performance. They prefer to avoid any situation that presents the possibility of disagreement or conflict, preferring to live in a fictitious Lake Wobegon world where all the children—and all the workers—are above average.

There is, however, a genuine need to communicate exactly what is expected, to assess accurately just how well people are doing, and to let them know honestly and straightforwardly exactly where they stand. Truthfully evaluating the quality of people's performance—and their potential—allows organizations to correctly make critically important decisions.

- How should rewards be allocated? Who should get a big raise, who should simply be kept whole, and who should be denied any increase at all?

- When a vacancy arises, who should be tapped for promotion? Do we already have excellent candidates ready and waiting inside the organization, or do we have to go outside to get the needed talent?

- What is the depth of our talent pool? Do we have the people we need to meet the demands of the future?

- What is the relative strength of talent across our organization? Are there pockets of excellence and pockets of mediocrity within the company?

- Do we have a level playing field in our talent assessment and performance evaluation practices? Are the criteria and standards used by different managers and different departments reasonably consistent across the company, or are some parts of the organization much tougher (or more indulgent) than others?

- What kind of training and development efforts should we invest in? Who should they be directed toward? Where will we get the biggest bang for the training buck?

- Who are our best performers, the people who are outstanding performers in their present positions with the potential to take on more demanding roles? Do we have retention strategies in place to make sure that they do not leave?

- Who are our worst performers and what do we need to do about them? Which ones can we salvage? Which ones should we cut loose?

ABSOLUTE AND RELATIVE COMPARISONS

Every member of an organization wants the answers to two questions: (1) What do you expect of me? (2) How am I doing at meeting your expectations? We answer the first question at the start of the year by setting goals, clarifying job responsibilities, and communicating clear expectations about the behaviors we expect of organization members. There are two ways to answer the second question. One way is to respond in terms of *absolute* performance, the approach used in conventional performance appraisal. The other way is to focus on *relative* performance, the approach used in forced ranking processes.

Absolute Comparison.   When a person's performance is appraised using an "absolute comparison" approach, he is evaluated in terms of what he achieved and how he went about achieving it—his results and his behaviors. This is the familiar approach employed by conventional performance appraisal processes. It is a person-to-standard comparison.

At its best, here is how it works: at the beginning of the year Sam and his boss sit down and review the key job responsibilities in Sam's position. They come to agreement on the goals that Sam will achieve in the upcoming 12 months. They discuss the competencies or expected behaviors that Sam needs to exhibit as he goes about meeting his responsibilities (typically including such attributes as communication skills, interpersonal skills, decision making, leadership and similar behavioral elements of effective organizational performance). They talk about what development plans Sam has in mind and discuss how Sam's performance will be measured.

During the year Sam and his boss meet for updates and feedback and informal reviews. At the end of the appraisal period, the manager formally evaluates how well Sam performed, how good a job he did in achieving the goals he was expected to achieve, the key job responsibilities that they identified, and the competencies or behaviors they discussed. With this *absolute comparison* approach, the question the manager answers is: "How well did Sam do against the goals and objectives that were set at the beginning of the year?"

Conventional performance appraisal procedures, the kind used by almost every organization, evaluate performance in this way. They operate on the basis of an *absolute* comparison by asking how well the employee performed compared with the goals set and the boss' expectations. The year-end performance appraisal rating depends then on two factors: how tough the goals were and how high or low the boss's expectations are. If the goals were easy and the boss's expectations are low, it is possible for everyone to get a superior rating.

Relative Comparison.   When employee performance is appraised using a "relative comparison" approach, people are evaluated in terms of how well they did compared with how well other people did. The question the manager is asking is no longer, "How well did Sam do in meeting his goals?" Instead, the boss now asks, "How good a job did Sam do as compared with how well Betty and George and Tom did?"

A relative comparison process requires the manager to evaluate the employee's performance compared with that of others in the organization. An employee who is rated superior in a conventional performance appraisal procedure may well be ranked toward the bottom in a forced-ranking, relative-comparison process when performance is compared with that of others who are more talented. It could be very accurate for a manager to rate an employee high in terms of meeting objectives, and at the same time give a low rank in comparison to peer performance. And the reverse may also be true: in spite of missing every target, Sam's performance was superior to the even more dismal performance turned in by others in the unit.

The Problems with Absolute Comparisons

The primary pitfall in using the traditional absolute comparison method for performance evaluation is obvious: if the expectations are set low enough, almost anyone can exceed them. Likewise, set the standards too high and everyone will fail.

Another problem with using absolute comparisons, the mechanism used in conventional performance appraisal procedures, is that the level of expectations may vary greatly across the organization. One manager may be a tough grader where no one ever performs at a level that earns a top rating. In other parts of the organization there will be supervisors who award superior performance appraisal ratings to everyone who shows up.

Another subtle difficulty with the absolute-comparison approach is that managers tend to set performance expectations at a level that they are reasonably sure their subordinates can meet. The situation then arises where every person, from the least talented member of the crew to the star, ends up exceeding expectations and there is no differentiation in terms of their performance. As a result, it is almost impossible to make valid pay-for-performance compensation decisions.

THE BUSINESS CASE FOR FORCED RANKING

Forced ranking is the antidote to the problems of inflated rating and the failure to differentiate. By making relative comparisons, and identifying the organization's A, B, and C players, companies can assure that increases and bonuses are awarded fairly and appropriately. They can identify where their bench strength is strong and where it is lacking. They can apply appropriate and necessary retention strategies to keep their most talented members. They can assure their solid, vital middle performers that they are recognized and valued. And they can get the message across to those who contribute the least that they need to either markedly improve their performance or find jobs that better fit their talents and preferences. Assuming that the system is wisely constructed and effectively executed, a forced ranking system can provide information that conventional performance appraisal systems cannot.

But just assuring differentiation, while valuable in itself, is not the whole reason companies use forced ranking systems. Creating a forced ranking system forces a company to articulate the criteria that are required for success in the organization. During Jack Welch's tenure, for example, GE identified a set of criteria called their 4 E's that they used to rank their managers and executives: high *energy* level, the ability to *energize* others around common goals, the *edge* to make tough yes/no decisions, and the ability to consistently *execute* and deliver on promises. These criteria were determined over a period of several years and were the result of serious deliberation. They also facilitated cross-department comparisons and allowed the performance of people doing widely varying jobs to be compared.

Another important business outcome that is often unrecognized is forced ranking's ability to provide the organization with useful data on the ability of managers to spot and champion talent. In one company I worked with, one of their criteria for their forced ranking system was the ability to make tough decisions. In the course of briefing the senior executive team I pointed out that one of the best sources of data would be the way that the vice presidents, their direct reports, went about making the forced ranking decisions during the sessions where they would all be together. Who is able to come up with telling examples of a subordinate's strengths and weaknesses? How well do various managers really understand the major strengths and development needs of their subordinates? A forced ranking procedure forces managers to think in far greater depth about the quality of talent in their unit than conventional performance appraisal systems typically require, and their ability to describe and verbalize their assessments provides a good indicator of a critical aspect of their leadership ability.

Another important reason for installing a forced ranking procedure is that it can alleviate some of the frustrations generated by the conventional performance appraisal system and the succession planning system. Forced ranking can provide an independent verification of performance appraisal and succession planning data. Significant variations in the information provided by the performance appraisal, succession planning systems, and the forced ranking process sets up a red flag. In addition, forced ranking can provide something of great value that even the best performance appraisal systems cannot—accurate cross-department comparisons. As larger groups are evaluated, and with criteria that can be applied equally across a variety of jobs, the forced ranking process may permit more accurate cross-department comparisons.

DESIGNING A FORCED RANKING SYSTEM

The first question any organization that is considering adding a forced ranking component to its talent management palette needs to ask is: What are our objectives? Clearly specifying why the company has decided to embark on a process that is inherently controversial will be helpful in coming up with good decisions about the ranking scheme to be used, what use will be made of the data generated by the system, whether to let people know how they came out in the forced ranking evaluations, and other critical issues.

A critical decision is the ranking allocation scheme to be used. Many options exist. Some organizations use Top 10/Bottom 10 (and one company that had long used a top 10/bottom 10 approach later moved to top 10/next 10/bottom 10). Years ago, when I worked for PepsiCo, we used quartiling; EDS used quintiling. Others attempt to make their distribution clusters resemble a normal curve: 5/20/50/20/5. One British company's unwieldy scheme allocated talent into 10/80/5/5 clusters, forcing an excessive focus on the poorest performers.

My recommendation of a ranking scheme of top 20/vital 70/bottom 10 has several advantages. The percentage allocations indicate that there are twice as many top performers as there are people at the bottom of the heap. It emphasizes the fact that the majority of people who are ranked in the middle are indeed *vital*. They are not average or mediocre; rather they are good solid performers. Finally, the top 20/vital 70/bottom 10 has the great advantage of simplicity.

A great many other questions must be raised and answered wisely for a forced ranking system to provide maximum value. These include:

- How will the ranking be done? What will the specific mechanics be?

- How will the ranking pools be constructed?

- Who will be in each ranking pool?

- Who will serve as rankers?

- How will the rankers be trained?

- What will the process be named?

- What will be the criteria against which employees will be ranked? Should we consider both performance and potential? How will we evaluate potential?

- How will the data be rolled up from individual departments to get valid company-wide information?

- How will the results of the forced ranking process be used?

- Should people be told how they came out in the ranking process? Who will tell them? What should they be told?

- How will the forced ranking process be linked with other performance management and talent management processes?

- How can the potential negative consequences of implementing a forced ranking procedure be minimized?

THE PROS AND CONS OF FORCED RANKING

The most common misunderstanding about forced ranking is that the primary reason companies implement a forced ranking system is to finger their poorest performers, and that the biggest benefit they get comes from terminating this bottom group—thus the term, "rank-and-yank." But this is false.

In spite of much media misinformation, it is actually uncommon for companies to automatically terminate the people who rank in the bottom group of a forced ranking procedure. Certainly there are some who do: General Electric and Sun Microsystems have been vocal about their routine replacement of employees ranked in their bottom category. But most organizations that use a forced ranking, relative-comparison process do not automatically terminate those who end up in the lowest group. They use the information to make good compensation decisions. They use the results of the forced ranking process to calibrate the data produced by their conventional performance appraisal system and their succession planning system. Some may advise those who are seen as making a lesser contribution of the need to change or move on to greener pastures. But rank-and-yank is actually unusual.

Another misunderstanding involves where the payoff to forced ranking lies. The biggest advantage of the process results from identifying the company's top talent, since they now are known to a much wider group of senior managers. Appropriate recognition and retention efforts can now be directed where they will have the biggest payoff. And surprisingly, the biggest benefit of all may be to those who serve as rankers, since not only do they get a much broader understanding of where the talent in the organization is, they understand the emphasis the organization places on talent management. In fact, not only are valuable data generated about the quality of performance of the population under review, but equally valid and important data are also generated about the people who are doing the reviewing:

- Are managers able to articulate exactly why one of their subordinates belongs in a particular category?

- Are they able to come up with convincing examples?

- Do they argue persuasively in favor of their best, or do they go through the exercise in a perfunctory manner?

- Do they argue excessively to protect a favored buddy from assignment to a low category? Do they yield their point of view too easily, or hang on too long to an obviously untenable position?

- Do they know their people well enough to apply the organization's criteria to their performance accurately by providing specific examples?

- To what extent have they gotten to know people in other parts of the organization?

- How much attention are they paying to talent in other departments?

- Do they remain engaged when the discussion shifts to individuals outside their chain-of-command?

- Are they sensitive to the importance of diversity and the nuances of language?

- Are they willing to challenge other managers who, they believe, are overinflating their assessments of their troops?

- Do they take the process seriously?

A forced ranking process requires managers to pay serious attention to talent management, and allows senior managers an opportunity to observe how well junior managers spot and promote talent.

Despite the benefits forced ranking offers organizations, there are some legitimate concerns and potential problems.

- *Some managers and some employees may resent and resist the process*—there is no question: forced ranking is a disruptive process. It may well be the kind of disruption that is necessary to jumpstart a high-performance culture, but there will be those who prefer to maintain the status quo.

- *Employees ranked in a lower category may be demoralized*—this too is true. But telling the truth trumps sparing people's feelings at the expense of honesty. And if there is to be "demoralization," better that it be in the ranks of those who contribute the least rather than among those who contribute the most.

- *Lower ranked employees who are members of a protected class may believe that the ranking procedure produced illegally discriminatory results*—this is the loudest charge leveled against forced ranking. However there is nothing legally that prevents a company from assessing one employee's performance and potential as greater than that of another and making employment decisions based on that assessment. The results of the forced ranking procedure (like the results of any other procedure that differentiates among employees) should always be checked for adverse impact. But recognize that the media reports have focused exclusively on the handful of companies that have been the target of discrimination lawsuits— many of which have been won or dismissed—rather than on the thousands that have successfully used a forced ranking or relative comparison process without any challenge.

- *The process may produce an excessively competitive environment where corporate goals are suboptimized*—this common objection to forced ranking argues that engaging in a relative comparison process will generate a dog-eat-dog, red-in-tooth-and-claw, every-person-for-themself Darwinian outcome. The truth is that simply making "teamwork" one of the primary assessment criteria can send the message companywide that playing well with others is the best way to get ahead.

- *Mistakes are inevitable—you are bound to miss a few late bloomers and over-rate a few glib duds*—this is certainly true. Performance evaluation procedures of any kind ask fallible and imperfect human beings to make difficult decisions that will affect the future of their colleagues. Sometimes mistakes are made.

FORCED RANKING AND FORCED DISTRIBUTION

There is little argument that those who contribute the most, have the greatest potential, and shoulder more than their share of the load should be more generously rewarded. Likewise, almost no one would argue that those who contribute the least should be encouraged to either increase the quality of their contribution or find employment at another organization where their talents and contributions are more in line with the organization's expectations. Here is the challenge: how do you figure out who is in which group?

If conventional performance appraisal systems were actually used as they were intended, the need for any more rigorous procedures like forced ranking would be minimal. Most appraisal systems ask managers to identify their distinguished performers, their solid performers, and their also-rans. But, as many companies have experienced, many managers prefer to fudge the facts and inflate the ratings rather than face having the hard conversations that truthful performance assessments often require.

To drive rigor and truth into talent management discussions and decisions, organizations employ techniques that involve using relative-contribution assessments in addition to the absolute comparison approach of conventional appraisal systems. One of these approaches is *forced ranking*, the process we have just explored. The other is *forced distribution*, the setting of maximums and minimums in performance appraisal ratings to assure that there is differentiation. These two processes are often confused.

FORCED DISTRIBUTION

One way to bring more truth into performance management involves tweaking the rules of the performance appraisal procedure to either request or require a certain distribution of performance appraisal ratings. For example, consider a company that has a five-level rating scale—distinguished/superior/fully successful/needs improvement/unsatisfactory. Unhappy with the fact that every year almost everyone in the firm is rated in the top two categories, management adopts a policy that restricts the number of people who can get the top rating and requires a certain amount of lower level ratings. Their forced-distribution scheme might look like Figure 36.1.

If rigidly enforced, the new policy will insure that there is differentiation in performance appraisal ratings. But two major problems immediately arise with the proposed distribution scheme illustrated above. First, there is no flexibility in the percentages of ratings allowed. As a result, the manager of a low-performing group is required to assign 5 percent of subordinates into the "distinguished" category and another 20 percent into the "superior" category when, in truth, hardly any of them deserve even a "fully successful" rating. Likewise, the manager of a

FIGURE 36.1   Forced distribution: a potential scenario

Distinguished	5%
Superior	20%
Fully Successful	50%
Needs Improvement	20%
Unsatisfactory	5%

group of all-stars is restricted from giving appropriately high ratings to his outstanding cadre of performers. And exactly half of the people in each group, regardless of either the relative or absolute quality of their performance, must be rated as "fully successful."

Another problem with the proposed distribution scheme above is that it exactly mirrors a bell-shaped curve. Regardless of how well people in the organization actually perform, in this example, the manager is required to allocate performance ratings to fit a Gaussian statistical model. But a pure bell curve is almost never accurate in describing the distribution of human performance. For a legitimate bell-shaped Gaussian curve to be valid, there must be a sufficiently large population and a random distribution. But the employee population of an organization is never the result of random distribution. Companies do not hire people at random, i.e., selecting every fourteenth applicant. They do not promote people at random, selecting people for advancement by lottery or on an alphabetical basis. And in spite of the complaints that they do not do it fast enough or soon enough, organizations still weed out and terminate some members of the workforce whose performance is unacceptable.

Thus a normal distribution curve is almost never an appropriate model for the distribution of scores in a performance appraisal system. The distribution must take into account the fact that there will always be a positive skew—an appropriate positive skew—caused by organizational efforts to improve the quality of the employee population.

A better approach might be to allow some flexibility in the allocation of ratings, and to allow a positive rating skew to reflect the reality that the members of the organization are not performing at random. A better distribution requirement might be illustrated in Figure 36.2.

Now, instead of requiring that exactly 5 percent of all employees be rated "distinguished" regardless of the actual level of their performance, the revised distribution scheme allows managers to place up to 5 percent in that category—but there is nothing that says that anyone must be rated "distinguished." At the other end of the scale, the requirement has also been adjusted to provide a range of 2–5 percent of employees who are expected to fall into the "unsatisfactory" category. "Unsatisfactory" appraisal ratings are still mandatory but the requirement has been significantly reduced.

Instead of the rigid and fixed percentages that were required for each of the three middle performance appraisal ratings in the initial model, ranges have now

FIGURE 36.2   Forced distribution: a more flexible scenario

Distinguished	5% maximum
Superior	20%–30%
Good Solid Performer	50%–60%
Needs Improvement	10%–15%
Unsatisfactory	2%–5%

been provided. This will increase the flexibility of the system and allow managers of particularly poor-performing or high-performing work units to reflect that fact in the appraisal ratings they assign to their team members. Finally, the rigid bell-curve requirement has been adjusted to allow twice as many people to be assigned to the rating category one step higher than the middle rating than the one a step lower than the middle. In other words, 20–30 percent of all employees can expect to receive a "superior" rating while only 10–15 percent of all employees— half as many—are expected to fall into the "needs improvement" category.

But some important questions still need to be addressed.

- Is the distribution scheme described above in reality appropriate for an actual organization?

- How well will the system actually meet the needs of the two managers described earlier, the first saddled with a bunch of goof-offs and goldbrick and the second blessed with a cadre of champions?

- How should it be applied to a work unit with a very small population? For example, if there are only three people in the department, does that mean that no one can be rated "distinguished"?

- Should the distribution percentages merely be suggested, with flexibility allowed for individual managers to vary from the ranges if they can present a compelling case for variance, or must the distribution requirement absolutely be met by all?

- When, if ever, should exceptions be allowed? If a manager can demonstrate through hard business results that her team has outperformed any comparable unit in the organization, should she be allowed to award a greater percentage of higher ratings? And if another manager's unit produces only mediocre results, should he be prevented from awarding a "distinguished" or "superior" rating to anyone on the team?

- How do you control for variations in the standards and expectations of various managers? In one department the manager may evaluate a subordinate with a 98 percent customer satisfaction score as "needs improvement"; in the next department the same 98 percent customer satisfaction score may earn the employee a "superior" rating.

- Who will police the system, making sure that the guidelines are followed? Is that line management's job? Is it HR's? And what happens if the police are asleep on the beat and allow variances to get by?

- What will happen when a manager (or a whole department) ignores the guidelines? Will managers have to take their appraisals back and assign a different rating (provoking morale-destroying, buck-passing whines from spineless managers to their subordinates that "I really rated you 'superior' but personnel forced me to lower it to 'meets expectations.'") And what will happen if the manager has already had the performance appraisal discussion with the individual when the variance from the guidelines is noticed? Will changes be made?

All these issues must be addressed if a forced distribution component to a company's performance appraisal system is going to be included.

Whether the distribution is indeed "forced" through a set of rigid requirements, or merely offered as a set of guidelines that managers are expected to follow, forced distribution can help drive the truth into the performance management process.

SUMMARY

The rationale of forced ranking seems unassailable—in every group there will always be those who perform better than others. Whether by retraining or reassignment or termination, removing C players and replacing them with, hopefully, A and B players will increase the overall vitality and competitiveness and success of the organization. And while it may initially be painful to those who are identified as being in the lowest category, ultimately they too will benefit, for they will either improve their performance and join their colleagues as fully successful members of the team, or they will leave the organization and seek more congenial employment opportunities elsewhere.

Of course, managers should be doing this pruning and weeding routinely, using the performance management tools that organizations have long provided. But too many managers are reluctant to make meaningful differentiations among the troops, preferring a Lake Wobegon cocoon where all the children are above average.

In a relative comparison or forced ranking process, the comparison is not to numbers-on-a-scale. Instead, the comparison is person-to-person. When people are evaluated in isolation, against numbers on a scale, it is easy to rate everyone about the same. When people are compared side-by-side, the relative differences in their performance become much more apparent. Both approaches—relative and absolute comparisons—are appropriate, and both are needed to get a well-rounded and fully accurate picture of employee performance.

However, requiring relative comparisons strikes many as somehow unfair. Is it not possible, they argue, for a manager to assemble a team of highly talented and highly motivated performers, and through exemplary leadership enable all of them to surpass the goals no matter how high they are set? And is it not just as possible for a skilled teacher, given a classroom filled with bright, motivated, and energetic students, to have demanding expectations and still discover at the end of the semester that every single student has in fact earned an A?

Certainly it is possible. But while it is possible, it is not common. What is common is the fact that the quality of performance varies, and varies significantly, in both the classroom and the workplace. What is being asked in relative-comparison approaches—forced ranking systems of any kind—is that managers look at the performance of their subordinates in both absolute and relative terms. There are good reasons to insist on differentiation, if for no other reason than to ensure the universal expectation that people get what they deserve. Forced ranking generates differentiation and accountability. Used well, it is a fair and valid way of making sure that those who contribute the most are recognized for what they have done, and those at the opposite end of the contribution continuum are also recognized appropriately.

37

THE BALANCED SCORECARD AND COMPENSATION

Paul R. Niven, President

The Senalosa Group, Inc.

O**VER 150 YEARS AGO WILLIAM THOMPSON** presciently noted: "When you can measure what you are speaking about, and express it in numbers, you know something about it; but when you cannot measure it, when you cannot express it in numbers, your knowledge is of a meager and unsatisfactory kind." Measurement is a subject that has been with us as long as time has been recorded (perhaps the first measurement?) and the notion of tracking results touches virtually every facet of our lives today. Whether it is counting the calories we vowed to curtail as we savored our last sip of champagne on New Year's Eve, or tracking the miles per gallon on our new car, we simply love to tally things. Of course, measurement has been a staple in the organizational world for centuries, but was refined dramatically in the twentieth century thanks to innovations by early industrial pioneers such as DuPont and General Motors.

WHY ORGANIZATIONS NEED A BALANCED SCORECARD

Using performance measures to gage success is vital to any organization, whether operating in the private, public, or nonprofit sectors. Sadly, despite the importance of the topic, measurement has been under siege for a number of years with cries for change coming from both pundits and practitioners alike. Perhaps speaking for the multitudes of critics, much revered management guru Peter Drucker once went on record as suggesting that few factors are as important to the performance of an organization as measurement, and measurement is among the weakest areas of management today. Just why is measurement in such a deficient state anyway? Let us consider three factors that may explain the problems we face when attempting to accurately monitor our success through measurement.

The Limitations of Financial Measures

Traditionally, the measurement of business has been financial, in fact bookkeeping records can literally be traced back thousands of years. But a traditional focus on something, no matter how "tried and true" it may have been in the past, does not mean that it is well suited for today's environment. Such is the case with financial measures. Organizations ranging from Fortune 500 companies to local nonprofits to the federal government are beginning to question our almost exclusive reliance on these not so dependable gages of success. The chief criticism levied at financial measures is that they are tantamount to driving our car by the rearview mirror. You get a great view of where you have been, but little guidance towards where you are headed. So it is with financial measures. A good quarter, or year, one filled with economic success, is no guarantee of future financial rewards—just ask the folks at Enron! Even so called "great" companies, those that once graced the covers of business magazines and were the envy of their peer groups, can fall victim to this unfortunate scenario. Witness the vaunted Fortune 500 list; two-thirds of the companies compiling the inaugural list in 1954 had either vanished or were no longer large enough to maintain their presence on the list's fortieth anniversary.[1]

Despite their flaws, financial measures will continue to be vital yardsticks used in assessing the success of any organization. Even public and nonprofit enterprises, once thought to be immune to financial monitoring, must balance their desire to achieve mission outcomes with the reality of taxpayer and donor demands for efficiency. What we need is a performance measurement system that balances the historical accuracy and integrity of financial measures with the drivers of future financial success.

The Rise of Intangible Assets

Think about any organization with which you are affiliated. It could be your workplace, the nonprofit where you volunteer, or even your own family. Now, consider specifically what drives the success of that organization. Is it the physical equipment you possess, such as buildings and machinery? What about your personal computer? Probably not. If yours is like the vast majority of modern organizations, what is driving your success is not tangible assets, but their far more valuable and sustainable cousins, intangible assets. Isolating our discussion to the world of business, it is things like employee knowledge, databases full of rich information, and cultures of innovation and change that really drive value. Some recent estimates peg the value of intangibles as high as 75 percent of an organization's true worth. Our traditional financial measures have a very difficult time tracking intangible assets—how do you put a price on a motivated, skilled employee operating in an environment that encourages growth and change? As we move into the twenty-first century it is clear that today's performance yardsticks were designed for yesterday's challenges. We need a new performance measurement system, one that sheds light on the value of intangibles and allows us to predict and drive future economic success.

The Challenge of Executing Strategy

During my career I have had the opportunity to sit in on a number of strategy setting workshops and have always relished the spirited debates, the "Aha" moments of breathtaking clarity, and of course the ever-present jugs of coffee and trays of gourmet cookies. The freshly minted strategy emerging from these often grueling sessions is a justifiably pride-invoking achievement; however, it is a far cry from producing this document to living and breathing it day in and day out. But to succeed in any business today that is precisely what we must do—bring the strategy to life with the unmistakable clarity necessary for everyone in the organization to act on it each and every day. Let us face it—we have to execute not only to thrive but to simply stay alive in a business world in which 84 percent of respondents in one recent poll said that competition in their industry had significantly increased in the last five years.[2] And leaders, you know how vital it is to execute your strategy quickly; an oft quoted Fortune magazine study from 1999 found that seventy percent of CEO failures came not as a result of poor strategy, but the inability to execute.[3] Need one last shred of evidence to get your blood pumping—or maybe boiling? A team of researchers recently discovered that companies, on average, deliver only 63 percent of the financial performance their strategies promise.[4] The good news is that strategy implementation has been proven to boost financial fortunes rather significantly—one study suggested a 35 percent improvement in the quality of strategy implementation for the average firm was associated with a 35 percent improvement in shareholder value.[5] Unfortunately, many organizations fall off the strategy execution track—frequently in dramatic fashion—simply because their measurement systems focus almost entirely on financial targets, ignoring the enablers of strategy implementation.

Given what we have covered thus far is it any wonder the measurement naysayers are striking such a resonant chord with organizational audiences around the globe? The challenges are profound and significant—the limitations of traditional financial metrics, the demands of a society of knowledge workers, and the absolute imperative of executing strategy. Fortunately, a tool has emerged which has proven capable of overcoming those and a host of other challenges along its path to the pantheon of business systems. That tool is the Balanced Scorecard, and in this chapter we will examine the fundamental principles of this revolutionary management system, and later I will introduce you to one of thousands of organizations around the globe that has reaped tremendous rewards from its Balanced Scorecard investment—Horizon Fitness.

THE BALANCED SCORECARD

The Balanced Scorecard was developed in 1990 by Robert Kaplan and David Norton. Interestingly, Kaplan is an accounting professor at Harvard University. Given his profession you might suspect that he had a vested interest in safeguarding the vaunted position of financial numbers. But Kaplan was a visionary; he realized that financial numbers alone would not be enough for organizations attempting to thrive, or even compete, in the twenty-first century. To that end, he and Norton organized a research study of a dozen companies, attempting to discern "best practices" in performance measurement. Out of that study the Balanced Scorecard was born.

The basic premise behind the Balanced Scorecard is a simple, yet profound, one. Financial measures are, and always will be, important, but they must be supplemented with other indicators which predict future financial success. With that as their goal, Kaplan and Norton developed the Balanced Scorecard framework. Strategy is the center of the framework. Unlike traditional performance measurement systems that have financial controls at their core, the Balanced Scorecard begins with an organization's strategy. We seek to *translate* the strategy into objectives and measures which can be tracked and used to gage our success in the successful implementation of strategy.

For profit driven enterprises, the *financial perspective* is placed at the top of the Scorecard model. The objectives and measures chosen here represent "the end in mind" of their strategic story and normally focus on profits, revenue growth, productivity, and asset utilization. With financial measures determined, the Scorecard poses an important question: how do we derive this profit or growth? Well, from customers of course. Thus we shift our focus to the *customer perspective*. Here we measure our performance from the eyes of our customer. What do they expect or demand from us—timely service, quality, a deeper relationship, accuracy, price, accessibility? By answering these questions we can derive measures that allow us to track our success from their perspective. Next we turn our gaze inward and examine our *internal business processes*. To meet customer demands there are core business processes at which we must excel. Every organization will have dozens if not hundreds of processes (manufacturing, order entry, branding, reporting, etc.) but in this perspective we are attempting to measure our performance on those that directly impact performance for our customers. If, for example, we determine that our customers demand a low price, we could measure price relative to our competitors in the customer perspective. Internally, we must excel at low-cost manufacturing in order to offer low prices, and therefore we measure our manufacturing cycle time in that perspective. Finally, the Scorecard forces us to grapple with the true value-creating mechanisms of modern organizations, intangible assets. We do so in the *learning and growth perspective*. Here we focus on measuring three things: human capital (employee skills, training, etc.), information capital (access to information for example), and organizational capital— the ability to change and sustain success (culture, teamwork, etc.). Sometimes considered "soft stuff," these measures are truly the enablers of everything else appearing on an organization's Balanced Scorecard.

The Balanced Scorecard Gets Results

I first met Bob Whip, CEO of Horizon Fitness, on a blustery December night in Madison, Wisconsin. The company had engaged me to assist them in the development of a Balanced Scorecard and Bob was kind enough to collect me at the airport on that chilly winter's night. As we drove to the hotel Bob gave me the Horizon story: a new company in 2000 they amassed $6.6 million of revenue in that first year, but Bob had a grand strategy as the manufacturer and distributor of fitness equipment, one that would see sales grow dramatically over the next few years. The strategy he laid out was sound, but the problem as we both knew was execution.

Using the Balanced Scorecard as their template for success, Bob and a team of senior managers at Horizon translated their strategy into a set of measures spanning the four Scorecard perspectives, and soon began using the results to drive the agenda of monthly and quarterly management review sessions. Additionally, they transformed the Balanced Scorecard from a mere measurement tool to a powerful strategic management and communication device by linking resource allocation decisions to Scorecard measures and communicating Scorecard objectives and measures to all employees in an effort to ensure they could define their unique contribution to the growing company's success. On the resource allocation link Bob notes,

> It definitely makes budgeting easier. For example, if the proposed expenditures are not in alignment with our strategy then the expense is rejected. This has given us a great deal of focus in settling our annual budgets as it tests our expenditures and takes a lot of the guess work and emotion out of budget decision making. It also makes it easier to justify expenditures to our board of directors.[6]

Horizon Fitness, now in just their fourth year of Balanced Scorecard use, has seen transformative results from their investment in strategy execution. The

Scorecard has become a powerful tool for training and orienting new employees to the company's strategy, has introduced a new level of accountability to the management ranks, is relied upon to communicate strategy to all stakeholders, and most importantly the focus it fosters has helped the company reach over $85 million of sales in its most recent fiscal year. Given those impressive results it is not surprising to hear Bob say, "We like the flexibility of the BSC system of management and would strongly recommend it to any company."[7]

Like Horizon Fitness, thousands of organizations have harnessed the simple, but not simplistic, principles embodied in the Balanced Scorecard model to achieve tremendous results. From an unrelenting focus on strategy, to employee alignment around a few key goals, to breakthrough financial results, these organizations have used the Balanced Scorecard as a powerful measurement and management system, one truly suited for the modern world we face.

LINKING THE BALANCED SCORECARD TO COMPENSATION

Some will argue that aligning rewards to Balanced Scorecard targets provides merely extrinsic motivation and could possibly hamper innovation, creativity, and fulfillment. A more optimistic, and pragmatic, view illuminates another possibility. Linking the Scorecard to compensation is simply an added benefit that completes a true win–win arrangement.

Simply developing the Balanced Scorecard and sharing it with employees across the organization holds the strong prospect of increasing intrinsic motivation. Employees, possibly for the first time, now have the opportunity to gain an in-depth knowledge of the company's strategy and define the role they will play in its achievement. Brainstorming performance measures and questioning the hypothesis underlying the Scorecard are intellectual tasks that serve to amply stretch the cognitive and organizational abilities of every employee participating in any level of Scorecard development. There is little doubt that knowledge and involvement are powerful levers in enhancing intrinsic motivation. The Balanced Scorecard offers the possibility of both.

Providing extrinsic rewards should not lead to the erosion of motivation produced by developing the Balanced Scorecard. Rather it acts as a laser, focusing the attention of all employees on the critical drivers of organizational success. The two motivational factors work together in this scenario. Involving all employees in the development of Balanced Scorecards increases intrinsic motivation, which is used to develop breakthrough solutions in the achievement of Scorecard targets. Exceeding the targets then translates into performance rewards to be shared by all those who made the valuable contributions necessary for success.

While the discussion above focuses mainly on theoretical considerations for linking the Balanced Scorecard to compensation, a more pragmatic inducement is represented by recent studies which find that top performers are focusing heavily on pay in their decision to leave employers. In a survey of about 1,100 U.S. employees, Watson Wyatt found that 71 percent of top performers listed pay among the top three reasons they would consider leaving their employer. Managers are fond of saying employees leave because of bad bosses or limited growth opportunities, but the research says otherwise. This should not come as a surprise, however, when you consider that pay increases have been modest in recent times and employee-borne health care costs have more than doubled since 2002.[8]

We will now examine how you can link a Balanced Scorecard system to compensation. We will begin by considering the attributes of such a link, and conclude with potential methods for the union.

DESIGN ATTRIBUTES TO CONSIDER

No two Balanced Scorecard implementations will be completely alike. Each and every organization choosing to use the Scorecard system will manipulate the tool to fit individual culture, current managerial processes, and the state of organizational readiness for such a major change initiative. Linking the Scorecard to compensation will result in even greater individual differences. Historical pay preferences, possible presence of union contracts, and the variety of job classes are but a few of the many factors affecting the incentive pay decision. Let your creativity soar here and you will be rewarded with a program that cements focus and alignment toward your overall goals, and when the going gets tough think of those traveling the Scorecard path before you, 86 percent of whom agreed or strongly agreed in a recent study that the Scorecard should be linked to compensation in order to help support appropriate behavior.[9]

To assist you in designing a system that is customized for you, here are a number of design issues for your consideration. Readers should note that all references to compensation contained thus far and in the remainder of the chapter signify "variable" or "incentive" compensation. Base salary is normally not affected by the Balanced Scorecard.

Planning the Compensation Link

- *Purpose:* What is the overall purpose of your linkage of compensation to the Balanced Scorecard? What specific behaviors are you attempting to encourage or discourage? How will the new pay plan affect the culture of the organization? Having an overarching purpose in mind will help guide your efforts in a direction that best suits your individual needs.

- *Communication:* Stephen Covey has referred to employee compensation as "rice bowl" issues. Messing with someone's rice bowl, whether in a positive or negative vein, is bound to stir up a lot of interest. There tends to be an air of controversy surrounding even the most well-intentioned compensation schemes, so it is in your best interests to communicate the specifics of the plan to your entire employee audience as soon as the plan is developed. Actually, even before the plan is developed it should be reviewed and discussed with employee focus groups. You must ensure the perception among employees is that the plan is fair and equitable. Communication efforts not only enlighten everyone as to the compensation plan but may also be used to demonstrate the value and benefits to be derived from using the Balanced Scorecard as a key component of your overall management system.

■ *Development:* Who will be involved in the development of the new program? As with all other aspects of the Balanced Scorecard, you should attempt to involve a variety of participants in the design of your new pay program. The different perspectives and functions represented will help ensure the new process is perceived as fair and equitable throughout the company. Perceived fairness is an issue that should not be taken lightly. Research on pay programs at a variety of companies has demonstrated that employees are more concerned with the equality and fairness represented by the program than they are with the actual amount of monetary rewards available.

■ *System Review:* There is a lot at stake with your compensation plan, and it is certain to be closely watched by all employees once up and running. Make it clear from the outset that you plan to review the entire program within 12 months of its initial launch. Stating this intention in a forthright manner from the beginning will send a strong signal that you are committed to making any necessary adjustments to ensure the plan functions as anticipated in a manner assuring everyone's best interests at heart. This way, if modifications must be made they will not be perceived as changing the rules in midstream or subjectively altering the program to stack the deck in management's favor.

Design Elements

■ *Timing:* You may be anxious to link rewards to performance and consider establishing the bond in the first year of your implementation. However, there are a number of issues you must ponder prior to launching the program. The primary concern relates to the measures you have selected for your initial Balanced Scorecard. Performance measures represent a hypothesis, or your best guess, as to what it will take to execute your strategy. Most organizations I work with will make changes to their original Scorecard objectives and measures as their implementation progresses along the path to maturity. Linking pay to measures that may or may not stand the test of time is a dangerous proposition. Employees will be motivated to achieve the targets you establish, and, as we have all heard, "you get what you measure." Can you afford to pay for results that do not necessarily assist you in fulfilling your strategic objectives? Another issue is data collection. The Scorecard will often result in developing brand new performance measures for which a reliable data source is currently unavailable. Obviously you do not want to link rewards to measures you cannot accurately report. In addition to the possibility of inaccurate data you may not have the requisite systems to manage the pay program. Variable compensation is among the least automated items on a typical profit and loss statement, but given the potentially volatile swings of payouts you need methods of accurately tracking your compensation liability.

- *Involvement:* Will every employee be eligible for participation in the new pay program, or is involvement limited to certain categories of your staff? Many organizations will pilot the linkage of compensation to the Balanced Scorecard with their executives. This approach certainly has merit since the senior team was most likely involved in the development of the Scorecard and has a vested interest in the outcomes of all performance measures. However, it is often the lower levels of the organization who lack awareness and knowledge of the Balanced Scorecard. Extending the pay program to all employees greatly enhances the likelihood of increasing knowledge and advocacy of the Balanced Scorecard. Related to the issue of involvement is the question of whether incentive pay should be awarded to individuals or groups. Awarding individuals recognizes outstanding achievement and can motivate excellent performance in the future. However, most organizations today rely heavily on interdependence and the sharing of information across the enterprise. Rewarding individuals in this environment could potentially impede the knowledge sharing and collaboration necessary to generate innovative solutions. This has been empirically demonstrated, as researchers have determined that information sharing is minimized when individual rewards are the norm.[10] Practitioners are mixed on this point. Some provide only group rewards in an effort to stimulate teamwork and collective accountability, while others provide a mix of individual and team rewards.

- *Number of performance measures included:* Psychologists suggest that we humans have difficulty concentrating on more than seven items at any given time. Have you ever noticed how many things seem to involve the magical number seven? The Seven Habits of Highly Effective People and seven deadly sins for example. Does this mean we should limit to less than seven the number of performance measures linked to compensation? Some would say yes, and suggest that a smaller number of measures is yet another method of sharpening focus on the critical drivers of success. No magic number exists, however. Most practitioners, when initially creating the Scorecard-to-compensation link, will limit the number of measures impacting pay, often choosing one measure from each of the four perspectives. Some will actually restrict the bond to one key metric. In the mid 1990s Continental Airlines determined the key to their turnaround was on-time departures and paid a $65 cash bonus to all nonmanagement employees in any month the company was in the top five of U.S. carriers on the measure.

■ *Perspectives of measures:* Not only is the number of measures linked to compensation an element for consideration, but the type of measure must also be contemplated. Will you attach rewards to the achievement of only the most verifiable and objective indicators, normally represented by financial measures. Or, will meeting targets of measures located in other perspectives also lead to rewards? In one study focusing on the linkage of compensation to the Balanced Scorecard it was discovered that leading Scorecard organizations are aligning rewards with measures from all four perspectives. However, the weights assigned to each perspective are not always equal. Most respondents applied a heavier weight to financial measures, which averaged about 40 percent of the potential reward. Customer, internal process, and the employee learning and growth perspectives were weighted approximately 20 percent each.[11] Deciding to include nonfinancial measures in your calculation can heighten the challenges associated with the process. While you would like your nonfinancial indicators to focus on outcomes, a key benefit of the Scorecard is the articulation of leading indicators of performance—measures predictive of future results—that are not always outcome-based. For example, you may hypothesize that "hours spent with customers" is a leading indicator of "repeat purchases." However, aligning compensation with "hours spent with customers" could lead sales people to amass unnecessary time with non-purchasing customers simply to boost the chance of receiving an incentive award. Incentives should be balanced so that both leading and lagging indicators of performance are appropriately represented and lead to the outcomes you desire.

■ *Measure timing:* Another measure-related consideration is whether rewards should be linked to short-term or long-term performance. Some argue the Balanced Scorecard is a tool for sustaining success over the long term, and thus a true indication of success is best measured by examining enduring accomplishment. Additionally, by linking rewards to long-term success there is no incentive to sacrifice long-term benefits for the sake of achieving a short-term gain. Others point to the motivational benefit of providing more frequent rewards along the path to long-term prosperity. Proponents of this camp will suggest that generating positive Scorecard results and sharing the rewards with employees on an annual, or even more frequent, basis serves to strengthen the commitment of all organizational participants to the achievement of strategic goals.

■ *Performance thresholds:* There are those who believe paying incentives on individual measure results when overall organizational objectives have not been met obscures the focus needed from all employees. For that reason some organizations will not distribute any rewards unless a predetermined standard or cap is met. Normally this hurdle will be represented by a high-level financial metric such as return on equity. This approach ensures that all employees know very well what the key driver of success is for the organization and helps them align their efforts in exceeding it. However, the problem with this course of action is that employees may feel bitter or resentful if for reasons beyond their control a high-level financial objective has fallen short while other performance goals are met.

- *Funding:* Do not forget this very pragmatic element of any compensation plan—from where does the money flow? Will the potential payouts associated with exceeding Scorecard targets be funded from the firm's budget, or do you expect savings generated from the Scorecard to "self-fund" the incentives? And just how much do you plan to offer in incentives? Involving both your executive team and the professionals in your human resources department will help you develop solutions to these issues.

METHODS OF LINKING THE BALANCED SCORECARD TO COMPENSATION

As noted previously, you have virtually unlimited choices when making a link from the Balanced Scorecard to compensation. The many permutations and combinations of award triggers, measures, and potential outcomes are staggering. Organizations pursuing this link will undoubtedly travel many different routes but all arrive at the same conclusion—aligning rewards with Scorecard results leads to increased attention on the critical drivers of the organization. Let us examine some of the methods used to combine Scorecard measures and compensation.

Basing Rewards on Overall Results

The simplest method of tying Balanced Scorecard performance to rewards is using the highest-level organizational Scorecard as the barometer of success and arbiter of bonuses. Under this scenario a certain percentage of incentive compensation is available to employees should the organization achieve some or all of its goals. Each measure on the high-level Scorecard is assigned a weight, with total weights across the four perspectives summing to 100 percent. Financial targets will often receive a higher weight, reflecting the value management continues to place on achieving fiscal success. As results are tracked, percentage payouts are calculated and distributed. Depending on the level of program sophistication, this allocation of rewards may take place monthly, quarterly, semi-annually, or annually. Here is an example of how the program might work.

Let us say an organization is willing to extend a 10 percent annual bonus (of base salary) to employees based on Scorecard results. The company tracks a total

TABLE 37.1   Balanced Scorecard Measures

Perspective	Measure	Target	Weight
Financial	Return on equity	15%	30%
	Revenue growth	25%	10%
Customer	Customer satisfaction	75%	15%
	Repeate purchase percentage	80%	5%
Internal processes	On-time delivery	90%	10%
	Manufacturing efficiency	85%	10%
Employee learning and growth	Competency attainment–percentage of employees gaining 3 new competencise	70%	12%
	Employee turnover	5%	8%

of eight measures across the four perspectives as shown in Table 37.1. Final results are reported at year-end, and the employee bonus is calculated as shown in Table 37.2.

The organization achieved its return on equity target and since it makes up 30 percent of the total weight of all measures employees will receive 3.0 percent of their base salary based on that result. Based on the positive Scorecard results achieved, the total award adds up to 7.5 percent of base salary. In this example the payout is conducted annually. However, to ensure employees remain locked in on overall goals, the organization would be wise to provide regular (perhaps monthly) feedback on Scorecard results.

TABLE 37.2   Balanced Scorecard Payout Based on Measures

Perspective	Measure	Target	Weight	Actual	Payout
Financial	Return on equity	15%	30%	16.5%	3.0%
	Revenue growth	25%	10%	20%	0
Customer	Customer satisfaction	75%	15%	77%	1.5%
	Repeat purchase percentage	80%	5%	75%	0
Internal processes	On-time delivery	90%	10%	85%	0
	Manufacturing efficiency	85%	10%	85%	1.0%
Employee learning and growth	Competency attainment–percentage of employees gaining 3 new competencies	70%	12%	75%	1.2%
	Employee turnover	5%	8%	4%	0.8%
				Total payout	7.5%

The simplicity of this method makes it very transparent and ideal for communication to the entire workforce. As Scorecard results are monitored throughout the year, they form the basis for strategic conversations from top to bottom within the firm. Issues associated with this technique include the degree of stretch involved in the targets, and the lack of any thresholds that must be achieved before bonuses are awarded. Using this method of incentive compensation it is conceivable that employees will receive a bonus whether or not the firm achieves its overall financial objectives. This could send a message inconsistent with the theory of the Balanced Scorecard, which asserts that positive results on measures in the lower perspectives will drive improved financial performance.

DRIVING THE LINK TO ALL LEVELS OF THE ORGANIZATION

Many Scorecard-adopting organizations put tremendous energy into establishing the all-important line-of-sight from individual action to overall goals. This process of cascading not only informs employees of how they can influence results, but also serves as a powerful mechanism for using the Balanced Scorecard as a true strategic management system. In this section we will discuss the use of cascaded Scorecards as the springboard for making a connection between the Scorecard and compensation. In contrast to the approach discussed in the previous section, which relied on overall corporate results to dictate bonus allotments, using the cascading technique aligns awards with results that hit closer to home for employees. Cascading displays how individual employees are able to influence higher-level goals, and the associated compensation link demonstrates the rewards that await outstanding performance at the business unit, department, or individual level.

Nova Scotia Power Inc., a Canadian electric utility, is one organization that used the cascading method of linking the Balanced Scorecard to compensation. The utility's Scorecard implementation had proven very successful even from the earliest stage of development. However, managers continually noted that until the new system was linked to paychecks it would never become "real" in the minds of most employees. Senior management took this advice to heart and developed a system of incentive compensation that aligned rewards with the successful achievement of Balanced Scorecard targets.

The first level of compensation cascading at Nova Scotia Power took place when each member of the executive team developed a Personal Balanced Scorecard based on the Corporate Scorecard. The weights assigned to each perspective and associated measures were relatively balanced; however, each executive overweighted those areas in which he or she was best able to contribute. For example, the Vice President and Chief Financial Officer developed a Scorecard with representative measures in each of the four perspectives, but the Financial perspective and related measures were assigned the greatest weight given the nature of the CFO's work and its impact on these critical indicators. Similarly, the

Vice President of Sales and Marketing overweighted the customer perspective. Scorecards developed at the executive level contained a mix of measures, some pulled directly from the Corporate Balanced Scorecard and others describing how the executive would influence the corporate indicators. Rather than using one target for each measure, three were developed, with each indicating increasing degrees of stretch. Percentages of base salary were linked to each, representing its degree of difficulty. A threshold target stood for minimum acceptable performance on the measure. No incentive compensation would be paid on a measure for which the threshold was not achieved. Midpoint targets represented better than average performance and therefore warranted increased rewards. Finally, stretch targets were considered best in class and required significant effort to be met. Therefore, additional incentives awaited their achievement.

Balanced Scorecards were then developed at the business unit, department, and individual level of the organization. As with the executive Scorecards, every group or individual assigned weights to each perspective, and developed corresponding threshold, midpoint, and stretch targets. All Scorecard measures and targets were reviewed and approved by management to ensure adequate coverage of corporate strategic themes, and achievable yet challenging targets. Nova Scotia Power wanted to leave no doubt in employees' minds that meeting their return on equity target was critical for the ongoing success of the organization. Therefore, they decreed that no incentive awards would be paid unless the corporation met this financial target. This message served to galvanize employees around meeting their own Scorecard targets, which they knew from cascading experience would help drive the overall corporate results.

COMPETENCY-BASED PAY

Towers Perrin has reported that, while only 8 percent of surveyed organizations currently use competency based pay systems, a whopping 78 percent plan to implement such a system in the near future.[12] As the world of work continues to evolve from machines to knowledge, the focus on competencies appears to make sense. Organizations have squeezed practically every last drop out of process improvement and reengineering. Nothing is left but the greatest source of productivity enhancements of all: human knowledge. Competency-based systems with their painstaking attention to the attributes and behaviors necessary to effectively compete in today's environment can drive the changes organizations require to succeed. Basing pay on competencies is a dramatic shift from the old world of seniority-dependent pay.

Assuming you cascade the Balanced Scorecard, all employees can use their individual Balanced Scorecard to track the addition of key competencies. As a logical extension, incentive compensation may be directed toward the acquisition of competencies. Employees who can demonstrate they have been able to add new competencies to their repertoire are allotted an incentive award. One potential drawback is the concern that an exclusive focus on competencies may lead to lesser concentration on actual performance results. Therefore, a caveat when considering this approach is that pay for competencies must be balanced with results, especially in the short term. Other measures on the Balanced Scorecard can be used to provide a balance between new skills and attributes and the results they collectively produce.

Gainsharing

Gainsharing is an improvement system that relies on employee actions to enhance organizational results. Key measures of performance are developed and targets for improvements or cost savings are agreed upon. Any savings generated from the improved results are shared with employees through incentive bonuses. Gainsharing experts suggest that organizations engaging in this technique

> must be willing to engage in at least some form of employee involvement that shares business information, educates employees in the economics of business, and encourages suggestions. Without moving information, knowledge, and power downward, it is unlikely that a significant line of sight will develop and that the plan will be successful.[13]

Sounds to me like they are describing the need for a Balanced Scorecard to make gainsharing work. The Scorecard involves employees in its design, provides unlimited educational opportunities, encourages suggestions through the questioning of assumptions, and creates a powerful line of sight.

Performance measures developed for the Balanced Scorecard can serve as the guiding force behind a gainsharing program. Each of the four perspectives may contain measures that have an economic element and can be used to drive cost savings throughout the organization. As Scorecard results are tracked over time, any savings can be distributed to employees in the form of incentive compensation.

Nonmonetary Rewards

A recent study conducted by Mercer Human Resource Consulting discovered that 70 percent of companies now use some type of nonmonetary recognition for incentive rewards.[14] As powerful as the lure of a pocketful of greenbacks can be, sometimes it helps to have a tangible reward in front of us to focus our attention on something we can see, feel, and grasp. That is what Goodyear found a few years back when they sponsored a campaign to improve tire sales. Two large employee groups were monitored; one was offered monetary rewards, and the other was offered merchandise. The group receiving tangible rewards outperformed the cash awards group by nearly 50 percent.[15] Programs of this nature appeal to a basic desire to want what we do not have. While a cash bonus is nice, chances are the prudent voice in our head will scream that paying down some debts with the windfall, or starting a child's college fund is the only thing to do. But when management dangles a flat screen television in front of us it is difficult not to picture ourselves curled up on the sofa channel surfing to our heart's delight, all the while marveling at the crystal clear images beaming forth. For some that physical product creates more desire and attention than the ephemeral joy of cash and fashions nonmonetary rewards a fulfilling supplement to cash bonuses.

For some companies the idea of a cash-based incentive program makes great sense but their union contracts prohibit the use of such tools. In these circumstances creative teams have developed innovative ways of recognizing employee and organizational success without distributing the usual monetary award. Scorecard architects Kaplan and Norton describe the case of Texaco Refinery and Marketing Inc. (TRMI).[16] Constrained by their union agreements, this organization turned to a points program to reward success. Points, each with a par value of $1, were awarded based on plant-wide, work-group, team, and individual results. The accumulated points could be redeemed for merchandise, travel, and retail awards. Results were swift and dramatic. In the very first year of the plan two plants set records for utilization, expense reduction, and safety.

SUMMARY

An anonymous sage once noted "Money is the root of all evil." To which George Bernard Shaw wittily retorted, "Lack of money is the root of all evil." I think we can probably all point to evidence of both. Regardless of where you stand on this issue, one thing is clear: organizations have in the past rewarded excellence with the allocation of monetary rewards, and will continue to do so in the future. This chapter investigated how the Balanced Scorecard can be profitably linked to your incentive compensation system. Summarizing the topic very nicely, Scorecard architects Kaplan and Norton note: "When all individuals understand how their pay is linked to achieving strategic objectives . . . strategy truly becomes everyone's everyday job."[17] When constructed with care, and executed with precision, the Balanced Scorecard and compensation link can create a situation in which everyone wins.

Note: Portions of this chapter are drawn directly from Paul Niven's book, Balanced Scorecard Step by Step: Maximizing Performance and Maintaining Results (2nd edn), *John Wiley & Sons, 2006. He has updated and adapted the work for the present publication.*

END NOTES

1. Thomas A. Stewart, *Intellectual Capital*. New York: Currency, 1999, p. xxi.

2. McKinsey Quarterly Global Survey of Business Executives, November 2004.

3. R. Charan and G. Colvin, "Why CEOs Fail," *Fortune*, June 21, 1999.

4. Michael C. Mankins and Richard Steele, "Turning Great Strategy Into Great Performance," *Harvard Business Review*, July–August, 2005, pp. 65–72.

5. Brian E. Becker, Mark A. Huselid, and Dave Ulrich, *The HR Scorecard*. Boston, MA: Harvard Business School Press, 2001.

6. From author interview with Bob Whip, October 10, 2005.

7. Ibid.

8. Erin White, "Opportunity Knocks, and it Pays a Lot Better," *Wall Street Journal*, Monday, November 13, 2006, p. B3.

9. Raef A. Lawson, William G. Stratton, and Toby Hatch, "Scorecarding in North America: Moving Toward a Best Practices Framework, Part I," *Cost Management*, July–August 2005, pp. 25–34.

10. Marshall W. VanAlstyne, "Create Colleagues, Not Competitors," *Harvard Business Review*, September, 2005, p. 24.

11. Todd Manas, "Making the Balanced Scorecard Approach Pay Off," *ACA Journal*, Second Quarter 1999.

12. Marie Gendron, "Competencies and What They Mean To You," *Harvard Management Update*, September, 1996.

13. Edward E. Lawler III, *Rewarding Excellence*. San Francisco, CA: Jossey-Bass, 2000.

14. Alix Nyberg, "Motivating the Middle," *CFO*, October 2005, pp. 63–70.

15. Adrian Gostick and Chester Elton, *Managing With Carrots*. Salt Lake City, UT: Gibbs-Smith, 2001.

16. Robert S. Kaplan and David P. Norton, *The Strategy Focused Organization*. Boston, MA: Harvard Business School Press, 2001.

17. Ibid., p. 271.

PERFORMANCE METRICS AND COMPENSATION

Mark Graham Brown, President

Mark Graham Brown & Associates

T HE FOUNDATION OF ANY SUCCESSFUL compensation plan is that it serves to drive the right employee behavior. The metrics or measure upon which compensation is based is the most important part of the system. Selecting the wrong measures can result in rewarding undesirable behavior and decision making. Following are 10 rules for creating effective performance measures that can then be linked to bonuses or compensation are discussed.

RULE 1: SELECT MEASURES THAT LINK TO KEY OUTCOMES EMPLOYEES CAN INFLUENCE

Process is a big word these days. Organizations are implementing approaches like Lean and Six Sigma to analyze and improve the processes used to get day-to-day work accomplished. Measures are often created around processes and improvements that are based upon human behavior. A good scorecard or set of performance measures should include a balance of leading and lagging or process and outcome measures. However, compensation should be based on outcome metrics, not process measures. Outcomes like sales, customer referrals, profits, projects completed successfully, and new products introduced on time are easily measured and important to the overall success of the organization. The problem with process measures is that they often do not predict success of outcome measures. This is especially true of processes that include a lot of human behavior. If a process is highly automated such as manufacturing aluminum, process measures and standards are based on solid research and directly linked to key product outcome measures. Most processes in today's organizations involve a great deal of human behavior and are not as much a science as manufacturing aluminum. For example, building a relationship with a customer is not a formula, and what works with one customer may alienate another.

The challenge when defining outcome measures upon which to base compensation is to ensure that the employees have the ability to achieve the outcome or at least contribute to it. Achieving most outcomes in an organization is a joint effort of a number of departments or units. The way to use these outcomes metrics for compensation is to assign a percentage weight to each group that contributes to the outcome measure, based on their level of influence. For example, a measure like sales of new products might be on the scorecard of R&D, sales, marketing, and manufacturing. Each of these four functions has some degree of influence over the measure, but some have more control than others. The weights of each of these groups might look like the example below:

R&D	50 percent
Marketing	20 percent
Sales	20 percent
Manufacturing	10 percent

Bonuses for R&D personnel might include other measures over which they have greater control, such as patents, products in the pipeline, or project milestones met, but the heavier weight should be on the outcome metrics, even though they must work with others to achieve good performance.

RULE 2: AVOID LINKING COMPENSATION TO OVERALL COMPANY PERFORMANCE

A common practice is to link employee bonuses to overall measures of company performance such as hitting a sales or profit target, stock price, or other high level financial measures of company success. While this is a good practice for compensating executives, it is not productive for most employees. The flawed logic is that everyone will then work harder to help the company stock price rise, or achieve some financial goal if their pay is tied to it. The reality is that the vast majority of employees see absolutely no connection between their own job performance and overall company performance. A sales manager might have her best year ever and beat her growth target by 15 percent, yet receive no bonus because the company had a big R&D project fail, eating up all potential profits. An individual employee in a call center was rated number three in the entire company for her customer service performance, but sadly receives no bonus because the company did not hit its customer satisfaction targets. Compensation should be linked to metrics for individual job performance, not company performance. The more control an individual has over performing well on certain measures, the more powerful the compensation based on those measures will be in driving desirable behavior.

RULE 3: AVOID BASING COMPENSATION ON METRICS THAT ARE EASY TO MANIPULATE

It is currently common to link performance-based pay to measures of customer satisfaction. This is a good idea. The problem with this in many organizations is that there is only one measure of customer satisfaction—the dreaded survey. Whether it is one question (a recent trend) or 50, survey data is easy to manipulate. A national real estate company I worked with counted on agents to hand out customer surveys at the end of a transaction to get buyers and sellers to rate their performance. When the agents knew that the transaction had not gone well and they were likely to get a bad score, they forgot to hand out the survey and ended up getting all high ratings. Car dealers are notorious for calling customers before a survey goes out and offering free detailing or other services in exchange for high ratings. I recently got a letter from my dealer after leasing a new car suggesting that I call the service manager first if I planned on marking anything less than the highest ratings regarding the sales process.

When you start linking pay to performance, people get very creative in coming up with ways of making the numbers look good without doing the work that the measure was intended to reward. Cheating on performance measures is not limited to surveys. All kinds of measures and data collection methods are subject to manipulation. Using an outside company to collect the data helps to ensure integrity in the data, but even that can be manipulated. A hotel I stayed in recently uses J.D. Power to do their customer satisfaction surveys. A letter in the room from the hotel manager informed me of the upcoming survey, asking for my feedback, and suggesting that if there was anything I was not 100 percent satisfied with, I should call guest services to get it remedied before I checked out.

RULE 4: AVOID OVERLY COMPLICATED COMPENSATION FORMULAS

In order to avoid driving behavior that is counter-productive by basing compensation on a single measure of performance such as sales or units produced, some organizations create indices or analytics that are a summary of several aspects of performance. This makes a lot more sense than trying to measure a complex dimension of performance with a singular measure. My most recent book (*Beyond the Balanced Scorecard—Improving Business Intelligence with Analytics*, Productivity Press, 2007) presents a number of examples from business and government of some of these index measures. The idea is that an overall measure of something like R&D might include some leading or process metrics like new products in the pipeline, patents, and project management metrics like milestones, along with lagging measures like industry firsts, sales, and profits from new products. Each of the subfactors in the analytic is assigned a percentage weight based on factors such as its importance, data integrity, and other factors. The summary gage or analytic then displays performance on typically a 0–100 scale. This approach allows you to combine unlike units of measurement such as number of patents, percentage of milestones met, and revenue in sales from new products into a single metric.

While these analytic metrics are an excellent way for senior management to measure various aspects of performance, these summary analytics or indices are often too complicated to use for determining compensation for all employees. Employees should be able to track through the year how they are doing at earning a bonus. If bonuses are paid frequently (e.g., monthly), this is less of a problem, but it is still important that employees see a connection between their own job performance and the payout they are going to receive. If employees are mostly in the dark regarding how much bonus they are likely to receive, or cannot explain the formula used to compute bonuses, you need to modify the metric to make it easier to understand.

RULE 5: SET REALISTIC AND ACHIEVABLE TARGETS

It is hard enough to come up with valid performance measures that are likely to drive the right behavior from employees. It is even more difficult to set realistic targets or objectives for those metrics. It becomes very frustrating to be given a target that is linked to your pay that is unrealistically high. Leaders often think that setting ridiculously high targets will motivate people to stretch and work as hard as they can to get the payout. What more often happens is that they become disgruntled and frustrated.

When setting targets for any metric it is important to consider:

- past performance averages
- best past performance
- competitor performance
- industry averages or typical performance
- customer and/or stakeholder priorities and needs

- resource constraints (time, dollar headcount, technical capabilities)
- links to other metrics

Targets should be set high enough so that the organization achieves high levels of performance, but should be realistic as well. A hospital I worked with had a target of 50 percent patient satisfaction, which sounds like a ridiculously low objective, but not when you consider that past performance was in the 30 percent range, and current performance was 42 percent patient satisfaction. For some metrics it becomes difficult to set a target that is less than perfection. For example, an airline would not set a target of 95 percent safe landings. A manufacturing organization would not set a target of only having 10 serious injuries or accidents this year. Achieving high levels of performance on one metric might result in poor performance on other related metrics, so that needs to be considered. For example, a corporate law department I worked with dramatically reduced their cycle time for processing company documents. However, as a result of rushing through each task, several mistakes were made that cost millions in lawsuits. Targets and metrics need to be balanced so as to not put too much focus on a single aspect of performance.

RULE 6: MEASURE PERFORMANCE AS OFTEN AS POSSIBLE

Whatever you decide to measure to assess the performance of your employees, try to select dimensions that can be measured on a daily, weekly, or at least monthly basis. The best scorecard measures are those that are tracked on a daily basis. With daily feedback, people can monitor and adjust their performance on an ongoing basis. You would not find any business that only measures financial performance once a year. Even the smallest of businesses tends to measure some aspects of financial performance daily, and at least once a month look at factors such as costs and profit and loss. Yet, some of the largest and most sophisticated organizations worldwide measure important things like employee satisfaction and engagement or relationships with customers via an annual survey. Annual metrics are close to worthless. If the last data point shows poor performance, you have to wait 11 more months to get another data point to see if any improvement strategies are working.

One of the best compensation systems I have seen is the piece-rate system still being used in many clothing manufacturing facilities. Workers get paid a set amount for each good quality component that they produce. Quality inspectors check each piece or component for errors and return those pieces to workers when rework is needed. The workers get paid more if they produce more, but only good quality products count, so they must also focus on quality. The system often creates some tension between the workers and inspectors, but some organizations put the inspectors on incentive-based pay as well, to encourage a more cooperative approach. The workers like the daily feedback and the compensation system ensures that the best performers can earn quite a bit more money than their average performing peers. Seniority and experience are also rewarded because the workers with the highest pay and productivity tend to be the more experienced ones.

RULE 7: BASE PERFORMANCE-BASED PAY ON INDIVIDUAL AND TEAM PERFORMANCE

Older compensation plans such as piece rate in the garment industry or commission for salespeople are based 100 percent on individual performance. The benefit of such approaches is that each individual has a great deal of influence over their own compensation and does not need to depend on anyone else. Individual compensation plans like this tend to separate the best performers from their more mediocre peers. Systems like this work the best in organizations where individual contributors are completely on their own and do not need other employees or departments to achieve their goals. However, most organizations today are not set up this way. In many jobs, performance is dependent on peers, bosses, other departments, and contractors or vendors. In a situation like this 100 percent individual performance-based pay systems tend to fail. Another problem with basing pay solely on individual performance is that these systems often create a culture of unfriendly competitiveness. The experienced worker will never help train a new worker or share tips for performing better with peers. Everyone is out for himself, and there are no rewards for cooperating and helping others do well.

A popular alternative compensation approach is not much better. Linking compensation to team performance sounds like a more valid approach for encouraging teamwork and a spirit of working together for common goals. What really happens is that some employees bust their butts and others slack off and everyone gets the same bonus. On any team there are some players who play better than others. With this team compensation system there is no differentiation in pay for the good vs average or poor performers. The good performers end up angry because they were better contributors than others and received the same pay. The poor performers are encouraged to slack off again next month or year because they are rewarded with a healthy team bonus.

The best compensation systems are a mix of individual and team performance. A good combination is 60 percent individual performance and 40 percent team performance. This rewards the individuals who perform much better than their peers, but also puts a strong weight on helping their peers to achieve high levels of team or unit performance.

RULE 8: PROVIDE EMPLOYEES WITH AN EASY WAY TO TRACK PERFORMANCE THROUGHOUT THE YEAR

A common way to report performance data is to use spreadsheets for reports and PowerPoint presentations for monthly review meetings. Neither of these methods is very effective for performance feedback. Spreadsheets are often very hard to read, and make it hard to spot important statistics or problem areas. I sit next to executives on airplanes often and watch them squint trying to read the hundreds of tiny figures in their spreadsheet reports. I have sat in countless monthly meetings as well where managers are droning on with their impossible to read PowerPoint charts that present data in charts and graphs that are impossible to decipher. A better approach is to give everyone access to scorecard software linked to important data bases of various types of performance data. An inexpensive tool called Xcelcius (from Business Objects) allows managers and employees to view performance in color-coded gages that look like the dashboard of a sports car. The inexpensive software extracts data from Excel Spreadsheets and coverts it to easy to understand graphics. The disadvantage of the software is that it does not allow any data analysis; it is strictly a presentation tool. For larger organizations or those in search of something more sophisticated, the best scorecard software is called PerformanceSoft from Actuate, a San Francisco company. This software not only has extensive analytical capabilities, but it is also incredibly easy to use. Training requires about 30 minutes and most users can figure it out without even going through the training because it is so intuitive. Many of my business and government clients have purchased this software to automate their scorecards and provide feedback to employees, and I have never heard any negative feedback about the product or the company. The software sits on top of your existing data warehouses and systems and can extract data from various sources, or allow you to hand-enter it each week or month.

The advantage of using software like this to give feedback to employees is that they can track how they are doing on a daily basis at their own desks, without attending meetings. Controls can be put in place to control access to sensitive data, and each employee can customize her own "briefing book" to look at her own performance measures in a format that she most prefers. Software like this also eliminates the need to prepare charts for monthly review meetings. Someone brings a laptop to the meeting, hooks it up to the company database where the software resides, and real-time performance data can be reviewed and analyzed. Of course, this software costs a bit more than a few hundred dollars, but it can pay for itself in the first year by no longer having staff work overtime each month preparing charts and reports for meetings.

RULE 9: BEWARE OF STRATEGY MAPS TO DEFINE METRICS

A popular approach for identifying metrics linked to key outcomes like profits or growth is to create strategy maps. These diagrams, typically constructed on flipcharts or white boards in small group meetings, are based on sound logic, but they are most often flawed. The idea is to begin by identifying some important outcome and then work backward by identifying important factors and measures that lead to that outcome. For example, a company might identify increasing sales by 15 percent as an important outcome goal (metric = percentage increase in sales from last year). The main strategy for improving sales is to increase loyalty from the best customers (metric = dollars spent per customer account compared to previous years). In order to get customers to spend more money, account managers need to get more face time with key players at each customer account (metric = hours spent per month in contact with customers). The strategy for spending time on the right activities with customers is implementation of a new customer relationship management (CRM) strategy (metric = milestones met on CRM implementation plan). The key to making the new CRM system successful is proper training of account managers and other sales support personnel (metric = percent of staff who have attended all required CRM training).

I am sure all of this sounds like it makes sense if you can follow the train of logic. The big problem with this logic chain and resulting metrics is that the links are all based upon a string of assumptions and opinions. Every one of these links need to be evaluated and tested to determine if an improvement in one factor leads to a concomitant improvement in the later measure. For example, there might be an inverse relationship between face time with your account managers and an increase in spending by customers. It could be that the more time your account manager spends with a customer the more disgruntled they become, the more they hate your company, and the more likely they are to switch their business over to another supplier who does not bother them as much. Another flaw in the logic chain might be that the new CRM software will actually make account managers more successful at account management. Most salespeople I know view the CRM software as a time-wasting distraction that encourages sales managers to second guess all their decisions and micromanage them.

A compensation system that is based upon process or activity measures developed using strategy maps is very dangerous. Unless all of the assumptions in the various links of the strategy map are tested, you may be paying for employee activity that does nothing to contribute to positive performance. One guaranteed benefit of strategy maps is that they increase the billable hours of the consultants running the meetings to create them. Whether or not the circles and arrows allow you to define valid performance measures is a big risk.

RULE 10: ELIMINATE CHICKEN EFFICIENCY MEASURES

Seventeen years ago when I started my own consulting practice, my second client was a company in the fast food business that sold fried chicken. At one time, they were one of only a handful of international chains that had a menu based on fried chicken. Their market share eroded as more and more companies like Popeye's, Church's, and others entered the business. The company asked me to conduct a study of their best performing restaurants to determine what the managers did to make the restaurants so successful. They were then going to give my findings to the training department to develop a workshop to teach the best practices to all of their restaurant managers.

After sitting in my first restaurant outside of Knoxville for half a day, I did not have many notes. After the lunch crowd came and went, I got time to talk with Roy, the manager. I asked him what the secret to his success was, since the company had identified him as one of the best managers in the country. He explained: "The secret to success in this business is something we call 'Chicken Efficiency'." Roy took me in the back room to show me his poster-sized graph of chicken efficiency. There was a little chicken sticker pasted on each day for his performance, which was often 99–100 percent so far that month. Now I was starting to see why he was selected as a great performer, but I was not sure what chicken efficiency was. Roy explained: "At the end of every day I calculate my chicken efficiency percentage on these worksheets they give me, and I peel off one of these chicken stickers and mash it on the chart for my performance for the day."

Still confused, I asked him what factors went into calculating chicken efficiency and he explained: "You take how much chicken you cook, subtract how many pieces you sell, and you get a percentage which shows you how much chicken you throw away or how much scrap we have. The bean counters tell me that this number directly links to a store's profits, so I try to make sure I sell every piece of chicken I cook. We also have tough quality standards for how long it can sit under the heat lights before I have to throw it away."

When I asked Roy how he got nearly perfect performance and sold practically every piece of chicken he cooked, he explained that he never cooked chicken and put it under the heat lights after 6:30 p.m. Customers who came in after 6:30 had to wait 15–20 minutes for Roy's staff to custom cook a bucket of chicken for them. That is a long time to wait with six hungry eight-year-old girls in the mini-van after a soccer game, so Roy explained that most of the people that came in after 6:30 pm were not willing to wait, and they left. The problem was that the company did not measure that, but they did measure chicken efficiency every day. They only measured customer satisfaction once a year, so that did not drive employee performance. Employees get promoted for having good chicken efficiency scores as well as receiving other forms of recognition. Because of the focus on this performance measure, employees and managers were purposely not cooking chicken and subsequently were making customers angry, in order to make this short-term financial metric look positive.

It may be hard to believe how a major corporation can do something this stupid, but I have seen chicken efficiency measures in many large businesses and government organizations. In fact, it is rare to find a scorecard or set of performance measures that does not include a few of these chicken efficiencies.

SUMMARY

The key to any successful compensation plan is that it is based on solid performance metrics. The metrics should be:

- few in number, 1–6 vs 20–30
- linked to individual and team performance
- tracked frequently (at least monthly)
- balanced to address the needs of key stakeholders like customers, shareholders, employees, and partners
- understandable to the employees being judged on them

In spite of how much care you put into defining the right measures that serve as the foundation of your pay-for-performance plan, you will need to continually fine tune it. That is good news for performance management consultants. As soon as you think you have the ideal systems that drive the right behavior, your situation will change, driving the need for new metrics and priorities.

CHAPTER

USING COMPENSATION
TO DRIVE WORKFORCE
PRODUCTIVITY

Christian M. Ellis, Senior Vice President, and
Summer F. Barnes, Senior Consultant

Sibson Consulting

OVER THE LONG TERM, PRODUCTIVITY is the only differentiating factor that defines the wealth of organizations. Writing in *The
Handbook of Industrial and Organizational Psychology*, Robert
Pritchard explains that, if the productivity of a firm is higher than that
of its competitors, that firm has a better chance of surviving because
it is more competitive. Productivity is the primary driver of long-term growth and
profitability. Just as there is no single way to define productivity, there is no single
way to measure it. The definition of productivity and the metrics used to support it
vary by business model, nature of work, and employee segment. Essentially,
however, productivity is how well a system uses its resources to achieve its goals.

One important and often underutilized driver of productivity is compensation, a
substantial resource in any organization. Fixed compensation can reinforce the
demonstration of the key capabilities that are critical for driving productivity. Variable

compensation can motivate and reinforce the achievement of productivity-based results.

Highly productive organizations have a *culture* of productivity and recognize it as the foundation of value creation. Developing a culture of productivity requires taking a systemic view of the organization's drivers of productivity and finding the right mix of investments that can be applied in an integrated and consistent manner over a sustained period. Regardless of what an organization produces—a service, a product, a piece of information, or a unit of wealth—the level of productivity of the organization ultimately determines the degree to which it can create value for its customers and stakeholders over the long term. In today's knowledge economy, where labor investment typically exceeds capital investment, labor—or employee—productivity is the most critical ingredient.

To build a culture of productivity, an organization must understand and define the nature of productivity. Start by considering the following questions:

- How does the organization define value creation for its customers and other stakeholders?

- How does the organization define productivity today? How does it measure productivity?

- To what extent are productivity metrics used in managing the performance of the enterprise?

- What are the organization's beliefs and hypotheses regarding its productivity?

- What is the organization's productivity growth strategy? What are the drivers of real productivity improvement?

- How do the organization's investments in people, including compensation, benefits, and development, drive productivity?

EXPLORING THE DRIVERS OF PRODUCTIVITY

Creating and sustaining a culture of productivity requires a comprehensive understanding of the mix of ingredients that drives productivity over the long term. Although this mix will vary by organization, the key drivers are relatively straightforward and constant. They are:

- *Process*—the business processes used to carry out the work of the organization

- *Capability*—the skills and knowledge needed to execute processes

- *Structure*—the design and organization of roles and jobs, functions, and units

- *Technology*—the tools, equipment, and technologies used to get work done

■ *Rewards*—the strategies used to motivate and reinforce the achievement of results

To drive productivity, an organization needs to examine all these categories and their interrelationships to find the optimal mix of investments in one or more of the drivers, given its business model.

Consider the following question: *If an organization has defined what productivity is, has identified the metrics to measure it, and wants to improve it by 10 percent, what investments should it make in one or more of the key drivers to achieve that increase?*

Although each organization would answer this question differently, one of the key drivers—rewards—is often overlooked or ignored.

There are many reasons organizations stumble when it comes to designing reward programs that drive real productivity gains. Some place too much emphasis on the process and technology drivers—almost every company has done a form of business process redesign and/or installed a large-scale information system. Another common problem is that rewards are unfocused and are tied to many other things: revenue, profit, management by objectives, quality, etc. A third reason is that some organizations simply do not believe in using compensation as an *active* driver of business results—it is not part of their philosophy or culture.

What forms of compensation offer the greatest opportunity? Many types of financial rewards, from gift certificates to stock grants, can be used to reinforce productivity. The balance of this chapter will focus on the two most prominent: fixed and variable compensation. Both represent significant investments for just about any organization and typically are underutilized in driving productivity.

USING FIXED COMPENSATION TO DRIVE PRODUCTIVITY

Most organizations view fixed pay (i.e., base salary compensation) as a cost of doing business without understanding what it returns beyond keeping bodies in chairs or on the line. Moreover, most employees and managers also think merit pay—the primary vehicle used to deliver an employee's annual pay increase—is a highly ineffective motivator. Nevertheless, there are ways to improve dramatically the effectiveness of merit pay by linking compensation opportunities to the drivers of productivity.

The first step is to define the role of fixed pay relative to other forms of compensation and rewards. Organizations that have done this are able to distinguish paying for *what gets done* from paying for *how it gets done*. Since fixed compensation is an investment—a base salary increase provides compensation going forward into the future—it should reinforce *how it gets done*: the behaviors and capabilities that will drive productivity gains in the long term. This is critical in creating a culture of productivity because it clearly links compensation opportunities with the potential to contribute to productivity improvement.

Over the years, we have done substantial research into what differentiates highly productive organizations. That and our own experiences in working with client organizations have revealed that highly productive organizations typically possess several of the following core capabilities:

- *Customer focus*—constant emphasis on creating value for the client

- *Execution*—rigor, discipline, accountability, and follow-through in getting things done

- *Communication*—clarity and transparency in how information is shared

- *Process orientation*—effective, efficient, and consistent processes

- *Simplification*—breaking down structure, complexity, and other obstacles to productivity

- *Continuous improvement*—relentlessly upgrading how work and processes are carried out

- *Long-term focus*—viewing results through short-term actions that accumulate over time

- *Agility*—real-time adaptation to the changing competitive landscape

- *Flexibility*—the ability to shift focus and change tasks based on changing operational needs

- *Attention to detail*—the discipline of focusing on many variables at once but not over-engineering through structure or complexity

While these categories provide a good start in defining the behaviors and capabilities that will drive productivity in the organization, once again, each organization will have its own nuances in how it defines and measures productivity and its drivers. Therefore, it is important to beware of generic "off-the-shelf" competency models. Although defining capabilities through behavioral descriptors is the most important and difficult step, it forces the organization to examine how people can and should affect the drivers of productivity. Once these specific behaviors are defined, fixed compensation can be used to reward people for their development and demonstration of those behaviors. In Table 39.1, we explore how fixed compensation can reinforce the drivers of productivity for the various segments of the workforce.

USING VARIABLE COMPENSATION TO DRIVE PRODUCTIVITY

As opposed to fixed compensation, which is an investment in the future, variable compensation is a reward for the achievement of results—*what gets done*. Effective variable pay programs have clear goals and metrics along with well-defined mechanics for basing rewards on performance. Despite what some critics suggest, we know empirically that incentives can and do have an impact on behavior

TABLE 39.1 Using Fixed Compensation to Drive Productivity

	Key Responsibilities in Driving Productivity	Key Capabilities in Driving Productivity	Implications for Base Pay Delivery
Executives	■ Set a clear, straightforward, and compelling direction and strategy ■ Provide leadership that helps builds a culture of productivity ■ Ensure the right people are in the right jobs to reinforce the culture and execute on the strategy	■ Customer focus ■ Execution ■ Communication ■ Simplification ■ Long-term focus ■ Developing people ■ Agility ■ Attention to detail	■ Tie most of the annual merit pay award to the degree to which the executive develops and demonstrates key capabilities ■ Consider the demonstration of capabilities in succession planning and advancement
Sales workers	■ Maximize return on investments in relationship and transactional selling ■ Sell the optimal mix of products and/or services for customers and the business	■ Customer focus ■ Execution ■ Process orientation ■ Attention to detail	■ Tie key capabilities to merit increase opportunities, to the extent that they are available ■ Consider the demonstration of capabilities in succession planning and advancement
Managers/ knowledge workers	■ Translate strategic direction into operational processes and activities ■ Constantly improve processes and break down and/or navigate through inhibiting structure/bureaucracy ■ Engage and develops others to ensure motivated and capable workforce	■ Execution ■ Process orientation ■ Continuous improvement ■ Simplification ■ Communication ■ Developing people ■ Agility ■ Attention to detail	■ Tie most of the annual merit pay award to the degree to which the manager develops and demonstrates key capabilities ■ Consider the demonstration of capabilities in succession planning and advancement

Continued

TABLE 39.1 *Continued*

	Key Responsibilities in Driving Productivity	Key Capabilities in Driving Productivity	Implications for Base Pay Delivery
Core workers	■ Make a product or deliver a service that can directly impact the customer ■ Know what really matters to the customer ■ Know the interplay of quality and productivity in how the enterprise makes money	■ Customer focus ■ Execution ■ Process orientation ■ Continuous improvement ■ Flexibility ■ Attention to detail	■ Design pay progression systems that define productivity-oriented capability requirements at each "level" or step of pay ■ Consider the demonstration of capabilities in promotions or job changes

SOURCE: Sibson Consulting.

and performance. For example, in *The Effects of Feedback, Goal Setting, and Incentives on Productivity*, Robert Pritchard found that group incentives increased productivity an average of 75 percent over the baseline. Nevertheless, this study stands out as one of the few that focus on productivity, and while we know a lot about what makes incentive compensation effective, there is limited information about how variable pay can reinforce productivity improvement.

Research on the effectiveness of variable pay, and, in particular, group-based incentives, yields insights into how compensation can best drive productivity. An effective incentive program that drives productivity improvement has the following characteristics:

- A balanced set of metrics with one to two measures focused on productivity or productivity drivers (for more on this subject, see "A Balanced Set of Metrics" at end of chapter)

- A unit-based tier of one to two shared metrics and goals that reflect an interdependent group's contribution to productivity

- A funding mechanism that directly relates award opportunity to financial gains for productivity improvement while also delivering a significant and measurable return on investment to the enterprise

Finding the right measures of productivity is a challenging but worthwhile endeavor. It first requires a good definition of productivity that is specific to the organization. Once that is developed, the organization can define the metrics and the drivers. Avoid developing yet another list of variable pay metrics; there is more value in identifying good measures of productivity and exploring their implications for variable compensation program design. Major categories of productivity-oriented metrics are:

- *Output vs input*—units produced per some investment variable

- *Return on investment*—revenue and/or profit per compensation dollar or per employee

- *Value creation*—the growth in what the enterprise is worth vs some baseline or expectation

- *Cycle time*—the speed to produce an output or a deliverable or make a decision

- *Customer satisfaction*—the level of service and satisfaction delivered to clients

- *Process control*—the degree to which business procedures are consistently and effectively executed

- *Employee ratios*—various internal ratios such as span of control, strategic jobs vs nonstrategic jobs, etc.

Defining the metrics that will reflect productivity improvement is just as important as defining the behaviors and capabilities that drive productivity in the organization. Once an organization defines these metrics, it can examine how people should affect the drivers of productivity and can start to design a variable compensation program that will reward those who achieve and/or surpass the metric-based goals. In Table 39.2, we explore how variable compensation can reinforce the drivers of productivity for the various segments of the workforce.

SUMMARY

Productivity is one of the most critical drivers of the long-term success of an enterprise. Although some organizations make the mistake of thinking that technology is the only tool that can be used to improve productivity, others have created a culture that reflects a more optimal mix of ingredients that contribute to constant productivity improvement. One important and often underutilized ingredient, or driver, is compensation. Fixed compensation can reinforce the demonstration of the key capabilities that are critical for driving productivity. Variable compensation can motivate and reinforce the achievement of productivity-based results.

In using compensation to drive productivity, it is important to understand that productivity is not the same thing as performance. Productivity should almost always be defined in some way *relative to inputs*, whereas performance is often defined *relative to expectations*. Achieving performance goals may or may not affect the productivity of an individual, a group, or an organization.

TABLE 39.2   Using Variable Compensation to Reinforce the Drivers of Productivity

	Key Responsibilities in Driving Productivity	Key Measures in Assessing Productivity	Implications for Incentive Pay Delivery
Executives	■ Set a clear, straightforward, and compelling direction and strategy ■ Provide leadership that helps builds a culture of productivity ■ Ensure the right people are in the right jobs to reinforce the culture and execute the strategy	■ Return on investment ■ Value creation ■ Customer satisfaction ■ Cycle time	■ Define specific productivity-oriented metrics for use in the annual incentive plan ■ Link the individual component of the incentive plan to one or more metrics of productivity
Sales workers	■ Maximize return on investments in relationship and transactional selling ■ Sell the optimal mix of products and/or services for customers and the business	■ Customer satisfaction ■ Process control	■ Ensure that sales incentives recognize more than just revenue or share growth ■ Factor in the productivity of sales: the inputs required to generate sales
Managers/ knowledge workers	■ Translate strategic direction into operational processes and activities ■ Constantly improve processes and break down and/or navigate through inhibiting structure/ bureaucracy ■ Engage and develop others to ensure motivated and capable workforce	■ Output vs input ■ Return on investment ■ Cycle time ■ Process control ■ Staff ratios	■ Define financial and operational-oriented metrics of productivity for use in the annual incentive plan ■ Define eligibility deep into the organization: almost everyone can affect productivity ■ Reinforce critical "white collar" barriers to productivity such as slow decision-making

Continued

TABLE 39.2 *Continued*

	Key Responsibilities in Driving Productivity	Key Measures in Assessing Productivity	Implications for Incentive Pay Delivery
Core workers	■ Make a product or deliver a service that can directly affect the customer ■ Know what really matters to the customer ■ Know the interplay of quality and productivity in how the enterprise makes money	■ Output vs input ■ Customer satisfaction ■ Cycle time ■ Process control	■ Develop group incentive programs for segments of employees who are interdependent ■ Define metrics of productivity for use in group incentives ■ Avoid individual incentives for productivity

SOURCE: Sibson Consulting.

With this in mind, using compensation to unleash greater productivity requires a clear and specific definition of productivity, the understanding of the organizational capabilities that drive it, and the definition of metrics that reinforce it. Moreover, the effort to build a productive culture takes time, commitment, and consistency of approach, but the return on investment will make it worthwhile.

A Balanced Set of Metrics

Capitalizing on Human Assets, a 1992 study conducted by the American Compensation Association (now WorldatWork), found that combination performance-reward plans, which use both financial and operational metrics, generate the greatest satisfaction among participants. Financial plans are defined as those that use "bottom-line" (P&L) measures, specifically profit, earnings and/or return calculations as the only basis for payouts. Operational plans use some combination of productivity, quality, attendance, safety, cost-reduction, project milestones, output or volume, or sales/referral measures to determine payouts. Combination plans combine financial and operational measures to determine payouts. Survey participants reported a 3.8 level of satisfaction with combination plans (on a 5-1 scale with 5 = very satisfied). This compares to 3.7 for operational plans and 3.4 for financial plans.

REFERENCES

Bossidy, L. and Charan, R., *Execution*. New York: Crown Business, 2002.

Jennings, J., *Less Is More: How Great Companies Use Productivity as A Competitive Tool in Business*. New York: Penguin Group/Portfolio, 2002.

McAdams, J. L. and Hawk, E. J., *Capitalizing on Human Assets*. American Compensation Association, 1992.

Pritchard, R. D., "Organization Productivity," *The Handbook of Industrial and Organizational Psychology*. Palo Alto, CA: Psychology Consultants Press, 1992.

Pritchard, R. D., Jones, S. D., Roth, P. L., Stuebing, K. K. and Ekeberg, S. E., "The Effects of Feedback, Goal Setting, and Incentives on Organizational Productivity," *Journal of Applied Psychology Monograph Series*, vol. 73, no. 2, 1988, pp. 337–358.

Sibson, R. E., *Increasing Employee Productivity*. New York: AMACOM, 1976.

Weisbord, M. R., *Productive Workplaces*. San Francisco, CA: Jossey-Bass, 1987.

C H A P T E R

RETURN ON INVESTMENT OF COMPENSATION EXPENDITURES

Fred Whittlesey, Principal Consultant

Compensation Venture Group, Inc.

THE INFORMATION REVOLUTION HAS ONCE again shifted the balance among categories of resources and their relative value. Just as the industrial revolution emphasized the value of physical assets—and stripped individual workers of their economic participation in the enterprise—the information revolution has had a similarly dramatic effect but in the opposite direction. Whether discussed under the heading of "human capital," the "new economy," or "ROI" it is clear that the individual worker is again the focus of value creation and business success.

The vast majority of businesses now find that the primary basis of their value resides not in tangible physical assets but in other types of assets—intellectual property, business processes, and people. A conversation with a financial accountant will quickly shape your thinking that these latter items, with few exceptions (e.g., a patent) are not assets at all and in fact are either expenses or just a concept with no financial tangibility.

This is at the heart of the continuing problem faced by human resources professionals seeking to attain business credibility. Virtually any recommendation coming from HR is deemed to "create an expense" which of course "reduces profit." Because most businesses exist to make a profit, the logic stream then continues that HR's ideas are detrimental to the business. Unlike other areas of the organization which are able to characterize their "expenses" as "investments" HR lacks in most cases both the financial acumen and the methodologies to win that debate.

For HR professionals to be true strategic business partners, there is a mandatory way of thinking, a way of gathering and presenting data, and a way of communicating. While the field of accounting is often called "the language of business," the true language of business is a multifaceted tongue of which financial accounting is an element but often an unproductive constraint. There is a broader, deeper way which is the core of all business decisions and cuts across all disciplines: return on investment (ROI). This material focuses on that way of thinking; the methods for gathering and presenting data, and a way of communicating concepts that will allow a good HR idea to make its way over the hurdles of "cost" and "expense" to a discussion of "value" and "return"—the basis of business success. This requires believing three central tenets of the ROI approach:

- Calculating ROI for HR requires no greater degree of estimates and assumptions than other financial measurement and reporting systems, including financial accounting

- Most organizations do not have the data collection and measurement systems required for calculating the true financial impact of HR transactions and HR bears the burden for accumulating the data

- Financial estimates are always better than mere quantification of subjective factors and a methodology which includes estimates and assumptions and proactively gathered data will provide a solid foundation for business decisions that is lacking today

METRICS AND VALUE

Lord Kelvin said "When you *cannot* express it in numbers, your knowledge is of a meager and unsatisfactory kind. When you *can* measure what you are speaking about and express it in numbers, you know something about it." He had a good point, but unless you are an engineer you probably rarely discuss the temperature in terms other than Fahrenheit or Celsius—when was the last time you sat in a room that was 294 degrees? Much of the HR literature today is filled with talk of

HR "metrics" and notions of "ROI" that have addressed neither return nor investment. Like Lord Kelvin's thermometer, we might know more than we did without it, but that is not the tool people use to decide if they need to wear a sweater today.

The fact is that managers make resource allocation decisions based on a variety of financial information, not just "numbers" or "metrics." Because in many organizations people expenses are the single largest financial category, HR costs have the highest effect of any cost category on value creation. That value is measured in dollars, dollars to be gained that exceed the dollars needed to generate those gains. Every HR communication must start and end in the context of ROI. If you ever heard your grandfather say "you have to spend money to make money," he was teaching you about ROI.

I often ask students this question: if I have $10,000 in my bank account, is that good or bad? To most students, that sounds pretty good. Then I ask: if I earned $800 interest last year on that bank balance, is that good or bad? The quicker ones note that an 8 percent return (as this chapter is written) is a very good interest rate, so that is good. Then I mention that the way I got the $10,000 was by taking cash advances on my credit card, $1,000 at a time with a transaction fee of $75 each time and I'm paying 21 percent interest on the balance. This instantly changes the assessment of how "good" my financial results are. Why? Because my return is lower than my investment cost and I am losing money. I did not make a profit of $800 last year, I lost $2,850. But until I gather and communicate all of the costs and outcomes and put them together in a meaningful calculation, I cannot get the right answer. Note that I had to go to several different sources for the data to understand that situation—several savings account statements, and several credit card statements; no single piece of paper gave me the answer. That is because no single party had an interest in the integrated answer. The savings bank does not care where the money came from, and the credit card company does not really care how the borrowed money was used.

Today, the field of compensation is experiencing an influx of new "experts" in pay, coming from a variety of backgrounds, but primarily from accounting and finance. Many of them are questioning the decision making process used by HR just as my students questioned the wisdom of borrowing money on credit cards. Here is a common conversation:

HR says,

"We need a merit increase budget of 3.8 percent for next year."

"Why?"

"To be competitive."

"Competitive with whom?"

"The other companies in the survey."

"How much, in dollars, is that 3.8 percent?"

(silence)

"What is the impact of that increase on our earnings per share?"

(silence . . . I wonder what "earnings per share" is?)

"What if instead we reduce salaries by 3.8 percent, lower our costs, and increase our profit?"

"People will leave."

"Really, all of them?"

"No, just some."

"How many?"

(silence)

"Which ones?"

(silence)

Meeting over.

Contrast the merit increase discussion with this one:

VP of Manufacturing,

"I need $50 million for a new piece of factory equipment."

"Why?"

"The current piece is declining in productivity, is breaking down a lot, we're missing customer delivery deadlines, and there are better technologies available now that will allow a higher quality product for a lower cost."

"How much is all of that costing us per year?"

"Here's my spreadsheet analysis. Using this series of 17 assumptions and calculating a 5-year discounted cash flow, our return would be approximately 24.55 percent per year."

"So this is actually going to save us a little over $12 million per year in today's dollars if I give you the $50 million."

"Yes."

Meeting over.

Every compensation practitioner has available to them the same methods, tools, and techniques to get a 3.8 percent merit budget approved as a "good investment" rather than an expense and have that desired "seat at the table" where decisions about machines and merit budgets are made.

DEFINING ROI

Compensation expenditures, like any business expenditures, must produce a return exceeding their true financial cost, and the "cost" of compensation expenditures must be measured and calculated in real financial terms rather than pursuant to only accounting, tax, or other mandated methods. The cost of compensation must produce a positive return both *internally* (we will call that iROI) and *externally* (eROI). Internally, the cost of delivering compensation should:

- not exceed the compensation delivered and the cost of delivering it—the relationship between the organization and the individual should be mutually advantageous financially; express mailing you a $10 bonus check at a cost of $12 dollars would not make sense

- not produce, for new programs, incremental costs exceeding additional pay; implementing a program that delivers $1 million in additional pay but costs $1.3 million to design, administer, and communicate would not make sense

  Externally, the cost of compensation should:

- produce a level of return on investment expected by the investors; this constitutes many of the media headlines today regarding executive pay for performance but applies to all employees

- be directly aligned with the return to investors (or other stakeholders); if employee pay goes up when investor return goes down we should revisit the pay structure

THE STATE OF COMPENSATION PLANNING TODAY

There is a compelling need to adopt a true financial ROI approach to compensation decisions. Major criticisms of pay design today are rooted in practices that were developed decades ago—with little improvement since then. I believe there are six driving factors that need to be fixed through the ROI approach, not all of which come out of the HR field but will nevertheless need to be repaired therein.

1. *Continuing failure of financial accounting to capture compensation-related costs and returns*—the fixation on financial reporting of stock options, based on questionable accounting rules which are based on even more questionable economic theory, has distorted the analytical processes of pay determination. By extending our analysis to capture more than the accrual accounting effects of a decision we improve decision-making.

2. *Continuing failure of cost accounting systems to capture compensation-related costs and returns*—the most sophisticated cost accounting systems still fail to capture the indirect and intangible, but very real, costs in the organization. I know Joe spent six hours working on this part. I do not know what Joe did for the other two hours, and I do not know if Joe could have made two parts rather than one in those six hours.

3. *Misleading "survey data" continuing to provide an inaccurate basis for decision-making*—50-year-old methodologies continue to guide compensation

decisions. We look in the book, there is the number, and that is often the end of the analytics.

4. *Use of misguided pay-for-performance "metrics" that focus on measures unrelated to value creation*—decades of research are the underpinning of recent investor reaction to executive pay that produces large payouts for results that have little or no relation to shareholder value. The extreme cases are when large bonuses are paid for "customer satisfaction" while sales plummet and losses accumulate. Where did those satisfied customers spend there money?

5. *Much attention to pay vehicle expense but not associated costs*—the recent gyrations from stock options to restricted stock and now to performance plans have been rooted in accounting expense with little attention to the aggregated costs of implementing these changes and, more importantly, the behavioral impact of such changes.

6. *Exacerbation of these issues by the all-or-nothing plan design mentality*—the question "Should we switch from options to restricted stock?" or "Should we replace equity with cash for the rank and file?" have been prevailing questions of the early part of this decade but, as this chapter will point out, we will find the same questions being revisited because inappropriate financial analytics were the basis for earlier decisions. We are already seeing and hearing these effects.

Understanding the above points requires a move toward meaningful ROI analysis and the identification of some of the semantic "traps" that trip up discussions about money and send decisions in the wrong direction.

THE BASICS OF ROI

At the root of the difficulty in dealing with the notion of ROI for compensation expenditures is a centuries-old mentality about where money goes and what it is called when spent.

Expenses, Assets, and Capitalization

By definition of the accountants, organizations only spend money on only two things: expenses and assets.

- *Expenses* are (the dollar cost of) goods or services used in the current period

- *Assets* are (the dollar cost of) goods or services used in one or more future periods

But among assets there are distinctions:

- Tangible assets are generally *capitalized*, that their cost is treated as a *value* on the balance sheet and the use of them recognized as a cost over the years of use. A building that costs $10 million and is expected to be used for 10 years will result in an expense to the business of $1 million per year over the next 10 years.

- Intangible assets—with a few exceptions—are generally *expensed* . . . or ignored altogether. A training program that costs $10 million that is expected to add value to employees over a 10-year period is expensed in the year of training. A $10 million expense to improve productivity by boosting morale due to a recent layoff appears on financial statements as an overhead expense, and only indirectly through other results.

Our problem in HR is that accountants treat virtually everything we do as an *expense* and/or an expenditure to acquire *intangible assets*. But as financial analysts we are not constrained by accounting rules and only must ensure that we identify the accounting impact as only one facet of financial impact.

A PRACTICAL MODEL FOR ROI IN HR

Addressing these challenges and getting the attention of the CEO and CFO require translating our ideas into a way of thinking and speaking that is their norm. Tourists often find that the easiest way to get directions in Paris is to be able to speak French, though they also quickly learn that speaking French poorly can lead not only to wrong directions but antagonism. HR practitioners that say "we really got a positive ROI on that new program" often mean "employees like the new program"—breeding antagonism with financial professionals due to the poor language skills.

If we follow a practical method for data collection and analysis, think like financial analysts, and produce dollar-denominated ROI outcomes, we will succeed. Here is that process.

Define the Hypothesis. First we must define our ideas in terms of business need. An idea is not a good one because 68 percent of the companies in the surveys do it, or the company across the street did it, or someone defined it as a "best practice." An idea has potential if it can be demonstrated to have a positive financial effect on the organization. Let us think through an example.

A VP of HR was concerned about turnover and upon delving into the details of exit interviews, market data, and discussions with managers concluded that the company probably was offering a substantially lower total pay value than its competitors. While recognizing that pay is not the only factor in retention and turnover, the differential here seemed to be a significant issue. The proposed solution was framed as:

"Increasing total compensation will increase our profitability."

HR's point was that low pay results in turnover (based on data from exit interviews); lower job satisfaction (as reported in employee surveys), leading to higher turnover and lower levels of employee engagement; and reduced productivity, resulting from those two effects. Intuitively, the senior management team did not find fault.

But the CFO had some compelling counterpoints regarding the projected financial impact of the recommendation.

"We can't afford to increase our compensation costs"

The proposal would result in higher compensation expense, which would reduce earnings per share and reduced operating cash flow; this would contribute to a reduced share price, lowering the value of employee stock options and executive compensation, and have a companywide ripple effect—a cure worse than the disease.

The CFO's thinking is illustrated in Figure 40.1.

But this savvy VP of HR had a graphic, too (see Figure 40.2).

The senior management team could not disagree with the logic of the VP of HR's points, but the CFO had hard numbers while the VP of HR had some potentially good ideas. The VP of HR took action: give me two weeks to demonstrate my numbers and I will show that my approach will have a greater financial return than a cutback approach. We are now off to demonstrate grandpa's point that you have to spend money to make money.

Develop the Types of Assumptions and Estimates Needed as Inputs for the Model. This step typically causes the most uneasiness as many HR professionals do not understand that even accountants routinely use estimates, projections, assumptions, and subjective judgment to produce what looks like impeccably precise financial statements. I often ask my students as a homework assignment to

FIGURE 40.1 The CFO's view of the compensation issue

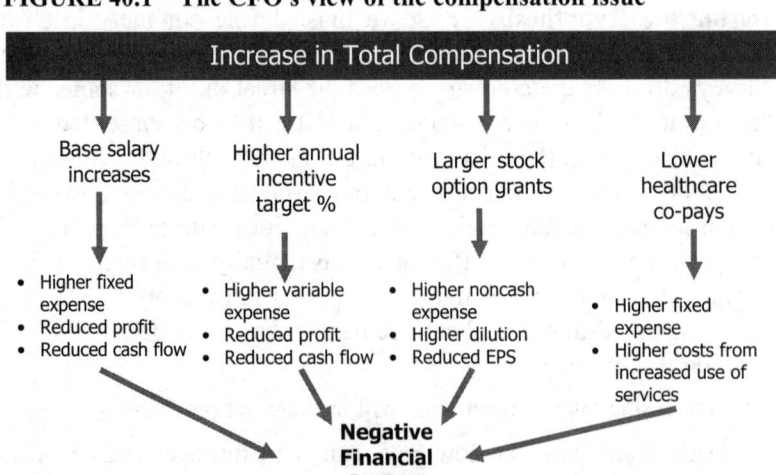

FIGURE 40.2 The VP of HR's view of the compensation issue

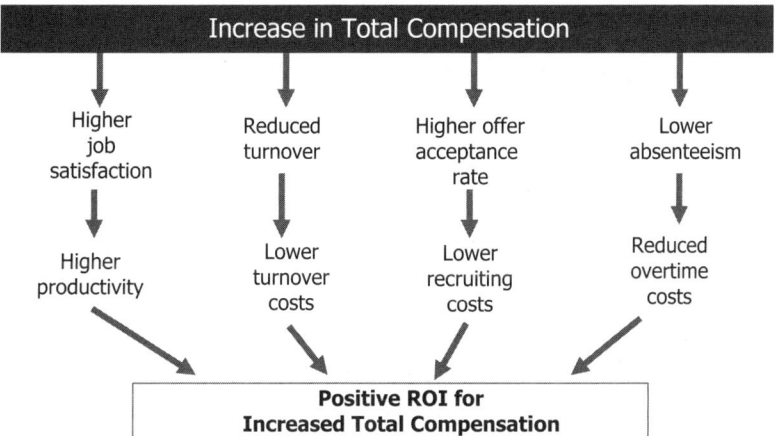

get the annual report of a company, turn to the footnotes following the four basic financial statements, and with a pink highlighter highlight each time they find the word "estimate," "projection," "assumption," "expected," "approximate," and "judgments." The exercise is self-explanatory and their highlighter runs out of ink half way through the financial statement footnotes. Understanding the financial results of an organization requires a series of subjective calculations, and financial analysis takes us beyond the somewhat more rigid confines of financial accounting.

We must define what types of assumptions and estimates are needed. If we project that turnover and productivity will be affected, we need to estimate those numbers, and make assumptions about why the estimate is what it is.

Gather the Data. Once we know the types of data we are seeking, we face what can be the most challenging and time consuming step because:

- the data may reside in many different locations (accounting, finance, HR, operations, market data)

- the data may reside in many different formats (spreadsheets, HRIS, paper files, managers' brains)

- the data may not exist (how unproductive, really, is a disgruntled employee?)

But if we dig we may find more data that we expected. We may find research that shows that the average employee could be 35 percent more productive than they are, if they had reason to be. We may find research that finds the top performers in some occupations are five to eight times more productive than the average performer. We may find that during the first four weeks of employment an employee is only 35 percent productive and during the last four weeks they are only 30 percent productive.

We also may find interesting circular data—that the managers with the highest turnover rates spend the most time interviewing replacement candidates and thus have the least time to do performance management tasks, which is the number one complaint of those leaving those managers' departments—no feedback, no clear goals, no timely performance review.

Develop the Financial Model of Pay and Return.   Through these data gathering tasks we get a solid understanding of the costs of various activities and situations. But it is here that we reach an understanding about the value corresponding to those cost situations: the question must be asked, "How much money do we make on each employee—each engineer, each salesperson, each receptionist, each attorney?" It is a question that must be answered because if we say "we don't make any money on them," then we have another HR task to do, called a termination, and maybe the CFO was right after all. We cannot allocate funds to any asset that does not produce an identifiable return for the business.

In Figure 40.3, we show how we might think about this for a salesperson, admittedly one of the easier positions for which to conduct an analysis.

At a minimum, we start in aggregate, allocate relatively higher and lower value by occupation category and level, and get to a rough starting point for thinking about value. For example, does it cost us more to lose a second-year engineer, or an executive assistant with 10 years' experience?

The estimates will be imperfect. All of the calculations will be imperfect—just like the income statement is imperfect. We are striving for a decision tool, not how to make the Space Shuttle intersect with the orbit of the moon.

Quantify the Assumptions.   Now we need to input real numbers. If we are calculating turnover cost, most would agree that the last week on the job a person is not at full 100 percent productivity. If nothing else, that last day they come in late, say goodbye to all their friends, attend the going-away lunch, and probably leave early for the farewell happy hour. But how long before that last day was that person less than 100 percent productive once they had decided to leave. Did they: take a

FIGURE 40.3   Calculating the profitability of an employee

• Salary	$70,000
• Commission target	$30,000
• Benefits (company cost)	$15,000
• Total Direct Employee Expense	$115,000
• Other SG&A Expenses	$35,000
• Total Employee Cost	$150,000
• Revenue target	$1,000,000
• Gross Margin (50%)	$500,000
• **Net Employee Margin**	**$350,000**

FIGURE 40.4   Life cycle employee productivity curve

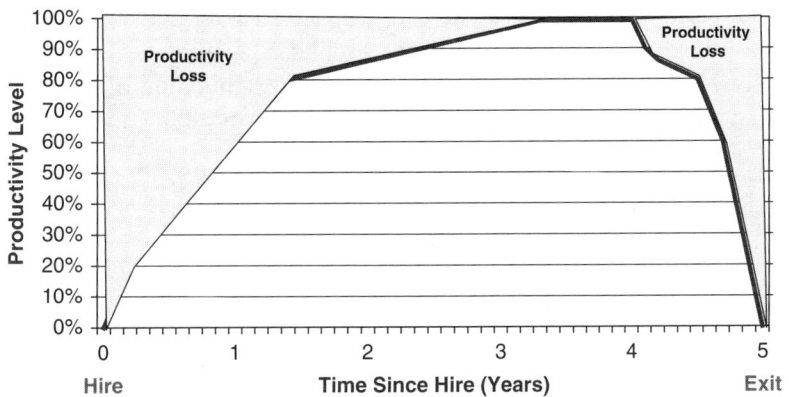

couple of extra sick days? Take long lunches for job interviews? Surf the job websites during work hours? (See Figure 40.4.)

We develop a page of assumptions that feed into the model, and we will find that, because there is conceptual agreement with the model (yes, there is a cost to turnover), we can focus our attention on the assumptions (no, it does not take eight weeks to fill the position, it takes only six weeks). Factually, human resource financial models are so highly leveraged that we find that the continual tweaking of assumptions leads us to a consistent conclusion: poor people management creates a huge money leak for the organization, and we need to plug it.

Calculate a Reasonable Range through Scenario-based Pay Planning.   Now that we have a model and some assumptions to play with, we introduce a fundamental decision making process. What is the worst case, best case, and middle case scenario. Maybe there are five with points in between those three. Let us resist the need to create 10. The worst case represents all of the variables going in the wrong direction for our business—for an airline, oil prices spiral up, the union strikes, a terror attack and/or economic recession reduce demand, but then the labor market softens, pressure on wage rates subsides, and so on. The best case is oil is down, traffic is up, business booms, but then wage demands return. We think through the effects of the end points and the middle. This allows us to understand the range of possibilities. Our stock price is at $50; it is unlikely to go under $25 and it is unlikely to go above $75. Now let us work in that range.

Calculate the Expected Value.   Then we have to make our crystal ball a little bit clearer. We can assign probabilities to each of the scenarios (20 percent chance of worst case, 50 percent chance of middle case, 30 percent change of best case) and calculate the expected value. Of course we will tweak that and end up backing into the numbers.

This is the step that allows you to say "allocating an additional 0.5 percent to the merit budget this year will *save* us somewhere between $12 million and $18 million dollars, most likely right around $14 million. The spreadsheet model allows variation of every variable and the examination of every scenario. I find that the more that people tweak the model the more the numbers converge. Yes, it is $14 million.

AND THEN WHAT?

And then the fun begins because the guy that wants $50 million for the new equipment with a five-year annualized return of 22.45 percent is in line behind you. You, too, have spreadsheets and data. You, too, have a crisp ROI calculation. You, too, have a value-adding solution for the business. And maybe because you are in HR, it is just a little more fun because your solution involves people instead of a piece of equipment. Remember how much fun all those people had at the company picnic last year. By the way, what was the ROI for the money spent on the company picnic last year?

Fun aside, you have demonstrated a financial return on a financial expenditure that adds value to the business. You and your team of financial analysts have figured out where the hidden costs and hidden value is in the business, things the accountants and financial analysts have not been able to articulate. You win.

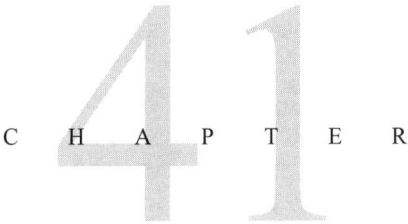

PAY-FOR-PERFORMANCE: NEW DEVELOPMENTS AND ISSUES

Mark D. Cannon, Ph.D., Associate Professor of Leadership and
Organizational Studies

Peabody College, Vanderbilt University

INTENSE COMPETITIVE PRESSURES AND THE NEED** for continual improvements have increasingly led organizations to turn to financial incentives to boost performance. Consequently, the use of various types of pay-for-performance programs today and the interest in understanding how to make these programs most effective is at a record high. Pay-for-performance programs are designed to accurately measure employee performance on an ongoing basis and then to align their pay such that it rises and falls in accordance with variation in their performance. More corporations have adopted pay-for-performance programs now than at any other time in history, and these plans are involving a greater percentage of workers than ever before. Even more dramatic has been the growth in instituting pay-for-performance programs in new areas of application. The growth of interest in such programs has been especially strong in health care, schools, and to some extent in government.

However, the burgeoning enthusiasm for pay-for-performance has not always been paralleled by the achievement of desired results from such programs.[1] This has led to an increasing recognition of the need to better evaluate and understand the complex dynamics of these programs in order to make them more effective.

In this chapter, we first examine the recent developments in pay-for-performance with a focus on the explosive growth of programs in new areas of application. Next, we identify a number of challenges that organizations must meet if they are going to maximize their benefits. Specifically, we identify and explore the challenges associated with learning from experience and identifying the best practices, design, implementation, and adoption of a strategic perspective. We also provide suggestions for meeting these challenges successfully.

CURRENT TRENDS IN THE USE OF PAY-FOR-PERFORMANCE

Hewitt Associates' 2007 annual survey reveals that the use of variable pay programs among companies has reached a historic high. Their survey shows that 90 percent of companies are using some kind of broad-based pay-for-performance program. This is up from 80 percent just last year and up from only 51 percent in 1991.[2]

Research shows not only that more companies are using pay-for-performance than ever before, but that these plans are also reaching a larger proportion of the employees within these utilizing companies. Between 1976 and 1998, the proportion of jobs covered by pay-for-performance plans rose from 30 to 45 percent.[3] These moves reflect a general trend away from providing across-the-board raises and towards performance-related bonuses. By focusing on bonuses, corporations hope to motivate workers, lower fixed costs, and reduce the sense of entitlement among the workforce.[4] Next, we examine the growth in new areas of application in health care, schools, and government.

Health Care

The United States spends more on health care per person than any other country, but the quality of care and the outcomes often fall short of what should be expected for the expense.[5] The rising cost and variable quality of health care have been significant concerns for employees, employers, and practitioners.[6] One of the leading causes of personal bankruptcy has been medical bills associated with serious illnesses. Surprisingly, an estimated 40 percent of these bankrupt families actually had some form of health insurance.

Providers.   Annual increases in health care costs have risen at a considerably higher pace than inflation. Employers paid an estimated 86 percent of the $1.6 trillion cost of medical insurance in 2002.[7] The extensive cost of health care and the desire for better quality have led many to push for greater use of pay-for-performance in the health care industry; consequently, the use of pay-for-performance in the health care field has grown dramatically. Recent research estimates that adoption of pay-for-performance programs in the health care sector has almost quadrupled over the last five years.[8] Over half of health maintenance organizations have adopted pay-for-performance programs.[9]

Britain has aggressively implemented its own pay-for-performance program for family practitioners. Their program sets aside 25–30 percent of practitioners' pay to be determined by their performance.[10]

Incentives to Employees for Managing Their Own Health. In contrast to the previous section, which describes how financial incentives are being used to influence the behavior of health care providers, it is also interesting to note that some organizations are offering financial incentives directly to their employees for managing their own health, which is the opposite end of the health care spectrum. To both slow the growth in health care costs and to encourage good health among their employees, some organizations are providing individual incentives to employees who engage in health-conscious practices. For example, a number of companies contribute to health savings accounts of employees who agree to engage in health-promoting activities.

Healthways has made a business of helping organizations manage health care costs by coaching individual employees with health risks and providing them with financial incentives to mitigate their risks. Employees receive a discount in their health insurance premiums through their companies for participating independently in the Healthways program. Healthways Center for Health Research[11] monitors and regularly feeds back to employees their scores on 11 lifestyle biomarkers such as nicotine levels, blood pressure, body fat, and cholesterol. These are associated with chronic disease and financial strain on the health care system. Employees who manage to keep these markers within desired ranges are eligible for additional financial incentives such as further reductions in health care premiums or contributions to health savings accounts.

Schools

Compared to other industrialized countries, American students score poorly on reading and towards the bottom of standardized tests in mathematics and science. Conversely, an Organization for Economic Cooperation and Development (OECD) study ranks the United States as tied for first place among industrialized countries in spending per pupil at approximately $11,000 each in 2005.[12] Between 1960 and 1995, per pupil spending in the United States increased 212 percent in real (inflation adjusted) dollars.[13] This dilemma may provide fertile ground for pay-for-performance programs in the field of education.

Many people are alarmed that teacher pay tends to be determined by years in the job and degrees held rather than any parameters of quality teaching. Under current systems, the worst teacher in a system could be paid exactly the same as the best teacher. Consequently, many have looked to financial incentives as a way to encourage better teaching and improved educational results.[14]

A number of states are making a significant investment in experimenting with pay-for-performance for teachers in schools. Florida, Minnesota, and Texas have taken a leadership role with combined annual funding of $550 million to provide performance incentives for high-quality educators.[15] The federal government has also made $99 million available to states to fund pay-for-performance programs to enhance education. Chicago was the recipient of a $28 million federal grant to improve its at-risk schools. Chicago schools may receive $500,000–750,000 per year to provide annual performance bonuses to teachers in amounts ranging from $1,000 to $8,000.[16] Other cities involved in developing and implementing new pay-for-performance programs in schools include Denver, Little Rock, and Nashville.

Government

The public sector is examining private-sector HR practices such as pay-for-performance programs. Although the work of state, local, and federal governments' employees may not yet have received the same attention as health care and schools, there appears to be a growing interest in experimenting with such programs. The General Accountability Office, for example, moved to a performance-based pay system in 2006. Other federal departments, including the Federal Aviation Administration, the Veterans Health Administration, and the U.S. Department of Labor's Employment and Training Administration, have also adopted an array of variable pay schemes.[17] Legislation has even been proposed to overhaul current pay programs for more merit-based plans; many proponents suggest that the current personnel system, designed over half a century ago, is outdated.[18]

REALIZING THE POTENTIAL OF PAY-FOR-PERFORMANCE

Thus, we see record interest in pay-for-performance in business, health care, education and the public sector with the possibility of a bright future for pay-for-performance. However, we should also note that, although pay-for-performance programs have generally been associated with positive outcomes, results have been mixed, and the programs often fall short of achieving their potential.[19] In some cases, new programs have even been known to do more harm than good.[20] For example, when executives finally decided to discontinue an experiment with pay-for-performance at Hewlett-Packard, the employees threw a party to celebrate.[21] The program had been seen as a nuisance, and maintaining the program took time away from tasks that employees perceived as having higher value added. When employees conceive of pay-for-performance programs (like other new initiatives), they are vulnerable to unreasonable optimism and thus may overestimate the likely benefits and underestimate the efforts required to build and maintain an effective program.

Despite the rapid adoption of pay-for-performance programs in health care, research reveals some cause for concern.[22] For example, a report from Price Waterhouse Coopers' Health Research Institute[23] was fairly critical of current pay-for-performance programs for health care practitioners. They concluded that many of them have done a good job of involving physicians, but that on many measures these programs "would barely receive a passing grade." Another study of the effectiveness of pay-for-performance programs in health care found that four out of the 17 programs studied produced unintended and undesirable consequences.[24] For example, some critics have charged that these programs can encourage physicians to avoid minority patients and patients with complex medical needs.[25] Pay-for-performance programs in health care have been critiqued for being burdensome to manage and producing only limited results, leading many to question their value.[26]

Of course, the administrators of these programs may smooth out these complications over time. One could argue that health care institutions are still scaling the learning curve and that these difficulties will be overcome as organizations learn from experience. However, pay-for-performance programs in industry also often have difficulty producing desired results and may even deteriorate over time. Gerhart and Rynes[27] conclude about the effectiveness of variable pay plans that they enhance performance the majority of the time, approximately two-thirds of the time. Although a two-thirds success rate is not bad, it does suggest that about one-third of the time the effort put into developing such plans either does not pay off or perhaps may even be damaging in some cases. Thus, there appears to be room for improvement.

Consider the recent critiques being made of top executive compensation. Although many have argued that high pay for executives is justifiable as long as it is based on performance, recent research has questioned the relationship between executive pay and performance. The book, *Pay Without Performance: The Unfulfilled Promise of Executive Compensation*, by law professors Lucian A. Bebchuk and Jesse M. Fried, has received a great deal of attention. Their book argues that executive pay is often not aligned with performance or with shareholder interests. In fact, they assert that executive power can be used to produce weak or even perverse incentives.[28] Dramatic examples of misalignment, such as Bob Nardelli at Home Depot, are often cited in the popular press. Nardelli walked away with approximately $250 million despite the fact that the company's stock dropped slightly during his tenure and he managed to alienate a number of organizational stakeholders and embarrass the company through his mishandling of their annual shareholders meeting.[29]

The history of pay-for-performance is characterized by both dramatic successes and resounding failures.[30] The ability of our society to make the most constructive use of financial incentives depends on our ability to understand and meet a distinct set of challenges that create vulnerabilities for pay-for-performance programs.

THE CHALLENGE OF LEARNING FROM EXPERIENCE
AND IDENTIFYING BEST PRACTICES

Despite decades of interest in study on financial incentives, we lack specific, definitive conclusions about the conditions under which different kinds of financial incentives are or will be most effective and what their impact will be. Reports on the efficacy of financial incentives are often anecdotal and lacking in scientific rigor. We have an insufficient amount of longitudinal research, and we have not had enough rigorously designed experiments.[31] Current research has not done an adequate job of assessing the impact of different types of pay-for-performance programs that are used in combination with each other.[32] Research has also done an inadequate job of assessing the costs vs the benefits of pay-for-performance programs and how they compare with other types of interventions that are designed to enhance performance, such as coaching, mentoring, and other types of professional development.[33]

As the popularity of pay-for-performance grows, the importance of learning from experience and identifying best practices increases in importance. Today, more sophisticated methodological and analytic tools are available than ever before. Thus, our ability to answer questions about the effectiveness of various types of pay-for-performance arrangements and the conditions under which they are most and least effective will be determined by whether we invest the effort to gather data in ways that enable us to answer those questions.

The National Center on Performance Incentives (NCPI) provides an excellent example of how this can be done. The motivation for the center grew out of the recognition that policy makers and educational leaders have little reliable information on the impact of financial incentives in education and how they should or should not be used. Without such information, they are stuck being guided more by intuition than by science as they work to develop constructive policies and practices.

Fortunately, the need for more definitive information on how pay-for-performance might be used in schools has been recognized and supported through a $10 million grant from the U.S. Department of Education's Institute of Education Sciences that was awarded to Vanderbilt University professors James W. Guthrie and Matthew G. Springer. The funding enabled the establishment of the NCPI, dedicated to the scientific study of how financial incentives for teachers, administrators, and schools affect the quality of teaching and learning.

One of their first initiatives is conducting a set of methodologically sophisticated experiments in which they are researching the impact of pay-for-performance on teaching. For example, they are assessing the impact of offering math teachers the possibility of earning $5,000–15,000 bonuses depending upon student improvement as measured by state exam score improvements. This and other studies supported by the center probe deeply into the impact of financial incentives, not only on the individual recipient, but also on colleagues and the institution as a whole. They measure both intended and unintended consequences and the comparative efficacy of financial incentives vs other interventions such as professional development opportunities and changes in class size. The center has also been involved in assessing the effectiveness of certain aspects of the pay-for-performance programs in Texas and Florida. Such evaluations enable states and the center to learn from their experience, address previously unanswered questions, and identify best practices.

The NCPI is sill early in its life, but its initial efforts are showing potentially impressive results. For example, one serious concern and significant unanswered question about using performance incentives in schools is whether they might encourage unconstructive competitiveness and lack of teamwork among teachers. Although there is more data to be gathered, the initial evaluation of the Texas pay-for-performance initiatives appears to suggest that these concerns are not materializing.[34] In fact, the limited data so far suggest that organizational dynamics are fairly positive, teachers' attitudes toward the program are becoming more positive, and that the incentives appear to be having a constructive impact on teacher and student performance.

Meeting the challenge of learning from experience and identifying best practices means understanding and taking advantage of what we currently know from research on pay-for-performance practices. It also means tracking the impact of pay-for-performance programs as they are implemented and sustained in order to understand their impact and learn what is or is not working well so that the organization can make adjustments as needed.

THE CHALLENGE OF DESIGN

The challenges associated with effectively designing pay-for-performance programs can be enormous. Plans with flawed designs fail to capture the potential benefits of pay-for-performance and may cause damage if they inadvertently reward counterproductive behavior or produce divisive relationships when cooperation is necessary. Practitioners tend to underestimate the challenges associated with designing effective plans and the intensity of employee reaction to the need to periodically adjust plans. Common design challenges include: difficulties in measuring performance, setting payouts at the correct level, managing factors outside the control of individuals being paid for performance, discomfort that managers and peers have with rating employees differentially, limited funding for payouts, resistance to adjusting payout levels as technology or market conditions change, and avoiding perceptions of unfairness.[35] As one example of the challenge of setting payouts at the correct level, British policy makers thought they had set physician pay-for-performance standards at the right level. However, they underestimated how quickly physicians would reach certain levels of performance, and they ended up owing physicians approximately $700 million more than they had budgeted for the program.[36]

Managers also need to balance out how simple vs complex to make the programs. If programs are too simple they appear to lack important nuances of performance or they may encourage employees to focus on just one measure at the expense of others that are also important to organizational performance. By contrast, if they are too complex, they risk becoming a source of confusion and frustration rather than a source of motivation.

Ineffective design of executive pay-for-performance is at the heart of much of the recent criticism. O'Bryne and Young[37] concluded from their study of pay packages from 702 publicly traded companies that there was a clear lack of sensitivity between the measures determining executive pay and those contributing to shareholder wealth. They also note that alternative designs which would correct this lack of sensitivity are available if boards can muster the will to enact them.

Pay at the highest managerial levels has it own unique complications that may be difficult to resolve. Fortunately, many of the other potential design problems described above can be managed if designers are realistic and thoughtful about the challenges associated with effective design, involve a variety of employees in the design process, and make time to pilot test and make adjustments prior to full-scale implementation.

THE CHALLENGE OF IMPLEMENTATION

Design is only part of the problem because the efficacy of a program also depends on the quality of implementation, and managers often underestimate the challenges associated with execution. One continuing challenge has to do with communication about how the program works and what is required to achieve rewards. One survey found that only 29 percent of respondents reported having clarity about the connection between their performance and rewards.[38] Similarly, the NCPI's examination of pay-for-performance initiatives in Florida schools revealed that less than half of the teachers reported having a clear understanding of what they would need to do to achieve rewards.[39] In reflecting upon her experience with pay-for-performance throughout her career, one human resources executive at American Express shared the perception that more often than not employees she observed in various companies lacked a clear understanding of how their pay-for-performance compensation was determined and that often led to suspicion and cynicism rather than motivation. When KeySpan Corporation (a New York gas-and-electricity company with about 9,700 employees) first initiated its new pay-for-performance program, workers were "demoralized" by it.[40] KeySpan had not taken the time to communicate and help employees understand the reasons for it and how it was designed to work. Subsequently, KeySpan Corporation managers made the effort to explain and were able to change perceptions of the program.

Another problem that often receives insufficient attention is the match between current management skills and the skills necessary to effectively implement the pay-for-performance program.[41] Programs often require that managers rate employees and deliver critical feedback. Often, employees are also asked to rate each other and sometimes to provide feedback. Managers and employees are often uncomfortable with the interpersonal tensions associated with the roles of evaluator and feedback giver and they lack the skills necessary to carry out these roles effectively.[42] Organizations often fail to assess what new skills will be needed and to provide appropriate training prior to implementing pay-for-performance programs. This was another reason that KeySpan employees were demoralized by their new pay-for-performance program. Supervisors were suddenly required to give critical feedback and manage performance in ways that they had not previously been required to do, and they were not prepared sufficiently for the transition. Thus, there was a rough implementation and KeySpan had to take corrective action after the fact.[43]

THE CHALLENGE OF ADOPTING A STRATEGIC PERSPECTIVE

The drive to use pay-for-performance comes from a simple desire to motivate more constructive behavior. However, compensation is a complex and multifaceted phenomenon that can impact organizational effectiveness in a variety of ways. Leaders need to be clear on the organization's purpose, strategy, and core competencies and consider how these might be affected by different types of compensation programs. Pay-for-performance programs should be designed to be consistent with and supportive of the organization's purpose, strategy, and core competencies. What might be good for one individual, group, or department might not be fitting for the organization as a whole.

Managers should consider the fit of pay-for-performance initiatives with their organization's culture and preferred management tools. Baron[44] observed that organizations tend to either cluster around "harder" management tools (i.e., "incentive systems, standardized processes, and use of metrics") or "softer" management tools (i.e., "enculturation, personal networks, and corporate strategy statements"). Introducing "harder" management tools into a culture that is dominated by the use of "softer" tools may prove to be a poor fit and produce undesirable results.[45]

In addition to considering the impact of pay-for-performance on motivation, managers are also advised to consider their impact on selection effects. Specifically, compensation systems influence not only motivation but also the types of prospective employees who are attracted to an organization and the types of employees who are likely to stay in vs leave a particular organization. This should also be a factor in determining the appropriate compensation system for an organization.

ROCKY FLATS ILLUSTRATION

When the challenges listed above are managed effectively, organizations can use financial incentives to achieve incredible feats. Consider the impressive results achieved at the Rocky Flats (one of the nation's toughest nuclear cleanup sites). Initial estimates were that it would take 70 years and $36 billion to clean up the site.[46] However, Kaiser–Hill set a goal of cleaning up the site in roughly 10 years and for less than $7 billion. In addition to the aggressive time frame, the leaders faced an additional challenge: the workers would be working themselves out of their jobs, so they would have a natural incentive to work slowly in order to prolong their employment. Thus, leaders at Kaiser–Hill had to figure out how to motivate workers to accelerate the pace at which they would work themselves out of their jobs. Despite the aggressive goal and significant labor obstacles, Kaiser–Hill completed the project within the self-set deadline and at a cost of just over $6 billion.[47]

How did they achieve this feat? Leaders at Kaiser–Hill successfully addressed each of the challenges described above. They adopted a visionary, strategic perspective that relied heavily on financial incentives but also integrated a number of other changes that were all designed to work in concert with each other. These included interventions designed to change the culture and build a supportive, collaborative working environment with the appropriate balance of structure and freedom. Thus, they encouraged initiative and innovation. Leaders also applied a number of organizational best practices and they learned from their experience and adapted to address various challenges that unfolded as they journeyed through their task.[48]

They carefully designed and implemented financial incentives in conjunction with other mutually supportive managerial tools. Incentives were thoughtfully designed to reward the key strategic outcomes necessary for success—speed, quality, safety, and innovation. Workers were involved in the process and all workers were given significant financial incentives. Financial incentives were provided both in cash and in "scrip" (safe units that acted somewhat like stock options). Leaders made available a generous bonus pool of roughly $90 million to be shared with the workers if they achieved their deadline. However, the percentage of this bonus pool that would go to the workers was designed to fall sharply if they were to exceed the deadline.[49] Specifically, 100 percent of the bonus pool would be paid to workers if they achieved the deadline. If they exceeded the deadline by as much as one year, the proportion of the pool available to workers would fall to 50 percent of the original. If they exceeded the deadline by more than one year, the bonus pool would drop to zero. This provided a strong incentive to work at a rapid pace.

Although $90 million may see like an extremely large bonus pool, one senior executive commented that the incentives more than paid for themselves through their immense impact on worker productivity.[50] According to this executive, Kaiser–Hill's eventual profit was far higher than it would have been without the incentives, despite the considerable expense.

SUMMARY

The use of pay-for-performance programs continues to grow both within the traditional arena of the corporation as well as in new areas of application such as health care, schools, and governmental institutions. Pay-for-performance programs will be most effective when they successfully address the challenges associated with learning from experience and identifying the best practices, design, implementation, and adopting a strategic perspective. Kaiser–Hill provides an example of the results that are possible when an organization effectively manages each of these challenges.

END NOTES

1. M. Beer and M. D. Cannon, "Promise and Peril in Implementing Pay-for-Performance," *Human Resource Management*, vol. 43, no. 1, 2004, pp. 3–48.

2. M. Kanter and M. Lucas, "Hewitt Study: While Salary Increases in 2008 Remain Modest, Variable Pay Awards Reach Record High," 2007.

3. T. Lemieux, Parent, D., and W. B. MacLeod, "Performance Pay and Wage Inequality," National Bureau of Economic Research Working Paper No. 13128, 2007.

4. E. White, "Theory & Practice: Employers Increasingly Favor Bonuses to Raises; Companies Aim to Motivate Workers, Lower Fixed Costs; Losing 'Entitlement' Notion," *The Wall Street Journal*, 2006, p. B.3.

5. V. Jablow, "The prognosis for U.S. health care: the health care system in the United States can provide technology advanced treatments, but it still struggles to cover the basics. An expert outlines how to ensure more citizens access to high-quality health care," *Trial*, vol. 54, 2006.

6. A. M. Epstein, "Paying for Performance in the United States and Abroad," *The New England Journal of Medicine*, vol. 355, no. 4, 2006, pp. 406–408.

7. K. Levit, C. Smith, et al., "Health Spending Rebound Continues in 2002," *Health Affairs*, vol. 23, 2004, p. 147.

8. A. Robeznieks, "P4P Programs Quadruple," *Modern Healthcare*, vol. 37, no. 35, 2007, p. 10.

9. M. B. Rosenthal, Landon, B. E., et al., "Pay for Performance in Commercial HMOs," *The New England Journal of Medicine*, vol. 355, no. 18, 2006, pp. 1895–1902.

10. Epstein (2006), see note 6.

11. Healthways Center for Health Research, "Measuring the Success of the Healthways myhealthIQ Program," Nashville, TN, 2006.

12. OECD, "Education at a Glance," OECD Publishing: Paris, France, 2005.

13. W. J. Bennett, "OECD calls for braoder access to post-school education and training," *School Reform News*. Chicago, IL: The Heartland Institute, 1999.

14. M. Podgursky and M. Springer, "Teacher Performance Pay: A Review," *Journal of Policy Analysis and Management*, vol. 26, no. 4, 2007.

15. B. Jacob and M. G. Springer, "Teacher Attitudes on Pay for Performance: A Pilot Study," National Center on Performance Incentives, 2007.

16. T. Dell'Angela, "10 Schools will Offer Teachers Merit Pay; High-performing City Educators could get $8,000 Bonuses," *Chicago Tribune*, Chicago, Ill., May 22, 2007, p. 1.

17. B. Trahant and S. Yearout, "Making Reward for Performance a Reality," *Public Manager*, vol. 34, no. 4, 2005, p. 49.

18. Ibid.

19. W. F. Cascio, *Managing Human Resources: Productivity, Quality of Work Life, Profits*. Boston, MA: McGraw-Hill/Irwin, 2006.

20. L. A. Bebchuk and J. M. Fried, *Pay without Performance: the Unfulfilled Promise of Executive Compensation*. Cambridge, MA: Harvard University Press, 2004. J. Pfeffer, "Six dangerous myths about pay," *Harvard Business Review*, vol. 76, no. 3, 1998, pp. 108–19.

21. Beer and Cannon (2004), see note 1.

22. J. B. Christianson, D. J. Knutson, R. S. Mazze, "Physician Pay-For-Performance. Implementation and Research Issues," *Journal of General Internal Medicine*, vol. 21, no. s2, 2006, pp. S9–S13. doi:10.1111/j.1525-1497.2006.00356.x

23. Price Waterhouse Coopers Health Research Institute, "Keeping Score: A Comparison of Pay-for-performance Programs among Commercial Insurers," 2007, p. 24.

24. L. A. Petersen, Woodard, L. D., et al., "Does Pay-for-Performance Improve the Quality of Health Care?," *Annals of Internal Medicine*, vol. 145, no. 4, 2006, pp. 265–72.

25. E. S. Fisher, "Paying for Performance – Risks and Recommendations," *The New England Journal of Medicine*, vol. 355, no. 18, 2006, pp. 1845–47.

26. A. T. Chien and R. A. Dudley, "Pay-for-Performance in Pediatrics: Proceeed With Caution," *Pediatrics*, vol. 120, no. 1, 2007, pp. 186–8.

27. B. A. Gerhart and S. Rynes, *Compensation: Theory, Evidence, and Strategic Implications*. Thousand Oaks, CA: Sage, 2003.

28. Bebhuk and Fried (2004), see note 20.

29. R. Kirkland and D. Burke, "The Real CEO Pay Problem," *Fortune*, vol. 154, no. 1, 2006, p. 78.

30. Bebchuk & Fried (2004) and Pfeffer (1998), see note 20.

31. R. A. Dudley, "Pay-for-Performance Research," *The Journal of American Medical Association*, vol. 294, no. 14, 2005, pp. 1821–3.

32. Gerhart & Rynes (2003), see note 27.

33. Beer & Cannon (2004), see note 1.

34. M. G. Springer, M. Podgursky, et al., "Governor's Educator Excellence Grant (GEEG) Program: Year One Evaluation Report," Austin, TX: Texas Education Agency, 2007.

35. M. B. Rosenthal and R. A. Dudley, "Pay-for-Performance: Will the Latest Payment Trend Improve Care?," *The Journal of American Medical Association*, vol. 292, no. 7, 2007, pp. 740–4.

36. R. Galvin, "Pay-for-Performance: Too Much of a Good Thing? A Conversation with Martin Roland," *Health Affairs*, vol. 25, no. 5, 2006, pp. 412–19.

37. S. F. O'Byrne and S. D. Young, "Why Executive Pay Is Falling," *Harvard Business Review*, vol. 84, no. 6, 2006, p. 28, 5/9p, 1 chart.

38. M. A. Stiffler, "Incentive Compensation Management: Making Pay-for-Performance a Reality," *Performance Management*, vol. 45, no. 1, 2006, pp. 25–30.

39. Jacob and Springer (2007), see note 15.

40. White (2006), see note 4.

41. K. S. Helgason and V. Klareskov, "When the Halo Wears Off," *Public Manager*, vol. 34, no. 4, 2005, p. 42.

42. M. D. Cannon and R. Witherspoon, "Actionable Feedback: Unlocking the Power of Learning and Development," *Academy of Management Executive*, vol. 19, 2005, pp. 120–34.

43. White (2006), see note 4.

44. J. N. Baron, "Commentary on 'Promise and Peril in Implementing Pay-for-Performance'," *Human Resource Management*, vol. 43, no. 1, 2004.

45. Ibid.

46. J. McGregor, "Rocky Mountain High," *Business Source Premier*, vol. 84, 2004.

47. K. S. Cameron and M. Lavine, *Making the Impossible Possible: Leading Extraordinary Performance—the Rocky Flats Story*. San Francisco, CA: Berrett–Koehler, 2006.

48. See Cameron and Lavine (2006), ibid., for a detailed account.

49. Ibid.

50. Ibid.

REFERENCES

Bebchuck, L. A. and Fried, J. M., "Executive Compensation at Fannie Mae: A Case Study of Perverse Incentives, Nonperformance Pay, and Camouflage," *Journal of Corporation Law*, vol. 30, no. 4, 2005, p. 807.

Bebchuck, L. A. and Fried, J. M., "Pay without Performance: Overview of the issues," *Academy of Management Journal*, 2006, pp. 5–24.

Rosenthal, M. B., Frank, R. G. et al., "Early Experience With Pay-for-Performance," *The Journal of the American Medical Association*, vol. 294, no. 14, 2005, pp. 1788–1793.

PART 7

Talent Management and Compensation

USING COMPENSATION TO WIN THE TALENT WARS

Deborah Rees, Director

Innecto Reward Consulting

IS YOUR ORGANIZATION WINNING THE war for talent? Are you incorporating more opportunities, more mentoring, more recognition? The premise of "growing your own" is attractive—but how effective are most HR and Reward professionals in ensuring that talent management processes and pay strategies are linked? We know that talent management has become a major discipline within HR in the last 10 years, rooted in the launch of the concept of "The War for Talent" following seminal research by the McKinsey Corporation in 1997. Organizations have made huge expenditures in developing talent management strategy processes to attract and retain key employees who hold the silver bullet to organization success. However, in reality there has been a significant disconnect between the investment in talent management processes and the reality of the success of "talented" individuals in organizations. The developed world is facing significant issues around demographic change, the retirement of the baby boomer generation, and the lack of new graduates in science and engineering.

For companies to build a sustainable future, there has to be significant changes in the way in which talented individuals are attracted, retained, and rewarded.

The "prevailing wisdom" in managing talented individuals has extensively focused on developing strategies in career management, building a compelling future, and linking development and job opportunities for individuals. This perception of what attracts and retains the cohort has been the case for many years. However, with the generational changes in the workforce, new research challenges that stance and reviews the success of talent management strategies, particularly when linked to reward.

DEFINE THE ISSUES

There are as many definitions of talent as there are books on the subject. However both Towers Perrin and Hay in their research in this subject have identified that an organization-specific definition of talent and the consistent delivery of talent management processes are essential to effective talent management practices. The CIPD (Chartered Institute of Personnel and Development) UK, in August 2007, has developed a definition stating:

> Talent consists of those individuals who can make a difference to organization performance either thorough their immediate contribution or in the longer term, by demonstrating the highest levels of potential.

By using the above as our working definition of talent, we can consider how to build a strategic pay and reward framework around these key individuals, rather than the tactical knee-jerk relation which often characterizes organizations' response to rewarding talent. It is clear that those individuals who make a difference to the organization "right here, right now" may need to be treated differently in pay terms than those who have the potential in the future to effect change. Hay, in their report *"Talent Management – what the best organizations actually do"*, make the point that "divergent notions of what talent management looks like across the organization" are a barrier for effective talent management. For pay and reward strategies to work there has to be clarity about the strategic requirements of the organization, and how this links to individual people who can deliver what the business needs.

IMPACT AND IMPORTANCE

It is hard to overrate the importance of attracting talent into an organization. Changing demographic issues, particularly around the retirement of key management and the falling numbers of younger people seeking degrees in high demand areas, have led 42 percent of organizations in the U.S. to believe that the aging workforce issue is significant to their future success. They highlight in particular the departure of senior management and the technical and talented individuals, and the issues of transferring their knowledge and skills through the organization.

Across the UK and Europe some of these issues emerged several years ago. Early retirement ages, favorable pension conditions, and discrimination by employers in employing men and women over the age of 50 led to a decline in the net retirement age. The consequence of this, not unforeseen, was fewer individuals at a senior level and possessing senior technical and specialist skills. As a result, the focus on talent management has shifted in several ways. The stereotypical talented individual, a white male, has now been replaced by a broader approach. It has become clear that the effect of wider acceptance of different working practices such as flex time, immigration, embracing diversity, and tackling age discrimination are approaches that have been successful in widening the talent pool. The United States faces significant issues between the years 2008 and 2015 and beyond as the baby boomer generation reaches the historic retirement age. Many of these aging workers are in senior management positions and there are insufficient employees with the developed competencies to succeed them. Simply put, too many organizations are chasing too few individuals.

In addition, in the UK and Europe forces driven by the European social equality agenda have driven organizations to focus on internal equity, equal pay issues and eliminating pay discrimination based on age, faith, race, and sexual orientation. This has, in turn, impacted organizations on their pay structures and choices on individual employee differentiation in pay.

STATE-OF-THE-ART THINKING

A great employer brand name, strong working practices, and clear value in adding experience to an employee's resume are all important, but organizations must be aware of all the bullets they can fire in the war for talent. Over the years of development of the theory of talent management, the concepts around what talented individuals seek as their reward have been based on surveys of the baby boomer population. This population is characterized as essentially very team-focused and historically has seen the rewards of staying with an organization over a long period of time.

However, the population that is now being courted as talent is significantly different. Innecto Reward Consulting's High Flyer Trend report found that the conclusions drawn from a group of younger employees (under 40) showed their drivers were significantly different from those of the previous generation, and that the old beliefs about managing and retaining talent may simply no longer hold true. By interviewing both HR managers and career-oriented individuals in the UK, the survey demonstrated that there is a clear disparity between the beliefs of these two groups. In addition, this difference is having a negative impact on talent retention with more than three-quarters of businesses admitting that they lose at least five talented employees every year.

Currently, the UK HR profession holds that career-minded employees are not primarily motivated by financial reward but by other factors such as quality of work, a good working environment, career opportunities, and personal development. The under-forties (Generation X) is the first generation without a "job for life" expectation. During the past 15 years society has fundamentally changed—working and resourcing practices have changed, and as loyalty to employees has withered, so has employee loyalty to their employer. It is as easy to compare salaries and packages on the Internet, as it locate the price of a stereo. With rising cost of living and housing costs affecting most young professionals across North America, Europe, and the UK, it is demonstrable that the focus for individuals to improve their standard of living overrides all other considerations.

The Innecto study established that the new generation of talent is focused on financial reward. Some 68 percent of those in the survey said that pay was their number one career motivator. By contrast, HR professionals identified personal pride as the number one motivator for talented individuals, followed by a competitive or challenging environment, and financial reward was only placed as the third most important motivator.

In high-performing organizations, HR and compensation professionals are recognizing that, in addressing the issues and needs of Generation X and Generation Y there needs to be a fundamental rethink of the way talent is rewarded in the organization. Deloitte identifies the impact of the experience of previous generations on Generation Y as they enter the workforce as focusing on adding value, making a difference, and CSR.

It has been demonstrated that high talent strategies can actually work against the success of the business. There have been assumptions that individuals can replicate their success in technical roles across wider management roles. Individuals have been promoted too quickly to levels where their skills do not support them. There is a lack of clarity about what talent looks like and a lack of process to maintain the talented individuals in different positions has been ascribed as a reason why organizations fail to retain the talent they wish to. In researching rewards, compensation, and talent, it is clear that there is little information on this key area available to the practitioner. Many books and journals on reward strategy do not touch on the subject. The focus of talent management strategy literature is about managing the process and often simply asks readers to consider that other factors may need to be adjusted, including reward. However, our premise is that reward is a fundamental component in talent management strategy and high attrition and the lack of success of some major talent programs can be directly ascribed to HR and compensation professionals being unable to link effective reward to the appropriate individual.

IDENTIFY OPTIONS AND SOLUTIONS

Linking talent management strategies and reward for individuals is a complex business. Michael Williams takes an uncompromising stance; "High performers almost instinctively expect reward systems based upon differentials that reflect achievement, contribution, and results."

But we recognize that, in day-to-day corporate life, the sometimes conflicting culture of the organization and how wider employee retention and motivation can be affected must be considered. Talented individuals do not exist in a bubble inside their corporations. Therefore aligning pay strategies (base pay, bonus or nonconsolidated pay, and long-term incentive plans) to talent management processes is key to attracting and retaining talent. Successful organizations that have been running talent management for a number of years have found that the longer term impact of making tactical decisions around pay, bonus, and long-term incentive plans (LTIP) have come back to haunt them in situations where individuals appear not to fulfil their originally identified talent.

Base Pay

Numerous organizations that would identify themselves as having effective base pay management have followed a path rooted in assessing how much the *job* is worth—both internally and externally. For many organizations the development of pay structures and strategies has been heavily driven by legislation across Europe and in the United States aimed at ensuring fairness and equity for all employees. The difficulty in developing a base pay strategy for talented individuals is that the pay for talented individuals is fundamentally about the individual and not the job, and requires extending salary differentials for individuals rather than pay convergence.

In considering the development of a pay strategy, it is helpful to separate out the two categories of talented individuals:

- talent making a difference through immediate contribution and *performance*
- talent with identifiable *potential* for the future

The two groups of talent should be treated differently for base pay purposes. The first group of talent, i.e. those who demonstrate their skills currently and are of immense importance to the success of the business, are likely to be a more unstable cohort. These individuals are vulnerable to poaching from other organizations and, with information on salaries readily available, it can be too late if an organization finds that they have let salaries drift behind the market. Therefore wider reward strategies such as interesting work, enjoyable culture, high levels of recognition and the employee feeling valued are important. Getting base pay wrong and underpaying employees can have a catastrophic effect on this group, and the longer-term success of the business.

Establishing appropriate base pay levels for high-performing talent can be complex—pay structures are too inflexible to adopt sufficiently adaptable practices on pay. Where pay movement is limited to a flat 3 percent cost of living rise per annum, based on union agreement, it can be difficult to "bend" sufficiently to reward individuals and create performance differentials.

In many organizations there is an inherent conflict between wanting to ensure that all employees give of their best and feel engaged and motivated by their work, and the reality of highlighting the group of individuals who are treated as special cases. Zingheim identifies the issues around paying base pay differently for the high-talent workforce (she describes them as "superkeepers"), and states that this 2–5 percent of employees must be "kept without regard for tenure or entitlement because they get your company through thick and thin." This uncompromising position makes business sense, and while Boards dither, key employees may not be able to withstand the blandishments of the hard-sell headhunter offering substantial improvements in pay and therefore lifestyle.

Key principles to bear in mind when developing a reward strategy for key talent are:

- Ensure that the individuals in the cohort are demonstrating through their immediate contribution that they are fundamental to your organization's success. Be vigilant—base pay changes are very difficult to undo.

- Consider the implications of the loss of these individuals and their skills, competencies, and the value they add to the organization, plus the costs of recruiting new hires to replace them.

- Focus on predicting external market movement and the growth in value of the talent base, and plan to manage pay proactively by developing a budget in advance to handle mid-cycle changes.

- Some organizations develop rules about breaking the rules, adopting a strategy around developing an upper quartile base pay position or even an upper decile base pay position for talented individuals in comparison to others in the organization.

In contrast, when looking at individuals with potential for the future, focusing on base pay movement is less successful. It is noticeably more difficult to identify those individuals who may be effective in the future; some inevitable crystal ball gazing is required regarding the requirements of both the organization and the matching abilities of the individual in future years. The intention with these individuals is to retain them in the organization and grow their potential into actual performance. There are key differences with the first group:

- this group have not yet demonstrated that they are able to turn raw material into actual deliverables

- they are less likely to be as attractive in the external market as they are not yet performing at the level which the organization has recognized they may in the future

- there is a possible long-term relationship with this type of employee that is mutually beneficial

This high-potential group of "talent" should probably not be directly rewarded for their talent in base pay differentials. The difficulty with base pay is that its very permanence can cause issues long-term for the management of this more volatile group, some of whom are likely to jump ship over time. While it is important that base pay is kept in line with the market, other ways of rewarding this group including the traditional "talent management" approaches of interesting work assignments, recognition, mentoring, sabbaticals, and wider project opportunities are all crucial in developing a mutually dependent relationship between the high-potential individual and the company. While it is important to recognize the increasing value of these individuals to the organization through calibrating base pay to the market, other forms of reward such as bonuses and long-term incentives can be more effective in retaining this group.

ANNUAL BONUS AND LUMP SUM PAYMENTS

Any form of variable pay is an attractive tool in attracting and retaining key talent. High-performing and high-potential individuals recognize in themselves the ability to make a difference in the workforce. They are frustrated by lack of recognition in the differentiation between their performance and that of their peers. If this is not adequately reflected in reward, then attrition is to be expected. For current high-performance individuals—the "superkeepers"—base pay plus performance based lump sums keep pay fresh and exciting, and ensure that the individual employee knows they are valued by the organization for what they deliver. However, we have already outlined the difficulty in rewarding high-potential employees in base pay.

Options for rewarding high-potential talent include compensation mainly through nonconsolidated payments rather than base pay. These lump sum payments may take the form of being targeted to reflect the achievement of a prior agreed objective or project and may be closely aligned to the changes in the value of the individual, both external and internal. The nimble and flexible approach of using nonconsolidated lump sum payments ensures the business is not making permanent changes to an individual's base pay when that individual has yet to prove their long-term worth to the organization. Lump sums can provide an attractive and exciting incentive for employees who recognize that their value to the organization is growing. From a management perspective, these payments can be offered mid-pay cycle allowing a closer link between deliverables and payment.

By linking lump sum payments to specific deliverables, the high-potential employee has the prospect of demonstrating how their potential is migrating to actual performance. It is also easy to identify and focus on those individuals who have failed to live up to their earlier promise and are not yet able to translate potential into output without compounding the problem with inflated base pay. This scenario demonstrates the flexibility and cost effectiveness of the lump-sum approach.

Using the current annual bonus system can be problematic—the eligibility rules may prevent some future talent from accessing bonus payments as they are too junior. Where annual bonus is specifically focused around the senior team, another option is to create a "group B" bonus pot where entry eligibility is offered to those employees who, while not yet residing in the senior levels of the organization, are identified as being of significant importance to the organization and its succession plan. The inclusion of an employee in group B in one annual bonus cycle does not necessarily mean their inclusion in future years. By putting a spotlight on these individuals relatively early in their careers, it gives the opportunity for employees to comprehend and be incentivized by the opportunities further up their career ladder. Towers Perrin also found that the amount of the bonus paid was less important to some individuals than the fact that they were eligible for a bonus.

LONG-TERM INCENTIVES

Long-term incentives are frequently used creatively in "state-of-the-art" organizations to reward talented individuals. The use of employee share plans and equity over the last decade was seen as extremely attractive. It was viewed as inexpensive, engaging the employee in the long-term success of the business, and sharing reward with those who have helped to create it. However, the changes to accounting rules on both sides of the Atlantic have meant that the share options or stock option has become a less attractive vehicle for the long-term retention of individuals. In addition, the dot-com boom and crash means that employees have a more realistic understanding that options may never translate into hard cash. However, stock still has a place in total reward compensation. From a rewarding talent perspective:

- It closely aligns the individual with the long-term success of the business

- It has a pleasing balance in that it allows the organization to repay and share some of the value that the individual has participated in building, and helps to share the financial benefits of success

- It acts as a reminder to both high-potential and high-performance individuals that the long-term sustainability and success of the company is critical

There are alternative approaches to be taken by creating cash LTIPs. Cash LTIPs can be beneficial for two reasons:

- They do not further dilute shareholder equity

- They are a more flexible and directly useful tool than stock plans that are based on the entire value of an organization

By linking a cash plan to the success of the specific business unit, there can be significant benefit in drawing a clear line-of-sight from the individual employee and the wealth and value that their efforts have helped to build. As Patricia K. Zingheim identifies "The goal of focusing the efforts of the individual on adding value to the organizational unit in which they work is often best accomplished with long-term pay that emphasises business unit performance."

SUMMARY

In creating a culture where high-performing and high-potential individuals are rewarded and retained by the organization, the organization has to face some significant adjustments to its "one size fits all" pay strategy. In the same way that organizations have become used to compensating sales professionals and senior management differently, for state-of-the-art performance management a new mindset is required to boldly challenge the reward strategy for talented individuals.

As senior management and senior technicians who hold key knowledge and skills about the organization's success gradually approach retirement, a new population of dominant individuals will have to emerge for sustained success. Finding key talent willing to take up residence in your organization is the future challenge for many current Boards and HR executives.

A majority of organizations understand the business requirements for key talent, and know that identifying and retaining the people who can deliver is essential to build a sustainable future. However many organizations have failed to make the link between the success of the organization and the personal opportunity and reward of the individuals concerned. While much talent management research has been conducted on the baby boomer generation, more modern research suggests that some of that received wisdom should now be turned on its head. Generations X and Y seek primarily to increase and maximize their reward using their talent. They have significantly less loyalty to an organization than previous generations, as in turn, the organization has to them. In this age of outsourcing, off-shoring, fixed-term contracts and short-term memories, it is clear that the enduring slow-build, slow-burn career pattern of the baby boomer generation is less likely to be replicated with the Generations X and Y of today's workforce. For the company to attract, retain, motivate, and engage these employees, it has to become more flexible, nimble, and smart in rewarding them in a way that is attractive to them.

Employees now have ways of accessing information about their salary and packages literally at their fingertips through the Internet. They have grown up with family members who have received significant amounts of money through the stock market growth. In short, they are aware of their own value and they wish to maximize it during the time period that they choose to work.

The traditional talent management approaches to reward employees, including offering interesting work, wider experiences, and new projects, all act as incentives to attracting and retaining individuals. However, "show me the money" is the cry that resounds from the upcoming generation of talent.

Our recommendations are wide ranging:

- Organizations have shown themselves to be significantly behind the wave in terms of their lack of flexibility, foresight, and ability to plan for what they know is inevitable. Organizations need to become more astute in matching the ability, aspiration, and agility of their talented employees. This involves being geared up in creating and setting pay budgets which anticipate the uplift in an individual's value to the organization and attractiveness to external companies. It involves recognizing that this value does not align neatly to the regulation annual pay cycle or company fiscal year, but opportunities, pay changes, and bonus payments may need to be made at different points through the year to ensure that the key individual is sufficiently recognized.

- Reward and HR directors are aware that by building a business case they can demonstrate the value of key individuals to the organization and the cost both financially and in terms of degree of difficulty in replacing these individuals. Our findings from state-of-the-art organizations show the breadth of the full gamut of reward opportunities available. These include:

  - the flexible and thoughtful use of base pay
  - interesting and exciting linking of annual or shorter term lump sum payments to direct performance and objectives
  - the creative use of long-term incentives not just around shares and stock, which may have a cloudy line-of-sight for the individual employee, but through the use of cash plans related to the particular business unit where the individual is employed
  - in addition, but not instead of pay, the traditional mainstays of reward in this area—recognition, new opportunities, mentoring, long-term career planning and the incentive of a seat at the top table—should be thoughtfully utilized

Having an effective reward strategy for talented individuals is part of the war chest for HR Directors in addressing new strategies for winning the war for talent, but it is an element that organizations, researchers, academics, and practitioners seem to have put to one side or filed in the pile marked "too difficult". For the majority of organizations who are complacently behind the wave in seeking to attract and retain individuals to support the future sustainability of their organization, a review and update of their pay structure and approach to rewarding talent cannot come too soon.

REFERENCES

Buck Consultants, "The Real Talent Debate: Will Aging Boomers Deplete the Workforce?", 2007.

Conley, P., Lassonde, R. and Larson, S., "Using Long Term Incentives to Retain Top Talent: Super Rewards for Superkeepers", *The Talent Management Handbook*, Berger, L. A. and Berger, D. R. (eds). New York: McGraw-Hill, 2003, pp. 399–413.

Deloitte Research, *It's 2008: Do You Know Where Your Talent Is? Why Acquisition and Retention Strategies Don't Work*. Deloitte Development LLC, 2004.

Deloitte Research, *Winning the New Talent Game*. Deloitte Development LLC, 2005.

Deloitte Research, *Generational Talent Management*, Deloitte Development LLC, 2006.

Hay Group, *Talent Management—What the Best Organisations Actually Do*. HayGroup Inc., 2005.

Hay Group, *Potential—For What? What Every CEO Should Know—New Insights into Selecting the Right Leaders to Secure your Competitive Future*. HayGroup Inc., 2006.

Hotopp, U., "Labour Market Trends" *The Employment Rate of Older Workers*, London: Office for National Statistics, 2005, p. 73.

Independent Writer, "Be Structured in Managing Talent," *Development and Learning in Organizations*, vol. 21, no. 3, 2007, pp. 31–4.

Kermally, S., *Developing and Managing Talent*, Thorogood, 2004.

Phoeniz, T., Craver, B. and Desai, A. H., "Workforce Analytics: Driving Talent Management Strategies through Workforce Data," *IHRIM.link*, April/May 2007, pp. 16–19.

Rees, D. et al., *High Flyer Trend Report*. Innecto Reward Consulting, 2006.

Thorne, K., *Managing the Mavericks*, Spiro Press, 2003.

Towers Perrin report, *How Leading Organizations Manage Talent*, Towers Perrin LLP, 2001.

Williams, M., *The War for Talent—getting the best from the best*, London: CIPD, 2000, pp. 16–17.

Winkler, V. and Clark, R., *Talent Management*, London: CIPD, 2007.

Zingheim, P. K., "Rewarding Scarce Talent," *Pay People Right!: Breakthrough Reward Strategies to Create Great Companies*, Zingheim, P. K. and Schuster, J. R. (eds). San Francisco, CA: Jossey-Bass, 2000, pp. 232–36.

Zingheim, P. K., "Winning the Battle for Superkeepers: Talent Your Company Needs to Thrive," *The Talent Management Handbook*, Berger, L. A. and Berger, D. R. (eds). New York: McGraw-Hill, 2003, pp. 365–84.

C H A P T E R

TALENT MANAGEMENT, ORGANIZATION TRANSFORMATION, AND COMPENSATION

Lance A. Berger, Chief Executive Officer

Lance A. Berger & Associates, Ltd

LOUIS PASTEUR STATED, "CHANGE FAVORS only the prepared mind." Compensation professionals have to proactively sift through best practices as well as current theories to incorporate into their collective body of knowledge the processes that will result in favorable results. The collective body of truthful knowledge is critical because it is the basis upon which we make important decisions that support the continual, sometimes rapid, transformation of organizations.

This material provides a conceptual framework or decision-making tool that incorporates the experiences of my colleagues and I, our research, focus groups, and interviews, as well as information garnered from existing compensation literature, including this book. It is not an elixir guaranteeing results, but with appropriate modifications, the framework can be a productive starting point in the creation of a compensation program.

WORKFORCE MANAGEMENT

In my experience, compensation programs are complex financial distribution systems serving a multitude of overlapping, conflicting, and frequently unclear purposes. Chapters in this book describe how compensation programs are used to attract, retain, motivate, and reward employees. Certainly these goals are worthy and justifiably have remained part of our psyche for decades. I have found, however, that the real purpose and use of compensation programs, under which the previous rubrics are subsumed, is workforce management. This goal is not effectively met because organizations are frequently clumsy and sometimes disingenuous in their application of both selective pay distribution and the support systems necessary to effect this activity.

My definition of *workforce management* is the *planned*, *selective* attraction and retention of specific individuals and classes of employees, derived from a human resources strategy, based on an organization blueprint or success model. A pay premium is assigned to an individual, or group of individuals, because of their performance, potential future organizational contribution, special talent group, or some other value-differentiating characteristic. A workforce assessment process must be conducted to determine premium individual and talent classes in order to effectively implement a viable compensation system. Such an assessment system clearly identifies high-potential and high-performing employees as well as critical replacements and "hot" talent markets.

When pay practices are ambiguous, inconsistent, or arbitrary, or perceived as such by employees, dysfunctional performance, unwanted turnover, and/or morale problems are triggered. Historically, organization compensation programs sought internally to minimize differences in external pay markets, choosing to establish a small number of salary structures favoring internal equity over market conditions. Typically, organizations selected the strongest pay markets as their reference points, or benchmarks. My experience indicates that in these situations more employees were overpaid than underpaid, and this overpayment was a major contributor to unaffordable payrolls. The overpay practices coupled with higher unemployment rates concealed the emerging pay gaps in certain talent markets and increased the likelihood of losing top talent and retaining mediocre performers.

The "peanut butter" approach of spreading dollars evenly over the workforce was destined for obsolescence as all sizes and types of U.S. businesses began to realign their strategies, operations, and human resources to effectively compete in a global economy. This natural alignment process, combined with a growing economy and changing workforce demography, led us to reaffirm what we already knew: there is no single approach to employee pay that works in all situations, and whichever approach is used will most likely require adaptation as an organization's business situation changes in a rapidly evolving business environment. Additionally, it is likely that one pay system will not work for all employee groups, let alone premium subclasses of these groups. The time, cost, and long-range credibility of an implementation plan must be carefully considered because it could become obsolete before it is completed and it may not be applicable to all covered employees.

Organizations are always transforming themselves. Most of the transformational changes are small but have large cumulative effects over time. Some transformations are major, and these are becoming more frequent. Given the transformational nature of organizations, and specifically the continual need for managing workforce transformation, the question of how to structure transformational compensation systems must be addressed. My experience and research confirm that the answer is found in the reconciliation of business phases (stage of growth), multiple external talent (pay) market demands, and pay techniques. Successfully reconciling these forces requires not only a high level of technical expertise but also a certain boldness and willingness to embrace change.

What is *transformation*? It is a situation that is created when an organization anticipates and responds to changes in its customer base, competitive environment, or internal capacity to deliver a service or product. Based on both external forces and internal capacity for adaptability, the magnitude and speed of change will vary within organizations. Internal change readiness is related to the alignment of a organization's strategy, operations, culture, and reward systems. Any perceptible change in one or more of the first three elements in any organizational unit should trigger a reassessment of compensation systems. When a change trigger destabilizes an organization, a snapshot of the organization's alignment of compensation with its existing strategy, operations, and culture should be taken and its targeted alignment or blueprint must be developed. The gap between current and future compensation becomes the basis for developing a transformational plan.

Both the snapshot and blueprint should contain the following elements of pay strategy: identification of pay aspects of *each* talent market based on sources of recruitment and turnover activities; mix of compensation (base salary, annual, and long-term incentives, benefits, and work–life factors); and competitive level. Within its total level of affordability, an organization will manage a portfolio of pay strategies that will allocate compensation to individuals and classes of employees based on their premium value to the organization. The goal is not to lose anyone that the organization cannot afford to lose, while encouraging turnover among individuals and employee groups that are not as essential to the long-range business and human resources plan.

Transformational compensation activities involve realigning one or more of the pay components that include external pay market, competitive level, mix, or pay technique (delivery system). Transformational compensation necessitates a willingness to alter programs when change occurs and to focus on greater customization of pay packages. To this end, this chapter presents a series of tools that may help practitioners better formulate their options for compensation decisions.

THE ALIGNMENT MODEL

In order to have all key elements of an organization operating in harmony with each other, an alignment model should be developed. Organizations experiencing sustained success practice a version of alignment that transcends functions and units. Their concept of alignment is a multidimensional approach that includes the following:

- Clear vision, mission, values, and goals

- A well-set deployment of process to help achieve the goals

- Key methods of measuring progress (and alignment), including process, results, and customer satisfaction

- Commitment within and throughout the organization on what the critical goals are, how the goals will be reached, and how employees will be involved, appraised, and rewarded

- Recognition of the outside world, including customers, suppliers, competitors, and benchmark performers

Organizations must not only be in alignment but must be able to maintain the alignment in the face of rapid change. Thus the organization that carries the concept of alignment to its broadest potential is the organization that maintains it while managing corporate transformation. Achieving successful transformation is contingent on the following:

- Current, accurate, and "customer-driven" data

- A well-conceived plan that is communicated throughout the organization

- A strategy to follow up, measure, and reinforce performance

- Adequate resources and training

- Leadership and accountability

- Recognition for those who perform well

Figure 43.1 illustrates an alignment model. This model should be customized to the industry of each business unit within a corporation.

The most difficult transformations occur when an organization rapidly shifts to a different phase of growth and its internal alignment is no longer appropriate. This is evident in the radical adaptations made by organizations through downsizing, mergers, and acquisitions. It is also true when smaller organizations

FIGURE 43.1 Alignment model

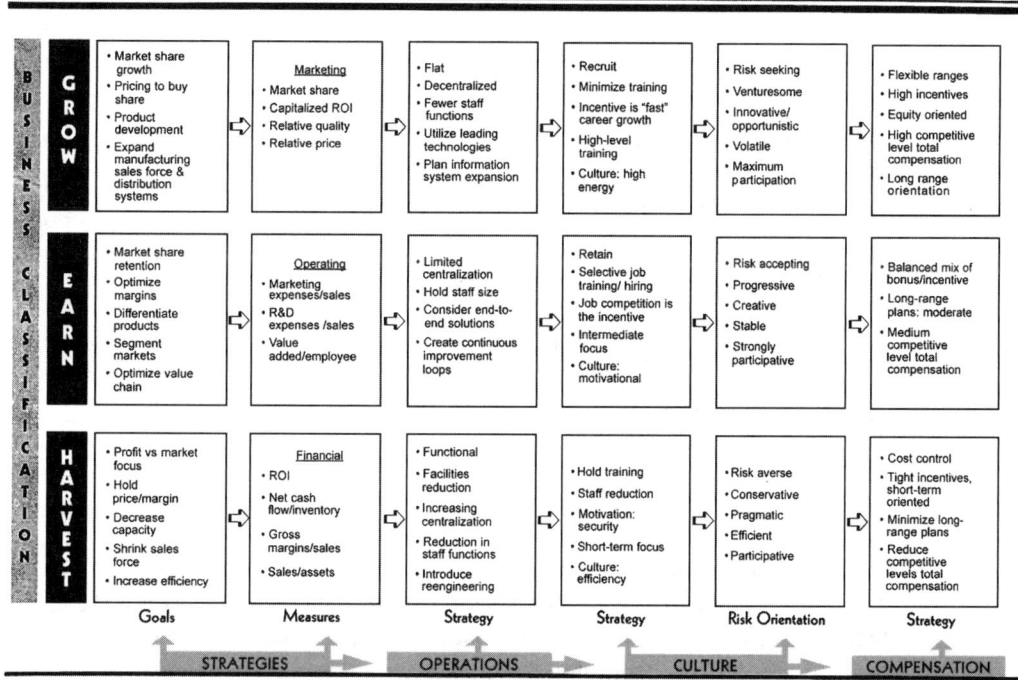

experience a deceleration in their growth rate and organizations of all sizes experience sudden growth. The alignment model suggests that radical and sudden change requires a different culture and, in turn, a different reward system. Regrettably, an existing culture may not support the new business scenario. Additionally, an organization may not be able to adjust its pay packages in accordance with the implications of customization in Figure 43.2. The success of the realignment of internal change elements (strategy, operations, human resources, and compensation) will determine the survival and effectiveness of the business.

The following tools were developed to assist in making an informed choice when change triggers affect internal alignment. The tools are intended to be illustrative and not exhaustive. For details of the various discussed techniques, see chapters throughout the book.

The tools are organized into three sections. The sections are as follows:

■ *Business situations and pay techniques* (see Figure 43.3)—this chart relates nine different business situations to 16 separate pay techniques. Each cell contains Xs reflecting the effectiveness of the technique associated with the business situation. For example, group, team, and opportunity sharing incentives are very effective in times of financial difficulty, and broadbanding is effective when there are current or expected frequent changes in job content.

FIGURE 43.2   Customizing a compensation system

Availability of Talent

		Low	Medium	High
Growth of Industry	High	Highly and Widely Personalized		
	Medium		Moderately Flexible Packages	
	Low	Selective Personalization		Highly Standardized Packages

- *Pay techniques, descriptive matrix* (Figure 43.4)—this chart summarizes four important characteristics associated with the pay techniques identified in Figure 43.3. For example, key contributor programs must be supported by a credible process for identifying must-keep employees, and profit sharing requires a communication process focusing on a common fate for all employees.

- *Culture and pay techniques* (Figure 43.5)—these charts summarize eight culture considerations involved in pay techniques. For example, profit sharing could add to employee dissatisfaction if trust in management were low.

Under the most successful scenario, a business should plan a compensation transformation before it is destabilized by market, competitive, or internal change triggers. An organization's potential for survival is increased by fast response and quick adaptation. The following simplified steps can be helpful during the transformation process:

1. *Determine the direction of the transformation, that is, the acceleration or deceleration of growth.* In general, the amount of *leverage* (percentage variable pay) will increase or decrease with the projected rate of business growth with the specific amount varying by individual, organization level, and work unit. There may be problems with employee cultures that are risk-averse or risk-oriented and that may not therefore fit a business shift. Poor culture fit may delay the complete and timely introduction of a new pay plan.

2. *Determine the amount affordable by the business unit over a two- to three-year period.* Annual increases must be distributed selectively to critical employees or classes of employees to avoid a crippling turnover.

FIGURE 43.3 Business situations and pay techniques

Business Situation/ Pay Techniques	High Cyclicality	Emerging Business	Financial Difficulty	Inflated Wages	Controlling Turnover	Down-sizing	Culture Change	Simulate Entrepre-eurship	Frequent Job Content Shifts
Profit Sharing	XXXXX	XX	XXX				XXXXX	XX	
Subjective Perf. Bonus	XXXXX	XXX			XX				
Opportunity/ Gain Sharing	XXXXX		XXXXX				XXXXX		XXX
Group/Team Incentive			XXXXX			Cancel Any Existing	XXXXX		XXX
Individual Incentive	XXX		XXX			Cancel Any Existing	XXXXX	XXXXX	
Key Contributor Programs	XX	XXXXX			XXXXX		XXXXX	XX	XXX
Competency, Knowledge or Skill-Based Pay			XXXXX				XXX		XXXXX
Broadbanding	XXX		XXX		XXXX		XXXXX		XXXX
Long-Term Plans	XX	XXXXX			XXXXX		XXXXX	XXXXX	
Pay Cuts			XXXXX	XXXXX		XXX			
Pay Freeze			XXXXX	XXXXX		XXXXX			
Two-Tiered Pay System *				XXXXX		XXXXX			
Lump Sum in Lieu of Increase			XXXXX	XXXXX					
Extended Pay Review Intervals			XXXXX	XXXXX					
Work-Life		XXXXX			XXXXX		XXXXX		
Non-Monetary	XXX	XXX		XXX	XXXX		XXXXX		XXXX

Xs indicate the effectiveness of the technique
* New employee at lower rate than current employees

3. *Identify the characteristics of each discrete pay market in which the organization competes for talent.* Remember that these competitors may not be business competitors. The list can be found in recruitment sources, turnover analyses, and internal promotion data. Initially each pay market should be discretely segmented, although they may converge or remain separate and then change over time.

FIGURE 43.4   Pay techniques: descriptive matrix

Pay Technique	How does this technique work?	What business situations lead companies to consider this technique?	What conditions are important for this technique to succeed?	What are the risks of using this technique?

Profit Sharing	• Share the profit once-a-year.
	• Profit can be taken as:
	  – Cash/stock
	  – Deferred for retirement
	  – Split between options above
	• Promotes employee involvement in improving profits.
		• Underachieving financial performance.
		• Need to lower relative labor costs.
		• Desire to create sense of common fate.
		• Shift from entitlement mentality to performance.
		• Quality orientation.
			• Sense of common fate.
			• Management credibility/trust.
			• Employee involvement/ participation.
			• Open communications.
			• "Accurate" financial statements.
				• Profitable years are rare.
				• Employees view plan as a benefit.
				• Link between individual payout and organization performance is weak.
				• Expectations are not met.
				• Management uses the plan as a low pay supplement.
				• Application is forced.
				• Employees focus on short-term results.
				• Uncontrollable factors exist (adversely impact profits).

Subjective Performance Bonus	• Unexpected bonuses. • Intent is to "present" behavioral models to the organization.	• Rapid change. • Trust, support, and commitment on everyone's part. • Good communications. • Use of reinforcement in addition to other alternative rewards.	• Credible performance. • Credible management judges. • Sound communication system.	• Weak selection. • Poor communications. • Inequity of awards. • Does not inspire most employees.
Opportunity/Gain Sharing (Small Group, Rucker, Scanlon, Improshare, Team)	• A group of highly interdependent workers is selected. • Piece rate or measured day, standard hours, sales, R&D, technical milestones or unit measures can be used.	• Need to work in groups. • Highly interdependent employees. • Group can influence its own work.	• Group must be able to collaborate and work together. • Measures must be group not individual. • All awards paid on group results. • Employees trust management. • Group identity.	• Group unable to influence end result. • Payouts may not relate to corporate performance. • Groups sometimes act to destroy another group. • Manipulation of standards.
Group/Team Incentive	• Rewards quality, production, project milestones or other financial or operational objectives. • "Shares" profit according to pre-determined formula. • Targeted incentive awards vary based on organization level, total targeted compensation.	• Need to improve productivity and quality. • Shrinking margins. • Focus on information sharing, employee commitment/ involvement and teamwork.	• Management credibility/trust. • Employee opportunity to impact/ improve. • Sufficient demand/market potential. • Workforce interdependence. • Adequate support systems. • Management acceptance of employee work. • Commitment to change. • Strong measures.	• People can't work together. • Lack of top management commitment. • Use as a "Band-Aid". • Inadequate information sharing/ employee involvement. • Inadequate design, administration, and follow-through. • Lack of understanding of risks. • Payouts for gains are not a result of employee efforts. • Weak measures.

Pay Technique	How does this technique work?	What business situations lead companies to consider this technique?	What conditions are important for this technique to succeed?	What are the risks of using this technique?

Targeted Individual Incentives	• Once a year:
	  – Develop a pool or fund based on affordability, performance, and pay.
	  – Distribute to employees.
	  – There is a threshold before a payout can be made.
	• Typical focus on financial measures resulting from cascading goals.
	• Formula for payout ties to corporate goals and measures.
	• Total value of pool ties to total compensation levels.
	• Allocate funds on the basis of individuals or groups.
		• Performance focus.
		• Affordability
		• Goals/measures focus.
			• Risk accepting or entrepreneurial culture.
			• Measurable results and good follow-up.
			• Attainable goals.
			• Individuals influence results.
				• Organization doesn't define performance measures.
				• Entitlement culture resists risk based pay.
				• Decisions are not under executive control.
				• Organization unable to objectively judge performance.

Targeted Individual Incentives – Piece Rate	• Pay individuals for each unit produced with predetermined amounts of money for each unit (typically sole performance measure). • Differentiate base rate on levels of production. • Create a clear link between pay and performance.	• Need to motivate employees in de-skilled environment.	• Simple, repetitive manufacturing process. • Results of the work are easy to measure. • Minimum amount of interdependence. • Minimum need for cooperation. • Trust • Job security.	• Employees create counter-productive behavior trying to "beat the system". • High costs to maintain the incentive system because every time a technological change is made or a new product is introduced, new rates need to be considered.
Targeted Individual Incentives – Measured Day	• Fixed pay assuming employees maintain specified level of performance. • Guaranteed incentive payment in advance. • Pay does not fluctuate in the short-term.	• Inappropriate condition for piece rate. • Long job cycles.	• Total commitment of management/employees. • Effective work measurement/control system. • Logical pay structure.	• Worker ingenuity has lowered the standard (used to create measured day work rate). • Relieves pressure to perform. • Escalates labor cost (additions to staff).
Key Contributor Programs	• Individuals with historical high performance are priced in plan (usually in technical or R&D). • Special compensation in addition to traditional pay is given (stock/cash). • There is usually a waiting period to receive the award.	• Strong need for innovation culture. • Retention is imperative for certain employees. • Business is in growth stage. • Special pay market conditions.	• Able to clearly identify "must keep" employees. • Environment must provide for individual contribution. • Employee has resources and can influence resources.	• Selection of recipients not credible. • Non-recipients may be discouraged.
Competency, Knowledge or Skill-Based Pay	• Determine pay progression based on competencies (skills, behaviors, knowledge) associated with superior performance.	• Large skilled, technical or professional workforce and/or presence of career ladders. • Focus on work teams and need for workforce flexibility. • Slower growth rates/fewer opportunities. • Linkage to broadbanding.	• Well-defined position competencies. • Value person, not job. • Well-developed training and assessment programs. • Willingness to pay for unused capacity.	• Weaken the pay-for-performance link. • Majority of employees with limited growth opportunities. • Unaffordable labor cost. • Investment on faith.

Continued

FIGURE 43.4 *(Continued)*

Pay Technique	How does this technique work?	What business situations lead companies to consider this technique?	What conditions are important for this technique to succeed?	What are the risks of using this technique?
Broadbanding	• Pay structures which consolidate large numbers of grades and ranges into a smaller number of "bands" (ranges) with wide salary spreads between minimum and maximum.	• Reengineering. • Downsizing. • Organization restructuring. • Fewer upward job prospects. • Need for multi-skilled employees. • Focus on career development.	• Current program is not credible. • Company has commitment, money, and time for major change. • High level of trust between management and supervisors/managers. • Viable/credible performance and career development systems are in place. • Workforce is change ready and a crisis is perceived.	• Lack of trust in management. • Poor understanding of broadbanding. • Poor implementation. • Loss of control over compensation. • Cultural resistance. • "Old wine in a new bottle." • Inadequate support systems (performance/management). • Low sense of urgency by management/employees.
Long-Term Plans	• Employees are provided with special forms of pay based on results over a 3 to 5 year period. • Stock options give employees the right to purchase shares at a fixed price over a time period, creating a long-term financial interest; alternative stock plans can be used. • Some long-term plans use cash instead of stock.	• Need to focus on strategic issues and measures. • Attraction of key talent. • Retention of key talent. • Need to create sense of common fate. • Need to align more closely with shareholders. • Encourage entrepreneurship, particularly in start-ups.	• Measures must be correctly established. • Employees must be willing to take risks. • Management/employee trust.	• Options "under water". • Limited participation in plan. • Windfalls can produce exaggerated payouts. • Poor measures of competitiveness. • Overly complex stock and surrogate programs.
Work-Life	• Package of benefits designed to help balance conflicting demands of family, personal life, and work. • Provide childcare, paid time off, family services, flexible work arrangements, eldercare, convenience services.	• Recruiting in tight market. • Meet specific needs of workforce. • Strategy is to become "employer of choice." • Employees wanting to make culture statement.	• Accurate determination of workforce needs (survey). • High levels of communication. • Cost/benefit analysis. • Employee/management trust. • Ongoing monitoring. • Pay at or above market.	• Inability of supervisors and managers to implement program. • Pay levels not competitive. • Low employee perception of value of benefits. • Insufficient management commitment.
Non-Monetary Awards	• Recognition of outstanding performance using non-cash awards. • Focuses on creating awareness of successful behaviors exhibited by recognized employees (role models). • Awards include: merchandise, travel, time-off, symbolic (trophy), praise. • Awards can be individual, group or team.	• Supplement to sound cash programs. • Retention of key people in tough market. • Helpful when goals change frequently. • Can apply across most employee populations.	• Recognized employee behaviors must be credible to organization. • Award "judges" must be credible. • Communications system explaining program before and after awards must be in place.	• Rewarding wrong behaviors. • Rewarding weak or wrong results. • Using non-cash in place of cash program.

FIGURE 43.5 Culture and pay techniques

Pay Technique	Role of Employee/Management Trust	Achievement Orientation	Capacity to Measure Performance	Current Compensation Issues
Profit Sharing	Could add to dissatisfaction if trust is low.	Culture must be performance oriented.	Can be used where accounting data is all that is available.	Consider total compensation effect.
Subjective Performance Bonus	Trust level varies with individual's relationship with management.	May be counter-productive in risk adverse organization.	Successful plans have good measurement.	
Opportunity/Gain Sharing	Most need neutral to positive level. Standards are an issue.		Requires good cost of goods and labor data.	
Group Incentive	Should be positive. Standards are an issue.		Varies with degree and focus desired.	An additive built on sound base salary, not a substitute.
Targeted Individual Incentive	Perceived attainability of goal is critical.	Works best with high achievement individuals. Largely dependent on culture.	Objectives must be measurable.	Consider total compensation effect.
Key Contributor Programs	If negative, participant backlash could be a problem.		Able to identify key contributors.	An additive built on sound base salary, not a substitute.
Competency, Knowledge or Skill-Based Pay			Must be able to assess level of knowledge or skill.	Can be expensive. Must be justified by impact on productivity.
Broadbanding	Aspects of application requires high levels of trust at all organization levels or could be perceived as arbitrary.	Lack of quality performance management system and performance culture will negate value approach.	Must have solid linkages between corporate strategy and performance measures down to individual and/or team level.	Can disrupt and distract organization or improve morale, performance, and organization strength when compared to existing system
Long-Term Plans	Trust in equitable assignment and appropriateness of measures is critical.	Achievement orientation must be focused over a longer term.	Must be able to select appropriate measures which satisfy all stakeholders.	Predicting long-term stock payouts can be a source of conflict.
Work-Life Benefits	Employees must believe management is sincere and supportive.			Compensation levels must at least equal and preferably exceed pay market.
Non-Cash	Potential for arbitrary decisions makes it important to make basis of reward explicit.	Does not require organization wide achievement orientation.	There should be clear measures of behaviors and results.	Compensation levels should approximate pay markets. Awards are taxable.

Continued

FIGURE 43.5 *(Continued)*

Pay Technique	Power of the Technique	Potential Impact on Employee Compensation	Organizational Issues	Culture Characteristics	Organizational Pressure For Performance
Profit Sharing	Diffuse unless backed by culture.	Can be demoralizing if no profit to share.	A good option where measurement capability is limited.	Most compatible with a group-oriented culture.	Can reinforce and help raise level of demand.
Subjective Performance Bonus	Arouses desire to do well, but does not focus employee in advance.	Unpredictable.	Often found where direction is unclear.	Focuses on individual accountability.	Can be successful if clearly defined.
Opportunity/Gain Sharing	Powerful if done right. Effective at focusing efforts.	Upside 5% - 15%. Downside varies by plan type.		Fits a group-oriented culture best.	Supports emphasis on performance. Adds peer pressure.
Group Incentive	Strongest with small cohesive group.	Upside potential controlled by group output.	Clear goal-setting needed.	Requires a group-oriented culture.	Fits medium to high demand.
Targeted Individual Incentive	Strongest if achievable cash award.	Opportunity must be at least 10 % – 15% to have an impact.	Clear goal-setting needed.	Totally focused on individual accountability.	Good for high demand situations.
Key Contributor Programs	Powerful for retention. Recognition can be motivational.	Must be sizable and not very variable.	Must be limited to "truly key" contributors.	Will culture accept "individual deals?"	Aimed at retaining proven performers.
Competency, Knowledge or Skill-Based Pay	Objective is workforce flexibility, not incentive.	Should be large enough to make acquiring skills worthwhile.			Most useful as part of a broader productivity effort.
Broadbanding	Relieves employee frustration over perceived loss of career opportunities and pay growth. Focuses on performance when support systems are in place.	Some redistribution of pay based on perceived individual actual/potential contribution. Need for adequate assessment tools.	Organization commitment to implement and support. Strong rationale is rapid organizational change.	Tolerance of ambiguity necessary or bands will be structured similar to grades. High commitment to communications.	Better for medium demand. Unproven in creating high performance demand.
Long-Term Plans	Driven by significant capital accumulation.	Maximize or minimize competitiveness of total compensation.		Executives must be able to collaborate and sacrifice unit for company performance.	High performance pressures optimize success.
Work-Life Benefits	Works best as loyalty and morale builder. Helps recruitment and retention.	Reduces employee out-of-pocket expenses.	Communications, supporting policies and procedures, orientation of supervisors is key.	Works best in IT, R&D and related cultures and in younger workforce.	Fits all situations.
Non-Cash	Role modeling and public recognition can be an incentive for future behavior.	Should make no impact.	Good option when goals are unclear or changing frequently.	Highly collaborative cultures might resist individual or group recognition.	Fits all situations (individual, group, or team).

4. *Within each pay market and within the organization as a whole, assess the competitive level of total human resources cost (include base salary, variable pay, benefits, training, education, work-life, and other relevant programs) of the workforce.* This will help further set the limits of affordability and the allocation of pay since the costs of some employee groups may be too high or low in relationship to their value-creating contribution.

5. *With each pay market, determine the difficulty of recruitment, time to recruit, turnover rate, skill levels required, and training necessary.* Difficulties in recruitment when combined with long recruitment times, high turnover rates, strong skill requirements, and high internal training costs will require a greater allocation of pay than is required for talent groups and individuals scoring low on these dimensions.

6. *Assess affordability based on the feasibility of basing more pay on incremental profits.* An organization can afford to pay a higher competitive level if variable pay is funded by incremental profit. However, the risk factor of greater leverage may not suit the business culture, and its introduction might further destabilize a workforce in transition.

7. *Assess change readiness.* If the culture will not support the requirements of business, organization, and human resources alignment, then the compensation transformation might have to be geared to the rate of actual culture transformation, or perhaps slightly leading it, to communicate a new business paradigm.

8. *Identify pay techniques relevant to each pay market.* Once preliminary competitive levels and degree of leverage are established for each market, consideration for specific pay techniques can follow. The outlined approach is as follows:

    a. identify pay techniques associated with your particular business situation (Figure 43.3)

    b. assess the nature of business techniques using Figure 43.4

    c. refine the assessment of pay techniques using the culture factors described in Figure 43.5

    d. use the final list of options to develop a more detailed understanding of implementation mechanisms using chapters in this book and other literature as appropriate.

9. *Utilize succession and workforce assessment to customize compensation programs for must-keep employees.*

10. *Develop customized pay strategies, administrative processes, performance management, and career management processes for each talent pay market by combining those with similar characteristics and segmenting others that do not fit together.*

11. *Communicate new programs.* Describe the basis of each employee's compensation clearly and honestly to your workforce.

SUMMARY

This section summarized some key compensation elements that have become part of our collective wisdom. The goal is to provide a prototypical framework and set of tools for compensation practitioners as a basis for developing their programs. The empirical basis is my experience and my colleagues' experiences, a study of 350 organizations of various sizes representing different industries and stages of development, focus groups, literature, and interviews. The only conclusion that can be drawn from our review is that different approaches will work under different circumstances, in different times, and in different places.

Compensation practitioners involved in organization transformation should be mindful of the words of Machiavelli, the great human resources professional, "It must be considered that there is nothing more difficult to carry out nor more doubtful of success nor more dangerous to handle than to initiate a new order of things."

WORK–LIFE EFFECTIVENESS AND TOTAL REWARDS STRATEGY

Kathleen M. Lingle, Director, Alliance for Work–Life Progress

WorldatWork

Three people were at work on a construction site. All were doing the same job, but when each was asked what his job was, the answers varied. "Breaking rocks," the first replied. "Earning my living," the second said. "Helping to build a cathedral," said the third. (Peter Schultz, CEO, Porsche)

DRAMATIC CHANGES IN THE WORKFORCE, the workplace, the way we work and the work itself are propelling a new discipline within people strategy onto center stage. It goes by the label *work–life*, an invented term that does not do justice to this emerging practice, since it is not at all descriptive, but simply indicates an intersection between the two primary domains of modern human existence. However inadequate, the name has "stickiness," to quote Malcolm Gladwell. Over time, it has become a place holder for "overall quality of life" (organizational and personal), so the phrase pops up with increasing frequency in books, articles and discussions about work and business, and is frantically pursued by people everywhere as if it were some twenty-first century incarnation of the holy grail. Even such a skeptic as Jack Welch has been reluctantly forced to write and speak on the subject, because as he travels around the world since his retirement from GE, his audiences deluge him with "slews of work–life [balance] questions."

The goal of this material is to define what work–life is in the organizational setting, to describe its body of knowledge (the work–life portfolio), and to demonstrate how it contributes to positive business outcomes. Its value as a powerful no-to-low cost resource that can help resolve today's most cogent human capital issues will be made explicit, from the rising cost of health care to the management of an increasingly diverse, multigenerational workforce. Its dynamic interaction with the more traditional elements of human resources strategy (i.e., compensation, benefits, performance management, recognition, development, and career management) will be explained within the framework of what WorldatWork refers to as Total Rewards Strategy.

Let me begin by setting the context, because the work–life portfolio has been forged in a crucible of extreme economic, demographic, social, technological, and political transformation over the past 30 years. It has responded by providing a steadily expanding set of creative, nontraditional and occasionally controversial solutions to employers' perpetual need to attract, motivate, and retain the best talent available.

IT IS NOT YOUR FATHER'S WORKPLACE

In today's 24–7 work environment, where people are working longer and harder in more demanding jobs than 25 years ago, the economic principle of scarcity dictates that time has literally become as valuable as money. The traditional employment contract has dissipated, along with the mutual loyalty it once fostered. The employment-for-life value proposition my father took for granted has been replaced by job insecurity, felt acutely by at least 30 percent of the workforce. By 1998, the median tenure that an employee spent with a single employer had dropped to 3.6 years, a dramatic shift from an average of 22 years in 1950. Pensions, retiree medical coverage, and heavy reliance on the security of base pay are relics of the past, supplanted by "the new pay" designed to encourage employees to fund their own retirement, contingent on successful performance. Cost sharing of benefit coverage and self-directed health care consumerism are rising tides; "paternalism" has become a pejorative term. Meanwhile, the compensation and perquisites of the chief executives of American corporations have multiplied handsomely in step with the growing pressures of their increasingly large responsibilities. One of their central challenges is to elicit employee engagement, which means finding effective ways to harness the discretionary energy of employees to go "above and beyond" towards achieving the organization's business objectives.

Meanwhile, employees are beset with their own concerns and responsibilities. They are under increasing pressure to perform faster and to continuously higher standards, to manage their financial options responsibly while paying for an ever larger share of the health and welfare safety net that supports themselves and their family, and to forsake unhealthy lifestyle habits while responding to work demands wherever and whenever they arise, even at home or on vacation. In fact, by 2002, almost half of U.S. workers (46 percent) reported that they were contacted about their jobs outside of work hours that averaged 45 per week, and a quarter (26 percent) were working at least one weekend day on a regular basis Not surprisingly, 44 percent of U.S. employees feel overworked and 33 percent can be categorized as chronically so As for engagement, Gallup's *Engaged Workers Index* (2003) suggests that less than a third (29 percent) of U.S. workers are engaged in their work; over half (54 percent) are not engaged, and 17 percent are actively disengaged.

Working conditions, compensation strategy, and benefits philosophy are not the only workplace elements that have radically altered over the past several decades in response to these profound changes. The workforce has been transforming itself with equal vigor. Three developments are especially relevant to comprehending today's employment value proposition:

- *Dual-earner couples (both partners working for pay) now comprise 78 percent of the workforce*, up from 66 percent five years ago, and rising.

- *A single-minded focus on work is giving way to a "dual-focus" mindset.* The traditional "work-primary" employee, whose first obligation is to the job no matter what the personal sacrifice, is being supplanted by a predominance of "dual-focus" workers. These are now the majority of employees who place somewhat equal weighting between work and family or other personal responsibilities. Out of necessity, they develop the ability to fluidly shift their time and energy between priorities at work and at home as needs arise in both domains. Ready or not, they *are* the new human capital.

- *Fewer high-performance employees are opting for positions of greater responsibility.* According to a study of global corporate executives by Boston College, Families and Work Institute and the Alfred P. Sloan Foundation, 21 percent of men and 34 percent of women executives said they have reduced their career aspirations. Why? The most cited reason was "the sacrifices I would have to make in my personal life." Additionally, there has been a 16 percent decline over the past decade among college-educated men in the overall U.S. labor force who are willing to move into jobs with more responsibility, and a corresponding 21 percent decline among their female colleagues.

Given these measurable shifts in values and attitudes, the effectiveness of work–life strategy in eliciting the full power of *intrinsic motivation* is highlighting its potential as a valuable participant in cutting-edge and integrative people strategies that go by such diverse labels as *human capital*, *talent management*, *employer of choice*, and *Total Rewards*.

WORK–LIFE EFFECTIVENESS DEFINED

Work–life effectiveness (the term preferred by Alliance for Work–life Progress) refers to the complex and continually evolving interplay between the worker, his career (which unfolds in a workplace or a series of them), the community, and the family (see Figure 44.1).

Worker is the most obvious part of this equation. *Workplace* is seldom as static as the word implies, since in our virtual world there may be no physical place where all workers gather to do their work. *Community* (whether local, national, or global) is where workers live and from which employers draw both customers and their labor force. Employer organizations also earn their reputation or good will within the community, the maintenance of which is vital to positive business outcomes. Thus, community is an important base of operations as well as a major stakeholder for both the employer and employee. *Family* is the core unit of society, the glue that holds civilization together, and the engine that creates the future supply of labor and customers, the pipeline and quality of which is of great interest to employers.

As a person moves through their career, predictable tensions or conflicts arise between these domains. There is inevitable spillover between what goes on at home and in the community and in the workplace and vice versa. These conflicts require active management for the mutual success of employees and employers.

FIGURE 44.1   Work–life effectiveness model

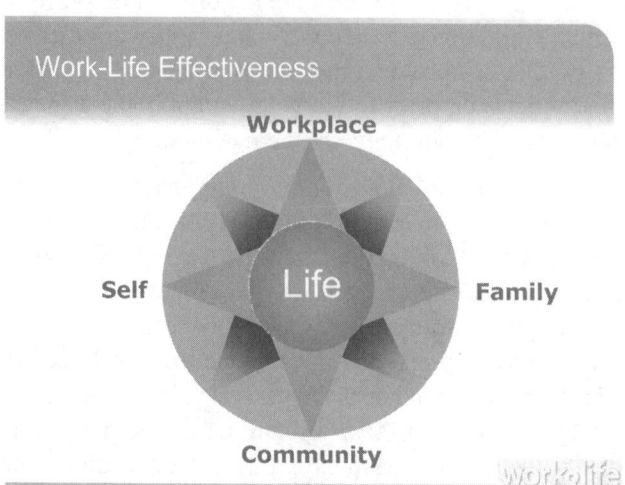

For example, having a child is a major life event that requires significant changes in the expenditure of time and energy, both off and on the job, especially (but not exclusively) for the primary caregiver. The declining health of an aging parent may have a similar impact. Everyone who works is a juggler, perpetually navigating his way through an ever-changing variety of often conflicting priorities at the critical intersections between work and other aspects of life.

ORGANIZATIONAL SUPPORT FOR WORK–LIFE EFFECTIVENESS: THE WORK–LIFE PORTFOLIO

Employers have responded to this reality, beginning three decades ago with the influx of great numbers of women into the paid workforce. The first work–life issue that employers had to address centered on childcare. Who was going to take care of the children when mothers were not at home? As the workforce has aged, dependent care has of necessity broadened into support for elders in the family.

Over time, employer responses to a wide variety of work–life conflicts throughout the career life-cycle have clustered into seven major categories of support, each defined by a robust suite of responses that weave together a number of related policies, programs, and practices:

- Caring for dependents (policies and services for reconciling parenthood and employment)

- Creative uses of paid and unpaid time off

- Proactive approaches to health and wellness

- Workplace flexibility

- Financial support

- Community involvement—*internal* (practices and policies that reflect caring for each other as a community) and *external* (outreach to the surrounding community)

- Managing cultural challenges

Each category or policy cluster has been shown to provide differential returns on investment over different timeframes. But accumulating research also demonstrates that the power of the whole is greater than the sum of the parts. That is, as employees use more and more work–life options across multiple categories in response to the numerous and predictable work–life conflicts encountered in the course of a typical career, the greater the benefits that can be documented for the business, workforce, and other key stakeholders, such as clients and shareholders, families and communities.[1]

It is also becoming increasingly clear that the categories are not linear, but interact with each other in powerful ways. For example, workplace flexibility is increasingly shown to exert a positive impact on health outcomes, and should therefore be widely regarded as an important part of the arsenal that human resources has at its disposal to combat the rise in health care costs.

In the aggregate, these clusters of practices and policies represent the work–life body of knowledge, and are the foundation upon which the first-ever certification for the work–life professional is being created by WorldatWork/AWLP.

I hasten to point out that the work–life portfolio does not correspond to organizational governance. By that I mean that not all of these programs, policies, and practices typically reside in one neatly organized and appropriately resourced department or function. Nor does the work–life professional independently "own" much of the terrain in which he operates. The work–life function is, therefore, a highly collaborative endeavor that helps connect the dots between many other human resources efforts. Properly deployed, it serves as a catalyst that, working in collaboration with other disciplines—such as compensation, benefits, and/or organization effectiveness—assists in driving the organization to measurably superior outcomes, such as maximizing employee engagement.

Commensurate with the growing recognition of its beneficial impact on business outcomes, work–life effectiveness should be appreciated as no mere repackaging of benefit offerings, but represents a major restructuring of the employment "deal" in alignment with new realities in the workplace that are contributing to the rise of the dual-focused worker.

"PROOF POINTS" FOR EACH CATEGORY OF THE WORK–LIFE PORTFOLIO

Category 1: Caring for Dependents (Children and Aging Parents)

The business impact of providing dependent care has been widely researched:

- A wide array of child care benefits enhanced retention at 94 percent of companies offering them

- A 2003 study by Circadian Technologies found that, when child care is offered, absenteeism, turnover, and overtime are reduced

- A 2001 General Services Administration study found that child care subsidies offered to low-income workers helped more than half (55 percent) to better concentrate on work, a fifth (19 percent) experienced lower rates of absenteeism and 75 percent of recipients felt the subsidy program had improved their job performance

Category 2: Creative Uses of Paid and Unpaid Time Off

Now that time has become the new currency, finding enough of it to spend with family, on one's self and in the community is the most fundamental work–life need. Some of the more innovative policies in this category include paid family leave for new fathers as well as mothers, sabbaticals, paid or release time for community service, responsive shift-work policies, paid time off leave banks, extreme travel compensatory time, and after-hours email policies.

Business Implications. The "vanishing vacation" means less productivity and more stress, according to the results of a Hudson survey.

- More than half of employees do not use all of their vacation time; 30 percent use less than half of it and 20 percent take only two or three days off in a year. Vacation deprivation is one reason workers make more mistakes and exhibit more anger and resentment toward coworkers. On the flip side, NASA scientists found that vacationers showed an 82 percent increase in job performance upon returning from vacation, and that two or three days did not result in the same benefits.

- A 2000 study by the Radcliffe Public Policy Center surveyed 1,008 male workers between the ages of 20 and 39 who reported that spending more time with their families was more important to them than challenging work or earning a high salary. In fact, 70 percent of respondents indicated that they would be willing to give up some pay in exchange for more family time.

- Aetna's extended maternity leave for new mothers resulted in an annual savings of approximately $1 million.

- A cross-industry study by WFD Consulting demonstrated that managers who work more than 60 hours a week are not more committed to their organizations than those who work only 45 hours. But there was one significant difference. The group working over 60 hours experienced a 230 percent increase in burnout.

- At a 24-hour command center of a pharmaceutical company, the staff monitoring a hazardous manufacturing process developed a schedule with more concentrated time off for each of the 30 individuals directly involved. After two years, the group had eliminated seven shifts, reduced error rates and overtime, and reduced shutdown time, in spite of an increase in the number of monitoring "hot spots" from 10,000 to 20,000 during the same timeframe. Productivity increased and the center became a magnet for transfers and new hires, given the availability of regular and predictable time off.

Category 3: Proactive Approaches to Health and Well-being

Reduction of stress is the central promise of work–life effectiveness. Since the negative impact of stress-related illness has been shown to eclipse the combined annual profits of the Fortune 100 companies, a focus on this category of work–life support holds the most promise of contributing to the reduction in the escalating cost of health care. The work–life practitioner adds distinctive value because of a focus on the family and knowledge of family systems theory. Today, many employers are trying to encourage individual employees to engage in behavioral change that includes healthier options. Most of this is done with (or to) the employee at the workplace, with minimal attention paid to the influence of the family or significant others. However, if the major influencers in any individual's life are not also changing their habits, the employee does not stand much chance of sustaining their own behavior change.

- A long-term evaluation of the financial and health impact of a large-scale corporate health and wellness program at Johnson & Johnson showed that participating employees had significantly lower medical expenses and achieved overall improvements in several health risk categories. The reduction in medical care costs averaged $225 per employee, resulting in an overall savings of $8.5 million annually.

- As the result of a workplace health promotion effort, DuPont experienced a 14 percent decline in days lost to disability claims over a two-year period. The resulting savings offset the program's cost during the first year, and resulted in an overall return of $2.05 for every dollar invested.

- A 2003 study of hospital workers in Finland found "attention to interpersonal treatment" decreased the risk of ill health. Male employees who felt they were treated unfairly were 41 percent more likely to take sick leave, and women were 12 percent more likely to take sick leave than those who felt respected.

Category 4: Community Involvement

This is one domain where employers' and employees' interests are spontaneously in close alignment, since both the labor force and customers come from the community in which the organization operates.

Business Impact.   Companies that help their employees volunteer their skills to nonprofits could have an advantage in recruiting younger talent, according to a Deloitte & Touche survey of 18- to 26-year-olds. However, only 26 percent said that idea was mentioned during their recruitment.[2]

- In an internal study at General Mills, supervisors reported an improvement in teamwork and other interpersonal skills for employees who participated in the company's volunteer program.

- According to a 2002 DePaul University study, socially responsible companies had more than a 10 percent higher sales, profit and return on equity growth than companies not in the "100 Best Corporate Citizens of 2001."

- A 1997 NYU Stern School of Business study of 216 socially responsible companies revealed that Fortune 500 companies with a good reputation are more profitable and enjoy higher stock prices.

Category 5: Financial Support (Self and Family)

Providing financially for oneself and family from career entry through retirement is basic to work–life effectiveness. In this arena, benefits, compensation, and work–life professionals collaborate closely to create relevant policies where appropriate, and find compelling ways to communicate the value of financial offerings. Some examples of programs and services of value to employees today include personal financial planning, adoption reimbursement, dependent and health care flexible spending accounts, discounted pet/auto/home insurance, mortgage assistance, group discounts on a variety of retail products, and workplace convenience services (dry cleaning, parking lot oil changes, etc.).

Business Impact. CF Industries (Long Grove, IL manufacturer) has been offering financial planning classes and counseling for many years. They have found that employees who gain the ability to make personal financial choices are more productive, have a greater sense of ownership, and engage in minimal absenteeism.

Category 6: Workplace Flexibility

Workplace flexibility refers to a leadership practice that facilitates the customization over when, where and how work gets done by individuals and teams. This practice has been empirically shown to increase engagement, retention, productivity and even wellness, and is thus the keystone of the work–life portfolio.

Workplace flexibility holds the promise of creating a work environment characterized by quick and efficient decision-making, short cycle times, high levels of employee engagement and empowerment, flexible leadership and management practices, high-performance teams and individual contributors that work well from anywhere in response to market demands. Thus, its implementation has as much impact on business outcomes as it does on the quality of life of employees—the ultimate win–win situation.

Flexibility practices are proving to be the most powerful single motivator in the work–life effectiveness portfolio, in large part because they fulfill a psychological need for what Robert Karasek (specialist in the psychosocial aspects of work and stress) describes as *job autonomy*—an optimal sense of control over one's job and working conditions. Karasek's research has shown that job control lowers stress and even health risks, while increasing job performance. This is shaping up to be the next frontier in management training—helping supervisors learn how to optimize the level of job control for teams and/or individuals in order to increase engagement.

Business Impact.   In 29 corporate examples in Corporate Voices for Working Families & WFD Consulting flexibility research study, 2006, work–life balance (40 percent) topped the list when 1,000+ financial services, law, IT, HR, sales, and marketing professionals were asked what would make them regard their place of work as a "great employer." Next in priority came a transparent career path (22 percent), followed by employer brand and corporate culture (15 percent), and in last place at a close 14 percent came benefits and salary package.[3]

Category 7: Managing Cultural Challenges

In order to implement some of the more culturally sensitive elements of the work–life portfolio (such as flexible scheduling), it is sometimes necessary to engage in specific culture change interventions to eliminate preexisting barriers to the full productivity of everyone in the workforce. Thus, there is a strong link between work–life effectiveness, diversity initiatives, women's advancement, multigenerational issues, mentoring, and networking.

THE WORLDATWORK TOTAL REWARDS MODEL

To illustrate how this integration of work–life effectiveness into the larger organizational context manifests itself in actual practice, let us examine WorldatWork's newly revised Total Rewards Model (see Figure 44.2).

The basic intention is to depict all of the major elements of human resources strategy that, collectively, provide the requisite tools to attract, motivate, and retain the

FIGURE 44.2   Total rewards model

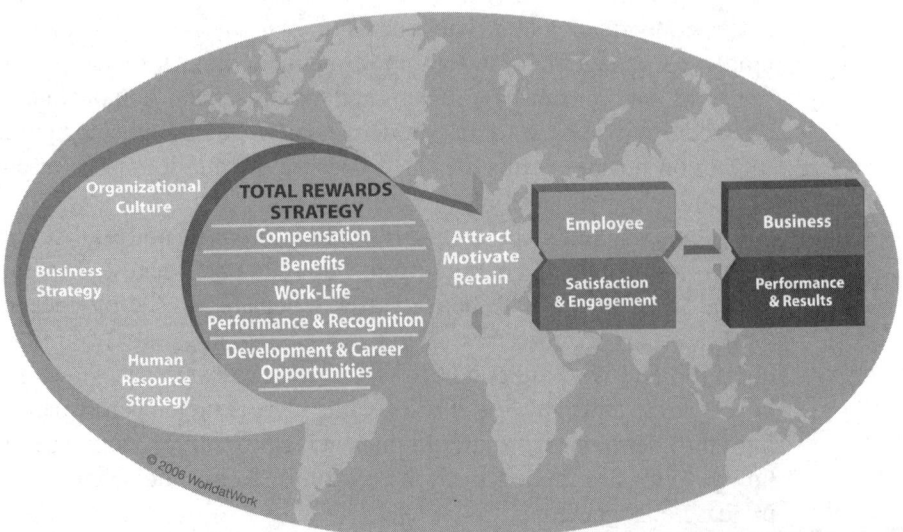

talent an employer needs to achieve business success. Following two years of thoughtful consideration by leaders primarily in the compensation profession, five major components were identified: compensation, benefits, work–life, performance and recognition, and development and career opportunities. This carefully selected set of tools, resources, and solution sets enables managers to leverage both *extrinsic* and *intrinsic* motivational factors simultaneously, which accurately reflects the complex and diverse needs of the contemporary workforce. The model serves as a framework for creating the kind of appropriately customized team or individual employment value propositions ("the deal") in great demand today.

For those to whom money alone is totally rewarding, there is a solution. For the growing segment of the labor force that values time (for themselves and/or with family) as much or more than money, there are several elements that can be blended to provide the proper level of both. For those who crave more control over when, where, and how they work as the ultimate reward, there is proper guidance and multiple resources.

The model further provides the organizational and environmental context in which these total rewards strategies and programs exist; i.e., organizational culture, business strategy, and the overarching human resource strategy—all of which operate in a specific geography.

Most notably, the model also incorporates the core work–life premise that business and personal success are interconnected, and do not operate to the exclusion or detriment of each other. It is work *and* life, not work *or* life. Truly successful people are often successful across several domains of life, and are great assets to their employer as well as their family and community. The opposite is equally true—successful companies provide valuable rewards to and enrich the lives of employees, families, and the communities in which they operate. This exchange relationship, which involves the reciprocity of respect and support between employees and their employer, is shown in the middle of the model. According to this strategic business perspective, the more success employees achieve in both the public and private domains of life, the more discretionary energy they will generate and devote to both, thus maximizing positive business as well as personal outcomes.

SUMMARY

It is the central premise of work–life effectiveness that respecting people for *who they are* (intrinsically) in addition to *what they do or produce* for the organization (extrinsically) that employs them is a necessary response to the new realities of the twenty-first century marketplace that we have briefly reviewed. The organizational consequences of doing so are beneficial to *all* stakeholders—employers, employees, customers/clients, shareholders, families, and communities. Furthermore, these positive outcomes are measurable, using a combination of quantitative and qualitative techniques. There is more than a decade of evidence to substantiate this bold claim.

REFERENCES

Burud, S. and Tumolo, M., *Leveraging the New Human Capital: Adaptive Strategies, Results Achieved, and Stories of Transformation.* Mountain View, CA: Davies-Black, 2004.

Crittenden, A., *If You've Raised Kids, You Can Manage Anything.* New York: Gotham Books, 2004.

Gallup Management Journal's Employee Engagement Survey, 2003.

Great Place to Work Institute. Press Release, 15 February 2005.

National Study of the Changing Workforce. New York: Families and Work Institute, 1997, 2002.

Pfau, B. and Kay, I., *The Human Capital Edge: 21 People Management Practices Your Company Must Implement (or Avoid) to Maximize Shareholder Value.* New York: McGraw-Hill, 2002.

Schor, J., *The Overworked American.* New York: Basic Books, 1991.

Schuster, J. and Zingheim, P., *The New Pay.* San Francisco, CA: Jossey-Bass, 1992.

Welch, J. and Welch, S., *Winning.* New York: HarperBusiness, 2005.

END NOTES

1. See *Categories of Work–life Effectiveness: Successfully Evolving Your Organization's Work–life Portfolio,* at www.awlp.org.

2. Press release, Deloitte & Touche, 16 April 2007.

3. HR Zone Ltd, 2 May 2007; Webwire, 30 April 2007, as cited in June 2007 issue of WFC Resources Newsbrief.

C H A P T E R

COMPENSATING AND MOTIVATING A DIVERSE WORKFORCE

Martin G. Wolf, Ph.D., President

Management Advisory Services, Inc.

THIS MATERIAL TAKES AN ICONOCLASTIC view of the traditional approaches to compensation. It proposes two alternative approaches to compensation delivery that would increase both the job satisfaction and the motivation of today's diverse, multicultural workforce without any increase in cost to the employing organization.

One approach challenges the current approach to payment. It proposes an alternative compensation vehicle that replaces cash for many aspects of the reward program. The other approach proposes a nontraditional method of tying reward to performance.

In regard to the first approach, after a brief review of what we know about employee motivation, a highly flexible form of compensation based on individual values is proposed. The concept of *credits* is used to individually tailor compensation packages to each employee within controlled cost limits.

These credits can be used as a delivery mechanism for both cash and noncash compensation. To keep things simple for both the organization and the employees, each credit would be equal to $1.00. Some of these credits might even have a vesting period to aid in retention (for example, the hiring bonus given to new MBAs).

In regard to the second approach, a system of *lightning strike bonuses* is proposed to break the predictable, time-bound method of compensation delivery that tends to create an entitlement mentality for variable compensation as well as for base salary increases.

CREDITS: A NEW PAYMENT VEHICLE

While much has been written about the values of "Generation X" and "Generation Y," about how the baby boomers' values are shifting as they approach retirement age, and about the value systems of women in professional and managerial roles, little if any of this has influenced the practice of compensation management. It is time to think beyond the simple financial carrot and to look at alternative forms of "reward."

After all, what is rewarding, like what is beautiful, is in the eye of the beholder. Given today's policy of inclusion and the resulting diversity in the workforce, what is perceived as rewarding is probably far more diverse than what is allowed under most organizations' reward system.

Depending on the values and life situation of the employee, true reward may be the opportunity to take a sabbatical, to have paid time off for a particular leisure pursuit or family situation, to learn a particular skill or develop an area of knowledge, to work in a different geographical or functional area, or to pursue any activities that have substantial value to them.

Even within the framework of performance-related pay, there is an opportunity to think creatively. Would a 55-year-old baby boomer be more motivated by the opportunity to earn an extra, performance-related, contribution to his 401k than by a current cash bonus?

WHAT WE KNOW ABOUT WORK MOTIVATION

Based on their research, Herzberg *et al.*[1] postulated that work motivation was based on two separate factors. One was called the job context factor; the other was the job content factor. Salary was found to be a mixed item, sometimes acting as a satisfier (content) and sometimes as a dissatisfier (context). Herzberg *et al.* classed it as a context item because its effects were more like the other context elements.

Content was held to tie directly and literally to the individual's level of work motivation, while context was felt only to affect dissatisfaction, i.e., the lack of satisfaction.

A flood of research and doctoral dissertations testing this provocative theory of work motivation followed, one of which lasted throughout the 1960s and into the 1970s. As might be expected, some studies supported the theory, some refuted it, and some partially supported it.

By focusing only on differences in the effects of the reward elements, Herzberg and these researchers overlooked differences in the perceived value of these rewards to individual employees. Both satisfaction or dissatisfaction and motivation (or the lack of it) depend less upon inherent differences in the nature of the various reward elements and more upon which of them are particularly important to a given individual. Those for individual X vary from what may be particularly important to other members of the same work group.

Further, what is important to that individual at that particular point in time may be quite different from what was most important to her last year, or what may be most important next year. Employees' needs and desires not only are quite different one from the other, but they also change over time.

Integrating the Herzberg-inspired research into a need gratification theory, Wolf concluded that

> Job motivation occurs when an individual perceives an opportunity to gratify an active need through job-related behaviors. The strength of this job motivation is a function of the individual's subjective probability estimate of the likelihood that the desired consequences will follow given job-related behaviors.[2]

What we should carry away from all of this is clear: one size never fits all! The key to motivating employees is the creation of a direct link between behavior and that employee's desired content and/or context element(s).

REWARD COST VERSUS REWARD VALUE

The implicit assumption underlying all compensation programs (including benefits, base salary, and all types of incentive plans) is that the employees' perceived value of the various elements of the program is at least equal to their cost to the organization. Unfortunately, this often is not the case.

Employees in general simply may not appreciate the true value of some elements of the compensation program, particularly in the case of noncash items ("fringe" benefits), while employees of a particular demographic group may be indifferent to one or more specific elements of their package. On the other hand, the saliency of a particular program element to some individuals may be such that its perceived value to them is much greater than its cost to the organization.

To maximize the return on the compensation dollar, one must structure the organization's compensation program to maximize the degree to which each employee receives the compensation program elements that are most salient to them. This means that each employee's compensation package should be tailored to his values.

CUSTOMIZING COMPENSATION

Given the ubiquity of computerized payroll and benefit administration programs, the mechanics of administering a customized compensation package for each employee are not a barrier. However, the design of such a program is complex in that it involves both costing the various nontraditional reward elements in each individual's package and effectively communicating the results to employees.

For example, how should a sabbatical be valued? The minimum value to be assigned is the salary paid for not working. However, there is an organizational opportunity cost that also might be considered since the employee presumably is contributing value over and above his direct payroll cost. Should all or part of this opportunity cost be included in the valuation of this reward element? If so, how is it calculated? Would the same additional percentage apply for everyone? More for line positions than for staff? Would there be more for supervisors than for individual contributors?

There is also the issue of allocating these reward elements in the appropriate amount for each individual employee. There must be a direct way for the organization to control the total cost of the various elements awarded to any employee and an equally direct way for the employee to understand both the value and the limits of the award. Overriding all this is the tax code and its definition of taxable (basically cash equivalents) and tax-free (mostly noncash) compensation.

TAX ISSUES ASSOCIATED WITH CREDITS IN LIEU OF CASH

If the credits carried a risk of forfeiture should the employee be discharged before redeeming them or should the organization be dissolved, it is likely they would be considered as not having been constructively received when granted. If so, rather than being taxable at the time of grant, they would be taxable only when actually used.

Another barrier to constructive receipt would be a restriction that use of credits was at the employer's discretion. The employee could ask to exercise them, but the employer would retain control. A vesting period before the credits could be used would defer constructive receipt at least until the end of the vesting period, but it would also tend to reduce the utility of the credits to the employees.

Many of the tax issues associated with credits in lieu of cash are complex and would probably require an IRS ruling. The following are some of the significant tax issues to be settled regarding the use of credits:

If an employee chose *to designate in advance* that a portion of any performance-based variable compensation he might earn in the coming year should be provided in the form of additional credits rather than in cash, would that compensation be income tax-free if used to "purchase" additional amounts of benefits nontaxable under the current IRS code?

If the employer established a performance-based variable compensation program that paid out *only* in credits, would this make that compensation income tax-free if used to "purchase" additional amounts of benefits nontaxable under the current IRS code?

If the performance-based compensation under either scenario were to be considered as income tax-free, how would this affect other benefits that are salary-based, such as retirement plans, disability insurance, social security, etc.?

If an employee *specified in advance* an amount to be withheld from salary each pay period to buy additional credits, would this be considered as a pretax payment for additional benefits coverage even if the exact benefits for which it was withheld were not specified in advance?

If the employee *designated differing amounts* of additional withholding periodically as he wanted additional credits, would this be considered as a pretax payment for additional benefits coverage? Would it matter if the exact benefits for which it was withheld were not specified in advance?

In the directly following sections of this chapter, some possible applications of credits to create individually customized compensation packages are offered.

USING CREDITS AS PART OF A TRADITIONAL BENEFITS PACKAGE

The use of *credits* to purchase additional amounts of traditional benefits should be relatively straightforward from a tax standpoint. The organization could supply a basic benefit package for each employee, perhaps differentiated by employee class (for example, nonexempt, exempt, executive). Such a package might consist of a limited health insurance plan that covers only the employee and a one-time salary life insurance program.

In addition, each employee would automatically receive a specified number of credits, also perhaps differentiated by employee class. These credits could then be used to "buy" additional traditional benefits, such as increased health insurance for the employee, dependent coverage health insurance, disability insurance, additional life insurance, etc., each of which would have a published "price" in credits.

Some aspects of this portion of the credit concept are covered by so-called flexible benefits programs. However, the credit concept is broader and even more flexible than such programs.

Since all such benefits would be denominated in credits, and since each credit has a value of $1.00, employees would understand both the cost to the organization of the basic benefits they are receiving and the "price" they pay for additional coverage. If an employee wanted more additional benefits than his available credits, the difference could be made up via payroll deduction, just as is currently done for optional benefits.

This process would allow each employee to customize his benefit package to meet his needs while at the same time controlling the cost to the company. The number of credits provided to each employee might even remain the same from one year to another as future benefit costs went up, thus providing a simple mechanism to shift more of the total benefit cost from the organization to employees, who would then have either to supplement their credits with payroll deductions in order to keep their same level of benefits or to accept a reduced level of benefits.

USING CREDITS IN LIEU OF CASH COMPENSATION

All existing cash compensation programs (annual incentives, sales commissions, special bonuses, long term incentives, etc.) other than base salary potentially could be delivered via credits. Employees could elect *in advance of earning them* to take these credits in cash or to use them to "buy" any of a number of alternatives as offered by the organization, such as an additional contribution to the employee's 401 k. Each alternative would be "priced" in credits.

Credits in lieu of cash would be more highly valued if they could be "banked" for some period, and then used when needed. If they were subject to constructive receipt and thus income taxable when granted, this alternative would be useless. The employee would be better off simply taking the cash, paying the taxes due, and literally banking the remainder for future use.

If these credits in lieu of cash can be banked before being constructively received, then they could be exchanged for additional paid time off at the employee's convenience. The exchange of credits for paid time off, coupled with a tuition reimbursement program that could be enhanced by the employee through the use of his credits, could offer employees a wide variety of opportunities. These opportunities might focus as much on furthering the employee's personal interests as on meeting current organizational needs.

The credits to "purchase" the paid time off presumably would be tax-free when earned by the employee, although the payments for the time off clearly would be taxable income when actually received by the employee.

LIGHTNING STRIKE BONUSES: A NEW DELIVERY VEHICLE

While most organizations overestimate the motivational effect of money, most also underestimate the communications effect of the reward system. What the organization pays for communicates its value system louder and more clearly than letters from the CEO or the mission statement on the wall in the lobby. "Actions speak louder than words" and "Put your money where your mouth is" are more than just old sayings.

Most compensation programs attempt to tie compensation to performance. An important part of the pay-for-performance concept is that this relationship will motivate employees to perform better to obtain increased compensation. While increased compensation, whether in cash or in credits as proposed above, has an intrinsic value, effectively tying compensation to performance also has a score-keeping value. That is, it can serve as a feedback mechanism to employees, communicating their degree of success in accomplishing their assigned objectives and enabling them to focus their efforts on those activities that are most valued by the organization.

The actual effect of most pay-for-performance base salary programs and of most variable compensation programs often is far from this ideal relationship. A key reason for this is the all too predictable results of these programs. Salary reviews come annually on an organizational or individual anniversary date. Increases cover a narrow percentage range, with a minimal percentage difference between average and outstanding performance. Bonuses are given out XX days after the end of the fiscal year, and either almost everyone or no one gets one. The net effect is to encourage an entitlement mentality, with employees expecting to get annual salary increases and at least a percentage of their incentive opportunity.

The Nature of a Lightning Strike Bonus

In keeping with its name, a lightning strike bonus (LSB) can happen to any employee at any time. Unlike the common myth about its namesake, LSB's can strike in the same place more than once, so that having received one does not preclude an employee from the opportunity to receive another.

To be effective, an LSB program must have several characteristics:

- Awards can, and do, occur at any time during the year

- Awards are large enough to have financial significance to the recipient

- Any employee at any level is eligible for an award, but only a select few will win one

- Its receipt by the honored individual is widely publicized within the organization

- It is clearly tied to a specific, identifiable accomplishment

- That accomplishment is significant enough that other employees clearly understand the appropriateness of granting an LSB for it

To be effective, an LSB program must avoid several pitfalls:

- The appearance that only certain categories of employees (supervisors, professionals, line, sales, etc.) can win an award

- The appearance that their superior's favorites will win an award, regardless of their performance or that of others, that what you accomplish is less important than who you know

- Reducing the impact of receiving an LSB by making it too common, thus becoming something that "everyone" wins rather than something truly special

Paying for the Lightning Strike Bonuses

All organizations have a compensation budget, whether formal or informal. That is, they all have only so much that they are willing or able to spend on employee compensation in all of its forms. Adding a new compensation element thus requires cutting an old one.

If one takes 0.2 percent of payroll from the compensation budget and forms an LSB pool, then it would be possible to give 4 percent of annual salary (two weeks' pay) to 5 percent of the total number of employees from this pool $(0.04 \times 0.05 = 0.002 = 0.2$ percent$)$.

For example, assume a salary increase budget of 3.0 percent of payroll, with no traditional bonuses to be paid. Rather than giving out the full 3.0 percent in salary increases, only 2.8 percent is given out. This leaves 0.2 percent of payroll in the LSB pool. Assuming that LSBs are fairly distributed across the various salary levels within this population, a grant of 4 percent of annual salary to 5 percent of this population approximately equals the 0.2 percent of annual payroll.

Setting up an Effective LSB Program

Given the "dos and don'ts" outlined above and also the need to keep program costs within the available LSB pool, an effective LSB program requires both formalization and a fairly strong degree of centralization. Nominees for an LSB should meet formal eligibility criteria.

A written nomination in a specified format should come from the employee's supervisor and be approved by the supervisor's supervisor. The approved nominations should go to an LSB review committee. This committee should consist of the highest ranking local managers at remote sites or of top officials at division or corporate headquarter sites.

The committee's responsibilities include:

- Insuring that a nominee's performance is fully documented and that the outstanding performance aspect is clearly understandable to the reader

- Insuring that LSBs are given only for performance that is truly outstanding and not as a reward to a favorite employee or in lieu of the ability to grant a larger salary increase to an employee threatening to leave the organization

- Insuring that LSBs in any one year do not go to more than 5 percent of the total employee population in the locales controlled by that committee

- Insuring that LSB awards are properly publicized within the organization

SUMMARY

This chapter proposed two nontraditional approaches to compensation delivery designed to increase both the job satisfaction and the motivation of today's diverse, multicultural workforce without any increase in cost to the employing organization. One approach (credits) challenged the current approach to payment, while the other (lightning strike bonuses) broke from the time-bound methods of compensation delivery. Whether or not either of these approaches offers something of specific interest, it is hoped that the reader will take from this chapter the need to challenge traditional assumptions about compensation design and delivery.

As organizational strategy continuously evolves to deal with the rapidly changing external environment, human resources strategy must continually evolve with it. As human resources strategy continuously evolves to deal with the rapidly changing organizational strategy, compensation strategy must continuously evolve with it. The challenges of globalization and of employee diversity are affecting every organization, and they require that we approach all of our cherished beliefs about how best to compensate our organization's employees with an open mind.

END NOTES

1. F. Herzberg, B. Mausner and B. B. Snyderman, *The Motivation to Work*, 2nd edn. New York: Wiley, 1959.

2. M. G. Wolf, "Need Gratification Theory: A Theoretical Reformulation of Job Satisfaction/Dissatisfaction and Job Motivation," *Journal of Applied Psychology*, vol. 54, 1970, pp. 87–94.

COMMUNICATING COMPENSATION PROGRAMS

John A. Rubino, President

Rubino Consulting Services

EFFECTIVE COMMUNICATION OF COMPENSATION PRO-GRAMS is the most important component in the development and implementation of pay plans. After all, the most elegantly designed compensation arrangements will not achieve their desired results unless employees and managers understand and, ultimately, buy into the program. What is surprising, however, is the lack of importance many companies place on communicating compensation. This is true despite the fact that it is easy for organizations to get the attention of their workforces when dealing with pay issues. Many studies show that pay is consistently cited as one of the primary reasons for accepting a position or staying with a company. Moreover, compensation can either be a powerful job performance motivator or an equally powerful demotivator, depending upon how it is used—and how well it is communicated to the workforce.

Nonetheless, the reasons many companies do not communicate are varied. Some companies, unfortunately, have compensation plans that are not designed properly or administered consistently, so communicating them would result in confusion or dissension among employees. Other companies with well-designed programs choose to maintain secrecy because "That's the way the culture is around here," or "It's management's responsibility to determine pay; the employees just have to accept it," or (an actual comment from a compensation professional), "The more communicating that I do, the more questions I get, and the more explaining and convincing I have to do. I don't have time to do my job!" It is important to remember, however, that a major part of every compensation professional's job is answering questions and clarifying the details of the compensation program and, most important, try to get management and employees buy-in.

In today's competitive business and human resources environment, many companies are beginning to change their way of thinking. They are finding that carefully designed and thoroughly communicated compensation programs are the key ingredients for motivating employees and increasing profitability. Because of this, many of them are abandoning an antiquated "mushroom" mentality of keeping employees in the dark and telling them nothing constructive about their compensation programs.

As a result, there are an increasing number of companies that devote a great deal of time and effort to communicating their compensation programs. However, many organizations do not approach the task in an organized manner. Some believe that the "medium is the message" and start the process by choosing the tools of communication, such as brochures, plan descriptions, videos, and the Internet/intranet. This is a mistake because a well-designed plan description, a beautiful, multicolored brochure, or an elegantly designed HR Web site may not communicate in a consistent or coherent manner—or worse, they may communicate unintended messages. Another common mistake companies make is to view communication as an after-the-fact exercise; that is, design the compensation program first, and then communicate. However, the most effective communication programs are developed and implemented *in tandem* with the compensation design project.

STEPS TO COMMUNICATING COMPENSATION, SYSTEMATICALLY

To avoid these problems and to help achieve success, it is important to develop a systematic, approach for communicating compensation programs effectively. I have found through my global consulting experiences that following the six steps below will help to ensure that compensation communication is accomplished in a systematic, "managed" way.

Step 1: Analyze the Current Situation

This first step includes analyzing the current state of the compensation system. This is to ensure that everyone involved in the execution of the program has a clear picture of what is working and what needs to be changed. Also, in situations where major changes will take place, the business case needs to be made for why a new compensation strategy is necessary. In addition, it is important to "play newspaper reporter" by answering the following questions: who, what, where, when, how, and why. That is, *who* will be affected by the new compensation strategy; *what* will be communicated; *where* will the communication take place; *when* will this happen; *how* will it get done; and, most importantly, *why* this needs to be accomplished. In this step, these questions should be answered in a general way, with more details provided in the steps to follow.

Step 2: Define the Objective and Key Messages

This next step may seem obvious; however, it is often overlooked. Defining the objective and key messages means figuring out what needs to be communicated, the major points to be emphasized, as well as what the company hopes to accomplish through the communication. This is very necessary in order to stay "on message."

When companies institute a new or revised compensation program, more often than not this involves some changes in compensation philosophy or approach. It is important that the communication program not only conveys new information, but also effects some change in employee attitude and behavior. Therefore, one key objective of the program should be not only to "tell them" but to "sell them." This "tell and sell" approach will affect every aspect of the design and implementation of the communication program.

The three "mega"-objectives of all compensation communication programs are:

- To ensure understanding

- To change perceptions and get buy-in

- To motivate the right behaviors

With slight variations, these objectives can be used in a variety of compensation communication programs. Furthermore, within the framework of these mega-objectives, it is important to customize the goals to fit the specific programs to be communicated and to support the objectives the company hopes to achieve. Next, the key messages are the content and action plans that are directly linked to the specific objectives. They are typically written in bullet format and number no more than three or four.

Step 3: Conduct the Audience Research

After the objectives and key messages have been identified, the next step is to collect information from executives, managers, and employees concerning their current understanding and perceptions of the compensation programs. This includes the attitudes they have regarding current programs, in addition to any knowledge they may have of anticipated changes. The use of this information, combined with the stated objectives and key messages, will ensure that the needs and concerns of the company as well as the employees will be addressed.

Asking employees for their opinions and perceptions, and assessing knowledge and attitudes (in effect, taking their temperature), indicate that the company cares about what and how they think. Moreover, the employees become involved in the design of the program and, as a result, feel a sense of ownership and commitment. This goes a long way towards ensuring a successful communication program.

Examples of questions to be addressed include:

- Who are the audiences?

- What is the current level of understanding regarding the compensation programs?

- Is there a perceived alignment of the compensation programs with corporate culture and philosophy?

- How does the compensation program fit with any other recent or upcoming changes?

- Are communication messages clear and consistent?

- Do managers have the necessary people skills?

- Do the employees know what is expected of them regarding job performance?

- Do employees believe there is a connection between performance and the reward system?

- How does senior management view communication?

- What is the current employee relations climate?

- Are global considerations an issue?

These questions represent general topic areas to be addressed, and are only an example of the type of information that needs to be collected and assessed. More detailed questions need to be articulated and more specific information needs to be obtained depending upon the particular compensation program being communicated.

Gathering as much information as possible on knowledge, attitudes, perceptions, and opinions is important not only in designing communications, but also in developing an anchor point from which to later evaluate the effectiveness of the communication program.

Research methods include questionnaires, focus groups, informal network, one-on-one interviews, and interviews with senior management.

Step 4: Choose the Media

As mentioned earlier, many companies inappropriately begin at this step when developing communication programs. However, only after analyzing the situation, defining the objective and key messages, and conducting the audience research can a company choose effective communication tools—that is, determine what would be the most appropriate media to use.

There is a wide variety to choose from, ranging from the relatively simple to the technologically complex. Most of the various types of media can be slotted into one of four major categories: audiovisual, print, personal, and electronic. It is important to note, however, that these categories are not mutually exclusive. Virtually every successful communication program uses a number of media methods in various combinations.

Audiovisual media include PowerPoint presentations, flip charts, videotape, and teleconferencing. Examples of print media are brochures, booklets, letters, memos, summary plan descriptions, compensation policy manuals, and paycheck stuffers. Personal communications can be large meetings, small gatherings, one-on-one counseling, and manager–employee sessions. Finally, all computer-based communication technology is in the category of electronic media. These include human resources Web sites/intranet, interactive PC programs, e-mail, and Web-casting, as well as personalized total compensation statements.

When deciding on which media (and media combinations) are most appropriate, it is important to consider the development and production costs as well as the media's communication effectiveness. In general, the most effective methods of communication are those that require a good deal of face-to-face human interaction (allowing for real time two-way communication), and also those that convey a personalized message. This is particularly important to keep in mind as computer-based technologies continue to play an increasingly greater role in communications. It is essential that the communication process does not become dehumanized.

In most instances, people absorb and respond to spoken messages better than they do the written word. More senses are at work, which, in turn, heightens attentiveness, improves retention, and increases buy-in. Also, tailoring a message to meet the specific needs of an individual or group virtually insures that it will be understood and accepted. However, some of these methods carry relatively high development, production, and/or time costs.

Step 5: Design and Implement the Strategy

The next step is to develop and implement a communication strategy within the framework of the defined objectives, and to incorporate the most aligned media techniques within that strategy. The following is a generic example of a communication strategy which can be tailored to other specific compensation situations:

- A memo from the CEO will be sent to all employees before the new compensation design project begins. The memo generally will outline the process as well as stressing the company's commitment to the project's success.

- Principal managers will meet to discuss specific responsibilities for the compensation project and subsequent communication sessions.

- To keep employees informed throughout the process, information will be communicated at key stages through live presentations and discussions, strategic e-mails, and through the human resources Web site.

- As the project progresses, all managers will participate in training courses on interpersonal and team-building skills. Also, important elements of the compensation project will be discussed; particularly the performance criteria and evaluation programs.

- Formal communication sessions will be conducted for all employees at the conclusion of the compensation project, which will include an extended questions and answers section.

Step 6: Evaluate the Communication Program

The final step in communicating compensation programs is evaluating the effectiveness of the communications effort. This statement is somewhat misleading because feedback should be obtained not only after the formal sessions, but also throughout the course of the communication program. For example, the company should be evaluating the extent to which the communication objectives and key messages are realistic and attainable; whether the information collected on employee attitudes and perceptions is valid and indicative; whether the strategies developed are effective; whether the media chosen are the must appropriate for conveying the message; whether the communication sessions are targeting the appropriate audiences; and, most importantly, whether the messages are being assimilated. Some of this information will become readily apparent as the communication program progresses, and ongoing adjustments in strategy and implementation may be required.

It is best to evaluate the effectiveness of the entire communication effort four to six months after the formal sessions. This allows time for employees to assimilate the information and adjust to the new system. Generally, the same approach can be used to evaluate the program as was used to conduct the audience research in step three. This includes the use of questionnaires (with additional questions relating specifically to the communication program), focus groups, interviews, and the informal network. Ideally, the employees surveyed should be the same ones who participated in the initial information-gathering process.

As a result, a comparison of the before and after responses to questions such as the following will provide a wealth of information on whether the communication program was effective:

- What is the current level of understanding regarding compensation and benefit plans?

- How well do managers and employees communicate with each other?

- Are consistent messages being communicated by top management?
- Do employees believe there is a connection between performance and the reward system?

MANAGED COMMUNICATION METHODOLOGY FOR A NEW COMPENSATION STRATEGY—A CASE STUDY SYNOPSIS

Analyze the Current Situation

The organization is transforming its reward strategy this year away from a traditional job-based system (merit increases) towards incentive compensation for all employees. This will require significant cultural change as well as the establishment of new behaviors that define success. The entitlement mentality will be abolished, and monetary rewards will be variable based directly on performance— a marked distinction between those who go above and beyond and those who do not. Executives and managers will model the new behaviors and establish performance goals that are discernable, valid, and measurable. The organization must make these changes in order to remain competitive, as well as to attract, retain, and motivate a top-quality workforce.

The communication will take place within the next six months in every company operation and location, and will utilize a combination of media methodologies and techniques to ensure effectiveness. To be comprehensive and to increase buy-in by everyone, a cross-section of executives, middle managers and human resources representatives will all be directly involved in the communication effort.

Define the Objective and Key Messages

Objective Statement.   To ensure understanding and acceptance by all employees of the changes in the organization's reward strategy, we will effectively communicate the benefits to both the employees and the organization of the new compensation incentive program. We will emphasize compensation variability based on performance and de-emphasize the entitlement mentality, for the purpose of aligning the new desired behaviors with the new organizational values.

Key Messages

- Communicate the new behavioral models that must be demonstrated by all employees. These behaviors are directly aligned with the articulated organizational values and core competencies.
- Communicate the importance of job ownership and personal responsibility with regard to work performance.
- Thoroughly explain the new incentive compensation reward mechanisms, emphasizing variability based on performance.

Conduct the Audience Research

Because the introduction of the new incentive compensation plan represents significant cultural change, it is imperative that management and employee acceptance and buy-in be accomplished in a complete and systematic manner. The first step toward achieving this objective is an audience research approach which casts a wide net and will serve both as an information-gathering exercise and an educational forum:

- A written questionnaire (paper- and/or intranet-based) distributed to all employees. The survey will capture the degree of understanding and acceptance by the employees of the new behaviors and reward strategies.

- Using the tabulated survey results, focus groups will be formed to delve deeper into topic areas of most concern.

- Manager and employees study groups will be formed to get brainstorming input on the implementation of the new reward strategies.

Choose the Media and Design and Implement the Strategy

To support the new culture, behaviors and reward strategies, the media and strategy must be thorough and human-oriented:

- A video, recognizing and demonstrating the emotionality of the subject matter.

- Written materials (plan documents)—a detailed explanation of the new incentive compensation program, with examples.

- Face-to-face meetings throughout the organization conducted by well-trained managers and assisted by program designers from human resources. In order to help achieve the stated objective, all employees will have an opportunity to participate in two-way, real-time presentations.

- Working, training, and education sessions for all managers and employees to help them establish performance goals and behavioral guidelines under the new reward strategies.

- Additional information and Q&A follow-up through additional live sessions as well as the human resources Web site.

Evaluate the Communication Program

Four to six months after the new incentive compensation plan goes live, we will resurvey the managers and employees and reconvene the focus groups in order to conduct a before and after comparison. Also, all managers will submit a written assessment to human resources on the degree of success of the communication effort.

Strategic questions should be answered by citing specific examples, e.g.:

- Are employees demonstrating and internalizing the new competencies and behaviors?

- Is the new incentive compensation program perceived as fair?

- Are the performance goals and criteria being adhered to and, most importantly, are they being accomplished?

- Are employees taking ownership of their jobs and career development?

SUMMARY

It is important to note that the compensation system must first be well designed in order for positive results to occur, i.e., improved employee motivation, increased productivity, etc. However, given that the system is sound, these and other positive results will *not* occur unless the communication program is successful.

TALENT MANAGEMENT AND COMPENSATION IN THE FAST FOOD INDUSTRY

Jerry M. Newman, Distinguished Teaching Professor and Chair, Department of Organization and Human Resources

State University of New York at Buffalo

THIS MATERIAL WILL PROVIDE CASE study illustrations of retention issues in occupations with lower barriers to entry. Through studies of the fast food industry, I will demonstrate how rewards other than money play prominent roles in employee turnover. Furthermore, I will contrast how high-performing fast food restaurants with lower turnover rates differ from their lower-performing competitors in the way they administer rewards.

I worked undercover in seven fast food restaurants over a 14 month period. One of my goals was to observe employees' behavior and ask what rewards work best to retain workers? Why, when the manager was not looking and things slowed down, did we play pickle Frisbee to cheers and jeers as these little green disks were alternately caught or dropped? Why did some managers work hard to build relationships among crew members, while others could not care less? As compensation people we normally think pay assumes a pivotal role in retention. But in the quick service restaurant (QSR) sector (i.e., fast food), pay levels are constrained by the need to support corporate strategy—to provide a low-cost, quality alternative to casual dining establishments (e.g., Denny's, Outback) and other players higher on the, if you will, food chain. Compensation professionals in this industry face unique challenges.

The sector is characterized by low barriers to entry—worker training is relatively low and from both the store and individual perspectives this encourages turnover. Historically, short training times mean lower turnover costs for stores. For workers, the short training entails minimum personal investment. Choices about where to work, whether to work hard, and how long to stay, may turn on compensation and reward decisions that are not easily documented in traditional survey research. In part this is the reason I went undercover to capture preliminary data about what makes labor "tick." How important is money, and what else matters when entry barriers are minimal.

As you read through these examples, consider how supportive they are of job embeddedness theory. Job embeddedness theory says that workers are less likely to turn over if they are selected for fit and if managers and workers make a concerted effort to develop social ties with these new employees. In turn, selection for fit means hiring people whose skills and interests match those of the job's and organization's unique requirements. As an example, do not hire someone who is detail-oriented and uncomfortable with thinking outside-the-box into a job and workplace where innovation is prized. Embeddedness also posits that managers and employees have mechanisms that act as "social glue." New employees become "stuck" to the organization because of social rewards that create friendship bonds.

Six of the seven stores I worked in provide anecdotal support for the concept of embeddedness. Interestingly, the methods for building bonds for new employees in three of the stores had some commonalities, but also differed in important ways. My final three examples illustrate stores that I believe failed at "embedding workers," with negative implications for turnover.

IMPROVING RETENTION: SIX CASE STUDIES IN THE QSR (QUICK SERVICE RESTAURANT) SECTOR

McDonald's 1

Chronologically, my second job was at a McDonald's. When the manager asked me what pay I was looking for, I gave her my research protocol answer: "Whatever you are paying the others would be fine with me." She responded: "$5.15 per hour is our standard starting rate." As a compensation guru, I am embarrassed to admit

I thought the minimum wage was $5.35. I sputtered that she could not pay that low and she took my ignorance for negotiation. I accepted the counteroffer of $5.50, red face and all.

We know why I took the job—I was writing a book. But in my time at Mickey D's I saw others accept the offer at similar wages. Why would people stay here when down the road, less than a mile away, was a Wendy's offering a dollar more an hour? On the surface, labor economists would call this illogical. Part of the answer links to this store's ability to create social ties. When I sat down for my job interview one of the crew members came over and offered me a soda—no higher paying store attempted to forge a social relationship this quickly. On my first day of work, less than five minutes into the form-completion process, a worker close to my demographic (i.e., old) proactively sought me out and talked about the three jobs he had. This job, he declared, was his favorite. Real nice people, he noted. Moments later I was watching a DVD, the sole purpose of which was to identify the many ways in which McDonald's was a fun place to work. Every other DVD I saw across the seven stores I worked in focused almost exclusively on skills training and harassment no-no's. This DVD offered no training, just a perspective on why I should work for Ronald McDonald.

This store also worked hard to make sure it could accommodate my specific needs. In the QSR sector hours of work are an important currency. If I cannot get and keep the hours I want, I will go to a store that is more flexible. This McDonald's was a corporate store using a unique (at least in my experience) software program requiring me to answer three questions: (1) what days did I want to work per week, (2) how many hours per day, and (3) during what timeframe. I got the hours I wanted. Other stores had managers develop schedules with far less satisfactory results. By being flexible and trying to accommodate my preferred work schedule, this store promoted systems that increased the chances that I would "fit."

Burger King 1

Of the seven stores I worked in, only two of my interviews lasted more than 10 minutes. Most were under five minutes. My best manager interviewed me for more than an hour. She admitted that her goal was to see if I would fit in with the existing culture. Fit to her was not about a fit between her skill needs and my skill profile. In low-barrier jobs this is not typically an issue. Rather she wanted to make sure that what mattered to me, my values and interests, coincided with those of her workers. Her crew got along well together and she did not want to spoil a team that had an enviable performance record (one of the top-rated stores in the northeast and with turnover hovering at just about 100 percent—very low for the QSR sector). I found out much later that I passed her scrutiny because it was evident that I was proud to be working in fast food and that I had a sense of humor that enjoyed give-and-take joking. This, she noted proudly, was a key characteristic of the people on her team.

Everything that Kris did, conveyed that she took our jobs seriously and viewed us as a team. She was heavily involved in my training, devoting more time than any other manager I encountered to giving me feedback and acted as a sounding board in my first days on the job. When she "handed me off" to a crew member for further training I already felt a bond with her. A manager's time is a valuable asset, and I knew that she had expended more time than was typical in prior jobs to help me weather the first days.

Kris also knew how to have fun. When a particularly grueling lunch rush was over she was one of the first to joke about some of the customers and their odd demands. And if a hacky sack happened to fly through the air in a brief game of hacky tag, well, she was conveniently looking the other way. The group who worked in this store knew when to work, and enjoyed each other's company when time permitted. Kris guarded this culture by hiring only people who fit, and nurturing them through the training process. This emphasis on the social side, approached differently in McDonald's than in this Burger King, nevertheless emphasized building social networks and enjoying each other.

Krystal

Krystal is a medium-sized chain located in the southeast with a business model much like White Castle in the midwest. I was scheduled for an interview with James at 3 p.m. James was 10 minutes late, rushing in while apologizing that he had to act as chauffeur to a crew member with car problems. Over the course of the next two days I found that this impromptu favor to a crew member was classic James behavior. Crew members informed me that James regularly worked uninterrupted 24 hour shifts. These weekly occurrences were the unavoidable outcome of trying to make sure his workers all get exactly the shifts they wanted. Someone had to pay for this flexibility, and James willingly assumed the burden.

It was my third day and I was in the walk-in refrigerator getting pickles. I dropped the container and pickle juice flew everywhere. Fifteen minutes later, pickle juice cleaned up, I emerged to what seemed an empty store. There were no employees. There were no customers. I wondered, was Stephen King at work? Had a virus felled everyone and I had survived because of the pickle juice antidote? As I walked to the front of the store I glanced out of the drive thru window. The entire missing crew was gathered around one of the cars, smoking and drinking sodas. Laughter flowed freely. Later I asked James what was going on. These "smoke breaks" were a regular part of James's strategy to keep workers socially linked.

Arby's

The manager here hired me because, in his words: "I want to change the store culture." Apparently there was a group of males in their early twenties who bonded around a death mctal band member who reveled in shocking people with his language and behavior. Because he was a superb employee with several years' tenure, the store manager put up with his sometimes borderline behavior. But the cadre attached to him was another matter. They all attempted to imitate his behavior, with sometimes hugely coarse outcomes. The profanity-laced language and sexual innuendo were textbook classics of a hostile work environment. The manager had warned these workers, but he was reluctant to terminate anyone because all of them might have exited at once. The cost of this indecision, though, was high. New employees endured a mild mix of initiation rights, usually centered on sarcastic critiques of mistakes we made in the first days. On my first day working I was put on the front counter. I mistakenly referred to a chicken fillet sandwich order as a "chicken filly." The group erupted into laughter: "what's a chicken filly? Are we serving horse sandwiches here? Nayyyyyyy," the wittiest of them said. I was mortified, and not the least bit amused. Later, a young female was subjected to similar rituals. After enduring them she whispered to me: "Is this all there is?" I interpreted this as a question about life addressed to someone who had eaten several slices. I was not prepared to answer such soul-searching questions in the middle of a lunch rush. Nor was I likely to bond with a group of males who could drive a teenager to such a desperate search for meaning.

McDonald's 2

The crew in this store was about evenly divided between Hispanic and white crew members. Hispanics had all the sandwich assembly jobs and the maintenance jobs. Only one of these workers appeared to speak fluent English. The white workforce occupied all the jobs interacting with customers—front counter, drive thru, and runners (carrying food from bins to pack into bags or place on trays). The two groups were separated not only by language, but also by the barriers of technology. Warmer and holding bins, drink dispensers, and heating lamps made it difficult for the two groups to converse even if the language barriers were not prevalent. Further reducing the ability to interact was a store manager who was uneasy in her role. She had not yet been to Hamburger University to receive managerial training. She admitted in a moment of nerves that she was scheduled to go the next week and she was very concerned about her ability to measure up. She also was not very good at her job! With this single exception most of the managers and assistants tended to be amongst the best workers in the store. They were fast sandwich assemblers, and adept at packing orders into bags or onto trays quickly. Sara was none of these things. For example, the runner usually is expected to fill drink orders and take meal items and place them into sacks. Sara regularly would get behind and angrily tell the crew on register that she needed help filling drink orders. This, of course, slowed down order-taking—a necessary outcome if Sara was to avoid getting even further behind. Sara's inability to work as quickly as those she managed made for a lack of credibility and little respect.

Her anger also further widened the social gap created by language and technology. Because she could go from benign to ballistic in a matter of minutes, most people did their jobs and avoided conversations that were not job-related.

Burger King 2

I had my worst employment experience here. I walked into the store around 3 p.m., a good time to find harried managers with a moment of free time to conduct an interview. The first words from the shift supervisor as he sat down to interview me were: "You don't want to work here!" Shocked that I might have misheard him I said "What?" He reiterated "You don't want to work here. It's a terrible place to work." Rubbing my hands gleefully at the thought of all these data points, I quickly accepted the job that was offered less than five minutes later. My first day of work was a Monday. Even though I worked the same shift as the store manager, I had no idea who she was. This continued through the third day. People approached me, barraging me with conflicting advice on how to do my job—none of them was Angela. She was, I was informed, one of the women up front. The design of fast food restaurants makes it, intentionally I think, difficult for customers to see the workers in the back sandwich assembly area. Equally, though, the technology barriers (warming lights, fry bins, drink dispensers, etc.) made it difficult to figure which of the three women were Angela. None wore name tags. In fact no one wore name tags. Through the third day I was referred to as "Hey You." On the fourth day my work area was underneath the central part of a leaking roof—the inevitable outcome of a flat roof combined with a heavy storm the night before. Worried that the floor was getting slippery, I put down a cloth to soak up the water. Not five minutes later I heard a booming voice say "Pick that up." I countered by explaining how this condition was a workers' compensation claim waiting to happen, and was about to explain OSHA requirements when I felt a jab in the back and heard a crew member behind me say "don't say another word. She fired someone last week for less than what you're doing." I quickly shut up, but I was angry. I deduced that I had finally met Angela, and it left me wishing I had not.

Two people in the store were in Angela's good graces—her sister and her best friend. Everyone else was treated as replaceable units expected to do their jobs without complaint or interaction. On one occasion the regional manager came to the store. It was a busy Friday and he rallied the crew to explain that drive times (a vital metric in fast food, measuring time from order-placed to order-filled at drive thru windows) were below acceptable levels and exhort us to work faster. As an intended demonstration of his concern, he stayed during lunch rush to work first sandwich board, akin to mission control in a moon launch—with orders coming in to his screen and him dictating what other crew members should assemble and in what order. Some two hours later lunch rush was over. I assumed this regional manager would let us know—if our efforts had paid off. Did we come together as a team to cut drive times? The regional manager went to the manager's office, conferred with Angela about the drive times showing on the computer screen in front of them, walked out of her office, and exited by the back door. Not a word to the minions. I took this as yet another sign that we were not valued. Nothing embedded here!

On what turned out to be my last day, I received a policy-prohibited cell phone call from my wife. I found that my daughter had to have a surgery with potentially serious consequences. I told the manager, losing a battle to fight back tears. She was nonresponsive to my emotional state, asking only if I wanted a leave of absence or if I was quitting. Until that moment I had intended to return. The coldness of her response, though, prompted an angry "I'm quitting."

SUMMARY

I do not believe that turnover in these stores was caused by money issues. Most stores paid similar amounts and offered increases on equivalent time schedules. As anecdotal evidence, one of the highest paying stores, my second Burger King, had 500 percent turnover. The other Burger King, part of the same corporation and paying identical wages, had turnover of just over 100 percent—about one-fifth that of the other store. I think a key difference between these two stores, and probably between the first set of three stores and the latter set, was the level of success in building a strong social environment where individual needs were attended to and friendships flourished. My first Burger King experience best exemplifies this. The manager selected me for fit with the personalities of crew members. She took no chances leaving my early socialization to others—most of my early training came from her. Despite being very focused on achieving good metrics, she knew how to have fun when lunch rush was over and she knew when to turn her back and let good-natured games prevail. Krystal and my first McDonald's also focused on creating camaraderie amongst crew members. The Krystal manager actually asked me if I smoked. Only later did I find out that he liked his crew to all break at once, usually in the parking lot, and usually over a cigarette.

Conversely, in my worst store I was referred to as "Hey You." Even though I had a name tag, it was too much of a bother to learn my name. After all, if history was any predictor, I would be gone before my name could be learned. This depressing view was most subscribed to by the store manager, a woman who spent time with only two crew members—her sister and her best friend. In my Arby's experience and in my second McDonald's, language and technology barriers further contributed to social distancing. Not understanding Spanish and being uncomfortable with profanity-laced conversations both added to social barriers and reduced embeddedness. The result was turnover.

REFERENCES

Allen, D. G., "Do Organizational Socialization Tactics Influence Newcomer Embeddedness and Turnover?," *Journal of Management*, vol. 32, no. 2, 2006, pp. 237–256.

Holtom, B. C., Mitchell, T. R. and Lee, T. W., "Increasing Human and Social Capital by Applying Job Embeddedness Theory," *Organizational Dynamics*, vol. 35, no. 4, 2006, pp. 316–331.

Milkovich, G. and Newman, J., *Compensation*, 9th edn. New York: McGraw-Hill, 2008.

Mitchell, T., Holtom, B., Lee, T., Sablynski, C. and Erez, M., "Why People Stay: Using Job Embeddedness to Predict Voluntary Turnover," *Academy of Management Journal*, 2001.

Newman, J., *My Secret Life on the McJob: Lessons from Behind the Counter Guaranteed to Supersize any Management Style*. New York: McGraw-Hill, 2007.

Global Compensation

EXPATRIATE COMPENSATION PRACTICES

Geoffrey W. Latta, Executive Vice President

ORC Worldwide

THIS MATERIAL PROVIDES READERS WITH a guide to the fundamental issues that organizations face in paying employees they send to another country to work. Unlike compensation systems and issues that operate in a single-country context, the principles that drive compensation design within one country break down in the face of the challenge of dealing with two labor markets at the same time. As a result, compensation systems for "expatriates," as such employees are often known, are complex and frequently expensive.

There might appear to be some simple answers to paying an expatriate. For those not familiar with the area, the first response might be to place the expatriate in the salary structure of the country in which the employee is working. Unfortunately, for the typical expatriate, working on a fixed-duration assignment of two to five years, this often does not work. An alternative response might be to simply pay the employee the same salary for the job as would have been paid at home and to make no other adjustments. Once again, this usually is not an equitable solution. Because neither of the obvious approaches is satisfactory, companies have over the years devised more sophisticated pay systems. While no two organizations pay their expatriates in exactly the same way, a pattern has emerged that allows generalizations about expatriate pay practices to be made.

EXECUTIVE SUMMARY

This comprehensive discourse on expatriate pay practices covers the following:

- The key issues that create the complexity in expatriate pay systems
- The major options for determining the base pay structure for assignees
- The most significant cost-related elements of expatriate package design
- The choices involved in the provision of incentives to assignees
- The issues related to benefits and pay delivery
- The underlying factors such as assignment length and pattern, the nationality of the assignee and the type of job involved that need be considered in choosing between alternative approaches

WHAT ARE THE ISSUES?

There are eight key factors that drive pay practices.

1. Gross and net compensation levels for the same job vary between countries
2. The purchasing power of any nominal salary varies from one country to another
3. Comparisons of home and assignment location income will be affected by changes in exchange rates between the two locations
4. Most expatriates are taken temporarily from one housing market and placed in another in conditions where they are not able to compete evenly with local nationals
5. Many employees (and their families) do not welcome the disruption to family and social life caused by an international move
6. Some locations to which employees may be transferred are not necessarily considered intrinsically desirable places to live
7. There are difficulties in addressing benefit provisions, especially in relation to pensions and social security, across two countries
8. There is a need to provide for certain special circumstances such as education for the children of expatriates and the need to assist the employee in returning to the home location periodically during the expatriate assignment

THE COMPENSATION OPTIONS: SALARY BASE

The key decision in compensation design is the designation of base salary. This decision impacts most other areas of the package in a very direct manner. The choices are to retain the employee in the home country salary structure, to put the employee into the assignment country structure, or to adopt some other salary base.

Option 1. Home Salary

Most organizations retain employees in the home salary structure, especially when they are on assignment for a limited duration and they are expected to return to their home country. Retention in the home structure makes it easier to bring the employee back at the end of the assignment as she has never lost contact, in practical or psychological terms, with her home salary. Most organizations also wish to retain employees in home benefit programs, and the home salary structure retention facilitates this.

The major drawback of retaining employees in their home structure is that, by definition, the expatriate will have a different income from comparable local peers and from expatriates of other nationalities working in the assignment location. A company with expatriates mostly of one nationality may not worry about this latter issue. Even when the nationality mix is greater, the degree of concern about comparability with local nationals varies by organization.

Retaining employees in the home country structure requires the company to review the base salary level while the employees are on assignment as they would have done at home. Failure to do this will mean that the employees are suffering a disadvantage from holding an international position.

Option 2. Host Salary

Fitting employees into the host salary structure is administratively straightforward and addresses the issue of comparability with other employees. The prime drawback is that, in many cases, the attraction for the employees to accept the assignment disappears. A move from the United States to Nigeria on local pay is unlikely to attract employees to relocate, but a move to the United Kingdom or Australia will lead to an American taking a pay cut in nominal pay terms. If the pay cut is accompanied by an equal reduction in living costs, it might be acceptable, but this is not necessarily the case. A move from the United States to the United Kingdom on a British salary represents a clear reduction in purchasing power. Even a move to a country with higher nominal gross salaries such as a move from the United States to Switzerland may turn out to be less attractive when the higher cost of living in Switzerland is taken into account. Thus, integration into the local salary structure works only where it involves an increase in real purchasing power. Thus a move from a low-wage country to a high-wage developed country is feasible on this basis, and many companies pay people a host salary in the case of transfers from Thailand or India, for example, to the United States. Even then, some companies keep a link to the home salary because it provides a base for benefits and it helps ensure that the employee keeps in mind the salary level to which she will return.

This problem of different purchasing power can be overcome if the employee is placed in the assignment salary structure but paid other allowances to compensate for the higher costs. However, this approach can become complex as it involves tracking the relationship of the home pay to the assignment pay level, and it undermines the value of equalizing expatriates with local employees.

Other Options

Some companies opt for an approach that is neither pure home nor pure host. A rare approach is to create an entirely separate pay scale for international employees. A few companies use this approach but usually only for a small group of their employees who are highly mobile and no longer have any real link to any home country. This approach is much more common in organizations like the United Nations in which almost all professional employees work outside their "home" country.

Another approach that is more common is to link all employees who are being expatriated to the salary structure of one country, usually the country in which the company is headquartered. This approach is used by some companies that have few expatriates other than those from the headquarters country. It is also used, however, by some companies with a large multinational workforce to overcome the problem of expatriates of multiple nationalities having different compensation packages in the same assignment location.

Another variant, particularly popular in Europe, is the so-called higher-of-home-or-host approach. In this model, the company calculates a pay package based on home pay plus allowances (see below) and compares the net pay of the employee with the net of the peer position in the assignment location. The higher of the two will be paid. The precise calculation methods used vary considerably, but the perceived advantage is that there is the potential for integration in the host pay structure but with a guarantee that the employee will not suffer a reduction in living standards. In many companies using this approach, the majority of employees are actually paid based on the home calculation, and so the advantage of integration into the host pay structure may be questioned.

COMPENSATION OPTIONS: COST ALLOWANCES

In conjunction with retaining the expatriate in the home country salary structure, most companies pay the employee a set of allowances designed to deal with additional costs that the employee could incur. The most significant of these costs is in relation to goods and services (food, clothing, recreation, etc.), housing, personal taxation, and education.

Goods and Services

Where the costs of purchasing a similar range of goods and services in the assignment location are higher than costs at home, most organizations pay a cost-of-living or a goods-and-services allowance, usually based on information from external consultants. There are numerous ways of comparing such costs, which need to be monitored regularly to reflect the impact of the exchange rate between the two locations. Typically the external consultant provides an index that compares costs in the two locations, where 100 indicates that costs are the same in the two locations. The allowance is usually doled at each pay period. The purpose of the allowance may be viewed in two slightly different ways. It may be seen as a protection against higher costs, or it may be seen as part of an attempt to ensure that the employee neither gains nor loses in living standards from accepting the assignment other than from changes in direct pay. The latter philosophy may be termed a *cost equalization approach*. The distinction is not just a semantic issue. A company that sees the payment in *protection terms* will not take any action when the employee moves to a country with lower costs; a company adopting the equalization approach may do so. Those who adopt the equalization approach argue that to do so avoids employees' receiving arbitrary variations in real living standards based on the location to which they are sent. Thus an employee sent to a much lower cost country will receive an additional windfall unrelated to the amount of money needed in the location; another employee sent to a higher-cost location is protected but does not enjoy any such windfall. If costs suddenly rise in the low-cost location, the employee may perceive a decline in living standards when, in reality, there has merely been a reduction in the windfall gain. Because of this, some companies that do not reduce the employee's pay in lower-costs locations choose to show the employee the windfall gain to avoid complaints if costs rise.

It should be emphasized that the above approach should be used in conjunction with retention in the home salary structure. If the employee is placed in the host structure, a comparison back to home costs is inappropriate because the local salary may reflect local living costs. If a higher (or lower) salary exactly reflects living-cost differences, no allowance would be needed. Unfortunately, the salary levels of two countries rarely precisely reflect differential living costs, hence one of the problems of a host pay approach: most commonly the cost differences are partially reflected and so a payment of a goods-and-services allowance in addition to host salary would still be overly generous.

Where a company uses a headquarters approach, the cost comparison should still be made but between the headquarters country and the assignment location. The result will be that the salary reflects the headquarters living costs, not the actual home location of the employee. It also ensures that expatriates of different nationalities receive the same pay, which is often the underlying objective of those using a headquarters approach.

Housing

Housing is affected by two considerations. Most companies prefer their expatriates to rent rather than purchase housing in the assignment location. This is felt to be administratively simpler, to protect against possible losses if the host housing market falls, and to provide greater flexibility in disposing of the home on return. Second, consideration needs to be paid to the employee's house in the home country. The most common approach is that the company encourages the employee to retain the home if the expectation is that the employee will return to the same location. In this case, the company usually provides assistance in renting out and managing the property. In the assignment location the company will assist the employee in finding a home and will pay the rental cost either directly to the landlord or as an allowance to the employee. Some companies pay an allowance equal to the actual rent of the property; others pay a defined amount but leave the employee to select the property and to keep any amount by which the housing allowance falls below the actual rent or to pay out of their own pocket any amount by which the rent exceeds the allowance. Whatever approach is adopted, companies need to decide how much they are willing to pay for the employee's housing. Many companies use external consultants to set housing allowance levels, which often vary by family size and by job level.

Most U.S. companies take a "housing deduction" to reflect the savings that the employee is realizing in home housing costs. European companies are less likely to take this deduction, largely because they do not assume that the employee will rent out the home property while on assignment. Once again, the philosophy of most companies is to equalize costs for the employee, and whether this is done by requiring a home deduction or not depends on the circumstances of the employee. Some companies will allow the policy to vary depending on individual circumstances; others choose a policy that reflects the majority of their expatriate population.

The payment of host housing costs is a policy that most companies adopt regardless of whether they use home, host, or headquarters pay as a base. Again, in one sense this undermines the logic of host pay systems because it represents a clear distinction between expatriates and local nationals. However, it is a pragmatic reflection of the need to help employees find and pay for housing when on limited-term assignments.

Personal Taxation

In the area of taxes, the equalization philosophy is firmly entrenched. Most companies use an external accounting firm to prepare expatriate tax returns. This is particularly important for U.S. citizens and U.S. permanent residents as they are taxed by the United States even when they are not resident. For most other nationalities, tax liability depends not on citizenship but on residence and the source of income. Thus, a British expatriate working in the United States is not taxed by the UK on U.S. earnings but only on residual British earnings (interest, etc.) as long as the expatriate is not in the UK for more than a certain number of days in the year. Despite this, the principle of tax equalization is usually followed for other nationalities although practice is more varied than for Americans.

For the employee, the normal approach is that the company will pay all personal taxes that arise from employment income; increasingly companies also pay all or a portion of the liability related to nonemployment income. In return, the employee pays the company through regular payroll deductions, an amount usually termed a "hypothetical tax deduction," equivalent to what would have been paid in taxes at home.

Education

An international assignment is disruptive for expatriates with children. Where the language of the assignment country is different from the home country, most expatriates want to send their children to a school in the assignment location that provides teaching in the home country language. Even if the language is the same, if the curriculum does not match that of the home country, it may disrupt the child's ability to progress through the home curriculum. This is especially true for children in secondary education.

Such international schools are usually private and therefore charge tuition and fees, and companies will generally meet at least the direct tuition costs and often other additional costs. For U.S. expatriates, this usually means the "American" schools that exist in many cities around the world; similar schools exist for French, Japanese, and British children, although in smaller numbers. If no school is available in the assignment location, most companies will pay for boarding schools in the home country or in a third location. The cost impact for companies is therefore quite high if they send expatriates with children on assignment. This has led some companies to seek to persuade expatriates to send children to local schools if the language of the assignment and home countries are the same. This is sometimes acceptable for younger children, but differences in the curricula and in university entrance requirements make this difficult for older children.

As with housing, most companies pay for education, regardless of the salary base for expatriates.

COMPENSATION OPTIONS: INCENTIVES

In addition to allowances to reflect specific costs, most companies pay direct cash incentives to expatriates that are unrelated to cost. Many companies make a payment to all expatriates going on assignment. Historically the most common form of payment has been a *foreign-service premium*, usually expressed as a percentage of base pay. The most common formula has been 15 percent of pay, sometimes capped at an upper level, paid along with each regular paycheck. An alternative approach consists of providing a lump-sum incentive payment, usually termed a *mobility premium*, paid in two amounts at the beginning and end of the assignment. This is seen to have three main advantages over the traditional approach:

1. It does not become buried in the ongoing salary, a situation that leads expatriates to forget why the payment is being paid and to perceive a pay cut when it is removed at the end of the assignment.

2. It associates the payment with the actual process of moving from one country to another. This is particularly important if the employee moves from one assignment country directly to another. If the premium is ongoing, the employee sees no change in pay despite the need to move; if a lump sum is paid, it is triggered by the move.

3. The payment can be made in the home country immediately prior to assignment and in the home country immediately after return. This minimizes taxes as the payments are not taxable in the assignment country.

Although the payment of a premium remains the majority practice, there has been a clear trend for companies to do away with this across-the-board incentive. Companies using a host pay approach are unlikely to pay a premium.

Most companies feel the need to pay an incentive if the employee is moving to a "difficult" location. Such payments are often termed *hardship premiums*, although some companies see this terminology as vaguely insulting to local employees in the assignment country and may use more neutral language like a *location premium*. The payment is usually expressed as a percentage of salary varying by location; a common approach is to make payments that vary in 5 percent increments from 5 percent for slightly undesirable locations to 35 percent (or more) for very problematic locations. It is rarely paid in lump-sum form. Because the type of locations that attract a hardship premium are not those in which a host pay approach could be used, the issue of paying hardship along with host pay almost never arises.

EMPLOYEE BENEFITS

For expatriates going on assignment for a limited duration, the main benefit issue that companies face is in relation to both company and state pensions. Most companies sending employees for limited-duration assignments try to keep employees in the home country company pension plan. This is usually feasible, although it may raise administrative and tax problems. It is also usually possible to retain an employee in the home social security program; in addition, companies would like to exempt assignees from required payments to the host country system. This is usually possible for up to 5 or 6 years when the home and assignment countries have a bilateral social security agreement (often termed a *totalization agreement*). Retention in home benefit plans is clearly consistent with retention in home salary structures, but not with host pay approaches. Notwithstanding the apparent anomaly, most companies using a host approach for base pay continue to opt for a home approach to benefits.

Issues also arise with other benefit plans, particularly medical plans. The company needs to decide how to cover the employee when on assignment; this may involve a special international plan or a plan on a home or host country base.

OTHER PAYMENTS

Most expatriates receive a number of other payments as part of their compensation package. Companies incur significant expenses from payments for actual relocation costs such as shipping goods to the assignment location or storage at home as well as miscellaneous additional relocation expenses. These may be reimbursed against actual expenses, or they may be covered by a lump-sum payment.

The cost of providing home leave for the expatriate and family, usually once a year, is significant. In addition, in difficult locations, many companies pay for *rest-and-recreation* (R&R) *leaves* to a third location.

PAY DELIVERY

Companies must decide how much of the compensation package to deliver in home currency and how much in host currency. Some companies, especially smaller ones, may lack the capability to deliver pay in local currency, and so they pay entirely in home currency, leaving the employee to decide when and in what quantities to exchange home into host currency. Other companies find that there are advantages to delivering, in local currency, the amount required by the employee to buy goods and services (and housing if the company does not pay this directly). This protects the employee against exchange-rate fluctuations and prevents delivering pay in constantly varying amounts. The rest of the pay package will then be delivered in home currency. This so-called *split-pay approach* is increasingly popular.

SUMMARY OF EXPATRIATE OPTIONS

From the preceding discussion, the most common approach to paying expatriates is the following:

1. To retain the employee in the home salary structure
2. To pay a cost-of-living allowance if costs in the assignment location are higher than at home
3. To pay the employee's housing costs in the assignment location, with or without a direct contribution from the expatriate
4. To use a system of tax equalization that ensures as nearly as possible that the employee pays no more and no less tax than if he or she had remained in the home country

5. To pay an incentive to the employee above base pay for accepting and remaining on the assignment

6. To pay a special additional incentive to employees transferring to designated "difficult" locations

7. To pay for private education in the assignment location for the children of expatriate employees

This combination of policies has become known in the compensation area as the *balance-sheet approach* to expatriate compensation, or in Europe as the *home build-up approach*. In recent years there has been much discussion as to whether this approach is the most appropriate, but it remains the dominant model.

The main alternative to a home approach in practice has been a headquarters approach. For all practical purposes, this makes the employee an "honorary citizen" of the headquarters country and then works in exactly the same way as a home approach. The host pay approach is a more fundamental change but some of its advantages are undermined by providing many of the elements that an expatriate employee paid under a home approach would receive.

The Underlying Variables

There are several variables that lead organizations to differing answers to the question of how to design an expatriate program. Some of these are factors that spring from the organizations' human resources strategy or from deeply entrenched cultural factors. Others have a more concrete origin. In designing your policy, you should look at all these factors and assess their impact.

Assignment Length. Most expatriate assignments fall in the range of two to five years, and most compensation systems are predicated on the assumption of this length. If assignments are intended from the outset to be much longer, an attempt should be made to place the employee in the assignment country salary structure. Unfortunately, this does not work in situations where the local salary structure is much lower than the home, and so it is not uncommon to retain elements of the more typical shorter-term expatriate package. In addition, many organizations find that what was initially intended as a shorter assignment turns into a longer one during the course of the assignment. The employer then faces the challenge of converting the assignee from one type of compensation package to another. Many organizations have a policy provision that states that employees should be "localized" after five years on assignment in the same location. This involves the removal in phases or in one single step of the expatriate package. Despite the policy provision, many organizations do not actually put this into practice unless the decision to remain on assignment is clearly the wish of the employee.

A different situation arises with short assignments of under one year. Such assignments have grown steadily for most organizations as a percentage of their total assignee population. As a result, many organizations have special policies for such assignments. A major factor is that many of these assignments take place without the whole family relocating to the assignment location, and this simplifies or alters some of the elements of package design in areas like education and housing.

Assignment Patterns.   In many companies, the typical assignment pattern is for an employee to go out on assignment and return to the home country, perhaps going on another assignment at some future point in their career. The mainstream solutions to expatriate policy design are based on this pattern. If employees are on a sequential assignment pattern, moving from one location to another but not necessarily back to a home country, the compensation design may need to be different. Many companies pay these "global nomads" by placing them on the salary structure of the headquarters country. Others use an international pay scale. Benefits may be funded on an offshore basis as one of the major concerns for this group lies in the provision of pensions.

Type of Assignee.   Some organizations have a strong philosophy that all assignees should be covered by one policy. Others distinguish among employees based on the type and/or level of job performed, on the business unit for which the employee works, or on the geographic pattern of movement. Thus some companies have one policy for management development assignments and another for technical transfers. Some distinguish between a European employee transferring within the region and one transferring out to another region. The advantages that derive from "multitier" policies are that they may help reduce overall costs by matching compensation elements to clear needs, and they may allow business units with different economic circumstances to reflect these in the level of compensation. The disadvantages are more complex administration and potential employee resentment if they are on a less generous package than some of their perceived peers. Companies that have used such an approach find that it works best when there is little movement of employees from one expatriate policy to another, when the economic reasons for differences can be clearly explained, and when the categories of policy can be clearly defined. The last is a problem where policy is based on assignment type for which there may be room for differences of view about the classification of a particular assignment. Assignment types also clearly influence the differences in policy from one organization to another. A company that sends only high-level executives may adopt a different strategy from one that sends primarily project engineers.

Country of Origin.   Established pay systems work well for assignees from developed countries, who have generally formed the overwhelming majority of expatriates. In recent years, however, there has been some increase in assignees drawn from countries like China and India. This can create specific compensation challenges as pay levels for more junior transferees may be too low to make the traditional balance sheet approach work effectively. On the other hand, the shortage of available talent at higher managerial levels means that some potential higher-level assignees from these countries are actually highly paid. In that case, if they come from a country where the cost of living is low, a combination of a high salary at home and low living costs as a base for the goods and services allowance may actually produce a compensation package on assignment that seems overly generous. Given these challenges, the design of an appropriate pay policy for transferees from less-developed countries requires a thorough analysis of the type of employees being moved and may require multiple pay policies.

Industry.   The industry in which an organization operates will have some impact on policy. The oil industry requires specialized expatriates to work in a variety of often remote locations; an investment bank is likely to send employees mainly to more developed locations.

Globalism.   An organization employing and transferring employees who are predominantly of one nationality faces a different set of challenges from those that are transferring employees of multiple nationalities.

SUMMARY

The dominance of the balance-sheet approach to expatriate compensation has been achieved in the face of frequent criticism that it is expensive and complex. The problem, however, is that the complexities are inherent in the process of transferring employees internationally, and no simple solution has been advanced that allows companies to attract employees to go on assignment and to pay them in a fair and cost-effective manner while there. Pay administration requires the company to track many more payments than it does for a domestic employee; moreover, such payments may be in two currencies, and some of them such as the goods-and-services allowance are subject to frequent change. Compensation professionals used to working with pay structures in a single country will find that expatriate compensation has unusual challenges. Addressing those challenges is, however, fundamental to those companies wishing to operate on a global basis.

REFERENCES

Herod, R. (ed.), *International Human Resources Guide*. Eagan, MN: Thomson/West, 2006.

Hsu, Y. S., "Expatriate Compensation: Alternative Approaches and Challenges," *WorldatWork Journal*, 1st Quarter, 2007.

Latta, G. W., "For Richer, For Poorer," *Workspan*, August 2000.

Latta, G. W., "Addressing Pay Issues for Nontraditional Expatriate Assignments," *Benefits and Compensation International*, March 2005a.

Latta, G. W., "High Mobility International Employees," *WorldatWork Journal*, 2nd Quarter, 2005b.

Latta, G. W., "The Future of Expatriate Compensation," *WorldatWork Journal*, 2nd Quarter, 2006.

Reynolds, C., *Compensating Globally Mobile Employees*. Scottsdale, AZ: WorldatWork, 1995 (reprinted 2006).

Schell, M. S. and Marmer Solomon, C., *Capitalizing on the Global Workforce*. Chicago, IL: Irwin Professional, 1997.

GLOBAL LOCAL
NATIONAL
COMPENSATION
PRACTICES

Paul Coleman, Senior Consultant

ORC Worldwide

WITH THE INCREASING GLOBALIZATION OF business, there has been a corresponding interest in the more effective management of local national employees and in rationalizing the ways in which they are compensated. *Local national employees* are defined as those who are employed within a given country and whose conditions of employment are established by the local organization. As such, a local national could be of any nationality as long as he were eligible to work in a given location. The conditions of employment for the local national employee typically reflect the local statutory requirements, local customs, and practices found in the marketplace. This is in contrast to the *expatriate*, who would be working with local nationals in a given location but whose compensation and conditions of employment are typically tied to a home location where he or she is expected to return at the end of the expatriate assignment. These assignments typically extend from three to five years, but long-term, or permanent, expatriate assignments typically have built-in processes to integrate individuals to the local national conditions of employment over a period of time. The other class of employee is defined as *international cadre* and typically represents those having a career path based on many global assignments. In this particular instance, organizations typically create a special employment policy providing for employee compensation, benefits, and retirement that are necessary to facilitate frequent relocations.

As organizations extend their global reach, the management of all of these types of employees becomes more complicated, forcing many organizations to reconsider their compensation strategy on a global scale. This is not without its challenges; the biggest of which is ensuring an appropriate balance between global consistency and local market compatibility. While a global compensation strategy offers internal equity and facilitates international mobility, it must also reflect and be responsive to the local market conditions in any given country that ultimately influence compensation.

Pay levels for local national employees vary based on the traditional compensation practices and values inherent in the concept of pay in that particular country, for example:

- Statutory requirements

- National and/or sector collective bargaining agreements

- The type and number of specific pay elements

- International work experience (which may carry a "pay premium" in the country)

The situation is complicated by the demand for and supply of labor in any local market—an excess of labor will cause pay levels to drop whereas a shortage of labor will cause pay levels to rise. This is further influenced by a number of factors, including the geographic location of the organization and the sector within which it operates.

The following section is an overview of the complexities and challenges associated with achieving a consistent and effective global compensation strategy whilst maintaining local compensation practices and culture. The management of both expatriate and local national employees is more critical then ever before as compensation and human resource practitioners are tasked with preparing their organizations to keep pace with a world of complex equity situations driven by the movement of talent within and across country borders.

THE NEED FOR LOCAL COMPENSATION DATA

The globalization of the marketplace and the attraction of low-cost labor towards the end of the twentieth century have caused the compensation of local national employees to become a major focus. In an increasingly competitive marketplace, the costs of equipment, materials, and labor are now all tightly controlled.

While an international pool of labor does exist for senior executive positions and certain highly skilled professional roles, the majority of other roles operate in local labor markets at either a national- or location-specific level. It is for this reason that the provision of compensation data at the local level is paramount in ensuring that organizations can be responsive to the external market in which they operate. Indeed, it has been estimated that, in the majority of multinational organizations, around 90 percent of their payroll is based on local national compensation.

Local compensation data allows organizations to determine their level of competitiveness in the local marketplace. This is important for a number of reasons; firstly, many organizations openly communicate a formal compensation philosophy which specifies who they define as their competition for talent and services, and where they position themselves relative to the global market. The most common statement is to "maintain competitive pay levels," usually expressed in terms of position relative to the 50th percentile of their specific market, therefore it is important for organizations to examine whether they are actually doing this or not at a local level. When "new" positions are created, organizations may not be familiar with their "market value," therefore accurate local compensation data is crucial in ensuring an appropriate and attractive level of pay is specified.

Another reason why reliable local compensation data is vital is in relation to talent management. The more competitive an organization is in relation to local pay levels, the greater the chance of attracting high calibre individuals and retaining them once they have joined. This is currently evident in the Indian market, where intense competition for scarce talent between organizations, particularly at the managerial level, has led to a poaching war and aggressive pay increases.

However, the provision of local compensation data is not always readily available. As a direct result of globalization (e.g., organizations establishing an office or site in a new country), many compensation and human resource practitioners find themselves in need of local compensation data in countries where this information has been difficult to obtain. This point is particularly true for not-for-profit organizations, which generally operate in developing or remote locations where, quite simply, no data exists. In these cases, there has been a significant rise in the development of customized surveys as this is often the only viable approach to gathering meaningful local compensation and benefit information.

VARIATIONS IN PAY ELEMENTS

Any discussion of local national compensation needs to consider the variety of pay elements that exist in any given country. There are three initial ways in which compensation is commonly defined across the world:

- *Cash compensation*—this definition specifically includes wage rates, salary, cash bonuses and short-term incentives, but excludes the value of employee benefits, special allowances, long-term incentives, deferred compensation, contributions to savings plans, distributions through profit-sharing plans, and noncash compensation such as equities (stock). In the United States this would typically include wage rates, salaries, and annual bonuses.

- *Gross compensation*—this definition typically includes the payroll costs of all employee benefits and allowances as well as the total of cash compensation as defined above.

- *Net compensation*—this definition is used when comparing the *net* (after-tax) calculation of compensation.

Ideally, each of these compensation definitions would identify each pay element so that items can be compared on a like-for-like basis. The following example is based on employment in Mexico and lists the typical pay elements associated with salaried employees in the country:

- Base salary (reported monthly and annual)

- Number of extra months of salary

- Christmas bonus (*Aguinaldo*)

- Profit sharing (*fundo de ahorro*, reported in currency and in number of days' pay)

- Vacation bonus (reported in currency and in number of days' pay)

- Transportation or car allowance (reported as a monthly allowance)

- Social provision (reported as a monthly allowance)

- Housing fund (*Infonavit*)—statutory requirement to individual accounts

Other benefits include costs associated with the following:

- Medical insurance

- Life insurance

- Pension and retirement

- Social security (*IMSS*) where the employer pays the *employee's* contribution

There is also considerable difference in the pay elements depending upon the class of employee. Hourly paid employees (craft or factory workers typically classified as "blue collar") have a range of additional allowances and benefits not applicable to salaried or executive employees. Again using Mexico as an example, the following pay elements are typically provided to this class of employee (however, variations exist depending upon the actual geographical location):

- Transportation provisions

- Clothing allowance

- In-house meal provisions

- Housing (in some locations for larger employers)

- Punctuality bonus

- Discounts on company products

- Seniority payments

- Cost-of-living allowance in some locations

If we now switch our attention to the Indian market, we find a different set of pay elements, many of which are used to reinforce various social values. A number of cash allowances are prevalent such as housing and conveyance (transportation) along with a unique "special allowance." This is simply the difference between the sum of the base salary and all other allowances and the total cash compensation rate in the local market. This "special allowance" pay element is traditionally used in older mature organizations where it is typically a large portion of the total cash compensation.

Further complication is provided by the increasing trend of new organizations in India to adopt an approach referred to as the "Cost to Company." In this instance, organizations determine the total cost of providing the base salary, allowances and benefits based on where they want the role to be positioned against the local market. The employee is then given a choice as to how they want the amounts distributed against the various pay elements. Organizations typically only determine the base salary amount in order to minimize their obligatory pension contribution and allow employees the freedom to allocate the balance based on their own individual preferences and tax concerns.

Executive pay elements also vary from country to country. Frequently, they are the result of the tax policy for a given country. Such executive elements of compensation that have been identified in the global marketplace include the following:

- Stock options

- Long-term deferred compensation

- Home entertainment allowances

- Housing supplements

- Low-cost or no-cost housing loans

- Company-provided car and driver

- Education allowances for dependents

In summary, there are considerable differences in pay elements throughout the world. These differences are driven by the economy, laws, and culture of the particular country which make cross-border pay comparisons extremely difficult.

Foreign exchange rates can be used for this purpose but in the global marketplace of today, exchange rates can be volatile and in a constant state of change. In any case, this approach is not ideal as it does not take account of factors unique to each country such as the demand for and supply of labor and the cost-of-living.

THE COMPLEXITY OF UTILIZING LOCAL COMPENSATION DATA

Using local compensation data is not as straightforward as you may think. The first step is to ensure that you have access to market data that individually lists all the appropriate pay elements for the role in the relevant country and provides unambiguous definitions. It is important to note that some surveys can be vague in their explanation of the various pay elements which can be confusing for compensation and human resource practitioners when trying to match roles accurately against the local market. For example, many countries in Europe, Latin America, and Asia have practices of 13, 14, and up to 18 months of "extra" salary, sometimes referred to as a "fixed bonus" or "seasonal bonus." Clearly, using base salary comparisons could potentially lead to misleading results as base salary may be defined as including some or all of the extra months' pay (depending on the survey). In an effort to make the comparisons more useable for analysis, off-the-shelf compensation surveys conducted by a number of leading consultancies report a base salary and a guaranteed base salary (including the extra months' pay either required by statute or provided by local practice).

Traditionally, local market comparisons have taken place at base salary level. However as variable pay or "pay at risk" becomes increasingly available to a wider employee population across the world, more organizations now require local compensation data at the total cash level in order to make meaningful comparisons against the marketplace. Again, as with base salary, it is important to ensure that comparisons are made on a like-for-like basis and that the information used is clearly defined in terms of the total cash components. For example, some surveys will include allowances and variable pay under a "total cash" heading whereas other surveys will report "total cash" as simply the addition of base salary and variable pay (excluding allowances).

This can all be further complicated by substantial pay differences (for the same role) between multinational organizations and local indigenous employers in the same country. This is usually driven by the background and work experience of the actual incumbent in the role. In China, for example, local national employees are paid significantly lower than "returning" Chinese nationals (i.e., those who have gained international experience in the United States or Western Europe), employees from other Asian markets (who have moved to China) and western expatriates. In the Middle East region, the working population is a mix of local nationals, western expatriates and contractors from the Indian subcontinent; again, there are marked differences in pay levels that are not necessarily segregated through off-the-shelf compensation surveys.

In an attempt to ease the pressure on compensation and human resource practitioners to understand all the compensation practices around the world, some consultancies produce individual customized market pricing reports based on local compensation data. By developing a composite of compensation data from a variety of published surveys for similar positions—within the same or similar industries and at similar revenue levels or organization types—these consultancies can arrive at a targeted view of compensation within a given local market.

CURRENT COMPENSATION ISSUES FOR LOCAL NATIONAL EMPLOYEES

The Emergence of Comprehensive Global Compensation Strategies

For many years, international compensation specialists have sought to develop a consistent and comprehensive compensation philosophy that would be applicable on a global basis. Due to the complexity of the marketplace, such efforts have resulted in clear pay philosophies for expatriates and, to a much lesser degree, for senior executives. Local national employees below the executive level have largely been ignored. Typically, such comprehensive pay philosophies have been so vague, flexible, and generalized as to not be very useful in the day-to-day work of compensation professionals. It has been easier and more practical to establish a strategy that encourages local compensation to be consistent with the local market practices and to ignore the inconsistencies between locations.

Traditionally, the key inhibitors to the development of comprehensive global compensation strategies have fallen into two categories. The first is in the definition of total compensation. Intercountry comparisons are difficult, especially when one includes long-term incentives and employee benefits. Efforts have included establishing guidelines for minimum levels of employee benefits on a global basis. The benefits would include both statutory requirements as well as private coverage. In terms of stock options for executives, efforts to establish global guidelines have been difficult due to the very high level of option grants typically given in the United States and the relatively low level of grants provided in other countries where the local cultural values make large grants impractical or illegal. Another factor is the tax requirements that vary as well. They range from countries in which grants are not permitted to those in which taxation makes grants less attractive. In some locations tax liability may occur at the time of the grant or over time, but it is not deferred until the time of exercise. Obviously this complicates the development of a consistent global policy.

Global compensation strategies that relate to a narrower definition of compensation are emerging—namely, limiting it to salary and short-term bonuses or incentives. Indeed, a number of recent studies suggest that approximately 85 percent of US and western European multinational organizations have a global compensation strategy in place with around 45 percent of these having had the strategy in place for less than four years. These global strategies establish guidelines as to how the marketplace is to be defined, where in the marketplace compensation is to be targeted, and how the mix of base salary and forms of incentive is to be determined. Furthermore, the strategy establishes an internal relationship of jobs classified into bands. The global strategy encourages local adaptation of the overall principles to the local marketplace. One of the substantial benefits is the communication of highly regarded benchmark practices that might be considered by local units who wish to challenge the traditional local practices.

Changes Occurring in Traditional Local Markets

The concept that each country has a fixed and consistent culture related to compensation has been a myth widely circulated and assumed to be accurate. As more compensation data is gathered and analyzed, it is clear that variations exist within locations and that the most traditional cultures are changing. An example is Japan, which has had a long history of unique pay values. These traditional values relate to the high correlation between compensation and age, pay related more to the person than to a specific job, and the concept of variable pay related to individual performance. All these concepts are changing as a result of considerable experimentation by the very large Japanese trading companies.

Many multinational organizations are finding that they can be innovative in local markets in a way that is nontraditional but that makes good business sense and is acceptable to local employees. Much of the data being generated on this subject is anecdotal, but it appears that best practices in compensation (especially the concept of variable pay) are being considered in locations where such practices were not considered a few years ago.

The emerging concept is that traditional local practices can be changed and that organizations need not be locked into them if alternative creative initiatives make good business sense. In most local markets there is more room for creativity than was previously believed to be the case.

The key question is whether a basic compensation approach might become more universally acceptable than it has been in the past. Clearly, many elements of the systems and innovations developed in the United States and many parts of western Europe are being adapted in many other locations across the world.

The Development of Regionally Identified Markets

Over the past decade, many analysts have believed that a single compensation market would begin to emerge in Europe. It has been hoped that the concept of supply and demand would create a single market in terms of pay levels as trade barriers have declined and the workers have been able to cross country borders. This has not occurred and appears to be inhibited by two major factors. The first is the difference in tax policies among country locations that impacts the level of pay and the way in which pay is delivered. The second is the differences in currencies, which make comparisons difficult. The introduction of the Euro makes comparison easier, but not all countries in Europe are included. This consolidation is likely to take a long time, and there are many factors that impact regionalization. In addition to tax policies, the design of and benefit levels associated with social security systems are also a factor.

Interest in the development of Asian regional compensation polices has been a topic of discussion, but the variations among countries are even wider than they are in Europe. Although the desire for regional offices in the area is to develop such policies to facilitate regional relocations, to date the common ground for such policies is not apparent.

Internal Equity Among All Classifications of Employees

The different levels of pay and conditions of employment among expatriates, international cadre, and local nationals residing in a single country location have been a constant concern in terms of internal equity. The differences in practices have been rationalized in terms of the different markets to which each group has been compared. Each classification had a policy designed to attract and retain the necessary talent based on business need. Although conceptually consistent, the perception has been that some classifications are treated preferentially. This is further complicated by expatriates who remain for long periods of time and expatriates who have home countries in high- and low-cost of living countries. The appearance is that the expatriates and international cadre live better and have a higher level of purchasing power than the locals.

Some approaches to minimizing the inequities relate to housing where a common standard of housing for a given location is targeted for all employees and policies are designed to permit access to a similar housing market. A tougher issue is to seek to equalize the perceived level of discretionary spending by the individuals involved. Traditionally, compensation professionals have avoided any such involvement.

Differences in conditions of employment become more apparent and less acceptable with the organizational principles of teamwork, employee involvement, and shared responsibilities. The longer-term strategy for many companies is to continually reduce the number of expatriates and to limit the time of the assignment. In addition, there is an increasing interest in the processes needed to "localize" expatriates as quickly as possible in order to minimize inequities with the local employees.

No single approach appears to be emerging, but to the degree possible, more expatriates are being asked to accept local practices in areas not directly related to salary. Where practical, expatriates are put into the local host pay system in order to minimize internal inequities.

ANTICIPATED TRENDS FOR LOCAL NATIONAL COMPENSATION IN THE FUTURE

There is no single trend that will impact all local national locations; each location is subject to pressures unique to its history and culture. However, there appear to be some power drivers of change that can be recognized.

- The concept of *meritocracy*, and specifically the vehicle of variable pay (variable in terms of the relationship of pay to business success), is widely accepted in market-driven economies. In some locations it may be in the form of statutory profit sharing, while in others it will follow the U.S. and European models of short- and long-term incentives. There is likely to be a corresponding decrease in pay systems that are related to tying pay to age, seniority, gender, and other non-performance-related criteria.

- *Traditional systems of compensation*, which have been unique to a particular country's set of values, are likely to encounter a broadening variety of nontraditional initiatives. This will be led primarily by multinational organizations but will provide a broader range of acceptable pay systems than has been the case in the past.

- *Employee retirement delivery vehicles* will shift gradually. Both social security and private plans will continue to move toward defined contribution plans rather than defined benefit plans.

- *Demands for market compensation data* for local national employees will create additional and improved survey designs, and there will be an increased level of participation. The survey technology will make surveys easier to complete, and they will be available more quickly as all-electronic surveys become the preferred vehicle.

SOURCES OF COMPENSATION SURVEY DATA

There is not a single source of data for local national compensation that covers all country locations. The quality and validity of market data vary widely, and care must be taken in assessing individual market data. The availability of data falls into three broad categories:

- Published data that can be obtained with or without cost

- Annual or ongoing customized survey data available only to survey participants

- Customized surveys conducted at a sponsor's request

The following is a listing of the most widely used data sources.

Published data

- Watson Wyatt, *Global 50 Remuneration Planning Report*
- Watson Wyatt, local reports on various countries
- William M. Mercer, *International Benefit Guidelines*

Custom reports

- Hay Associates, local reports on various countries
- Towers Perrin, local reports on various countries
- AON Consulting, local reports on various countries
- U.S. Chambers of Commerce in various country locations
- The U.S. State Department, surveys of U.S. embassy locations

The above listing is primarily focused on gathering data from multinational organizations. This reflects a bimodal market that exists in most countries. The "local" local market, which is composed of organizations that operate only within the country location, are typically smaller and represent a lower-paid market than exists for the larger multinational organizations. Care should be taken to ensure that the appropriate market has been identified and that the survey data is appropriate.

In many countries, market data shows a fairly wide distribution frequently without a strong central tendency in the data. This is a common situation in locations that are unstable from a compensation perspective or are experiencing high rates of inflation. Examples include Russia (and the Baltic States), Brazil, Venezuela, Turkey, and Indonesia. The effective date of the survey data is critically important and must be carefully "aged" to approximate current levels of compensation where the inflation rate is high.

CONSULTING SERVICES RELATED TO LOCAL NATIONAL JOB PRICING

All of the above consulting organizations offer job-pricing services. These consultants can provide clients with compensation, benefits, and pay-related policies and practices for a number of country locations using various survey sources. Typically, these services use public and custom-designed surveys for the purposes of job pricing. They will also conduct specialized surveys when requested. Compensation consultants who offer job-pricing services typically have access to many local consulting organizations in various countries that conduct specialized data gathering activities.

C H A P T E R

GLOBAL COMPENSATION PROCESSES

Robert Mattson, Product Marketing, and
David Turetsky, Director of Product Management

Workscape

DESIGNING, PLANNING, AND MANAGING COMPENSATION on a global basis is highly challenging as companies scale and expand to new markets or attempt to create consistent processes in multiple countries. When it comes to compensating a globally dispersed workforce, organizations need to manage intricate data privacy regulations, differing cultures, currencies, time zones, and languages while aligning employees across various regions toward common goals. Employees need to be equitably rewarded, both competitively within their regional market, as well as internally for their contributions to the organization's success.

Global organizations that take this centralized approach to compensation can universally realize the benefits of standardization across their entire operation. A survey by Watson Wyatt Worldwide of 275 companies with operations in two or more global regions revealed that half of them are already taking a centralized approach to their companies' global compensation structure.[1] However, even with implementing a centralized compensation structure, there are other challenges that global organizations need to navigate when crossing continents and countries.

Understanding the issues and options for accommodating variations in compensation structures, differences in local data privacy laws, and local customs—and even holiday schedules—is necessary to improve an organization's ability to compete in a global world.

BENEFITS OF A CENTRALIZED APPROACH

According to the Watson Wyatt Global Compensation Practices survey, respondents with a centralized compensation structure noted that key drivers for taking a more centralized approach were having a consistent link between rewards and results and maintaining a consistent position concerning market and internal equity. There are two facets of a centralized approach: first, the creation of a centralized compensation structure that provides consistent guidelines while maintaining flexibility for use in multiple regions, and second, providing an automated system that helps manage the compensation structure. Having a centralized system also offers greater budgetary control, increased visibility into compensation and performance review processes, the ability to consistently enforce policy throughout the organization, shorter compensation cycles, reduced IT expenses, and audit trails to demonstrate compliance. While it is theoretically possible to manage global compensation without automation, doing so in the real world has shown that it is virtually impossible as manual processes defeat the goal of centralization by creating thousands of process and information islands.

One immediate benefit of a consistent, global system and a centralized approach is to shorten the compensation cycle by automating workflow and enabling managers to see who has taken action as well as quickly identify process bottlenecks. The planning process is inherently more efficient when managers have access to online guidelines and decision support tools such as automatic calculations and auto-allocations based on budget availability, performance ratings, or other criteria. Another benefit is the ability to lower IT costs by streamlining systems. Companies that maintain separate systems require distinct yet sometimes duplicate skills and schedules to support islands of technology that are performing similar tasks and functions. As a result, they incur increased costs whether they are supporting these systems using internal IT resources or external vendors. In addition, they also have to manage multiple service level agreements and pay for separate hardware, operating systems, and databases.

Even with a centralized system in place, there are still challenges to be faced when competing globally. One obstacle is maintaining equity globally while accommodating market-specific practices such as allowances and whether to meet government regulations or local market expectations. While increased visibility through a centralized system enables insight into whether or not a region is conforming to corporate policy, there are variations in terms of allowances when operating around the globe that need to be accommodated. Another challenge is accounting for differences in local data privacy laws and options for managing the compliant sharing of information. Local currencies, languages, and cultures also need to be considered and managed through a system that offers the flexibility to account for these variations. Organizations that understand the issues can then begin strategizing the most effective solutions to operate across multiple countries.

BEYOND COMPENSATION—NAVIGATING DATA PRIVACY AROUND THE GLOBE

One key issue that organizations wrestle with is the differing data sharing and privacy regulations that vary from country to country. For businesses that operate in the United States, organizations tend to focus on U.S. or industry-specific data and reporting requirements such as Sarbanes–Oxley and HIPAA. A shift in processes and thinking is required when facing the challenges of operating in other countries that embrace an entirely different set of standards.

Organizations that do business in Europe need to meet requirements set forth by the EU. The EU's Data Protection Directive sets restrictions on how elements of personal information can be collected, stored, and shared. One reason managing data privacy is so cumbersome for organizations is the variations in stipulations between European data privacy requirements and those in the United States.

Under the EU directive, the focus is heavily on protecting the individual and their identifying information such as race, political affiliation, sex, name, or even seemingly standard business information such as office phone extension number. These types of data are restricted from being shared unless explicit employee permission is given or procedures put in place to properly protect this information. Organizations must be aware that personal data that is protected under EU privacy directives could be the same data that could be requested under U.S. law such as the Patriot Act. It is these types of conflicts that require scrutiny once a U.S. company goes abroad and needs to adhere to new rules and requirements when it comes to their employee data.

The EU restricts the transfer of data to those countries that it deems do not have rigorous data privacy regulations, including the United States. However, there are a few countries within which companies are free to share information under the EU requirements. Those countries include Argentina, Canada, Guernsey, the Isle of Man, and Switzerland. To manage the transfer of data to other countries, multinational employers need to adopt compliance strategies for data.

One option, albeit very limiting, is local processing. This local storage format and processing of data needs to happen within the country of origin and restricts the movement of data. Organizations embracing this strategy may want to partner with a vendor that has local hosting facilities that will keep data within EU boundaries for services like payroll. This option would have to include controls on who accesses data, as all accessing personnel would have to be considered "local" to that country. Under this option, managers in countries outside the approved set would not have access to compensation data for employees in those countries.

Arrangements can be made to have a local manager act as proxy in compensation decisions.

Derogations are another compliance option for organizations managing information globally. Derogations make specific provisions or exemptions for data sharing and require individual consent. The challenge with relying on derogations is that, for them to be valid, a company cannot require employees to give individual consent and must allow individual employees to opt out at any time. As a result, companies need to be prepared for individual compensation data to be blocked from being viewed when permission has not been given or is withdrawn.

Safe Harbor guidelines are another strategy for organizations to meet privacy standards. Safe Harbor standards were agreed upon by the EU and the United States and ensure protection of personal data consistent with EU policy specifications. The Safe Harbor framework offers a clear set of steps to comply with the EU data privacy directive. Organizations that participate in Safe Harbor are required to obtain certification and adhere to its principles. U.S. organizations adhering to Safe Harbor are subject to audits by the U.S. Commerce Department. By adopting Safe Harbor practices in each country in which employee data is accessible, organizations will be deemed compliant and able to share data and conduct business without interruption.

Model contracts are another strategy for data sharing compliance. These contracts contain standard clauses that are accepted throughout the EU and require organizations to adhere to established terms before data can be shared between them, even in the case of corporate subsidiaries. One key point to make is that these standard contracts cannot be modified in any way, and must be signed as-is. Any change invalidates the model contract.

Large organizations may want to consider binding corporate rules to manage the cross-border use of their data. Binding corporate rules are multinational data protection standards that are adopted by a corporate group. In 2005, General Electric was the first organization ever to be granted permission in the UK for its binding corporate rules to export data. A benefit to binding corporate rules is the ability to negotiate content, reporting, and compliance mechanisms with the data privacy regulators in each country. Many countries, like Germany, require data privacy regulations to be approved by local works councils, which can extend the time it takes to become compliant.

Although there are challenges with managing data privacy regulations from country to country, heightened awareness of the various options will enable effective compliance and adherence to varying data protection requirements. Because many data privacy options can take months or years to achieve compliance, many companies focus initially on getting employees to sign consent forms. In the case where consent is not given, it is important to have a compensation system where access is easily restricted based on geography and status of consent. Also, the compensation system should make it easy to implement proxies so a manager in the employee's country can act on behalf of an actual manager who resides in another country.

VARIATIONS IN COMPENSATION STRUCTURES AND LEVELS

In addition to navigating various data privacy regulations, maintaining equity globally is another challenge for organizations that operate in multiple countries. Performance-driven compensation is already changing the way organizations align individual, group, and company goals to determine business outcomes. By implementing a consistent global HR strategy, organizations can more effectively reward their workforce for reaching their goals.

While a centralized compensation system may help enforce global consistency, it must be able to easily accommodate when there are variations in terms of salary and allowances that differ from market to market. What constitutes base salary in one area of the world may differ dramatically from what defines base salary in another region. For example, in Australia, base salary is the guaranteed rate paid to every employee, regardless of his or her performance. Commissions, incentives, car allowances, and other bonuses are not included as part of an employee's base pay. In Taiwan, base salary is inclusive of bonus or other contractual payments. In France, base pay may also encompass vacation pay and overtime payments. These regional differences need to be built into the compensation rules.

One of the issues for global organizations is having a strategy in place for managing the differences in salary and bonus ratios. While the EU is moving to be more like the U.S. where there is a heavy emphasis on bonus and incentives, areas such as Asia put more weight on salary vs bonus.

Managing environmental pay issues is another area for concern for organizations that operate globally. In some emerging markets, there simply is not enough adequate market data available for organizations to have the intelligence to make competitive compensation decisions. Compensation experts are advising companies operating in countries such as Russia, where compensation data is scarce and unreliable, to privately fund studies for a small sample of key jobs.

As employees become aware of differences in compensation structures by region, some will campaign for similar rewards. For example if an organization generally supplies car allowances to employees in Australia, that same benefit may not be offered to employees holding the same position in the United States. Companies that give in to employee pressure for homogeneity may end up with a very expensive plan. First and foremost, you need to establish appropriate total compensation levels that are competitive with the market. Then, ensure that the delivery mechanisms are appropriate and rewarding for the job, culture, and local law.

For example, total compensation for engineers in Silicon Valley may be high, relative to other areas of the world, but a smaller percentage of their pay is in salary or bonus with more emphasis placed on long-term incentives to help improve employee retention. In New York, that engineering job has a higher base salary, a higher bonus percentage, but fewer long-term incentives. All in all, the same total compensation, just structured differently. That same engineering job in India may have a higher bonus percentage but total compensation may be less with no long-term incentive eligibility due to local laws.

ACCOMMODATING LANGUAGE, CULTURE, AND CURRENCY

Another point for consideration is accommodating the various languages, cultures, and currencies global organizations need to manage. Cross-cultural communications with respect to compensation are much more effective when received in the local language. How organizations handle multilingualism can make a difference in improving employee morale, as well as the ability to effectively deliver content to their workforce. For a country where English is not the official language, organizations need compensation systems that enable managers to access the same, centralized systems simultaneously, but in their local languages.

Managing cultural differences is another issue for global organizations. For example unlike the more casual U.S., most other cultures put greater emphasis on titles and surnames. In many cultures, honorifics indicate either social status or noteworthy achievements. In Japan, the—san suffix is a sign of respect bestowed on someone with higher social standing, such as the boss. In China, honorifics are slightly different than their Japanese counterparts. Employees expect that their total reward statements will address them appropriately. Whether earned or not, ignoring someone's honorific can be insulting. Also, some titles are not gender-neutral and can lead organizations to communication faux pas. A proper understanding and use of socio-cultural titles can play an important role in communicating with a global workforce and boosting morale.

Setting and paying compensation in local currencies is another element needing to be managed for global organizations. We cannot translate market rates for one country to others by using currency conversions, nor can we use cost-of-living indices. The valuation of individual jobs is a deeper economic rule called "comparative advantage." This rule asserts that there may be advantages that a country will have in producing goods and services over another country. This could be based on natural resources or technology.

Comparative advantage may also relate to the availability of capital, whether human or financial. This advantage creates supply and demand movements that make changes to the value and price that can be received for the scarce products in demand. In the case of software developers, India has been producing a large supply of development talent owing to its educational systems and the tendency for a high ratio of the population being drawn to opportunities in the engineering profession when compared to other countries.

These advantages translate directly to the market forces that govern compensation rates in various markets. While an engineer working in the United States may command an $80,000 per annum salary, that same position in India may only warrant the equivalent of U.S.$11,000 per annum.

Managers planning salary and rewards need to be able to understand the market rates for each job they are planning for and be able to understand the relative value of compensation in the employees' currency—even when members of the manager's team reside in different countries—as well as in the manager's currency and the headquarters' currency. This will enable managers to feel comfortable with and be able to make good decisions.

PROVIDING A FRAMEWORK THAT IS FLEXIBLE, YET WORKS GLOBALLY

One of the more important challenges on a global basis is having a process that enables flexibility, yet maintains a consistent global framework. The hard part is not designing a system that will work with all of the differences in plans on a global basis. The hard part is ensuring that the processes are coordinated in a way that gives the corporate compensation function the opportunity to provide consultation and governance over decisions that have been made. This is true of small and large global organizations. It is either the "out-of-sight/out-of-mind" approach or unintentional ignorance that corporate compensation uses to dismiss their lack of understanding and governance to international compensation plans.

Trends show that the top global companies are shifting more of their compensation spent outside the United States. That trend will continue with the growth of outsourcing and off-shoring. With higher amounts of compensation being spent outside the United States, compensation groups should have a solid understanding of the needs of global programs.

Knowing what the programs offer is just one part of the problem. The other is having the right data to judge whether or not the programs are effective, rewarding, and being adjudicated correctly. Most global companies do not have one HRIS/ERP with all of their HR data stored centrally. Even if the data is stored centrally, it may not be accurate. Accuracy of HR data is generally relative to its use with payroll, as this data is constantly reviewed by not only the compensation staff, but by the finance staff, and each individual employee when they review their pay stub.

The best example of the diversity of the global corporate world is to view how differently payroll is completed around the globe. In the United States, different states have different taxation, reporting, and data privacy rules. Outside the United States, those rules vary as well by region within each country. This makes the one global payroll system with clean data a fantasy. Many large companies try to have one global database, but are generally forced to admit defeat and scale back their ambitious plans to limited data sets. This makes the job of ensuring compensation governance difficult, but not impossible.

So, with the data and compensation plans in place, the next step is to create a common process structure and timeline that works with vacations, schedules, and other company-specific support activities (e.g., budgeting exercises, closing, and reporting statements), again, no small task. Other complications include reporting structures or employee hierarchies, workflows, and technology aptitude. In order to make all of this work together, compromises need to be made that allow the organization to utilize a technology to bring all of the data, programs, and differences together.

What is the result? A manager in New York can plan for his employees globally from his desk. An executive in South Africa can review the compensation planning for her entire division from the comfort of her office. One system can contain all of the global eligibilities, guidelines, and other rules that are inherent in the company's processes. It can send out alerts for managers who have overspent their budgets and collect reasons for the overage. Compensation staff can spend less time working with spreadsheets and more time working with managers.

FOUR BEST PRACTICES APPROACHES TO GLOBAL COMPENSATION CHALLENGES

Find a Data Privacy Strategy that Best Meets your Organizational Needs. One size does not fit all. With multiple options for managing data storage and sharing, choose one that delivers the flexibility you need and enables you to remain compliant in the areas where you operate.

Accommodate Local Cultures. If you are trying to determine when to schedule your planning cycles, take local customs into consideration. In Israel, employees may take extended time off during the Jewish high holidays. During the European summers, many organizations close down for seasonal vacations. When operating globally, scheduling a common focal planning period becomes much more challenging.

Target your Focus for Market Data to Meet Specific Needs. Salary surveys may not be available for new or emerging markets. In areas such as Brazil, China, and Russia that have a shorter history of U.S. companies with established business operations, be prepared to go out and do individual surveys. Instead of pricing 150 jobs as you may in more developed markets, focus on the top 20 jobs that you will have operating in this emerging area to determine the cost of talent.

Have a Centralized System for Compensation Management. A centralized system provides more stringent budgetary control and the data visibility necessary to make informed decisions.

PLAN AHEAD AND BE PREPARED

Organizations in the new global economy need to prepare for these additional levels of complexity when running their business. To succeed, multiple divisions must effectively manage processes that span different operating units or global regions and address multiple local demographic challenges.

When it comes to global compensation systems, be sure to look not only for one that can scale to handle the volume of users you have but one that also accommodates the requirements for multiple languages, currencies, and local cultures. And, even after making this wise investment, be prepared to proactively manage the ever-changing ancillary issues surrounding data privacy and other geographical nuances by having strategies in place to position your organization for success—anywhere in the world.

EXAMPLE 1: SELLING CENTRALIZATION INTERNALLY

One global company in the manufacturing industry was suffering from a classic case where they operated in 15 countries and each area had their own policies, procedures, and processes. Compensation was handled on a regional basis that took into account multiple countries in a region. As is the case in many large companies, the only true control was based upon cost center budgets where countries in the same regional cost center would tend to do things in a fairly similar manner.

The only way to tame this multicountry problem was to consolidate the processes and the technology to drive consistency across the company, but still take into account the specific needs of each region. The decision was to implement a best of breed compensation planning solution.

While the corporate management team had defined the strategy for consolidating a single software as a service (SaaS) technology platform for compensation planning and implementing a standard set of practices, each region would be required to pay for their use of the new system from their own operational budget. The question was how to internally sell this new process and technology to each region?

The answer, while relatively straightforward, was far from simple to achieve. The vice president of worldwide compensation had to become a salesman, build a "sales team" and travel from region to region discussing the solution, the new policies and how both would improve the lives of the HR staff and frontline managers of each country. Each region was different due to their history, culture, level of technical sophistication, and unique needs.

When building such a team the members identified in Table 50.1 must be included. Once the team is assembled it must travel from region to region presenting benefits, listening to objectives and addressing issues. Each country will have concerns over the loss of autonomy and how their specific needs will be met. Primary issues include:

- How will multiple data sources supply references and employee data per region?
- Will the local currency be supported?

TABLE 50.1   Sales Team to Promote Best of Breed Compensation Plan

Team Member	Purpose
Executive sponsor	■ Outline purpose of initiative ■ Supply credibility for the program
Technology representative	■ Address core technology and functionality issues (this could either be supplied by an internal technology resource or potentially by the vendor that is supplying the solution)
Implementation representative	■ Address implementation and change management issues
Compensation specialist	■ Communicate program details and process changes

■ Will compensation statements be supplied to employees in the local language?

■ What will be the effect of standardization of global compensation processes and methods on the local unit?

■ How will data integrity and consistency of cross-regional, multisource information be assured?

■ How will multifaceted, regional business unit and employee-specific bonus plans and elements be addressed?

The answers to each question can vary depending upon the audience and the solution and processes being implemented. However, putting the right team in place, prepared to address concerns and to drive buy-in from regional management, is the key to project success by transforming challengers into champions.

EXAMPLE 2: DATA PRIVACY, EUROPE, AND SaaS

A technology services firm was consolidating their global compensation processes to a single technology platform that would support divisions in the United States, Latin America, Europe, and Asia. The challenge was accommodating EU data privacy regulations while supporting the needs of matrix managers that had dotted line relationships to employees in the EU.

Selecting the right technology and application turned out to hinge on more than just a selection based on features and functionality. While as a global technology company there was discussion about building a solution internally, the management team decided that building a compensation application was not a core competency of the company and that selecting a best-of-breed solution would better serve the company.

Finding the right vendor and solution was initially based on meeting the functional needs of the organization, but as the direction was finalized to search out a hosted solution, the location of the hosting center and how the vendor would meet the data privacy requirements for the company employees in Germany became a potential stumbling block.

Supporting a globally dispersed community with members inside and outside the EU is both a legal and a technical challenge. The vendor must employ some acceptable method of ensuring data privacy compliance to address legal stipulations and have technology that has sufficient flexibility to limit access to sensitive data. For example, if a manager in the United States has dotted line responsibility for a German employee, that United States manager must be restricted from viewing that employee's compensation details to meet the stipulations for EU data privacy. The compensation system must have the flexibility to both grant and limit access based on a number of various criteria and rules.

END NOTE

1. Watson Wyatt Global Compensation Practices, WorldatWork Survey, 2006.

Index